THE GREENWOOD ENCYCLOPEDIA OF WORLD POPULAR CULTURE

The Greenwood Encyclopedia of World Popular Culture

General Editor
GARY HOPPENSTAND

Volume Editors
MICHAEL K. SCHOENECKE, North America
JOHN F. BRATZEL, Latin America
GERD BAYER, Europe
LYNN BARTHOLOME, North Africa and the Middle East
DENNIS HICKEY, Sub-Saharan Africa
GARY XU and VINAY DHARWADKER, Asia and Pacific Oceania

THE GREENWOOD ENCYCLOPEDIA OF WORLD POPULAR CULTURE

NORTH AFRICA AND THE MIDDLE EAST

Gary Hoppenstand
General Editor

Lynn Bartholome
Volume Editor

GREENWOOD PRESS
Westport, Connecticut • London

Library of Congress Cataloging-in-Publication Data

The Greenwood encyclopedia of world popular culture / Gary Hoppenstand, general editor ; volume editors, John F. Bratzel ... [et al.].
   p. cm.
   Includes bibliographical references and index.
   ISBN-13: 978-0-313-33255-5 (set : alk. paper)
   ISBN-13: 978-0-313-33316-3 (North America : alk. paper)
   ISBN-13: 978-0-313-33256-2 (Latin America : alk. paper)
   ISBN-13: 978-0-313-33509-9 (Europe : alk. paper)
   ISBN-13: 978-0-313-33274-6 (North Africa and the Middle East : alk. paper)
   ISBN-13: 978-0-313-33505-1 (Sub-Saharan Africa : alk. paper)
   ISBN-13: 978-0-313-33956-1 (Asia and Pacific Oceania : alk. paper)
   1. Popular culture—Encyclopedias. 2. Civilization, Modern—Encyclopedias. 3. Culture—Encyclopedias. I. Hoppenstand, Gary. II. Bratzel, John F. III. Title: Encyclopedia of world popular culture. IV. Title: World popular culture.
   HM621.G74 2007
   306.03—dc22   2007010684

British Library Cataloguing in Publication Data is available.

Copyright © 2007 by Lynn Bartholome

All rights reserved. No portion of this book may be reproduced, by any process or technique, without the express written consent of the publisher.

Library of Congress Catalog Card Number: 2007010684
ISBN-13: 978-0-313-33255-5 (Set)
ISBN-10: 0-313-33255-X

ISBN-13: 978-0-313-33316-3 (North America)
ISBN-10: 0-313-33316-5

ISBN-13: 978-0-313-33256-2 (Latin America)
ISBN-10: 0-313-33256-8

ISBN-13: 978-0-313-33509-9 (Europe)
ISBN-10: 0-313-33509-5

ISBN-13: 978-0-313-33274-6 (North Africa and the Middle East)
ISBN-10: 0-313-33274-6

ISBN-13: 978-0-313-33505-1 (Sub-Saharan Africa)
ISBN-10: 0-313-33505-2

ISBN-13: 978-0-313-33956-1 (Asia and Pacific Oceania)
ISBN-10: 0-313-33956-2

First published in 2007

Greenwood Press, 88 Post Road West, Westport, CT 06881
An imprint of Greenwood Publishing Group, Inc.
www.greenwood.com

Printed in the United States of America

The paper used in this book complies with the Permanent Paper Standard issued by the National Information Standards Organization (Z39.48–1984).

10 9 8 7 6 5 4 3 2 1

To Becky and Hop, who love me no matter what
And to my sister SueSue, who arrived just at the right time

CONTENTS

FOREWORD: POPULAR CULTURE AND THE WORLD   ix
   Gary Hoppenstand

INTRODUCTION: POPULAR CULTURE IN NORTH AFRICA AND THE MIDDLE EAST   xi
   Lynn Bartholome

ARCHITECTURE   1
   Matthew R. Hachee

ART   27
   Rosemary Gallick

DANCE   45
   Stasia J. Callan

FASHION AND APPEARANCE   61
   Elizabeth D. Johnston

FILM   95
   Susan Booker Morris

FOOD AND FOODWAYS   107
   Heather L. Williams

GAMES, TOYS, AND PASTIMES   133
   Mary Findley

LITERATURE   157
   Kathryn Knight

LOVE, SEX, AND MARRIAGE   187
   Rihab Kassatly Bagnole

MUSIC   205
   Rihab Kassatly Bagnole

PERIODICALS   225
   Lynn Bartholome

RADIO AND TELEVISION   245
   Rihab Kassatly Bagnole

Contents

SPORTS AND RECREATION *Kathleen J. O'Shea*	263
THEATER AND PERFORMANCE *Ann Tippett and Michael Doolin*	287
TRANSPORTATION AND TRAVEL *Holly Wheeler*	307
GENERAL BIBLIOGRAPHY	351
ABOUT THE EDITORS AND CONTRIBUTORS	353
INDEX	357

FOREWORD

POPULAR CULTURE AND THE WORLD

GARY HOPPENSTAND

Popular culture is easy to recognize, but often difficult to define. We can say with authority that the current hit television show *House* is popular culture, but can we say that how medical personnel work in hospitals is popular culture as well? We can readily admit that the recent blockbuster movie *Pirates of the Caribbean* is popular culture, but can we also admit that what the real-life historical Caribbean pirates ate and what clothes they wore are components of popular culture? We can easily recognize that a best-selling romance novel by Danielle Steel is popular culture, but can we also recognize that human love, as ritualistic behavior, is popular culture? Can popular culture include architecture, or furniture, or automobiles, or many of the other things that we make, as well as the behaviors that we engage in, and the general attitudes that we hold in our day-to-day lives? Does popular culture exist outside of our own immediate society? There can be so much to study about popular culture that it can seem overwhelming, and ultimately inaccessible.

Because popular culture is so pervasive—not only in the United States, but in all cultures around the world—it can be difficult to study. Basically, however, there are two main approaches to defining popular culture. The first advocates the notion that popular culture is tied to that period in Western societies known as the Industrial Revolution. It is subsequently linked to such concepts as "mass-produced culture" and "mass-consumed culture." In other words, there must be present a set of conditions related to industrial capitalism before popular culture can exist. Included among these conditions are the need for large urban centers, or cities, which can sustain financially the distribution and consumption of popular culture, and the related requirement that there be an educated working-class or middle-class population that has both the leisure time and the expendable income to support the production of popular culture. Certainly, this approach can encompass that which is most commonly regarded as popular culture: motion pictures, television, popular fiction, computers and video games, even contemporary fast foods and popular fashion. In addition, this approach can generate discussions about the relationship between popular culture and political ideology. Can popular culture be political in nature, or politically subversive?

Foreword

Can it intentionally or unintentionally support the status quo? Can it be oppressive or express harmful ideas? Needless to say, such definitions limit the critical examination of popular culture by both geography and time, insisting that popular culture existed (or only exists) historically in industrial and postindustrial societies (primarily in Western Europe and North America) over the past 200 years. However, many students and critics of popular culture insist that industrial production and Western cultural influences are not essential in either defining or understanding popular culture.

Indeed, a second approach sees popular culture as existing since the beginning of human civilization. It is not circumscribed by certain historic periods, or by national or regional boundaries. This approach sees popular culture as extending well beyond the realm of industrial production, in terms of both its creation and its existence. Popular culture, these critics claim, can be seen in ancient China, or in medieval Japan, or in pre-colonial Africa, as well as in modern-day Western Europe and North America (or in all contemporary global cultures and nations for that matter). It need not be limited to mass-produced objects or electronic media, though it certainly does include these, but it can include the many facets of people's lifestyles, the way people think and behave, and the way people define themselves as individuals and as societies.

This six-volume *Encyclopedia of World Popular Culture*, then, encompasses something of both approaches. In each of the global regions of the world covered—North America, South America, Europe, the Middle East, Sub-Saharan Africa, and Asia—the major industrial and postindustrial expressions of popular culture are covered, including, in most cases, film; games, toys, and pastimes; literature (popular fiction and nonfiction); music; periodicals; and radio/television. Also examined are the lifestyle dimensions of popular culture, including architecture; dance; fashion and appearance; food and foodways; love, sex, and marriage; sports; theater and performance; and transportation and travel. What is revealed in each chapter of each volume of *The Greenwood Encyclopedia of World Popular Culture* is the rich complexity and diversity of the human experience within the framework of a popular culture context.

Yet rooted within this framework of rich complexity and diversity is a central idea that holds the construct of world popular culture together, an idea that sees in popular culture both the means and the methods of widespread, everyday, human expression. Simply put, the commonality of national, transnational, and global popular cultures is the notion that, through their popular culture, people construct narratives, or stories, about themselves and their communities. The many and varied processes involved in creating popular culture (and subsequently living with it) are concerned, at the deepest and most fundamental levels, with the need for people to express their lifestyle in ways that significantly define their relationships to others.

The food we eat, the movies we see, the games we play, the way we construct our buildings, and the means of our travel all tell stories about what we think and what we like at a consciously intended level, as well as at an unintended subliminal level. These narratives tell others about our interests and desires, as well as our fundamental beliefs about life itself. Thus, though the types of popular dance might be quite different in the various regions of the world, the recognition that dance fulfills a basic and powerful need for human communication is amazingly similar. The fact that different forms of popular sports are played and watched in different countries does not deny the related fact that sports globally define the kindred beliefs in the benefits of hard work, determination, and the overarching desire for the achievement of success.

These are all life stories, and popular culture involves the relating of life's most common forms of expression. This *Encyclopedia of World Popular Culture* offers many narratives about many people and their popular culture, stories that not only inform us about others and how they live, but that also inform us, by comparison, about how we live.

INTRODUCTION

POPULAR CULTURE IN NORTH AFRICA AND THE MIDDLE EAST

LYNN BARTHOLOME

The Middle East is frequently referred to as the "crossroads of the world." It is a gateway to the Far East, sub-Saharan Africa, southeastern Europe, and India. The Greeks call this part of southwest Asia the Near East, to distinguish the territory from China and Japan. The *Concise Encyclopedia* states that it is the geographic region where Europe, Africa, and Asia meet.[1]

The region is a bastion of cultural diversity, being the birthplace and spiritual center of the Baha'i faith, Judaism, Christianity, Islam, and Zoroastrianism. Ethnic groups include Africans, Arabs, Assyrians, Azeris, Berbers, Chaldeans, Druze, Greeks, Jews, Kurds, Maronites, Persians, and Turks. Languages spoken include Arabic, Turkish, Persian, Kurdish, Azeri, Armenian, Assyrian (also known as Aramaic or Syriac), Hebrew, and Yiddish. Historians also assert that part of the geography that is today modern Iraq is one of four possible sites for the "cradle of civilization" (the others being the lands surrounding the Nile River in Africa, the Indus River in South Asia, and the Huang-He and Yangtze Rivers in China).

The Middle East defines a cultural area, and as such, it does not have precisely drawn borders. For purposes of this volume, it includes the territories around the southern and eastern shores of the Mediterranean Sea, stretching from Morocco to the Arabian Peninsula and Iran. Countries include Egypt, Jordan, Israel, Lebanon, Syria, Iraq, Iran, Turkey, Bahrain and the United Arab Emirates, Kuwait, Qatar and Saudi Arabia, Oman and Yemen. Since the North African nations of Libya, Algeria, Morocco, and Tunisia are often linked as well, they too are included.

The region as a whole has experienced periods of both relative tolerance and calm and upheaval and confrontation. During the late twentieth century and early twenty-first century the Middle East has been at the center of world affairs. The focus is even more dramatic since the catastrophic events of September 11, 2001. On that day, often referred to as "9/11," a series of well-planned suicide attacks were carried out on targets in the United States. Nineteen terrorists, all with Middle Eastern connections and members of the fringe group al-Qaeda, hijacked commercial airlines just after they had taken off from U.S. airports.

Introduction

Two of the jetliners crashed into the World Trade Center and a third smashed into the Pentagon Building outside of Washington, D.C. A fourth airliner was intended to strike the U.S. Capitol, but brave passengers on board attempted to retake control; the hijackers instead crashed this plane into a field in Somerset County, Pennsylvania. All on board were killed. Besides the 19 hijackers, 2,973 others died on that day—and another 24 are still missing and presumed dead.

These attacks set into motion a flurry of political events, the repercussions of which are still being felt around the world. Within a month after 9/11, the United States and a coalition of her allies invaded Afghanistan in order to topple the fundamentalist Taliban regime that had harbored the al-Qaeda terrorist organization. The Taliban were quickly driven from power; however, the United States still maintains a force there to protect its interests. Counterterrorism expert Richard A. Clarke maintains that internal political struggles within the Muslim world are the primary cause for the attacks of 9/11. In particular, al-Qaeda's Osama bin Laden and other Islamic extremists believe that the majority of governments in the Middle East are apostate governments; as such, the collective religiosity of these governments does meet bin Laden's measure of Muslim piety. Influenced by Egyptian theologian and writer Sayyid Qutb, bin Laden contends that, as a dutiful Muslim, he must instead establish a caliphate in the Middle East.[2] Thus bin Laden conceived a plan to attack the United States in order to establish this caliphate. Calling the United States the "Far Enemy," bin Laden orchestrated the September 11 attacks in order to force the United States to increase its military and cultural presence in the Middle East.[3] In bin Laden's mind, once Middle Eastern Muslims meet head-on the evils of an imperialist, nonsectarian government, they will support a social and political movement to establish conservative and fanatical fundamentalist governments throughout the land.[4] Coupled with the current U.S. occupation of Iraq and the ongoing conflict between Israel and other constituents of the Arab world, this region continues to be both mesmerizing and frustrating to both participants and world observers.

The next installment in the Middle East saga has yet to be written. Perhaps by exploring the popular culture of this diverse "crossroads of the world," we can begin to understand the complexity of the Middle Eastern situation. We may also be able to propose some antidotes for the current state of affairs.

The Chapters in This Book

Matthew R. Hachee, in his chapter on Middle Eastern and North African **Architecture**, suggests that the buildings and architectural techniques and designs most characteristic of the region continue to be the outcome of a cross-cultural struggle to balance ethnic tradition against the influence of Western styles and building methods. Western culture and ways of organizing everyday life have come to the Middle East and North Africa through such things as Western plumbing techniques, bathroom design, and choices of building materials just as much as they have from television, film, and other media. In most of the countries of the region, however, the strong influence of Islam and Arabic nationality is still reflected in the most important structures of daily life. A return to the conservative remains the norm.

Rosemary Gallick relates in the chapter on **Art** that the visual arts of the Middle East and North Africa reflect the creative impulses throughout turbulent times. The art is historically rooted in religion and politics, and there is an especially rich expression in the pictorial arts. The art in these countries continues to venerate and perpetuate past traditions.

Stasia J. Callan, in the chapter on **Dance**, reports that in the desert lands of the Middle East and along the north coast of Africa, dance has undergone a fascinating evolution.

INTRODUCTION

Through the ages, dance has lost its religious significance and become a secular activity. Now considered entertainment, dance is an art form performed for Middle Eastern spectators rather than a participatory activity. In North Africa dance is an ancient tradition that has been an essential part of births, rites of passage, harvest, and marriage ceremonies. Ceremonial, recreational, and religious dance forms are found in traditional, neotraditional, and contemporary proceedings. Callan further states that African dance is humanistic and has for centuries been the chronicler of history. The dances of Egypt, Morocco, Algeria, Tunisia, and Libya mirror similar motifs found in Middle Eastern dance forms.

Elizabeth Johnston explains in the chapter on **Fashion** that styles in the Middle East and North Africa are largely dictated by four facts: secularization, commercial development, wealth, and the youth population. The influence of the West on Middle Eastern and North African trends is unquestionable; since 1980 over 200 Western-style malls have opened, with dozens more to be built over the next five years in the Persian Gulf area alone. Many countries, nonetheless, continue to adhere to strict religious guidelines concerning physical appearance and adornment. These dress codes are designed to draw attention away from the body and restrict personal expression.

In her chapter on **Film**, Susan Booker Morris points out that film production in the Middle East has been scarce in countries such as Syria, Iraq, Lebanon, and Jordan and that it consists mostly of small productions on old technologies such as 16-mm film. For example, *Today and Tomorrow*, which debuted at the Osians-Cinefan Eighth Festival of Asian Cinema in New Delhi, India, in 2006, was the first feature-length film made in Saudi Arabia. She puts forward the view that film is a product of technology that functions as a commodity, whether as an art form or as an object of popular culture. Any consideration of film in this region must reconcile the fact that technology and commodification (Morris's term) are Western impositions on an area that has a long history of tension with European and American colonialism and political influences. Another complication is religious resistance to production and distribution based on a cultural belief that Islam is in opposition to Western art, modernization, and technology.

Heather L. Williams's chapter on **Food and Foodways** will definitely whet the reader's appetite. Middle Eastern cuisine is characterized by strong Mediterranean, Persian, and various North African traditions; Middle Eastern food reflects the depth and breadth of its ethnic influences with distinct spices, nuts and olives, fish, coffees and anise, grains and breads, fresh herbs and seasonal produce, yogurts and goat cheeses, all adapted to specific customs and locales. No matter what the occasion, food serves as a critical mechanism for building and binding familial and larger social bonds within these cultures. A significant influence on the cuisine of the Middle East and North Africa is religious doctrine, which dictates some of the preparation and consumption of certain foods. Primarily, this includes the halal and kosher traditions of the Islamic and Jewish faiths, respectively.

Mary Findley states that **Games, Toys, and Pastimes** in the Middle East have existed as long as children have been around. Before toys were manufactured, they were fashioned out of any material available, even mud. The current culture of toys in countries such as Iraq, however, has changed dramatically because of the prevalence of violence, war, and government upheaval. Toys such as Galimotos, handmade push toys made out of string, wire, and other available waste products, have a universal presence in North Africa. Other popular favorites, such as Legos, are as popular in the Middle East as they are in the rest of the world.

In her chapter on **Literature**, Kathryn Knight provides a concise history from the classical period to the present day, discussing both prose and poetry. One of the most intriguing motifs in the literature of this region is that of the city. Bustling with life and sophistication,

Introduction

themes relating to the modern metropolis have become a staple of Middle Eastern poetry. Palestinian poets have utilized the image of the city to express the feeling of loss and rootlessness and to emblemize victim, hero, and resistance.

Rihab Kassatly Bagnole presents a compelling portrait of the Middle Eastern cultural experience in the chapter on **Love, Sex, and Marriage**. Marriage in the Middle East and North Africa is the most important goal in the life of young people. Marriage allows a woman increased freedom and power, determined primarily by her education or background. Although more women are pursuing an education and working outside the home, their essential role is to support their husbands and take care of their children. The husband fulfills the expectations of his society by marrying a woman who is able to bear him children, preferably sons who carry his family name and inherit his assets. All Middle Eastern and North African countries are primarily patriarchal societies. Marriage is an event that impacts the entire family, not just the bride and groom. Romantic relationships are frequent in urban settings, while the countryside still adheres to more traditional ways. Premarital sex is not publicly condoned in the Middle East and North Africa, because a woman's virginity is highly valued. Because the cities do tolerate a freer lifestyle, however, some couples do have sex before marriage, even if it is risky.

In the chapter on **Music**, Rihab Kassatly Bagnole relates that music is indispensable to Middle Easterners and North Africans because it is woven into the mystical and secular aspects of people's lives. While music continues to be a part of religious ritual, it also serves as a mechanism to soothe the souls of average men and women as they live their busy lives. The imprint of the West is evident in the music of this region—contemporary songs from many of these countries are now released via music videos produced by large-scale production companies. In places such as Cairo, Egypt, satellite channels are used to advertise and commercialize the artists and sell their creative products around the world.

In my chapter on **Periodicals**, I examine the press industry in the Middle East and North Africa at present. While Israel implements relatively few governmental curbs on subject matter, many of her neighbors receive their daily news and information from sources that are closely monitored by government censors. Journalists are threatened with fines and jail time for objectionable story content. This is stunningly illustrated in the recent furor in several Muslim countries over the publication of allegedly blasphemous cartoons of the Prophet Muhammad.

Rihab Kassatly Bagnole's chapter on **Radio and Television** explores the notion that radio and television are natural extensions of the oral tradition of Middle Eastern and North African cultures. Citizens of these countries like to listen, watch, and discuss news of local and international events. Considering the strong allure of the spoken word, radio and television offer natural outlets for mass communication in a region steeped in oral tradition.

In her chapter, Kathleen J. O'Shea reports that **Sports**, especially team sports, are increasingly becoming a part of Middle Eastern and North African cultural life. Sports that typically attract the wealthy, such as golf, sailing, powerboat racing, rallying, and horse racing, are booming. There are now over 100 sports associations at national levels for Olympic sports, football, basketball, horse racing, rugby, volleyball, golf, motor sports, and water sports. At least ten Middle Eastern countries have national soccer teams. Every nation has local and national radio and television stations; these stations are imitating Western practices in sports-related coverage. National satellite channels also provide wide-ranging exclusive coverage of sporting events.

Ann Tippett and Michael Doolin, in their chapter on **Theater**, reflect that drama is not a native Arab art. Western theater was unknown to this part of the world until the nineteenth century. Before this time, comedic presentations and storytelling stood in for theatrical arts. Similar to the passion plays of the West, Muslim faith was promoted through the Taziya (literal translation, *consolation*). The main purpose of Taziya was to present the suffering and death of Muhammad's descendants and their followers. The plays were performed to the accompaniment of music in theaters, mosques, or the open air. Today drama prospers in the more stable countries and struggles in others. It is the object of censorship; nowhere is this more apparent than in Saudi Arabia, which has no current dramatic or theatrical efforts, and Iraq, which has a cultural tradition of live theater, but now has very little theatrical activity because of the current occupation by U. S. forces. Puppet Theater thrives in Iran. The country hosts the International Puppet Theater Festival every two years. Additionally, eight Middle Eastern countries participate in a current UNESCO initiative called the International Theater Institute.

Written by Holly Wheeler, the chapter on **Transportation and Travel** illustrates that, although Westerners tend to group all Middle Eastern countries together, the countries making up this region have more differences than similarities. Diverse traditions, conservative versus modern views, and varied topography separate these lands into distinct entities. Tourism is alive and well and developing rapidly in this region. From the smallest of nations, Bahrain, to giant Saudi Arabia, a country comparable to the size of Indonesia, people from all over the world are traveling to the Middle East.

NOTES

1. Encyclopaedia Britannica Online, "Middle East," October 12, 2006, http://britannica.com/ebc/article-9372091.
2. Richard A. Clarke, *Against All Enemies* (New York: Free Press, 2004), pp. 122–124.
3. Peter Bergin, *The Osama bin Laden I Know: An Oral History of al Qaeda's Leader* (New York: Free Press, 2006), p. 229.
4. Bergin, pp. 233–235.

ARCHITECTURE

MATTHEW R. HACHEE

The popular architecture of the contemporary Middle East and Northern Africa—its prominent housing styles, commercial and cultural buildings—reflects the complex cultural and economic changes that have swept over the region since the first oil concessions were bought in Iran in 1901, sparking the last century's race for oil. The building and architectural techniques and designs that are most characteristic of the region during this period continue to be the outcome of a cross-cultural struggle to balance ethnic tradition against the influence of Western styles and building methods. The struggle is more than just symbolic, as changes in the architecture of daily life can and do have a real effect on culture by making some ways of living and organizing activities more likely to be chosen than others. Consequently, Western culture and ways of organizing everyday life have increasingly come to the countries of North Africa and the Middle East through such things as Western plumbing techniques, bathroom design, and choices of building materials just as much as they have from television, film, and other media.

In most of the countries of the region the strong influence of Islam and Arabic nationality is still reflected in the most important structures of daily life. Starting as early as 1950, designers and architects from across the region began to take seriously the influence of Western styles and designs, determined to prevent an unwitting wholesale adoption of Western lifestyles. Rather than reject all things Western, however, Islamic and Arabic architecture has, from the beginning of its modern engagement with the West, attempted to find a peaceful accommodation with Western design standards and styles. At the end of the twentieth century, this kind of accommodation has increasingly turned toward attempts to synthesize nearly all details and advancements of Western building techniques, accoutrements, and styles with the traditional cultural architectural motifs, symbols, and layout unique to the region. Whether in Iran, Egypt, or Morocco, the story of popular architecture in the region over the twentieth century is generally the same: how is it possible to borrow from Western influence and culture without compromising the traditional forms of ethnic and cultural identity of the particular country and region more generally? This debate has taken place among Middle Eastern and African architects themselves, but also within the halls of government, where the questions about the cumulative effect of years of unplanned wholesale adoption of Western architecture are being asked for the first time, as are questions of the desirability of nearly exclusive reliance on Western architectural firms for all large-scale building and design work. And these questions have increasingly motivated lawmakers to become more self-conscious in housing design and urban planning.

In the early years of the twenty-first century, architects, designers and urban planners of the region have increasingly returned to themes that are unmistakably traditional, whether they be traditionally Arabic, Islamic, or (in Israel exclusively) Judaic. Although this return does not apply to some cities, such as Dubai City, with its massive, cutting-edge hotel and resort complexes, it seems that in general these Westernized "pleasure cities" are the exception to the rule, and that a return to the conservative in architecture remains the norm. As relations between the Islamic and Arabic countries and the West continue to be tense, we are likely to see an increasing number of attempts to temper the desire for rapid development using primarily Western design practices and constructional expertise in order to preserve or retrieve the traditional domestic, religious, and commercial structures that have been characteristic of the region for centuries. For much of the mid- to late twentieth century, many of the new buildings and construction projects were direct imitations of Western models. Today it is more common to find urban planners and architects who are seriously concerned that the economically driven imitation of past years has resulted in the creation of an environment that is strange and alien to local people. Consequently the most recent examples of large popular architectural projects in the region are targeted attempts to turn the tide against the cumulative effect of years of design without regard for local culture and environment.

The specific details of contemporary popular architecture in the region have never been fully studied, and many significant details remain unknown at present. However, in each country of the region, it is possible to put together a basic picture of the structures of everyday life, which tend to be a mix of the old and the new. Even common homes and markets being constructed today tend to be interesting and ingenious structures and spaces in which function, Western ideals and designs, and local custom and religious belief are interwoven as in a rich tapestry. For example, enclosed spaces, defined by walls, arcades, and vaults, are traditional elements of Arabic and Islamic architecture found throughout the region. Incorporating many of these elements into even the simplest dwelling or high-rise commercial building has been made significantly easier with the introduction of Western construction techniques and materials, such as concrete. At the same time, though, Western techniques and methods, with their general tendency toward exterior embellishment and ornamentation, tend to run up against the sensibilities of many in the region. With the exception of the dome and the entrance portal, decoration in the region's architecture is typically reserved for the interior.

The typical major cities in the region, which in many places are direct descendants of earlier military forts or compounds, are built around five common structures: the *souq*, or marketplace; the *madrassa*, or religious and legal school; the *mosque*; the *hammam*, or bath; and the private home. Throughout the twentieth century, wherever Western-oriented architecture has not been simply adopted wholesale in these important buildings, it is typical to find designs that called for taking modern Western forms of popular design and grafting traditional-looking "facades" such as arches and domes onto them (such as in the modern hybrid high-rise buildings of Cairo, or Cairo's steel high-tension power lines designed to resemble date trees). In the 1990s and in more recent years, new generations of planners and designers have worked to take advantage of opportunities that new materials and mass production techniques make possible, trying to create a new architecture that is consistent and expressive of tradition and yet which is radically new and distinctive, using local materials and local building methods in exciting new ways. Even in the contemporary state of Israel, where the influence of Islam is regionally weakest, the popular architecture and the structures of daily life show a strong influence of the traditions and themes of the region.

COMMON MIDDLE EAST STRUCTURES

The Souq

As the focal point of commerce, the traditional market of the region has a long history in Persian and Arabic culture. The original international trading posts, the souqs of North Africa and the Middle East, began as places where caravans from as far away as India and China could exchange their cargo and bargain with other traders. Prior to the twentieth century, these bazaars were constructed out of the haphazard intersection of many narrow lanes with little or no central planning. Structures contained stalls occupied by various vendors, with particular souqs coming to be associated with particular goods and services. This tradition continues today with a steady growth in specialty souqs, especially gold, spice, and jewelry souqs in urban and tourist hot spots. By the end of the twentieth century, however, this tradition of specialty souqs had become increasingly anachronistic, as the urban souqs had increasingly come to resemble Western-style shopping malls and supermarkets both in terms of their organization and in basic physical appearance.

The Madrassa

This unique type of religious building has long been a part of Islamic civilization. As a school for the training of spiritual and legal leaders, the madrassa has been a familiar part of Arab and Islamic civilization from the twelfth century. And today, just as in previous centuries, most madrassas are seen as public institutions, even though they are endowed through the use of private funding called a *waqf*. In many cases important private donors are buried on the grounds in adjoining mausoleums. Given their important function as a means for private memorialization, it is not surprising that the basic design and layout of these important cultural centers has changed little even with the introduction of new materials and construction methods.

The most visible features of the madrassas are typically their portals and minarets, but the traditional interior design and layout are equally intricate and complex. Most madrassas are centered on a court with one or more *iwans*—large, three-sided, vaulted halls used for teaching and living. In many madrassas four iwans are present, representing each one of the four rites of Islam in the madrassa's functional design. The halls often include dwellings (*riwaq*) for the students and teachers. Syria and Egypt have the largest number of madrassas per capita today, with some dating back to the thirteenth century and growing into enormous complexes, like the madrassas of Barsbay and Oaytbay in Cairo. With gateways 20 meters high and minarets approaching 70 meters, these madrassas share a vertical design, with exterior walls that are almost entirely bare, that is common in many madrassas in the region. All that one can see from the outside are simple cornices that run the entire length of the buildings and recessed portal windows.

Architecture

The Mosque

As houses of the ritual of daily prayer in Islam, mosques are the center of religious community life for most people who call North Africa or the Middle East home. In Islam, however, there is no clear distinction between the sacred and the profane. Therefore, it is not completely false to say that wherever one prays, that place is a mosque. Mosques, just like madrassas and hammams, are best understood in terms of their social function as a place for gathering and an anchor of a neighborhood. Traditional mosque architecture is known for its classic exterior, and for its use of painted decorative tiles such as mosaic on the interior openwork, pillars, and walls.

At the same time, the style and design of the mosque is flexible and has been adapted in many ways even within the region. Many of the mosques built since the 1960s make use of explicitly modern architectural motifs, such as the construction of symbolic minarets. This flexibility in mosque design goes hand in hand with a basic nondirectional planning common to Arabic and Islamic architecture more generally. The availability of modern construction materials and methods gives the designer of today's mosque a large amount of freedom to play with the repetition of such individual elements as bays, columns, arches, and courtyards so that in the architecture of the mosque it is hard to find any specific focus or central direction.

The Hammam

Building off the example of Roman baths found in Northern Africa and Mesopotamia, the hammam is a place of ritual washing and ablution. And yet, like mosques, hammams need to be understood in terms of the social function they perform as places of gathering. From this point of view, modern hammams appear more like a corner café or the neighborhood barbershop. In fact, even the earliest Islamic hammams of the seventh century were often built close to residential complexes for this very reason. Over the centuries hammams have been built in urban neighborhoods, stately houses, palaces, and suburbs.

Originally men-only facilities, women gained access to the hammams centuries ago. As early as the twelfth century, a man's refusal to let his wife visit the baths qualified as grounds for divorce in many cities. The typical hammam consists of four interconnected chambers, beginning with a cooler, less humid antechamber, which is followed by a series of connected hot rooms for stretching, exercising, and reclining. Next a narrow passage leads into what is usually the hottest of the rooms, which functions as a vapor bath with a swimming pool in its center. A hammam bather completes the ritual by returning to the first antechamber and relaxing on couches while refreshments are taken. Some historic hammam antechambers still display some of the most decorative surface treatments in world architecture. Even today this tradition of decorative interior design in the antechamber or "cold market" section of the hammam continues. Hammams in Jordan and Morocco are particularly famous for their decorative designs ranging from geometric shapes to floral patterns. A significant feature of the exterior of many hammams, even as they have become smaller and more moderate in size over the centuries, is a distinctive dome or vault.

The Home

Traditional homes in the region are variations on rectangular structures organized around inner courtyards. Called by many in the West the "architecture of the veil," the domestic architecture of the region begins with a facade common to many traditional homes across North Africa and the Middle East.[1] This exterior consists of high, windowless walls with only a single nondescript door to mark the entryway. In many instances, only rooflines were decorated.

In the home as in the mosque, regional architecture reflects a tendency to disdain inherent directional patterns and layouts, which can be quite confusing to foreigners. Because there is no requirement that structures be symmetrical, additions to original structures are relatively easy and inexpensive undertakings. As families grow, for example, new buildings can be added to the traditional courtyard-house complex with minimal disturbance to daily life and routine. If space permits, the traditional homes of wealthy and poor alike have been known to grow into mazes of structures that eventually even engulf the original building. These multistoried courtyard houses are often clustered together with others into walled complexes shared by extended families. These housing complexes are considered by many as multigenerational projects that will never be complete.

Entrance through the front door typically leads to a passageway through which most of the individual rooms of the home can be reached. In traditional homes of the region, for example, a double circulation system can be found in the rest of most domestic structures. Traditionally a guest reception room located near the entrance lobby limits access of unrelated visitors to the female household. This convention is even upheld in ethnic traditions of rural nomadic groups, which make use of a screen or cloth across the center of a tent when unrelated male visitors are present. This guest reception room commonly serves as a place to mark the economic and social success of the family, and is therefore often intricately and ornately decorated; typically it is the most decorative room in the entire house. It is also quite common to find displays of family heirlooms in the guest reception room.

With very little furniture used in traditional Islamic life, decoration and design are used by individuals living within a traditional dwelling to express themselves publicly. Surface decorations, such as cushions and carpets, as well as ceiling and wall decorative schemes that repeat themselves throughout the home, have always been common elements in the traditional home. The traditional courtyard house design and structure is also especially suited to the climates of the region. The open-air interior courtyard performs an important function as a moderator of temperature in hot, arid areas. The typically flat roof and plain exterior walls serve to withstand severe elements such as annual hot sand- and windstorms.

REGIONS OF THE MIDDLE EAST

Tunisia, Algeria, Morocco

Tunisia, located in Northern Africa between the Mediterranean Sea and the Sahara desert, borders Algeria in the west and Libya in the southeast. The north is mountainous with a temperate climate marked by mild, rainy winters and hot, dry summers; the desert is in the south. With a population of just over 10 million inhabitants and a total land area of roughly 164,000 square kilometers, Tunisia has a population density of about sixty-one persons per square kilometer.[2]

Tunisia has four distinct demographic regions: a well-watered, fertile north; a semiarid central plain; the east and coastal olive-growing regions; and a desert south that has little to no vegetation. In the central and southern regions, there are still people who have preserved some cohesion in their communities by following a traditional quasi-nomadic way of life. In the north and along the coast, the population is mixed, especially in cities that have become incredibly crowded over the last century.

Architecture

In fact, Tunisia's few urban centers had effectively absorbed more than three-fifths of the country's population by the late twentieth century. By itself Tunis is home to one out of every nine of the country's residents. Recent attempts by Tunisians to give expression to cultural tradition while using modern materials and designs have drawn inspiration from important historical buildings of the region, such as the Great Mosque of Qairawan. Begun in the eighth century, the Mosque of Qairawan has a plain exterior highlighted by a square, massive minaret. Entrances are cut through a stone wall and lead to a courtyard. In the back of the courtyard is a large hall with two cupolas.

The influence that the Great Mosque has had on architecture in North Africa and the Middle East has been great, and this is particularly true of the popular architecture of Tunis. Today middle-class and wealthy residents typically purchase homes that resemble an ideal implicit in the Great Mosque, for example—little exterior decoration and the interior decoration includes proper ornamentation, such as the extensive use of luster tile and mosaic artwork. The University of Tunis (founded in 1960) is the country's major institution of higher education, and its design has been characterized as chiefly utilitarian and modern. Its basic design was carried over into later higher-education building projects from the 1970s and 1980s, such as the universities opened at Al-Munastir (near Susah) and Safaqis.

Algeria, located in Northern Africa, encompasses 2,381,741 square kilometers of land and lies between Morocco and Tunisia. It is the second largest country in Africa, after Sudan. Algeria's population is roughly 31 million inhabitants, with a population density of about thirteen persons per square kilometer.[3]

Northern Algeria is in a temperate zone and enjoys a comparatively mild climate, typical of the Mediterranean coast. To the east, average temperatures are lower, and on the high plateaus in the central and southern regions, winter temperatures approach freezing. Commercial and domestic structures must all be built to survive the seasonal gale-force sirocco winds that blow inland from the desert.

Chronic housing shortages have plagued Algeria for much of the latter half of the twentieth century. Uninterrupted rural-urban migration and unrestrained population growth has produced the proliferation of urban shantytowns. Traditionally rural domestic architecture in Algeria consisted of widely scattered hamlets and the isolated dwellings of the nomads who live in parts of the Sahara and its fringes. As in other places in Northern Africa, rural settlements are sometimes found at oases as well as around the Aurès Mountains and in other hilltop villages known for their traditional way of life. In 1986 the Algerian government began encouraging local and private housing initiatives in these rural areas. These government-subsidized housing starts were aimed at being affordable for lower-class Algerians so as to address the region's urgent need for housing. These important projects minimized construction costs by working from large prefabricated housing kits.

By contrast, the city of Algiers, which faces east and north, forms a large amphitheatre of dazzling white buildings that dominate the harbor and the bay. The old Turkish section of Algiers is especially notable for the preserved architectural character of its plain walled houses built along the upper slopes of the hills. Narrow and winding streets serve to connect all of the crowded neighborhoods of Algiers. A prominent feature of this part of the city's skyline is the illuminated fortress of the Casbah, which was the residence of the last two Turkish governors of Algiers. In the Muslim section of the city, the construction of the Ketchaoua Mosque in 1962, out of the Cathedral of St. Philip, was an early symbolic attempt by local architects to refuse much of colonial tradition.

Modern attempts at Algerian native architecture can be found in the French section of Algiers. This section extends along the lower slopes of the surrounding hills toward the harbor, and its recent additions include many public squares and wide boulevards, as local architects draw on French colonial inspiration while marking their projects with distinctly Algerian themes and style. Situated in the center of the modern part of the city is the first major modern construction project in Algerian history—the University of Algiers (1879). The newer commercial sections of the city host a number of distinguished foreign embassies and even a few skyscrapers and television towers. Football is the pastime of the region, just as it is in many countries across the world. In many working- and middle-class homes, football is considered to be a family sport. The demand to watch contests has grown steadily since the 1960s and has been a significant driving force in the growth of satellite television across the region. Increasingly modern sports centers have been built that allow locals to do more than participate in a pickup football game with friends; these facilities offer accommodations for hiking, running marathons, and, in some cases, even playing golf and windsurfing.

The city of Oran's Spanish quarter contains the former Cathedral of Saint-Louis (rebuilt by the French in 1838), the Porte de Canastel (reconstructed in 1734), and the fountain in the Place Emerat (1789). The Turkish section of the old town is built around the Great Mosque (1796) and contains several important Algerian architectural structures including the town's citadel built around an old Spanish castle. The former French section of Oran exists outside the second city wall (built in 1866; now largely demolished) and is home to many mid-rise apartment buildings and offices.

Located in Northern Africa, and bordering the Mediterranean Sea and Spain to the north, the Atlantic Ocean to the west, and Algeria to the east, Morocco's area covers roughly 450,000 square kilometers. Most of the coastal terrain north of the western Sahara—where most of the region's 33 million inhabitants reside—experiences a typical Mediterranean climate, with dry, searing summers and mild, wet winters. This area's wet winter season extends from October to April. The general concentration of Morocco's population in and near coastal regions brings its population density to seventy persons per square kilometer.[4]

In rural areas, some Moroccans still reside in *ksour* (fortified adobe villages) and agricultural villages. For many years the government tried to discourage the development of bidonvilles ("tin can cities") and other spontaneous settlements that often appear on the boundaries of many urban areas in the region. Toward the end of the twentieth century, this trend of governmental opposition to shanty housing shifted significantly in the direction of providing basic resources to existing structures. The largest of the Moroccan government bidonville projects to date have succeeded in bringing water, electricity, and basic service facilities to many of these areas. In addition, as in other countries in the region, the Moroccan government has offered attractive special financing arrangements as incentives for encouraging local residents to improve their buildings. The highland areas surrounding the Rif and the Atlas mountain ranges are home to about a fifth of the population and are perceived as centers of traditional Moroccan culture. Local villages were originally built out of a need for tribal defense, so it is not uncommon to find villages built into the sides of hills. Dwellings in this region are often multistoried, built of adobe and stone, and constructed in tight clusters for extended family. During the 1990s and continuing today, private developers have worked in tandem with government officials on the promotion of new housing construction starts in this area of Morocco, as well as in the populous coastal region. Most of these housing starts have been middle-class prefabricated dwellings that continue to remain outside the financial reach of many of the country's working poor.

Since 1980, many of Morocco's cities have undergone public projects to preserve at least some of their traditional character. Preserving this character has become increasingly difficult because more than half the population now lives in urban areas. Rabat, for example, is the national capital and sits on the Atlantic coast and the Bou Regreg River. Its "Old Town,"

Architecture

or medina, is still surrounded by ramparts. Within its walls a visitor can still find its ancient Muslim center or medina as well as its equally historic Jewish quarter, the millah. Southeast of the old town are a number of outstanding historical structures that give the Rabat skyline its signature look. The twelfth-century tower of Hassan minaret can be seen across the city; and the ruins of the mosque of Abu Yusuf Yaqub al-Mansur serve as excellent examples of Moroccan traditional style, as does the ar-Rouah city gate. The Casbah des Oudaia, a nearby seventeenth-century fortress, remains an important architectural influence in the country, with images of its iconic twelfth-century gateway and garden repeating themselves in local contemporary designs. In addition to the famous Almohad gateway, the Casbah is also home to a madrassa that houses a museum of Moroccan art.

The modern sections of Rabat remain partly enclosed behind the historic fortified wall, and local architecture in relatively recent times has moved toward more modern structures, with examples such as the royal palace (built in the 1950s), Muhammad V University (built 1956–57), a national library, and various administrative buildings. These modern construction projects have entirely reshaped the southern outskirts of this ancient city. Casablanca, Morocco's most famous city, is like Rabat in that it remains partially enclosed by its original rampart walls. Here the mazes of narrow streets that are common in North Africa are lined with whitewashed brick houses that give many local buildings an ancient look. A diverse mixture of traditions and materials, including, most recently, the long French colonialization, have gone into making modern Casablanca what it is today. Traditional stone architecture exists literally next door to nineteenth-century wide colonial boulevards; Art Deco town houses and Art Nouveau film palaces sit next to Neo-Moorish, palm-lined colonnades. Casablanca's skyline is dominated by the 656-foot minaret of the Mosque of Hassan II. Along with the title of world's tallest minaret, the Hassan II Mosque also has the distinction of being the third largest mosque in the world. Finished in 1993, the Hassan II Mosque required that nearly 10,000 skilled artisans and craftsmen work for over six years.[5] Many of the commercial construction projects started in Casablanca since 1990 have been aimed primarily at resurrecting revered structures and bringing money back into the city's aging center and neighborhoods by converting existing structures into cafés and specialty boutiques.

Nightlife in Morocco is split between the flourishing club scenes of Marrakech and Casablanca; this activity keeps areas of these cities alive with both new commercial development and resurrection of the old. In Casablanca's Gauthier district, Art Deco buildings in various conditions abound. And, in the city's downtown, the Art Deco Rialto Theater and Hotel Transatlantique remain important landmarks. Marrakech is widely viewed as the "Entertainment Capital" of Morocco. In general, the city lacks significant historical architecture, but as a vibrant metropolis, Marrakech is also the hottest spot in the country to purchase a home at this time. Villas and apartments, as well as traditional courtyard homes, are the most popular new housing starts. Both Marrakech and Casablanca have experienced a boom in luxury hotel construction as well, with nearly 80,000 new hotel rooms scheduled to be built by 2010—the projected year Morocco will enter into the Euro-Med Free Trade Zone agreement. This growth in luxury resort and tourism, and the construction of six new coastal resorts, is predicted to create approximately 600,000 jobs over the course of the next four years.[6]

Libya

Libya's terrain is mostly barren, marked by flat to undulating plains punctuated by plateaus and depressions. Because of its size and varied terrain, it is divided into at least five different climatic zones, but the dominant climatic influences are Mediterranean and Saharan.

The old walled city of Tripoli, one of Libya's most important urban centers, is a picturesque maze of narrow alleyways leading to traditional mosques, small inns, and private houses. Turkish, Maltese, Spanish, and Italian influences can be found throughout the architecture of everyday life in Libya, which is to be expected in light of the country's turbulent history and many foreign occupiers. Known for its many vibrant souqs, especially around the medina or city center, Tripoli has also set an important example in North Africa in its attempts to restore and incorporate relics of architecture from the city's important past into the modern metropolis it is becoming. Important structures such as the ancient Marcus Aurelian Arch and the Al Nagha mosque have undergone attempted restorations with varying degrees of success and have been become part of modern Tripoli's tourism and cultural life. In most of Libya's modern urban housing developments, functionality has been stressed above detail. The end products are largely featureless homes and apartments. These public building projects dot Libya's urban areas and are distinctive for the plainness of their design, which leaves the structures looking like simple cement boxes.

Outside of the major population centers that exist along the valley, close to the Mediterranean, the architecture of everyday life changes substantially. Ghadames, for example, has been called the "Pearl of the Desert" and is located in a desert oasis town 500 miles southwest of Tripoli. This small, ancient town's architecture is famous for the broad, whitewashed mud walls that surround it, as well as the covered walkways lit by skylights and open squares that cut a labyrinth out of the homes, stores, and stalls.

The vast majority of Libya's rural population lives in coastal oases and is engaged in farming based on irrigation; plots of land are generally held in individual ownership and are often small. Land ownership in these areas is no longer exclusively tribal, and three to four individual tenant families typically share smaller farms that average five to seven acres per unit. Along the lowlands of the coast, Libyan farmers typically live on their own land while maintaining rights to graze their stock and cultivate grain on community-shared land. In contrast, in both the east and the west, Arab farmers occupy large, formerly European estates, in which individual units range from 12 to 600 acres.

Libya's libraries and museums include the Government Library and the Archives in Tripoli, the Public Library in Benghazi, and the university libraries. In the major urban areas such as Benghazi and Tripoli, shopping, entertainment, and social gatherings are often focused around cafeterias and coffee shops, as well as restaurants accommodating both local and international tastes. In addition, there are now many completely modern indoor and outdoor theaters and amphitheaters that are used primarily for sporting events, as well as for special music concerts.

Egypt

Typically divided between its upper and lower regions, Egypt covers 1,001,449 square kilometers of land, with a landscape dominated by desert terrain. Almost half of Egypt's nearly 68 million residents live in urban areas along the banks of the Nile. Population density estimates of these Egyptian urban centers, which approach 1,100 persons per square kilometer, mark these areas as some of the most highly dense regions in the world.[7]

Lower Egypt's landscape is dominated by the Nile Delta. The delta region is well watered and crisscrossed by channels, canals, and marshes. The climate is milder than the climate in Upper Egypt, with the Nile Delta region receiving more rainfall than the entirety of Upper Egypt. The mild climate has made Lower Egypt the historical center of population growth.

ARCHITECTURE

HASSAN FATHY (1899–1989)

Hassan Fathy is perhaps the most influential popular architect for all of North Africa and the Middle East during the twentieth century. In his designs and architectural philosophy, he worked for the benefit of the poor in Upper Egypt and the more wealthy in Lower Egypt. His architecture was well received by international critics, but he received praise at home only more recently, in the years following his death. The driving force behind much of Fathy's work was the need to develop human solutions to the problems of housing shortages that especially hurt the working poor of developing nations. Climate, insisted Fathy, must be a central factor in all design. In Egypt and elsewhere in Northern Africa and the Middle East, Fathy's designs returned to the iconic dense brick walls around traditional courtyards as a way to take advantage of the passive cooling effects of channeled wind. His work continues to be the subject of much scholarship and debate, and his ideas on urban architecture have influenced many countries and development projects in the region. Fathy's practicality led him ultimately to favor the creation of "indigenous" structural environments (both domestic and commercial) that cost as little as possible. To create such indigenous environments, Fathy made use of traditional design methods and materials whenever possible. He even trained the inhabitants of local areas to construct their own buildings from native materials. These efforts were part of his general philosophy; he saw his architectural projects as part of a larger effort to improve the economy and standard of living of the world's poor.

This trend has continued in more recent years with Lower Egypt becoming the focus of much of Egypt's industrialization and commerce with the rest of the world.

Faced with serious continuous urban housing shortages since World War II, the housing problems of Egypt have been aggravated in recent years by increased immigration from rural to urban areas, resulting in extreme overcrowding. In these overcrowded urban areas, there is little evidence of town or city planning or of adherence to building regulations; often mud village houses are clinched within the confines of city walls. Private homes in smaller cities and villages are typically two-story houses or apartment blocks four to six stories high. The more wealthy residents' homes are often identified by a distinctive lime washing and flat roofs with numerous balconies. In working-class and poor neighborhoods, these private dwellings are often constructed of unpainted concrete and red brick.

Telling the complete story of Cairo's architecture would require a history lesson of more than 1,000 years. Contemporary Cairo is complex and crowded. It is also Western and metropolitan in appearance. In contrast to its modern skyscrapers and high-rise residential complexes, it is still possible to find preserved examples of traditional Egyptian elegance, even if they have contemporary touches, such as modern communications, lighting, and heating. A shady courtyard in a fine *Mamluk* house in Cairo is the epitome of desirable townhouse architecture in many of the largest commercial centers across North Africa. Typically constructed of fine verdant stone ashlar, these courtyards repeat many of the elements of the traditional Arabic private house.

By contrast, an Egyptian rural settlement is usually a compact village surrounded by heavily cultivated fields. Village populations vary from small communities of no more than 500 to impressive small towns of more than 10,000 residents. In these rural villages domestic architecture remains much as it has for the last millennium. Across these villages there are basic commonalities of physical appearance and design, but it is typical for particular villages and communities to exercise shared local variations in building materials, design, and decoration. The villages located around the Nile Delta region contain houses that are typically one or two stories high. These structures are generally built from local materials such as baked mud bricks and mud and straw plaster in the north and stone in the southern Nile valley. Often these homes are joined together in a continuous row. These row houses are often constructed with few openings in order to control the flow of light and air. The distinctive flat roofs are used to store corn stalks as well as provide outdoor sleeping quarters at certain times of the year. Constructed out of dried date leaves and palm rafters, the roofs of these rural homes often have silos that can be sealed built on top.

The private homes of the area's poorest residents typically consist of a single bedroom, a passageway, and a courtyard; part of the courtyard may be used as an enclosure for farm animals. Mud brick ovens are built into the wall of the courtyard or even inside the house. The oldest homes still occupied in the oases areas of Egypt can reach up to six stories in height. Made of packed mud, these fortified homes were originally clustered close together for defense. More modern private homes in these same areas today are usually no more than two stories high and are built much farther apart than the earlier structures, with ample room for courtyards and even small pools.

In wealthy and affluent villages, houses are built of burnt bricks reinforced with concrete and are generally more spacious than older homes. Extended family members often live under one roof. Running water, multiple bathrooms, electricity, and contemporary furniture are increasingly commonplace and are no longer signs of special prosperity. Even modern building standards and requirements have reached the most isolated settlements of Egypt through government-planned "combined service units." In these remote and often desolate settlements, one can find a number of modern buildings, such as a health station, a school, a social service unit, and a cooperative marketplace. Many travelers have remarked on the striking contrast one feels upon seeing these modern facilities amid the mud houses of the village.

Shopping centers, resort projects, and entertainment districts in major cities in Egypt have been following Western design theory and principles since the 1950s. In more recent years, many prominent Egyptian architects and designers have denounced this practice as nothing more than a bald appeal to Western investors. In response, there has been a growing movement in the commercial architecture of major centers like Cairo toward surface treatment architecture intended to cover-up the telltale signs of Western commercial construction. This practice, often called "facade architecture," began seriously in the 1970s and continues today, although it does not occur as frequently as it once did. "Facade architecture" is a commercial developmental strategy that attempts to excite public imagination through the construction of building fronts that graft some distinctive local flavor and symbol onto the shell of a building constructed in a predominantly Western style. Once a very common practice—such as in the Cairo and Alexandria shopping malls or strategic building renewal projects in other urban areas—facade architecture has increasingly been criticized by contemporary Egyptian architects as being silly and heavy-handed and not at all authentically Egyptian.

The cooler temperatures of Alexandria during the summer have made the city an increasingly popular resort destination for wealthy locals and tourists alike. In 2002 the Bibliotheca Alexandrina opened near the site of the ancient Library of Alexandria following a vigorous international design competition. The design that was selected called for a colossal structure embodying Fathy's "indigenous architecture." The bibliotheca consists of a complex of libraries, art galleries, and museums, as well as a planetarium and an ancient document preservation laboratory. The main library is built to contain 8 million volumes over eight levels, with a distinctive main reading room whose walls jut out toward the sea, supporting a 32-meter-high, glass-paneled ceiling. The walls of the library are distinctive gray granite from the Aswan area. Much like Alexandria, Sharm El Sheikh continues to transform itself into a modern Red Sea beach-resort community with a modern airport and hospital, as well as shops, hotels, and restaurants, all in a modern style. Property investment has increased in the Red Sea resort centers for the last several years.

Jordan

Sharing borders with Syria, Iraq, Saudi Arabia, and Israel and the Palestinian Territories, Jordan has an area of about 90,000 kilometers. With a population of nearly 6 million residents and a population density of about sixty persons per square kilometer, the country can be divided between the western highlands that share a Mediterranean climate similar to the countries of the Levant, and the rest of the country that shares a dry, arid climate with hot summers and cool winters.[8]

Like many of its neighboring countries, Jordan's newest housing developments have left its urban areas a curious mix of the modern and the traditional. In today's Jordan, overcrowded urban buildings that are jumbled together serve as the primary residences for much of the lower- to middle-class and poor people. At the same time, these large and decaying buildings coexist alongside luxuriant stone villas, supermarkets, and specialty boutiques.

Many of Jordan's existing hotels were developed in the late 1970s and early 1980s to serve the needs of business travelers. Unlike comparable Israeli resorts, however, Jordanian hotels have only recently begun to attract leisure visitors. A recent wave of speculative development during the late 1990s brought in many new international hotel chains; many investors see Jordan as a potential center of regional and international recreational tourism, when and if the threats in the region subside. The Swiss group Mövenpick has been particularly active in Jordan since the turn of the twenty-first century, with new hotels under construction or planned in Petra, the Dead Sea, Amman, and Aqaba. South of Aqaba a major tourism development zone has been planned for several years. This zone will include major world-class resorts that in some cases will accommodate up to 5,000 rooms. Tourism development and planning has also reached the Dead Sea region, with recent construction on a "Lowest Park on Earth." When completed, this second tourism zone is slated to include several major Western hotel projects by important international corporate chains such as Hilton and Holiday Inn.

For example, the Mövenpick Resort and Spa in the Dead Sea area has been designed to nearly disappear into its surroundings, including the vast expanses of the Jordanian desert. Its exterior architecture was inspired by traditional Jordanian stone fortresses, and the resort was built to closely follow this traditional style, complete with the use of local materials. The scarcity of water has guaranteed that water symbols and motifs will have a prominent place in traditional Islamic interior ornamentation, and in many Jordanian resorts, these features abound. The Mövenpick Resort reflects this traditional motif through the repeated use of waves and similar designs built into many of its interior surfaces such as tables, lamps, and walls. In the more luxurious hotels and resorts, ornate mosaics and wooden shades serve both as decorative room treatments and as ways to regulate temperature and control light. Increasingly common in Jordan's finest hotels, and even in some of its "not so finest," are indoor/outdoor pools that combine massage jets and variable salt concentration control.

Israel

Israel borders the West Bank to the east and Egypt and the Gaza Strip to the south, and, with a population of roughly 7 million, has a population density over 300 persons per square kilometer.[9] Israel's coastline and northern sections are marked by a Mediterranean climate, whereas its eastern and southern areas are characterized by subtropical aridity.

Israel's rural population constitutes less than one-tenth of the nation's total inhabitants.[10] Only a tiny fraction of Israel's Arab population lives in rural areas, and those who do are either Bedouins or residents of small agricultural villages. The Jewish rural settlements are organized into two different types of agricultural cooperatives known as kibbutzim and moshavim; a small number of Jewish agricultural communities also exist, and there are a scant number of individually owned farms engaged in private production.

Kibbutzim are marked by communal living and cooperative agricultural work (although a few have ventured into other types of manufacturing). Many kibbutzim have modern kitchens, swimming pools, and gymnasiums, and also boast art galleries, concert halls, and cultural centers. A moshav also functions as a collective, although residents are more independent than those of a kibbutz, with each family owning its own farmland and home. Still, purchasing and selling are both done cooperatively. The moshav is typically designed so that a number of small villages surround a central town, which functions as an administrative center. These central towns also boast schools, concert halls, and theaters.

The great majority of the population, both Jewish and Arab, reside in urban areas. The government has made great efforts to prevent overpopulation of these areas, overseeing in both the north and south the development of new towns occupied largely by the country's most recent immigrants. Israel's massive wave of building in recent years, stemming mainly from the need to house new immigrants from the former Soviet Union, threatens to permanently alter the landscape. Increasingly land previously zoned for agricultural use has been designated for new building use. The neighborhoods constructed in these areas are now increasingly established and are easily recognized as a sea of red-roofed homes (sometimes three or four levels). Many of these neighborhoods can be found both in the hill country of Judea as well as along the seacoast.

In Afula and "Upper Nazareth" (twin to the predominantly Arab old town of Nazareth), both built on fairly steep hillsides in Galilee, massive eight-story apartment buildings mark the slopes, with concrete bridges reaching out from the entrance on the fourth or fifth floor of each building to connect with the sidewalks. On the ground floors of lower, more massive buildings, shops are built. In the 1960s ambitious government-sponsored architectural projects were undertaken across the country. In many cities such as Beersheva, groups of apartment buildings were organized in squares around small, district shopping centers, with some of the stores and passageways for pedestrians located in the bottom of the apartment houses themselves. Each apartment has a private patio, and common areas are marked by pyramid-enclosed covered walkways and play areas. Many of these large-scale projects and experiments in communal living failed to produce the kinds of results desired and were canceled by the 1970s.

One-third of Israel's population lives in the commercial and cultural center of Tel Aviv, and the city bustles with restaurants, art galleries, museums, and beaches. Tel Aviv's most distinctive buildings have led many to call it an open museum of the International style in architecture. Tel Aviv was a budding population center at the same time the modernist movement in architecture had reached its peak in Europe and the United States; as a result many of the architects working in the new city center were drawn to the architectural theories of Le Corbusier and the Bauhaus School. For example, the Herzliya Gymnasium in Tel Aviv, designed by Yosef Berski in 1910, displays features from Mesopotamia and local Arabic elements inside the contours of a monumental European building.

A serious attempt to come to grips with the local building tradition is apparent in the Supreme Court Building in Jerusalem, designed by Ram Carmi and Ada Carmi-Melamede and opened in 1992. The structure moves beyond function and incorporates a wide-range of references to many different traditions and motifs in Israeli building. With open-air atriums offering a striking contrast between human made and surrounding natural beauty, this much celebrated building is a complex, almost baroque structure that is both straight and round, as well as narrow and wide. As if to suggest that the structure was built entirely in contrast, the open-air walkways and atriums produce distinct geometrical patterns of light and shade across the concrete and marble flooring through the course of the day.

Tourism in Israel has increased significantly in the past decade, and visitors are drawn to numerous religious, archeological, and historic sites. The Hyatt Regency Jerusalem (designed by David Resnick) and the Eilat Princess Hotel are two of the most architecturally interesting of the newer mega-hotels in Israel. The Eilat Princess Hotel, for example, opened in 1993 and is built into a hillside facing the Red Sea, a few miles south of downtown Eilat. The Princess is billed as a self-sufficient tourist haven, and like many other modern hotels in Israel, it was designed to include all modern recreational facilities, as well as restaurants, swimming pools, and even a nightclub. The growth of regional mega-hotels has started to establish a new level of style in Israeli hotel design, calling for buildings that are at home in their surrounding natural environment while providing hundreds of guest rooms complete with all modern amenities, including the Internet.

The Palestinian Territories: The West Bank and Gaza Strip

The area of the Palestinian Territories is a little more than 6,000 square kilometers: 5,640 square kilometers in the West Bank and 365 square kilometers in Gaza Strip. The Gaza Strip, with a flat to rolling, sand- and dune-covered coastal plain, has a population of about 1.5 million residents and features a temperate climate. The West Bank, with just over 2 million residents, is marked by a rugged dissected upland with some vegetation in the west, although it is mostly barren in the east. The West Bank climate is temperate, although rain and annual temperature do vary with altitude.[11] Gaza's population density is nearly 3,000 persons per square kilometer, which is the highest rate in the world; in the West Bank, the density is just under 300 persons per square kilometer.[12] In light of limited access to resources such as land, the area's high population density has resulted in stagnant economic conditions, and internal and external political events have continued to keep the local economies at or near subsistence levels. With its particularly high population density, the economy and architectural infrastructure of the Gaza Strip has suffered even more than similar institutions in the West Bank.

Seventy percent of West Bank and Gaza Strip Palestinians live in villages of 5,000 inhabitants or fewer. Fifteen percent live in refugee camps, and about 15 percent live in cities; the number of Bedouins who still live in tents and rely on grazing cattle is small. The region encompasses more than thirty municipalities, but only fourteen of these can be called "cities," with populations of more than 20,000 persons. A modest middle-class home typical of housing in the region (although such a home is an increasingly rare find in Palestinian Authority-controlled territories) would cost, in U.S. dollars, $42,000 in the West Bank, $37,000 in Gaza, and $28,000 in Jordan.[13] The standard design averages 120 square meters, divided between a living room, three bedrooms, a kitchen, and bathroom, for a household of six to seven persons. In established settlements, even poorer families aspire to such a "typical" dwelling, saving their resources over time and building additions onto their structures incrementally.

Any discussion of the popular architecture of the Palestinian territories must include reference to the region's ongoing refugee crisis. Over half of the population of the region is composed of refugees sent away from their family homes as an immediate result of the 1948 war with Israel. The refugees constitute 77 percent of the Gaza Strip population and 37 percent of the West Bank population. More than 500,000 refugees still live in overpopulated camps with minimal services that can only be maintained with the periodic assistance of United Nations relief agencies. More than 350,000 refugees live in eight camps in the Gaza Strip.[14] The camps have grown over the past 50 years and have become midsized and citylike with schools, clinics, and markets, but life circumstances are still very bad. The camps are severely overcrowded, and the spread of intestinal diseases due to the absence of drainage systems prevails. In most camps, water flows in the streets in open ducts.

Camps range from those in which there is only an old rudimentary water reticulation system, no piped sewerage, unpaved roads and footpaths, and no surface drainage system, to those with water, sewerage and drainage systems, and paved and drained roads and footpaths.

The middle zone is one of the most highly populated areas in the Gaza Strip, with more than 200,000 residents. Here, there is one stadium, al-Dora, and one closed athletic hall, Hassan Salama, although both offer only the most rudimentary accommodations. The athletic clubs of the middle zone suffer from lack of playgrounds, and most of the clubs do not offer anyplace to train teams for current or upcoming competitions. The clubs cater to men of all age groups, although more cater to adults than youth. The Ministry of Sport and Youth is working to put an end to this situation and is trying to find the space to build new stadiums and athletic halls. Financial needs, lack of grounds, and Israeli seizure of land are all hindrances to this goal. Another problem is lack of security for sports club members, as clubs have been attacked by Israeli settlers. At times attacks have turned to the demolition of facilities, with major sports stadiums and surrounding buildings becoming the accidental object of Israeli missile strikes.

The small resort, hotel, and entertainment industry of the region has succeeded in experiencing minor growth even where more commercial developments have not. After the establishment of the Palestinian Authority in 1995, beach clubs, resorts, and even a few modern Western hotels started to open along the sunny Gaza coast. The Palestinian Authority has pushed through special tax laws to encourage local and foreign investors to build even more. The Nawas Beach Club, owned by Palestinian writer Abdel Karim Sabaweh, screens movies in a plain utilitarian building. In contrast, the Al Kasaba Theatre and Cinematheque, located in Ramallah City, are wonderful examples of the playful use of bright colors that are typical in Palestinian culture. Due to its long-standing conflict with its neighbor Israel, access to popular entertainment structures in the Palestinian Territories has been severely limited, with the Al Kasaba remaining one of its only fully equipped professional theaters. Combining Art Deco and Mediterranean design, the Al Kasaba is an important cultural site in the territories, screening Egyptian and European films and hosting local musicians and theatrical productions.

Although it is difficult to estimate tourist statistics, Gaza presently boasts twelve hotels and beach resorts. Most of Gaza's resorts are situated on the dunes at the northern coast, between Gaza City and the Israeli border. In recent years, there has been talk about developing the archaeological sites in and around Gaza as a fuel for tourism. Many of the local archaeological digs date back to at least the Byzantine period, and public officials hope that historical tourism will increase as sites such as the Byzantine cemetery and basilica near a resettlement camp at Jabalya become fully restored. Two historic harbors have also been excavated for tourism. These sites exhibit the beautiful traditions of Palestinian ethnic design, such as the use of colorful mosaic.

Architecture

Lebanon

Lebanon borders the Mediterranean Sea on the west, Israel on the south, and Syria on the east and north. Its population is approximately 3,900,000.[15] Most of the population (more than 2 million) lives in and around Beirut. Like Israel, Lebanon's coastline has a Mediterranean climate, but its eastern areas are more arid.

Like other countries in the Middle East, Lebanon contains impressive buildings of antiquity. Beirut, often described as the Paris of the Middle East, is a beautiful and sophisticated city, but it also suffers from urban crowding and decaying and destroyed houses and buildings. After the civil war in Lebanon ended in 1990, a plan for reconstruction began, especially in Beirut, but reconstruction has been hampered by even more strife, including, most recently, damage from the 2006 war between the Hezbollah in Lebanon and Israel. This situation will only exacerbate the housing shortage already in existence, especially for those who cannot afford to live in the more expensive housing erected in the urban areas in the last 10 years.

Pierre El Khoury of Beirut is perhaps the best known of current Lebanese architects. His career of more than 50 years has included more than 200 projects, including museums, libraries, public gardens, universities, office buildings, and more.

Iraq

Located in southwestern Asia, Iraq shares borders with Saudi Arabia and Kuwait to the south, Jordan to the west, Syria to the northwest, Turkey to the north, and Iran to the east. It encompasses the northwestern part of the Zagros mountain range and the eastern part of the Syrian desert. Iraq's population is approaching 23 million, and its population density stands at just under fifty-two people per square kilometer.[16] Much of the country is characterized by mild to cool winters and dry, hot, rainless summers. In the northern mountainous areas of the country, cold winters with occasional heavy snows are common. Average temperatures in July can get higher than 120 degrees Fahrenheit and drop to below freezing in January. Most of the rainfall occurs from December through April.[17]

The modern history of Iraq is dominated by war, colonial invasions, and political instability, and war continues to ravage daily life in contemporary Iraq. Following the second Persian Gulf War that began in 2003, there are few aspects of daily social life that can be said to be unaffected by shortages of water and electricity, as well as damaged infrastructure and postwar guerrilla violence. Even so, the twentieth century has been a time of rapid development in Iraq, with urban growth accelerating social change and the increased assimilation of secular and largely Westernized lifestyles.

The availability of adequate housing remains a problem in Iraq at the beginning of the twenty-first century. One source of this housing shortage has been the large number of ethnic Shiites who have fled from the south of Iraq into an already overcrowded Baghdad; also, large groups of Kurds and Assyrians had been displaced by government policy during the 1970s and 1980s. Access to adequate water, electricity, and sanitation remains perhaps the most serious problem both in new housing construction and in existing residences. As increasing numbers of immigrants make the move from rural areas to urban ones, many people have been forced to live in large urban slums that exist on the boundaries of the urban centers. These urban slums lack almost every modern convenience. Even those persons displaced in the north by government policy in the 1970s and 1980s often had to live in less than desirable residences, including tents and shantytowns.

Domestic architecture of the region shows distinct variations, but the basic house types are similar to those of neighboring Arab countries. Mud brick continues to be common throughout the south, with stone used more extensively in the north. Some of the larger villages are surrounded by mud-brick walls. Unique to Iraq are the traditional reed houses, with their barrel-vaulted roofs, of the marsh dwellers of the Al Amarah area.

The Baath political party, which held power in Iraq from 1968 to 2003, attempted to influence the direction of the urban development and popular architecture of the region through sponsorship of architects, engineers, artists, sculptors, and others. The central goal of these programs was to encourage builders and designers to clearly highlight the cultural connection between the modern Iraqi people and the ancient peoples and civilizations of Mesopotamia. As a result, impressive museums, especially archaeological museums, were built in every governorate. Even more, a European-style version of Babylon was built on that civilization's ancient ruins as part of this general government program. The government also funded such metropolitan projects as the Babylon International Festival, held every September in a reconstructed Hellenistic theatre.

Other notable museums and cultural buildings of Iraq are the Iraq Museum (built in 1923), the National Library (built in 1961), and the Central Bank of Baghdad (built in 1985). This high-rise concrete structure surrounds a large interior courtyard and sits in the center of the city near the Emir's Palace. Despite sustaining damage during the first and second Gulf Wars, these buildings strongly exhibit the original Baathist cultural plan of highlighting the Mesopotamian heritage of the region. Baghdad also has some excellent examples of buildings from the golden age of Abbasid architecture in the eighth and ninth centuries, as well as from the various Ottoman periods. During the 1970s, the government undertook an extensive effort to renovate many of these historical buildings—and even whole streets.

Modern Iraqi architects, such as Mohamed Saleh Makiya and Rifat Chadirji, have exerted influence inside Iraq and in the Arab countries of the region more generally. And yet, in a trend that holds throughout the region, many of the major public building projects of the last 80 years have been designed by foreign architects. Even in the years following the second Gulf War and the U.S. occupation aimed at liberating Iraq from the Baathists, broad areas of planning and large-scale construction remained in the hands of architects from the United States, Greece, England, and Scandinavia.

Perhaps more than any other single Iraqi, Mohamed Saleh Makiya is responsible for the look and design of the commercial and residential buildings of modern Iraq, including bank buildings in Basra and Mosul (both built in 1966), and Kerbala and Al-Kufa (both built in 1968). As an illustration of Makiya's vision that historical elements must be synthesized with

> **MOHAMED SALEH MAKIYA (1914–PRESENT)**
>
> Makiya's work stands out in the modern history of architecture not just in Iraq, but across the region generally. Like Hassan Fathy in Egypt, Makiya incorporated Iraq's historical patterns and symbols in his very contemporary architectural designs. The author of several books on Arab architecture, Makiya was educated in both Baghdad and Liverpool, in the United Kingdom, leaving Iraq and taking up permanent residence in London in 1975. Makiya's work inside Iraq centered on a theme of cultural harmony and stressed Iraq's unique traditions as the source of its citizens' cultural identity and unity. Some of his major projects in Iraq included Baghdad University (1965), the Theology College or madrassa in Baghdad (1966), and the ceremonial parade grounds in Tikrit. In each of these examples, Makiya treats the traditions of the Iraqi people as living and growing entities and not as simple ornaments for modern structures. A shared ideal of many mid- to late twentieth-century Iraqi architects has been the quest for a "continuous architecture" linking past and present.

modern building materials and styles, these buildings exhibit traditional motifs, such as the setback windows and the use of blue tiles on exterior walls on the bank building of Kerbala. As a reminder of Iraq's current wartorn history, this renowned commercial building was completely demolished in the first Gulf War.

Other telling examples of significant commercial and cultural buildings constructed in modern Iraq include the Baghdad Conference Palace (built between 1978 and 1982), the Baghdad Island Recreational Area (built in 1984), and the Al-Karame General Hospital (built in 1980).

Iran

Located in Southwest Asia and bordering the Gulf of Oman, the Caspian Sea, and the Persian Gulf, Iran is one of the world's most mountainous countries. Iran's 1,648,000 square kilometers place it sixteenth in size among world countries. Given its size and distinctive terrain, the climate of the country is variable, with cold winters and heavy snowfalls in the northwest and mild winters and hot summers (average daily temperatures in July exceeding 100 degrees Fahrenheit) in the south.[18]

With a population approaching 70 million, Iran has a relatively low population density.[19] Persian culture is dominant in Iran, and yet Iran remains a multiethnic state with small minorities of Armenians, Kurds, and Azerbaijanis who continue to keep alive their own unique traditions (including their architectural ones). An increase in public literacy has been a major trend in twentieth-century Iran, with four-fifths of Iranians able to read and write in 2006.[20]

The flow of population to the cities following the creation of major railways and highways has created serious housing shortages, and only in the 1990s did the Iranian government begin to address the housing crisis. It has attempted to accomplish this largely by providing government credits for private-sector development. However, most of the nation's energies have been devoted to urban development—mostly in the larger cities, particularly Tehran—and habitation in rural areas remains austere in both design and ornamentation.

In major Iranian cities, construction of broad avenues and ring roads to accommodate modern traffic, shopping, and daily life has changed much of the appearance of the traditional population centers with their old labyrinthine crooked and narrow streets and cul-de-sacs. Yet, as an example of the integration of the old and new, Iran's popular architecture continues to make use of structures such as the arched porches and openings called *iwans* in even the most recent construction of mosques, schools, and private homes.

In urban Iran, housing styles of the rich and poor alike follow many of the basic principles that characterize the country. Wealthy apartment complexes are often built with main halls leading to private apartments that further open out into smaller courtyards and ceramic and stucco baths. Increasingly town houses are being built in many places, such as in important historical cities like Isfahan. Despite the use of modern construction methods and materials, these town houses attempt to incorporate the elements of Middle Eastern and especially Islamic architecture into the design of the domestic environment, including sheltered courtyards with trees, pools, and sparing use of outdoor furniture. Many modern dwellings both urban and rural continue to follow a traditional style, with domed-roof structures constructed of mud brick or stone that are built around closed courtyards with a garden and a pool.

Public baths are found in all sections of cities. Recent trends in the design and construction of the hammam are well illustrated in the restoration of the Ali Gholi bathhouse in downtown Isfahan. Isfahan is considered one of the most significant architectural centers in all of Iran, with its "Imam's Square" (measuring 1,674 by 540 feet), located at the center of the city, and its "Royal Mosque," begun in 1612 and decorated with enameled tiles that have been faithfully restored in recent years.

Iran's only gallery devoted solely to art, the Tehran Museum of Modern Art, opened in 1977. As with other regional museums, such as the National Museum (built in 1937) and Negarestan (built in 1975), this museum's architecture is striking for the way it attempts to straddle two diverse cultural influences of the area. A central concern of contemporary Iranian architects—especially after the Islamic revolution of 1979—centers on whether they will be perceived as too "Western" in their attempt to express an authentic Iranian identity that makes sense in light of contemporary history and events.

In rural Iran, population groups are separated from one another by deep gorges, deserts, and *kavirs*, producing insularity among local people. In these secluded areas, felt yurts, the black tents of the Bakhtyari, and the osier huts of the Balochi are typical, as they allow local tribespeople to roam from summer to winter pastures.

Oasis settlements stretch across the central plains of Iran. From 1950 onward, the migrations of local nomadic people in this area ended, leaving permanent settlements of iconic hemispherical huts. The structures of these rural villages continue to follow a traditional pattern: high mud walls with corner towers form the outer face of the houses, which have flat roofs of mud and straw supported by wooden rafters. In these rural areas, houses are often two-story, square, windowless structures made of mud brick. A single hole in a flat or domed roof allows for light and ventilation. Additionally, a mosque is often situated in the open center of the village and also serves as the madrassa. Villagers along the Caspian Sea live predominantly in small hamlets that serve as a primary private dwelling. Small self-contained units, these hamlets typically consist of a series of outbuildings (such as silkworm houses and barns) that, along with a two-story wooden house, form an open courtyard.

United Arab Emirates, Kuwait, Bahrain

Covering approximately 83,000 square kilometers and divided among seven states, the United Arab Emirates (UAE) is characterized by a mountainous eastern border and a flat coastal plain that merges into a nearly uninhabitable desert region. Annual rainfall is minimal and mostly occurs between November and March. Temperatures are very high between May and September and warm to mild for the rest of the year.[21]

Boasting over 2.5 million residents, the population of the UAE is one of the fastest growing in the world; it has more than quadrupled over the past 25 years. Its population density stands at just over twenty-eight persons per square kilometer. Of particular significance to the development of the popular architecture of the region is the fact that nearly three-fourths of UAE residents are noncitizen guest workers.[22]

Today the UAE is the location of some of the world's most ambitious architectural projects, including modern shopping complexes, resorts, and large residential buildings such as the Three Palm Islands, the Dubai Marina, and Jumeirah Lake Towers. Like other countries in the Middle East, UAE popular residential and commercial design and construction must take into consideration the extremes of climate and the frequent sand and dust storms typical of the region. For example, air-conditioning is commonplace both in private residences as well as commercial centers.

During the winter and early summer months, winds called the Shamal bring dust and sand into the business and population centers from the north. As a consequence, as the residents have migrated to urban areas, construction of private homes and dwellings has been increasingly replaced by large residential parks and towers strategically located near major retail projects. Examples of these largely self-contained "cities within cities" are found particularly in the state of Dubai, but they are also increasingly found in other parts of the country. Examples include The Palm, Jebel Ali, Jumeirah Lake Towers, Jumeirah Islands, and The Gardens. When it is completed in 2008, the Burj Dubai Tower will be the world's tallest building, and it will also integrate great spirals of metal and glass into its metal frame to give it the distinctive look of the modern Islamic and Arabic world.

In strict contrast to the religious traditionalism of Saudi Arabia, as industrialization and urbanization have increased in the UAE, new sites of popular entertainment have appeared. From massive citylike shopping centers to theme and adventure parks and world-class golf courses, the UAE has made a name for itself across the world as a tourist destination. One of the most breathtaking examples of modern commercial architecture in the UAE is the Ibn Battuta Mall. Originally conceived to serve as the jewel in the crown of Dubai's shopping district, Ibn Battuta was specifically designed to reflect the embrace of traditional Arabic life and cosmopolitanism that is distinctive of local culture. Marketed as the world's largest themed mall, the Ibn Battuta Mall takes the traditional idea of souq and explodes it in all directions by incorporating retail shopping, entertainment (including several megaplex cinemas that make use of cutting-edge technology, wall-to-wall screens, stadium seats, and stylish lobbies to serve nearly 3,000 moviegoers), dining, and family activities in a single massive structure of nearly a million square feet. The complex was named for the legendary Arab explorer Ibn Battuta, and the mall attempts to join the traditional and the modern by surrounding the retail and entertainment center with six separately themed "courts" that are based on his travels and adventures across Asia and the Middle East.

Another example of the explosion of retail and commercial construction in the UAE is the largest gold souq in the world, located in the equally impressive Dubai Mall. The mall—which has set for itself the mission of becoming the "next fashion capital of the world"—includes the souq, as well as an ice rink, the world's largest three-story aquarium, a cybercafé, and a supermarket. Covering just over 2,500 square meters, the gold souq houses several hundred major gold retail houses intricately linked via oblique shopping streets that are decorated in traditional souq architecture. The central focal point of the souq is the breathtaking 50-meter-high dome that is detailed in the historical decorative traditions of classical Arab architecture.

A final example of the integration of the old and the new in the commercial and retail buildings of the UAE is the ongoing attempt to develop a replica of the ancient Khan Murjan souq. Set to open in early 2007, this new commercial center in Dubai was designed by a team of architects working in collaboration with local archaeologists and historians. It will include artist retreats, cafés, meeting rooms, and restaurants within a structure of over 50,000 square feet, including two subterranean levels.[23] The architecture of the souq will draw on elements of Islamic and Arabic architecture from Andalusian Spain to Afghanistan.

New trends in the design and building of hotels and resorts in the UAE and Bahrain are also evident, and these sumptuous structures are approaching the size of small cities. Here (and in the Gulf states more generally), increasingly one sees attempts to break away from the small, traditional, popular architecture of Islam, to turn toward Western ideals of first-class holiday resorts that cater to an exclusive clientele. The Kempinski Hotel Emirates Palace in Abu Dhabi required nearly 2.5 years and the work of nearly 12,000 workers and craftsmen (working in 24-hour shifts), to complete. Its royal suites measure nearly 1,200 square meters.[24] Another important example of the massive resort hotels that dot the landscape of the emirate states is the Al Maha Desert Resort in Dubai. Designed to be reminiscent of the traditional Bedouin style, the Al Maha is the first eco-resort built in a blossoming oasis. All the Gulf States' resorts are increasingly being designed and built to fit this popular contemporary style, offering a refined mix of Arabian ambiance, luxury, and breathtakingly massive architecture.

Bordering the Persian Gulf, Iraq, and Saudi Arabia, Kuwait is a small state of nearly 18,000 square kilometers. Its population stands at nearly 2 million residents, with a population density of nearly 112 persons per square kilometer. With average summer temperatures between 110 and 115 degrees Fahrenheit and cold winters with temperatures dropping as low as 40 degrees Fahrenheit in some places, Kuwait is an entirely desert country interspersed with small hills and sparse vegetation. Notable also are the dramatic northwesterly dust storms that cover many Kuwaiti cities with sand during the long summer months of June and July.[25]

Housing in Kuwait is heavily subsidized by the government. Because the government has invested large amounts of money in development since the oil boom, housing standards are generally high. The traditional housing of the country—one- or two-story dwellings built of local materials such as mud walls—has been replaced in recent decades by modern apartments, duplexes, and single-family homes in most parts of the country. The private homes of traditional Kuwaiti society people are variants on the Islamic courtyard home. As in Bahrain and other Arabic and Islamic cultures of the region, the heart of the traditional Kuwaiti home is the space set aside for gatherings (typically among men), usually in a separate room or even a separate tent off from the main house. Modern homes in Kuwait continue this important tradition, although increasingly this traditional "men's only" gathering space has become more of a family gathering space, in which family members can enjoy refreshments, talk, and play games.

After the discovery of oil in the 1930s and the oil industry's rapid expansion after World War II, Kuwait City, in particular, underwent a dramatic transformation. Sudden increases in urban population have produced significant changes in the old city, such as the destruction of the semicircular city wall (its gates had been preserved as a reminder of Kuwaiti ethnic history). And even the new Western-style suburbs of the city are the result of formal planning and design, laid out in advance by city planners. With the stated goal of turning small Kuwait into a modern metropolitan center, the government continues to invest large portions of oil revenues in infrastructure and urban development.

The Kuwait State Mosque is a clear example of how the traditions of the past have continued to give way to contemporary standards and requirements inside Kuwait. With an original cost of 13 million Kuwaiti dinars, this decidedly modern structure makes use of straight-line architecture and imported modern construction materials and can accommodate over 7,000 of the faithful.[26] Other examples of public architecture include Kuwait's traditional souqs, which feature conventional Bedouin architecture and design (although few Bedouins now inhabit Kuwait), with a special emphasis on the intricately woven fabrics made on Bedouin looms.

As a direct result of the country's high oil revenues, sports, entertainment, and cultural building projects have long enjoyed strong government support. Today Kuwait is home to a number of modern stadiums and amphitheaters that are capable of hosting international competitions. The country's two most widely played sports are football and golf, so majestic and sweeping golf courses and massive modern stadiums are found throughout Kuwait (especially in and around Kuwait City). And while the invasion of the Iraqi army in 1990 had a disastrous effect on many of Kuwait's entertainment and cultural institutions, with many significant works of art stolen by the Iraqis and some buildings severely damaged, a number of enormous state-sponsored rebuilding projects have almost eliminated any trace of the invasion. Two examples are the National Museum of Kuwait and the Tareq Rajab Museum, which once housed collections of regional art, jewelry, pottery, and musical instruments,

Architecture

and were important Kuwaiti architectural landmarks in their own right. Both museums were looted and burned during the Iraqi invasion. Dedicated public revitalization projects in the years following the invasion and the subsequent partitioning of Iraq by the United Nations have produced near complete renovations, and repairs have been made to most of these structures, allowing them to be reopened to the public.

Saudi Arabia

The largest country on the Arabian Peninsula, Saudi Arabia borders Iraq, Jordan, Kuwait, and the United Arab Emirates. As is typical of countries in the region, the climate of Saudi Arabia is hot and dry, featuring extreme temperatures and a great deal of uninhabitable sandy desert with very limited vegetative growth in scattered oases.

The total population of Saudi Arabia is just over 26 million inhabitants. With less than 2 percent of the total area of Saudi Arabia suitable for cultivation, population distribution in the 1990s has come to vary greatly among the towns of the eastern and western coastal areas and the densely populated interior oases. Before the 1960s, however, most of the population of the region was nomadic or seminomadic. Rapid urban and economic growth in the intervening years has produced a population that is more than 95 percent settled.[27]

Although most Saudis are ethnically Arab, many members of the region's working class are Arabs and Muslims from other countries, including a significant number of Indians, Pakistanis, and Indonesians, as well as the Filipinos. With almost no exception, these non-Arab groups live together apart from mainstream Saudi society, in compounds or gated communities.

Following the strict Islamist traditions of the region, there is not much diversity in traditional architecture of the private Saudi home. Some typical features include decorative designs on doors and windows and a wide use of the motif of fortification in wall design. During the 1960s, however, exposure to Western housing and commercial building styles began to show itself more clearly, with a wave of construction of office and residential buildings that made use of stark linear motifs strongly reminiscent of Western commercial urban centers.

Given the cultural predominance of strict Islam, many efforts are made to preserve the country's religious purity, including proscriptions of behavior and dress, as well as general prohibitions on the development of public theaters and cinemas. As in other countries of the Middle East and North Africa, Saudi Arabia's system of markets, or souqs, serves as a primary public space and hence reflects attempts at developing commercial buildings that are modern and Western in building methods and techniques and yet distinctly Arabian.

An excellent example is the recent attempt to renovate the Souq Al-Hijaz in Jeddah. This ancient market has been upgraded in recent years to attract new customers through the addition of modern parking facilities and remodeling of the existing shopping center and the exterior facades. The updating has included the extensive removal of existing traditional building fronts and the addition of a prefabricated "second skin" using the linear smooth lines of Western architecture. The renovated exterior of the souq incorporates traditional Arabic patterns of color, panels, and inlays in decorative patterns that aim to be visually appealing in their complexity. At the same time, borrowing from the European and American "shopping mall" model, the Souq Al-Hijaz has been upgraded to include the use of electronic bulletin boards and a system of escalators leading through the shopping complex.

The distinctive Islamic architecture of the region is also expressed through the design and construction of educational facilities, including madrassas and King Saud University in

Riyadh. King Saud University, for example, is fronted by an impressive entrance gate designed to appear as imposing open books (the "Books of Faith and Knowledge") with interlocking pages, suggestive of the interrelation between the Islamic faith and knowledge of the natural world.

It is impossible to consider the architecture of daily life in Saudi Arabia without briefly considering the holy sites in the history of Islam and their current status. The Kaaba at Mecca—the holiest of the great shrines of Islam—serves as the locus of the *hajj*, or pilgrimage tenet of Islamic tradition. The Kaaba is famous for the circular lines inscribed in its pavement that guide the rite of circumambulation. And, although the present dimensions of the Kaaba have changed little over the last several centuries, the same cannot be said of the second holiest site of Islam, the Mosque of the Prophet Muhammad in Medina, which was recently completely renovated and enlarged by King Fahd. Originally built by the Prophet himself in 622, and now his place of burial, this important mosque functioned as a standard for almost all subsequent Islamic buildings. Today the decorative marble and mosaics inlaid with gold and glass that cover the rectangular walls of the open courtyard and south colonnade have been completely restored to their original beauty, as have the existing five minarets and the famous green great dome.

Modern Western hotels, resorts, and conference centers are increasingly commonplace in major population centers across the country, but especially in the port of Jeddah and the capital Riyadh. Even so, attempts have been made in both of these cities to infuse modern construction with traditional style. The best examples are found in the world-famous design of the airport terminals at both Jeddah and Riyadh.

RESOURCE GUIDE

PRINT SOURCES

Barrucand, Marianne, and Achim Bednorz. *Moorish Architecture.* Paris: Taschen, 2002.
Bowen, Donna, and Evelyn Early, eds. *Everyday Life in the Muslim Middle East,* 2nd edition. Bloomington, IN: Indiana University Press, 2002.
Braude, Joseph. *The New Iraq: Rebuilding the Country for Its People, the Middle East, and the World.* New York: Basic Books, 2004.
Cleveland, William. *A History of the Modern Middle East,* 3rd edition. London: Westview Press, 2004.
Creswell, K. A. *A Bibliography of Muslim Architecture in North Africa, Excluding Egypt.* Alexandria: Librairie Larose, 1954.
Deplazes, Andrea. *Constructing Architecture: Materials, Processes, Structures.* Princeton, NJ: Princeton Architectural Press, 2005.
Grube, Ernst. "What Is Islamic Architecture?" in *Architecture of the Islamic World.* London: Thames and Hudson, 1978.
Hakim, Besim-Selim. *Arabic-Islamic Cities: Building and Planning Principles.* London: Kegan Paul, 2001.
Hutt, Antony. *North Africa: Islamic Architecture.* London: Scorpion Publishing, 1998.
Ibrahim, Abdelbaki Mohamed, ed. *Contemporary Architecture in Egypt.* Vol. 199, Government Publication Newsletter. Cairo: Center for Planning and Architectural Studies, 1998.
Kultermann, Udo. *Contemporary Architecture in the Arab States: Renaissance of a Region.* New York: McGraw-Hill Professional Press, 1999.
Kunz, Martin. *Luxury Hotels: Africa/Middle East.* New York: Te Neues Publishing, 2006.
Lampugnani, Vittorio, and Vittorio Mangnano, eds. *Mediterranean Basin.* Vol. 4, *World Architecture 1900–2000—A Critical Mosaic.* Princeton, NJ: Princeton Architectural Press, 2003.
Pirani, Khalil. *Understanding Islamic Architecture.* New York: Routledge, 2003.

Architecture

Schofield, C. *Middle East and North Africa.* Vol. 2, *World Boundaries.* London: Routledge, 1994.

Shyrock, Andrew. "The New Jordanian Hospitality: House, Host, and Guest in the Culture of Public Display." *Comparative Studies in Society and History* 46.1 (Spring 2004): 35–61.

Steele, James. *Architecture for People: The Complete Works of Hassan Fathy.* Darby, PA: Diane Publishing, 1997.

Watenpaugh, Keith. *Being Modern in the Middle East: Revolution, Nationalism, and the Arab Middle Class.* Princeton, NJ: Princeton University Press, 2006.

Wharton, Annabel. *Building the Cold War: Hilton International Hotels and Modern Architecture.* Chicago: University of Chicago Press, 2001.

WEBSITES

ArabianEye. http://www.arabianeye.com/library/default.asp?CategoryCode=STOCK. Regularly updated libraries of contemporary architectural photographs from across North Africa and the Middle East.

ArchInform—International Architecture Database. www.archinform.net/. Contains over 14,000 searchable images of actual buildings as well as a number of designs and proposals, many of which are North African and Middle East entries.

Art & Architecture—Courtauld Institute of Art. http://www.artandarchitecture.org.uk/. An extensive image library available for public use.

Art and Architecture: Links. Updated December 28, 2005. NITLE Arab World Project. http://arabworld.nitle.org/links.php?module_id=12. Links to fine arts in the Arab world, including sites for Arabs Art.com and IraquiArt.com, and sources for Lebanese art and Palestinian and Israeli poster art.

Basic Principles of Arabic/Islamic Architecture. National Institute for Technology and Liberal Education. http://arabworld.nitle.org/introduction.php?module_id=12.

City and Building Database. University of Washington. http://content.lib.washington.edu/buildingsweb/index.html. This Website contains over 10,000 images from all major countries in the world.

Contemporary and Ancient Arab and Islamic Architecture. http://www.al-bab.com/arab/visual/architecture.htm.

International Style in Tel Aviv. http://www.interart.co.il/bauhaus/. Several photographs documenting the legacy of the International style movement on the architecture of Israel.

The Negatives Collection of G. Eric and Edith Matson. http://rs6.loc.gov/pp/matpchtml/matpcabt.html. This collection of historically important photos depicts the early years of urbanization in North Africa and the Middle East.

Shechori, Ran. *Architecture in Israel 1995–1998.* Israel Public Council for Arts and Culture. 1998. http://www.mfa.gov.il/MFA/MFAArchive/2000_2009/2002/7/Architecture%20in%20Israel%201995–1998.

Willis, James. *Bibliotheca Alexandrina: Images.* http://www.jwillisphoto.com/flash.html. This Website contains sixty high-quality art shots by of the library's inspiring architecture by photographer James Willis.

World Housing Encyclopedia. http://www.world-housing.net/index.asp. Updated statistics on housing conditions and access to resources.

NOTES

1. Pirani, 2003 (in Resource Guide), p. 23.
2. Central Intelligence Agency. *The World Factbook—Tunisia Population.* Accessed October 5, 2006.https://www.cia.gov/cia/publications/factbook/geos/ts.html#People.
3. Central Intelligence Agency. *The World Factbook—Algeria.* Accessed October 5, 2006. https://www.cia.gov/cia/publications/factbook/geos/ag.html.
4. Central Intelligence Agency. *The World Factbook—Morocco.* Accessed October 5, 2006. https://www.cia.gov/cia/publications/factbook/geos/mo.html.

5. Architecture About.Com. *Hassan II Mosque 1986–1993*. Accessed August 29, 2006. http://architecture.about.com/library/blhassanIImosque.htm.
6. Office of the Prime Minister, Republic of Turkey. *The EURO-Mediterranean Free Trade Area*. http://www.dtm.gov.tr/ab/ingilizce/euromed.doc.
7. Central Intelligence Agency. *The World Factbook—Egypt Population*. Accessed October 5, 2006. https://www.cia.gov/cia/publications/factbook/geos/eg.html#People.
8. Central Intelligence Agency. *The World Factbook—Jordan*. Accessed October 5, 2006. https://www.cia.gov/cia/publications/factbook/geos/jo.html.
9. Central Intelligence Agency. *The World Factbook—Israel*. Accessed October 5, 2006. https://www.cia.gov/cia/publications/factbook/geos/is.html.
10. Central Intelligence Agency. *The World Factbook—Israel: Population*. Accessed October 5, 2006. https://www.cia.gov/cia/publications/factbook/geos/is.html#People.
11. Central Intelligence Agency. *The World Factbook—West Bank*. Accessed October 5, 2006. https://www.cia.gov/cia/publications/factbook/geos/we.html.
12. Central Intelligence Agency. *The World Factbook—The Gaza Strip*. Accessed October 5, 2006. https://www.cia.gov/cia/publications/factbook/geos/gz.html.
13. Palestinian National Information Center, *Geography and Population of Palestine*. http://www.pnic.gov.ps/english/tourism/tour2.html.
14. *Palestinian Refugees: An Overview*. Palestinian Refugee ResearchNet (PRRN). http://www.arts.mcgill.ca/mepp/new_prrn/background/index.htm.
15. Central Intelligence Agency. *The World Factbook—Lebanon*. Accessed October 9, 2006. https://www.cia.gov/cia/publications/factbook/geos/le.html.
16. Central Intelligence Agency. *The World Factbook—Iraq Population*. Accessed October 5, 2006. https://www.cia.gov/cia/publications/factbook/geos/iz.html#People.
17. Central Intelligence Agency. *The World Factbook—Iraq Geography*. Accessed October 5, 2006. https://www.cia.gov/cia/publications/factbook/geos/iz.html#Geo.
18. Central Intelligence Agency. *The World Factbook—Iran Geography*. Accessed October 5, 2006. https://www.cia.gov/cia/publications/factbook/geos/ir.html#Geo.
19. Central Intelligence Agency. *The World Factbook—Iran Population*. Accessed October 5, 2006. https://www.cia.gov/cia/publications/factbook/geos/ir.html#People.
20. Ibid.
21. Central Intelligence Agency. T*he World Factbook—United Arab Emirates Geography*. Accessed October 5, 2006. https://www.cia.gov/cia/publications/factbook/geos/ae.html#Geo.
22. Cleveland, 2004 (in Resource Guide), p. 211.
23. *Wafi Property announces development of historical souk, Khan Murjan*. AME INFO. Accessed August 29, 2006. http://www.ameinfo.com/72908.html.
24. *Kempinski Hotel Emirates Palance, Abu Dhabi, United Arab Emirates*. Hotels Europe.Com. Accessed August 29, 2006. http://www.hotels-europe.com/kempinski-hotels/uae-emirates-palace.htm.
25. Central Intelligence Agency. *The World Factbook—Kuwait Geography*. Accessed August 29, 2006. https://www.cia.gov/cia/publications/factbook/geos/ku.html#Geo.
26. *Kuwait State Mosque*. ARCHNET. Accessed August 29, 2006. http://archnet.org/library/sites/one-site.tcl?site_id=605.
27. *Settlement Patterns (from Saudi Arabia)*. Encyclopaedia Britannica. Accessed August 29, 2006, http://www.britannica.com/eb/article-45202/Saudi-Arabia.

ART

ROSEMARY GALLICK

North Africa and the Middle East have a tradition of rich expression in the pictorial arts. Historically rooted in religion and politics, and expressed in ornate script, the visual arts of these various countries reflect the creative impulse through turbulent times. Although this vast territory called the Middle East and North African includes additional countries, this chapter will focus on the traditional and contemporary art of Egypt, Jordan, Israel, Lebanon, Palestine, Syria, Iraq, Iran, Saudi Arabia, Sudan, and the United Arab Emirates.[1] The art in any country, including the countries of the Middle East and North Africa, is a reflection of society at a particular time in a specific geographical location. Most of the land in this area is semiarid or desert. The region is separated by deserts and mountains that extend from sub-Saharan Africa to the Indo-Pakistani subcontinent. As a result, influence from other cultures on art styles of the region has been severely limited.[2] By examining the art, it will be clear that art in these countries continues to venerate and carry on past traditions, making popular art a regeneration of images in a technological format.

Popular arts are those traditions, customs, and rituals that have concrete designs and that last over time. In general, popular culture has been defined as "the everyday world around us: the mass media, entertainment, diversions; it is our heroes, our icons, rituals, everyday actions, psychology, and religion—our total life pictures."[3] Pop art (a term credited to British art critic Lawrence Alloway) is an abbreviation for popular art and addresses the conversion of elements of mass culture into works of art.[4] The artwork covered in this chapter will include the popular art forms that range from fine art to folk arts and crafts, including painting, sculpture, billboards, cartoons, ceramics, jewelry, graphics, metalworking, pottery, woodwork, and photography. Globalization and technology have enabled cultures around the world to have glimpses of the popular culture aspects of these North African and Middle Eastern societies.

THE ISLAMIC WORLD

The religion of Islam, an Arabic word translated as "submission to God," plays a significant role in the Middle East and North Africa, even though there is much diversity regarding culture, class, and religion.[5] Originally, the Arabs were nomadic herders and merchants who traveled over large desert regions. Muhammad, an Arab trader, began to preach the submission to one God in the seventh century (around 610 CE) in Mecca. Because of political and religious pressure, Muhammad fled to the city of Medina in 622. This event became known as the Hegira (meaning emigration in Arabic) and marks the starting date of the Islamic calendar.[6] Within a century, Islam had dominated the Middle East and replaced Persian control. By 640 Muslims ruled Palestine, Iraq, and Syria. The Muslims had conquered Lower (northern) Egypt by 541. All of North Africa had succumbed to Muslim control by 710. The following year, Muslim armies entered Spain.[7] The Muslim triumph had lasting implications for art and architecture. Islamic art replaced the style known as Late Antique in the Middle East and North Africa.

Although there are a few exceptions, human imagery does not appear in Islamic religious art. There is a religious taboo on the representation of human figures. Muslims believe that artists who render human figures are imitating God, who alone is the sole creator of life.[8] In very recent times, the Western media was in an uproar after a Danish press printed twelve caricatures of the Prophet Muhammad in September 2006. The Muslim world reacted strongly, vehemently asserting that representation of Allah and his prophet is strictly forbidden. On the other hand, the Danish and Norwegian press claimed the right to print blasphemy is one of their democratic rights of free speech.[9] Most political analysts agree that printing the cartoons added fuel to an already volatile situation, which further alienated increasing numbers of Muslims living in European nations. Protests opposed to the European newspapers that had published these depictions continued to gain momentum, and boycotts by Muslims against Danish products resulted in economic loss.[10]

To put this latest political outrage into historical perspective, it is interesting to note that throughout the centuries, art has acted as a powerful tool for the masses. Painstaking effort can go into the preservation of customs, artifacts, and the traditional folk art of a culture. On the other hand, equal energy can be expended on destroying art when one country is in conflict with another. During the seventh and eighth centuries, Christian icons were a major source of conflict. Some Christians considered devotion to these images as sinful and as promoting pagan idolatry, which sometimes led to the destruction of art pieces. During this same time period, Arabs invaded Byzantium, Constantinople, and Persia, professing the religion of Islam. Iconoclasm—from the term "iconoclast," meaning destroyer of images—existed for a century, and many historically valuable religious icons were destroyed.[11] During World War II, Nazi Germany intentionally destroyed ancient Byzantine religious icons as well as monuments during the Nazi occupation of Russia. Even in modern times, art continues to be lost in conflicts, as seen in events in the Muslim world today.

It is not entirely true to assert that Muslims did not depict figures in art. Usually, however, images of Muhammad were not rendered in traditional Islamic religious painting.[12] This custom not to render figures notwithstanding, Persians in centuries past did not believe this rule applied to their miniature paintings. Despite the limited figurative representation, creativity was and is abundantly expressed in decorative forms based on geometric shapes, intertwining lines, repetition of patterns, and calligraphic forms to achieve a unified artistic style.[13] Decoration provides a significant tool across the various Islamic art forms. Decorative patterns are used to add surface detail to interior and exterior walls, floors, and mosaics. These geometric motifs are used endlessly in textiles, rugs, and calligraphy, and are incised into metal vessels as well as jewelry.

The use of metal was a key element in Islamic artwork. Iron and bronze were used for weapons; silver and gold were used as well but less extensively. For example, Islamic craftsmen used an inlaying technique whereby threads of gold, silver, or copper were incorporated into the surface of various objects: bowls, vases, jugs, candlesticks, and sculptures. Most artworks were decorated with arabesques and geometric patterns.[14] This distinct pattern elevates common objects to items of distinction through the decorative rhythm of the plant forms, stems, leaves, and tendrils. A sculpture dated from 796, *Ewer in the Form of a Bird* by Sulayman, provides an excellent example of the sophistication of sculptural forms and shows the etched lines and decorative patterns that can be found on Islamic textiles, pottery, and architectural decoration.[15] Today, replicas of such pieces, which follow tradition and use metalworking techniques from the past, are available for purchase. By recycling these great achievements of the past through present-day replicas, contemporary popular art is a re-creation of the past.

Another art form, ceramics, illustrates a second great Islamic artistic achievement. Islamic pottery connected the ancient world to Europe in the Middle Ages. The Islamic craftsmen elaborated on the Egyptian technique of glazing and applied their knowledge of Mesopotamian colored-enamel techniques to pottery. They incorporated more ornamentation and incisions, resulting in the creation of ceramic objects characterized by a metallic sheen with an array of many colors.

Jewelry was also an important form of art in Islamic societies. Women and men frequently wore objects such as anklets, necklaces, bracelets, earrings, rings, and turban ornaments. Sometimes, jewelry would be a portion of the woman's dowry.[16] Following Middle Eastern and North African tradition, gold was usually reserved for royalty. In terms of vessel creation, copper and brass were the materials of preference, but more commonly, artisans used iron, steel, or bronze. Jewelers also used gemstones such as emeralds, lapis lazuli, jade, topaz, turquoise, and rock crystal to embellish surfaces.

Silk and wool carpets illustrate the fine skill of Islamic artisans. The work is painstaking and very intricate. Silk is very fragile and thus difficult to preserve over the centuries. The arabesque and geometric patterns are also evident on movable furnishing such as tapestries. Rugs and carpets also have a prominent place in Islamic art. Islamic rugs typically have a border design. The center may vary from a number of squares of floral patterns. Under certain regimes, royalty had carpets created for display rather than for function. These carpets were categorized by their designs. For example, if the carpet had a floral motif, it fell into the garden carpet variety. Rugs were made for both private homes and mosques. There are primarily three types of rugs: knotted, woven, and chain-stitched.[17]

Script has been sacred in the Arab culture for centuries. In its earliest form, script was the graffiti of its day. The intricate relationship between religion and Arabic script endures today. As part of the exposure to Arabic popular art, the British Museum sponsored a show in 2006, called Sacred Script, which explored the relationship between the written word and identity, politics, religion, and tradition. The importance of calligraphy in Islamic art is paramount since this ornamental script has been applied to all of the art forms and architectural embellishments. Because of the customary ban on figurative and animal representations, creative expression turned to undulating plant forms and elaborate scripted designs. The stylized scripted patterns and floral repetition provide a continuity of themes and motifs across various aspects of art in the Islamic world.

REGIONS

Egypt

Even though more than 2,500 years have passed, the splendor of Egypt's royal tombs is well-known. The stability of Egypt is based on the annual flooding of the Nile River that has supported the prosperity of the region. Throughout the centuries, Egypt has enjoyed the reputation of a land of intrigue, with mysterious hieroglyphics, glorious monuments, and an abundance of gold decorations. Europeans rediscovered Egypt in the late eighteenth century, when Napoleon Bonaparte, fascinated with this ancient culture, led a military expedition to the land.[18] As a result of Napoleon's invasion, Egypt became the first Arab country in the nineteenth century to be exposed to Western artistic expression on a grand scale.[19]

Unlike many of the other Middle Eastern cultures discussed in this chapter, Egypt has a rich history of figural depictions both in painting and in sculpture. The artistic designs were carefully regulated by a grid system called "canons of proportion," which established rules for figurative representation. This system of depicting objects and figures on square grids provided a stylistic unity that remained unchanged over centuries.[20] With the uncovering of the tomb of Tutankhamen in 1922 by Howard Carter, a feverish new interest in ancient Egypt was unlocked. A glimpse into the contents of the "boy king" Tutankhamen's tomb revealed a vast quantity of objects representing the minor arts, including chariots, furniture, games, and all forms of golden jewelry. Exquisite necklaces, bracelets, and rings served as inspiration for replicas in modern society. Artworks paid homage to the pharaohs while depicting motifs such as the scarab, a symbol of resurrection; the wings of Isis; or the eye of Horus. The tomb paintings, pottery, sculpture, and jewelry remain popular today.

Jewelry has and continues to be a great source of artistic pride and skill in Egyptian culture. From the earliest times, men and women were adorned with jewelry such as elaborate gold necklaces, bracelets, and earrings. Hair wrapping with decorative beads is depicted on several ancient relief sculptures, and this tradition continues to be popular today as well.

In terms of contemporary Egyptian art, there have been an abundance of styles. Easel painting in Egypt, as in most Arab countries, was a relatively recent development, starting in the mid-nineteenth century. For example, French artist Jean-Leon Gerome relocated to Cairo in 1857 and influenced the notion of easel painting.[21] In 1908 Prince Yusuf Kamal started the School of Fine Arts in Cairo. The institution hired several Western artists as teachers, and the introduction of Western ideals permeated this course of study.

There have been significant developments in contemporary art. Specifically, a yearly festival called PhotoCairo was started in 2002. The event displays photographic exhibitions and provides panel discussions, seminars, workshops, and film showings. The intended audience for this festivity is general and diverse.[22] Also in Cairo, the Townhouse Gallery of Contemporary Art has sponsored an ongoing Open Studio Project, where approximately twenty local and international artists are provided studio spaces. Egyptian artists have also been participating in the Venice Biennale under the direction of curator Gilane Tawadros. There has been an attempt to bring the contemporary Egyptian art scene to an international level through the Wasla Contemporary Art Workshop.[23] Egypt hosts the International Cairo Biennial, which was founded in 1984 and was opened to non-Arabs in 1986. Three main exhibition buildings are used: the Akhenaton Gallery, the Gezira Arts Centre, and the Opera House. Based on the show's regulations, social, economic, and political implications are evident: the show abides by Article 3 of the United Nations Charter, which prohibits countries that violate the sovereignty of others or that occupy a foreign territory by force to participate in the Biennial. As a result, Israel has never been a participant in the Biennial. Nevertheless, at the 9th Biennial the United States had its own pavilion and promoted its exhibition as an important way to create a dialogue between the Islamic world and the United States.[24]

Royal Dutch Shell's oil and gas companies play an important role in Egyptian artistic sponsorship. Shell Egyptian has developed numerous Websites to sponsor contemporary Egyptian artists. Particularly noteworthy are the works of painters Abd El Aal Hassan, Abdel-Wahab Mosi, Adel Thabet, Ahmed El Rashidi, Abd Al-Hadi Al-Gazzar, Ahmed Hussein, and Antoun Hanna; sculptors Abdel Aziz Saab, Amr Heiba, and Halim Yacoub; and Egyptian ceramic artist

Gamal Abdel Ghani.[25] These artists represent many institutions, such as the Syndicate of Plastic Artists, and show the expanding Egyptian art world to the international market.

Popular culture in Egypt promotes astounding landmarks of civilization and reintroduces past treasures to the world through technology. For example, sculptural and architectural landmarks are promoted in numerous ways as posters, billboards, calendars, and greeting cards to markets around the world. The advent of the computer has made graphic designs of the pyramids, the Sphinx, and other icons of Egyptian culture available for purchase, even on eBay. Also noteworthy are the numerous billboards that promote contemporary cinema; their subjects range from lightweight romances to traditionally clad portraits of the actors. The use of the elaborate script calligraphy on billboards indicates that, although the images seem somewhat Westernized, the culture is not Western.

Sudan

Sudan is the largest country in Africa; it extends from Upper Egypt to the forests of Uganda and Zaire. The inhabitants of this area are diverse. There are approximately nineteen major ethnic groups, with Arabs comprising about 60 percent of the total.[26] Islam is the official religion of Sudan; in 1988 about 70 percent of the population was Muslim. Attracted by gold and slavery, Muhammad Ali of Egypt successfully invaded Sudan in 1820. Islam spread at a swift pace and engulfed much of North Africa and the Middle East. As a result, the art of Sudan has a rich cultural history that embraces the diverse styles of the region and the distinctive calligraphic style of Islam. Figurative representation was discouraged in Islamic art, which resulted in a highly refined, aniconic motif, characteristic of this distinct style.[27]

During the nineteenth century, Sudan became subject to slave traders and European missionaries. By World War II, there was a growing nationalism in Sudan; however, it was not until 1954 that Sudan became independent of both Egyptian and British rule. Thereafter, periods of political unrest unfolded and have continued into the present.

Because of external Islamic influences in this North African region, the art of Sudan has very limited representation of human or animal forms; instead, it focuses on elaborate decoration.[28] Much of the contemporary art in Sudan was made by expatriates who had been trained at the Khartoum School of Fine and Applied Arts. In the 1950s many Sudanese artists studied abroad and later returned to Khartoum with hopes of creating a distinctive Sudanese style. One well-known artist was Ibrahim El Sahali, regarded as a modern artist, who worked to express both his Islamic and African identities. El Sahali studied at the Slade School of Art in London; upon returning to Sudan, he combined his modern style with repetitive decorative patterns. One of his important drawings, *Allah and the Wall of Confrontation,* used geometric shapes and decorative calligraphy.[29]

Rashid Diab, a second-generation Khartoum artist who studied in Spain, departs from Islamic tradition and uses calligraphic designs, animal and human imagery, and African mask motifs in his artwork. Also noteworthy is expatriate Hassan Musa, who lives in France and is a performance artist.[30] Prior to the nineteenth century, the most significant influence on culture outside of Africa was Islam. In the Sudan region, artists have tried to maximize the rich cultural traditions of Islam as well as the countries they have experienced.

Jordan

The first Arab-Israeli war occurred in 1948. After that time, more than 100,000 Palestinian refugees fled to the East Bank. Another large number of Palestinians, approximately

310,000, arrived after the 1967 war. Prior to 1948, Jordan's population was composed mostly of peasants and nomads, most of whom were of Palestinian or Syrian descent. World War I had significant implications for this area. The San Remo Conference in 1920 awarded the Mandate for Palestine to Britain, and Syria was placed under French rule. By 1928 Great Britain had signed a treaty that gave Transjordan more independence; however, World War II delayed full independence. Later, Jordan was granted independence by the Treaty of London in March 1946,[31] even though Britain was allowed to maintain troops in Jordan. The area that is now Jordan became Muslim after 636; the majority of those residing in the East Bank today are Sunni.

A time of rapid political change ensued after World War II. Jordan participated in the first Arab-Israeli war in 1948. Later, the Jordanian army occupied much of East Palestine, which had been given to the Arabs under the United Nations' partition of land. This area, known as the West Bank, became formally incorporated in April 1950. During this time period, militant organizations that much later became known as Hamas, Islamic Jihad, and Al-Aqsa Martyrs Brigade had their beginnings.[32] A time of relative stability continued between the second Arab-Israeli war in 1956 and the third Arab-Israeli war in 1967, when Jordan actively engaged its troops alongside Syria's and Egypt's. The Arabs were defeated, and Jordan lost the territory of the West Bank. The Palestine Liberation Organization, previously regarded as an extension of Egyptian foreign policy, became militarized and more radical in political actions. There was a period of reconciliation among the Arab nations. However, Jordan was not a participant in the 1973 war with Israel.

The 1980s marked a period of political stability under the power of King Hussein. Jordan has been a supporter of Iraq against Syria and has benefited from an alliance with its former rival, Saudi Arabia.[33] An interesting promotion of the arts in Jordan started in 1979, when a nonprofit organization, the Royal Society of Fine Arts (RSFA), was established. Its goal was to promote cultural diversity in contemporary art. The RSFA opened in 1980 and currently houses over 1,800 works that include sculpture, photography, paintings, prints, installations, ceramics, and weavings by over 700 artists from forty-five countries.[34] The individual primarily responsible for this contribution to the arts was Princess Wijdan Ali, the first woman to be part of the Ministry of Foreign Affairs in Jordan; she also served at the United Nations. She left the diplomatic position to become a founder and spokesperson for the arts. Her original intentions were to create a place for Islamic and Arab artists to show their work according to their own aesthetics. Initially, her gallery was one of the first venues to display the modern art of the Islamic world. In an interview, Princess Ali stated, "We have to reach out in order to attain a basic and exigent goal: the promotion of world peace through the advancement of the arts and eradication of cultural apartheid."[35]

Another art institution, Makan—The House of Expression, was founded in 2003 by Ola Khalidi, an artist who had worked and completed her studies at the University of Surrey in England and had worked in Beirut, Lebanon. In addition to showcasing artists' styles, the Makan House broaches topics such as politics, sexuality, and socioeconomic issues as legitimate avenues for artistic expression.[36] The fine arts in Jordan are very progressive and experiment with a variety of techniques. There are many activities happening in the Jordanian art world, such as the expansion of the Jordan National Gallery of Fine Arts that opened in May 2005 as well as the video installations of Suha Shoman in an exhibition titled Of Time and Light.[37]

Contemporary art from Jordan is also featured in international exhibitions. For example, the *Fondation Arabe pour L'Image* (FAI) is based in Beirut. The goal of the FAI is to preserve, collect, and display photographic images from all over the Middle East and North Africa. Housed in the Starco Building in Beirut, its collection includes over 75,000 photographs by artists from Lebanon, Syria, Palestine, Egypt, Iraq, Morocco, and Jordan.[38]

Israel

Israel, the newest of the countries and cultures under discussion, certainly has had a turbulent history that continues today. The Jewish people have a long tradition of artistic achievement. To briefly summarize chronologically, Israeli artwork evolved from calligraphy and illustrations in religious manuscripts to the emergence of popular portraits of rabbis. During the nineteenth century, these portraits were popular and plentiful throughout Eastern Europe, and miniature replicas were often hung on the walls of homes. Throughout, Jewish artists have excelled in metalworking and have been particularly skilled in using silver and gold. The period from 1920 to the 1940s has been described as the heroic period of Israeli artistic achievement, and Palestine was the hub of this creative explosion.[39]

> **POPULAR ART AS A REFLECTION OF ISRAELI CULTURE**
>
> What would the viewer expect to see in Israeli art today? Art is a reflection of what is current, what is considered popular culture at that moment. By merely observing the news, viewers have a sense of struggles, explosions, thoughts on the political climate, extreme reverence for religious ideology, promotion of leaders, and establishment of ethical dialogues. Examining the art of any country, however, will show the visual expression of what is in the minds, hearts, and souls of individuals in society, and the art will provide insights into the news as well.

Jewish influence on popular art and culture in America is a direct result of the anti-Semitic atmosphere before and during World War II. To avoid persecution, Jewish artists such as Marc Chagall, Jacques Lipchitz, and Chaim Soutine fled to the United States to escape Nazi persecution. The center of art transferred from Europe to New York at this time mainly because of this massive Jewish exodus. Over time, the Star of David became a symbol used in graphic design for various purposes, both for promoting nationalism and as a badge the Nazi government required Jewish citizens to wear. Another popular theme depicted in Israeli art was the Arab village; this type of landscape motif continued until the 1960s. Images of the Holy Land persist in Jewish art. Posters depicting the Holy Land and monuments such as the Dome of the Rock can even be ordered on eBay.[40]

When tracing the tumultuous patterns of Israeli history in modern times—from the Six Day War in 1973, to the War of Attrition from 1969 to 1971, to the Yom Kippur War in 1973, to the Lebanon War in 1982, to the Gulf War in 1991, to the events of the year 2006—it is easy to see why art produced during these periods would reflect a chaotic social and political climate. Such an environment produced "radical" Israeli art, particularly from 1970 to 1980. Much of the artwork during this time demanded social and political reform.[41] From 1980 to the present, Israeli art has responded to these wars as well as depicting modern and postmodern themes. With their use of abstract designs and patterns in painting, ceramics, jewelry, and other art forms, Israeli artisans are very contemporary and produce popular arts that are internationally recognized. Given the effects of globalization and the fact that Israel is a modern, progressive state, it makes sense that Israeli popular art would be in keeping with Western aesthetics.

Lebanon

Lebanon is part of the Arab League, which was established in 1945. The Arab League was founded to encourage unity and coexistence among the Arab nations.[42] Over time, there have been several stumbling blocks along this path. In Lebanon, violence starting in 1975 has impacted all aspects of Lebanese society. Interestingly, Lebanon is regarded as the birthplace of newspapers in the Middle East, which naturally contain visual images to support the stories being reported.[43] In spite of all the political unrest, Lebanon is still a major promoter of the fine arts. For example, the Lebanese American University (LAU) supports discussion of new ideas in education and the arts. A 2004 lecture by Natalie Fallaha called "Design Talks" was held at the School of Architecture and Design in Sharjah, in which she discussed the multireligious communities in Lebanon that comprise the educational system.[44] Ricardo Mbarak has also lectured on art and media in Lebanon at the Lebanese Academy of Fine Arts, noting that religion, war, and politics have inevitably affected the Lebanese population.[45] In Lebanon today, a complex variety in artistic styles reflects the country's cultural diversity in visual form.

Palestinian Territories and Syria

The Palestinian Territories and Syria have been associated with ancient Mesopotamia because of the importance of trade routes along the Khabur River valleys and the Euphrates River. Syria and Palestine became important parts of the Achaemenid empire prior to being conquered by Alexander the Great in 333 BCE.[46] In terms of the evolving advances in ancient art, the location of the Euphrates River cannot be overlooked. A distant town called Dura-Europos (located in contemporary Syria) that overlooked the Euphrates provides insight into the complexity of the religious differences of that time that still prevail today. The Sasanian victory over Dura-Europos proved to be important because this town was evacuated with its ancient buildings left untouched. These architectural structures and the decor within have provided outstanding clues to the polytheistic religions of the Middle East and the Mediterranean. Equally noteworthy, archaeologists also discovered the existence of monotheistic houses of worship for Judaism and Christianity, both religions that were banned under the Roman empire.[47] Figurative murals found in the synagogue at Dura-Europos depicted several scenes that surprised scholars since they appeared to defy the biblical Second Commandment, which prohibits making images for worship. Scholars were similarly astonished when they assessed the newly discovered paintings and sculpture. They found that portrait sculpture of Roman emperors had continued, but the creation of statues of pagan gods and mythological figures had decreased.

A second-century philosopher and convert to Christianity, Justin Martyr, expressed the biblical warning of the Second Commandment that prohibited idol worship in his *Apologia*. At the time, Christians regarded these kinds of sculptures as idols or cult statues. Monumental figurative Christian sculpture did not become prominent until the twelfth century. During the eleventh through the thirteenth centuries, vast numbers of Christians made pilgrimages to Islamic lands, particularly to Jerusalem and Bethlehem. Many of the wealthy travelers commissioned Islamic artists to create custom pieces, in addition to purchasing less expensive items. An example of a custom piece is a brass canteen with inlaid silver, dated 1240–50, that depicts scenes from the life of Christ (housed in the Freer Gallery of Art in Washington, D.C.).

The Islamic artistic tradition swept from Arabia to India to North Africa and to Spain, leaving a lasting legacy that continues to affect modern art.[48] For Palestinians today, art is an emotional subject and serves as a vehicle to preserve a national identity. Even in the twenty-first century, the concept of prohibited representation of religious icons looms large and is a catalyst for unrest. Artistic expression and freedom of speech can be in direct conflict with the prohibition against the creation of religious images of designated prophets. The political climate and the occupation of Palestine continue to create issues for artistic expression.[49]

The National Museum in Damascus, Syria, contains a vast collection of archaeological treasures. The west wing contains preclassical, Islamic, and Arabic works. One room of the museum is dedicated to Mari, the Bronze Age site that was previously located on the Euphrates; in addition, Islamic jewelry, coins, and armor are proudly exhibited. The east wing displays classical and Byzantine objects. Fragments of the museum's facade are pieces of the twin-towered gates of Qasr al Heir. Reputed to be one of the most popular sections of the National Museum is the reconstructed second-century CE synagogue. These reconstructed walls have been decorated with Talmudic inscriptions and human figures from the Bible. In addition, the museum houses the Dura-Europos room.[50] Visitors to the museum can expect to witness ancient history come to life.

Iraq

Mesopotamia was known as the land between two rivers, namely, the Tigris and Euphrates. Today it is the approximate area known as Iraq. Mesopotamia is at the base of the region called the Fertile Crescent. This crescent forms a large landmass stretching from the mountainous border between Syria and Turkey through Iraq to the Zagros mountains of Iran. This land is thought to be the location of the Garden of Eden.[51] This region also is the birthplace of the three major monotheistic faiths: Judaism, Christianity, and Islam. Mesopotamia was rediscovered after 4,000 years when treasures were uncovered in the 1920s by Leonard Woolley in the royal cemetery at Ur. These excavations produced golden objects, jewelry, and musical instruments. The discovery at Ur was approximately simultaneous with the uncovering of King Tutankhamen's tomb in 1922.

In ancient times, Sumerian art in Mesopotamia encompassed many pieces of sculpture, primarily of worshippers. Characteristics of these statues are large eyes, frontal position, clasped hands, and tufted skirts. Sumerians are credited with creating cuneiform, a method of wedge-shaped picture writing, and for development of the wheel. Another major contribution to the field of art was the cylinder seal. The successors of the Sumerians were numerous and included the Akkadians, Babylonians, Assyrians, and Persians. Artwork flourished during this time period. The Akkadians were known for their bronze royal portraits. Hammurabi's Code of laws, an example of a carved stone stela from 1780 BCE, dates from the period under Babylonian rule. The palaces of the Assyrians, whose artwork reflects themes of war and hunting, house huge doorways that were protected by human-headed, winged bulls. These guardian figures are called *lamassu*. All these examples of artwork show the historical climate of the era and the advancement of artistic skills.

A new Persian empire originated in 224 BCE with the crowning of the first Sasanian king, Artaxerxes I, who defeated the Parthians. Artaxerxes established Ctesiphon, which is located near modern Baghdad in Iraq, as the capital. This empire lasted until the Arabs drove the Sasanians out of the Mesopotamian region in 636 CE, just four years after the death of Muhammad, the founder of Islam. In terms of artwork, Sasanians excelled at metalworking and at portraiture, as evident in the piece *Head of a Sasanian King (Shapur II?)* from 350 CE (housed in New York's Metropolitan Museum of Art).[52]

Iraq in the Twentieth and Twenty-First Centuries

By the end of World War I, Ottoman rule over the Arab nations ended. In 1918 the region now known as Iraq was taken over by Great Britain. A French mandate was issued in 1919 that established French power over Syria and Lebanon. At the same time, Jordan and Palestine were placed under British rule, and Egypt became a British protectorate. Western archaeologists, who had previously worked with Iraqis to preserve artifacts of their past, now had erratic relationships with the native people. Bouts of nationalism also impaired the work of Western archaeologists.[53]

In terms of fine arts, Iraqi artists began painting in oils on easels at the turn of the twentieth century. These artists, who were trained at military schools in Istanbul, introduced Iraqis to Western painting. During the 1930s, the government actually encouraged training in the arts. Many Arab countries gained their independence from France and Great Britain after World War II and during the mid-1950s. Not until the 1960s, however, did widespread Western art exposure in Iraq take place. Western exposure primarily resulted from modernization of the school system and the existence of scholarships to study art in foreign countries.[54] Because of the political and economic turmoil since that time, the traditional arts have been viewed as declining. Conversely, because of the lack of stability and artistic custom, globalization has increased exposure to many artistic styles, including those of the West. Since the 1960s, there has been an increase in the number of artists from the Arab nations, including Iraq, making their statements in the world.[55]

The period from 1980 to 1988 marked a time when Western archaeologists joined with Iraqi museum staff and shared a common interest in preserving the treasures of antiquity. For example, Americans in Baghdad were considered guests of the British School of Archaeology. In the 1990s, however, this peacefulness came to a halt when Iraq invaded Kuwait. A prominent archaeologist at the University of Chicago, McGuire Gibson, expressed his opposition to the war that not only killed people but also destroyed ancient artifacts so carefully preserved at the museums.[56] In 1991 there were local uprisings in Iraq against Saddam Hussein, and local museums were looted. By the late 1990s, the Iraqi regime once again was luring Western archaeologists back into the country.

After 9/11, a different state of affairs emerged. Archaeologists sent an unheeded warning to U.S. President George W. Bush, pleading for consideration of the detrimental outcomes to the study of ancient treasures and urging the need for protection. The official day of retaliation was March 19, 2003, when the new war began. On April 10, 2003, the media reported the looting at the National Museum in Baghdad, claiming that over 170,000 items of antiquity were missing.[57] Within a few days of these alarming accounts, media outlets were reporting the possibility that the looting had been staged by professionals within the museum itself. Later it was discovered that 170,000 pieces was a gross overstatement of the loss. To show dissatisfaction with Western ideology, political cartoons of George Bush emerged frequently during protests against the 2003 war.[58]

Meanwhile, contemporary artistic expression continues to surface, even as a repressive climate continues to exist. Exhibitions such as Between Legend and Reality: Modern Art from the Arab World, held at the Jordan Gallery of Fine Arts, addressed issues important to politics, gender, and concern for human conditions. Abstract styles and a pride in reviving Islamic calligraphy have surfaced. Iraqi calligraphic artists, whose work is displayed in this exhibit, include Taha Boustani, Raad Dulaimi, and Issam El-Said. The exhibition represented forty-six artists from fourteen countries.[59] This gallery was established in 1980 and attempts to give viewers a glimpse into modern Arab art that expresses the creative side of their culture.

Iran

Early revolutionary rulers in Iran outlawed certain types of artistic freedom and censored printed works and the media. Although figurative representation has been frequently labeled as sacrilegious, artistic expression has flourished in photography, cinema, and video. Apparently, the restrictions do not apply when a mechanical device such as a camera is involved in portraying the human figure and condition.

Television satellites have been banned since 1994 in order to limit the exposure to views from other parts of the world. However, satellites and video recordings are available. Also in the 1990s, the arts were burgeoning with young people studying the visual arts. As a result, Iranian art encompassed a variety of styles from miniatures to traditional calligraphy, from paintings to sculptures, and sometimes a combination of the above.[60]

Contemporary artists representing the variety in styles are listed in the *Artists' Directory* that provides a source of information on the latest trends. For example, the work of Parastou Forouhar is reviewed. Forouhar's installation art criticizes the social situation in her homeland of Iran. The work of Shirin Neshat features two film installations that were exhibited in Berlin and Salzburg. An exhibition titled Far Near Distance was held in 2004 in Berlin and presented expressions of contemporary Iranian Artists. *Tavoos*, a journal and online magazine, provides a wealth of information on the current art scene in Iran.[61]

Saudi Arabia

Prior to World War II, the land called Saudi Arabia was poor, and its revenues were derived from the Hijaz customs and pilgrim dues. In 1933 the first oil concession to Standard Oil was made, and the future and wealth of Saudi Arabia changed dramatically.[62] Today the General Presidency of Youth Welfare has an active role in determining the production of art in Saudi Arabia.[63] The Presidency prepares annual and five-year plans to develop artistic forms. Saudi Arabia is the home to many exhibitions and artistic competitions. It promotes an international forum and has tried to build connections with other countries. The Presidency also has been a participant in the Kuwait Exhibition for Formative Artists, the Arab Youth Festivals, and the Biennial Arab Exhibition that is controlled by the Arab Formative Artists Union. In 1972 the Saudi Arabian Arts Society was created by royal decree. The name later was changed to the Saudi Arabian Society for Culture and the Arts. The Plastic Arts Committee is the most important branch for promoting art at this center. The society is also responsible for monitoring and developing a cultural video film and recording library.[64] Because of international exposure to the Western world and the kingdom's own promotion of the arts, the work of contemporary Saudi artists such as Shadia Alem, Reem Al Faisal, Zaman Mohammed Jasim, Bakr Sheikhoon, and Faisal Samra possess an international flair.[65]

United Arab Emirates

The geographic location of the United Arab Emirates (UAE) is strategically situated: it provides direct access to the Indian Ocean and is inside the Persian Gulf and on the Gulf of Oman.[66] Until 1971 this area was known as the Trucial States. In the nineteenth century, Britain had a major interest in the Trucial States in order to ward off piracy and to police the sea route to India. In 1939 Britain sent a political officer to reside in Sharjah as a result of growing interest in oil and civil aviation. Beginning in 1935, the Iraq Petroleum Company began its search for oil, and its subsidiary was granted concessions from the sheikhs of Dubai, Sharjah, Ras al-Khaima, and Kalba. The oil expeditions were halted as a result of the outbreak of World War II. After the war, development of Gulf oil fields focused on Kuwait and Qatar, where oil had already been discovered. However, oil was later found in the Emirates in

> ## THE ROLE OF CLASS DISTINCTION IN ARAB ART
>
> In all the cultures under discussion in this chapter, the distinction between high culture and low culture in the Arab world has emerged. Class distinction continues to play a major role. Artistic traditions continue and are regenerated into accessible images for a wider global market in numerous popular forms. Because of the deep roots in religion, much of the artwork continues to be portraits of rulers, who are venerated as having godlike status. An example of this genre of art is a mural of Saddam Hussein depicted as the ancient Babylonian ruler, Nebuchadnezzar.[69] By marketing images of the past and replicas of ancient treasures, the art of the past can now decorate both the body and hang on the walls of individual dwellings. Much artistic expression is emerging in the Arab countries, primarily in cinemagraphic form. The popular art found today, overall, is a continuation of past traditions in technologically enhanced formats. Art is controlled by governmental entities and, therefore, new art and ideas can be suppressed or promoted as propaganda.

1958. The official founding of the UAE was in December 1971. The UAE was based on a provisional constitutional that could be renewed every five years.[67]

The UAE has been a cultural center for art of the Gulf region. While Dubai is the center for commerce, Sharjah is considered to reign as the cultural capital of the UAE. Since 1993 Sharjah has hosted an international art biennial. Also impressive is the fact that Sharjah was the location of the UNESCO cultural capital. The Sharjah Art Museum opened in 1995 and continues to expand.[68]

In 1987 Hassan Sharif founded the Art Atelier in Youth Theater and Arts, located in Dubai. An active member of the National Artists' Association, Sharif runs workshops, organizes exhibitions, and reaches out to the community. Photographer and video artist Mohammed Kazem is another popular in this area. Painter and videographer Khalil Abdul Wahid is known for his extreme close-ups. Summer workshops are sponsored by the central UAE Ministry of Education. The goal of these programs is to visually train students to look at the outside environment with a discerning eye. The instructors use art history slides, promote book discussions, and encourage exposure to a variety of visual forms. Since art is not taught in the public schools, these founding artists hope to create an interest in the public and especially in the youth to learn new means of artistic expression.[70]

Sharjah is also known for its contemporary photography. Ebtisam Abdul Azia was born in Sharjah and has a degree in mathematics and science. In the early 1990s she began experimenting with various art forms. A member of the Emirates Fine Arts Society, she has frequently translated art essays and art history from English into Arabic to increase the availability of art research. Two of her works were featured at the Sharjah Art Museum during the biennial exhibition. Her video called *Vision and Illusion* used her science background and showed an optician's light box (used for testing sight) while the patient and optician engaged in a repetitive dialogue.[71] Her other works shown at the museum were two photographs of hands, which she believes reveal the essence of the individual.

Another interesting female artist whose work was exhibited at the seventh Sharjah Biennial (2005) was Nuha Asad. Her project titled *Faces with One Feature* shows photographs of heads wrapped in red satin. The only body parts that are revealed are hands and feet, which serve to provide clues as to what lies beneath the surface. Her photographs are placed in their cultural context and explore the customs and the dress code of veils and covering bodies and female faces.[72] By concealing most individual identity within the clothing, Asad wants to be free of racism and class distinctions.

RESOURCE GUIDE

PRINT SOURCES

Al-Farsy, Fouad. *Modernity and Tradition: The Saudi Equation.* New York: Kegan Paul International, 1990.
Ali, Wijdan. *Modern Islamic Art: Development and Continuity.* Gainesville: University of Florida Press, 1997.
Armbrust, Walter, ed. *Mass Mediations: New Approaches to Popular Culture in the Middle East and Beyond.* Berkeley: University of California Press, 2000.
Bailey, David A., and Gilane Tawadros. *Veil: Veiling, Representation and Contemporary Art.* London: Institute of International Visual Arts and Modern Art Oxford, 2003.
Balaghi, Shiva, and Lynn Gumpert, eds. *Picturing Iran: Art, Society and Revolution.* New York: I. B. Tauris, 2003.
Barthes, Roland. "Rhetoric of the Image." Pp. 32–51 in Stephen Heath (trans.), *Image, Music, Test.* New York: Hill and Wang, 1978.
Biale, David, ed. *Cultures of the Jews—A New History.* New York: Schocken Books, 2002.
Bohrer, Frederick, ed. *Sevruguin and the Persian Image: Photographs of Iran.* Seattle: University of Washington Press, 1999.
Browne, Ray. "Internationalizing Popular Culture Studies." *Journal of Popular Culture* 30.1 (Summer 1996): 3–20.
Bryson, Norman, Ann Holly, and Keith Moxey, eds. *Visual Culture: Images and Interpretations.* London: Wesleyan University Press, 1994.
Chowdhry, Prem. *Colonial India and the Making of Empire Cinema: Image, Ideology and Identity.* Manchester: Manchester University Press, 2000.
Dabashi, Hamid. *Iranian Cinema Past, Present and Future.* New York: Verso, 2001.
Dalmia, Yashodhara. *Contemporary Indian Art: Other Realities.* Mumbai: Marg, 2002.
Davis, Craig S. *The Middle East for Dummies.* New Jersey: Wiley Publishing International, 2003.
Douglas, Allen, and Fedwa Malti-Douglas. *Arab Comic Strips: Politics of an Emerging Mass Culture.* Bloomington: Indiana University Press, 1994.
Dempsey, Amy. *Styles, Schools and Movements.* London: Thames and Hudson, 2002.
Esposito, John, ed. *The Islamic World: Past and Present*, vol. 1. Oxford: Oxford University Press, 2004.
Falk, Toby, ed. *Treasures of Islam.* London: Sotheby's/Philip Wilson, 1985.
Freedberg, David. *The Power of Images.* Chicago: University of Chicago Press, 1989. http://www.universes-in-universe.de/islam/eng/2005/11/abdulaziz/index.html.
Hammond, Andrew. *Pop Culture in the Arab World! Media, Arts and Lifestyle.* Santa Barbara, CA: ABC-CLIO, 2006.
Hourani, Albert. *A History of the Arab Peoples.* New York: Warner Books, 1991.
Keddie, Nikki R. *Modern Iran Roots and Results of Revolution.* New Haven: Yale University Press, 2003.
Khalaf, Rami. "Review of *Pop Culture in the Arab World!*" *Journal of Popular Culture* 39.2 (2006): 330–331.
Kleiner, Fred S., and Christin J. Mamiya. *Gardner's Art Through the Ages.* 12th edition. Belmont, CA.: Thomson/Wadsworth, 2005.
Lazzari, Margaret, and Dona Schlesier. *Exploring Art: A Global, Thematic Approach.* Belmont, CA: Thomson/Wadsworth, 2005.
Limbert, John W. *Iran at War with History.* Boulder, CO: Westview Press, 1987.
Mackey, Sandra. *The Iranians: Persia, Islam and the Soul of a Nation.* New York: Plume, 1998.
Mandel, Gabrielle. *How to Recognize Islamic Art.* New York: Penguin Books, 1979.
Mirzoeff, Nicholas, ed. *Diaspora and Visual Culture: Representing Africans and Jews.* New York: Routledge, 2000.
Moore, Molly. "Offending Cartoons Reprinted European Dailies Defend Right to Publish Prophet Caricatures." *Washington Post* (2006, February 2): A17.
Moore, Molly, and Faiza Saleh Ambah. "Tension Rises over Muslim Cartoons." *Washington Post* (2006, February 3): A1, A16.

Mostyn, Trevor, ed. *The Cambridge Encyclopedia of the Middle East and North Africa.* New York: Cambridge University Press, 1988.
Munier, Gillis. *Iraq: An Illustrated History and Guide.* Northampton, MA: 2004.
Nashashibi, Salwa Mikdadi. *Forces of Change: Artists of the Arab World.* Lafayette, CA: International Council for Women in the Arts & Washington, D.C. National Museum of Women in the Arts, 1994.
Patai, Raphael. *The Arab Mind.* New York: Hatherleigh Press, 2002.
Perani, Judith, and Fred T. Smith. *The Visual Arts of Africa.* New Jersey: Prentice Hall, 1998.
Roraback, Amanda. *Israel-Palestine in a Nutshell.* Santa Monica, CA: Enisen, 2004.
Stokstad, Marilyn. *Art History.* 2nd edition. New York: Prentice Hall, 1999.
Walter, Lynn, ed. *Greenwood Encyclopedia of Women's Issues Worldwide; The Middle East and North Africa.* Westport, CT: Greenwood Press, 2003.
White, David Manning, and John Pendleton. *Popular Culture.* San Diego: University of California Press, 1977.
Willett, Frank. *African Art.* New York: Thames and Hudson, 1993.
Zuhur, Sherifa, ed. *Images of Enchantment: Visual and Performing Arts of the Middle East.* Cairo: American University in Cairo Press, 1998.

WEBSITES

Aaronovitch, David. *Lost from the Baghdad Museum: Truth.* 10 June 2003. Guardian Newspapers Ltd. http://www.guardian.co.uk/Iraq/Story/0,2763,974193,00.html. David Aaronovitch reports on the false allegations that were made regarding the 170,000 items missing from the Baghdad Museum.
About Shell. 2003. http://www.egyptart.org.eg/misc/events.asp. Egypt Art. This site provides information about ways the Shell companies are trying to promote art events in Egypt. This site lists various galleries such as Arabesque, the EFPAC Gallery, the Asmara Gallery, and the Espace Karim Francis Gallery.
Ali, Wijdan. *Modern Art from the Arab World.* January 2004. Institute for Foreign Cultural Relations. December 28, 2005. http://universes-in-universe.de/islam/eng/2004/01/jngfa/wijdan-ali-text.html. This site provides the catalogue text for the exhibition Between Legend and Reality: Modern Art from the Arab World, extracted from the permanent collection of the Jordan National Gallery of Fine Arts.
Art and Architecture: Links. 2006. NITLE Arab World Project. December 28, 2005. http://arabworld.nitle.org/links.php?module_id=12. This site promotes fine arts in the Arab world, including sites for ArabsArt.com, IraquiArt.com, and sources for the art of Lebanon and poster art of the Palestinians and Israelis.
Art and Architecture: Readings. 2006. NITLE Arab World Project. January 2003. http://arabworld.nitle.org/texts.php?module_id=12. This site provides a list of suggested readings about Islamic art and architecture as well as popular culture.
Art Museums Worldwide. http://www.artcyclopedia.com/museums.html. This site is an online guide to art museums and art spaces in the Middle East.
Asia Book Room. www.asiabookroom.com. August 11, 2006. This is a repository that sells old, out of print, and new books on Asia.
Carver, Antonia. *Fondation Arabe pour l'Image.* August 2003. http://www.universes-in-universe.de/islam/eng/2003/03/fai/index.html. This site describes the Fondation Arab pour l'Image (FAI). The organization's mission is to archive photography from the Middle East and North Africa. The photographs preserved by this group are chosen for artistic rather than historical value. The site provides information on exhibits as well as information about contacting the FAI.
Contemporary Art from the Islamic World: Egypt. 2006. Institute for Foreign Cultural Relations. 10 March 2005. http://www.universes-in-universe.de/islam/eng/archiv/egy/index.html. This site contains multiple listings for exhibitions of contemporary Egyptian art from 2003 to 2005. The site provides a link to an interview with Mai Abu El Dahab, an independent curator, on the

recent developments in Egyptian art. The October 2005 issue of this online magazine focuses on contemporary artists in Saudi Arabia.

Contemporary Art from the Islamic World: Iraq—Artists. Institutes for Foreign Cultural Relations. November 25, 2003. http://universes-in-universe.de/islam/eng/artists/irq/index.html. This site lists contemporary Islamic artists and their works. The site also discusses issues regarding artistic representations in the Arab world.

Contemporary Art from the Islamic World: Palestine. 2006. Institute for Foreign Cultural Relations. http://universes-in-universe.org/eng/islamic_world/countries/middle_east/pse. This site lists a directory of contemporary artists in Palestine; it also provides a link to a project by Palestinian and Israeli photographers who are opposed to the occupation of Palestine and seek peaceful coexistence.

Contemporary Art from the Islamic World: Palestine. Institute for Foreign Cultural Relations. June 2004. http://www.universes-in-universe.de/islam/eng/archiv/ps/index.html. This site is specific to issue 10 of the online magazine, focusing on Palestine. There are articles about contemporary Palestinian artists, including a review of a project by Israeli and Palestinian artists who call for a peaceful coexistence.

Delahunt, Michael. *Islam and Islamic Art.* 2006. ArtLex. http://www.artlex.com/ArtLex/ij/islamic.html. ArtLex is a valuable site that serves as a general art annotated dictionary as well as a source for specific information on various art pieces, including those found in Islamic culture.

Encyclopaedia of the Orient: The Only Encyclopaedia for North Africa and the Middle East. August 9, 2006. LexicOrient. January 2003. http://I-cias.com/e.o/. This site is based on the *Encyclopaedia of the Orient* and contains background information on the Middle East and North African countries and cultures.

Fallaha, Natalie. *Local Flavor: Teaching Graphic Design in Lebanon.* September 2004. Institute for Foreign Cultural Relations. http://universes-in-universe.de/islam/eng/2004/04/lau/index.html. This site describes the process and approach of the artist Natalie Fallaha as she attempts to teach art courses within the Lebanese educational system. She discusses the challenges faced because of culture, language, and the political nature of Lebanese society.

Godlas, Alan. *Academic Islamic Studies and Middle East, Central Asian, and other Area Studies Sites.* August 18, 2005. University of Georgia. http://www.uga.edu/islam/MESCenters.html. This site provides a listing of world scholars specializing in Islamic, Middle Eastern, and Central Asian studies.

Hafidh, Hassan. *Priceless Treasures Lost at Baghdad's Museum.* April 13, 2003. http://www.rense.com/general37/pice.htm. The text of this statement by Hassan Hafidh criticizes the Americans' promise to protect the Baghdad Museum prior to the fall of Saddam Hussein's government.

Joffe, Alexander H. *Museum Madness in Baghdad.* April 16, 2003. Middle East Forum. http://www.meforum.org/article/609. In this text, Alexander Joffe provides insights into the looting that occurred after the collapse of Saddam Hussein's government and the damage that was reported to the Iraq National Museum in Baghdad. This site also contains a valuable bibliography on events in Baghdad during this time period.

Khasawnih, Diala. *Makan—The House of Expression.* November 2005. Institute for Foreign Cultural Relations. http://universes-in-universe.de/islam/eng/2005/025/index.html. This site describes Makan, the cultural hotspot in Jordan. It is a place where artists of all kinds gather to perform, exhibit, and network. It has become a key location for many Middle Eastern artists interested in promoting their ideas to the local public.

Marshall, Andrew. *Iraq Museum to Reopen Displaying Lost Treasure.* June 8, 2003. Ancient Worlds LLC. http://www.ancientsites.com/aw/Post/151377. This article reviews what items will be on view in the museum, such as gold Assyrian jewelry and other priceless artifacts from Nimrud.

Mbarak, Ricardo. *Art and New Media in Lebanon.* March 2005. Institute for Foreign Cultural Relations. http://universes-in-universe.de/islam/eng/2005/10/mbarak/index.html. This site contains lists of events, exhibitions, and lectures, as well as a directory of artists from Lebanon. It also contains the text of a lecture by Ricardo Mbarak, a media artist and art professor at the Lebanese Academy of Fine Arts, who spoke on media art in Lebanon at the Berlin "transmediale" festival.

MENIC: Arts and Humanities. 2004. University of Texas–Austin. January 2003. http://menic.utexas.edu/menic/humanities.html. This is the site for the University of Texas–Austin's resource center on the Middle East.

Middle East and North Africa. August 7, 2006. U of California–Berkeley. http://www.lib.berkeley.edu/MRC/MidEastVid.html. This site is an excellent source for reviews of videotapes on the Middle East and North Africa; it is part of the Media Resources Center at the University of California–Berkeley. Overviews of the videos cover the following regions: Afghanistan, Algeria, Cyprus, Egypt, Ethiopia, Iran, Iraq, Israel, the Kurds, Lebanon, Morocco, Palestine, Saudi Arabia, Syria, Turkey, and Yemen. Copyrighted 1996.

Middle Eastern Cultures Research Guide. January 5, 2006. College of DuPage Library. January 2003. http://www.cod.edu/library/libweb/kickels/middleeast.htm.

This site provides a bibliography of books, audio visual resources, and other Internet resources on the Middle East and North Africa.

Middle Eastern Popular Culture. April 24, 2002. The International Association for Middle Eastern and North African Popular Culture. http://www.orinst.ox.ac.uk/nme/nesp/middle.htm. This site gives pertinent information about the first and second international conferences on Middle Eastern Popular Culture and lists the participants and contributors.

Museum Guide. http://www.wadsworth.com/art_d/templates/student_resources/0155050907_kleiner/museumguide. This is the companion site to the Gardner *Art Through the Ages* (12th edition). This site provides links to museums all over the world, including the Iraq Museum in Baghdad, the Louvre in Paris, the University of Pennsylvania's Archaeology and Anthropology Museum, and the Metropolitan Museum in New York.

Painting. 2003. Egypt Art. http://www.egyptart.org.eg/galleries/default.asp?mt=1.

This site contains a listing of contemporary Egyptian artists and provides extensive interviews with these individuals. The artists include painters, sculptors, calligraphers, and those who create ceramics.

Routledge: Miltary, Strategic and Security Studies. 2006. Taylor & Francis Group. January 8, 2006. http://www.routledgestrategicstudies.com/. This site contains information on the development of art and its historical evolution in the Middle East.

Serwach, Joseph. *Theme Semester Will Spotlight "Cultural Treasures of the Middle East."* January 7, 2005. University of Michigan. 20 December 2004. http://www.umich.edu/~urecord/0405/Dec13_04/theme_semester.shtml. This site discusses the University of Michigan's sponsorship of semester programs that focus on Middle Eastern popular culture, social issues, arts, language, cinema, literature, and history. The theme of the semester is "Cultural Treasures of the Middle East."

ORGANIZATIONS (MUSEUMS, SPECIAL COLLECTIONS, AND LIBRARIES)

British Museum, Great Russell Street, London, WC 1B 3DG. http://www.thebritishmuseum.ac.uk/.

Iraq Museum, Karkh Museum Square, Baghdad 361215. http://www.baghdadmuseum.org/.

Jordan National Gallery of Fine Arts, PO Box 9068, Amman 11191, Jordan. http://www.nationalgallery.org/. Established by the Royal Society of Fine Arts (RSFA); current director is Dr. Khalid Khreis.

Metropolitan Museum of Art, 5th Avenue at 82nd Street, New York, NY10028. http://www.metmuseum.org/.

Middle East Studies Association (MESA), University of Arizona, 1219 N. Santa Rita Avenue, Tucson AZ 85721. http://www.mesana.org/.

Musée du Louvre, 75068 Paris, France. http://www.louvre.fr/llv/commun/home.jsp.

Museum of Archaeology and Anthropology, University of Pennsylvania, 33rd and Spruce Street, Philadelphia, PA 19104. http://www.museum.upenn.edu/.

National Museum, Shoukry al-Qouwatly Street, Damascus, Syria. http://www.syriagate.com/Syria/about/cities/Damascus/museum.htm.

Oriental Institute, University of Chicago, 1155 East 58th Street, Chicago, Illinois 60637. http://oi.uchicago.edu/OI/default.html.

Oriental Institute, University of Oxford, Pusey Lane, Oxford, OX1 2LE, UK. http://www.orinst.ox.ac.uk/.
Sharjah Art Museum, P.O. Box 19989, Sharjah, United Arab Emirates. http://www.sharjah-welcome.com/html/ch_art_museum.htm.
State Hermitage Museum, St. Petersburg, Russia. www.hermitagemuseum.org.
University of Michigan, Department of History of Art (Attn: Sussan Babaie), 519 South State Street, Ann Arbor, Michigan 48109 (Marya Ayyash, Center for Middle Eastern and North African Studies-UM). http://www.umich.edu/~iinet/cmenas/.

NOTES

1. See http://www.universes-in-universe.de/islam/eng/archiv/geo-start.html.
2. Lynn Walter, 2003 (in Resource Guide), p. 2.
3. Ray Browne, 1996 (in Resource Guide), p. 22.
4. Fred S. Kleiner and Christin J. Mamiya, 2005 (in Resource Guide), p.1051.
5. Lynn Walter, 2003 (in Resource Guide), p. 3.
6. Gabrielle Mandel, 1979 (in Resource Guide), p. 3.
7. Fred S. Kleiner and Christin J. Mamiya, 2005 (in Resource Guide), p. 357.
8. Gabrielle Mandel, 1979 (in Resource Guide).
9. Molly Moor, 2006 (in Resource Guide), A17.
10. Molly Moore and Faiza Saleh Ambah, 2006 (in Resource Guide), A1,A16.
11. Margaret Lazzari and Dona Schlesier (in Resource Guide), p. 144.
12. Mandel (in Resource Guide), p. 4.
13. Raphael Patai, 2002 (in Resource Guide), p. 178.
14. Mandel (in Resource Guide), pp. 36–37.
15. Kleiner and Mamiya (in Resource Guide), p. 367.
16. Mandel (in Resource Guide), p. 53.
17. Ibid., p. 58.
18. Kleiner and Mamiya (in Resource Guide), p. 56.
19. Wijdan Ali, 2004 (in Resource Guide).
20. Trevor Mostyn (ed.), 1988 (in Resource Guide), p. 217.
21. Ali (in Resource guide), p. 2
22. Mostyn (in Resource Guide).
23. See http://www.universes-in-universe.de/islam/eng/2003/03/wasla/index.html, p.1
24. Iolanda Pensa, *The 9th International Cairo Biennial: Pass Me a Balloon*, http://www.universes-in-universe.de/islam/eng/2004/01/cairo-bien/index.html, pp. 2–3.
25. *Painting*, 2003 (in Resource Guide).
26. Mostyn (in Resource Guide), p. 416.
27. Marilyn Stokstad, 1999 (in Resource Guide), p. 344.
28. Frank Willett, 1993 (in Resource Guide), p. 239.
29. Judith Perani and Fred T. Smith, 1998 (in Resource Guide), p. 304.
30. Ibid., p. 305.
31. Mostyn (in Resource Guide), p.360.
32. Amanda Roraback, 2004 (in Resource Guide).
33. Ibid., p. 362.
34. Mostyn (in Resource Guide).
35. Ibid.
36. Diala Khasawnih, 2005 (in Reference Guide).
37. See http://www.universes-in-universe.de/islam/eng/archiv/jor/index.html.
38. Antonia Carver, 2003 (in Resource Guide).
39. David Biale, 2002 (in Resource Guide).

40. See http://www.art.com/asp/search/products-asp/.
41. See http://www.questia.com/PM.qst?a=o&d=4947987.
42. Mostyn (in Resource Guide), p. 484.
43. Ibid., p. 151.
44. Natalie Fallaha, 2004 (in Resource Guide).
45. Ricardo Mbarak, 2005 (in Resource Guide).
46. Mostyn (in Resource Guide), p. 47.
47. Kleiner and Mamiya (in Resource Guide), p. 301.
48. Ibid., p. 378.
49. Ali (in Resource Guide), p. 4.
50. See Website for National Museum, Damascus, Syria (in Resource Guide).
51. Kleiner and Mamiya (in Resource Guide), p. 31.
52. Ibid., p. 52.
53. Alexander Joffe, 2003 (in Resource Guide); from *Middle East Quarterly* XI (Spring 2004).
54. Ali (in Resource Guide), p. 3.
55. Ibid., p. 4.
56. Joffe (in Resource Guide), p. 3
57. Ibid., p. 5.
58. Hammond (in Resource Guide), p. 93.
59. Mostyn (in Resource Guide).
60. Nikki Keddie, 2003 (in Resource Guide), p. 302.
61. See http://www.universes-in-universe.de/islam/eng/archiv/irn/index.html.
62. Mostyn (in Resource Guide), p. 403.
63. Fouad Al-Farsy, 1990 (in Resource Guide), p. 241.
64. Ibid., p. 242.
65. See http://www.universes-in-universe.de/islam/eng/artists/sau/index.html.
66. Mostyn (in Resource Guide), p. 442.
67. Ibid., p. 447.
68. See http://www.universes-in-universe.de/islam/eng/2004/03/art-sharjah/index.html.
69. Hammond (in Resource Guide), p. 93.
70. See "Establishing a New Generation—Interview with Mohammed Kazem and Khalil Abdul Wahid," http://www.universes-in-universe.de/islam/eng/2004/03/abd-kazu/index.html.
71. See http://www.universes-in-universe.de/islam/eng/2005/11/abdulaziz/index.html.
72. See http://www.universes-in-universe.de/islam/eng/2005/11/asad/index.html.

DANCE

STASIA J. CALLAN

> Dancing is the loftiest, the most moving, the most beautiful of the arts, because it is no mere translation or abstraction from life; it is life itself.
>
> —Havelock Ellis, *The Dance of Life*

Dance is one of the oldest human activities in the world. Its movements convey the rhythm of the universe re-enacted through motions of the human body. Its gestures manifest enchantment.

All dance comes from life. Dance facilitates self-expression and helps us ease the burdens of existence, among other functions. Dance satisfies many basic needs besides celebration. It helps release the pent-up stresses of daily life and facilitates joyful affirmation of both self- and group identity. The word "dance" comes from the Sanskrit *tanha*, meaning "joy of life." Dance has always been therapeutic for the individual and often has served as an activity used to attract a partner. In tribal communities, dance was an application of sympathetic magic, a ritual created to evoke human, animal, and plant fertility. In some parts of the world, it still plays such a role, pointing to the presence of powerful ancient mysteries in today's tribal cultures. These are forces that reach beyond conscious understanding.

As a fundamental element of human behavior, dance has evolved from the primitive movements of early civilizations to traditional folk dances, classical ballet, and several genres of modern and contemporary dance. In the twenty-first century, dance includes ballroom dancing, jazz, tap, break dancing, aerobics, belly dancing, and many other varieties. Such diversity is an outcome of the multimillennial evolution of dance throughout world cultures.

Over the millennia, dance underwent numerous changes before it reached its present-day diversification. When it ceased to function as a means of communal ceremony and ritual, it was taken up and refined by professional performers, and it became a secular entertainment. With the transition from sacred to secular, lines were drawn between what was acceptable and unacceptable. Dance forms using the hips, which are often highly sensual and erotic as well as an expression of goddess worship, celebrated fertility and the dynamism of life in ancient times. In patriarchal cultures, these forms of dance became bound up with the role of women in society and with what was permitted and forbidden to them. On the acceptable side was dance as a social pastime done mainly in one's home. On the unacceptable side was professional dance done by Gypsies, starving artists, and poorer members of the community. People such as these were distrusted for their free and easy ways, and for not conforming to the moral standards of the community at large. However, professional dancers were invited to perform at public festivals and some social events for wealthy community members; nevertheless, dancing in front of strangers was not considered an acceptable activity for respectable women.

In the desert lands of the Middle East and along the north coast of Africa, dance underwent a fascinating evolution. Dance movements remained the same, but the dance lost its religious significance and became a secular activity. At first an entertainment, dance later became an art form created for the purposes of observation rather than for participation. In the Arab-Islamic world, the secular art of dance requiring great skill and variety emerged from harems. Most often, it had and has no conscious connection to the ancient fertility dance from which it was derived, but a powerful residue of its ancestry is still embedded in it.

A rare biblical reference to dance is expressed in the New Testament through the story of Salome, Christianity's adaptation of a pagan myth. This story is based on the myth of Ishtar, the Babylonian goddess of love and fertility. In an allegorical rendition of the cycle of death and rebirth in nature, Ishtar's lover, Tumuz, dies and is taken to the underworld, which represents the womb of the Mother Earth. As the distraught Ishtar enters the most secret chambers of the underworld, she has to pass through seven-times-seven gates. In order to be admitted at each set of gates, she has to leave one of her jewels and a veil. While she is absent from the earth, no crops grow, and the earth is engulfed in sorrow. Upon her return from the underworld with her lover, nature is resurrected to new life after barren months of winter. The "Dance of the Veils of Ishtar" from her descent to the underworld became the "Dance of Shalome" (from the Hebrew greeting *Shalom).*

In addition to myth-based dances and belly dancing, there are many other vibrant dance forms performed today in the Middle East. They include the meditation dances of the Whirling Dervishes and the *dabkah*, a line dance enjoyed at festive celebrations in Palestine, Lebanon, Syria, and Iraq. Israel is teeming with folk dancing, ritualistic dancing, ballet, and modern dance.

In North Africa, as on the whole continent, dance has an ancient and venerable tradition. It has been an integral part of births, rites of passage, harvest celebrations, and marriage ceremonies. Masked, stilt, ceremonial, recreational, and religious dance forms are found in traditional, neotraditional, and contemporary dance. The pulse of African dance is humanistic, and for centuries it has been the chronicler of history, traditions, and aesthetics. The dances of Egypt, Morocco, Algeria, Tunisia, and Libya manifest indigenous strands as well as motifs found in Middle Eastern dance forms.

Middle Eastern Dance

The Middle East is the region of some of the oldest civilizations in the world. This extends to dance forms as well. There is a rich variety of dance forms, and some, like belly dancing, may be among the oldest in the world. The Middle Eastern spinning dance of the Whirling Dervishes is a ritualistic dance, a form of meditation leading to spiritual awakening. The dabkeh is a line dance enjoyed at community celebrations and festivals in Lebanon,

Syria, Iraq, and Palestine. There are also tribal men's and women's dances performed in Yemen. Israel is known for the *hora* and for highly stylized, choreographed folk dances performed to melodies from Spain, Russia, or Eastern Europe. Israel also features impressive modern dance and ballet troupes and performances.

The Middle Eastern dances have undergone many changes in their social and cultural contexts through the unending upheavals typical to the history of the region. Dance meanings have ranged from the sacred to the profane, from the spiritual to the sexual. The cultural view of dances has depended on the social system that was in power at a given period in history. In matriarchal (female-dominated) societies, dance was a form of goddess worship, with strong sexual and reproductive characteristics. In patriarchal cultures, such as Jewish, Christian, or Islamic, males dictated what was appropriate for women's behavior. For example, in matriarchal societies the belly dance had been viewed as a form of goddess worship. In patriarchal cultures, it was regarded as a form of lower behavior deemed unworthy of respectable women. The cultural interpretation of dance has been and still is gender based. By its very nature, dance stimulates the senses and lowers inhibitions. For this reason it is viewed by some with suspicion and disrespect. Yet, despite people's reservations, dance in the Middle East, as well as elsewhere in the world, has remained an indispensable means of animating both private and public celebrations. In this context, a conscious consideration of technique and aesthetic values emerged and became the art of the individual as well as an expression of virtuosity and innovation.

Belly Dance: Once an Ancient Ritual Is Today's Nightclub Entertainment

The dance most often associated with the Middle East is called the belly dance. It is believed to have originated in the Paleolithic era. Its history reflects as much the history of women as the history of the dance itself. Originally, dance was part of religious ritual, and religion was a part of everyday life. The rising and setting of the sun, the cycles of harvest, birth, and the death of the body were seen as manifestations of powerful forces beyond conscious understanding. The natural order of life evoked wonder, mystery, and sympathetic magic, which were exercised through rituals. Dance had a central role to play in ancient rituals, and over the years it grew to embody the value systems of the cultures that shaped it.

The Middle East gave rise to powerful goddess worship. The great regional goddesses such as Innana, Ishtar, Astarte, Aphrodite, and Isis—among others—were often imaged as mothers, the agents of life. Since the role of the male in reproduction was not fully understood until much later, the mysterious ability of women to give birth inspired both fear and wonder. Women's dances, captured in the ancient image of the "Dance of the Veils of Ishtar," became viewed as sexually evocative and threatening to male societies that established themselves in the Middle East in later periods of history. Thus, the ancient ritual of the belly dance was suppressed or permitted by males on their own terms, but its exotic appeal and stigma lived on.

The purest form of the belly dance may have been lost, but its current versions most likely retain some of its original elements. Ancient artifacts and descriptions of the dance focus on movements of the abdomen, with legs and arms gracefully enhancing the swaying, rotating, and undulating movements of the torso and hips. Such movements were once performed for women in labor, thereby rendering the birth less painful. This custom is still practiced in some parts of the Middle East and North Africa. Saudi Arabian women to this

Dance

> ### WHO BELLY DANCES?
>
> Today in the Middle East, as well as around the world, belly dancing is not restricted to the young. Mature women can celebrate their lives, maturity adding beauty to their performances. Many of the professional belly dancers work through their forties or fifties, and some well into their sixties.

day cry out sympathetic laments to the movements of belly dance at the time of childbirth. The belly dance had been and still is performed at weddings.

The history of belly dancing reflects different aspects of its cultural evolution in the countries of the Middle East. In the later eighteenth century, the Egyptian culture supported female performers, the *awalim*, or learned women, who were also called "savants." They were a celebrated community within the country because they were painstakingly educated.

An awalim had to have a beautiful voice, strong language skills, knowledge of poetry, and the ability to improvise spontaneously both lyrics and melody suitable to an occasion. At first, awalim performed mainly for women in harems, but in later times, no festival took place without them. They were acceptable in the male culture because they veiled themselves and observed other requirements of modest demeanor in public. Their counterparts were the *ghawazee*, the Gypsies. In Egyptian villages, Gypsies were regarded as professional dancers. The important role of Gypsies in the development of secular dance is reflected not in the Egyptian but in the Turkish word for female dancer: *cengi*, which is rooted in *cingene*, or Gypsy. The Egyptian word "ghawazee" means invaders, or outsiders, the meanings often associated with Gypsies.

The Gypsies of all lands share a common origin in India. In the past, they were the low-caste tribes that found no place in society and were forced to live a nomadic life, a lifestyle that has survived into the twenty-first century. In Hindu belief, the patroness of Gypsies is Kali, consort of the god Shiva. Kali is often imaged as the "Black Madonna," whom the Gypsies call "Sarah, the Egyptian." Yousef Maazin, father of one of the most famous ghawazee who lived by the temple of Luxor, admitted that the Gypsies were driven out of their homeland because of their stealing and bad reputation. Having few options for employment, Gypsies became entertainers in order to settle in Egypt and to survive in other countries. The ghawazee performed unveiled in public places. They fraternized with spectators and were not regarded as decent women. Some of them combined dancing with prostitution.

In time, the line between the highly educated and respected awalim performers and the ghawazee dancers blurred. At the end of the eighteenth century, the Egyptian government imposed many restrictions on both types of dancers and taxed them heavily. These measures drove many dancers out of Cairo to parts of the country where governmental controls were less effective. At that time, foreigners were coming to Egypt in increasing numbers, and these foreigners provided new employment opportunities for performers. Foreigners were mainly interested in dancing, so the awalim became known as singers and dancers; the ghawazee became dancers and prostitutes.

The development of the Egyptian nightclub scene in the late nineteenth century enabled the government to institutionalize and regulate entertainment. In connection with the British presence in Egypt and the expansion of tourism, the existing forms of entertainment were transformed into the nightclub scene, which began to mirror Western cabarets. Thus, belly dancing, the sacred dance of the Middle East, assumed a secular identity characterized more by its social role, its sensuality, and its aesthetics rather than by its spirituality.

Today, belly dancing is present in some form in every country of the Middle East. In Turkey, Israel, Palestine, and Egypt, belly dancing is largely part of the nightclub scene. In countries such as Syria, Jordan, Kuwait, Bahrain, Qatar, United Arab Emirates, Yemen, Oman, Iran, and Iraq, belly dancing is often practiced by women as they get together to relax and socialize. They bring along their children, who learn to imitate the dancing without conscious effort. Those who learn quickly are often invited to perform for adults. The skilled ones are praised for their grace and technique. In such settings, there are no clear divisions between the performers and spectators since they take turns dancing. Each woman shows her own style, which reflects her personality. This form of belly dancing is also practiced at weddings, births, and parties.

The Sufi Meditation Dance of the Whirling Dervishes

Similar to the belly dance, the Sufi meditation dance is uniquely Middle Eastern and rooted in the early history of the region. The founder of this branch of Sufism, a form of Islamic mysticism, was Mevlana Jalaluddin Rumi, the greatest Sufi Islamic mystic and poet in the Persian language. He was born in 1207 in Balkh, Persia, located in today's Afghanistan, but to escape the threat of the approaching Mongols, he settled in Konya, Turkey, with his family. The decisive moment in Rumi's life occurred when he met a wandering dervish (Persian *darvis*, meaning "poor" religious man), the holy man Mehmet Semseddin Tebrizi, also known as Shams. For months the two men lived closely together and developed a deep friendship. Shams revealed to Rumi the mysteries of divine majesty and beauty, and inspired him to new levels of poetry. The closeness of the two men was threatening to Rumi's family and disciples, so they forced Shams to leave town. Then, one night in 1247, Shams disappeared forever. He had been murdered, and Rumi's sons buried him.

Rumi expressed his experience of loss, longing, and love in about 30,000 quatrains (four-line verses). The various stages of love led Rumi to experience what his son wrote about him: "He found Shamas in himself, radiant like the moon." Thus, Rumi achieved complete identification between lover and beloved. It is believed that most of Rumi's verses were composed in a state of ecstasy induced by the music of a flute, the sound of a drum, the hammering of a goldsmith, or the sound of the watermill in Meram, where Rumi used to go with his disciples to enjoy nature. He often accompanied the recitation of his verses with dancing. It is said that one day, hearing the sound of a hammer in front of a shop in Konya, Rumi began a whirling dance. This, in turn, inspired some of the townsmen to participate in this dance of meditation and ecstasy. After Rumi's death in 1273, his successors organized the loose fraternity of his disciples into the Mawlawiyah, also known as the Whirling Dervishes because of the mystical dance that constitutes their ritual.

The practice of spinning or whirling, called *sema*, is central to Mawlawiyah worship. It involves spinning counterclockwise (right to left, toward the heart). The ritual begins with the chanting of prayers, followed by the beating of the kettledrum symbolizing the divine order. The prayers and the drums are followed by musical improvisation on a reed flute to represent the breath of life. The dervishes wear ceremonial cone-shaped hats, which represent tombstones, and their full-skirted white robes represent burial clothes. The black cloaks worn over the white robes symbolize tombs, and the whole costume is meant to reflect the death of their egos.

The leader of the ceremony leads the dervishes around the room. As they pass the main ceremonial part of the room, they bow to each other to show respect for the soul of each participant. Having completed three circles, they drop their black cloaks. This symbolizes that they have given up their attachment to the world. With arms crossed over their chests, the dervishes approach the master one at a time, kiss his hand, and begin to spin. Opening their arms, they raise their right arms to receive blessings. With their left arms down, they pass those blessing to the earth. Eventually, all the dervishes are whirling. As the whirling comes to an end, the leader reads a verse from the Qur'an reminding everyone that all directions belong to God, and that wherever one turns, God's face is there. The sema ends with the prayer for the peace of souls of all the prophets and believers.

Today, authentic sema is still practiced, but it is not to be confused with the many imitations presented as secular entertainment. As performed for tourists in many Middle Eastern countries, dancing based on the Sufi meditation ritual requires a high degree of balance and agility. The secular dancers wear wide, brightly colored skirts. When they whirl, the skirts rise and display a marvelous kaleidoscope of movement and color. The music of the dervishes is beautiful and haunting. It is sacred music, and it should to be treated as such.

Dabkeh (also Debke): The Folk Dance of the Levant

The *dabkeh* (the word means to stomp the foot joyfully) is a line or circle dance common to several Middle Eastern countries formerly called the Levant: today's Israel, Palestine, Lebanon, and coastal Syria. Considered the national dance of Lebanon, the dabkeh is also much beloved by Jordanians, Turks, and Syrians, and it is sometimes danced in Iraq. The dabkeh is currently danced by people of all ages at private parties, weddings, community celebrations, and night clubs. In Palestine, it is most often danced at weddings. The dabkeh is also performed by professional dance troupes in the Levant and around the world. Recreational folk dancers worldwide delight in dancing the dabkeh and its variations.

The earliest form of the dabkeh may have been introduced by the Turks during the Ottoman empire, when they ruled most of the Middle East. Its traditional costume reflects Turkish folk designs. However, the costume from each area may have distinctive features that identify it as being from a particular place. According to folk traditions, the joyful stomping of feet on the ground connects people to each other and to the earth, the mother of all life. This characteristic of the dance is common to all regions. The dabkeh has been central to village life because it is a dance that bonds a group of people together, but the way it has been incorporated into the community varies from village to village.

The dabkeh can be danced by men only, women only, or in a mixed formation. If it is danced in a line, the line may break off into formations. Dancers usually join hands, and for some formations, they clasp their hands at hip level, holding their arms straight, shoulder-to-shoulder, giving the formation an interesting appearance as they sway their bodies in synchrony while performing uniform footwork. The steps may involve hopping, skipping, fancy footwork, and rhythmic stomping. The leader, called the *ras*, is usually the most talented and experienced dancer in a group. The ras is always at the right end of the line (the top) and determines the pattern of the dance by twirling a handkerchief or a scarf overhead in time to the music. The ras begins to move the line smoothly in proper form, and then may break away from the line and demonstrate personal skill and style of leaps, quick turns, shoulder shimmies, and intricate footwork, challenging other dancers to join, match, or challenge these improvisations.

There is a particular type of music played for the dabkeh. The traditional music usually has six beats to the measure; while some modern pieces have eight beats to the measure, they are still danced in six-beat patterns. The mood of the dance is set by the musicians, particularly the flutist, and the ras. The flutist, while playing, is able to join the dance. At times, the flutist's playing seems to put the dancers into a trance as they shuffle and joggle along endlessly, without changing pace. At other times, the flutist may inflame the dancers into leaping, shouting, and early exhaustion. A very skilled drummer may also be able to participate in the dance while drumming, adding another dynamic to the dance. For centuries, the dabkeh symbolized the strength of the people of the mountain villages, who were accustomed to tough life. It was a way to energize them and bring relaxation to their stressful lives. Today, the dabkeh enlivens all who dance it: the people living in the Levant, those who migrated from that region to other parts of the world, and those who have never stepped on Levantine soil but like to stomp to the dabkeh tunes.

> **KLEZMER MUSIC**
>
> Although it had its origins with Eastern European Jews, klezmer music is not strictly Eastern European. It is a uniquely Jewish rendition of music from that region, but it has spread in popularity around the world, and folk dancers from the United States to Japan enjoy dancing to klezmer music. The word "klezmer" means "a musical instrument" in Yiddish, but it has also come to mean traditional Eastern European Jewish music or a musician who plays it. Klezmer music may be wailing, laughing, or sob-like, the melody carried by the coronet, clarinet, and violin, while such traditional musical instruments as the valve trombone, alto horn, and piano provide the underlying rhythm.

Hora: The Unofficial King of Israeli Folk Dancing

Originating in Romania, the hora was once a circle dance with social significance. The *hora mare*, or great hora, was danced on special occasions, such as weddings, and for relaxation. But it was also a metaphor for the community: the circle opened to admit sexually mature and suitable-for-marriage young women, adolescent boys entering manhood, and those ending their mourning. It was also the dance that facilitated shouting at anyone who had violated local moral standards. The Israeli hora, imported from the Balkans, does not carry any social significance other than serving as an expression of happiness. It has been regarded as the national dance of Israel since the nation's founding in 1948.

The Israeli hora is danced in a circle. The dancers put their arms on each other's shoulders, or hold hands, and move to the left, using grapevine steps. A dancer starts by stepping forward toward the right with the left foot, then follows that step by swinging the right foot to the left. The dancer then brings the right foot back and repeats the same movement with the left foot. The hora can be danced slowly and solemnly, or fast and furiously. In Israel, and around the world, it is danced to the melody of "Hava Nagila," a popular Israeli song. The hora can also be danced to many of the traditional *klezmer* melodies.

The Women's Hair Dance

This dance is danced in the Persian Gulf states and on the Arabian Peninsula in the countries of Saudi Arabia, Kuwait, Bahrain, Qatar, United Arab Emirates, Yemen, Oman, Iran, and Iraq. The harsh desert climate in this region necessitates napping or resting in the afternoon to escape the exceedingly high temperatures. As a result, the inhabitants are inclined to entertain at night and well into the morning hours when the weather is pleasant. The women tend to socialize separately since they are still excluded from men's circles. Thus, singing, dancing, and storytelling are the ways women entertain themselves and deepen their relationships. One of the women's dances is the hair dance.

Long hair has always been a symbol of female beauty in the Middle East. Even though some of the Arab women today cut their hair short, there are still many long-haired females available to preserve the hair dance, and their long hair is still greatly admired in that culture.

The skilled dancers grow their hair at least to the waist, or even to the knees or longer. As they dance, their hair spreads out in breathtaking circles and figure eights as they sway in time to the music. The sight of rows of long-haired, costumed women performing this dance is an inspiring and unforgettable experience.

The footwork of the hair dance is relatively simple. The dancer takes small steps forward, stepping on the flat of one foot while staying on the ball of the other foot, which is locked in place just behind the flat foot that leads forward. The feet are then reversed so that the other foot leads forward. This produces a gentle hopping or limping look as the dancer bobs along to the music. There are also steps that produce a smooth, gliding illusion, especially when the dancer's feet are hidden from view. The hair dance is danced to Khalid music. It is known as Saudi music, characterized by simple melodies and punctuated with percussion, which makes it rich, layered, and syncopated.

Al Ardhah: The Saudi Sword Dance

The *al ardhah* of Saudi Arabia is a men's dance rooted in the chants and melodies of the poets and singing swordsmen of its ancient Bedouin past. Considered to be the dance of the Najd, the central region of the vast desert kingdom, it shares some characteristics with the *ayyalah* of the United Arab Emirates. The shared features include the use of singers, dancers, and narrator-poets. In ancient times, al ardhah was a war dance, and women held the swords to encourage the men to show their courage and strength in battle. Today, it is performed at important community events, and women are no longer part of the dance.

Today's al ardhah features men carrying swords. They stand shoulder-to-shoulder in two long lines that face each other, one toward the north and one toward the south. On the eastern and western ends, there are two lines of men holding drums. At the center of the formation stands a man holding a flag. Nearby is the poet-narrator, who begins the dance by singing a verse to prepare the men for battle. The dancers repeat the chant; then the drummers begin to beat slow, stately rhythms, and the dance begins. The lines of men take turns advancing and retreating. The flagman then accompanies a prince or some dignitary to the center of the square so that his dance can be showcased. This may last for hours, with each dancer having the opportunity to display his virtuosity but all the while being part of the group.

Prominent members of the Saudi royal family have been seen participating in the sword dance. In the recent past, the current king Abdullah and his brothers, as well as important statesmen, have delighted spectators by joining their countrymen in swinging swords in this dance.

The Middle East is a curious conglomeration of countries: while some live more by Western cultural values, including Israel, Turkey, or Palestine to some extent, other countries honor the Islamic tradition and live by its values. Just as with other aspects of life, dancing in countries of the Middle East is permitted, or forbidden, by the cultural values honored in that country. In Israel, couples can enjoy ballroom dancing, modern dance, tap dancing, or ballet; the young people can engage in disco dancing, and people of all ages participate in folk dancing. In Turkey, a Muslim country, there is enough cultural freedom for the people to participate in Western ways of life, including dancing. Palestine also has pockets of Western cultural freedom, which permits both couple and disco dancing. In all three countries, folk dancing is open to both genders. Sometimes folk dances are danced in mixed formations; other times, they are danced in single-gender lines or in circles, and they attract dance lovers of all age groups.

In other regions of the Middle East, such as the Persian Gulf states and the Arabian Peninsula, Muslim culture promotes male dances at public and private events. The women in some places may appear publicly as entertainers, but most often their dancing takes place at single-gender social gatherings at homes where they relax by viewing other women dance, where they dance themselves, or where they teach their daughters to dance. Couple dancing is not practiced in the Islamic culture, so ballroom and disco dancing are forbidden. In such a cultural setting, the traditional regional single-gender dances, such as belly dancing or men's battle dances, are performed at public events and parties. These dances thrive and delight the postmodern world with their aesthetic and historical components.

NORTH AFRICAN DANCE

To this day, dance is central to artistic, social, and spiritual life in North Africa. African dance is also the bridge between the dead, the living, and the unborn. It is an essential part of daily life. On the social level, it commemorates births, deaths, weddings, state events, and rites of passage as well as happenings in nature such as celestial events, harvest times, fertility rituals, and healing sessions.

There is a great variety of indigenous dances in Africa, but they generally fall into the following categories: stilt dances, mask dances, martial arts dances, story and myth dances, social and ceremonial dances, healing dances, funeral dances, religious and spiritual dances, ethnic identity dances, and others. Some of these may overlap; they are not mutually exclusive. In most African cultures, the dancer represents the culture rather than the self. The signature of the performer is inherent in the re-creation of the supernatural presence in the world for the community. It is understood that the artist is the conduit of the divine creator and seemingly not responsible for the greatness of the dance; nevertheless, the responsibility is awesome. Acceptance of the responsibility as a conduit is what the spectators acknowledge in their applause after a performance. The dancer is considered "chosen" for such an important cultural function. The rejection of this role is considered sacrilegious.

In North Africa, which includes Morocco, Algeria, Tunisia, Libya, and Egypt, the characteristics of the African indigenous dance culture may have been altered by cultural influences from the Middle East. Just as in the Middle East, these are largely Muslim countries. To a great extent, the population of North Africa consists of Arabs; therefore, there is a strong presence of dances from the Middle East in this region, and some indigenous dance rituals coexist with Middle Eastern dance forms.

Whirling Dervishes

The Whirling Dervishes, known as the Mevlevi Order of Sufi Muslims, practice their spiritual meditation dance, sema, in Middle Eastern countries and also in countries of North Africa such as Morocco, Tunisia, Libya, Sudan, and Egypt. Sometimes the dance is performed for tourists, but often it is practiced privately as a religious ritual. Occasionally, the Whirling Dervishes will allow nonmembers to watch their authentic sema if the people are genuinely interested in Sufism. Otherwise, they turn tourists away since gawking, whispering, and picture taking detract from the spiritual essence of their dance. The dervishes' style of tilting their heads to the right and stretching their arms as they spin round and round in a precise rhythm in order to achieve meditative trance is much the same as the style of the original Whirling Dervishes from Turkey. Their white robes are also much like the robes of the Middle Eastern Sufi dancers. (Information about their origin and style of dancing can be found in Middle Eastern Dances under The Sufi Meditation Dance of the Whirling Dervishes.)

Baladi: The Belly Dance

The belly dance, best known in North Africa by the Egyptian word *baladi*, is performed at weddings, birthdays, private parties, and public festivals. The baladi is also performed in nightclubs, hotels, and theaters. Often, it is a part of a larger program of entertainment. The dance has a few patterns that include "snake hands" that create smooth, wavelike motions, "side hips" that produce shimmering, the "hip roll," chest movements, and chest and shoulder shimmies. Usually a vocalist, live music, and a drummer accompany or lead the baladi dances. Other instruments used in addition to the drum include the *ud* (lute), *nai* (flute), and *mazmar*, an oboe-like wind instrument. The dancer is also the musician since she expresses the melody through her body movements.

The baladi is loved but not held in high regard because it is not performed by wealthy women but by those who must support themselves, who are trying to escape poverty. The baladi is not meant to be sexual, but the belly dancer carries a stigma because she uses her body to earn money, and this is considered immoral. In some nightclubs and cabarets, belly dancing is associated with prostitution. This is contrary to the original purpose of belly dancing, which once was regarded as sacred, honoring the fertility of the womb and of the soil, and also honoring the great goddess, who was believed to support these functions in nature. (For more information on the history of the baladi, see Middle Eastern Dances, The Belly Dance: Once an Ancient Ritual Is Today's Nightclub Entertainment.)

Razha: The Dance of the Arab Warriors

The *razha* warrior dance in North Africa resembles the al ardhah, or the sword dance of Saudi Arabia. It is danced with naked swords. Its original purpose was to strengthen the muscles of the sword arm. *Chaupo* and *vumi* drums provide the beat for the razha dance, which consists of two rows of men who dance facing each other. They advance slowly, keeping time to the drumming. The dancers hold their swords in their right hands, perpendicular to their bodies. While holding the hilt of the sword in perfect balance between the thumb and the first and second fingers, each dancer gives the base of the sword's hilt a precision blow so as to make the sword quiver. The highly polished, quivering blade reflects light in a spectacular way, adding drama and beauty to the performance. The dancers move forward until they are about eight feet apart. Then, to the beating of the drums, they bend their knees and bow their bodies slightly forward toward each other in unison. Razha is a dance of male solidarity performed at public ceremonies. It may have regional variations.

Tahtib: A Battle Dance

Tahtib is the best known variation of a popular Egyptian folk dance called *saidi*. Paintings and carvings on monuments and tombs in Luxor point to its ancient origins. It is danced with bamboo staffs four to twelve feet long, which originally were used by Saidi men for herding animals and for protection. The thrusting and swinging of the staffs imitates real combat. Tahtib is a high-energy male dance full of battle drama. It may be performed in large groups, but the dancers usually divide into pairs for the combat movements that are the basis of this dance form. The dancers circle one another in search of an opening for attack, all the while maintaining defensive postures and, whenever possible, exchanging mock blows. In earlier times, the dance was performed on horseback with the twelve-foot staffs. Today's dancers, dancing on foot and carrying the four-foot-long staffs, create bobbing motions that give the appearance of a battle fought from horseback. There is much strutting and posturing as the dancers show off their strength and virtuosity. Like the razha, the tahtib is a dance celebrating the male culture at public events.

Guedra: A Dance Delivering Blessings

Regarded as the dance delivering blessings and peace to others, or giving oneself to God, the *guedra* dance reflects characteristics of indigenous African dances. It is attributed to the Blue People of the nomadic Taureg Berber tribes of southwest Morocco. They are known as the Blue People because they live in the desert and have limited access to bathing. Their robes are dyed with blue powder, which colors their skins. They view the color blue as attractive, and the dye serves as a natural moisturizer and sunscreen. The women of the Blue People are not required to cover their faces with veils since they are regarded as divinely protected givers of life, who bring children into the world. However, in the guedra dance, some dancers begin completely covered by a black veil called *haik*. Other dancers cover themselves with remnants of the blue cloth left over from their everyday garments. Their attire signifies the darkness and mystery of the unknown.

A genuine guedra is usually danced by one woman in the firelight or inside a tent, with a circle of spectators who become participants by chanting and clapping their hands to the hypnotic rhythm of drum. The unique feature of guedra is that it is usually performed on the knees (if the dance is performed in a standing position, it is called *t'bal*.) The spectators first notice the dancer's hands, colored with henna, as they shyly emerge from the sides of her dance attire. The dancer begins by blessing the four cardinal directions: east, west, north, and south. Then she blesses the elements of nature: air, earth, fire, and water. Finally, she touches her heart, head, and abdomen, and then with a flick of her fingers, she sends a blessing to the spectators from the depth of her being. Since the rest of her body is covered, hand movements are the essence of the dance, and it is believed that the dancer's soul is channeled through her fingers as she sways to the beating of the drum.

As the rhythm rises to a crescendo, the audience becomes more enthusiastic and louder. Then the drum falls silent, and the dancer, still in her trance, collapses to the ground. Soon she is followed by another dancer. Guedra combines a social event with an aesthetic and spiritual experience.

Moroccan Tea Tray Dance

The tea tray dance is a Moroccan version of an acrobatic dance performed in some countries of the Mediterranean. It involves balancing an object on one's head while performing fancy footwork, bending to the floor forward or backward, kneeling and crouching, twisting and turning to the tunes of local music. In Greece the object held on one's head may be a bottle of beer or a glass of water. In Turkey, it may be a small tray or a large tray with lit candles and/or tea glasses. In Morocco, it is literally a tea tray dance: the tray on the dancer's head is laden with candles, glasses, and often a tea pot, too. The dance is quite spectacular; it is performed by male or female dancers in tea houses or in nightclubs, and at social celebrations such as weddings, birthday parties, and commemorative events.

Zar, the Trance Dance

The *zar*, or trance dance, is believed to have originated as a form of ancient African deities worship in pre-Islamic times. Because it honors pagan gods, the dance is prohibited by Islam but is still practiced privately or secretly despite the prohibition. Most of the leaders of the zar dance are women; occasionally, men are permitted to help with the drumming, with the sacrificial slaughter of animals, or with the making of offerings to the possessing spirits. The dance is usually held in an area where there is an altar. This place is separate from the living quarters. A round tray with offerings such as fruits and nuts is placed in the center of the room. Animal sacrifices, ranging from small birds like a pigeon to large animals like a camel, were once standard sacrifices at the zar, but they are seldom part of modern-day dances.

Before the dance begins, the leader positions herself with her musicians on one side of the room. The rest of the space is filled by the participants, who are expected to make a donation to the leader. The monetary offerings from the participants are then used to help women in the community who are in need. After the dance, all those present share a meal and a level of connection, or spirit, generated by the trance dance.

The dance starts with small, rhythmic, jerk-like movements. The leader responds to the music as she feels it. Her small movements become larger, progressing to flinging her upper body from side to side. Her arms may be raised but relaxed so they can follow the swaying motion of the body, which reaches a level of wild abandon before she collapses, freed of negative energies. As contemporary world cultures explore alternative treatments for illnesses and depression, they study ritualistic trance dances like the zar and experiment with them to explore possible benefits.

The Bori Demon-Dancing

Another North African healing dance is the *bori* demon-dancing practiced by the Hausa people of Tunisia. They believe that the human visible body houses a soul that resides in the heart and also in the energies of life that wander at will over the body and sometimes step outside of it. The energies are perceived as the bori spirits; these may represent the second soul that relates to specific stages in life and changes according to one's life circumstances. Bori spirits are believed to be the intermediaries between the human host and the *jinn*, who are viewed as intelligent spirits of lower rank than angels. The jinn can appear in human or animal forms to possess humans. The Hausas believe that they have different bori at different stages of their lives. From puberty until marriage, they have a bori of the opposite sex; when a boy or a girl considers marriage, he or she must consult their bori of the opposite sex because the bori does not like to be replaced by a human rival. The Hausas are especially preoccupied with the negative energies of life, the evil bori, and have practices to combat them.

The bori demon-dancing is the Hausa way of exorcising the evil bori. The dancers in such rituals are seen as being in a dangerous state, and they must be attentive or suffer immediate punishment. Through movements of the dance, the dancers become the visible channels of the bori spirits. If a male is controlled by a female bori, the audience remarks that she dances well, despite the dancer's gender. Either male or female can be controlled by any bori in whose mysteries they have been trained. In some areas, the bori are summoned through incense and drumming; in other areas, an animal, most likely a he-goat, will be sacrificed.

Then, having summoned the spirits, the dancers begin to perform. Their movements are involuntary, coming from the unconscious, reflecting the state of being possessed. As the dance begins, each bori is impatient to be addressed, so no dancer performs for very long, no matter how powerful he or she may be. Each dancer goes into a seizure, during which the bori spirit leaves. The dancer, or the vessel of the bori spirit, slowly recovers after being given a few sips of water. The ceremony ends with a meal of meat and couscous.

Bori dancing is used as a treatment for insanity. The actions of the performers simulate different states of psychological disorders, which seem to be neutralized as the dancer achieves peace after the trance dance. On anther level, the body movements of the bori demon-dancers represent the worship of ancient nature gods still residing in the depths of the human psyche.

The countries of North Africa are less technological than, for example, are countries in North America, Europe, or Asia. Television is not so omnipresent as in other parts of the world, so the people have more time for socializing, dancing, and singing. Whether in Muslim or African social groups, people dance for enjoyment and relaxation, for healing, or to re-enact rituals. In African cultures, dancing is a deep, multilevel essential experience of life involving community gatherings of both genders. Its impact on world-wide dancing is profound, whether through drumming, some tango steps, or a wide variety of patterns. In Muslim settings, women in single-gender groups dance the baladi, the hair dance, and others at home. Men usually dance at public celebrations. People are initiated into single-gender dancing by their families and friends. Couple dancing is seldom seen since it is forbidden by Islamic fundamentalism. However, in tourist areas, Western social dancing is practiced. Whether ballroom, disco, or rock and roll, these dances can be enjoyed in some hotels, night clubs, or at international universities.

Parallel to that, in the same places, indigenous dance performances are in high demand by tourists who want to experience local cultures. In fact, the local people earn money from tourists by dancing for them and sometimes from teaching them how to do the dances. The tourist interest in authentic indigenous cultures and their dances may contribute to their survival in the postmodern world.

RESOURCE GUIDE

PRINT SOURCES

AlZayer, P. *Middle Eastern Dance.* Philadelphia: Chelsea House, 2004.

Asante, K. Welsh. *African Dance.* Philadelphia: Chelsea House, 2004.

Asante, K. Welsh, ed. *African Dance: An Artistic, Historical, and Philosophical Inquiry.* Trenton, NJ: Africa World Press, 1996.

Ashkanani, Z. "Zar in the Changing World: Kuwait." In I. M. Lewis, A. Al-Sa, and S. Hurreiz (eds.), *Women's Medicine: The Zar-bori Cult in Africa and Beyond.* Edinburgh, UK: Edinburgh University Press, 1991.

Beckwith, C., and A. Fisher. *African Ceremonies.* 2 vols. New York: Harry N. Abrams, 1999.

Buonaventura, W. *Serpent of the Nile: Women and Dance in the Arab World.* New York: Interlink Books, 1998.

Cheshire, G., and P. Hammond. *Cultures and Costumes: Symbols of the World. The Middle East.* Broomall, PA: Mason Crest Publishers, 2002.

Cooper, L. *Belly Dancing Basics.* New York: Sterling Publishing, 2004.

Deagon, A. "Dancing on the Edge of the World: Ritual, Community and the Middle Eastern Dancer." *Arabesque* 20 (September–October, 1994): 8–12.

Dils, A., and A. Cooper Albright, eds. *Moving History/Dancing Cultures: A Dance History Reader.* Middleton, CT: Wesleyan University Press, 2001.

DANCE

Friedlander, S. *The Whirling Dervishes*. Albany: State University of New York, 1992.
Huet, M. *The Dances of Africa*. New York: Harry Abrams, 1994.
———. *The Dance, Art and Ritual of Africa*. New York: Pantheon Books, 1978.
Kaschel, E. *Dance and Authenticity in Israel and Palestine*. Brill Academic Publishers, 2003.
Ohanians, D., and O. Ohanians. *Latin Dancing*. New York: Sterling, 2002.
Sharif, K. *Bellydance*. Crows Nest, Australia: Allen & Unwin, 2004.
Stephenson, R., and J. Iaccarino. *The Complete Book of Ballroom Dancing*. New York: Broadway Books, 2001.
Thompson, R. *Tango: The Art History of Love*. New York: Pantheon Publishers, 2005.
Torstrick, R. *Culture and Customs of Israel*. London: Greenwood Press, 2004.
Tremearne, M. *The Ban of the Bori: Demons and Demon-Dancing in West and North Africa*. London: Frank Cass, 1968.
Wright, J. *Social Dance: Steps to Success*. 2nd ed. United States: Human Kinetics, 2003.
Zuhur, S., ed. *Colors of Enchantment: Theater. Dance, Music, and the Visual Arts of the Middle East*. Cairo: American University in Cairo Press, 2001.

WEBSITES

African Dance and Drum Classes, Tribal Music, and African-American Art. 2005. Ethnic Arts Network. http://www.ethnicarts.org/.
AfriCan Dance Conference. 2003. Dance Immersion. http://www.griots.net/archives/focus/dance.html.
African Dance Groups. http://dir.yahoo.com/Arts/Performing_Arts/Dance/Folk_and_Traditional/African/Groups/.
African Dance Tradition and Philosophy. February 25, 2004. Institute of African Dance, Research, and Performance. http://umfundalai.com.
Dances from the AVAZ International Repertoire. 1999. AVAZ International Dance Theater. http://www.avazinternationaldance.org/intldances.htm. This site describes and showcases different dances of the Middle East.
Finkelstein, Richard. *African Dance Resources*. May 18, 2004. Artslynx International Arts Resources. http://www.artslynx.org/dance/afro.htm.
Folk Dances of the Middle East and North Africa. July 20, 2006. http://www.chelydra.com/folkdance.shtml.
Middle Eastern and North African Dance. The International Academy of Middle Eastern Dance. http://www.bellydance.org/.
North African Dance. 2005. Khalidah's North African Dance Experience. http://www.khalidah.com.
Sa'id, Aziza, and Megan Marti'n. *Aziza Sa'id's Mid-Eastern Belly Dance Site*. March 11, 2003. http://www.zilltech.com/.
Shira. *The Art of Middle Eastern Dances*. December 31, 2004. http://www.shira.net/.
Suhaila. 2005. Suhaila Productions. http://www.suhaila.com/. This is the official site of dancer, choreographer, and instructor Suhaila Salimpour.
Wesley, Honey. *Discover Belly Dance—Costumes, Videos, etc.* http://www.discoverbellydance.net. This Website contains a directory that offers links to many other Websites dealing with the many different aspects of belly dancing.
Yasmina's Joy of Belly Dancing. August 1, 2006. http://www.joyofbellydancing.com.

VIDEOS AND FILMS

Middle East

Adam Basma Middle Eastern Dance Company: Live in Concert 2005. 2005. Directed by Nick Havinga; performed by the Adam Basma Dance Company.
Classics of Samia Jamal, Taheia. 1999. Contains performances by famous Egyptian dancers recorded in 1999.

DANCE

Egyptian Folkloric Dances. Egyptian folk dance troupe of five male and five female dancers performs a variety of dances with masterful renditions of the ghawazee and tahtib dances. 105 minutes.

Fifi Abdo Concert in Al Esmailia. Performance by a famous Egyptian belly dancer known for masterful shimming.

The Goddess Workout. Performance by Dolphina. GoddessLife. December 1, 1998. A Yemenese video, based on ancient belly-dance techniques, provides an innovative cardiovascular exercise routine demonstrated by Dolphina.

Iraqi Variety Folk Dances. A large folk troupe performing a rich variety of Iraqi dances; wonderful music and costumes. 50 minutes.

Mezdeke Show and Super Oriental. Turkish belly-dance performances displaying top Turkish talent.

Son of Sinbad. 1955. Directed by Ted Tetzlaff; performances by Vincent Price and Sally Forrest. RKO.

Sufi Soul: the Mystic Music of Islam. 2005. Directed by Simon Broughton. Songlines/MWTV.

Tamra Henna. 1957. Directed by Hussein Fawzi; performances by Naima Akef and Rushdy Abaza. A film showing an Arab version of *My Fair Lady*, with dancing.

Valley of the Kings. 1954. Directed by Robert Pirosh; performances by Robert Taylor and Eleanor Parker. MGM.

North Africa

African Dance: Sand, Drum and Shostakovich. 2002. Directed by Ken Glazebrook and Alla Kovgan.

Dances of Egypt. Directed by Aisha Ali. 1991. Association for Research in Arabic Folklore.

Dances of North Africa, vol. 1. 1998. Directed by Aisha Ali.

Egypt Dances. 1980. Produced by Magda Saleh. William Patterson College TV.

Marrakesh Folk Festival and More. 2005. A video of an entire festival showing authentic tribal dancing under the stars. 60 minutes.

Morocco & the Casbah Dance Experience at Riverside Dance Festival. 1986. Full concert that won four awards. 120 minutes.

FASHION AND APPEARANCE

ELIZABETH D. JOHNSTON

In the eighteenth century, and throughout the nineteenth, European society was fascinated by the Middle East, simultaneously seduced and threatened by its exoticism. Elements of its culture—its art, philosophies, myths, and literatures—made their way into European society; among these elements was fashion. We see this fascination with Eastern fashion as adopted in Western clothing styles,[1] and as it is represented in Western literature and art. For example, in order to seduce various men, the English-born heroine of Daniel Defoe's *Roxana* dons the clothes of a Turkish woman. Travel literature of the period, such as Lady Mary Wortley Montagu's *Turkish Embassy Letters*, routinely describes Middle Eastern women's fashions. Many paintings, too, depict the dress of exotic-looking men and women from the Ottoman empire.[2] More recently, following the terrorist attacks of September 11, 2001, such Middle Eastern–born designers as Raf Simons and Bernhard Willhelm have experimented with notions of terrorism and war in their designs, using dark colors, *kafiyehs* (a man's headscarf), veils, turbans, and the like. The fashion world calls this the "muslimization" of fashion. Currently, the Middle East is ranked fourth in the world league of fashion and clothing accessories exporters, accounting for nearly 5.5 percent of global trade.[3]

Just as Eastern fashions once fascinated Western minds, so too have Western notions of beauty penetrated Eastern cultures. Charlotte Jirousek, tracing the history of the mass fashion industry in the Ottoman empire, notes that the rate at which fashion changed in the Ottoman empire began to speed up in the eighteenth century and by the nineteenth century had "burgeoned into a mass fashion system of dress."[4] This growth was largely due to industrialization and an increasing number of families with disposable incomes. Jirousek notes, however, that Ottomans were slower to adopt European-style clothing and were, instead, largely influenced by other Eastern styles with which they came into contact as trade expanded. Following the nineteenth-century Tanzimat reform movement, Western fashion became increasingly common in the Ottoman empire. Today Western fashions continue to influence Middle-Eastern and North African styles, in large part because of mass media, such as satellite television and mass-circulated newspapers and magazines featuring the latest fashions.

FASHION AND APPEARANCE

Fashion, or what is considered fashionable, in the Middle East and North Africa is largely dictated by at least four factors often difficult to extricate from each other: the degree to which the region in question is secularized, its commercial development, its wealth, and whether it has a large youth population. Because of commercial globalization, the increasing influence of the West on the Middle East and North Africa is unquestionable, especially among youth culture and in urban areas (and thus a source of great tension); since 1980, 200 Western-style shopping malls have opened in the Persian Gulf region alone, with another 100 slated for construction in the region in the next five years. By 2010 the shopping mall industry is expected to grow by 140 percent.[5] However, many countries in this region continue to adhere to strict religious guidelines concerning physical appearance and adornment. Thus, one might argue that a description of these dress codes is not a description of *fashion,* because the dress codes are designed to downplay physical appearance, to draw attention away from one's body, and to curtail personal expression. While important variations exist between countries and within regions of the same country—distinctions this article will address—many of the fashion and appearance choices made by Middle Easterners and North Africans can be generalized because a large percentage of these populations are Muslim and therefore follow similar lifestyle guidelines. Unlike in the United States, where church and state are ostensibly separated, in many Middle Eastern and North African countries religion continues to direct both law and cultural choices. Thus, before detailing distinctions between regions, a description of these general guidelines applicable to those practicing the Islamic religion is in order.

MIDDLE EAST AND NORTH AFRICA: HISTORY AND OVERVIEW

Clothing

Although many inhabitants of the Middle East and North Africa battle poverty, many also have the money and leisure time to spend on finding and wearing what is most fashionable. In 2004 Middle Eastern and North African clothing and accessories imports were valued at $4.1 billion, while the region's exports topped out at $11 billion.[6] What one wears, however, is largely determined by whether one practices fundamentalist Islam.

Fundamentalist Islamic men usually cover everything from their navel to their ankles. They tend to wear sandals and loose-fitting, off-white pants or a long, loose robe. They grow a full beard, which they keep trimmed short; mustaches are optional. Although the dress code mandates that hair be kept shoulder-length, most modern Islamic men wear it shorter.

For fundamentalist Islamic women, wearing the *hijab* is common practice. In the West, the hijab is commonly misunderstood as a veil or head covering worn by Muslim women; however, in the Islamic world, hijab refers to a set of rules governing physical appearance, and it applies to both men and women, although the rules for modesty are greater for women. Most scholars agree that the Qur'an (or Koran) offers no explicit clothing guidelines; most notions about veiling come from other sources. Specifically the Qur'an states, "And say to the believing women that they should lower their gaze and guard their modesty; and that they should not display their beauty and ornaments except what must ordinarily appear thereof; that they should draw their veils over their chests and not display their beauty except to their husbands, their fathers" (24:30–31). In the most rigid interpretation of this dress code, Muslim women cover everything but their face and hands in the presence of anyone who is not a direct family member. More liberal understandings of the code require Muslim women to practice veiling, but this might mean wearing a simple headscarf.

The veil predates Islam by several centuries; it was initially used by harem women of Assyrian kings, and later in Greece, Byzantine Christendom, Persia, and India. According to scholar Lyn Reese, "Muslims in their first century at first were relaxed about female dress. When the son of a prominent companion of the Prophet asked his wife, Aisha bint Talha, to veil her face, she answered, 'Since the Almighty hath put on me the stamp of beauty, it is my wish that the public should view the beauty and thereby recognize His grace unto them. On no account, therefore, will I veil myself.'"[7] As Islam expanded, however, and came into contact with other cultures, they began to incorporate their practices. By the second century, wealthy Islamic women were using veils as a signifier of power and caste, but women who lived in rural areas and nomadic women rarely covered their faces. It was only during the Middle Ages that the veil became part of Islamic culture and, in some cases, law. In the nineteenth century, with increasing attention to women's rights in the West, these laws fell under scrutiny as scholars debated whether the injunction to cover women *really* was dictated by the Qur'an.

Arguments denouncing the veiling of women often occurred in conjunction with nationalist movements that linked women's emancipation to a more civilized state for all. Some of the women engaged in the nationalist movements preferred, instead, the *litham*, a smaller, triangular scarf made of silk. In the mid-twentieth century, however, the hijab once again became popular, a symbol of a growing rejection of Western ideas and culture. Both the politics and the history of the veil are complex and have been the subject of much critical discussion and media focus.[8]

What women wear with the veil also varies; it can be traditional costume underneath a body-length robe or Western name-brand jeans and T-shirts, with robe optional. Traditional costumes are often beautiful and ornate. Situated in the midst of busy trade routes for centuries, the Middle East and North Africa have had access to a wide variety of diverse and beautiful fabrics and designs. Traditional dresses worn by Arabic women could vary from region to region and from occasion to occasion. A number of traditional costumes are on display at the Palestine Costume Archive exhibition entitled "Secret

BODY ART—HENNA

A common practice in North African and Middle Eastern body art is the use of henna. Not exclusive to these two regions, the art has been practiced for medicinal and cosmetic purposes for at least 5,000 years by Hindus, Sikhs, Jews, Christians, pagans, and others. Scholars believe that the earliest practitioners of the art were the Babylonians, Assyrians, Sumerians, Semites, Ugaritics, and Canaanites, but the term originates from the Arabic word *Al-Hinna*. Henna is made from grinding up the plant *Lawsonia inermis* into a fine powder, which is then mixed with hot water; this mixture is then used to stain the skin. The stain lasts until the skin exfoliates, usually one to twelve weeks. Mixing the powder with other plants and fruits, such indigo or coffee, can create variations in its color. It has been used for centuries to die hair a reddish or deep brown tint, but mixing it with sugar and oil can produce the lasting effects needed to use it as body art. Arabic uses of the art tend toward floral or vine-like designs on hands and ankles, whereas North African designs favor geometric or abstract shapes. Henna is often applied in conjunction with celebrations such as weddings or religious holidays. The use of henna in the West became popular in the 1990s, although the U.S. FDA has not approved its use for skin applications.

Splendours: women's costume from the Arab world." The exhibition's Website describes this collection:

> There are village and oasis costumes (from Egypt, Syria and Jordan) and nomadic *bedouin* costumes (from the deserts of Egypt and Saudi Arabia). There are everyday dresses (from Jordan, Egypt, Oman and Syria) and special occasion and wedding dresses (from Egypt, the Gulf and Jordan). There are children's dresses from the Gulf, covered with glitter and sequins, and from Kuwait, designed in the colours and shape of the Kuwaiti national flag. There are silks and velvets and handwoven linens, *ikats* and *atlas* cloths from Damascus. . . . Choices in fabric reveal social status (wealth buys imported fabrics and silk threads for embroidery) while choices in decoration may reveal marital status (for example, the choice of embroidery colour among the *bedouin* tribes of the Sinai Desert), age, religion, or even the number of children in the family. . . . Through the language of costume—handwoven fabrics, silken threads and gold and silver couching, silver beading, tassels and plaited silk, red and pink cross stitch, appliqué, coined headdresses and facemasks, silver bells and blue beads, mother of pearl buttons and sea shells, indigo and sumac dyes, embroidered motifs such as birds, moons, cypress and palm trees, khol pots and pasha's tents, griffins and human figures (embroidered with handbags and high heels!)—we must come to understand that each costume tells us a story about its creator and its wearer, and about the cultural heritage.[9]

Clearly, both the veil and traditional costumes operate not simply as articles of clothing, but as signifiers with important cultural and historical contexts, some of which will be discussed at greater length in the sections to follow on each country or region.

Cosmetic Use and Hairstyles

In 2004 the Middle East and Africa accounted for $10.12 billion in sales in cosmetics and toiletries, $5 billion of which is estimated to be on beauty aids alone. The Gulf states of the Middle East—Iran, Iraq, Kuwait, Saudi Arabia, Bahrain, Qatar, United Arab Emirates, and Oman—together accounted for $2.1 billion sales in cosmetics and fragrances in 2005; per capita spending on cosmetics in these states averaged out at $334 annually.[10] These modern notions of beauty in the Middle East and North Africa are deeply rooted in a rich tradition of self-decoration and adornment.

Historically, Arabic inhabitants used a process called *threading*, or *khite*, to remove unwanted hair; this involved pulling leg hair through a circle of thread to rip it out. Today, threading is still practiced by many in Indian and Middle Eastern cultures to remove unwanted facial hair. Islamic law dictates that men and women should remove armpit and facial hair at least every forty days; women are discouraged from reshaping eyebrows for cosmetic purposes. Islamic law disallows women to shave their heads, although they are allowed to cut it to decrease volume. At last count, there were some 30,000 hair salons open for business in the Middle East and North Africa.[11]

Most scholars agree that alcohol-based perfumes derive from the Middle East, made from burning gum and resins to create incense, or by combining animal and vegetable oils with fragrant plants. When King Tut's tomb was opened in 1922, archaeologists could still smell the perfumes and oils that had been used to scent his body. Wealthy Egyptians used scented oils to soften their skin and make it more sexually appealing. Frankincense and myrrh were especially popular. Soap, too, is thought to have originated in the Middle East.

Makeup has long been intertwined with both cosmetic and medicinal purposes. Ancient Egyptians used minerals to color and define their faces, a practice dating back to

10,000 BCE that is discussed in such texts as the Old Testament and is seen on wall art. Mummies, too, were often buried with their makeup, considered an essential in the afterlife. Ancient Egyptians also used henna to tint fingernails, and they used rouge, made from safflower or from a clay called red ochre, on their cheeks and lips. Paints were used by women to color their breasts and nipples. Both sexes used kohl, made of crushed antimony, to line their eyes and darken their eyebrows, and blue paint to draw attention to their veins.

Scholars of Islamic law are divided about the use of cosmetics. Some argue that strict adherence to Islamic law requires that women wear cosmetics only in the presence of other women, their husbands, or their immediate male relatives. Others suggest that kohl is permissible around the eyes, but that rouge, lipstick, or nail polish is excessive. Since the U.S. invasion of Iraq in 2003, studies show that cosmetic and perfume use has declined markedly in such countries as Morocco because of a return to fundamentalist Islamic values. Use of kohl eyeliner and mascara, however, has increased because many scholars argue that Islamic law permits these.[12]

Physical Fitness and Cosmetic Surgery

Obesity is a growing health problem among adults and children alike in these countries and regions—arguably because of globalization and the introduction of fast food restaurants to these regions. In turn, eating disorders among youth are on the rise. Physical fitness equipment and spas that offer physical fitness programs have become increasingly popular in wealthier countries. Strict Islamic law does not permit cosmetic surgery for beautification purposes; however, cosmetic surgery is available in many Middle Eastern and North African countries and has become increasingly popular. However, breast augmentation and liposuction, so popular in the West, occur infrequently in Islamic countries, probably because women's bodies tend to be hidden by their robes. Instead, rhinoplasty (nose reconstruction) is the most popular cosmetic surgery, no doubt because faces generally are revealed.

Celebrity Influences

Satellite television and glossy fashion magazines have brought Western ideas of beauty to the East. One of the influences of female perceptions of beauty has been, as in the United States, Barbie. In 2002 the female Sara and her male counterpart Dara doll were released. Created in China but marketed in Iran, the dolls—a male and female set of twins first appearing on an Iranian children's show—are fashioned to be approximately eight years old and provide an alternative to the Western Barbie and Ken dolls at half the price. Each of the four Sara dolls comes with a white scarf that children can use to cover the dolls' hair. Another popular Barbie-doll imitator is Fulla, created by a Syrian-based company and launched in many Middle Easter countries in 2003. Fulla, like her two friends Yasmine and Nada, comes complete with a hijab and a pink prayer rug, and a variety of matching accessories, including a spring *abaya*, are sold separately. Her wardrobe has also been modernized for an Egyptian market. She sells for a shocking $16 in Damascus, where the average monthly income is $100; even at this high price, she is quickly rivaling Barbie dolls, selling 2 million dolls in the first two years of her arrival. But the twenty-two-member Arab League's much-talked about design for its own version of a Muslim-appropriate Barbie doll called Laila was shelved as inappropriate.

Fashion Magazines

Arabic women in Bahrain, Saudi Arabia, Qatar, Kuwait, Oman, and the United Arab Emirates possess increasing spending power; thus it makes sense that advertisers want to target them. They do this, as in the United States, largely through fashion magazines. In the last decade, censorship has been relaxed in many Middle Eastern countries, yet both the content and advertisements of the magazine articles continue to remain fairly traditional. Photos of women sporting the latest fashion trends tend to avoid displays of nudity or seminudity. Advertisements are, however, culturally specific. An ad for a watch, for example, might portray a hand decorated with henna designs. Products most often advertised in these magazines include perfumes, jewelry, and watches, followed closely by clothes and cosmetics. The major women's magazines circulated weekly are the Gulf magazine *Sayidaty* (142,157 sold weekly), the Egyptian *Kolennas* (109,934 sold weekly), Kuwaiti *Al Yakaza* (97,605 sold weekly), and the multiregional *Zaharat Al Khaleej* (86,760 sold weekly) and *Saydaty Saadati* (75,600 sold weekly). In Algeria, *Dzeriet*, the first woman's magazine featuring fashion and cosmetics, began publication in 2004.

REGIONS

Western Sahara

Few studies of the culture of this North African region, 95 percent of which is desert, have been conducted. There is no census information. The country has no FM radio stations and no television broadcast stations, so, as one might imagine, it has no fashion industry. However, it is well-known for its male beauty pageants, which take place during the ancient festival Gerewol. Men who participate in and win these contests signify the tribal Fulanis' ideals of beauty. These men adorn their bodies with jewelry and have long, slender bodies, white teeth and eyes, and straight hair. These notions of beauty derive, no doubt, from medieval times in which whiteness signified wealth.

Clothing is generally handmade by nomadic tribes. Tuareg men, who are part of North Africa's nomadic Berber population, famously practice veiling, wrapping their heads with an indigo veil to mark the end of boyhood. They consider it highly indecent for a man to expose his mouth to anyone deserving of formal respect; moreover, it is considered improper for a man to reveal his face to anyone of a superior class.

Mauritania

Mauritania is officially an Islamic Republic. Most of its population is either nomadic or seminomadic. Nearly half the population is under 14 years of age, and many belong to the Qadiriyya brotherhood.

One of the country's few manufactured goods is clothing. Mauritania has given the world a few world-famous fashion designers, among them Salamata Ba and Oumou Kane Sao. Its famous models include Khady Diop. Fatimetou Mint Sid'Ahmed Ould Mouguoya, alias Le Matt, is president of the Mauritanian women entrepreneurs and business owners (UMAFEC) and is considered one of the most powerful women in the region. Most Mauritanians, however, tend to wear traditional clothing, such as their *malhafa* robes or the *mouchtiya*, which is a cape-like shawl worn by married women. Most shopping is done at markets, and bartering is still common.

Obesity was once revered by Mauritanians. In fact, some young girls are force-fed before marriage in an often brutal ritual called *gavage.* This fattening up of girls begins when they are nine or ten, since they wed as early as twelve. Some may be taken to medical facilities, or fat farms, where professionals tailor for them fat-rich diets. Others are fed horse pills. Some are required to drink mass quantities of milk. The reasoning behind this tradition is that obesity is a sign of wealth, as well as a sign that a husband cared enough for his wife to provide for her. This is especially important in an otherwise impoverished nation. With Western ideals of beauty seeping into North African popular culture, however, fat has become less fashionable. A generation ago, one-third of the country's girls suffered this treatment; now the number is closer to one in ten. The government has officially banned the practice.[13]

Morocco

There is no national dress code in Morocco, where traditional clothing is deemed unfashionable. Dawn Marley writes, "If fashion mirrors society, then, Maghrebian society is a veritable melting pot of East and West, where women can feel comfortable in a variety of styles. Maghrebian women's magazines reflect this in their fashion pages, where the same unwearable Western fashions which grace the pages of European women's magazines alternate with 'special issues' on new designs in caftans and jellabahs (e.g., *FDM, Citadine,* Jan 1998)."[14] Men prefer Westernized fashions and are very brand conscious, rejecting the traditional *djellaba.* Older men, however, still wear *kaftans,* djellabas, and the traditional Moroccan *fez* hats (which came from Turkey). The djellaba, which replaced the *burnoose,* or *sulham,* is a hooded garment made of wool with neutral stripes and edged with vibrant tassels. Urbanites favor blue cloth. Beneath this is worn the kaftan, or *farasia,* a short dress with wide sleeves that buttons down the front and is belted. These garments tend to be wine red, olive green, light blue, or brown. The *djebba,* a completely square kaftan with holes for arms and neck, and *kamis* (or *gamis*), which has added sleeves, are worn only by men. Wearing silk is considered effeminate, but it can be worn by urban "punks" who are anti-establishment. These "punks" might also wear gold and earrings or sport piercings and tattoos, also indicators of their rejection of mainstream Moroccan society. However, men avoid showing bare skin; even their shoes are closed and worn with ankle-high socks. Notably, shoe polish is an extremely popular item in Morocco.

Fashionable men keep their hair short and undyed; men who dye their hair or wear it at an unfashionable length or in a messy style are called *m'shekek*. Most men are clean shaven, although some wear a goatee. Wearing a beard marks one as an extremist; only devout Muslims wear beards.

Clothing for women is more conservative. Muslim women wear loose clothing. Those who are strict Muslims wear a kaftan beneath the djellaba and must reveal no skin; they are not allowed to dye their hair or wear makeup. However, many women, mostly young, urban women, *do* wear Western-style clothing, which can be both tight and revealing. Many also wear makeup and dye their hair; blonde hair is considered very fashionable. Of course, during Ramadan even these women dress conservatively. However, as the country becomes decidedly more religious, its clothing fashions seem to follow suit. One reporter notes that, "More and more women are wearing headscarves, even in Casablanca's western fashion enclaves and Rabat's gleaming shopping centers. The designers of expensive caftans— creations of brocade and silk, embellished with gold thread, are now selling their products as luxury couture for the next party, and their clientele is no longer limited to wealthy tourists."[15]

FASHION AND APPEARANCE

Because of relaxed legislation, many foreign companies, such as Lacoste, Christian Dior, and Gucci, have moved into Morocco. Morocco offers shopping in over 1,000 souqs (or outdoor markets) and a number of supermarkets and hypermarkets. In 2003 Morocco boasted 14,135 clothing outlets and 1,345 jewelry stores, and its citizens spent $1.21 billion on clothing.[16] Famous Moroccan designers are Fifi Talsi and Samir Ben Fadoul, who hope to base their label, Talsi London, in Morocco. Moroccan-Nigerian fashion designer Seidnaly Sidhamed, also known as "Alphadi," launched a successful 2005 African fashion caravan in Casablanca that featured works of a number of young African designers, among them five Moroccans. In 2004 per capita expenditure on clothing and footwear was about $44.[17]

Moroccans also buy many cosmetics, spending $6.5 million on health and beauty supplies in 2003 and boasting 4,572 stores devoted to health and beauty. Taking care of one's skin is understood as important, and although still considered a luxury by most, is fast becoming a trend among working women. Concerns about sun exposure rank high. In 2001 consumers, mostly comprising wealthy women, spent a total of $10.7 million on skincare: $9.3 million on face care, $677,000 on body care, and just over $767,000 on handcare. Oriflame and Avon products dominate this market, although many Moroccans continue to use local herbs and minerals. Local cosmetics companies are Azbane Cosmetics, Crystal Lesieur, and UWS Huileries Du Meknes. Studies show, however, that since 2003 there has been a decline in growth in the area of cosmetics; many Moroccans have shifted toward Islamic products. Still others have refused to wear cosmetics and fragrances in public, possibly signifying a return to traditional, anti-Western values.[18] Nevertheless, eye makeup, mostly mascara and kohl eye pencils, remains very fashionable, totaling $17.7 million in consumer expenditures in 2003.[19] Further, even though men seem increasingly concerned about their appearances, their purchases are limited to shaving products. However, Morocco offers over 100 four- and five-star hotels, such as Le Pacha, which are beginning to offer such luxury treatments as manicures, pedicures, and anti-aging skin care, targeting, in particular, wealthy, appearance-conscious male customers.[20]

Algeria

The fact that 50 percent of Algeria's population is considered "youth" means that fashion is growing in importance, as is Western influence; however, the fact that 99 percent of its population is Sunni Muslim means that this influence remains largely contested.

The traditional dress of Algerians is much like that of its neighboring Islamic nations. Before 1830 all Algerian women were veiled, covering their head, hair, upper body, and face. In the late 1800s, because of Westernization, many women rejected veiling, but in the early nineteenth century, women took up the veil to protest the French Occupation. Today, because of Islamic influence, modern women's fashions tend to be modest; only half of all urban Algerian women wear Western-style clothes. Those who prefer traditional dress often wear the *Karakou*, a traditional jacket with silver and gold embroidery, paired with traditional trousers, called *saroual* or *sserual*, and the *Blousa*, a full-length, straight-cut dress, sometimes ornamented with lace and sequins. Alternatively, women wear the *Djeba Fergani*; in eastern Algeria this is a velvet dress, sometimes with lace sleeves, embroidered with gold and silver; on the western side, it is usually made of cotton and embroidered at the neck, bodice, and wrists. Another style involves a tunic, called a *habayah*, or djebba, which can be worn with a vest, a *ssedria* or *firmia*, and trousers. Traditional dresses come in a variety of colors, and vary regionally; women from the east prefer dark colors, whereas those in the west and central regions favor white. More conservative women will wear over these dresses a long overcoat made of light cotton, which covers them from head to foot. Traditional dress is not required, and many do choose Western fashions. However, most women cover their heads with a scarf when they are out in public. Very few women wear a face veil. Hairstyles tend to be very traditional for women; few cut their hair, but wear it braided down their back.

Men's clothing styles, as in most Islamic countries, is less rigid. Most urban men wear Western-style clothes. Those from more rural regions (and urban men who wish to dress traditionally) wear a *gandoura*, a white woolen cloak, which they pair with a long cotton shirt. Sometimes they wear over this a cape called a *burnous*, in the summer made of linen and in the winter, wool. This cape can be plain or ornately embroidered, an indication of the wearer's wealth. Traditionally, men wear a red head covering, a *fez*, which they wrap with white cloth. There are, of course, variations. Tuareg men wrap indigo cloth into a turban, or *Tarbush,* on their heads; this cloth extends over their robes and covers them entirely so that only their eyes are exposed. Interestingly, the Tuaregs are the only culture in Islam where women dominate the men. Therefore, it is the men in this society who are veiled. Algerian men usually sport a mustache, a symbol of masculinity.

Algerian fashion continues to be influenced by French fashions, although Mediterranean and African styles are also dominant. French garment companies constitute 17 percent of the Algerian market. Italian garments, however, predominate, claiming 22 percent of sales. While the fashion scene has been slow to make it to Algeria, indications exist that the market is growing. In 2005 Algerian women had access to their first monthly Algerian woman's magazine, *Dzeriet,* published in French. One of the articles in its first issue discussed how wives might deal with husbands who did not wish them to use cosmetics. Another article dealt with women's health.

According to 2003 World Health Organization statistics, 8.85 percent of men and 21.4 percent of women in Algeria, ages 25 to 65, were obese. No doubt, the health and fitness industry will soon experience a growth in Algeria. In 2004 Algerians spent a little more than $6.00 per capita on cosmetics and toiletries (the per capita wage is just over $2,000 per person), and a total of $204.8 million countrywide. They spent the most on color cosmetics, haircare, and face makeup, respectively.[21]

One of the world's most renowned fashion designers, Yves Saint Laurent, is an Algerian native. Born in 1936, he is credited with the creation of, among others, the 1960s Beat look, the first see-through clothes, the Jumpsuit, the Dinner Jacket, the Smoking Jacket, and the Reefer jacket. In 1983 his work was featured in the New York Metropolitan Museum, the only fashion designer ever to receive such an honor. He is best known for popularizing ethnic designs and for men's wear–inspired female fashions.

Tunisia

In 2000 Tunisia ranked in the top ten of world consumer expenditure on clothing and footwear, Tunisians spending on average 12.5 percent of their salaries on clothing. In 2004 Tunisians had the highest per capita income in North Africa, and since an estimated 80 percent of the population is considered middle class, people in this class have a lot of disposable income and are known for their conspicuous consumption. Further, 55 percent of the population is under 25; two-thirds live in urban areas; and two thirds have satellite television. All these factors work to make them more fashion conscious.[22]

Traditional national dress for Tunisians includes a lightweight cotton jacket, or *ghlila*, paired with trousers or *sserual,* a vest called a *ssedria* or *firmia,* and cap *shishia*. Men's shoes are traditionally yellow, whereas women's are red or green. The working class tends to wear the *kasabia* or *gasabia* and a hooded jacket. The first two are usually neutrally colored, made of a rough material such as wool or cotton, and decorated with white wool borders; the jacket, which replaces the *burnoose*, is worn on top. An alternate clothing choice is the *kandura* or *gandura*. Urbanites prefer this in wine red with green or yellow borders, while the wealthy prefer gray blue, pink, or lilac gray.

However, most people in Tunisia prefer Western clothing, readily available at local shopping centers and malls. In 2005 Tunisia opened its newest mall, Tunis City, featuring eighty brand-name stores. Levi jeans are popular, as is Guess. Plus size clothing, however, is not sold, as most Tunisian women are thin and do not wear sizes over 10. Biannually since 2005, Tunisia hosts a fall and spring "fashion week" celebration in one of its major cities, premiering the clothing lines of its top designers. Another exhibition is TEXMED Tunisia, a trade show that boasts 200 exhibitors and is split into four sections, one of which highlights ready-to-wear fashions. Since 1996 the Ministry of Commerce and Handicrafts has held the Golden Khomsa Award ceremony in Tunis, dedicated to promoting traditional clothing elements in modern fashions; one award goes to a designer of women's work clothes and another to evening gowns. Tunisia is also part of the "Fashion in Africa" project, the pilot for which was launched in May 2006. The project is designed to celebrate traditional African fashions, to build Africa's fashion export industry, and to unite African countries. It began with a fashion show featuring new designs based on traditional clothing from the cities of Twshane, South Africa, and Tunisia's capital, Tunis; the show's theme was "When North Meets South." In 2005 Azzedine Alaia, one of Tunisia's fashion designers, was honored in San Francisco. Another Tunisian fashion designer making news is Hedi Slima, a men's wear designer currently working for Dior in Paris. Fatma Ben Abdallah is another well-known Tunisian designer. Many European countries import from clothing manufacturers based in Tunisia. In fact, clothing is the number one export for Tunisia, representing half of all its exports and earning the country nearly $800 million each year.[23]

Libya

United States, sanctions against Libya were lifted in 2003, enabling its economy to grow. Still, Libya remains rather impoverished with an underdeveloped fashion industry. Ninety-seven percent of the population is Sunni Muslim. Thus, Libyan women tend to wear Westernized clothing but remain covered in long skirts and headscarves. Although the scarf is entirely voluntary, it has become more fashionable since the 1980s. Young women, in particular, will match their shoes and purse to their headscarf. Older women wear the *burnoose*. Men can wear anything, but they prefer Western styles. Some favor the *jelaba*, a knee-length shirt worn over baggy pants. Some men in Tripoli, the nation's capital, continue to wear the traditional *fez*, a felt cone or cannister-shaped hat with a tassel, once a sign of masculine intelligence. Most clothing for sale at the traditional souqs is not made in Libya, but imported from Turkey or Italy. Although some traditional clothing made in Libya can be bought at these souqs, these clothes are generally worn only to celebrations such as weddings.

Libya also hosted its first beauty pageant: Miss 2002 Net World. Twenty-two countries participated in the pageant, whose theme was "Beauty will save the world." Contestants were not allowed to wear bathing suits, but instead wore jeans and shirts, designed by Italian fashion icon Roberto Cavalli, featuring the heart-framed face of Libyan leader Colonel Muammar Gaddafi. They also strutted down a catwalk wearing Libyan army uniforms. Seven hundred thousand people voted online for contestants, and the final ceremony was held in Tripoli. A documentary of the ground breaking event, directed by Pieta Brettely, was released in 2004 by Commonwealth films.

Also held in Tripoli is the annual Hair and Beauty Exhibition, a trade show sponsored by Saker Expo, an organization that sponsors trade exhibitions. The show is held in the summer months because this is when weddings usually occur, and it is customary for Libyan brides to receive presents of clothes, perfumes, and cosmetics.

Egypt

Interestingly, Egyptian cotton was not worn by ancient Egyptians, who wore linen and sometimes wool instead. Silk came to Egypt in the sixth century, and cotton, first made in America, did not come to Egypt until the nineteenth century. Ancient Egyptian men seem to have been more fashion-savvy than the women; according to archaeological findings, the average man owned at least forty different garments. Men's clothing, on average, tended to be more decorative than women's; women preferred a simple, sheath dress. Both, however, wore jewelry that indicated wealth and often incorporated religious motifs. As is typical, the wealthier men and women tended to distinguish themselves by how ornate their clothing was.

Ancient Egyptians also preferred clean-shaven faces and used depilatory creams, razors, and pumice stones. Women waxed or used depilatories on their legs. Some tweezed their eyebrows. Both sexes shaved their heads and wore wigs instead. Because shiny, healthy hair signified virility and eroticism, wigs were the most important fashion accessory. Wigs served a practical purpose, too, as thick *natural* hair could prove both too hot for its wearers and a magnet for lice; most Egyptians who shaved their heads preferred removable hair. The most expensive wigs were made from real human hair. Very wealthy Egyptians also hired personal hairdressers.

Egyptians continue to be very fashion conscious. In 2003 consumers in Egypt spent $12.2 billion on health and beauty products. As of 2003 there were 23,845 health and beauty stores in Egypt. The most recent market research specific to cosmetics and hair care, conducted in 1999, shows that the growth in color cosmetics was highest among the middle classes and the wealthy. No doubt this was because of the pressure to keep up with current trends, as well as the fact that cosmetics were readily available for purchase in the growing number of supermarkets and high fashion boutiques in urban areas.

The increasing number of women in the workforce has also led to heightened beauty awareness, as have aggressive advertising campaigns in the region. Most of the products are Western brands manufactured locally, led by Procter & Gamble, Unilever, Johnson & Johnson, and Colgate-Palmolive. In 1999 the cosmetics and fragrances market in Egypt was valued at $2,363 million, and was predicted to rise 34 percent by 2004. Of this value, face makeup was worth $86.9 million, eye makeup $43.9 million, lip products $52.6 million, and nail products $217.2 million.[24]

Hair care is a dominant sector. Three-quarters of Egyptian men and women use shampoo regularly, and because it is manufactured locally, its prices stay fairly low. In 1998 shampoo sales, led by Unilever and then by Procter and Gamble's Pantene and Head and Shoulders, were $154.2 million; styling agents were $23.8 million; and hair coloring totaled $70.4 million. Shaving products for men are also popular, in particular because beards are increasingly associated with religious fundamentalism. Pre-shave gels and lotions are the most popular shaving products, earning $91 million of a total $189.9 million in shaving-product sales.[25]

Egyptians also love their clothes, in 2004 spending about $31.90 per person annually on clothing and footwear, about 2 percent of their total income.[26] Those who wear traditional costumes don the *yelek,* which is a woman's kaftan, worn over a shirt and open at the neck to the breast. The yelek is usually made of silk, adorned with many buttons, lace, and gold and silver brocade, and it fits closely at the waist. It has a high side slit that shows trousers worn beneath, and it can be girded with a cloth shawl. Over this women often wear a jacket or overcoat called a *djubbeh* or *binish,* which can be made of velvet or silk and which is embroidered with gold braiding. Historically, upper-class men wore the kaftan, or *kuftan,* which was belted and could be made of striped cotton or half-silk fabrics. The kaftan is very bright, often crimson or violet-red with white and yellow stripes, and is worn in combination with a vest, shirt, and trousers. Other popular traditional clothing choices include the *tob,* or *sebleh,* a wide cotton garment worn by women with stitching around the neck, and the *kalaba,* worn by men; both are paired with pants called *sserual.* Men who wear this costume also wear caps with blue silk.

Dressing in traditional costume is generally looked down upon as being too ornamental in what is a largely Islamic country; ironically, it is European haute couture that has often adopted the Egyptian "ethnic" look. So what kinds of clothes do modern Egyptians wear? Many Egyptians follow Western fashions, which were initially adopted by the Turco-Circassian aristocracy following France's invasion of Egypt in 1798–1801 and the reign of Mohamed Ali (1805–48). At this time, Egypt entered the global capitalist system and began to import many goods, including clothing, from Europe. The ruling elite imitated Western styles, and the middle class soon followed, abandoning traditional styles that came to be associated with the poor. Today, designer fashions like Gucci and Prada can be seen throughout the urban areas of Egypt. In poorer areas, people tend to buy clothes from local manufacturers or imports from China. In 2003 Egyptians spent $16.3 billion on clothes, most of which were imported. Clothing sales, including footwear, headgear, leather, and accessories (non-jewelry), constituted 46 percent of all retail sales. Nationwide, women, girls', and children's clothing brought in $1,267 million; men's and boy's wear sold $1,095 million; and footwear constituted $457.6 million in sales.[27]

This growth was due, in part, to an increase in average incomes and an influx of international retail businesses such as Nike, Timberland, and Adidas, with a corresponding increase in advertising. Most urbanites shop at department stores and shopping malls; only small stores exist in rural areas, and inhabitants from rural areas travel to cities to purchase clothing for such special occasions as weddings. In 2003 there were 89,952 clothing stores and 5,881 jewelry stores open for business in Egypt, sales from which showed a 30 percent growth between 1999 and 2003. In 2004 City Stars, at 170,000 square meters one of the Middle East and North Africa's largest shopping malls, opened in Cairo. In the last days of 2005 Ramadan, a time of heightened shopping, the mall saw 78,000 visitors per day. Among its stores are Gucci, Guess, Esprit, Levi, the United Colors of Benetton, and the Turkish design landmark, Beyman.[28]

Despite such big-name Western influences, Egyptian women continue to wear the headdress, or hijab and, according to Islamic guidelines, shun short skirts. In fact, the veil became fashionable again in the 1970s among urban college students; wearing it marked them as part of a grass roots movement to reestablish an Islamic identity. The 1980s witnessed a preference for a more fashionable turban than the traditional *khimar*. Although discouraged by the government, the wearing of the turban and veil in the latter part of the twentieth century signified many things, including Islamic nationalism and a rejection of Western ideas. In 1993 education minister Husain Kamal Baha' al-Din tried unsuccessfully to ban veiling at universities.

There are other ways in which Egyptian culture makes its way into Western fashions worn by those in Egypt. Ralph Lauren's polo shirts, for example, include a variation that displays a camel rather than a horse. The hijab is often fashionably coordinated with matching accessories.

Local celebrities influencing Egyptian culture include Egyptian pop princess Ruby, who was banned from Egyptian television for pushing the envelope of Muslim modesty with her daring music videos. Ruby's midriff-baring clothes are being imitated by fashion trends; young girls can purchase similar clothes in shopping malls, much to the ire of Muslim conservatives. Egyptian singer Nancy Agram's fashions have also influenced current trends; sequined *gelabiyas* like those worn in her video have become a hot-ticket item. Egyptian girls also tend to copy these women's hairstyles and makeup. Another clothing item made popular by television shows broadcast on satellite is lingerie; many brides-to-be are purchasing increasingly sexier lingerie. Interestingly, belly-dancing costumes are also quite popular in lingerie stores.

Children's tastes in fashions, like those of adults, are mediated by their culture. Toy makers recognize this, and one local manufacturer in Cairo has developed a Barbie-like doll, Laila, to appeal to young girls as a role model. She is a preteen, with dark hair and lashes, wears both Western clothes and traditional dresses, has a brother rather than boyfriend, and sells for $10 (versus the higher priced, $30 Mattel version).

Jordan

Inhabitants of the Hashemite Kingdom of Jordan are 95 percent Sunni Muslim. The region has long struggled with poverty, the most recent statistics estimating 40 percent of its population is unemployed.[29] Thus, for the average citizen of Jordan high-fashion clothing is not a top priority. However, Jordan's top export is clothing, and the textile and clothing industry is Jordan's top producer, accounting for more than 40,000 jobs in 2003. In 2002 Jordan exported $483 million in clothing while it imported $379 million in textiles and fabrics.[30]

Jordanian embroidery is both a cultural tradition and well known worldwide. Hotels in Jordan run fashion shows celebrating the country's rich fabrics and elegant needlework. In March 2004 the Jordan-United States Business Partnership initiated the Jordanian Garments, Accessories and Textiles Exporters' Association (JGATE), hoping to turn Jordan's textile industry into a world-class fashion industry. Its slogan is "Stitching Jordan to the World," and its aim is to fortify its international export business and to introduce fashion design to Jordan. There are already a number of designer boutiques in such urban centers as Amman, Sweifieh, Abdoun, and Jabal al-Hussein. Amman shopping malls include the Abdoun Mall, Amman Mall, Mecca Mall, and the Zara Shopping Centre. Amman also offers its world-famous Gold Souq. These stores, however, tend to cater to European fashions.

Jordanian women usually wear loose-fitting clothing and headscarves, although these remain optional. Like many other Middle Eastern countries, clothing in rural areas is conservative. The overcoat worn by more traditional women is the Jordanian *jilbab*, a Westernized substitute for the abaya, the traditional garment that covers the entire body except for the face, feet, and hands. Tunic tops are also often worn with pants called *salwar kameez*. Some women prefer a pants suit instead. Colored abayas are very popular in Jordan. Jordan's top celebrity influence on fashion is Queen Noor, wife of the late King Hussein, who frequents global best-dressed lists and is often favorably compared to Jackie Kennedy and Princess Diana. Queen Noor, who grew up in Washington, D.C., the daughter of a prominent politician and businessman, even has her own Website, www.noor.gov.jo. Also a fashion icon, and the world's youngest queen, is Queen Rania, married to Hussein's son, Abdulla II; she refuses to veil for sociopolitical reasons.

Jordan is also considered one of the best countries in the region for health care; it offers many spas and health centers for its wealthier citizens and tourists. Two five-star resorts in Jordan offer Dead Sea therapies. Also, Arabic-style communal bathhouses are a popular leisure and wellness activity. These baths consist of three main rooms: Frigidarium, Tepidarium, and Calidarium—the cold, warm, and hot rooms.

Israel

Israel is a fairly secular and cosmopolitan society. Hairstyles are very Westernized, with women coloring their hair and using hair extensions. Similarly, most Israelis wear Western clothing, although some Ethiopian Israelis wear traditional costume. In 2003 Israelis spent 3.4 percent of their total consumer expenditure on clothing and footwear.[31] In 2004 there was a 4.3 percent increase in consumer expenditure on clothing and footwear, to $1.67 billion, or $241 per capita.[32] Although many Israeli fashions are imported, including such name brands as Zara, Kouka, and Mango, Israel is well-known for its home-grown fashion industry. The local manufacturer and designer brand Castro has done quite well and now has sixty stores. Online shopping has also become quite popular among consumers wishing to buy the latest Israeli fashion trends; Mavensearch is the first online Website directory of clothing stores dedicated exclusively to Israeli women. In 2005 fashions in Tel Aviv were influenced by the roaring 1920s and Charleston styles. For a comprehensive listing of clothing, footwear, and health and beauty stores in Israel, one can visit ShopinIsrael.com, a nonprofit Website dedicated to highlighting Israeli products.

Israeli clothing exports brought in $716 million in 1999. Among its most popular export is the swimwear line, Gottex, by famous Israeli fashion designer Leah Gottlieb; this line alone brought in $44 million in 1999.[33] The government also sponsors The Israel Export Institute, which is in the process of training such up-and-coming fashion designers as Dorin Frankfurt, Gershon Bram, and the Hagara Fashion company. In 2005 Canada hosted "Fashion for Passion" in Vancouver, Montreal, Ottawa, and Toronto, a tour that showcased six of Israel's leading designers: Doreen Frankfurt, Ronen Chen, Sasson Kedem, Segal Dekal, Mirit Weinstock, and Zoe and Yael Orgad. Further, many Israeli fashion and design schools, such as Bezalel Academy of Art and Design in Jerusalem and Shenkar College of Textile and Fashion Technology in Ramat Gan, attract both national and international students.

In addition to being known for its vibrant fashion industry, Israel has also long been a popular resort destination because of its proximity to the healing waters of the Dead Sea. In 1993 Israel began its Dead Sea Research Centre, a nonprofit organization founded by the Ministries of Health, Science and Tourism, the Jewish Agency, the Regional Councils of Tamar and Megilot, and the Dead Sea Hotel Association. The organization studies the natural resources and health benefits of the Dead Sea environment. While most of its research is for medicinal purposes, the Dead Sea region is considered a national health spa center, and the Dead Sea Research Centre is dedicated to promoting its therapeutic potentials. The Dead Sea region offers a variety of spas and resorts that feature such health and cosmetic treatments as mud packs, salt massages, and salt water pools. Israel is one of only two countries that produce Dead Sea cosmetics, producing 92 percent of such products (Jordan is the other). In 2003 it sold 29.6 million tons of the product, which accounted for $5 million in sales.[34] Ahava is Israel's most popular brand of Dead Sea cosmetics. In 2000 it opened an online store to target international consumers. Belmont LTD is another popular distributor of cosmetics and perfumes using Dead Sea products.

Like many other Western and Middle Eastern countries, Israel has a growing cosmetics and cosmetic surgery industry. In May 2006 Tel Aviv will host a large cosmetics tradeshow, BeautyPharm. Israel is projected to spend $715.9 million on cosmetics and toiletries in 2006.[35] In 2005 there were 120 board-certified cosmetic surgeons operating in Israel, which has one of the highest per capita rates of cosmetic surgery in the world: an estimated 15,000–20,000 surgeries each year. Most of those seeking plastic surgery are teens or women in their early twenties, although male plastic surgery is on the rise.[36]

Palestinian Territories

The Palestinian Territories are composed of two areas: the West Bank and the Gaza Strip. Unlike the cosmopolitan Israel, 99.3 percent of the population of the West Bank/Gaza Strip is Sunni Muslim. Most living in the Palestinian Territories are poor; 63.3 percent live under the poverty line, according to the 2003 Palestinian Central Bureau of Statistics. According to a 2004 World Bank Report, 600,000 Palestinians could not afford to meet basic needs, spending only $1.50 per person per day, and 37 percent of the youth are unemployed. Thus, clothing and cosmetics expenditures are not high in these areas.

The textile industry of this region is small and underdeveloped, although it has played a major role in the country's economic development. The most recent statistics are from 1994, at which point there were 1,533 clothing stores that accounted for $107.2 million in sales and 576 shoe stores accounting for $26.8 million in sales. These stores, however, are very small; most have eight or fewer employees; half of these stores employ fewer than five workers. Most of what is produced is for export; local markets account for only 15 percent of production.[37] The most recent survey of household expenditures on clothing was conducted by UN Special Coordinator in the Occupied Territories (UNSCO); it found that in 1996 the West Bank spent more on average than those living in the Gaza strip. In their survey, seven-person households in the West Bank spent an average of $71.75 per month on clothing and those in the Gaza Strip spent $52.58 per month.[38]

The demand for cosmetics, however, is very high in this region because of its large youth population. Those in the West Bank also spent about 45 percent more on health and beauty products, including cosmetics and toiletries, than their Gaza neighbors. A 2003 market survey estimated the toiletries market to be $10 million annually, 40 percent of which is constituted by imports from the United States. Brand-name products are highly valued, and shaving creams, shampoos, and hair colorings are top sellers.[39] There are two shopping malls in Ashqelon, near Jerusalem, which is where many do their clothes shopping; here there are also a hair salon and a department store featuring clothing and cosmetics. There is one two-story shopping mall in the West Bank, in Ramallah.

Interestingly, fashion and beauty have been key players in trying to unite the highly vexed Israel/Palestinian regions. In 2005 Israel and the Palestinian Territories joined to co-host the Israeli-Palestinian Territories beauty pageant. The pageant, entitled "Miss Seamline" was hosted in the highly disputed Jewish Jerusalem neighborhood of Gilo in a southeastern suburb of Jerusalem. Seventeen Israeli women and three Palestinian women competed, with a seventeen-year-old Palestinian woman winning the title. Also in 2005, an Israeli fashion house staged a highly controversial demonstration/fashion show at the West Bank barrier, an 8-meter concrete wall separating Jerusalem from the West Bank. The owner of the fashion house, Sybil Goldfinger, claimed that she was trying to raise awareness of the barrier and to pull

Fashion and Appearance

Palestinian and Israeli women together. While Goldfinger said she was unable to recruit Palestinian models, models from Slovenia, Russia, Poland, France, and Israel paraded her summer line in front of cameras and angry Palestinian citizens.[40] The Palestinian Territories did, however, have an opportunity to parade their own fashions at the First Palestinian Fashion Show hosted in Dubai in February 2006, proceeds from which went to the Palestinian Cultural Foundation.

Lebanon

Lebanon, composed of a population that is 70 percent Muslim and 30 percent Christian, was once a major trading post prior to its civil war. Hence, it is a fairly cosmopolitan society. It is one of the few Middle Eastern countries that allow women to enter local beauty pageants, such as Miss Lebanon, Miss Zahle, and Miss Lebanese Expatriates. In 2003 it also hosted a Mr. Lebanon pageant, the winner of which went on to participate in the Mr. World pageant. Lebanon also participates in the Miss World Beauty Pageant.

Cosmetic surgery is popular in Lebanon. In 1965 Lebanon had only six plastic surgeons; today, the number is closer to forty. One Lebanese surgeon estimates that he has performed more than 22,000 operations in the last 36 years; 6,000 of these were nose jobs. The popularity of this procedure has led Cherine Fahd, a Lebanese artist and photographer, to create her "nose project," displayed in 1999 at the Sydney-Beirut/Beirut-Sydney Continental Art Exhibition. The exhibit included plaster casts of 200 noses, a celebration of diverse notions of beauty.[41]

There are no particular rules regarding clothing, although visitors to the country should avoid wearing revealing clothing in souqs of Tripoli or Sidon. Headscarves are also worn by those attending mosques. Otherwise, clothing is fairly Westernized and partially influenced by French styles, since Lebanon was a French colony until 1943. Clothing styles are also influenced by Lebanese celebrities, such as pop singer Nancy Ajram. While older men may wear a headdress or *kufiyah,* younger generations are very fashion savvy and adopt many European styles. In 2003 Lebanon imported $71.5 million in footwear and hats; $34.3 million in skins, leathers, and furs; and a combined $433.8 million on other textiles. Textile imports, on the other hand, accounted for only $64.7 million. In 2003 Lebanon had a $1.3 billion retail market, and more of its citizens are shopping in Lebanon rather than traveling to Europe for upscale products.[42]

Before its 1975–92 civil wars, Beirut was called "The Paris of the Middle East" because of its high fashion. Interestingly, the traditional kaftan and abaya became part of Lebanon's high-fashion world. As early as the 1960s, one Beirut fashion designer had found that the abaya sold well "for the bath, the beach and the boudoir," with short versions adapted "for wear as debonair smoking jackets and even as cozy apres-ski wear," and that the kaftan, "which is as elegant open as closed, is the perfect thing for hostesses to slip into for dinner on breezy penthouse patios or cocktails in cool mountain gardens."[43] The violence of the wars destroyed much of Beirut's cosmopolitan shopping centers; however, in 2003 the 450,000-square-foot ABC mall opened, the region's first European style mall. In 2004 ABC mall was followed by the launching of Souks of Beirut, a $100 million shopping center with 200 shops. Downtown Beirut offers a number of designer boutiques, including that of renowned fashion designer Ellie Saab. Other Lebanese designers known worldwide include Robert AdiNader, Camille Chamoun, Pierre Katra, Zuhair Murad, Abed Mahfouz, and Hanna Touma.

In September 2006 Lebanon hosted the trade show exhibition Beirut Fashion 2006: The Elegant Style Event. Beirut Fashion 2005 attracted over 8,000 trade visitors from thirty-three countries. Another popular fashion show routinely held in Beirut is the Lux Fashion Show. Beirut also holds its annual fashion week, featuring clothing lines from the top Middle Eastern fashion designers.

So great is Lebanon's love of fashion that Sophie Jabbour, a Lebanese woman interviewed by a Lebanese newspaper, recounts leaving bomb shelters in the midst of the civil wars to take death-defying excursions to designer boutiques. Jabbour, an owner of a high-end fashion boutique, says that "Lebanese people like to be very elegant. It's very important to have the nicest handbag, perhaps something from Chloé or Dolce & Gabbana, even if they can't afford more. Even if they're only able to buy one or two good pieces a year, they will still come here."[44] And one reporter notes that "Exact figures are hard to come by, but observers of the Lebanese scene agree that Beirut dwellers tend to spend an extraordinary percentage of their incomes on luxury products, and that they derive a great deal of prestige from choosing international brands and paying full price for them."[45] Another fashion designer concurs that it is customary "to find people earning $2,000 per month who were capable of buying $1,000 shoes."[46] The easy accessibility of credit cards has enabled their purchasing power. Brand names are important, as in Prada, Fendi, and Gucci purses. In fact, over 80 percent of clothing in Lebanon is imported. This preference for foreign brands can make it difficult for local shops to sell home-grown fashion, although traditional Lebanese costumes and designs are making their way onto international catwalks.[47]

Turkey

Although Turkey is 99 percent Muslim, it separates church from state in both law and practice and is therefore a rather secular country, and many consider it a part of Europe. Residents of Turkey spent over $6.3 billion on clothing and footwear in 2004, which means they spent $88 per capita on clothing and footwear (with a $7,400 per capita income) and $124.36 million on vitamins and dietary supplements.[48] In 2000 clothing and footwear accounted for 22 percent of non-food retail expenditure. Also in 2000, there were 121,500 clothing, footwear, and accessory outlets.[49] Further, Turkey is now the fourth largest exporter of ready-to-wear clothing in the world, totaling $2 billion.[50]

There is no national dress in Turkey, and the Republic of Turkey's Ministry of Culture and Tourism maintains that it is "inadvisable for the art historian, sociologist, folk dance arranger or designer to speak in terms of 'Traditional Turkish costume'" because so many variations exist. The Ministry is planning to publish the results of its study of clothing in twenty-five Turkish provinces. More information can be obtained at its official Website.[51]

Historically, Turkish fashion is perhaps best known for its headgear. In 1925 the fez, which had replaced the turban as national symbol in 1826, was banned.[52] Historically, Turkish women have worn veils. In today's secular Turkey, however, religious dress in public is banned, which means Turkish women are not allowed to wear veils. However, some (about 30 percent) choose to wear a headscarf and robe called *tesettür*. Universities and government offices, however, prohibit even the headscarf, a ban that was upheld in March 2005 by the European Court of Human Rights.

There are at least four different groups and four different meanings associated with wearing headscarves. Traditionalists, who tend to come from rural communities, believe it is invested with shamanistic powers to ward off evil; it can also signify marital status, as well as abstract ideas such as female modesty. It is worn at the onset of puberty to signify adulthood. Traditionalists also wear it for practical reasons—to keep hair clean and to provide protection from the sun—as well as for its decorative purposes. The middle class associates headgear with modesty, but many also wear scarves that sport modern and historical prints to make fashion statements. These headscarves are mass-manufactured and mass-marketed in a range of materials. A third group, the fundamentalists, many of whom are refugees of the Iran-Iraq war, choose either to veil their head or to completely obscure their bodies. For this group, veils signify their allegiance to Islamic political groups as well as a renunciation of Western influences. Finally, a fourth meaning for veils is understood by the secularists, who wear the scarf as an ornamental accessory.[53]

Today, those living in rural areas of Turkey continue to dress conservatively, wearing Turkish pants called *salvar* with long-sleeved tops. However, modern Turkey is fairly Westernized and its fashion industry is growing. It is one of the world's largest exporters of ready-to-wear garments, its top local brand names being Vakka, Beymen, and Mithat. However, the bulk of its domestic and export sales is in non-name-brand clothes. Dedicated to celebrating and promoting awareness of Turkish fashion, the Istanbul Textile and Ready-to-Wear Exporters Union run fashion shows featuring such world-renowned Turkish models as Atil Kutoglu and Dicey Kayek. The Union also produces the Young Stylists Competition, which chooses ten finalists among novice designers for a fashion show, three of whom are also recipients of scholarships to top fashion schools. Additionally, each year Turkey hosts the International Istanbul Fashion Fair. Istanbul is the second-largest exporter of clothing to Europe, and this fair provides Turkey the opportunity to showcase its latest fashion trends. Istanbul also held its first "fashion week" in February 2006. A number of fashion design programs are available at Mimar Sinan University and Marmara University in Istanbul, 9 Eylül University and Ege University in Izmir, Uludag University in Bursa, Pamukkale University in Denizli, Dumlupınar University in Gediz, and Mersin University in Tarsus.

Istanbul is Turkey's fashion hub. It is home to a fashion public relations (PR) company and a fashion magazine, *34*, which distributes in thirty-one countries and has a circulation of 60,000. Turkish designers Arzu Kaprol, Hakan Atil Kutoglu, Rifat Ozbek, Cemil Ipekçi, Vural Gokcayli, Yildirim Mayruk, Sadik Kizilagaç, Hakan Elyaban, and Bahar Korcan have begun to enjoy international fame; many of these designers have shops in Istanbul. Other Istanbul shopping destinations for the latest fashions include the world-famous Covered Bazaar, a maze of sixty-one streets, the 226-unit Akmerkez, and the Galleria, which in 1990 was named the world's outstanding shopping mall. Those looking for more traditional fashions can shop at Turkey's largest Islamic clothing chain, Tekbir Giyim, or "Allah Is Great Clothing." For a detailed description of the many faces of Istanbul fashion, see fashion reporter Suna Erdram's *New York Metro Travel* report, "Istanbul, Turkey."[54]

Ankara, Turkey's capital, is also known for its fashion. In 2006 it hosted a fashion show dedicated to the history of police uniforms in the Ottoman empire, by designer Farouc Sarac. Images of the show can be seen at the Website *A Documentary Fashion Show—Police Uniforms.*[55] In 2003 Ankara was at the center of a fashion controversy when it held a fashion show featuring models wearing Islamic clothing, despite the ban on headscarves in public. Ankara also holds its annual two-day capital fashion festival, featuring the works of contemporary Turkish designers.

Turkey is, of course, famous for its Turkish baths, or hammam. These baths were once communal baths with three rooms: a hot room, or caldarium, for steaming and massage; a warm room, or tepidarium, for washing and soaking; and a cool room for resting and napping. Today, many Turkish citizens still visit these weekly to relax; they are popular tourist sites as well. The baths are used for both therapeutic and cosmetic purposes and are often offered in combination with other spa services, such as facials and oil massages.

Beauty is also important to Turkey. Cosmetic surgery is popular in Turkey, nose-reshaping topping the list. In 2004 Turkey spent $1.06 billion on cosmetics and toiletries. Of this, color cosmetics accounted for $81 million, and hair care was $313 million. Other top products were men's grooming products, which brought in $110.9 million in 2003 and men's hair care products, which reached $5.9 million, suggesting that Turkish men are increasingly conscious of their appearance. Beauty Eurasia, a cosmetics trade show, is held annually in Istanbul. Another trade show, Konya Beauty and Personal Care, is held annually at the Konya Fair, and in 2006 Bursa sponsored the Bursa Beauty and Personal Care exhibition. Because of hard economic times, Turkish consumers are demonstrating less brand loyalty than in the past. Unilever is a leading manufacturer, with its Dove products very popular among consumers. Procter & Gamble is also a major player; its Pantene hair products are very popular.[56]

Syria

Traditionally, women of Syria wear the *aba,* which can vary in style. Wealthy women wear the aba as a multicolored, gold-embroidered gala dress that can be made of wool or silk. The common aba tends to be brown and white striped. Bedouins wear a version that is white and black striped. Unicolors are also favored. The aba can be accompanied by the *mashla,* which is a two-piece, tapestry-like overjacket worn by both men and women. Men wear it over their kaftans, women over their shirts.

Youth in urban areas such as Damascus, however, favor Americanized clothing, although they do tend to dress up. They like T-shirts with logos, but colors tend to be conservative. "Cool" Syrian male youth, called *shebab,* a bit more fashion conscious than American men, wear well-fitting jeans or pants and button-up shirts or sweaters. Shorts are never worn. Men also are very conscious of their hair, which they keep short and gelled back. However, they do have a lounging outfit called the *banjaamat,* which means "pajamas of sport." Usually these are sweat suits, Adidas for example. Women may or may not wear the hijab, but most do, as Syria is largely Sunni Muslim. However, these hijabs vary dramatically, from a black headscarf and matching robe, to a glittery headscarf paired with denim and a T-shirt.

In 2006 the Syrian government lifted its ban on clothing, cosmetics, and footwear imports. This has meant greater competitive pressure on Syria's local fashion designers and companies, as they now compete against such U.S. companies as Polo. Thus, Syria has been making efforts to build its fashion industry. In 2003 ten Syrian textile companies participated in, at that time, the world's largest fashion fair, held in Damascus. There were 450 exhibitors and seventeen countries represented, and products featured included men's, women's, and children's clothing. In 2004 Syria held its first Top Model fashion show, which was held again in 2005. Damascus also holds, annually, the Damascus Leather Fashion Activities exhibit, the largest trade show in the Arab world featuring leather goods and shoes. Shoppers in Syria head to Damascus or to Aleppo, its second largest city, which boasts a 7-kilometer labrynth-like souq. In fact, two-thirds of the industry in Aleppo is textile production.

Iraq

Years of economic sanctions and war have impoverished Iraq, where the per capita income in 2005 was $3,400.[57] This does not make for a thriving fashion industry. Between 1960 and 1990, Iraq boasted a vibrant artistic scene, but in the 1990s the early secularism of Saddam Hussein's rule gave way to increasing fundamentalism, and artists as well as fashion designers suffered from censorship. Moreover, following the 2003 U.S. invasion, the government-owned House of Fashion, Dar al-Azia, which since 1970 had held fashion shows and served as a museum celebrating Iraqi costumes, was looted and vandalized, and the elaborate costumes it housed were burned. It later became the interim headquarters of the new Ministry of Culture, which oversees the culture and heritage of the Iraqi people. According to its members, the former activities of the House of Fashion conflict with Islamic values.

Prior to 2003 many young, urban women had taken to wearing the "French hijab," a headscarf that covers only part of the head and hair, pairing it with jeans, denims, or capris. Since 2003 the once fairly secularized and Westernized dress of the Iraqi people, and women in particular, has turned to traditional styles. Making a fashion statement by choosing *not* to wear the headscarf can actually endanger one's life. Fundamentalist vigilantes have increasingly reprimanded women who forgo the hijab, at times using physical violence. Since 2003 there have been eighty such attacks involving four deaths.[58]

In traditional Iraqi dress, women tend to cover themselves completely. This means wearing the abaya, a billowing black cloth, over an overcoat, which in turn covers a *jupeh*, a long gown or housedress. Of course, they also wear a headscarf, hijab. The fabrics of these clothes are often dark; light-colored gowns or coats that button down the front are considered unlawful hijab. Of course, traditional styles vary depending upon one's religious and cultural affinities. One observer describes these variations: "Shiite women wear long, black, bell-shaped garments that cover the head but expose the face, and Sunni women typically wear long-sleeved cotton dresses with optional head coverings . . . Kurdish women are known to wear scarves and brightly colored baggy pants under long dresses and bold-patterned shawls."[59] In Karbala garment designers have tried to make black veils more desirable for young girls by stitching into the sleeves of pint-sized abayas cartoon characters such as Donald Duck.

Men wear a long-sleeved one-piece garment called a *dishdasha* or *thoub*, which is made of white cotton in the summer and heavier, darker fabric in the winter. Men also wear a three-piece head covering that consists of a white cap called a *thagiyah*, over which they wear a scarflike head covering—either a white *gutrah* in the summer or a red and white checked *shumeg* in the winter. Around this is wrapped a black band, the *ogal*. Kurdish men, who make up the largest ethnic group in Iraq, traditionally wear loose pants combined with a shirt, jacket, and cummerbund. On their heads they wear a skullcap and, over that, a turban. For many Iraqi men, head coverings are a sign of manhood, and young boys look forward to wearing them. Clothing colors are important signifiers as well, indicating the tribe or political party to which the wearer belongs.

As can be expected, fashion designers in Iraq have found it difficult to market their clothing lines since 2003. Many have complained that top clients have fled the country. One designer, Salim al-Shimiri, claims that fashion flourished in Iraq in the 1980s. Prior to the U.S. invasion, he had done thirty fashion shows, each of which featured an average of fifteen models. Since 2003, however, he has done no shows. A shop owner, he once employed fifteen models and fifteen tailors; now he employs only five models and three tailors.[60] Other clothing stores and fashion houses have been vandalized and looted in recent years.

The economic sanctions in place since the 1990–91 Gulf War have also been hard on the cosmetics industry, as has the current war. However, beauty continues to be important to Iraqi women, who have found creative cosmetic uses for everyday household items. One reporter writes, "Because of a lack of beauty cream, for example, they started making their own beauty masks from a mix of snake-oil and cloves and they use vaseline as beauty cream. For toning lotion they use watermelon juice and for cleansing their skin they apply a mixture of yogurt and honey. Poverty has also driven many of them to sell their hair. . . . 'They sell a pigtail for around 30 dollars,' [an Iraqi beauty salon owner] says. 'It's sad, but we use it for other women who want to have longer hair. We sew it onto their natural hair.'"[61] Iraqi women can also find cheap, but poor quality, cosmetic imports from Syria and Egypt at local souqs. They also rely on outdated perfume samples, Christian Dior, for example.

On October 10, 2005, National Public Radio reported on an increasing trend in cosmetic surgery among both the wealthy and middle-class Iraqis—largely tummy tucks and rhinoplasty.[62] A prominent Baghdad cosmetic surgeon boasts that he schedules at least three cosmetic surgeries a day, on both men and women. Apparently, Lebanese pop singer Nancy Asham has had quite an influence on standards of beauty; she herself has undergone multiple highly publicized cosmetic surgeries.

Iran

According to archaeologists who unearthed an ancient "state-of-of-the-art textile industry" in Burnt City, a historical site in the southeastern part of Iran, Ancient Iranians were highly concerned with clothing, accessories, and cosmetics. Inside the graves of young women, dating to 5,000 years ago, archaeologists found necklaces, bracelets, dresses that would show off bared shoulders, and makeup boxes.[63] Iran, today, however, is much more conservative. It is an Islamic state, and since the 1979 Islamic Revolution, women have been forced by law to cover themselves under either a *chador*, a black, head-to-toe wrap that means "tent," or long, dark coats called *manteaus* that cover their entire body to their knees. Trousers or dark stockings are worn beneath this overcoat. Interestingly, the *chador*, along with turbans and beards, was once banned by the Shah in an attempt to Westernize the country, but returned following the Islamic revolution. At age nine, girls are required by law to wear a veil. Some schoolgirls wear a veil called a *magheneah*, a hoodlike covering. Black veils are considered more modest than colored ones.

Beneath these long robes, however, Iranian women may wear more Westernized clothes—designer jeans, backpacks, and trendy shoes. In fact, shoe styles are one way in which Iranian women demonstrate their individual fashion sense. Sandals are increasingly popular, although wearers dubbed "fashionable fundies (fundamentalists)" risk being arrested and flogged for practicing bad *hejeb*. Morality police have been known to seize women's lip gloss and to flog women for letting their hair slip out from beneath their veils. When Iran's reformist president, Mohammad Khatami, came to power in 1997, Iranian women began to challenge these dress codes. Wrote one reporter in 2003, "Women are ditching the *chador* and dowdy coat for head scarves designed by Versace or Dior and tailored pea coats, subtly nipped in at the waist. This spring Tehran's most stylish women are wearing red for the first time."[64] Iranian fashion designer Mahla Zamani has been at the forefront of this challenge, funding five women-only fashion shows in Iran and publishing Iran's first fashion magazine, *Lotus*, in 2003. The magazine went through five issues, all government approved. However, in 2005, the newly elected Mahmoud Ahmadinejad banned fashion shows, shut down Zamani's magazine, and refused to allow her to go to Italy to present her designs. Yet women continue to seek out fashion. Another reporter writes, "Fashion [in Iran] is most girls' sole weapon of self-expression, so finding loopholes in the law is what it's about. The *roopoosh*, the mandatory coat for women, has shortened considerably, the hemline having risen from ankle length to something bordering on a mini-skirt. Headscarves, too, have been transformed into stylish accessories that highlight the features they were once meant to cover. Logo-centric labels like Hermès and Louis Vuitton are the most coveted, and the girls often paint their nails and lips to match the scarf's colour."[65] Fendi purses and Prada shoes are also very popular. Another hot fashion name brand is Gucci, whose label also appears on women's scarves.

Facial beauty is equally important. Women in Iran visit salons once or twice a week to shape their eyebrows. Plastic surgery, especially rhinoplasty, is also increasingly popular; in fact, Iran has the highest rate of nose cosmetic surgery in the world. Says Dr. Reza Moltaji, an Iranian cosmetic surgeon, "Today it's no longer 'chic' to redo one's nose, it's routine."[66] Also trendy is wearing plaster casts on one's nose to signify that one *has* had a nose job, even if one has not. Other procedures include chin operations, fingernail implants, planting fake diamonds in gums, and tattooing eyebrows. MAC cosmetics are especially popular. However, strongly opposing this trend are strict fundamentalists. In 2004 Islamic vigilantes seized "improper" clothes from fashionable shopping stores and have been known to beat women whom they consider to be immorally dressed.

Iranian men tend to wear Western-style clothing. The mustache is once more fashionable, as are men's slippers, some of which are high-heeled. Ties are a controversial signifier of Western values and have therefore all but disappeared. Clerics and older men wear turbans, usually white.

Mass media certainly influence Iranian fashion trends. Googoosh, a 1950s and 60s Iranian music and film icon who popularized short haircuts for women prior to the Islamic Revolution, is currently making a comeback in film after years of fundamentalist-imposed silence. Top Iranian fashion models include Yasmin Le Bon, male supermodel Cameron Alborzian, Shermine Sharivar (Miss Germany 2004), Nadia Bjorlin (on the U.S. serial *Days of Our Lives*), Sarah Racey-Tabrizi (*America's Top Model* reality show), and Nazanin Afshin-Jam (Miss World Canada 2003). Top and emerging Iranian fashion designers include Shirin Guild, Maryam Mahdavi, Shadi Parand, Michael Soheil, Laya Torkaman, Behnaz Sarafpour, Jasmin Shokrian, Hushidar "Hushi" Mortezaie, and Massoud Ansari. Iran's version of Barbie, the veiled Fulla, has been outselling her Western competitor at nearly 2 million dolls since her debut in 2004.

Kuwait

In 2000 Kuwait held the title of sixth-largest spender in the world on clothes and shoes; in fact, clothes account for 10.58 percent of Kuwaiti consumer expenditure.[67] Kuwaitis are very fashion conscious. As in many other Middle Eastern countries, modern shopping malls have become popular in urban centers such as Salmiya. Souk Sharq City is a new, highly modernized shopping center in Kuwait City, which is also the home of the popular Salhiya and Zahra complexes, the Laila Galeria, and the Marina Mall.

In general, there are three types of dress for Kuwaiti women: Western (which became popular in the 1960s), traditional, and Islamic; all must be modest, however. Many Kuwaiti women wear the traditional abaya over their clothing, whether traditional or Western. However, those who dress in traditional styles might also choose to wear the more colorful, more ornamental *thobe*. Beneath their robes, Kuwaiti women may wear Western clothes or the *dara'a*, a long-sleeved, practical dress that falls in a straight line from the shoulder to the ankle. Instead of the *dara'a*, they might wear a long, flared skirt, long-sleeved blouse, and tailored jacket or loose coat. Many Kuwaiti women also wear the hijab, or *Al Malfa'a*, usually made of silk or rayon. Bedouin women will wear the *burqa*, which covers their entire face except for slits for eyes, or the *bushiya*, which is a black, transparent veil which covers the face completely.

Kuwaiti men wear either Western clothes or the *dishdasha*, a long, usually white, one-piece robe. When in public, Kuwaiti men who follow the traditional dress code also wear a head covering called a *ghutra,* which is kept in place by a black rope called the *egal* or *oga*; a third component of this headdress is the *gahfiah,* a skullcap worn to keep the headdress from slipping. The wearing of this headdress at the onset of puberty signifies a young Kuwaiti boy's passage into manhood. Some men may also wear a cloak called a *bisht*, made of camel hair or wool, under the *ghutra.* A man's national identity, as well as his fashion preferences, can be represented through the headpiece, whether centered on the head and pulled down to cover his forehead, or off-center and tilted over the forehead. Shebabs—"cool" young Kuwaiti men—are known to spend much time on positioning their *ghutra.* During winter, the white *ghutra* is exchanged for the *shumag,* a red and white checked head covering, and darker, heavier robes are worn. Shebabs prefer leather, wool-lined jerkins to the *bisht.*

Brand names are important to Kuwaitis, a full one-quarter of whom hail from oil-wealthy families and have a lot of disposable income. In fact, in Kuwait (as in Saudi Arabia and the UAE), consumer spending has grown by 10 percent every year for the past five years.[68] Italian and French imports are especially popular, such as Christian Dior, Chanel, and Versace. Many stores also carry labels such as Timberland, Adidas, and Wrangler. In 2002 president and chairman of the Villa Moda, Sheik Majed Al-Sabeh, produced his limited-edition Prada caftans with matching bags and shoes for his exclusive shop in Kuwait. Al-Sabeh's Villa Moda empire, a 100,000-square-foot luxury boutique he began in Kuwait City in 2001, amassed $20 million its first year. The mall boasts ten stand-alone boutiques, including Prada, Fendi, and Gucci, two multibrand stores, a men's club, a health spa, and a botox clinic. Consumers at Villa Moda spend on average $600 per visit. According to one report, in the spring of 2005 "Dolce & Gabbana's entire fall denim line sold out in one day. Marni's $800 fringed belt had a waiting list 25 women long. Among last season's top sellers: Fendi Ostrik bags ($1,000 to $3,500) and YSL caftans ($4,500)."[69] Traditional souqs also continue to remain popular, and carry non–name brand clothing and accessories at reasonable prices.

In 2004 cosmetic sales in Kuwait were up 28 percent.[70] In 2007 Kuwait City will host two large trade shows dedicated to cosmetics and toiletries: the annual Autumn Fair and the International Perfumes and Cosmetics Exhibition.

Bahrain

Because Bahrain is an island nation, situated in the Persian Gulf between Saudi Arabia and Qatar, it has long been a favored trading spot and a site of urban civilization. It has historically been called the "Life of Eternity," "Paradise," and the "Pearl of the Persian Gulf." Like many other countries in the Middle East, Bahrain is Islamic, with 70 percent of its population Shia and 30 percent Sunni Muslim. However, at least one-third of its population is non-national, which means that Bahrain, especially in its urban areas, is a more moderate society. Although its villages continue to retain the conservatism of Islam, 85 percent of Bahrain's population lives in urban areas. Bahrain has a sophisticated communications and travel network and thus is host to many international visitors and businesses. For a time, Michael Jackson talked of making a permanent home in Bahrain. For all these reasons, Bahrain is more cosmopolitan than its neighbors.

Bahrain has been struggling economically, however. Bahrain began to manufacture its own clothes in 1980, opening up twenty-one ready-to-wear factories. However, sales have decreased, and clothing exports in the recent years have dropped. Since 2001 twenty garment factories have closed; now there are about fifteen clothing factories in Bahrain.[71] In

2005 it exported $182.7 million worth of apparel and textiles (mostly trousers) to the United States, only 0.2 percent of all products imported into the United States.[72] Bahrain tends to import most of its clothes, which are then sold in local shops or, in the newest Middle Eastern trend, at large shopping malls.

Many people in Bahrain continue to wear traditional Arab attire, but many have also adopted Western-style fashions. Bahrain is considered the fashion hub of the Middle Eastern and North African world. Its capital, Manama, has been host to the only international trade event dedicated exclusively to fashion jewelry, Jewellery Arabia, which brought in over 500 exhibitors in 2006.[73] Fashion trade shows Bahrain has hosted include the Middle East International Beauty show, Beauty Arabia, Syrian Products Expo, and Fashion Arabia, all of which targeted manufacturers, buyers, and designers in the world of beauty. Bahrain also hosts the annual Autumn Fair, which features textiles, apparels, and cosmetics, and the Middle East International Designer Fashion Flair. So popular is fashion that Bahrain held a fashion show as part of its National Day Celebrations. The show featured Indian Haute Couture by Hermant Trivedi, eighteen models, and TV veejay and Indian style icon Rakshadha Kaham.

Bahrain is also home to many big, air-conditioned shopping malls and private stores. Seef Mall contains 220 stores, including Liz Claiborne, Vogue, and United Colors of Benneton. In 2007 Bahrain will be opening Bahrain City Centre, an 11,200-square-meter mall that will have thirty shops, including Virgin Megastore, Massimo Dutti, Pull & Bear, Promod, and Zara, as well as such new brands as Bershka, Oysho, Salsa Jeans, and Bijoux Terner. Sitra Mall, on Sitra Island, opened in 2006.

Western ideals of beauty, although increasingly popular, are often in conflict with Bahraini culture. One of these areas of conflict is in body weight. Thirty-two percent of women and 25 percent of Bahraini men are overweight or obese. In another study, 15 percent of boys and over 17 percent of girls were found to be overweight or obese. An estimated 3 to 9 percent of preschool-aged children are obese. Experts suggest that one of the reasons might be that obesity is considered a sign of wealth. Another is modernization, which has brought with it fast but unhealthy food choices and a sedentary lifestyle.[74] The health profession has brought much attention to the dangers of obesity, and this attention is perhaps one of the reasons why the spa and wellness industry is growing at such a rapid pace in Bahrain.

Qatar

Daily clothing worn by men is the traditional long, white shirt, or thobe, paired with white trousers, and a head covering called the *ghutra*, which is worn with four black, braided tassels. Women wear the black abaya and some wear veils.

Shopping in Qatar can be done at the traditional souqs or at any number of shopping malls. In fact, City Center in Doha is the largest mall in the world, with five levels and 250 shops and an estimated 50,000 visitors annually. In 2006 the Doha Hyatt Regency hosted a Fashion Expose at its shopping concourse. The collections come from the stores on its concourse: Oltre, Evans, Milano, Mothercare, Lilica and Tigor, U2, List, Lilac, Signe, Nayomi, Bossini, Mr Price, Nine West, Aldo, Paris Gallery, Giant Stores, Bench, Orchestra, Marzooq Al Shamlan, and London Lady. Two of Qatar's own top designers are Noor Hamad Al Thani and Noor Jassim Al Thani, both of whom launched their commercial collections for a new Qatari fashion house at a 2006 fashion show in Salam Plaza. To encourage the large number of women entering the Qatari work force, Qatar boasts a women's-only school of design at the Virginia Commonwealth University School of Arts–Qatar.

UAE (United Arab Emirates)

Dubai is the UAE's recognized fashion capital, and because it offers tax-free shopping, it welcomes many international shoppers. Dubai itself hosts many international fashion houses, such as Gucci and Armani, most of which set up shop in Dubai's numerous shopping malls. In fact, Dubai was host to the first Western-style mall in the Middle East. The Mall of the Emirates, at 2.7 million square feet, recently opened in Dubai, and Festival City opened on March 1, 2007, and when completed will have 550 stores. By 2008 the UAE will boast two of the world's five largest malls, one of which will be in Dubai and offer 3 million square feet of retail space. Also of note is that the UAE has welcomed two Saks Fifth Avenue outlets, the only two outside North America. Three more are in planning stages.

Dubai is also well-known for its annual and very large fashion shows and exhibitions. These include Prestige Dubai, Fusion, BeautyWorld Middle East, Motexha, the Bride Show, and ICFS (Islamic Countries Fashion and Styles). In January 2005 the cellular giant Nokia sponsored Dubai's first fashion television show, "Strike a Pose," featuring international models wearing clothing from the JJ Valaya fashion line.

Every year Dubai hosts a forty-three-day shopping festival, at the heart of which is an emphasis on beauty and fashion. The Dubai Fashion event runs for the better part of a month and features work from top designers in the world of clothing, jewelry, cosmetics, perfumes, and accessories. In 2007 the festival attracted 1.6 million visitors and over 2 million residents. In a two-day extravaganza, big-name fashion lines premiering at Dubai Fashion 2006 were Christian Dior, Christian Lacroix, Emanuel Ungaro, Sonia Rykiel, and Kenzo, who came straight from their Paris launches, hitting Dubai before heading to New York.

An event immediately following Dubai Fashion 2006 was Creations 2006, which highlighted the works of regional designers. Up-and-coming fashion designers are encouraged through such awards as The UAE Fashion Design Award, supported by the Sharjah Ladies Club Chairperson and the head of the Supreme Council for Family Affairs, Her Highness Sheikha Jawaher Bint Mohammad Al Qasimi, wife of His Highness Dr. Sheikh Sultan Bin Mohammad Al Qasimi, Supreme Council Member and Ruler of Sharjah. Another fashion design award is the Swarovski Young Designers Award, which goes to emerging jewelry designers in the UAE.

Meanwhile the textile manufacturing industry is also growing. Dubai Textile City, which can house up to 250 manufacturing units and is valued at $60 million, opened in the fall of 2005 following an eight-year ban on establishing new, ready-made garment and textile factories. The Emirates Industrial Bank estimates the UAE's textile industry to be worth $4 billion, with 150 ready-made garment factories, mostly in Dubai and Sharjah, and a combined capital of nearly $69 million. In fact, the UAE is the fourth-largest buyer of clothing in the region, accounting for 11.42 percent of total consumer expenditure in 2000.[75]

Physical beauty is important to those living in the UAE, 40 percent of whom are youths. In 1999 the UAE spent $354.9 million on cosmetics and perfume imports, most of which was imported through Dubai. Of this total, $146 million was in perfumes, largely from France, the United States, Italy, Germany, and Switzerland. In 2004 perfume and cosmetic sales were up 48 percent over the previous year.[76] There are about 2,000 cosmetic companies and 2,300 hair salons in the UAE.[77] Most products are sold at souqs or private outlets and bought by middle-class consumers; there are seventy Christian Dior outlets alone. Products targeting male consumers are rapidly growing; in fact, 80 percent of men in the UAE use aftershave. The average man also possesses at least seven different fragrances. Skin care products, specifically anti-wrinkle treatments, facial scrubs, and shaving foams, are the most recent trends.[78]

Dubai consistently hosts the popular and very large Gulf Beauty Exhibition. In 2001, 6,020 people visited the exhibit; there were 300 exhibitors representing twenty-four countries and 450 manufacturers. The number of exhibitors was up to 544 in 2005. In 2006 Dubai also hosted an international beauty and wellness week in addition to Gulf Beauty 2006. Exhibits included cosmetics, dietary goods, fragrances, toiletries, health and fitness equipment, hair care, salon equipment, wellness and spa facilities, and wellness and spa equipment. Exhibitors of cosmetics were the largest numbers, followed by toiletries and salon equipment.

Saudi Arabia

Clothing in Saudi Arabia is very conservative. Men and boys wear the traditional, ankle-length shirt called a thobe, white in warm weather, darker colored in colder weather. Alternatively, they may wear the *dishdasha*. For special occasions, they may also wear the *bisht* or *mishlah*, long white, brown, or black cloaks trimmed in gold, over the thobe. Men also wear the traditional headdress: a small, white cap called a *taiga*, over which is worn the *ghutra*, a square piece of white, or red and white checked cloth, that is folded into a triangle, centered on the head, and held in place by the *igal*, a black cord. The igal is optional. Saudi men wear sandals with their traditional dress.

Saudi Arabia is one of only two countries that dictate women's dress (Iran is the other). In public, Saudi women are required to cover themselves with the abaya, a long, loose, and flowing body-length robe. They also wear a headscarf and face veil. Some wear the *boshiya*, a veil that covers their face from the nose down, or the *niqab*, which covers everything but their eyes, is optional. Underneath, however, they may wear very fashionable and ornate clothing, like an intricately decorated thobe and *surwal*, cotton or silk trousers. Alternatively, they may prefer Western clothing, like jeans and spandex tops, beneath their abaya. Jewelry, for both men and women, is popular. Ear and nose piercing have long been traditions. Generally, infant girls' ears are pierced at birth. Some tribal men who live in the desert wear a silver earring to designate social status. Henna tattoos are also popular for special occasions such as weddings.

Traditionally, Saudi fashion was best identified by its intricate embroidery work. Traditional Bedouin dress is waning in Saudi Arabia as more clothes are mass-produced. For a vivid description of Bedouin dress and Saudi Arabia's history of ornate embroidery, see Heather Colyer Ross's article, "Fashion in the Sand." For more contemporary fashion, Saudis can attend Fanshawe College, which has a three-year fashion design program. Famous fashion designers from Saudi Arabia include Summer Olayan, Yahya al-Bishri, and Adnan Akbar, who is described as the "Saint Laurent of the Middle East."

Because of government-imposed restrictions on entertainment, shopping has become a national hobby; most experts agree that Saudi Arabians spend more on shopping per capita than do their Western counterparts. Under construction in Saudi Arabia are the Red Sea Mall project, The Mall of Arabia, and Dammam Shopping City. Because of increasing oil revenues and relaxed trade agreements, Saudi Arabia is also importing many clothes and fashions. In fact, it is the largest purchaser of clothing and among the top ten countries in the world in per capita footwear purchases.[79] In 2000 consumers spent a little more than $5.3 billion on clothing and $1.1 billion on footwear. In 2000 clothing accounted for 9.92 percent of consumer expenditure. In 2004 Saudis spent $323 on clothing and footwear per capita, with the United

States exporting $257 million in clothing to Saudi Arabia.[80] Most consumption of clothing is by women and children. Brand names such as Ralph Lauren, Tiffany, Coach, Guess, Max Mara, and XOXO are popular and can be found in shopping malls.[81] However, there exist stark ironies. For example, only headless mannequins in clothing stores are legal, women's fitting rooms are not available (women must try on clothes in women's restrooms), and only male guest workers may work in "mixed sex" clothing stores. In 2006 men were banned from owning stores that sell women's lingerie and apparel. However, The Kingdom Center, a shopping mall in Riyadh, offers a third floor exclusively for women; men may not even ride the elevator to it, and on that floor, all salespeople and security guards are female. Here, customers can even check their abayas in the abaya coatcheck room.

Cosmetics are important to Saudi Arabians. In 2004 its cosmetics and toiletries industry was worth $1.33 billion, a 26 percent growth since 1999, and sales are expected to reach $1.6 billion by 2009. Hair care and skin care were the products most often bought, accounting for 20 percent of total sales. Eye makeup was the most popular item for women. Women prefer dark-colored eye makeup, lip color, and nail polish. Whitening creams are also popular. Men's grooming products, however, constitutes the most dynamic field. In 2004 Saudi men spent just under $29.9 million on cosmetics.[82] The first Saudi Beauty Expo took place in September 2006 in Jeddah and targeted salons, spas, and cosmetic shops, among others.

Saudi Arabians also love their fragrances, often buying two or three perfumes at one time. Many continue to use incense imported from India, Oman, Malaysia, Indonesia, and Vietnam among others. These imported fragrances are sold at souqs and are permissible because of their medicinal purposes. Women tend to be the main purchasers of fragrances and demonstrate little brand loyalty. The average Saudi woman owns five or six different brands and tends to use more at one time than most Westerners. This delight in fragrances can be attributed to Saudi women's desire to differentiate themselves from other women since many cover themselves entirely with the abaya. Men also love colognes; 2004 saw a growth of 5.6 percent in sales of fragrances. While unisex fragrances are not popular, Saudis do demand new brands. European products are the most popular, followed by Asian and then American brands. The brands that did the best in 2004 were LVMH, Loreal, and Unilever. A local producer, Mahmoud Saeed, was fourth in sales. Recent fragrance trends include a desire for high-tech packaging, extensions of original brands (such as Dunhill Desire and Dunhill Xcentri, both extensions of Dunhill by Alfred Dunhill), and his and hers fragrances such as Givenchy for Women and Givency Pour Homme for men.[83] Researchers expect sales of cosmetics and perfumes to rise by 7 percent, to $1.4 billion, in 2007.[84]

Oman

Omani men wear the traditional white *dishdasha* gown with a tassel called a *furakha* sewn into the neckline. They also wear the *Kashmir Mussar* turban. While the turban has been replaced in most Arab countries by the *ghutra* or *shumag,* it is still a strong tradition in Oman. Underneath this, they may wear the *kummar* cap. They also often wear a silver dagger called a *khunjar,* which is held in a long strip of cloth called a *shal.* They might also choose to carry a stick called an *assa,* which has both practical and fashionable purposes. Over the *dishdasha* they may also wear a long black or beige cloak called a *bisht,* which is embroidered with gold or silver stitching. Men generally wear sandals.

Women's national dress, usually vibrantly colored, varies regionally and denotes tribal affiliation. The basic components are the *dishdasha* or a knee length tunic worn over trousers called *sirwal,* which are embroidered with silver stitching at the ankles. In public they wear the *abiyah,* an overcoat which is called the thobe or *hatheeyah* outside the capital. However, clothing underneath the abiyah can be quite elaborate, including sequins, silver lacing, and intricate embroidery. They favor bold, primary colors. They also wear a veil called a *lihaf.* In the desert, many practice total veiling with the *birka,* or face mask. Women favor intricately engraved gold jewelry. Cities such as Muscat boast large malls that house high-end stores such as Chanel, Versace, and LaCoste, as well as such large department stores as JC Penney's. Muscat City Centre is the first "supermall" in Oman, with over 44,000 square meters of shopping space. Other options are the traditional souqs, where customers still bargain for goods. Ibra Souk, which opened in 1990, is a popular marketplace; dedicated exclusively to women, it sells cosmetics, fragrances, lotions, and henna.

Cosmetics and fragrances have historically been important to Omani women.[85] They tend to use kohl eyeliner and indigo as a skin wash; for special occasions, they apply indigo to their face in decorative patterns. Henna is used similarly. Both men and women also use a natural oil extracted from shoo seeds to condition their hair and prevent early graying; a widely used shampoo is made from sidr and ipomoea nil leaves. Fragrances are also very important to Omani women. Of note, Oman is the home of the frankincense tree, *Boswellia sacra,* whose fragrant crystals have traditionally been given as wedding presents. Other popular fragrances include rosewater, jasmine, and oudh, which is imported from Cambodia, India, and Malaysia and, because of its expense, used only for special occasions. Oudh oils are given to brides as part of their dowries.

Yemen

Female and male dress in Yemen is modest. Traditionally, most women wear the *kanis,* an indigo-blue shirt made of shiny cotton. The shirt has wide sleeves that narrow at the wrists, and it is embroidered with white, red, and yellow cotton stitching. Long trousers are worn beneath the kanis. Shorts are not acceptable for either men or women, nor are sleeveless T-shirts. In North Yemen, veiling became the fashion after the 1962 republican revolution; then, middle-class women began to imitate the elite women of the *sayyid* strata, wearing the *sharshaf,* a full, formal black veil, the adoption of which symbolized freedom from labor. Otherwise, much clothing style is determined by climate-but even in the hottest of regions, the heavy *sharshaf* is adopted as a signifier of fashion and wealth. In South Yemen, following the unity agreements of the 1990s, it became fashionable to adopt the hijab, usually worn over European-inspired fashions. Yemen is one of the poorest countries in the Arab world; thus, it does not offer much in the way of cutting-edge fashion. As Sheila Carapico astutely notes, "Beneath their shabby polyester sharshafs, ordinary women worried about economics, not fashion. In the deep recession precipitated by the return of Yemini migrants from Saudi Arabia and the loss of the bulk of its foreign oil due to the Gulf War, exacerbated by low oil prices and bad public management, the growing urban underclass and the increasingly impoverished rural majority's standards of living have declined."[86] Most people are employed in agriculture or herding, while services and industry account for less than one-quarter of the country's labor. In 2003, 45 percent of the population was unemployed.

Shopping is fairly limited in Yemen, although like many other countries in the region, it is growing. There is currently one indoor shopping mall in Yemen, in Sanaa; already at five stories, further expansion is expected. Also popular in Sanaa are beauty centers that provide customers skin treatments, beauty makeovers, dieting assistance and exercise facilities, physical therapy, and even some cosmetic laser surgery—although these operations are not approved of by the Ministry of Health.[87]

RESOURCE GUIDE

PRINT SOURCES

Bailey, D. *Veil, Veiling, and Contemporary Art.* Cambridge, MA: MIT, 2003.
Breau, M., and R. Marchese. "Social Commentary and Political Action: The Headscarf as Popular Culture and Symbol of Political Confrontation in Modern Turkey." *Journal of Popular Culture* 33.25 (2000): 25.
Carapico, S. "The Dialectics of Fashion: Gender and Politics in Yemen." In J. Suad and S. Slyomovics (eds.), *Women and Power in the Middle East.* Philadelphia: University of Pennsylvania Press, 2001.
El Guindi, F. "Veiling Resistance." *Fashion Theory* 3.1 (1999): 51–80.
Hassan, S. "Henna Mania: Body Painting as Fashion Statement, from Tradition to Madonna." Pp. 103–129 in *Art of African Fashion.* Trenton: Africa World Press/Prince Claus Fund, 1993.
Icon Group. *The 2000–2005 Outlook for Women's and Children's Clothing and Accessories in the Middle East.* San Diego: Author, 2003.
Jirousek, C. "The Transition to Mass Fashion System Dress in the Later Ottoman Empire." In Donald Quataert (ed.), *Consumption Studies and the History of the Ottoman Empire, 1550–1922: An Introduction.* Albany: SUNY Press, 2000.
Koslin, D., and J. Snyder. *Encountering Medieval Textiles and Dress: Objects, Texts, Images.* New York: Palgrave Press, 2002.
Lindisfarne, N., and B. Ingham. *Languages of Dress in the Middle East.* Richmond, Surrey: Curzon, in association with SOAS, 1997.
Losleban, E. *The Bedouin of the Middle East.* Minneapolis: Lerner, 2003.
Quataert, D. *Consumption Studies and the History of the Ottoman Empire, 1550–1922: An Introduction.* Albany: SUNY Press, 2000.
Remer, A. *Enduring Visions: Women's Artistic Heritage Around the World.* Worcester, MA: Davis Publications, 2001.
Ross, Heather Colyer. "Fashion in the Sand." *Saudi Aramco World* 31.6 (Nov.–Dec. 1980) www.saudiaramcoworld.com/issue/198006/fashion.in.the.sand.htm.
Rugh, A. *Reveal and Conceal: Dress in Contemporary Egypt.* Syracuse, NY: Syracuse University Press, 1986.
Scarce, J. *Women's Costume of the Near and Middle East.* London: Unwin Hyman, 1987.
Suad, J., and S. Slymovics. *Women and Power in the Middle East.* Philadelphia: University of Pennsylvania Press, 2001.
Tortora, P., and K. Eubank. *A Survey of Historic Costume: A History of Western Dress.* New York: Fairchild, 2004.

WEBSITES

CosmeticMagazine. http://cosmeticmagazine.com/frontpage.asp. Regularly updated consumer statistics in cosmetics and fragrances.
CosmosWorlds—Europe Style Portal. http://www.cosmoworlds.com/trade_shows-middle_east.html. Regularly updated information on Middle Eastern trade exhibitions, shows, and conferences.
The Countries and People of Arabia. http://www.hejleh.com/countries/index.html. Has extensive links to information and other Websites pertaining to Middle Eastern and North African culture.
Demircan, Piraye Yüksel. *Turkish Fashion Design.* Mimar Sinan University. http://sanat.bilkent.edu.tr/interactive.m2.org/Fashion/piraye.html. This site offers a concise, if generalized, history of Turkish fashion.
Dewitt, Karen. "All the Perfumes of Arabia," *Saudi Aramco World,* September/October 1974. http://www.saudiaramcoworld.com/issue/197405/all.the.perfumes.of.arabia.htm.
Ead, Hamed. *Cosmetics in Ancient Egypt.* http://www.levity.com/alchemy/islam23.html.
Economist Intelligence Unit. http://www.eiu.com/. Regularly updated consumer statistics and forecasts.

FASHION AND APPEARANCE

Euromonitor International. http://www.euromonitor.com/. Regularly updated consumer statistics and forecasts.

"Fashion Show?" *Adventure Divas Dispatches.* http://www.pbs.org/adventuredivas/iran/dispatches/fashion_show.html. PBS slideshow of various ways in which Iranian women interpret the hijab.

"In Pictures: Saudi Designer Fashion," *BBC News,* April 27, 2004. http://news.bbc.co.uk/2/hi/in_depth/photo_gallery/3664401.stm. Slideshow of contemporary fashion show.

Iranian Fashion Show. Ahmad Anvari, 1999–2006. http://www.anvari.org/cols/Iranian_Fashion_Show.html. Collection of photos from contemporary fashion designer in Iran.

Israel Export Institute: Cosmetics and Toiletries Sector. http://www.export.gov.il/Eng/SubIndex.asp?CategoryID=288. Has extensive information about Israel's exports in Dead Sea Cosmetics.

PersianMirror. http://www.persianmirror.com/culture/fashion/fashion.cfm. Has images of links to information about Iranian fashion and beauty.

Personal Hygiene and Cosmetics. April 2006. http://nefertiti.iwebland.com/timelines/topics/cosmetics.htm.

Saudi Aramco World. http://www.saudiaramcoworld.com/. Bimonthly magazine, archived online, designed to broaden knowledge about the Arab and Muslim worlds.

Turkish Clothing. http://sanat.bilkent.edu.tr/interactive.m2.org/Fashion/piraye.html. Mimar Sinan University Website detailing history of Turkish clothing, and with further links to organizations, institutions, and recommended readings.

Women's Clothing and Fashion in the Middle East. http://users.ox.ac.uk/~sant1114/Fashion.htm#Clothing. A useful annotated bibliography of print articles and books on a wide variety of subjects relating to fashion in the Middle East.

VIDEOS/FILMS

Beauty Will Save the World. (New Zealand 2003). Directed by Piettra Brettkelley. A documentary that follows the American contender for the crown in the first beauty pageant held in Libya.

Boom. (India 2003). Directed by K. Gustad. A fictional tale of three undercover Hindi fashion models in Dubai.

Covered. (Egypt 1991). Directed by T. Kamal-Elden, a Her Way Production. A documentary that examines the reasons for increased veiling in Egypt.

Middle Eastern Costumes. (University of Texas–Austin, 1985). Slides produced by center for Middle East Studies featuring clothing and costumes in the Middle East.

Our Heritage and the Land: Traditional Palestinian Costume Show. (USA 1991). Directed by Farah Munayyer, Hanan Munayyer, and Basel Sakkab. Features nineteenth- and twentieth-century Palestinian jewelry and costume.

Palestinian Costumes and Embroidery: A Precious Legacy. (USA 1990). Produced by Palestinian Heritage Foundation. 35 minutes. Features over 250 groups of costumes, representing towns and villages in the areas around Jerusalem, Bethlehem, Ramallah, Al-Khalil, Majdal, Gaza, Jaffa, Galilee, and the Naqab desert dating back to 1860s.

Portraits of Ordinary Muslims: Turkey. (USA: Frontline Documentary, PBS). Discussion of the banning of headscarves in Turkey, including interviews. Accessible online at http://www.pbs.org/wgbh/pages/frontline/shows/muslims/portraits/turkey.html.

ORGANIZATIONS AND MUSEUMS

American University of Beirut—Museum of Archaeology, Ancient Arab Textiles Collection. P.O.B. 236–9, Beirut, Lebanon. http://almashriq.hiof.no/ddc/projects/museum/. Contains a collection of jewelry artifacts.

Central Missouri State University Archives and Museum, Nance Middle Eastern Collection. JCKL Room 1470, Warrensburg Mo 64093. http://www.cmsu.edu/archmusm/. Artifacts from Saudi Arabia and Southeast and Southwest Asia.

Columbia College Chicago, Ethnic Costume Collection, Hugh Manning, Curator. 600 S. Michigan Avenue, Chicago, IL 60605. http://www.colum.edu/. Contains 1,500 articles of clothing.

The Dead Sea Research Centre. http://www.deadsea-health.org/new_html/about_us.html. A center for research and development concerning the relationship between health and the waters of the Dead Sea. It is a highly regarded center and recognized by prominent scientists from around the globe.

Egyptian Museum, Exhibition of the Perfumes and Cosmetics in Ancient Egypt. Tahrir Square, Cairo, Egypt. http://www.egyptianmuseum.gov.eg/.

Fine Arts Museums of San Francisco, de Young Textile Collections. Golden Gate Park, 50 Hagiwara Tea Garden Drive, San Francisco, CA 94118. http://www.famsf.org/deyoung. A total of 12,000 pieces from the Middle East and Africa.

Jordan Folklore Museum. Amman, Jordan. Tel: +962 (0) 6 465 1742. Displays traditional costumes and jewelry.

Jordan Museum of Popular Tradition. Amman, Jordan. Collection of traditional costumes in five exhibition halls.

The London Middle East Institute. Room B318, SOAS, University of London, Russell Square, London WC1H OXG, United Kingdom. Tel: 020 7898 4442; email: lmei@soas.ac.uk. Website: http://www.soas.ac.uk/lmei/. London-based organization promoting knowledge of Middle Eastern Culture, including gallery exhibits, lectures, and conferences.

Metropolitan Museum of Art, Exhibit: Western North Africa (The Maghrib), 1000–1400 AD.1000 Fifth Avenue at 82nd Street, New York, New York 10028-0198. http://www.metmuseum.org/toah/ht/07/nfw/ht07nfw.htm.

The National Museum of Bahrain. PO Box 2199, Manama, Bahrain. Tel: +973 292 977.

Palestine Costume Archive. PO Box 98, Lyneham, Canberra, Act 2602, Australia. Tel: 612-6248-0114. http://www.palestinecostumearchive.org.

The Palestinian Heritage Foundation. P.O. Box 531, West Caldwell, NJ 07007-0531. http://www.palestineheritage.org/. An organization focused on educating the public about Arab and Palestinian cultures and traditions. Houses a large number of costumes from the region as well as an online gallery.

Tareq Rajab Museum. PO Box 6156 Hawelli, Kuwait. Tel: 5317358; Fax: 5339063. http://www.trmkt.com/. This museum houses many costumes, weavings, and embroideries from areas such as Afghanistan, Palestine, Jordan, India, the Ottoman Empire, Yemen, and other parts of the Arab/Islamic world. Most items are dated from the nineteenth and twentieth centuries.

The Topkapi Palace Museum, Palace Attire and Garments: The Costumes of the Sultans. Sultanahmet, Eminonu, Istanbul, Turkey. Tel: +90 212 512 04 80.

Victoria and Albert Museum. London, UK. Tel: +44 (171) 938420. http://www.vam.ac.uk/.

NOTES

1. For images of Eastern style fashions adopted by Western cultures, see the Metropolitan Museum's online exhibit, *Orientalism: Visions of the East in Western Dress*. The Metropolitan Museum of Art, 2000–2006, 25 March 2006, http://www.metmuseum.org/toah/hd/orie/hd_orie.htm.
2. For a collection of nineteenth-century European images of the Middle East, see the online collection, Fink, Rick. 2000. 23 March 2006. *Orientalist Art of the Nineteenth-Century*, http://www.orientalistart.net/index.html.
3. See *TextileExpoDubai*, 20–23 March 2005, http://www.fibre2fashion.com/textile-expo/textile-expo–dubai-news.htm.
4. Jirousek, 2000 (in Resource Guide).
5. See "Middle East Vending and Kiosks Expo to be Held in May," Strategiy.com.
6. See "Textiles and Clothing," *Enterprise and Industry*, February 16, 2005, http://europa.eu.int/comm/enterprise/textile/euromed.htm.
7. See Lyn Reese, "Historical Perspectives on Islamic Dress," *Women in World History Curriculum*, 1996–2006, http://www.womeninworldhistory.com/essay-01.html.
8. For further discussion of this tension, see many of the sources cited in the Resource Guide.

9. See www.palestinecostumearchive.org/other_areas.htm.
10. "The New Fragrance Mecca," *Global Cosmetic Industry,* April 1, 2006, http://www.highbeam.com/library/docfree.asp?DOCID=1Y1:92249880&ctrlInfo=Round19%3AMode19a%3ADocG%3AResult&ao=; Messe Frankfurt, *BeautyWorld Middle East Gulf Beauty,* 2005, http://www.gulfbeautyexpo.com/beautynews.html; "Middle Eastern Beauty Market Boom Leads to Massive Growth in Trade Fair," *AME Info,* January 31, 2006, http://www.ameinfo.com/76830.html.
11. Messe Frankfurt, *Beauty World Middle East Gulf Beauty,* 2005, http://www.gulfbeautyexpo.com/market.html.
12. "Moroccan Market for Eye Care Products," *Market Research Monitor,* April 2006.
13. See Pascal Harter, "Mauritania's 'Wife-fattening' Farm," *BBC News,* January 24, 2006, http://news.bbc.co.uk/2/hi/africa/3429903.stm.
14. Dawn Marley, *Interactions between French and Islamic Cultures in the Maher,* www.surrey.ac.uk/LIS/MNP/may2000/Marley.html.
15. Helene Sober, *Spiegel Online,* January 9, 2006, http://service.spiegel.de/cache/international/spiegel/0,1518,394869,00.html.
16. "Moroccan Structure and Aspects of Retailing," *Market Research Monitor,* December 2005.
17. Ibid.
18. "Moroccan Market for Skin Care," *Market Research Monitor,* February 2003.
19. "Moroccan Market for Eye Care Products," *Market Research Monitor,* April 2005.
20. "Moroccan Market for Skin Care," *Market Research Monitor,* February 2003.
21. See "Economic Indicators: Middle East: Algeria, 1999-2004, *Euromonitor.com,* http://www.euromonitor.com/pdf/Consumer_Middle_East_2006_Samples.pdf.
22. "Agra-Food, Past, Present, and Future Report: Tunisia," *Agra-Food Trade Service,* December 2005, http://atn-riae.agr.ca/africa/4093_e.htm.
23. "Clean Country Profile: Tunisia," *Clean Clothes Campaign,* December 2005, http://www.cleanclothes.org/news/newsletter20-11.htm.
24. "The Egyptian Market for Cosmetics and Toiletries," November 2000, *Market Research Monitor.*
25. "The Egyptian Market for Cosmetics and Toiletries," November 2000, *Market Research Monitor.*
26. "The Egyptian Structure of Retailing," April 2005, *Market Research Monitor.*
27. Ibid.
28. Ibid.
29. *The World Fact Book: Jordan,* May 2, 2006, http://www.cia.gov/cia/publications/factbook/geos/jo.html.
30. See "Country Profile: Jordan (Sample)," *Economist Intelligence Unit Online Store,* 2006, http://store.eiu.com/index.asp?layout=show_sample&product_id=30000203&country_id=JO.
31. See "Retailing in Israel," *Euromonitor International 2006,* http://www.euromonitor.com/reportsummary.aspx?folder=Retailing_in_Israel&industryfolder=Retailing&print=true.
32. "Israel's Economy Shows Growth in 2004," *Israel Ministry of Foreign Affairs,* February 21, 2005, http://www.israel-mfa.gov.il/MFA/Israel+beyond+politics/Israel+economy+shows+growth+in+2004+-+Feb+2005.htm.
33. Shoshanna Solomon, "Facets of the Israeli Economy: Textiles and Apparel," *Israeli Ministry of Foreign Affairs,* July 1, 2001, http://www.mfa.gov.il/MFA/MFAArchive/2000_2009/2001/7/Facets%20of%20the%20Israeli%20Economy-%20Textiles%20and%20Appare.
34. "Dead Sea Cosmetics," *Unido Exchange,* http://exchange.unido.org/main2.asp?menu=MenuePopup6&ID=376&lan=en.
35. "Israel," *Euromonitor International, 2006,* http://www.euromonitor.com/factfile.aspx?country=IS
36. Gail Lichtman, "Vanity Growing among Israelis," *Jewish Independent,* December 16, 2005, http://www.jewishbulletin.ca/Archives/Dec05/archives05Dec16-11.html.
37. "Textile and Clothes Industry in Palestine," *Palestinian National Information Centre,* Palestinian National Authority, 1999, http://www.pnic.gov.ps/english/industry/Industries_in_Palestine/Industries_in_Palestine_1_1.html.
38. Expenditures and the Level of Living," *UNSCO Quarterly Report,* United Nations, 1 April 1997, http://www.arts.mcgill.ca/MEPP/unsco/qr2/qr2s3.html.

39. Market Research-Cosmetics and Toiletries," *strategis.gc.ca,* February 2, 2006, http://strategis.ic.gc.ca/epic/internet/inimr-ri.nsf/en/gr118559e.html.
40. "Fashion on Israel's Frontline," *BBC News,* March 4, 2004, http://news.bbc.co.uk/2/hi/middle_east/3531149.stm.
41. Anne Renehan, "Facing Extinction: The Lebanese Nose," *The Daily Star Beirut*, February 22, 1999, http://almashriq.hiof.no/lebanon/600/610/617/lebanese_nose.html.
42. Sascha Brodsky, "Peace Mongers," *ICSC. Org,* International Council of Shopping Centers, April 2005, http://www.icsc.org/srch/sct/sct0405/around_the_globe_1.php.
43. "High Fashion from the Arab World," *Saudi Aramco World,* September/October 1968, http://www.saudiaramcoworld.com/issue/196805/high.fashion.from.the.arab.world.htm.
44. Katherine Zoepf, "Lebanese Defiantly Make Lifestyle a Priority," *International Herald Tribune at Home, Abroad*, December 5, 2005, http://www.iht.com/articles/2005/12/04/opinion/rleb.php.
45. Ibid.
46. Ibid.
47. Ibid.
48. "Turkish Consumer Segmentation," *Market Research Monitor,* January 2006.
49. "Turkish Retailing, Parts 1 and 2," *Market Research Monitor* January/February 2002.
50. "Turkish Exporters Maintain Success in Foreign Markets," *TAIK,* http://www.turkey-now.org/default.aspx?mID=7&pgID=353.
51. See http://www.kultur.gov.tr/EN/BelgeGoster.aspx?17A16AE30572D313AC8287D72AD903BECA1229EB5DBEC2BB.
52. See Jeremy Seal's *A Fez of the Heart: Travels around Turkey in Search of a Hat* (Harcourt, 1996) for more on this history.
53. Jirousek, 2000 (in Resource Guide).
54. See http://www.newyorkmetro.com/nymetro/travel/features/situations/2005/11830/index.html.
55. See http://www.thy.com/en-INT/corporate/skylife/article.aspx?mkl=77.
56. "Turkish Market for Cosmetics and Toiletries: An Overview," *Market Research Monitor,* October 2003; "Turkish Market for Men's Grooming Products," *Market Research Monitor,* May 2004.
57. *CIA World Fact Book: Iraq,* 2 May 2006, http://www.cia.gov/cia/publications/factbook/geos/iz.html.
58. Diane Dees, "Iraqi Women without Headscarves Threatened, Attacked, and Killed," *Mother Jones*, March 7 2006, http://www.motherjones.com/mojoblog/archives/2006/03/iraqi_women_wit.html.
59. Christine Crabb, "A Woman's Place in Iraq," *The Iraq Journalism Project,* May 23, 2003, http://courses.washington.edu/com361/Iraq/ethnic_differences/cc4.htm.
60. Mona Mahmoud, "War Wears on Fashion Industry," *USAToday.Com,* October 27, 2005, http://www.usatoday.com/news/world/iraq/2005-10-27-iraq-fashion_x.htm.
61. See "Iraqi Women Get Creative As They Battle for Beauty," *Daily Times Pakistan,* May 3, 2003, http://www.dailytimes.com.pk/default.asp?page=story_3-5-2003_pg9_15.
62. See "Pop Culture Drives Desire for Nose Jobs in Iraq," by Deborah Amos, *Morning Edition,* NPR, October 10, 2005.
63. Jennifer Viegas, "Iran: Prehistoric Fashion Center?" *Travel Channel News,* March 20, 2006, http://travel.discovery.com/news/afp/20060320/iran.html?source=rss.
64. Catherine Taylor, "A Designer Tugs at Iran's Fashion Straitjacket," *Christian Science Monitor,* April 15, 2002, http://www.csmonitor.com/atcsmonitor/specials/women/mirror/mirror041502.html.
65. "Behind the Veil," Telegraph.co.UK, January 22, 2006, http://www.telegraph.co.uk/fashion/main.jhtml?xml=/fashion/2006/01/22/stiranian22.xml.
66. Ibid.
67. "Country Profile: Kuwait (Sample)," *Economist Intelligence Unit Online Store*, 2006, http://store.eiu.com/index.asp?layout=show_sample&product_id=30000203&country_id=KW.
68. Ibid.
69. "Shopper's Mecca," *Travel and Leisure,* October 2002, http://www.travelandleisure.com/articles/invoke.cfm?page=2&objectid=39981501-C747-11D6-82BC0002B3309983.
70. "Regional Sales of Perfume and Cosmetics Boom," *Cosmetic Magazine,* November 11, 2004, http://cosmeticmagazine.com/managearticle.asp?c=390&a=634.

71. "Indians among Sacked Workers," *The Tribune*—Chandigarh, India, November 8, 2005, http://www.tribuneindia.com/2005/20051109/world.htm.
72. *The CIA World Fact Book: Bahrain*, May 2, 2006, http://www.cia.gov/cia/publications/factbook/geos/ba.html.
73. *Jewellery Arabia 2006 Show Report,* http://www.aeminfo.com.bh/ja2006/showreport.htm.
74. Faisal Al-Mahroos, "Obesity among Adult Bahraini Population: Impact of Physical Activity and Educational Level," *Annals of Saudi Medicine* 21.3–4 (2001): 183–187.
75. "Country Profile: United Arab Emirates (sample)," *Economist Intelligence Unit*, 2006, http://store.eiu.com/index.asp?layout=show_sample&product_id=30000203&country_id=AE.
76. "Cosmetics and Perfume Industry in the UAE," *strategis.gc.ca*, March 8, 2006, http://strategis.ic.gc.ca/epic/internet/inimr-ri.nsf/en/gr109278e.html.
77. *BeautyWorld Middle East Gulf Beauty Brochure*, Epoch Messe Frankfurt, 2006, http://www.makowski.pl/upload/2006beauty-dubai/GulfBeauty2006.brochure.pdf.
78. "Cosmetics and Perfume Industry in the UAE," *strategis.gc.ca*, March 8, 2006, http://strategis.ic.gc.ca/epic/internet/inimr-ri.nsf/en/gr109278e.html.
79. "The World Leather Footwear Market," *The World Leather Market*, Investor Services, 2000, http://www.factbook.net/leather_components.php.
80. "Consumer Lifestyles in Saudi Arabia," *Euromonitor International*, 2006.
81. "2003 Saudi Arabia Apparel Industry Sector Analysis," *strategis.gc.ca*, February 28, 2006, http://strategis.ic.gc.ca/epic/internet/inimr-ri.nsf/en/gr109515e.html.
82. "Cosmetics and Toiletries in Saudi Arabia," *Euromonitor International*, 2006, http://www.euromonitor.com/reportsummary.aspx?folder=Cosmetics_and_Toiletries_in_Saudi_Arabia&industryfolder=Cosmetics_and_toiletries.
83. "Saudi Arabian Market for Fragrances," *Market Research Monitor*, February 2004.
84. "KSA Cosmetics Sales Boom," *AME Info: Saudi Arabia,* February 19, 2006, http://www.ameinfo.com/78183.html.
85. See "Regional Sales of Perfume and Cosmetics Boom," *Cosmetic Magazine,* November 11, 2004, http://cosmeticmagazine.com/managearticle.asp?c=390&a=634.
86. Carapico, 2001 (in Resource Guide).
87. Amel Mohammed Al-Ariqi, "Sana'a Beauty Centers: Business and Therapy," *Yemen Times*, 14, no. 1918 (2006), http://www.yementimes.com/article.shtml?i=918&p=health&a=1.

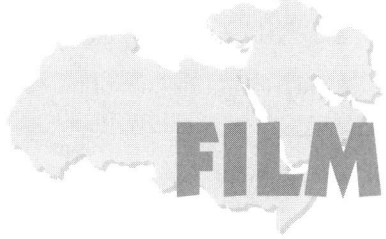

FILM

SUSAN BOOKER MORRIS

The legendary American film *Casablanca*[1] takes place in Morocco during World War II. The footprints of good and evil are clearly demarcated in this version of the political complexities of the war and the region, and love is merely a bother. It has taken decades for the film lens to turn toward these same events, and those that followed, from the point of view of the people who were living in the Middle East and North Africa, not as exiled political (or amorous) cynics, but as inheritors of long lineages of time and place. Even today, after a governmental campaign to support filmmaking in Morocco in the 1990s and the early years of the twenty-first century, only about seven films are made there each year.[2] The Maghreb area (Algeria, Morocco, and Tunisia) still produces only a handful of films each year, although interestingly, between 2000 and 2002, seven of fifty films made in the region were directed by women.[3] In most of the Middle East, filmmaking has been scarce in countries such as Syria, Iraq, Lebanon, and Jordan, and constitutes mostly small productions using old technologies such as 16-mm film. The first feature-length film in Saudi Arabia, titled *Today and Tomorrow,* debuted at the Osians-Cinefan 8th Festival of Asian Cinema in New Delhi, India, in 2006.

Fundamentally, film is a product of technology that functions in cultures as a commodity, whether as an art form or as an object of popular culture. As a result, any consideration of film in the context of the Middle East and North Africa must come to terms with the fact that both technology and commodification are Western impositions on a region that has a long history of tension over European and American colonialism and political influences. A further complication affecting film in the region is the religious resistance to its production and distribution, based on an Islamic position that sees itself in opposition to Western art, modernization, and technology. In this context, film raises concerns since its powerful reproduction of images draws the viewer's attention away from the sacred and from the contemplation of God.[4] The preferred Islamic arts traditionally have been architecture and calligraphy, seen as not being in competition with the worship of God because "the former take[s] pride of place with the building of sanctuaries and the latter act[s] as a perfect decorative geometric accompaniment."[5] A significant aspect of Islamic theologians' objections to film rests on their more general objection to representation. Dabashi describes the resistance as resting on four objections:

Film

The first objection is to the supposition that through any kind of creative visual representation the imaginative faculties will overcome one's reason. The second objection is based on the assumption that sustained reflection on visual representations of real things prevents us from examining the realities they represent. The third objection stems from the historical opposition of the Prophet of Islam to idolatry. Finally, the fourth objection is based on the belief that any act of creation that simulates the original creation of God is blasphemous.[6]

As a result of this kind of political-religious worldview, films have been routinely banned or restricted throughout the region. Although current restrictions are less severe in many Middle Eastern countries, the production process could not be described as free, and it often involves a state committee that allows production only after consideration of the project. As a result, many Middle Eastern filmmakers primarily produce and/or distribute their films outside the region.

From the invention of the moving picture in Europe and the United States in the late nineteenth century and the creation of the U.S. film industry in the early twentieth century, film has been viewed by local governments and often local peoples in the Middle East and North Africa as a Western influence and even as an imposition on local cultures. In fact, the notion of "the Middle East" is from the perspective of Europe and the United States; in addition, many Middle Eastern nations were established after each of the "world wars," which could more rightly be described as European-American wars. The notion of nationalism is not a worldview that grew out of local Middle Eastern cultures, so the idea of the film of the "nation" of Iran or of Egypt is not a simple matter.

The introduction of film into many Middle Eastern countries occurred either as a European cultural element or as a mechanism of regional or national propaganda. As an element of culture, cinemas were opened primarily to serve populations of Europeans in Middle Eastern countries, especially in Egypt. There were very few cinemas opened and little interest in establishing film industries in the less populated regions. Films were seen by local people as a European and American cultural form and were often held as suspect as a result. Throughout most of the twentieth century, the production of films in Middle Eastern and North African regions and countries was often limited to those holding official political control. Since film production requires groups of people and significant outlays of money in advance, private citizens were not encouraged or even allowed to establish production studios, which would essentially have constituted production companies. Since there was no way to sustain a consumable entertainment product, the only reason for film production in most of the Middle East was as a means of communicating political and religious doctrine to citizens.

In Iran, for example, officially produced films were carried out into the villages and offered as official screenings. Even after cinemas were established, the medium was used for propaganda purposes, as Dabashi recounts from his experience as a young man in Iran: "There was something palpably political about the cinema, even in its most innocent and entertaining moments. The Shah used the cinema as the most effective form of propaganda. At the beginning of every screening, the audience was forced to rise and stand to attention while the national anthem was played and pictures of the glories of Pahlavi regime were paraded on the screen."[7] Although the content and screening conditions were controlled, the impact of such an unusual experience of technology and visual presentation inspired interest in the cinematic form and encouraged political expression.

Many directors and film technologists were taught the trade in official production houses. Even today, regional cinema is still an idea in the making as actors, directors, and technicians apply their skills in what is only becoming a more open production system. Because of its ties to Europe and America, for example, Israel has produced and distributed films since the establishment of the state of Israel. Filmmakers in the rest of the Middle East and North Africa operate under the emerging Arab Cinema, which often functions as a conglomerate for film artists to produce and distribute films and to work collaboratively with film artists from other countries. The Iranian director Babak Payami, for example, is a resident of Toronto, grew up in and directs films about Afghanistan, and works in Italy.

For most of the countries of the Middle East and North Africa, production and distribution of Western films and regional films is negligible. Some feature-length films have been made, however, especially as countries gained their independence. In the decade following independence, one or two films a year were made in Algeria, Syria, and Lebanon.[8] On the other hand, film has a significant history in Egypt, Israel, and Iran, and there is increasing and significant current filmmaking in Turkey, Palestine, Iraq, and Lebanon (supported especially by the establishment of the International Beirut Film Festival), although production support and film distribution often take place outside directors' home regions. Because of the harsh political conditions in the area and the long history of censorship, many of the films produced currently through Arab Cinema are overtly political and are often not viewed by the people about whom the films are made. This raises the question of whether or not these films could be seen as popular culture and as consumable commodities; if they are consumable commodities, the question arises as to which populations consume them. Film in countries with older film histories, however, like Egypt and Israel, emerged primarily as a commodity; these countries have a significant variety of popular film genres in addition to what could be considered art or political cinema.

As a result of the varied production in the region, only those countries with significant film production history will be detailed.

REGIONS

Egypt

The first production industry in the Middle East and North Africa was established in Egypt, and films were screened in that country as early as 1896.[9] Since there was a significant population of Europeans in Egypt in the late nineteenth and early twentieth centuries, distribution of Western films was meant to target Europeans, particularly working-class audiences looking for entertainment.[10] Films were produced in Egypt by outsiders, who used the locations and actors in films that were made for Western consumption. The first film company in Egypt was established in 1917 by Italians, and short films were directed and shot by Egyptians by the 1920s.[11] The first Egyptian feature film was *Layla*, released in 1927; it was produced, although not directed, by a native Egyptian after the creation of the Egyptian Company for Cinema and Performance.[12]

The production of films in Egypt was modeled on the emerging Hollywood industry products, and a lively variety of popular Egyptian films was produced and distributed. The most popular genres were the melodrama, the musical, the gangster film, and the farce. Musicals such as *Widad* (1936), *Mermaid* (1948), *Lady Ghost* (1949), *Song of Eternity* (1952), *Taxi of Love* (1954), and *Woman on the Road* (1958) were distributed in Egypt and were exported to other countries in the region and to the West. Although musicals declined in popularity in the 1960s and 1970s, the 1990s saw a reemergence of music in Egyptian cinema as popular singers were integrated into such films as *Crabs* (1990), *Ice Cream in Glim* (1992), and *Abracadabra America* (1993).[13]

Although melodrama was an important element of the musical, melodrama was also its own genre, usually focusing on love. In such films as *Zaynab* (1930), *al-Wards al-Bayda*

(1933), and *Mortal Revenge* (1954), the melodramatic love story commented on arranged marriages or marriage despite family conflict. Plots involving the moral ruin of a female character became popular in the 1940s and 1950s, as in *Cry of the Plover* (1959), and the topic of women in danger or under threat continued into the 1990s in such films as *Rape* (1989) and *The Forgotten* (1993).[14] Although Middle Eastern film in general, and Egyptian film in particular, is known for melodrama, the genre has become less popular in recent times.

In the 1950s artists in Egypt, as elsewhere, became influenced by European realism. After the fall of the kingdom in 1952, realism marked Egyptian cinema more significantly and focused on social injustice.[15] Some of Egypt's most acclaimed films, such as *The Closed Way* (1958), *The Open Door* (1963), *I Want a Solution* (1975), and *Mouths and Rabbits* (1977), were influenced by realism. Issues addressed in these films included class difference, divorce, marriage, and political commitment. Other political films were made, but these were always subject to censorship, so often the political message was encoded in storylines and images. Examples of such films include *A Girl from Palestine* (1948), *Land of Peace* (1957), and *Naji al-Ali* (1992).[16]

Important Egyptian directors emerged in the era of realism and the new wave movement of the 1960s. The best-known Egyptian director of this type is Youssef Chahine (b. 1926), who released his first film, *Father Amin*, in 1950. An important early work of realism is his *Cairo Station* (1958), a "portrayal of the psychological breakdown of a crippled and sexually frustrated newspaper vendor, played with remarkable force and intensity by Chahine himself."[17] Other films include *The Land* (1969), *The Sparrow* (1973), and *The Return of the Prodigal Son* (1976). Chahine's work is overtly political, and *The Sparrow* was banned for two years in Egypt.

Selected Egyptian Directors

Abd al-Wahlab, Fatin (1913–72): Known primarily for comedy. Directed fifty-seven feature-length films.
Abu Seif, Salah (1915–96): Especially known for realism. Directed forty feature-length films.
Barakat, Henri (1914–97): Important popular filmmaker. Directed eighty-five feature-length films, including *Song of Eternity* and *Cry of the Plover*.
Chahine, Youssef (b. 1926): One of Egypt's most important filmmakers. Directed thirty-one feature-length films.
al-Dighidi, Inas (b. 1954): Most accomplished female director of mainstream Egyptian film. Worked under Henri Barakat and Salah Abu Seif.
Galal, Nadir (b. 1941): Known particularly for mainstream movies. Directed forty-one feature-length films.
al-Imam, Hasan (1919–88): Known for melodrama. Directed ninety feature-length films, the most of any Egyptian director.
Mustafa, Niazi (1910–86): Produced popular films in all genres. Most prolific Egyptian director with 107 feature-length films.
Washbi, Yusuf (1898–1982): Directed the early famous film *Zaynab* (1930) and twenty-nine other feature-length films.

Selected Egyptian Films

Bloody Destinies (1982; DVD/VHS unavailable in the United States)
The Dawn of Islam (1952; DVD/VHS unavailable in the United States)
The Eternal Song (1952; DVD/VHS unavailable)
Excuse Me Law! (1985; DVD/VHS unavailable)

Hunger (1986; DVD/VHS unavailable)
Land of Fear (1999; DVD/VHS unavailable in the United States)
Lashin (1939; DVD/VHS unavailable in the United States)
Layla (1927)
Mission in Tel Aviv (1992)
The Mummy: The Night of Counting the Years (1969)
Shafiqa and Mitwalli (1978)
The Sparrow (1972)
The Terrorist (1994; DVD Fox Lorber, 2000)
Visitor at Dawn (1975)
Widad (1936)
Zaynab (1930)

Israel

The development of Israeli film paralleled the creation of the Zionist state; until the 1960s, it functioned as a tool of propaganda to promote positive views about the state. The first movements toward any filmmaking other than that promoted by the government were influenced by émigrés from Arab countries, Europe, and the United States.[18] Commercial Israeli film was formed though the influence of many sources. In the 1960s, a popular form of film entertainment, inspired by the success of *Shallah Shabbati* (1964) and called *bourekas* after a cheese snack, began to be produced. According to Pappe, these films portrayed Palestinians and Mizrahi Jews in a degrading fashion,[19] perpetuating a kind of propaganda in the popular arena. Influenced by European realism, what was called the Israeli new wave cinema also began in the 1960s, stylistically running counter to the popular bourekas. A more original film style, called the "new sensibility," was inspired by two films made in the early 1960s: *In Jerusalem* (1963) and *Hole in the Moon* (1965).[20] The style, typified as "rough" and "tackl[ing] marginal themes," produced such films as *Three Days and a Child* (1967), *A Woman's Case* (1969), and *The Dreamer* (1970).[21]

After the Six Day War in 1967, the government funded film production, and Israeli cinema took off. Many new sensibility films were made during this productive period before a more political turn emerged in the 1980s and 1990s. According to Ne'eman, "The political cinema of the late 1970s and the 1980s articulated a radical critique of Zionism."[22] Such films include *Hamsin* (1982), *On a Narrow Bridge* (1985), and *Beyond the Walls* (1984). "The 1980s war films," explains Ne'eman, "re-examine the national ideal of self-sacrifice for the homeland that was at the core of the 1950s–60s heroic-nationalist cinema."[23]

More recently, and continuing in full force through the 1990s, a movement developed that reevaluated the ideology of the Zionist period.[24] Since the early 1980s, Israel has been in a pattern of shifting political orientations, moving from the leftist politics of its formative years to a period of critique followed by the current move to the right. Although the period of critique, referred to as post-Zionism, began in intellectual communities, it spread to the more popular arenas, particularly film.[25] The popular, nationally supported cinema had typically depicted a Jewish hero championing the efforts of the Jewish state; however, a film called *Hiuh Hagedi* [The Smile of the Lamb] was released in 1983, after the Lebanon War, which raised questions about the relationship between Israelis and Palestinians. An era of cinema followed that raised political and ethical questions about the Zionist ideology, the treatment of Palestinians during the settlement, the depiction of Mizrahi Jews, and the current relationship between Jews and Arabs through such films as *Bread* (1985), *Roveh Huliot* [A Wooden Gun] (1979), *Kaddim Wind* (Akedia Productions, 2002), and *House* (1998). It will be interesting to see what type of political films emerge from the more recent Israeli-Hezbollah conflict and how Arab filmmakers generally will respond to what are viewed by many as extremist views and actions on the part of Hezbollah.

Selected Israeli Directors

Agadati, Baruch (1895–1975): Director of the important early Zionist film, *This is the Land* (1935).
Golam, Yoram (b. 1943): Highly productive producer-director. Known for directing popular bourekas.
Loevy, Ram (b. 1940): Made over fifty documentaries and dramas and is especially known for the 1986 film *Bread*.
Mizrachi, Moshe (b. 1931): Directed thirteen feature-length films while also being a producer, writer, and teacher.
Shles, Julie: Primarily a director of documentaries, she won best director for her feature-length film *Pick a Card* (1997; DVD, Vanguard, 2001)

Selected Israeli Films

First Love (1982)
Hiuh Hagedi (1983)
House (1998)
I Love You Rosa (1972)
Kurdania (1984)
Land of Promise (1934)
Letters from Lebanon (1997)
Lovesick on Nana Street (Lovesick Limited, 1995)
My Father's House (1947)
Pick a Card (1997)
Shell Shock (1988)
Slow Down (1968)
Springtime in Palestine (1928)
A Thin Line (1981)
Through the Veil of Exile (1992)
Under Western Eyes (1996)
Work (1935)

Iran

Although Egyptian cinema is the oldest form of Middle Eastern cinema, Iran has produced what is considered to be the most accomplished set of films in the Middle East and in the "developing world" generally. As in Egypt, the influence of Western technology has been present as an important feature of Iranian culture. The early filmmakers often sought education either in Europe or America and became familiar with media in the West. Many came from non-Muslim religious minorities, such as Baha'i and Judaism, traditions with fewer restrictions on political and social expression.[26] The first film company in Iran was the Sun Cinema established by Roman Catholic missionaries in 1900, and according to Naficy, this sociocultural admixture, its "rhizomatic web of connections," is an important feature of the creation of Iranian film, as evidenced by the work of the early important cinematographer and official photographer to the Shah of the Qajar era, Akkasbashi, who was Christian, an ethnic Armenian, upper class, and supported by the French.[27] This complexity of cultural markers and affiliations continued to prove important to Iranian film as it developed. The first Iranian film, *The Lor Girl* (1933), made in India and directed by Ardeshir Irani, met with great success.[28]

Iran is known for its traditions and achievements in the poetic arts, and Iranian film has relied on poetic stories and also, importantly, translated the poetic into visual form. Dabashi explains, "As a quintessentially verbal culture, we exploded into a visuality that made our cinema a particularly powerful art."[29] As a result, Iranian film is known for its stunning cinematography, emphasis on color and lush landscapes, and reliance on visual beauty to communicate the value of human life. For example, in the film *Gabbeh* (1996), by acclaimed film director Mohsen Makhmalbaf, the storyline centers on the simple events of an elderly couple cleaning their cherished gabbeh rug. Much of the power of the film comes through its use of the imagery of the rugs, which depict stories, and the placing of the characters in an open, natural landscape as well as within the landscape of the rug's "plot" and the couple's memories. The colors for the rugs come from the plants in the landscape, but it could also be said that the characters' lives are colored by a close and necessary relationship to the natural world, such that life's meaning is expressed through the appreciation of nature and color itself, a connection produced through the film's attention to the vibrancy of light and the saturation of color.

In addition to the traditions of Iran, there had been a sustained impulse toward modernity in the twentieth century, especially during the time of the Shah's monarchy leading up to the 1979 Islamic Revolution, when modernism, secularism, and the West in general were renounced. Perhaps more than any other country in the region, the contemporary culture of Iran has been forged out of a sustained nexus of traditional elements, a complex of ethnicities, and the influences of colonialism and modernity.[30] As a result, cinema has developed as an impulse toward modernity; as an element of culture both resistant to and complicit with Persian, nationalistic, and/or Islamic traditions; and as a means of expression by marginalized ethnicities that otherwise have very little in the way of acknowledgment or influence.

In 1979 the Islamic Revolution threatened to destroy what was seen as a secular Iranian cinema. The Ministry of Art of Iran required closure of all cinemas in 1980, but the value of film was re-envisioned based on the centralized power of the religious clerics. Film was placed under the strict control of a new government agency and was used to spread Islamic ideology.[31] According to Egan, the revolution relied on as well as renounced film, thereby creating a "dual revolutionary cinema": "The first is defined as that employed by the government, serving the goals of revolution and acting as a form of Islamic propaganda. . . . In contrast, and as a type of reaction to this format, there has emerged a socially committed cinema . . . that politically and philosophically reflect[s] the complexities of Iran and its society."[32] The shifting representations of political "truth" and of Iranians themselves in the media have left the notion of "the Iranian" in film both complicated and contested. As a result, to view Iranian cinema is to witness questions of subjectivity, a notion so crucial to modernity and so foreign to Iranian traditions. "At its best," says Dabashi, "[Iranian] cinema has succeeded in resubjecting the Iranian self where the project of modernity has failed." The best of Iranian cinema, therefore, puts the human being at its center, presenting observable subjects to the rest of the world, but first, most importantly, to Iranians themselves. "The visual observation of a historical (as opposed to a biblical/Qur'anic) person," says Dabashi, "made the mere potentiality of 'Iranian' subjectivity possible."[33] This subjectivity is also evidenced in a generation of acclaimed film artists, particularly directors, who have been acknowledged in Iran, throughout the Middle East, and around the world.

Selected Iranian Directors

Baizai, Bahram (b. 1938): Baizai is a director, screen writer, editor, and university professor who began making short films in 1970. After a series of films, he was expelled from his university post during the Islamic Revolution and could no longer get his own films made in Iran.[34]

The Stranger and the Fog (1975; DVD/VHS unavailable in the United States)
Tara's Ballad (1978; DVD/VHS unavailable in the United States)
Bashu, the Little Stranger (1985; DVD International Home Cinema, 1990)
Travellers (1990)
Killing Rabid Dogs (2000)

Farmanara, Bahman (b. 1942): Farmanara's film *Prince Ehtejab* (1974), along with Mehrjui's *The Cow* (1969), made an important impact on the development of Iranian cinema, integrating European realism with Iranian landscapes and individuals. Farmanara was educated in London and the United States; after making *Prince Ehtejab* and because of the Islamic Revolution, he lived for many years in Canada. After returning to Iran in the mid-1980s, he made *Smell of Camphor, Fragrance of Jasmine* (2000), his first Iranian film in over 20 years.

Prince Ehtejab (1974)
Smell of Camphor, Fragrance of Jasmine (2000)

Kiarostami, Abbas (b. 1940): Kiarostami is one of the most widely acclaimed of Iran's film directors. He writes and edits many of his films, as well as writing for others (for example, *The Key*, 1986). He is considered a humanist and a director who experiments with film form. *Taste of Cherry*, for example, exhibits such stark realism that it almost appears to be a documentary. The camera movements and narrative events are minimal as the film follows a man around for a day while he attempts to convince someone to promise to bury him after he kills himself. The film ultimately proves to be a celebration of life, while still acknowledging the potent despair of life.

The Traveler (1972)
Suit for a Wedding (1976)
The Solution (1978)
Fellow Citizen (1983)
Homework (1990)
Close-up (1990)
Taste of Cherry (1996)
The Wind Will Carry Us Away (1999)
Ten (2003)

Makhmalbaf, Mohsen (b. 1957): The importance of Mohsen Makhmalbaf as a cinematic artist and as an influential voice in the shifting grounds of Islamic politics cannot be overestimated. Makhmalbaf is unique in having made films first that championed those who boldly criticized the "Islamic regime" and "fundamentalist, doctrinaire beliefs,"[35] starting in 1988 with *The Marriage of the Blessed*.[36] Many of his more recent films have been banned in Iran. In 1996 Makhmalbaf opened a film school called the Makhmalbaf Film House. It caught the attention of people in the Iranian Ministry of Culture, "who feared the emergence of a new generation of Makhmalbafs making politically engaged and socially critical cinema."[37] The filmmaker responded by involving his family members, and his daughter, Samira Makhmalbaf, has established herself as an accomplished filmmaker in her own right. The Film House has gone on to offer study programs in the various cinematic arts and trades and is influential in creating a new generation of Iranian filmmakers. Makhmalbaf's most recent film, *Kandahar* (2001), offers a surreal, cinematically rich, and referentially dense film about the effects of war and tyranny on the people of Afghanistan. The film follows a woman who is attempting to persuade people to take her to Kandahar where her sister risks death. The woman is met with complexity upon complexity as she, and viewers, enter further into a world of absurd despair.

Nasuh's Repentance (1982)
Two Sightless Eyes (1984)
The Cyclist (1988)
The Marriage of the Blessed (1988)
A Time to Love (1990)
Gabbeh (1995)

The Bread and the Vase (1995)
Silence (1997)
Kandahar (2001)

Makhmalbaf, Samira (b. 1977): Samira Makhmalbaf provides a view of the heightened political tensions existing in current Middle Eastern political traumas, emphasizing the oppression of the people of Afghanistan. Her style is one of realism, so she clearly steps into the Iranian cinematic tradition, using the techniques of Iranian cinema as established by the generation of filmmakers before her, including her father. Her subject matter focuses on the injustices done to women and children. *Blackboards*, for example, takes a realist/documentary approach, following two teachers as they seek out students to teach. The men carry large blackboards on their backs and walk into the desert landscape. The resistance of the people to the men's plea for education points out the losses incurred as a result of political upheaval and how humans are reduced to struggling for mere subsistence. In this situation, education becomes superfluous.

The Apple (1998)
Blackboards (2000)
September 11 (2002)
At Five in the Afternoon (2003)

Mehrjui, Daryush (b. 1939): Mehrjui was committed to French new wave cinema and was central in the creation of Iranian film, particularly by way of his influential film *The Cow* (released in 1970). He directed films both before and after the Islamic Revolution and is thought to be making social comments in this films, although in a poetic and symbolic form. *The Cow* is the story of a man's devoted and pure love for his cow. Various social forces are depicted as invasive and restrictive in contrast to this simple relationship. The experience of the individual is championed against the press of the social groups around him.

The Cow (1969; DVD First Run Features, 2004)
Mr. Gullible (1970; not available)
The Postman (1970; not available)
The Cycle (1974; not available)
The Tenants (1987; not available)
Sara (1993)
The Pear Tree (1998)

FILMS SINCE 2000

The Middle East has undergone remarkable changes in recent years. Partly as a result of political events and changes and partly because of the general globalization of popular cultures, the work of film artists outside Europe and the United States has garnered more attention than has been the case in the past. With recent wars and military actions in Afghanistan, Iraq, and the West Bank, cinematic artists of the Middle East have found their work included in the commodity marker of the West. It is possible for a Westerner, for example, to go to film retail and rental markets (like amazon.com, bn.com, and netflix.com) and buy recent films by Iranian, Israeli, or Egyptian directors. In general, Western popular culture has grown to embrace filmmakers from all regions of the world, with those from Iran, China, Japan, and India at the forefront. The term "foreign film," as used by cinematic art houses in the United States since the mid-twentieth century, has given way to terms such as world cinema or international film as a result of the shift away from reference to European films and the inclusion of work of filmmakers around the world. This is not a mere nod to inclusiveness: film is being produced around the world in ways never before imagined. Following is a list of some recent titles from the Middle East:

Baran (2001; DVD, Miramax, 2002). Directed by Hamsey-e Khoda. An Iranian girl masquerades as a boy to work at a construction site. Her male friend must eventually decide his loyalties when he finds out.

The Circle (2000; DVD, Fox Lorber, 2001). Directed by Jafar Panahi. This film analyzes the status of women currently in Iran.

Dreams of Sparrows (2005; DVD, Go-Kart Records, 2005). Directed by Hayder Daffar. This Iraqi director looks at Baghdad citizens as they wait for the U.S. invasion. This is the first historic documentary made by the Iraqi/American collaborative group EYE Group.

Kandahar (2001; DVD, New Yorker Video, 2003); Directed by Mohsen Makhmalbaf. This stunning film is about a woman, legally unable to travel alone in Afghanistan under Taliban authority, trying to get help to travel to Kandahar to save her sister from suicidal depression.

Or [My Treasure] (2005; DVD, Kino Video, 2006). Directed by Keren Yedaya. First film by Israeli director Yedaya; it tells the story of a sixteen-year-old girl who tries everything she can to get her mother out of prostitution.

Osama (2003; DVD, MGM 2004). Directed by Siddiq Barmak. Acclaimed Afghanistan film about a young girl who must pass as a boy in order to get work to support her mother and grandmother, who, as women, are unable to work under the Taliban.

Ten (2002; DVD, Zeitgeist Films, 2004). Directed by Abbas Kiarostami. Famed Iranian director Kiarostami's film recounts a few days in the life of a female bus driver as she picks up people. The film reveals the social complexity of life in today's Iran.

Yossi & Jagger (2002; DVD, Strand Home Video, 2004). Directed by Eytan Fox. Two male Israeli soldiers fall in love.

RESOURCE GUIDE

PRINT SOURCES

Abileah, A. *The Filmmakers and Film Production Services of Israel.* Jerusalem: Israel Film Center, Ministry of Industry and Trade, 1974.

Armes, R. *Postcolonial Images: Studies in North African Film.* Bloomington: Indiana University Press, 2005.

Arzooni, O. G. *The Israeli Film: Social and Cultural Influences, 1912–1973.* New York: Garland, 1983.

Asfour, N. "The International Beirut Film Festival." *Cineaste* 24: 2–3 (1999).

Cinematograph Film Research Group. *The 2000 Import and Export Market for Cinematograph Film in the Middle East.* San Diego: Icon Group International, 2000.

Culhane, H. *East/West, an Ambiguous State of Being: The Construction and Representation of Egyptian Cultural Identity in Egyptian Film.* New York: Peter Lang, 1995.

Dabashi, H. *Close Up: Iranian Cinema Past, Present and Future.* London: Verso, 2001.

Darwish, Mustafa. *Dream Makers on the Nile: A Portrait of Egyptian Cinema.* New York: Columbia University Press, 1998.

Egan, E. *The Films of Makhmalbaf: Cinema, Politics & Culture in Iran.* Washington, DC: Mage Publishing, 2005.

Kindem, G., ed. *The International Movie Industry.* Carbondale: Southern Illinois University Press, 2000.

Kronish, A., and C. Safirman. *Israeli Film: A Reference Guide.* Westport, CT: Praeger, 2003.

Leaman, O, ed. *Companion Encyclopedia of Middle Eastern and North African Film.* New York: Routledge, 2001.

Loshitzhy, Y. *Identity Politics on the Israeli Screen.* Austin: University of Texas Press, 2002.

Mansfield, P. *A History of the Middle East.* New York: Penguin Press, 1991.

Naficy, H. "Iranian Cinema." Pp. 130–222 in O. Leaman (ed.), *Companion Encyclopedia of Middle Eastern and North African Film*, New York: Routledge, 2001.
Ne'eman, J. "Israeli Cinema." Pp. 223–363 in O. Leaman (ed.), *Companion Encyclopedia of Middle Eastern and North African Film*. London/New York: Routledge, 2001.
Nowell-Smith, G. *The Oxford History of World Cinema*. Oxford: Oxford University Press, 1999.
Pappe, I. "Post-Zionism and Its Popular Culture." Pp. 77–95 in R. Stein and T. Swedenburg (eds.), *Palestine, Israel, and the Politics of Popular Culture*. Durham: Duke University Press, 2005.
Sacerdoti, Y. *The Israeli Cinema*. New York: Writers Collective, 2003.
Shafik, V. *Arab Cinema: History and Cultural Identity*. Cairo: American University of Cairo Press, 1998.
Shayegan, D. "A Taste of My Cinema." Pp. 81–95 in L. Zanganeh (ed.), *My Sister, Guard Your Veil; My Brother, Guard Your Eyes: Uncensored Iranian Voices*. Boston: Beacon Press, 2006.
Stein, R., and T. Swedenburg, eds. *Palestine, Israel, and the Politics of Popular Culture*. Durham: Duke University Press, 2005.
Thabet, M. *Egyptian Film Industry*. Cairo: Ministry of Culture, Foreign Cultural Information Dept, 1998.
Woffenden, R. "Egypt: The Arts in View." *Arts & the Islamic World* 35 (2001): 2–68.

WEBSITES

1-World Films. http://www.1worldfilms.com/. This is a worldwide resource of available films on DVD. It includes an exhaustive list of film festivals.
Araboo. http://www.araboo.com/dir/arabic-movies. Provides a searchable resource for Arab films.
Film Festivals. http://www.filmfestivals.com/index.shtml. A site for festivals and film news.
Iranian Cinema History. http://www.iranchamber.com/cinema/articles/critical_history_iranian_film.php. An excellent discussion of the history of Arab film.
Makhmalbaf Film House. http://www.makhmalbaf.com/. The home site of Iranian director Makhmalbaf and his cinematic school.
Moroccan Films. http://www.mincom.gov.ma/cinemaroc/. Provides history and information on Moroccan film; in French.

INTERNATIONAL FILM FESTIVALS

All the following film festivals have, more than others, shown or emphasized Middle Eastern films; this is a new phenomenon since international film festivals have traditionally focused on European films. Some of these international film festivals are located in countries with Arab cultures. See http://www.1worldfilms.com/international%20film%20festival.htm for an exhaustive list of film festivals around the world, including locations and dates when available.

Bahrain Film Festival
Berlin International Film Festival
Cannes Film Festival
Cairo International Film Festival
Dubai International Film Festival
Eilat International Film Festival
Human Rights Watch International Film Festival
International Beirut Film Festival
San Francisco International Film Festival
Seattle International Film Festival
Tirana International Film Festival
Toronto International Film Festival
Zanzibar International Film Festival

NOTES

1. Warner Brothers, 1942; DVD Warner Home Video, 2000.
2. Armes 2005 (in Resource Guide), p. 75.
3. Ibid., p. 74.
4. Egan. 2005 (in Resource Guide), p. 71.
5. Ibid., p. 71.
6. Dabashi 2001 (in Resource Guide), p. 14.
7. Ibid., p. 6.
8. Shafik 1998 (in Resource Guide), p. 20.
9. Ibid., p. 10.
10. Armes, 661.
11. Shafik, p. 11.
12. Ibid., p. 24.
13. Ibid., p. 48.
14. Ibid., p. 56.
15. Ibid., p. 59.
16. Ibid, p. 64.
17. Armes, p. 664.
18. Ne'eman, "Israeli Cinema," in Leaman 2001 (in Resource Guide), p. 227.
19. Pappe 2005 (in Resource Guide), p. 86.
20. Ne'eman, p. 228.
21. Ibid., p. 230.
22. Ibid., p. 230.
23. Ibid., p. 232.
24. Pappe, p. 77.
25. Ibid., p. 78.
26. Naficy, "Iranian Cinema," in Leaman 2001 (in Resource Guide), p. 130.
27. Ibid., p. 131.
28. Ibid., p. 133.
29. Dabashi, p. 4.
30. Ibid., p. 13.
31. Egan, p. 20.
32. Ibid., p. 19
33. Dabashi, p. 13.
34. Naficy, p. 204.
35. Ibid., p. 208.
36. Egan, p. 19.
37. Ibid., p. 189.

FOOD AND FOODWAYS

HEATHER L. WILLIAMS

Middle Eastern cuisine is characterized by strong Mediterranean, Persian, and various North African traditions. Foods characteristic of the Middle East, a region that proved to be the hub of some of humanity's earliest civilizations and their trade routes, reflect the depth and breadth of its ethnic influences. Distinct spices, nuts and olives, fish, coffees and anise, grains and breads, fresh herbs and seasonal produce, and yogurts and goat cheeses are all adapted to specific customs and locales, continually amended and revised as they are passed from generation to generation while maintaining, at heart, their traditional core, which still serves as the foundation for contemporary dining and world-renowned hospitality. Whether celebrating a holy union or a new year, or welcoming a stranger, food serves as a critical mechanism for building and binding familial and larger social bonds within these cultures. Some of the more definitive traditions of the region include Lebanese, Moroccan, Turkish, and what is generally referred to as Arabic.

One of most significant influences on the cuisine of the Middle East and North Africa is the millennia-old religious doctrines that dictate some of the preparation and consumption of certain foods. Primarily, this includes the *halal* and kosher traditions of the Islamic and Jewish faiths, respectively.

SPECIAL CONCERNS ABOUT FOOD, WATER, AND TRADE FOR MIDDLE EASTERN PEOPLE

Halal and Kosher

Dr. Mian Riaz summarizes the halal tradition efficiently by clarifying that

> Muslims use two major terms to describe food: *Halal* and *Haram*. *Halal* is an Arabic word which means permitted or lawful. There are no restrictions on consumption or use of *halal* food. *Haram* is an Arabic word which means forbidden or unlawful. There are prohibitions on consumption and use of *haram* food. Other terms used are *makrooh*, *mashbooh* and *dhabiha*. *Makrooh* is an Arabic word meaning "religiously discouraged" or "disliked." It covers any food

and liquid which are disguised or harmful to the body. *Mashbooh* is also Arabic word meaning "suspected." It covers the gray area between *halal* and *haram*. *Dhabiha* is another Arabic word meaning "slaughtered" according to Islamic method.[1]

The halal market for food is of significant importance for both domestic and foreign companies. In Egypt, Halwani is the company with the strongest sales for processed meat.[2] Friboi, a Brazilian meatpacking company, ships nearly 20 percent of its exports in halal meat.[3] In fact, Brazilian companies export to several Middle Eastern countries including Iraq, Jordan, and Egypt.[4] Sadia is a company in its third decade of halal business; it is considered the "leading family favorite Halal brand," offering over 800 products.[5] In fact the increasing popularity of halal products is even beginning to affect international retailers, which have begun offering such items in their "exotic foods" sections. This is most noticeable in countries such as France, Belgium, and the Netherlands.[6]

Many of the details regarding kosher strictures are found in the books of Deuteronomy, Leviticus, and Exodus of the Torah, which include forbidden foods, slaughtering practices, the draining of blood, the separation of meat and dairy, and the care and use of utensils. These rules have been aptly summarized by a follower of the faith as follows:

> Kashrut is the body of Jewish law dealing with what foods we can and cannot eat and how those foods must be prepared and eaten. "Kashrut" comes from the Hebrew root Kaf-Shin-Resh, meaning fit, proper or correct. It is the same root as the more commonly known word "kosher," which describes food that meets these standards. The word "kosher" can also be used, and often is used, to describe ritual objects that are made in accordance with Jewish law and are fit for ritual use. Contrary to popular misconception, rabbis or other religious officials do not "bless" food to make it kosher. There are blessings that observant Jews recite over food before eating it, but these blessings have nothing to do with making the food kosher.... The short answer to why Jews observe these laws is: because the Torah says so. The Torah does not specify any reason for these laws.[7]

Kosher food is another area of serious interest for domestic and foreign companies. One of the world's leading providers of kosher food is Orthodox Union Kosher, which certifies more than 400,000 products.[8] Since it is a thoroughly modern company, the Website offers not only the products available for sale but recipes; general information, including the steps for certification; and a weekly column on kosher-related topics.

Water

Another unchanging aspect of the area is the concern regarding the region's ability to support itself. One key issue is water. The emphasis that civilizations from these lands place on water predates some of the cultures currently found in the area. The erratic tides of the Tigris and Euphrates, and the seasonal ebb and flow of the Nile, are reflected in the mythologies of the Sumerian and ancient Egyptians, respectively. These stories, the oldest known to humanity, and the accompanying rites and rituals, attest to the power water has always held over the Middle East and North Africa. With the population's growing demands, this power has only increased.

There are varying reports regarding current agriculture, and the demands for grain-based products by global markets, but many experts agree sustainability and self-sufficiency are pressing issues. An area newspaper recently quoted forecasts predicting a serious gap between supply and demand in relation to available food supply because of increased population and increased income availability per capita.[9] More specifically, the Council of Arab

Economic Unity has estimated a 61-million-ton difference between what the region can produce and what domestic consumption will require by 2010.[10] The situation has been further complicated by a recent drought, considered the worst in decades, which has affected farm production in Jordan, Iran, Iraq, and Syria.[11]

There are discrepancies in expert accounts as to the impact water resources will have in terms of native agriculture; the effect limited fresh water supplies may have on the domestic and international sociopolitical arenas; and the degree to which the typical resident is invested in the matter, which may be difficult to measure in terms of interest or the effect on daily lives. Nevertheless, the issue of water is unavoidable when discussing the foodways of the region. In fact, in 2002 the Gulf Cooperation Council (GCC) countries decided to celebrate an official water week from March 22 to 29 each year, timed to coincide with the UN's World Water Day, celebrated annually since 1993. The goal of both events is to increase awareness of the necessity for a fresh water supply.[12] Whether it involves a tribe's decision to settle at a particular oasis, consideration of where to locate a dam, or the possible ramifications of particular international sanctions or trade agreements, ready access to ample fresh water plays a critical role in the practical realities of the region.

The area is surrounded by several seas, including the Mediterranean and Black seas, and the southeastern-most coast on the region meets the Indian Ocean. And yet, less than 10 percent of the land can support agriculture—for food, livestock, and trade—without artificial irrigation and increasing desalinization efforts. While there are a few fresh water rivers and underground reserves, the available resources are limited and often become the point of potentially heated contention.

For instance, the Euphrates and Orantes rivers, the sources of which originate in Turkey, supply Syria with most of its water. Jordan's two main sources of water are the Jordan River, the headwaters of which begin in Lebanon, and the Yarmouk River, which borders Israel, Jordan, and Syria.[13] After Jordan and Algeria recently signed a Memoranda of Understanding (MoU) regarding such issues as culture, education, and medicine, Jordan further suggested there be a future MoU addressing water resources.[14] Iran has also expressed interest in signing a MoU with Syria regarding food security and agriculture.[15] The allocation and dam construction issues related to fresh water have even affected bodies of salty water such as the Dead Sea, which serves as a major tourist attraction, the surface area of which has decreased by a third (its depth has decreased by 25 meters) over the last 50 years.[16]

The issue of water has become a political leveraging tool directly affecting international relations and trade, two critical elements that for millennia have governed the exchanges that continue to shape the culture, the people, and their cuisine.

Trade and International Relations

While always a hub for international trade—from the medieval Silk Road and the sailing routes that extended to China, East Africa, and the South Pacific[17]—contemporary Middle Eastern and North African cultures still rely on exchange with others to enhance and supplement their native cuisines. In 2004 the Gulf States imported $12 billion in food.[18] By 2006 imports were estimated at $15 billion, a $3 billion dollar increase.[19] As Hilal Said al-Mari, the general manager of the Dubai International Trade Center, declared in January 2006, the Gulf States import approximately 90 percent of their food and drink.[20] In 2005 alone, Great Britain exported $160 million worth of food and beverages just to the United Arab Emirates (UAE).[21] Brazilian companies are also looking to the Middle Eastern and North African sweet and drink markets.[22] Kazakhstani companies have also made agreements with Iranian markets regarding milling wheat.[23] In the interest of self-sufficiency, Iran has even begun working with the United Nations regarding a hybrid rice program, and with Afghanistan to address their respective food industries, among others.[24] However, the exchange does flow in two directions, as exports of beef and poultry of the region increased to 689,000 metric tons, and exports of fish increased to 67,000 metric tons.[25]

So large is the market for Middle Eastern and North African food industries that the Gulfood 2006—the 11th Gulf Food, Hotel, and Equipment Exhibition and Salon Culinaire, a trade-only exhibition—included food suppliers and restaurant and hotel chains from seventy countries.[26] About 30,000 visitors from 120 countries attended, including participants from Denmark, Serbia, South Africa, Australia, Cyprus, Greece, South Korea, Taiwan, and the United States,[27] including representatives from the South Australian Wine Industry Association.[28] This is largely the result of Gulf Cooperation Council targeting Saudi Arabia, Qatar, and the UAE as some of the most critical food and drink markets in the world.[29]

Professionals use such events as the Iraqi Business Networking Event, Buyers-Sellers Meeting on Horticultural and Agricultural Products, the 3rd Middle East Food Marketing Forum during Gulfood 2005, and the Wine & Spirits event at Gulfood 2006 as chances to network trade opportunities; they also use these meetings to explore concerns regarding the production, preparation, and consumption of food, such as during the food safety conference at Gulfood 2006.[30] And this was not their only opportunity to take advantage of unique exchanges. In December of 2005, for example, the Middle East Natural and Organic Products Expo was held in Dubai.[31]

The West and Westernization

During the twentieth century—and continuing into the twenty-first—the foreign cultures that have had the greatest influence on Middle Eastern cuisine are those of the West, albeit more so in the Middle East than in North Africa, a fact especially true for those with the financial resources to enjoy the cuisine. As Bernard Lewis stated, "In most cities outside the Arabian peninsula, the rich now wore different clothes, ate different food, and lived by different social rules from the unmodernized mass of the population."[32] Regardless of class, however, the influence of the West can be felt in many aspects of larger society, especially in urban areas, as an influence that has been governed in equal parts by commerce and hospitality, molding the region's cuisine and blurring but not erasing cultural boundaries.

An urban teenager in the Middle East may have thyme-flavored potato chips, in contrast to the sour cream and onion flavors enjoyed by his or her Western counterparts, but the Middle Eastern teenager is equally likely to wash that snack down with a Pepsi. In major cities in more open countries such as Dubai or the UAE, or in Kuwait City, one will be able to enjoy restaurants serving all ranges of Western-style fast food and casual dining—Fuddruckers, Benihana, Trader Vic's, Popeye's, and McDonald's—to five-star gourmet fare based on local and foreign cuisines.[33] This cultural mix has provided some rather culturally diverse business arrangements, as illustrated by the licensing agreement covering such countries as Kuwait, the UAE, Bahrain, Egypt, Turkey, Jordan, and Lebanon, through which the Louisville, Kentucky, restaurant chain Tumbleweed Southwest Grill plans to open nine restaurants in the Middle East over a period of five years. The Tumbleweed Southwest Grill franchises are to be operated by Jamil Sultan, owner of Sultan Center Food Products of Kuwait.[34] The influence is also evidenced by the baggies of kabobs and other foodstuffs purchased by foreign military forces currently in Iraq, and by vendors displaying handmade signs bearing the names of various Western chains purely in the interest of marketing, not as a reflection of the food available for purchase—a surreal juxtaposition of external influence and the street fare that has long been a staple of Middle Eastern foodways, and arguably the first "fast food." In this particular context, the West has even had the ability to import itself, as evidenced by the Burger King that opened in the "military-controlled" Baghdad International airport, which reported selling approximately 6,500 burgers per day in 2003, largely to foreign solders stationed in the area.[35]

Some countries are adapting Western fast food–eating habits, such as the concept of the food court as seen in American shopping malls, to better reflect immediate regional tastes. In Dubai, for example, Ibn Battuta Shopping Mall, advertised as the "world's largest themed mall," has enlisted the talents of Future Food to revamp the current food court to include more fresh food items and to allow customers to watch the food being prepared.[36]

A byproduct of Western influence, however, is that certain restaurants occasionally become targets for those wishing to express their distaste for the international diplomatic/political policies of certain Western nations, particularly those of the United States. This is exactly what occurred in 2002 when a Saudi man entered a McDonald's near a U.S. air force base and started a fire with gasoline.[37] Interestingly, while part of the larger Western chain, these individual restaurants are locally owned and operated, making what may seem to some as a simplistic, violent act far more culturally complex in its implications and consequences.

Other easily recognizable trends include the increasing popularity of pre-packaged foods, again more so in the Middle East than in North Africa, which varies depending on the level of disposable income. According to Euromonitor International, in 2004 alone Israelis consumed US$686.70 million per capita in packaged foods, Saudis US$323.80 million per capita, and the Turkish population enjoyed US$247.80 million per capita.[38] Also in 2004, combining off-trade and on-trade estimates, the same groups collectively consumed over US$12,144 million in soft drinks.[39]

While this Western staple has gained popularity, soft drinks are far from intrinsically Western. Gazoz, a Turkish lime soda much like fizzy lemonade, has been wildly popular throughout the Middle East and North Africa since the middle of the twentieth century. While Gazoz is still prominent in certain countries such as Algeria, the Western brands of Coca-Cola and Pepsi have taken over much of the indigenous market. For example, while Gazoz was the most popular drink in Israel by the 1950s, and even called the national drink by some, it had already begun to disappear by the 1960s and is now comparatively absent.[40]

All of the culinary traditions of the Near East, Middle East, and North Africa can be grouped into six geographically and culturally similar regions.[41] These regions are North Africa, including Algeria, Morocco, Tunisia, and Libya; Egypt; the Fertile Crescent, including Israel, the Palestinian Territories, Lebanon, Syria, and Turkey; the Tigris-Euphrates area, including Iraq; Iran; and the Arabian peninsula.[42] The following information will be arranged largely in terms of these regions.

REGIONS

North Africa

In addition to countries such as Libya, this region also includes and area traditionally referred to as the Maghreb region, which means "furthest west." This North African area includes such countries as Algeria, Morocco, and Tunisia.

Food and Foodways

Algeria

Algeria is one of the North African countries having a clear cultural perspective and identity into which minimal Western influence has been introduced, although there have been a few changes. As a local resident stated, "Algeria was once the granary of Rome, and now it has to import cereals to make bread. It is a land of flocks and gardens, and it imports meat and fruit."[43] The sociopolitical forces that have affected the original agricultural wealth can also explain the slight degree to which outside, particularly Western, aspects have altered Algerian cuisine. An illustrative example of this is the soft drink market.

While much of the rest of the world, including large areas of the Middle East and North Africa, have absorbed and adopted soft drinks such as Coke and Pepsi, Algeria is still defined by its immediate context. Gazoz, hugely popular throughout the greater region several decades ago, has yet to be replaced as the local favorite by the Western labels as in other countries, even though carbonated drinks are still the preference.[44] The next most popular types of drinks include various fruit juices and mineral waters, many of which are produced by government-owned corporations such as Entreprise Nationale des Eaux Minerales de l'Agerois (EMAL) and Enajuc. However, Coca-Cola had begun to be produced and manufactured locally by 1993–94.[45]

Marketing and sales of such items are also largely limited to the single government-owned television and radio stations, and to small, independent stores and cafés; larger, Western-style supermarkets are rare. Of the two major supermarket chains, Monoprix and Souk el Fallah, the later is also government owned.[46] Western fast food chains are not present. The other major reason for limited exposure to, or acceptance of, external influences rests with the poverty level experienced by much of the populace.

Morocco

Of the nearly 25 million Moroccans, 80 percent are Berber (indigenous people who are Islamic, although not ethnically Arab), although the strong Spanish, Jewish, and Arab influences combine to create a culturally diverse mix.[47] Favorite spices of Moroccan cuisine include cinnamon, cumin, turmeric, ginger, cayenne, paprika, anise and sesame seed, and black pepper. Key herbs are parsley, coriander, marjoram, mint, and basil. Other common flavors come from such ingredients as buttermilk, olives, oranges, lemons, prickly pear, shad, pomegranates, almonds, dates, walnuts, chestnuts, honey, barley, cherries, and melon. Main dishes often feature seafood, lamb, and poultry.

The largest meal occurs at midday and is likely to include any of the country's favorite entrées such as couscous (semolina grains over a variety of toppings), *mechoui* (roasted lamb), or *djej emshmel* (chicken roasted with lemon and olives). A preferred main dish, often reserved for special occasions, is *bastila* or *bisteeya*, from the Spanish word for pastry (*pastilla*) and "the Latin *pastillum*, from *panis*, meaning 'bread.' This layered pastry pie is often filled with chicken, or more traditionally, pigeon."[48]

Family dinners are often prepared and presided over by the *dada*, or mistress, of the home.[49] When entertaining guests, a hostess may spend up to a week in preparation, or she may employ a chef. The host tends to oversee rather than participate in the preparations, and no women are present at the meal. Guests are usually seated on pillows or mattresses situated around low tables, and hands are washed before the meal begins. The dinner may well begin with bastila, then brochette or kebab. This may then be followed by *tajine* (a spicy meat stew) served with *khubz* (flat bread), after which courses of *batinjann* (eggplant with chopped tomato salad) and couscous will likely come in succession. The meal is often finished with honey and almond pastries, melon wedges, and mint tea.[50]

Morocco is fortunate to be a highly agrarian society with ready access to fresh products, the preferred foundation of its cuisine. It is also a country with a scarcity of modern conveniences such as freezers and microwaves since there is limited availability of electricity.[51] For this reason, the popularity of such contemporary staples as pre-packaged frozen foods is marginal. In fact, power resources also influence the concerns regarding sufficient fresh water supplies, as was evidenced when Morocco hosted an international conference on nuclear energy, which was proposed as a possible source of power to meet desalinization needs.[52]

Tunisia

Tunisia's spicy cuisine blends European, Oriental, and Mediterranean traditions, drawing from many of the cultural influences that once dominated the land, such as the Phoenician, Roman, Arab, Turkish, French, and the native Berber cultures. Tunisia is a highly modern society: two-thirds of its 10 million inhabitants live in urban areas, and almost 20 percent of the population resides in the city of Tunis.[53] Eighty percent of the overall population is middle class and represents the highest level of purchasing power in the North African region.[54] Each household spends approximately $2,400 on food annually.[55] And while rural households spend almost 65 percent less than urban households, Tunisians on average spend 40 percent of the household budget on food.[56] These expenditures included purchases of $1 billion worth of imported agricultural products, $74 million of which came from the United States.[57]

Staples of the cuisine include breads such as the baguette and *tabouna* (baked in a clay domed oven), and meats such as lamb or beef. Seafood is also an important part of the Tunisian diet, and a favorite meal includes fried or grilled *rouget* (red mullet). The most distinct spice of choice may be *harissa*, a red pepper and garlic sauce/paste, the use of which can be traced back to the seventh century and whose name comes from the Arabic word *harasa*, meaning "to pound or crush."

Couscous is often cited as the national dish. Other favorites includes appetizers such as *mechouia* (grilled sweet peppers, tomatoes, and onions mixed with oil, lemon, tuna fish, and hard-boiled eggs), soups such as *chorba* (heavily peppered) and *lalabli* (chick-peas seasoned with garlic), stews such as *guenaoia* (lamb or beef seasoned with chilies, okra, sweet peppers, and coriander), and various tajine. Meals may end with many of the preferred sweets such as *bouza* (sorghum and hazelnut cake), *makroud* (semolina cake stuffed with dates, cinnamon, and grated orange peel), *mhalbya* (cake made with rice, nuts, and geranium water), *samsa* (a layered pastry with ground roast almonds and sesame seeds, baked in lemon and rosewater syrup), or *yo-yo* (deep fried donuts made with orange juice and then dipped in honey). In fact, few special occasions shared by family and friends would be complete without sweets. *Zgougou*, a sweet pudding of ground pine seed served with vanilla ice cream and grated nuts, is served throughout Tunisia. Eid al-Fitr, the celebration that marks the end of Ramadan, often includes dishes, favorite pastries such as *bakloua* or makroud. Indeed, the absence of sweets at a wedding, christening, or dinner party would be sorely felt.

Libya

Restaurants and cafés are largely the territory of tourists; many Libyans prefer to eat at home. Meals are served communally on platters; after the last dish is eaten, drinks are served from a communal *guerba* (a vessel holding milk or spring water). Meals then often end by enjoying coffee and tobacco.[58]

Favorite dishes include couscous (boiled cereal served with potatoes and mutton or chicken), *sherba* (spicy soup), *k'ak* (biscuits), spiced sausage, marinated chick-peas, and pickled eggplant or sardines. Since traditional Islamic law forbids the consumption of alcohol, popular drinks are more often bottled mineral water, soft drinks, fruit juices (especially orange), and thick Libyan tea. Coffee is available, however, if requested.

Egypt

Daily eating habits in Egypt generally consist of a light breakfast of beans, eggs, and cheese, followed by a large, starchy lunch and a nap. Then a tea is enjoyed in the late afternoon, with a light supper in the evening.[59] Staples of the diet include bread, rice, potatoes, *gibna* (a native cheese), tomatoes, eggplant, chick-peas, okra, bananas, dates, oranges, and melons.[60] Egyptians have also been taking increased interest in making healthy choices regarding their produce. In fact, Egypt has become one of the largest markets for organic products in the developing world, a trend that can be traced back to 1985 when Sekem began to offer a line of herbal drinks and remedies. This puts Isis teas sales just under the sales totals of the leading tea producer, Lipton.

In terms of popular dishes, *koshary* is a general favorite. A blend of chick-peas, pasta, onion, lentils, rice, chili sauce, and garlic sauce, it is available on the streets and can be made inexpensively in the home.[61] In fact, pasta has become one of the most popular dried foods consumed by Egyptians, second only to rice, both of which provide the bulk to koshary.[62]

Other favorites include shish kebob, whole wheat pitas, *hamaam* (pigeons), and *torly* (stew or mixed vegetable casserole). Another well-known specialty is Egyptian falafel, or *ta'miyya*, whose name stems from the Arabic word for nourishment and which uses hyacinth instead of fava beans. Also popular is *surbah*, a soup made from meat, fish or vegetables, a version of which uses *molokhiyya* (an Egyptian leafy vegetable).[63]

However, it is *ful* (a recipe made with a fava bean base) that is acknowledged by some as the national dish of Egypt. There are various varieties, all flavored according to the region and the cook's taste: *ful hammam* (bath fava, so named for the Princess Bath of the Middle Ages), *ful rumi* (large, kidney-shaped beans), *ful nabit* (bean sprouts), *ful akhdar* (fresh beans), and *ful madshush* (crushed beans) are some of the variations.[64]

Egyptian desserts are often pastries or types of pudding; perhaps the best known is baklava. Others include *fatir* (stuffed pancakes), *basbousa* (semolina pastry soaked in honey and topped with hazelnuts), *umm ali* (a raisin cake soaked in milk and served hot), *kanafa* (batter, stuffed and fried), and *mahallabiyya* (rice pudding). Another popular sweet is *halawa*, made from sesame paste, sugar, and spices. Western-style chocolate bars are also beginning to gain popularity. Critical differences exist, however, between rural and urban communities.

In rural Egypt much of the cuisine is defined by the lifestyle of the *fellahin* (farmers of various ethnicities).[65] For farmers, main meals consist of rice, fruit, and vegetables, with bread serving not only as the main staple but often as the primary utensil. Two such examples are *aysh* (unleavened bread baked in clay ovens) and *aysh sham* (bread made from dough set out in the sun to rise). On special occasions, and when available, meat is prepared often as *fattah* (a dish containing a mixture of bread, rice, and meat, seasoned with vinegar and garlic, and garnished with yogurt and nuts). Another critical component of the fellahin lifestyle is pigeons. These birds not only provide meat for their dishes but also fertilizer for their crops. In some small villages, the importance pigeons serve is clear from the elaborate coops built near fellahin houses.[66]

Because of the necessities of farming, the production and preparation of food is a full family affair. Boys as young as ten years old begin to learn how to work the land they will one day inherit.[67] Young children help out by herding sheep and goats. Young girls feed chickens, milk goats and *gamoosa* (water buffalo), and learn to carry loads on their heads. The women of the family are responsible for the preparation of the daily meals, and on days of feasts and celebrations, the women of the village will work together to cook elaborate meals.

In the country, groceries are still obtained primarily through weekly souqs (traditional Arab markets) or from independent food stores.[68] Purchases are based on daily needs and are made from limited funds. The success of such markets is based on the ability to buy on credit, as well as on the loyalty and trust shared between the merchant and the customer.

When eating out in more urban areas, Egyptians often patronize street vendors or small shops where customers stand at counters to enjoy roasted chickens, *shawirma* (gyros), or a quick snack of nuts.[69] Restaurants are usually open from 1:00 PM to 4:00 PM for lunch, and from 8:00 PM to midnight for dinner. Dishes offered in small local establishments are inexpensive and rooted in meat and fava beans. Western-style salad bars are popular in urban areas, as are Western food chains such as McDonald's and Kentucky Fried Chicken.

When shopping for food in cities, upper-middle-class and affluent patrons take advantage of Western-style supermarkets.[70] These are expected to continue to gain in popularity because of their convenience as the number of working women increases and households experience the time restraints of a modern urban lifestyle.

Just as in other areas of the Middle East and North Africa, the concept of packaged foods is present, although not as prominently here as in other countries. Part of this can be attributed to concerns regarding health and to the limited financial resources of the area residents. Also, there is a great appreciation for artisanal foods (made by a skilled craftsperson) over mass-produced foods. The general opinions regarding the international policies of some Western countries, and United States policies regarding Iraq and the Palestinian Territories in particular, also keep many from purchasing outside brands. However, sometimes even indigenous companies face challenges even though they are more closely tied to the immediate culture.

A case in point is the Faragello Group, a company established in 1974 which has had great success in the healthy packaged-food market with such products as frozen and canned meats and vegetables, and instant meals. Even so, the company changed its name in September 1999 from Faragella to Faragello to remove the name of Allah, which had inadvertently been embedded in the title.[71]

One element of Egyptian cuisine that does seem to aid in breaking down ideological lines is sweets. Of the Western companies making headway, Cadbury is described by Wallace Garland, the managing director of for the Middle East and North Africa region, as the "largest confectionery supplier to the [Egyptian] market."[72] Nestle is also making headway.[73] This explains why one of the exceptions to the packaged-food market resistance can be found in ice cream sales. Partially as a result of the numbers of tourists, this frozen treat is a favorite in the heat of Egypt.

Drinks accompanying any meal include teas, coffee, and juices. There are also flavored milks (e.g., strawberry, banana, and chocolate) and fruit-flavored yogurt drinks (e.g., apricot, raspberry, and mango). In terms of alcoholic beverages, Stella is a local beer enjoyed in large bottles.[74] Diluted brandy and local rum are also available, as is *zibib* (similar to Greek ouzo).[75]

A favorite time for Egyptians to enjoy their unique foodways, whether rural or urban, is easily during one of their many festivals and celebrations, and some even consider Cairo the "entertainment capital of the Arab World."[76] Some of the most important observances include Ramadan (Islamic month of fasting), Coptic Easter Monday, *eids* (festivals), *moulids* (birthdays), and *sebou* (week after birth). Easter Monday is celebrated regardless of religious affiliation or lack thereof, and people rush to the countryside for family picnics including hard boiled eggs and pickled fish. Eid al-Fitr is a festival that ends the fasting of Ramadan, the first day of the month of Shawwal. The day begins with quick nibbles and prayers, leading to large family picnics. One of the favorite sweets for this occasion is *kahka/kahk* (nut-filled cookies with a powdered sugar coating). During Eid al-Adha, a festival held at the end of the annual pilgrimage to Mecca, a lamb is slaughtered, when finances permit, to feed friends, family, and the poor to represent Abraham's sacrifice of a sheep for his son. The moulids are days to honor Christian and Muslim saints, dictated by the lunar Islamic calendar. This is a custom not strictly held according to religious tenets, and they are times for special treats. Two of these include Halawet el-Moulia, for which special sweets are made, and Aroussa al Moulia, during which children receive candy dolls. For sebous, a lamb is slaughtered and gifts of sweets and candies are distributed.

However, all is not celebration. One particularly contemporary concern impacting modern Egyptian cuisine has been the bread and import market crisis, which was particularly difficult in 2003. A poor wheat harvest, difficulties with milling, and rising costs of imported wheat created a national bread shortage. This was further exacerbated by the population explosion, an increase of 30 million that had occurred since 1981.[77] Another critical factor was the devaluation of the Egyptian pound, which caused a 10 to 20 percent cost of living increase.[78] This drastically affected import markets, on which Egypt is dependent—for example, Egypt imports 100 percent of its tea and 70 percent of its wheat and sugar.[79] The sharp increase in prices had some vendors reducing their orders by two-thirds over the previous year.[80] And while subsidies for staples such as tea, sugar, and cooking oil aided the immediate situation, they added to concerns regarding the government's budget deficit. Overall, the situation reminded many of the 1977 "bread riots" instigated by reduced government subsidies.[81] This serves as a critical example of the delicate relationship between agriculture, water, and trade that defines the foodways of the Middle East.

Another more recent concern affecting Egyptian cuisine includes issues regarding the poultry industry and avian influenza. Poultry is a staple enjoyed by both rural and urban peoples alike. In fact, Egyptians consume roughly 800 million birds annually. Now, however, it is estimated that the industry loses $1.7 million per day.[82] While most cases of the deadly H5N1 strain of avian influenza have been traced back to domestic farms beyond the direct control of officials, the government has "banned the transport of poultry between the country's twenty-six governorates, about half of which are affected by the epidemic."[83] The overall situation has affected restaurants, supermarkets, and egg and mayonnaise sales, despite the efforts of authorities to keep fears and rumors in check. In response, corporations have conducted a media campaign to increase awareness and trust. Two critically positive effects the crisis has had, however, are an increase in the market for fish and red meat as well as a growth in optimism that the situation will speed the modernization of the overall farming industry in the country.

Fertile Crescent

In addition to countries such as Turkey, this area includes a region traditionally referred to as the Levant—an indefinite region largely recognized as including such countries as Israel, Jordan, Lebanon, the Palestinian Territories, and Syria. They are distinct yet inextricably bound, with the sociopolitical relationships between them complex and sometimes strained as seen during the events of July 2006. However, there are several common aspects of their cuisine that permeate the entire region, often crossing specific national boundaries.

Jordan

Jordan has its own rich culinary traditions, ranging from grilled cuisine (shish kebabs, *shish taouks*) to stuffed vegetables (e.g., grape leaves and eggplants), meat, and poultry.[84] Meals are often communal, as an extension of classic Middle Eastern hospitality, with family and friends. The meals often begin with appetizers commonly know throughout the region as *mezze*, the most popular of which is hummus. Others include *ful moudames* and *koubba maqliya*. Favorite main dishes include *mansaf*, *freekie*, and stuffed or whole lamb, as well as *maglouba* (meat, fish, or vegetable stew served with rice) and *musakhan* (a baked chicken dish with onions, olive oil, and pine seeds).

It is mansaf, however, which is widely recognized as the national dish of Jordan. Mansaf is prepared using Arabic rice, *jameed* (rich broth made from dry sour milk), and chicken or lamb. It is often enjoyed communally as a celebration, for a condolence, or when making amends among friends or family.

However, as elsewhere in the region, Jordan has recently experienced economic and agricultural difficulties. While trade with such countries as the United States (from which the U.S. Department of Agriculture has authorized the export of $20 million worth of wheat, or about 107,500 tons) remains strong, local shortages have given rise to concern.[85] In fact, in 2003 the royal family offered aid to over 21,000 families during a recent difficult economic environment that had occurred because of rising fuel prices and suspected price gauging by shopkeepers during Ramadan, and to forgo their typically lush celebrations of *iftar* meals (evening meals used to break the daily fast during Ramadan).

Israel

Israel is a fully modern country of approximately 7,279,000 people, which incorporates multimillennia-old culinary traditions of the Hebrew, Christian, and Muslim faiths as well and contemporary global trends.[86] The cuisine draws from Oriental and Western culinary traditions. As the Israeli Ministry of Foreign Affairs has stated, "Despite its Biblical association with milk and honey, Israel lacks a long-standing culinary heritage. Only a few years ago, Israelis even doubted the existence of their own authentic cuisine. Today, most people agree that there is a distinctive Israeli cuisine, though like many aspects of the society, it is uniquely multifaceted. It reflects the various communities in the country and their diverse geographical and cultural origins."[87] For example, stuffed cabbage, traditionally a Jewish dish, is common in Eastern Europe. Blintzes and knishes are familiar to all Germans, not just German Jews. Couscous originally comes from the Maghreb nations of North Africa, falafel can be traced back to Egypt, and *shishlik* originated in Turkey. Favorite dishes include mansaf, humus, tahini (a sesame seed paste), kebabs, and gefilte fish (a Jewish white fish dish). Preferred drinks include regional wines, Gold Star and Maccabee beer, *arak* (a drink made with anise), and *sabra* (a chocolate and orange liqueur). Western-style soft drinks are also a favorite, and considered by some as a market indicator.

In 2006 alone, Israelis spent over $11,871.9 million on food consumption, including the purchase of 1,376 million liters of soft drinks.[88] While their overall expenditures for foodstuffs showed little increase (up only $2,381.7 million from the $10,490.20 million spent in 2002), there was some evidence to a shift in consumption style, as indicated by the 442-liter increase in soft drink sales during the same period.[89] Regardless, the food sector accounts for about one-quarter of local industry revenues and only 17 percent of its work force (59,000 workers).[90]

Meals in the home usually begin with a large breakfast, including such dishes as salads, cheeses, olives, Israeli bread, juice, and coffee. Lunch occurs at noon and is usually the largest meal of the day. Dinner is often light, consisting of salad, eggs, and dairy products.

Weekly food shopping is done mostly at supermarkets, which first appeared in the 1980s and 1990s, causing local independent markets to lose ground to larger stores such as Supersol, Co-op, and Co-op 1.[91] Convenience is increasingly the primary consideration affecting food buying and eating. However, specialty shops such as fishmongers, green grocers, and bakers have grown in popularity because of the uniqueness and quality of their products. The sales of packaged foods and alcohol reflect the trend toward larger shopping centers, with their variety and lower prices, especially as economic, political, and employment concerns press the population.

Another critical concern, as it is throughout the Middle East and North Africa, is that of water resources. In Israel and Jordan, large subsidies are offered to farmers who use water from the Jordan River. Unfortunately, this practice of fostering domestic crops has directly impacted the critical tourism industry by affecting the water level in such bodies of water as the Dead Sea, which host popular resorts.[92]

The Palestinian Territories

The Palestinian Territories, while sharing some of the same affinities regarding preferred dishes and spices. as evidenced in *musakhkhan* (baked chicken wrapped in bread and onions with sumac), and enjoying ful for breakfast, also shares the issue of foodways begin affected by sociopolitical challenges. Concerns have been present since the Palestinian-Israeli conflict that began in September 2000.[93] By 2002 the United Nations Agency for Palestinian Refugees (UNRWA) estimated that more than a fifth of Palestinian children in Gaza and the West Bank were suffering from malnutrition.[94] In addition the once strong fishing tradition has been complicated by the intricacies of the relationship with neighboring Israel.[95] Bakeries have been affected as well: because of Israeli closures of certain territories, difficulties have been experienced regarding sufficient supplies of, or access to, such staples as wheat flour, rice, cooking oil, and sugar, with bakeries often running short of supplying local demand.

Lebanon

Contemporary Lebanese cuisine tends to combine the foods of Europe, the Middle, and the Far East. Diet is characterized by bread, an abundance of other starches, fruits, vegetables, and fresh fish and seafood. Meat is consumed occasionally, although poultry is eaten with more frequency than red meat (usually lamb). Common ingredients include yogurt, cheese, cucumber, aubergines (eggplants), chick-peas, nuts, tomatoes, burhul, and sesame (seeds, paste, and oil). Garlic and olive oil are favorite seasonings, but parsley, mint, lemons, and onions can be used as well. Grilling, sautéing, and baking are preferred cooking methods, and vegetables are usually served raw, cooked, or pickled.

Meals often begin with mezze such as pickled vegetables, hummus, and bread. These may be followed by grilled marinated seafood, skewered meats, salads (cooked or raw), and a variety of desserts. Popular dishes include baba ghanoush, falafel, *lahma bi ajeen*

(Arabic pizza), musakhan (a chicken casserole with sumac and cashew seasoning), *sayyadiya* (spiced fish served with rice), and *oawrama* (small pieces of braised mutton or beef served with onions and tomatoes). Others include tabouleh (bulgur wheat, parsley, and mint salad), *fattoush* (toasted bread salad), and chicken with rice. *Kibbeh*, however, is widely recognized as the national dish of Lebanon.

Kibbeh is a paste made from lamb and bulgur wheat. It can take many forms including *kibbeh nayee* (raw), *kibbeh bil-saneeya* (baked), and *kibbeh rass* (fried), all of which may be served with yogurt sauce. This dish is usually reserved for special occasions because of the elaborate preparation it requires.

Regardless which main dish is served, bread is the key staple and often main utensil at every meal. The two main types of bread are the pita (a small pocket of flat bread) and *marcook* (thin bread baked over a fire). At breakfast, it is often flavored with *zahtar* (thyme-sumac seasoning).

At the end of meals, fresh fruit, coffee, and possibly dessert such as Lebanese baklava (made with pistachio nuts and topped with a rose-water syrup) are served. Other popular desserts include *kunafi* (a "shoelace" pastry with sweet white cheese, nuts, and syrup), *ma'a-mul* (date cookies) and mahallabiyya (semolina pudding served cold). Yet despite this rich tradition, here, too, foodways are directly tied to domestic and foreign policy.

In recent years the people of Lebanon have been wrestling with concerns regarding increased taxes, specifically VAT taxes, and a public debt that had reached $25.8 million by 2002, which directly affected food sales and consumption.[96] Additionally, some within the country have also expressed their disapproval of the activities of some foreign entities, specifically the United States and its policies regarding Israel and the Palestinian Territories, by violently attacking Western chains such as Kentucky Fried Chicken, an instance of which occurred in Tripoli in 2002.[97] Overall, the tensions caused by the dependency on outside resources and the country's own internal struggles directly complicate Lebanese culinary habits.

Syria

Syria, too, has experienced the challenge of negotiating between tradition and external influence. There has been a rise in popularity of Western brands such as Coca-Cola, Pepsi, and most recently Kentucky Fried Chicken, despite a strained political history with the United States.[98] However, here as elsewhere in the Levant, cultural and culinary identity continues to be rooted in consistent, familiar favorites such as the Syrians' cookie, *biscochos*.

Turkey

While some see Turkey as part of Europe geographically, Turkish cuisine is distinctly Middle Eastern. More precisely stated, Turkey, as the last stop on the Silk Road, is often cited as the bridge between East and West. Even though only 20 percent of the land is arable, the volcanic soil and extensive trade have helped foster a rich culinary tradition, which is generally broken down into seven separate regions encompassing all of the territory between the Black Sea, the Caucasus Mountains, and the central region of Anatolia. Indeed, it can be argued that it was in the grand kitchens of the Ottoman empire, wherein hundreds of specialized cooks served tens of thousands a day with platters of culinary dishes, that the staples of contemporary culinary favorites were perfected.

Breads and grain still play a key role in Turkey, as they have since wheat was domesticated there approximately 7,000 years ago. Other significant starches that persist in Turkish diets include potatoes as well as corn, which came to the region over 400 years ago from Mexico and now serves as the main grain of the mountain region.[99]

The tradition of sweets in the region is rooted in such fruits as pomegranates and apricots. Honey and nuts, such as hazelnuts and chestnuts, are also often combined in traditional candies, especially in autumn.[100] In fact, Turkey supplies 75 percent of the world's hazelnut crop. However, the country's main export is tea, which has grown to a production of approximately 800,000 tons since 1924.[101]

The consumption of animals includes the meat of goats, sheep, and lamb (the oldest known recipe in Turkey is believed to be one for lamb stew), as well as the dairy byproducts of goats and sheep such as milk and yogurt. However, as in other areas of the Middle East and North Africa, Turkey has begun to experiment more with the benefits of fisheries, specifically trout farming.[102]

Staples of contemporary cuisine are rooted in favorite traditional dishes including various dolmas ("stuffed things") such as peppers, and *yufka* (thin, flat unleavened bread that is filled with cheese, meat, or veggies and then fried). These are often complemented by lentils and spiced with paprika. However, here, too, the influence of Western habits is evident. Turkey today is challenged to "achieve . . . continuity in a time of genetic engineering, high-tech mass production, and a growing number of convenience-oriented households."[103]

The street vendors that have been an ever-present aspect of Turkish cuisine, in addition to selling their world-renowned breads, kabobs, and region-specific delicacies such as lamb entrails, can also now be seen offering New York style hot dogs.[104] The convenience of prepackaged foods has also been embraced.

The three most common forms of these edibles include dried, canned/preserved, and frozen foods. Of the dried items, ready meals such as bulgur *pilavi* (rice pounded from wheat) with vegetables are popular. Of the canned/preserved foods, ready meals are also prominent, the clear preference resting with vegetarian meals such as *fasulye pilaki* and *barunya pilaki*. Of the frozen items, traditional *manti* dumplings and *borek* (a bakery product with meat or cheese) are favorites, although newer items such as sea food ready meals have been introduced as well. Frozen pizzas are a clear favorite. All of these are available through both supermarkets and independent small *bakkals* (stores) and mini-markets.

In terms of snack foods, Turkish cuisine has always included what is arguably the original version of the Western fruit roll-up. Here they come in the form of sheets of mashed and dried apricots and grapes.[105] The idea of trail mix is also an old tradition, dating back to the culture's mythology and still practiced by mothers who provide school treats for their children, usually in the form of a mix of raisins and nuts, often hazelnuts.

The people most likely to spend money on these and other nonessential food items are the "tweens" (children between the ages of 10 and 14) and retirees, or "pensioners" (adults 60 years of age and older).[106] As in many cultures, it is these two groups that have the most disposable income and the fewest pressing necessities.

Tigris-Euphrates

Iraq

Traditional Iraqi food, much like elsewhere in the Middle East and North Africa, is rooted in a pluralistic culture defined by the highly social sharing and swapping of dishes and hospitality. Lunch often serves as the main meal, and stew and rice are eaten almost daily. There are favorite staples and dishes such as *kubbat mosul* (flattened bulgur dough), *misaqua'at betinjan bil laban* (browned eggplant with yogurt), *timman abyadh* (white rice made with a crust of yogurt and oil), and various *kleicha* (the "national cookies of Iraq").[107] Kleicha, which can be a bit dry, is spiced with cardamom and occasionally rose water, and coated in egg wash. It is made in a variety of shapes (discs, half moons, and molded) and with many different fillings (nuts, sugar, and dates).

However, as a result of events that came to a head in the 1990s and continued to color Iraq's political situation well past 2000, arguably one of the most definitive facets of contemporary Iraqi cuisine was the United Nations Oil-for-Food program, during which foodways were directly tied to international relations. Introduced in 1996 to help "soften the impact of sanctions" on Iraq as a result of its invasion of Kuwait in 1990, the Oil-for-Food program allowed Baghdad to obtain food and medicine with part of the revenue earned from exporting crude oil under UN supervision.[108] Free trade agreements were signed with countries including Oman, Algeria, Egypt, Lebanon, Sudan, Syria, Tunisia, the United Arab Emirates, and Yemen. Oman sent 67 percent of its exports to Iraq, making that country Oman's largest Arab client. Egypt soon became Iraq's third-largest trading partner, and its primary trading partner in the Middle East, with bilateral trade reaching $1.7 billion in 2001.[109] This includes consideration of the breach between the two countries when Egypt joined coalition forces in 1991, which was resolved in November of 2000. Relations have improved in recent years.[110] Unfortunately, the UN program was also soon embroiled in scandal regarding charges of corruption.

During the Oil-for-Food program, six out of ten Iraqis had to rely on public food rations, according to the United Nation's Food and Agriculture Organization (FAO) and the World Food Program (WFP).[111] Chronic malnutrition persisted among 100,000 refugees and approximately 200,000 internally displaced residents.[112] At this time, American wheat growers accused the Australian Wheat Board (AWB), Iraq's largest wheat supplier at the time, of paying kickbacks to Saddam Hussein's family to establish a "pre-war dominance" of the market.[113] The AWB initially insisted it was willing to compete in a free market and threatened to sue over the allegations.[114] However, it was later established that the AWB had indeed paid approximately $220 million in kickbacks to Saddam Hussein's regime under the Oil-for-Food program in exchange for $2.3 billion in wheat contracts. It was one of 2,200 companies found to have done so.[115] A U.S. Senate panel later stated that up to one-third of the amount paid to the Iraqi government from 1996 through 2003 was not distributed to humanitarian relief efforts.[116]

All of this continued to negatively impact the foodways of the Iraqi people, many of whom were dependent on aid. To address this, in 2004, after the Iraqi Red Crescent came to an agreement with coalition forces, thousands of Sunni and Shiite Muslims peacefully marched food and medical supplies to Fallujah.[117] According to the United Nation's WFP, 60 percent of the Iraqi population relied on rations before the war. By September 2004, 25 percent of the population was still dependent, and another 14 percent would be without a comfortable food supply if the rationing system were discontinued.[118]

Iran

In Iran, food is approached in three ways: medicinally, philosophically, and culturally.[119] Preparation and consumption are based on the idea of achieving balance between weakness and strength by way of the intrinsically cold or hot nature of the food. For example, animal fat, poultry, wheat, sugar, some fresh fruits and vegetables, and all dried vegetables and fruits are considered to be hot, while most beef, fish, rice, dairy products, and most fresh vegetables and fruits are viewed as being cold.[120] Presentation and fragrance are also given particular attention by chefs, the best of which are often women.

Food and Foodways

Iranian cuisine is rooted in familiar Middle Eastern staples such as lamb, wheat bread, eggplant, and yogurt. Dishes unique to the region are derived primarily from the Persian culinary tradition that uses long grain white rice and seasonal fruits and vegetables. Which of the ingredients are the scarcest, and therefore priciest and enjoyed only by the affluent few, is determined by the natural wealth of an immediate region (i.e., the availability of wheat or fish).

Arguably the best example of this situation is Iranian caviar, considered by some to be the best in the world.[121] In fact, the natural wealth of the surrounding bodies of water—the Persian Gulf, Oman Sea, Indian Ocean, and Caspian Sea—is an area of intense interest, as exhibited by the 4th International Fisheries, Aquaculture & Seafood Exhibition, held in the fall of 2006.[122]

Favorite Iranian dishes include *chelo* (plain rice), *chelo-kabab* (usually served with grilled tomatoes and herbs such as mint), *abgoosht* (literally "meat water," resembling a soup and containing boiled fatty pieces of lamb, potatoes, tomatoes, dried peas, and beans, with dried lime), *aash* (thick soup made with cereals, vegetables, herbs, and sometimes with meat), and *mahi dudi* (smoked fish). Snacks like toasted nuts, dried seeds, and roasted beans are also popular, especially *ajeel* (salted nuts and seeds with lime juice) and *miveh*, which can be purchased from vendors. Sweets are also a favorite and often include pieces of almonds, pistachios, and hazelnuts as well as dried fruits. Iranians also enjoy ice cream.

Here as elsewhere in the Middle East and North Africa, bread plays a significant role in regional cuisine. The four main types of bread are *taftoon* (fresh flat bread eaten at lunch), *barbary* (chewy bread served at breakfast), *lavash* (crispy, thin bread), and *sangak* (bread baked on hot pebbles).

And while Western soft drink brands have made their mark, such as those offered by Coca-Cola and Pepsi, drinks native to the region are still preferred. Some favorites include *doogh* (yogurt and mineral water), fresh juice from street vendors, or strong Iranian tea enjoyed with a sugar cube between the teeth. While alcoholic drinks are illegal, they can be found, although discretion is advised.

Meals in Iran begin with a basic breakfast of hot tea, bread, and feta cheese, which may be enhanced with milk, butter, jam, honey, eggs, fruits, walnuts, and pita bread. Lunch usually occurs between noon and 2:00 PM and is usually the largest meal of the day. It often consists of rice and *khoresht* (curried meat in a thick sauce served with vegetables, fruits, nuts, or legumes). The meal may also include kebab and soups, salad, appetizers, yogurt, and seasonal fruit.

A midday tea is often served around 4:00 PM. The tea is presented in small glasses and enjoyed with a sugar cube between the teeth. Other favorite beverages include *sharbat* (fruit and sugar served with ice and water), *sekanjebin* (mint, vinegar, and sugar served with ice and water), and *sharbat-e albaloo* (sour cherry syrup).

Dinner is light, usually served around 9:00 PM. Dishes are enjoyed while seated on cushions on carpets, and food is eaten with the fingers of the right hand.[123] When guests are entertained, the world-renowned hospitality common in the Middle East and North Africa is evident and embodied in the Persian saying *Mehman Hediyeh Khodast*, which means, "A guest is God's gift."[124] Thus, a host will often prefer to stay in the background to supervise and give the guest the most desirable seat and dishes.[125] This also explains why so much of Iranian cuisine is rooted in recipes that can be easily increased to accommodate unexpected visitors.[126]

Eating out in urban areas such as Tehran affords individuals much the same variety as any other metropolitan area in the region. Pizza, sandwich, and coffee shops are abundant, and their names often adopt or amend names pulled from various external traditions, such as Shiva and Tehran Fried Chicken.[127] However, traditional Persian restaurants, or *sofreh khaneh*, dominate.

FOOD AND FOODWAYS

Arabian Peninsula

Saudi Arabia

In the sense of commerce, Saudi Arabia is one of the more open countries of the Middle East. Here there is a large influence of Western corporate giants such as Pepsi and Proctor & Gamble. There is also a large youthful urban market for such items as snacks and soft drinks, as well as for a wide range of adult refreshments.

Although a relatively new concept in Saudi Arabia, chip snacks now account for 43 percent of the savory snack market, enjoyed primarily by young adults and children. The marketplace is dominated by brands such as Lay's, Tasali, and Cheetos. Much of the increased popularity can be attributed to increased television marketing and promotions aimed specifically at the young adult audience.[128] The most popular flavors include salted/plain, ketchup, pizza, chili, and barbeque as well as herb-flavored varieties such as *zahtar* (thyme).[129]

The most popular snack food, however, may be dried dates, both the seedless and nut-filled varieties, accounting for 67 percent of the sweet snack market. These are particularly popular when eaten to break the daily fast during Ramadan.[130] Other favorites include nuts and popcorn, although the latter is largely enjoyed only in the home.

One of the most persistent misperceptions of contemporary Saudi foodways is that because of the strict Islamic law that governs much of the society, the country is entirely free of alcoholic beverages. This perception is understandable since Saudi Arabia's constitution is based on Shariah law.[131] Derived from the Koran, these laws prohibit consumption or sale of alcohol, and the punishment usually involves some degree of flogging.[132] In practice, however, a lucrative illegal trade exists. This is often facilitated by wealthy and influential nationals and expatriates. Purchases can be made in Bahrain, while 80 percent of smuggled alcohol comes from the United Arab Emirates using such methods as empty gasoline cans, mouth wash containers, or diplomatic bags.[133] It is also not unheard of for expatriate compounds to distill their own beer in-house.[134]

For the general population, there are popular versions of low- or zero-level alcohol malt beverages by famous beer brands such as Amstel, Barbican, Budweiser, Holsten, Moussy, and San Miguel.[135] These are considered a sophisticated alternative and are available plain or in various fruit flavors, mainly in large cities in the western and central regions through supermarkets, groceries, and various self-service stores. Vigorous television and print marketing aimed at perpetuating the associated mix of sophistication and fun plays a role in the popularity of these drinks.[136]

A uniquely contemporary concern that has affected Saudi Arabian cuisine is connected to bovine spongiform encephalopathy (BSE), or "mad cow" disease. In 2000 Saudi Arabia banned beef and beef product imports from the United Kingdom, France, the Netherlands, Germany, Belgium, Austria, Portugal, Luxemburg, Switzerland, South Africa, and Denmark.[137] In 2001 Saudi Arabia banned beef, mutton, and lamb meat imports from European Union (EU) countries.[138] In 2004 the country banned cows and cow semen from the state of Washington, although this did not significantly impact the $10 million of U.S. beef exported to Saudi Arabia each year.[139]

Oman

Traditional Omani food is simple but uses marinades, spices, herbs, onion, and garlic to infuse the food with distinct flavors that differ greatly by region, with the areas of the south (Salalah) and north (Muscat) having the most unique characteristics.[140]

FOOD AND FOODWAYS

> ### SAUDI ARABIA: OPERATION DESERT STRAW
>
> In the process of embracing staples of Western cuisine, such as potato chips and fast food, the tensions associated with international diplomacy have created unique commercial challenges, and with those, unique solutions. One of the more entertaining may be the relationship between Coca-Cola and Saudi Arabia.
>
> At the end of the twentieth century, the Kingdom of Saudi Arabia, along with many other Middle Eastern and North African countries, mounted a boycott of Israel and, by association, its allies such the United States (anti-American sentiment was further bolstered for some in the region in the wake of Iraq's invasion of Kuwait and Operation Desert Storm, the resulting military action headed by the United States and its international coalition of allies). During this boycott, Coca-Cola was banned from Saudi Arabia.
>
> Upon its return to the country in 1993, Coca-Cola launched a vigorous marketing campaign to claim its share of the carbonated beverage market, which by the 1990s had grown to account for almost 60 percent of the soft drinks sold, in order to increase awareness of the brand and distinguish it from Pepsi in the public consciousness.[142] In March 1995, the company launched its main campaign dubbed, with a typically irreverent American sense of whimsy: "Operation Desert Straw" involved the use of eighteen different advertising formats, not including the TV and radio campaigns.[143] In fact, during Ramadan in 1996, Coca-Cola gave away 1 million free cans to needy people after workers agreed to work additional shifts without pay.

Throughout the country, the largest meal of the day is eaten at lunch, with a light dinner in the evening.

Rice often serves as the base and can be steamed or prepared with meat and vegetables. Bread is also a critical starch, and *rukhal* (a thin, round bread baked over palm leaves) may be included in any meal, served with curry at dinner or with honey at breakfast. Breads may be plain or baked with dates, sesame, thyme, or garlic.

Everyday meals can include soups (vegetable, lentil, lamb, or chicken), salads (vegetable, eggplant, tuna, dried fish, or watercress), kebabs, and barbecued, grilled, or curried meat. There are also favorite main dishes such as *marak* (a vegetable curry), *maqbous* (a saffron rice dish cooked over a spicy red or white meat), or *mashaui* (spit-roasted kingfish with lemon rice).

Preferred drinks include cardamom- and pistachio-flavored yogurt drinks, as well as *laban* (salty buttermilk). However, soft drinks are gaining in popularity. In fact, by 1996 the carbonated drink market alone was worth US$108 million, with 64 percent of that total attributed to the sale of colas.[141]

In the home, families may be greeted with a cola drink. Cola may also be served at social functions. Other important soft drinks include fruit juices and mineral waters (the popularity of which is derived at least in part from the fact that tap water is largely unfit to drink), all of which tend to see a slight increase when religious celebrations such as Ramadan, Eid al-Fitr, and Eid al-Adha take place. The impact seen in street cafés, local shops, hotels, and restaurants, including such Western fast food chains as Burger King, is substantial. By 1996, in these venues alone, 46.63 million liters of soft drinks were purchased.[144]

Pepsi, with products distributed through the privately owned Oman Refreshment Company, is the most significant supplier of colas, offering such brands as Pepsi Regular, Mirinda, Mountain Dew, Shani, and Pepsi Max.[145] The other major Western brand, Coca-Cola, is only now beginning to see success in Oman; it had been banned from the region for political reasons because of its ties with Israel until 1990 and is still only available by import through Al Ahlia Gulf Line General Trading in the UAE.[146]

Regardless of particular preferences or restrictions, however, it is during the religious celebrations when Omani cuisine is enjoyed to its fullest. Favorites include *aursia* (mashed rice with spices), *ruz al mudhroub* (cooked rice with fried fish), *maqdeed* (tripe and pluck with cinnamon, cardamom, cloves, black pepper, ginger, garlic, and nutmeg), *arsia* (lamb served with rice), and *mishkak* (grilled meat on skewers).[147]

During Ramadan, two of the most popular iftar foods are *sakhana*, a thick, sweet soup made with wheat, dates, molasses, and milk, and *fattah*, a meat and vegetable dish, mixed with *khubz rakhal*.[148] During Eid, lunch on the first day is usually *harees* (wheat made with meat), on the second *mishkak*, and *shuwa* on the third. To create shuwa, the entire village helps prepare a whole cow or goat. The meat is marinated with red pepper, turmeric, coriander, cumin, cardamom, garlic, and vinegar; wrapped in sacks made of dry banana or palm leaves; and then roasted for twenty-four to forty-eight hours in an oven prepared in a pit dug in the ground.[149]

Such a rich culinary tradition is not without its effects, and in recent years Omanis have moved toward more healthy choices to address the fact that 50 to 70 percent of married women and 30 to 50 percent of married men in the Gulf States are obese.[150] This is largely the result of generally poor nutritional habits, further complicated for women by frequent pregnancies.

The popularity of fruit juices is far more dynamic than that of colas, which are now banned in schools. By 1996 such brands as Al Khaleej, Suntop Fruit, and Top Fruit were responsible for contributing to the 32.8 million liters of fruit juice consumed in Oman, worth US$38 million.[151] The healthier trend is seen in other aspects of the culture as well. As an example, some Omani women have established a practice of taking an evening walk during Ramadan, after the iftar and the reciting of holy verses, in part to counteract the possible effects of the sweet foods enjoyed during the religious festival.[152]

RESOURCE GUIDE

PRINT SOURCES

Held, C. C. *Middle East Patterns: Places, Peoples and Politics*, 4th ed. Boulder, CO: Westview Press, 2006.
Mazda, M. *In a Persian Kitchen: Favorite Recipes from the Near East.* Boston: Tuttle Publishing, 1960.

WEBSITES

ArabNet. "ABC of Arabic Cuisine." http://www.arab.net/cuisine/. A glossary of Arabic cuisine.
Arab Water World. Chatila Publishing House. http://www.awwmag.comhttp://www.awwmag.com/index.aspx?all_lk_id=15&magazine_id=1. Online magazine dealing with the water, wastewater, irrigation, and energy industries in the Middle East and North Africa.
Bradmans. Ink Publishing. http://www.bradmans.com/middleeastafrica. An online travel guide to the region.
Culinary Kingdom. "Festival Foods and Religious Influences in the Middle East." DrewMCA. http://www.culinarykingdom.com/articles_festivalfoods_religious.htm. A site dedicated to articles about cooking and the sale of culinary products.
Dirks, Robert. *Food and Culture: Middle East, North Africa, and West Asia.* Illinois State University. http://lilt.ilstu.edu/rtdirks/MIDEAST.html. A bibliography of articles on food and culture in the region.
Food in the Arab World. http://www.al-bab.com/arab/food.htm. A collection of Arab recipes.
Eidlitz, Eliezer. *Kosher Quest.* http://www.kosherquest.org/. The Website of the Kosher Information Bureau.

Modern Egyptian Culture. InterCity Oz. http://www.touregypt.net/magazine/modernegyptculture.htm. A series of articles on Egyptian culture.

Orthodox Union. http://www.oukosher.org/. A complete guide to certified kosher products.

Star-K Online. Star-K Kosher Certification. http://www.star-k.org/. A comprehensive Website covering almost all aspects of kosher food, including certification.

Traditional Omani Food. Ministry of Information, Sultanate of Oman. http://www.omanet.om/english/culture/omani_food.asp?cat=cult. A guide to food cultures of Oman.

NOTES

1. M. N. Riaz, "*Halal* Food—An Insight into a Growing Food Industry Segment," International Food Marketing & Technology, 1998, accessed April 25, 2006, http://www.icbcs.org/halal.htm.
2. See "Egyptian Market for Packaged Food: Market Overview," *Market Research Monitor*, October 2005, accessed March 3, 2006, http://www.euromonitor.com/.
3. See "Food Company Friboi Exhibits in Dubai for the First Time," accessed March 3, 2006, Info—Prod Research (Middle East) Ramat-Gan: February 23, 2006. http://www2.lib.purdue.edu: 2048/login? url=http://proquest.umi.com/pqdweb?did=992407081&Fmt=31343&RQT=309&VName=PQD.
4. See "Cattle Beef Exporters after Emerging Markets in 2006," accessed March 3, 2006, Info—Prod Research (Middle East) Ramat-Gan: December 22, 2005. http://www2.lib.purdue.edu:2048/login?url=http://proquest.umi.com/pqdweb?did=946127461&Fmt=3&clientId=31343&RQT=309&VName=PQD.
5. See "Sadia Sponsors Salon Culinaire at Gulf Food 2006," accessed March 3, 2006, Info—Prod Research (Middle East) Ramat-Gan: February 22, 2006. http://www2.lib.purdue.edu:2048/login?url=http://proquest. umi.com/pqdweb?did991559441&Fmt=31343&RQT=309&VName=PQD.
6. See M. Follain, "Halal Market, Lucrative for Firms," October 24, 2002, accessed June 8, 2006, http://www.middle-east-online.com/english/Default.pl?id=2956.
7. See T. R. Rich, "Judaism 101—Kashrut: Jewish Dietary Laws," 1995–2002, March 3, 2006, http://www.jewfaq.org/kashrut.htm.
8. "Welcome to the Orthodox Union," *Orthodox Union*, accessed March 3, 2006 (in Resource Guide).
9. See "Increase in Gap between Food Product Supplies in 2010," accessed March 3, 2006, Info—Prod Research (Middle East) Ramat-Gan: February 14, 2006. http://www2.lib.purdue.edu:2048/login?url=http://proquest.umi.com/pqdweb?did 986607371&Fmt=3&clientId= 31343&RQT=309&VName=PQD.
10. See "Arab Food Gap Estimated 61 Million Tons by 2010," accessed March 3, 2006, Info—Prod Research (Middle East) Ramat-Gan: December 17, 2005. http://www2.lib.purdue.edu:2048/login?url=http://proquest.umi.com/pqdweb?did=948491971&Fmt=3&clientId=31343&RQT=309&VName=PQD.
11. See "FAO Rings Alarm Bells over Mideast Food Situation," March 7, 2002, accessed June 8, 2006, http://www.middle-east-online.com/english/Default.pl?id=413.
12. See O. al-Wadwwa, "GCC Could Face Water Shortage Due to High Rise in Population," March 29, 2002, accessed June 8, 2006, http://www.middle-east-online.com/english/Default.pl?id=1168.
13. See H. A. Choen, and Steven P. Quenching, "The Levant's Thirst," *Middle East Quarterly*, March 1995, accessed September 27, 2005, http://www.meforum.org/article/239/.
14. See "Jordan, Algeria Sign Executive Programs, MOUS," accessed March 3, 2006, Info—Prod Research (Middle East) Ramat-Gan: February 7, 2006. http://www2.lib.purdue.edu:2048/login?url=http://proquest.umi.com/pqdweb?did=982775551&Fmt=3&clientId=31343&RQT=309&VName=PQD.
15. See "Syria Discusses Agricultural Cooperation with Iran and India," accessed March 3, 2006, Info—Prod Research (Middle East) Ramat-Gan: February 7, 2006. http://www2.lib.purdue.edu:2048/

login?url=http://proquest.umi.com/pqdweb?did982775201&Fmt=3&clientld=31343&RQT=309&VName=PQD.

16. See M. Patience, "Action Call over Dying Dead Sea," *BBC News*, May 4, 2006, accessed May 4, 2006, http://news.bbc.co.uk/go/pr/fr/-/2/hi/middle_east/4968942.stm.
17. Held 2006 (in Resource Guide).
18. See "Extent of Operations in Food Sector," accessed March 3, 2006, Info—Prod Research (Middle East) Ramat-Gan: February 27, 2006. http://www2.lib.purdue.edu:2048/login?url=http://proquest.umi.com/pqdweb?did=994213701&Fmt=3&clientld=31343&RQT=309&VName=PQD.
19. See "$15 Billion Food Imports," accessed March 3, 2006, Info—Prod Research (Middle East) Ramat-Gan: January 26, 2006. http://www2.lib.purdue.edu:2048/login?url=http://proquest.umi.com/pqdweb?did=976513911&Fmt=3&clientld=31343&RQT=309&VName=PQD.
20. See "The Food Industry," accessed March 3, 2006, Info—Prod Research (Middle East) Ramat-Gan: February 27, 2006. http://www2.lib.purdue.edu:2048/login?url=http://proquest.umi.com/pqdweb?did=994213761&Fmt=31343&RQT=309&VName=PQD.
21. See "DH 600 Million Food Imports from UK," accessed March 3, 2006, Info—Prod Research (Middle East) Ramat-Gan: February 20, 2006. http://www2.lib.purdue.edu:2048/login?url=http://proquest.umi.com/pqdweb?did=990340391&Fmt=3&clientld=31343&RQT=309&VName=PQD.
22. See "Producers of Food Seek New Arab Clients," accessed March 3, 2006, Info—Prod Research (Middle East) Ramat-Gan: February 5, 2006. http://www2.lib.purdue.edu:2048/login?url=http://proquest.umi.com/ pqdweb?did=981528321&Fmt=3&clientld=31343&RQT=309&VName=PQD.
23. See "Kazakhstan-Iran Trade Cooperation Discussed in Tehran," accessed March 3, 2006, Info—Prod Research (Middle East) Ramat-Gan: December 14, 2005. http://www2.lib.purdue.edu:2048/login?url=http://proquest.umi.com/pqdweb?did=981528321&Fmt=3&clientld=31343&RQT=309&VName=PQD.
24. See "Iran, FAO to Expand Hybrid Rice Farming," accessed March 3, 2006, Info—Prod Research (Middle East) Ramat-Gan: December 12, 2005. http://www2.lib.purdue.edu:2048/login?url=http://proquest.umi.com/pqdweb?did=940273021&Fmt=3&clientld=31343&RQT=309&VName=PQD.
25. See "Increase in Export of Food Products," accessed March 3, 2006, Info—Prod Research (Middle East) Ramat-Gan: February 6, 2006. http://www2.lib.purdue.edu:2048/login?url=http://proquest.umi.com/pqdweb?did=982044851&Fmt=3&clientld=31343&RQT=309&VName=PQD.
26. See "Gulf Food Fair 2006," accessed March 3, 2006, Info—Prod Research (Middle East) Ramat-Gan: February 27, 2006. http://www2.lib.purdue.edu:2048/login?url=http://proquest. umi.com/pqdweb?did=994213631&Fmt=31343&RQT=309&VName=PQD.
27. Ibid.
28. See "South Australian Food and Wine Gets Middle East Showcase," *Al Bawaba*, February 20, 2006, accessed March 3, 2006, http://www2.lib.purdue.edu:2048/login? url=http://proquest.umi.com/pqdweb?did990231921&Fmt=31343&RQT=309&VName=PQD.
29. See "Middle East Food Market Offers 'Major Opportunities' for Producers and Distributors in 2006," *Al Bawaba*, January 18, 2006, accessed March 3, 2006, http://www2.lib.purdue.edu:2048/login?url=http://proquest.umi.com/pqdweb?did=971913161&Fmt=3&clientld=31343&RQT=309 &VName=PQD. See also "Gulf Food Imports Worth over US$12 Billion a Year:[1]," *Al Bawaba*, January 11, 2006, accessed March 3, 2006, http://www2.lib.purdue.edu:2048/login?url=http://proquest.umi.com/pqdweb?did=965567501&Fmt=3&clientld=31343&RQT=309&VName=PQD.
30. See "'Regional Food Safety is a Critical Health Issue,' Say Experts:[1]," *Al Bawaba*, January 23, 2006, accessed March 3, 2006, http://www2.lib.purdue.edu:2048/login?url=http://proquest.umi.com/pqdweb?did=975762881&Fmt=3&clientld=31343&RQT=309&VName=PQD.
31. See "Italian and Indian Companies to Have Major Presence at Middle East Natural and Organic Products Expo in Dubai," *Al Bawaba*, November 22, 2005, accessed March 3, 2006. http://www2.lib.purdue.edu:2048/login?url=http://proquest.umi.com/pqdweb?did=929831281&Fmt=3&clientld=31343&RQT=309&VName=PQD.
32. See B. Lewis, "The Middle East, Westernized Despite Itself," *Middle East Quarterly*, March 1996, September 27, 2005, http://www.meforum.org/article/290/.

33. "Middle East 2006—Restaurants," *Bradmans* (in Resource Guide), 2006, accessed June 8, 2006.
34. See "Tumbleweed to Open Middle East Restaurants," April 26, 2004, accessed June 8, 2006, www.bizjournals.com/louisville/stories/2004/04/26/daily9html.
35. See N. Parker, "Burger King in Baghdad," *Middle East Online*, July 15, 2003, accessed 2006 June 8, 2006, http://www.middle-east-online.com/english/Default.pl?id=6389.
36. See "World Experts 'Court' Ibn Battuta Mail with "Food Theatre," *Al Bawaba*, 2005, accessed 2006 June 8, 2006, http://www.Albawaba.com/en/countries/187762/&mod=print.
37. See "Armed Man Torches McDonald's in Saudi," *Middle East Online*, November 21, 200, accessed 2006 June 8, 2006, http://www.middle-east-online.com/english/Default.pl?id=3338.
38. See "Economic Indicators—Middle East: 1999–2004," *Euromonitor International*, 2006, accessed May 15, 2006, http://www.euromonitor.com/.
39. Ibid.
40. See "Philogos," *Forward*, October 24, 2003, accessed June 8, 2006, http://www.forward.com/issues/2003/03.10.24/arts3.philologos.html.
41. See P. Heine, *Food Culture in the Near East, Middle East and North Africa* (Westport, CT: Greenwood Press, 2004).
42. Ibid.
43. See B. Lewis, "The Middle East, Westernized Despite Itself," *Middle East Quarterly*, March 1996, September 27, 2005, http://www.meforum.org/article/290/.
44. See "Algerian Market for Soft Drinks," *Market Research Monitor*, July 1998, accessed April 13, 2006, http://www.euromonitor.com/.
45. Ibid.
46. Ibid.
47. See E. Sosa, "Morocco," 2006, accessed June 8, 2006, http://www.Sallys-place.com/fod/ethnic_cusine/morocco.htm.
48. Ibid.
49. See "Morocco," 2006, accessed 2006 June 8, 2006, http://www.Africa.upeen.edu/Cookbook/Morocco.html.
50. Ibid.
51. See "Moroccan Market for Frozen Food," *Market Research Monitor*, April 2004, accessed April 13, 2006, http://www.euromonitor.com/.
52. See "Drinking Water from Sea via Nuclear Energy," *Middle East Online*, October 18, 2002, accessed June 8, 2006, http://www.middle-east-online.com/english/Default.pl?id=2882.
53. See A. Sma, "Retail Sector Shepherds Tunisian Food Industry," October 2004, accessed June 8, 2006, "Attache Reports," http://www.fas.usda.gov.
54. Ibid.
55. Ibid.
56. Ibid.
57. Ibid.
58. See D. Rogov, "Libyan Cuisine—Simple but Tasty," accessed June 8, 2006, http://www.stratsplace.com/rogov/israel/libyan_cuisine.html.
59. See "Food and Drink," 1996, accessed June 8, 2006, http://www.touregypt.net/food.htm.
60. Se J. Carta, "Egyptian Food," 1999–2003, accessed June 8, 2006, http://www.touregypt.net/featurestories/food.htm.
61. See H. Bizzari, "Koshary," 1999–2003, accessed June 8, 2006, http://www.touregypt.net/featurestories/koshary.htm.
62. See "Egyptian Market for Packaged Food: Market Overview," *Market Research Monitor*, October 2005, accessed March 3, 2006, http://www.euromonitor.com/.
63. See "Food and Drink," 1996, accessed 2006 June 8, 2006, http://www.touregypt.net/food.htm.
64. See C. Wright, "Some Facts about Mediterranean Food History: Ful—The Egyptian National Dish," 1999–2004, accessed June 8, 2006, http://www.cliffordawright.com/history/ful.html.
65. See "The Fallahin," accessed June 8, 2006, http://www.Agrisport.com/egitto.htm.
66. Ibid.

67. Ibid.
68. See "Egyptian Market for Packaged Food: Market Overview," *Market Research Monitor*, October 2005, accessed March 3, 2006, http://www.euromonitor.com/.
69. See "Food and Drink," 1996, accessed 2006 June 8, 2006, http://www.touregypt.net/food.htm.
70. See "Egyptian Market for Packaged Food: Market Overview," *Market Research Monitor*, October 2005, accessed March 3, 2006, http://www.euromonitor.com/.
71. Ibid.
72. Ibid.
73. Ibid.
74. See J. Carta, "Egyptian Food," 1999–2003, accessed June 8, 2006, http://www.touregypt.net/featurestories/food.htm.
75. See "Food and Drink," 1996, accessed June 8, 2006, http://www.touregypt.net/food.htm.
76. See "Culture, Customs, Conduct," 1996, accessed June 8, 2006, http://www.touregypt.net/Culture.htm.
77. See A. Assaad, "Egypt's Bread in Deep Crisis," *Middle East Online*, September 19, 2003, accessed June 8, 2006, http://www.middle-east-online.com/english/Default.pl?id=7059.
78. See el-Beblawl, "Egypt Promises to Brake Rising Food Prices," *Middle East Online*, September 25, 2003, accessed June 8, 2006, http://www.middle-east-online.com/english/Default.pl?id=7139.
79. Ibid.
80. See M. A. Rehim, "Muslims across Mideast Shop for Ramadan," *Middle East Online*, July 15, 2003, accessed June 8, 2006, http://www.middle-east-online.com/english/Default.pl?id=6389.
81. See el-Beblawl, "Egypt Promises to Brake Rising Food Prices," *Middle East Online*, September 25, 2003, accessed June 8, 2006, http://www.middle-east-online.com/english/Default.pl?id=7139.
82. See J. Bassoul, and A. Simon, "Bird Flu Hit Egypt's Poultry Industry Hard," *Middle East Online*, February 21, 2006, accessed June 8, 2006, http://www.middle-east-online.com/english/Default.pl?id=15808.
83. Ibid.
84. See "Traditional Meals Feasting: Jordan's Gastronomic Adventure," accessed June 8, 2006, http://www.gondol.com/English.food.htm.
85. See "USDA Amends P.L. 480 Purchase Authorization to Jordan," May 1, 2006, accessed May 15, 2006, http://www.fas/.usda.gov/info/newsevents.asp.
86. See "Country Factfile—Israel," 2006, May 15, 2006, http://euromonitor.com/factfile.aspx?country=IS.
87. See "Beyond Milk and Honey," *Israel Ministry of Foreign Affairs*, December 29, 2002, accessed August 8, 2006, http://www.mfa.gov.il/mfa/facts%20about%20israel/israeli%20cuisine/beyond%20milk%20and%20honey%20-%20israeli%20recipes%20-%20jan-95.
88. Ibid.
89. See "Country Factfile—Israel," 2006, accessed May 15, 2006, http://www.euromonitor.com/factfile.aspx?country=IS.
90. See "Israel's Food Industry," December 6, 2004, accessed August 8, 2006, http://www.industry.org.il/Eng/Publications/Item.asp?CategoryID=3235&ArticleID=763.
91. See "Israeli Food Retailers," *Market Research Monitor*, October 2004, accessed March 3, 2006, http://www.euromonitor.com/.
92. See M. Patience, "Action Call over Dying Dead Sea," *BBC News*, May 4, 2006, accessed May 4, 2006, http://news.bbc.co.uk/go/pr/fr/-/2/hi/middle_east/4968942.stm.
93. See "UNRWA Warns over Palestinian Children's Malnutrition," *Middle East Online*, November 18, 2002, accessed June 8, 2006, http://www.middle-east-online.com/english/Default.pl?id=3299.
94. Ibid.
95. See B. Lecumberri, "Gaza Fishermen Dream of Freedom on High Seas," *Middle East Online*, February 6, 2002, accessed June 8, 2006, http://www.middle-east-online.com/english/Default.pl?id=245.
96. See S. Yassine, "'How Much for the Olives?'—Learning to Live with VAT in Lebanon," *Middle East Online*, February 6, 2002, accessed June 8, 2006, http://www.middle-east-online.com/english/Default.pl?id=245.

97. See "Bomb Blast in Lebanon's KFC Outlet," *Middle East Online*, May 9, 2002, accessed June 8, 2006, http://www.middle-east-online.com/english/Default.pl?id=1168.
98. See "KFC Opens in Syria," *Middle East Online*, January 23, 2006, accessed June 8, 2006, http://www.middle-east-online.com/english/Default.pl?id=321.
99. See "Hidden Turkey," Public Broadcasting Station, Houston Texas; January 3, 2006, 8:00 PM.
100. Ibid.
101. Ibid.
102. Ibid.
103. See "Turkish Cuisine: Diet and Health," 2004, accessed June 8, 2006, http://www.turkishcook.com/Turkish_food_ cuisine/Diet_Health.shtml.
104. See "Hidden Turkey" Public Broadcasting Station, Houston Texas; January 3, 2006, 8:00 PM.
105. See "Turkish Cuisine: Diet and Health," 2004, accessed June 8, 2006, http://www.turkishcook.com/Turkish_food_cuisine/Diet_Health.shtml.
106. See "Turkish Consumer Segmentation," *Market Research Monitor*, January 2006, accessed March 3, 2006, http://www.euromonitor.com/.
107. See N. Nasrallah, "Vegetarian Appetizers and Salads," in *Delights from the Garden of Eden: A Cookbook and a History of the Iraqi Cuisine* (Bloomington, IN: AuthorHouse, 2003), accessed June 8, 2006, http://www.iraqicookbook.com/contents/appetizers.html. See also N. Nasrallah, "Rice," in *Delights from the Garden of Eden: A Cookbook and a History of the Iraqi Cuisine* (Bloomington, IN: AuthorHouse, 2003), accessed June 8, 2006, http://www.iraqicookbook.com/contents/rice.html.
108. See "Egypt Is Iraq's Biggest Trading Partner in Arab World," *Middle East Online*, February 25, 2002, accessed June 8, 2006, http://www.middle-east-online.com/english/Default.pl?id=321.
109. Ibid.
110. Ibid.
111. See "Half of Iraqis Remain Mired in Poverty, Hunger," *Middle East Online*, September 23, 2003, accessed June 8, 2006, http://www.middle-east-online.com/english/Default.pl?id=7099.
112. Ibid.
113. See "Gulf War Allies Clash over Iraq Wheat Market," *Middle East Online*, June 6, 2003, accessed June 8, 2006, http://www.middle-east-online.com/english/Default.pl?id=5851.
114. Ibid.
115. See "PM: Australian Wheat Exporter's Monopoly at Risk," *Middle East Online*, January 20, 2006, accessed June 8, 2006, http://www.middle-east-online.com/english/Default.pl?id=15535. See also "Australian Firm 'Bribed' Saddam," *BBC News*, May 18, 2006, accessed May 18, 2006, http://news.bbc.co.uk/2/low/asia-pacific/4993376.stm.
116. See S. Griffith, "Galloway Vehemently Denies Profiting from UN Oil-for-Food Program," *Middle East Online*, May 15, 2005, accessed June 8, 2006, http://www.middle-east-online.com/english/Default.pl?id=13523.
117. See "Iraqis Head to Fallujah with Supplies," *Middle East Online*, April 8, 2004, accessed June 8, 2006, http://www.middle-east-online.com/english/Default.pl?id=9561.
118. See "One in Four Iraqis Still Dependent on Food Rations," *Middle East Online*, September 29, 2004, accessed June 8, 2006, http://www.middle-east-online.com/english/Default.pl?id=11410.
119. See "Culture—Food," accessed August 8, 2006, http://bestintravel.com/culture/food/food.html.
120. Ibid.
121. See "Iranian Food & Iran's Dining Online," accessed August 10, 2006, http://www.iranian.ws/travel/travel-dining.htm.
122. See "Iran's 4th International Fisheries, Aquaculture & Seafood Exhibition," accessed August 10, 2006, http://iranseafoodexpo.ir/.
123. See "Iranian Traditions—Meals and Customs," accessed August 8, 2006, http://www.digist.com/fod/4d.html.
124. Mazda 1960 (in Resource Guide).
125. See "Culture—Food," accessed August 8, 2006, http://bestintravel.com/culture/food/food.html.
126. Mazda 1960 (in Resource Guide).

127. See "Best Tehran Restaurants and Coffee Shops," February 3, 2006, accessed August 10, 2006, http://www.ghazayab.com/.
128. See "Saudi Arabian Market for Sweet and Savory Snacks," *Market Research Monitor*, February 2005, accessed March 3, 2006. http://www.euromonitor.com/.
129. Ibid.
130. Ibid.
131. See "Saudi Arabian Market for Alcoholic Drinks," *Market Research Monitor*, May 2003, accessed March 3, 2006, http://www.euromonitor.com.
132. Ibid.
133. Ibid.
134. Ibid.
135. Ibid.
136. Ibid.
137. See J. H. Wilson, "Foreign Agricultural Service GAIN Report—Livestock and Products: Saudi Arabia Imposes Ban on Imports of Beef and Dairy Products from Denmark," 2000, Foreign Agricultural Service/USDA, Saudi Arabia/Washington, http://www.fas.usda.gov.
138. See H. Mousa, "Foreign Agricultural Service GAIN Report—Livestock and Products: Saudi Arabia Bans Beef, Mutton and Lamb Meat Imports from EU Countries," 2001, Foreign Agricultural Service/USDA, Saudi Arabia/Washington, http://www.fas.usda.gov.
139. See Q. Gray, "Foreign Agricultural Service GAIN Report—Livestock and Products: Saudi Arabia Bans Washington State Cows and Cow Semen," 2004, Foreign Agricultural Service/USDA, Saudi Arabia/Washington, http://www.fas.usda.gov.
140. *Traditional Omani Food* (in Resource Guide), accessed June 8, 2006.
141. See "The Omani Market for Soft Drinks," *Market Research Monitor*, November 1997, accessed March 3, 2006, http://www.euromonitor.com/.
142. See "Saudi Arabian Market for Soft Drinks," *Market Research Monitor*, May 1998, accessed March 3, 2006, http://www.euromonitor.com.
143. Ibid.
144. See "The Omani Market for Soft Drinks," *Market Research Monitor*, November 1997, accessed March 3, 2006, http://www.euromonitor.com/.
145. Ibid.
146. Ibid.
147. *Traditional Omani Food* (in Resource Guide), accessed June 8, 2006.
148. Ibid.
149. Ibid.
150. See M. Bellouchi, "Omani Women Burn Fat in Ramadan," *Middle East Online*, October 7, 2005, accessed June 8, 2006, http://www.middle-east-online.com/english/Default.pl?id=14721.
151. See "The Omani Market for Soft Drinks," *Market Research Monitor*, November 1997, accessed March 3, 2006, http://www.euromonitor.com/.
152. See M. Bellouchi, "Omani Women Burn Fat in Ramadan," *Middle East Online*, October 7, 2005, accessed June 8, 2006, http://www.middle-east-online.com/english/Default.pl?id=14721.

ARCHITECTURE

ARCHITECTURE: The Wailing Wall and the gold-covered Umar Mosque, or Shrine, also called the Dome of the Rock, at night in Old City, Jerusalem. The dome continues to be an important element in modern mosques. Courtesy of Shutterstock.

ARCHITECTURE: This private residence in Algeria illustrates the level of luxury that can be found in the region. Courtesy of Shutterstock.

ART

ART: The tradition of depicting past rulers as godlike is demonstrated by this mural of Saddam Hussein as Nebuchadnezzar. It's even been suggested that Saddam was the reincarnation of the Babylonian ruler. © Francoise de Idder / Corbis.

ART: The detail of weaving and the vibrant colors in this Persian carpet ensure its desirability not only in the Mideast but worldwide. Courtesy of Shutterstock.

DANCE

DANCE: A bride (center) dances with relatives during her wedding party in Algiers, 2006. © Fayez Nureldine/AFP/Getty Images.

DANCE: Two men perform the War Dance, or *Razha*, ca. 2002. In Saudi Arabia, a similar dance is called *al ardhah*. © Arthur Thévenart/CORBIS.

FASHION AND APPEARANCE

FASHION: A model wears a creation by Lebanese designer Hanna Touma during the Beirut Fashion Week in Beirut, Lebanon, 2006. © AP Photo/Dalia Khamissy.

FASHION: A variety of silk scarves Islamic women use to cover their heads for sale at a market in Istanbul. Courtesy of Shutterstock.

FILM

FILM: Mohsen Makhmalbaf's 2001 film, *Kandahar*, also known as *Safar é Gandehar*. Courtesy of Photofest.

FOOD AND FOODWAYS

FOOD AND FOODWAYS: Food stands at night in the Djemaa el Fna Square in Marrakech, Morocco. © Art Directors/Simon Reddy.

FOOD AND FOODWAYS: A Starbucks Coffee kiosk in the Ibn Battuta Shopping Mall, United Arab Emirates, Dubai. © Jochen Tack / Alamy.

FOOD AND FOODWAYS: Exotic spices on display at a market in Morocco. Courtesy of Shutterstock.

FOOD AND FOODWAYS: The popularity of street falafel stands ensures they can be found throughout Israel. Courtesy of Shutterstock.

GAMES, TOYS, AND PASTIMES

GAMES, TOYS, AND PASTIMES: A veiled Iranian woman looks at Dara and Sara dolls dressed in traditional outfits. Iran unveiled the long-awaited Dara and Sara in 2002, twin national dolls that seek to preserve and promote Iran's culture and replace the American Barbie. © AP Photo/Vahid Salemi.

GAMES, TOYS, AND PASTIMES: These Saudi children find video games just as appealing as their Western counterparts. © Art Directors/Maggi & Doug Beaumont.

GAMES, TOYS, AND PASTIMES: An Egyptian girl inspects the Muslim Fulla dolls at a toy store in Cairo, 2006. Fulla is now thought to be the best-selling girl's toy in the Arab world, two years after it first came on the market. © Khaled Desouki/AFP/Getty Images.

GAMES, TOYS, AND PASTIMES

MARY FINDLEY

Answering the question "What was the first toy or game to be used in North Africa or the Middle East?" is the equivalent of answering the question "Which came first, the chicken or the egg?" The exact origin of toys and games—and which came first—not only in North Africa and the Middle East but in all regions, is largely a mystery. There is speculation, however, that toys and games, in their most basic forms, have existed for as long as children have existed. These basic forms equate to toys carved from sticks, rocks, bones, ivory, and other natural materials, in addition to toys created by the imagination: large leaves that, when folded correctly, dart and float in the wind; stones that roll in the dirt; and strong, pliable branches that can be bent into dolls of various sizes and shapes. These toys, along with games exhibiting either athletic or intellectual prowess, dexterity, and strength, had the same function and importance in ancient times as do the toys and games of today: to amuse, to teach, and to surprise.

It is easier, in many respects, to trace the history and popular culture of toys in North America and Europe, as opposed to that of North Africa and the Middle East. The more industrialized the nation, the more homogenized and culturally accessible toys and games tend to be. In other words, it is easier to trace the popularity of manufactured toys and games, as opposed to toys and games that are fashioned by individual children's imaginations. With that said, however, archeological evidence suggests that toys date back thousands of years, the earliest of which appeared in ancient Egypt. The excavation of a child's tomb dating back to the Predynastic period (5500–3100 BCE), for example, revealed small, carved wooden boats.[1] Toys like these, carved of wood, stone, ivory, mud, and clay, were quite common in ancient Egypt, in other regions of North Africa, and in the Middle East, where the materials to make them were readily available and accessible. This also holds true today, especially in impoverished regions such as Saharan Africa, or in regions where a nomadic lifestyle is typical.

Without the ability to purchase manufactured toys, children will fashion toys out of whatever is available. The Petrie Museum of Egyptian Archeology in London houses a number of archeological finds from ancient Egypt, including gaming boards carved from limestone and ivory, terracotta dolls, wooden dolls with jointed legs, and toy animals made of mud.

Many of them, like a limestone serpent-game board, date back to the Early Dynastic period (3100–2700 BCE).[2] While some of these toys look basic in design compared to the manufactured toys readily accessible in urban regions of the world today, it is important to note that a considerable amount of craftsmanship, as well as time, went into fashioning the intricate details and artwork on even the most basic toy or gaming board. This indicates that a high value and importance were placed on toys and games by ancient civilizations in Egypt and, it is thought, throughout North Africa and the Middle East. Some of the mud toys were even made by the children themselves, offering even the youngest members of society the opportunity to learn the importance of craftsmanship and pride in their work, as well as a chance to exercise their imaginative and creative powers.

Games, whether athletic or played on small boards, have always existed alongside toys, but their exact origins also are difficult to pinpoint. The History Channel's Timeline of Toys and Games indicates that a precursor to modern chess and checkers was played in Babylonia approximately 4000 BCE, and that a game similar to backgammon appeared in ancient Sumeria about 3000 BCE. It is also believed that stone marbles were used in Egypt during this period, and that kites appeared in China and stone yo-yos appeared in Greece in about 1000 BCE. In addition, the first iron skates were used in Scandinavia in 200 CE. It is believed, however, that much like toys, these or similar games had been played thousands of years before they were discovered or recorded in history. The earliest recorded games from the Middle East were based on archeological finds of paintings on tomb walls. One five-thousand-year-old drawing found on the wall of the Saqqara tomb, for example, depicts what might have been an early version of handball. According to the Egypt State Information Service, "The ball was made of leather and stuffed with plant fibers or hay, or made of papyrus plants in order to be light and more durable."[3] Although this particular drawing poses little challenge for historians and archeologists to understand, many games depicted on the walls of ancient tombs, along with their rules of play, are not recognized or understood today. Drawings of people, mostly men and boys, engaging in different activities that appear to be games are difficult to decipher from the perspective of contemporary culture. It is possible that some ancient games and their rules will never be recovered.

While archeological finds in ancient Egypt provide a wealth of information about the earliest and most basic toys and games of the region, tracking the history and current trends of toys, games, and hobbies in North Africa and the Middle East proves to be no easy task. In some regions poverty, warfare, and tribal or nomadic lifestyles preclude the purchase of manufactured toys and games that, by their very nature, leave a more easily traceable track on the cultural landscape. Computer and electronic games, for example, are virtually nonexistent in some war-torn regions like Gaza and the West Bank, where Internet users total little more than 60,000. The current culture of toys and games in Iraq has changed dramatically because of the prevalence of violence, government upheaval, and the influx of toy-carrying soldiers from the United States and other countries, who arrived in connection with the overthrow of Saddam Hussein. Beanie Babies, for example, which were once unknown to Iraqi children, have now grown in popularity. The diversity of the North African and Middle Eastern landscape and people, the prevalence of warfare in some regions, and the limited existence of documented research on the current toy, game, and hobby culture of the region make the gathering of this type of information challenging at best, and virtually impossible at some junctures. However, some games seem to cut across cultures and regions, enjoying popularity with children and adults throughout North Africa and the Middle East. Before looking closely at the uniqueness of the toy, game, and hobby culture of each region, it is important to discuss the games and toys that enjoy a more universal popularity.

COMMON TOYS AND GAMES

Galimoto

The first toy that could be said to have a universal presence in North Africa is known as *galimoto*. The word "gali" means wire, and "moto" means wheels. Galimotos are handmade push toys made by children in North Africa out of wire, string, and other available waste products or natural resources.[4] These toys take the shape of cars, bicycles, helicopters, and other vehicles, and they are often sold by children as a way to raise money to help support their families.

Mancala and Owari

The game of *mancala*, sometimes spelled *mankala*, is one of the oldest and most commonly played games in North Africa and the Middle East. The game board can be as basic as lines in the dirt, with stones and pebbles as playing pieces, or as elaborate as an intricately carved board or a manufactured board made of gold. There are numerous variations of this game, but the most common is played on a board with seven pits, six of which are used for play and one of which is used for scoring. At the start of the game, a set number of stones are placed in each pit. The number can be anywhere from three to five, but the same amount must be in each pit. Players then take turns "choosing a pit on their own side. When a pit is selected, it is emptied of its stones, which are then distributed counterclockwise to all pits and stores (except the opponent's store), one per pit/store. If the last stone of a move is placed in the moving player's store, that player may move again. If the last stone of a move is placed in an empty pit on the moving player's side, both the last stone and all of the opponent's stones in the pit opposite the previously empty pit are placed in the moving player's store. This is called a 'capture.'"[5] The first player with no stones left in the pits on their side of the board loses.

Owari is in the same family of games as mancala. It is a count and capture game played throughout North African and the Middle East. The game board is similar, but the rules differ slightly. Each player has six pits. The first player picks up the beads from any of the player's own pits and distributes them counterclockwise. The number of beads in the last pit to receive a bead determines the player's next move. If there are fewer than two or three beads, the player's turn is over, and it is the next player's turn. If there are two or three, these beads are collected and the adjacent pit is looked at. If that pit has two or three beads, these are also collected, and so on. Play continues until one player has all the opponents' beads.[6]

Legos

Although Legos are not native to North Africa or the Middle East, the Lego Group is the number one toy company in both regions. The company's success is largely the result of strong advertising campaigns, as well as the availability of a wide range of toys such as Bionicles, construction toys for infants and preschool children, and Legos such as those based on the literary character Harry Potter.[7] These toys enjoy popularity in the more urban areas of North African and the Middle East where the existence of toy stores and markets make manufactured toys easily accessible.

REGIONS

North Africa

Algeria

Algeria is one of the largest countries in Africa, but prior to March 1, 2005, it did not have a television station dedicated to children's programming until Algerie Premier hit the airwaves. The station currently "broadcasts its programmes from Luxembourg via satellite via the French La Locale television channel."[8] Whether classified as a hobby or simply as a pastime, television viewing is definitely a form of entertainment for children of all cultures, and Algerie Premiere fills a void that had existed for Algerian children. Along with entertainment, the station is also dedicated to the promotion of both Algerian and Maghreb culture, thus offering educational and cultural value as opposed to mere entertainment.[9]

Also popular with Algerian children is the game of soccer. Not necessarily played as a competitive sport among young children, soccer is more of an informal type of amusement, a game that is usually played in the streets for fun.[10]

Board games that are popular with both teenagers and adults, especially with Algerian men, include checkers, chess, and dominoes, which are frequently played at public coffeehouses as opposed to being played in the privacy of the home.[11] Algerian women are more apt to socialize and visit at home, while men socialize and relax in more public venues. One such form of recreation for men includes frequenting the Haaman, a public bath house with saunas, steam rooms, and massage facilities.[12]

In addition to playing chess for recreational purposes, the people of Algeria are supportive of their national chess team. The team consists of young players, with Aimen Rizouk currently holding the title of Algeria's number one player. His twin brother, Ryad Rizouk, is also a current member of the team.[13]

Card games also enjoy popularity in Algeria. Similar to those played in Morocco and elsewhere in Africa, popular Algerian card games include ronda, bezga, qezzet, nufi, and chkoubba, which are played with Spanish-suited cards, not with traditional decks of cards.[14]

The popularity of Internet and computer games is a bit more difficult to gauge. Estimates as recent as 2005 indicate that less than 10 percent of the population use the Internet.[15] Given these figures, it seems a reasonable assumption that the popularity and growth of computer games and of a gaming community will increase as Internet use becomes more prevalent.

Because of the number of coastal resorts in Algeria, as well as the miles of beautiful beaches, hobbies or recreational pastimes for many people include the simple joys of swimming, water skiing, and spending time at the beach. A large Algerian handicraft industry, however, also indicates the prevalence of more structured and artistic forms of recreation or hobbies, including the creation of pottery, ceramics, leather goods, and silver work.

Morocco

Since nearly half of the population of Morocco resides in urban areas that attract tourists, the types of games, hobbies, and toys enjoyed by the urban residents of Morocco differ from those enjoyed by people in more remote regions. Gambling casinos, for example, are virtually nonexistent in most locations in Morocco, or in North Africa, but their presence is becoming more prevalent in Moroccan cities. The seaport city of Agadir houses three casinos—Casino le Mirage, Shem's Casino d'Agadir, and the Sheraton Agadir—while Cabo Negro, Marrakech, and Tangier each have one. Slot machines, American roulette, video poker, blackjack, Caribbean stud poker, and punto banco are the most prevalent and popular casino games, indicating a strong American influence.[16]

Card games are not only popular in Moroccan casinos, but they also have enjoyed staying power throughout Morocco for more than a century. Ronda, a fishing game played with a traditional fifty-two-card deck, is popular with both children and adults and is often considered the most popular card game in the region. In this two-to-four player game, similar in theory to the American game of Go Fish, each player is dealt three cards and must match his or her cards with a layout of cards on the table. Each match becomes a capture, and each unmatched card remains as part of the layout. Other commonly played card games include venta, nouffi, tres, ch'kamba, el bazga, and sotta. Ch'kamba is "a simple Ace-Ten play and draw game," and sota is a kind of "coarse strip poker."[17]

In addition to the luck-of-the-draw games, Moroccans are also fond of games that are more strategic in nature, like chess. Currently, Hichem Hamdouchi heads the Moroccan national chess team and has enjoyed a ranking as Africa's top player.

Since 1989, Hamdouchi has played in 198 professional matches, including the 2005 Gibraltar Grand Masters.[18] The prevalence of chess is clear from the popularity and success of Hamdouchi, and the game is played throughout Morocco, along with other games of strategy such as backgammon.

The popularity of various toys in Morocco largely depends upon the geographic location of the people. In urban areas, for example, the Moroccan toy company Maxitoys offers a variety of popular children's toys, many of which are influenced by American or European culture and often do not display distinctly Moroccan cultural influences. Toys such as Dora the Explorer, Winnie the Pooh, Scooby Doo, Hot Wheels, Spiderman, Star Wars, Disney Princess, and Teletubbies, along with companies such as Mattel, Crayola, Fisher-Price, Hasbro, and Leapfrog, are heavily represented, indicating the strong popularity and resonance of these toys with Moroccan children. Action toys, such as those boasting various types of remote-controlled vehicles, and action figures, such as Batman, Power Rangers, and the Fantastic Four, are also strongly represented.[19]

Even though Maxitoys carries American Barbie accessories, Mattel created and marketed a Moroccan Barbie in 1998. In a manner similar to what has happened with its distant cousin Fulla in the Middle East, this Moroccan version has largely replaced Barbie, not only as a toy for young girls but also as a model of Moroccan female values. Dressed in a long orange and pink traditional Moroccan dress, the Moroccan Barbie has a distinct veil and headdress. The accessories also differ from the American version; they include a large gold coin hanging from the center of the headdress, and a gold chain necklace boasting a similar gold coin.

Children in more sparsely populated and rural areas of Morocco, however, are not as greatly influenced by the influx of American and European toys. These toys would, undoubtedly, enjoy popularity if they were readily accessible, but lower incomes and remote geographic locations play a large role in the types of toys these children play with. In smaller villages located throughout Morocco, children are more apt to play with self-created toys made from natural materials, such as reeds and vines for the hair of homemade dolls, and waste products such as various colored rags, copper wire, buttons, and other available materials for the doll's body. Moroccan boys may use "summer squash, pieces of potatoes and sticks to make human and animal figurines. They use clay, mud and gypsum to make human and animal figurines, small houses, toy utensils, all kinds of vehicles and even a telephone."[20]

Hobbies in Morocco, or any region of North Africa, are as varied as the people. Swimming tends to be near the top of the list of active hobbies in Morocco, as are watching and participating in various sports such as soccer.

Tunisia

Although situated on the Mediterranean coast, bordering Libya to the east and Algeria to the west, and boasting beautiful resort cities that attract thousands of tourists each year, Tunisia also includes a portion of the Sahara desert, which sets up an interesting dichotomy. The 10 million people of Tunisia are as culturally diverse and different as are the coastal blue waters and the dry desert sand. As a result, the games, hobbies, and toys of this region are not easily categorized and identifiable. With only 630,000 reported Internet users however, it is logical to conclude that computer and Internet gaming, even in urban, middle-class locations such as Carthage and Tunis, do not enjoy the same popularity experienced in the United States and Europe. The prevalence and popularity of computers and Internet-savvy adults and children is not yet to the proportion necessary to sustain popularity for computer and Internet games; however, with 75 percent to 80 percent of the population now considered predominantly middle class, the standard of living in Tunisia is expected to rise and produce a boom in the popularity of computer and Internet games.[21]

Unlike other countries in North Africa, where the toy and play culture is largely unresearched, extensive research has been done by Jean-Pierre Rossie, professor of African history and philology, regarding the toy and play culture of the once seminomadic and now completely settled population of the 5,000 Ghrib people of the Tunisian Sahara. Rossie's research on the Ghrib people offers insight into the evolution of toys and games through three generations as these people shifted from nomadic to seminomadic to completely settled lifestyles. According to Rossie, although changing times have brought about changes in the toys, hobbies, and games of children around the world, certain characteristics of the toy and play culture of the Ghrib people still hold true: "characteristics such as being mostly outdoor activities, collective activities, autonomous activities without adult interference, activities only slightly dependent on external resources such as the toy industry, and realistic play activities that are linked to real life not to worlds of phantasy."[22]

These characteristics, it seems, also hold true for many of the play cultures of children in impoverished areas of North Africa and the Middle East as well. It is interesting to note that impoverished regions, or nomadic and seminomadic lifestyles, dictate the need for imagination, not money, to create toys. In fact, Rossie notes that "the toy industry with its sophisticated female and male dolls, Tamagochis and electronic toys, has not yet been able to really infiltrate the play world of most African children, except those of the upper class."[23]

Although it may be true that the manufactured toy industry has not influenced the toys and games of many African children, the changing times definitely have. The evolution of the doll in the Ghrib society is reflective of generational changes in education and future expectations. For example, between 1975 and 2000, Rossie notes that the traditional doll, with two crossed sticks for a frame, braided hair, a kerchief, and pretend jewels made of iron wire and tin, represented a bride. The clothes, often made of rags and other available material, individualized these faceless dolls. Later, as the boys in the family attended school, they added facial features to the dolls, a change that soon became accepted. The new sophistication that they had attained from their education made their creations more intricate. More recently, however, young girls are adding facial features to their dolls as they are now becoming educated and able to do so themselves. In addition, girls are now using waste products, such as flasks and cut-out cardboard, for heads and other textiles to create the bodies of these once stick-figure dolls.[24]

Songs are also an important part of Tunisia's play culture. One game, Old Mother Tambo, believed to be "derived from a Phoenician sacrifice to the goddess Tanit," in exchange for rain during times of drought, consists of children carrying a stick-figure doll from house to house while singing the following song:

> Your old Mother Tambo, my children,
> Asked God to give her flowers
> Your old Mother Tambo, my little ones,
> Washed her djebba in the river
> Your old Mother Tambo, my children
> Asked God to sustain her
> By bringing the rain.
> Dear God, dear God
> If it is our will,
> Make this rain fall;
> Give us beans in the dewy morning;
> God, give us pepper in the hot morning,
> And corn too for a full stomach.[25]

While the children are singing, women of the house come out and throw a bucket of water on the doll and the children. The children must keep singing—without flinching—to break the drought and bring the rain.[26]

Another singing game, teeta, teeta, teeta, is similar to the American version of patty-cake. The song is as follows:

> Teeta, Teeta, Teeta
> Pappa brought a little fish,
> We're going to eat it in olive oil.
> My frying pan is sputtering.
> The cat's already nibbling the bones,
> Papa washed his hands, but found
> The Asaida prayer was finished.
> So he clapped his hands to his face.
> Teeta, oh Aneba
> What did Papa bring us?
> He brought us lots of henna
> So I'm going to put on henna
> And give the rest so Shoosena.[27]

As in many cultures, games also play a prominent role in Tunisia. Some games, again more prevalent in the Tunisian Sahara or other rural and impoverished areas, revolve around the imaginative use of common animals. One animal in particular, the dromedary, which is a member of the camel family, is popular in a number of children's games called "'ej-jmel,' the dromedary, sometimes also 'el-akkeri,' the saddle-cushion . . . and the dromedary with tied legs then called 'gid ej-jmel.'"[28] These games involve at least one child pretending to be the dromedary: the child is either led around by a shepherd, carries another child on its back, or is led around with its back legs tied together. When playing gid ej-jmel, two children will often portray tied-up dromedaries and fight each other, but the fight is "simulated and should never lead to a scuffle."[29]

Most games of strategy are also enjoyed in Tunisia, including dominoes, played primarily by men in urban cafes, and chess, played by amateurs and professionals alike. "Tunisia produced the continent's first chess Grandmaster in GM Slim Bouaziz (Morocco's Hichem Hamdouchi was the second). Although GM Bouaziz is still an active player, another Slim has emerged. Slim Belkhodja recently earned the country's second GM title."[30]

Card games are also popular throughout Tunisia with, chkoubba, a game "played with a 40-card French-suited pack lacking all 8s, 9s and 10s," being the most prevalent.[31] The game quarante de roi is also popular. This game is played "by four players in fixed partnerships using a 32-card pack ranking K-Q-J-A-10-9-8-7 in each suit. There are scores for having a set of three or four kings, queens or jacks in your hand, and for each king, queen or jack taken in a trick."[32]

While it is difficult to ascertain the hobbies of those in the Tunisian Sahara, hobbies for those in more urban or coastal areas include various sports such as soccer, handball, golf, tennis, and hiking as well as water sports such as sailing, surfing, and diving.

Libya

It is estimated that the African toy market for children is at an all-time high, equivalent to approximately US$800 million, with an expected annual growth rate of 6 percent.[33] With that said, Libya, which has traditionally been a culture lacking a strong focus on toys and children's entertainment, was host to the groundbreaking Toy Trade Fair in Tripoli in December 2006. An advertising campaign media blitz, which included national and regional advertising in newspapers and on television, radio, billboards, and the Internet, as well as direct advertising campaigns to various Libyan companies and parties of interest, garnered at least 3,500 visitors, many of which were parents with their children.[34] The types of toys highlighted and on view at the Toy Trade Fair said much about the growing popular culture of toys in Libya. Developmental toys, educational toys, children's books, bicycles, scooters, outdoor sports toys, roller skates, riding toys, tricks and magic products, video games, mechanical toys, electronic toys, children's computer games for fun and educational purposes, party toys, and group toys were represented. This trend toward more educational and learning-development toys, as well as computer games and technological toys, shows a strong focus on education and preparing children for the global market.[35]

Although the cultural shift in children's toys and games is in progress, informal and inexpensive games are still the most prevalently played games throughout Libya. Street soccer is popular with children, teenagers, and young adults; a basic game of tic-tac-toe played with sticks and marbles in the sand is a popular game with the Bedouin children of the desert regions; and isseren, a game in which children split sticks, throw them in the air, and garner points for ones that land split side up, is also popular. In addition, men tend to gather in public for games of chess and dominoes, although these games are played for mere entertainment value and no money changes hands.[36]

The card game chkoubba is also popular with Libyan men. Also played in public without the exchange of money, chkoubba is "derived from the Italian card games called Scopa and Scopone and its rules are very similar. It is played with a 40-card French-suited pack that is lacking all 8s, 9s and 10s."[37] In this game, each player is dealt three cards, and four cards are placed face up on the table. The object of the game is to capture as many table cards as possible. Captures, however, do not have to be identical matches. For example, a player with a 7 can capture the cards 4 and 3, or 5 and 2. If no captures can be made, the player must lay one card face up with the other cards on the table.[38]

In the realm of professional games, Libya has shown a growing interest in chess and hosted "the 2004 African Junior Championship and the 2004 FIDE World Chess Championship."[39] The country has also produced four top players, and there is speculation that the interest and support of chess as a national game will continue into the future.[40]

Hobbies in Libya are similar to those of other coastal regions in North Africa and include swimming, boating, scuba diving, and trips to the beach. Residents of larger cities also enjoy bowling, tennis, and other games and sports typically found in large urban areas. The thriving handicraft industry in both the coastal regions and the larger cities also indicates that Libyan hobbies continue to include various artistic trades, whose intricate craftsmanship is handed down from generation to generation. Libyan markets boast a host of regional handicrafts such as pottery, silver and gold jewelry, and leather goods.

The Middle East

Egypt

Located in both North Africa and southwestern Asia, Egypt also borders the Mediterranean Sea and is one of the most populated countries in the world, with more than 77 million people. As a result, the toys, games, and hobbies enjoyed by modern Egyptians are quite diverse.

As noted earlier, Egypt has a long-standing history with toys and games. Archeological finds in ancient tombs have unearthed a treasure trove of toys and game boards dating back thousands of years BCE. These toys, many of which were fashioned out of easily accessible materials, include animals, boats, dolls, and gaming boards carved or molded out of wood, limestone, mud, and ivory. Paintings on tomb walls also indicate that ancient Egyptians had a penchant for games. It is believed that men and boys engaged in games such as, archery, wrestling, boxing, and fencing.[41] Racing of all types—long distance, short distance, on the knees, or while carrying another person or child on the back—was also popular, as was wrestling another opponent while both wrestlers sat atop others, who were on all fours, until one or the other wrestler fell off.[42]

The board game senet, a possible ancestor and precursor to the modern game of backgammon, also originated in ancient Egypt. Through archeological finds, "more than 40 [game boards] have been discovered, some in very good condition with pawns, sticks or knucklebones still intact. The oldest known representation of Senet is in a painting from the tomb of Hesy (Third Dynasty circa 2686–2613 BCE)."[43] The senet game board consists of three rows of ten squares for a total of thirty squares. Some squares contain symbols believed to have a beneficial meaning for the players, and others contain symbols with a negative meaning. "Other elements found with the game boards were pawns. The Hesy painting shows a game with seven pawns for each player. Then, some time after 1600–1500 BCE, the players were represented with seven or five pawns. Some games have even been found with ten pawns per player. The movement of pawns was probably decided by the throw of four, two-sided sticks (as depicted in the Hesy painting) or, later, knucklebones might have been used to determine the moves."[44]

Although these ancient games may seem outdated, the fact remains that children in Egypt today still enjoy games played by Egyptian children of the past. Two games that still enjoy popularity are Egyptian tug of war and the game of foot grabbing. Unlike American tug of war, the Egyptian version involves only four players, as opposed to an entire team. One player draws a line in the dirt, and two players face each other with their toes pressed to the line and up against the opponent's toes. They then hold hands and lean back. The two remaining players, each from opposing sides, stand behind their leaders, grab the leader's waist, and begin pulling. The first side to successfully pull the other side across the line wins.[45] In the game of foot grabbing, players sit on the floor in a circle with one person sitting in the middle. They then gently nudge the middle person with their feet. The player in the middle tries to grab and hold onto the foot of another player. Once he or she has done this, the captured person sits in the middle, and the game begins again.[46]

Another game enjoyed by children in the more remote desert regions of Egypt is called seega, a game that has endured for centuries. Its staying power is largely because it is simple, requires few materials, and involves a great deal of strategy, concentration, and thought.[47] Similar to checkers, this game requires a playing board such as a 5 × 5 board similar to a checkerboard, or simple divots in the sand, and twelve playing pieces for each player. Playing pieces can be created out of anything handy and available, such as stones or pieces of broken pottery. Much like the idea of checkers, the object is to capture the opponent's pieces. The setup for the game differs from any form of checkers, however, and involves one player laying down two pieces in squares designated with an X, while the other player lays down two pieces in squares designated with an O. Players alternate laying down pieces until all pieces are laid and the center square is left open. Pieces can only be moved to open squares, and diagonal moves are not allowed.[48]

The rules of the game are a bit more complicated and involve the following:

A piece is captured when it is in between two other pieces either horizontally or vertically on the board. In order to be captured, the piece must be sandwiched by the opponent. Moving a piece in between two pieces of one player by the person whose turn it is does not result in a capture. Captures can only be the direct result of an opponent's move. When a player is blocked and unable to move, an opponent's piece is removed to clear play. In addition "a second move in a single turn is allowed if the first move yielded a 'take' and an additional move of the same piece will yield another 'take.' If a whole series of such moves are possible, then several moves in the same turn are allowed."[49]

Jumping rope and playing games involving balls are popular with Egyptian girls. One such ball game, abaliy, involves two players. One girl stands facing a wall, throws a ball against it, and claps her hands before the ball bounces back. The object is to clap as many times, and in as many creative ways as possible, without letting the ball fall to the ground. The player with the ball sings the following song while playing:

> Abaliy Abalandi . . . hey kids.
> French bread . . . for money.
> The daughter of an Effendi
> Sleeps while I play.
> I feared she'd beat me
> I scored (one) against her.[50]

A player scores one point for each time she finishes the song while clapping and keeping the ball from hitting the ground.[51]

Children also play games surrounding special events, holidays, or occasions such as the religious month of Ramadan. On the last day of Ramadan, for example, songs are sung to bid farewell to the month. One such song is sung by boys while engaged in play:

> O Ramadan O month of uncertain end
> Eat your predawn meal tonight
> O Ramadan O month of the copper basin
> O month present in all countries.[52]

One of the most popular games played during Ramadan is a clapping game called The Feast: My Rope is Long. This is typically played by girls who are not allowed to get their clothes dirty during this time. The girls face each other and alternately clap their hands together, right to right, and left to left, while singing the following song:

My rope is long O mama
It fell in the well O mama
I descended down to get it O mama
The Bey met me O mama
He gave me a pound O mama
What shall I buy with it O mama?
I shall buy a duck with it O mama
And the duck is shouting O mama
And it says: O my thighs O mama
O things of bad omen O mama
Abd al-Qayyum O mama
Grows lemons—O mama
His lemons are sour O mama
The sound of guns O mama
On the day of the feast O mama
The candles are lighted O mama
And I played then, O mama![53]

Casinos and typical casino games are also popular in Egypt. Of the twenty-four casinos in Egypt, twenty of them are located in the capital, Cairo, the largest city in the Middle East and North Africa. Games include American roulette, punto banco, blackjack, poker, and slot machines. American roulette is played on a wheel with thirty-eight numbered slots that alternate between even and odd numbers, and black and red. Slots number from 1 to 36, 0 and 00. The English version of roulette, played in some casinos, does not have a 00 slot.[54] "The table is designed so that the numbers, not including 0 and 00, are lined up into three columns, each of twelve numbers; the first row is 1, 2, 3; the second row is 4, 5, 6; and so on. The rest of the table is devoted to the myriad of bets the game entails. Betting is broken down into two major categories, inside bets and outside bets. There is no limit to the number of bets one can play."[55]

Inside bets include straight bets; split bets; a street bet, trio bet, or three-number bet; a corner bet, square bet or four-number bet; a five-number bet; and a six-line bet. Straight bets are just what the name implies: a player bets that one particular number will come up on the wheel. If so, the payoff is 35 to 1. With split bets, the player bets that one of two numbers next to each other will come up. If so, the payoff is 17 to 1. Following suit, in a street bet, trio bet, or three-number bet, the player bets that one of three numbers in a row will come up. The payoff for this bet is 11 to 1. A corner bet wagers that one of four touching numbers will come up on the wheel, and a five-number bet wagers that 0, 00, 1, 2, or 3 will come up. A corner bet pays 8 to 1, and a five-number bet pays 6 to 1. In a six-line bet, the player hopes that one of six numbers hits on the wheel. The numbers must, however, be in two adjacent rows of three, and the payoff is also 6 to 1.[56]

Outside bets include red, black, even, odd, low bet, high bet, dozen bet, and column bet. With red and black bets, the player wages that the next number to come up on the wheel will be black or red. These bets pay 1 to 1. Even and odd bets wager that the next number to come up will be either even or odd, and the payoff is also 1 to 1. Low bets wager that the number will be between one and eighteen, and high bets wager that the number will be between nineteen and thirty-six. The payoff for these bets is also 1 to 1. Dozen bets split

GAMES, TOYS, AND PASTIMES

> ### COOKING: AN EGYPTIAN HOBBY
>
> Egypt's unique geographic location has aided in the creation of a cuisine that has turned from hobby into art form and then into thriving businesses. The variety and scope of fresh produce and local ingredients have helped Egypt's cuisine emerge as unique, tasty, and popular with locals and tourists alike. The most authentic and culturally reflective food is found from street vendors and includes grilled pigeon, whole wheat pitas with various dipping sauces such as tahini, babaganoush, and hummus. Babaganoush is primarily made of mashed eggplant, which is also the main ingredient in another favorite, Egyptian moussaka.[59]

the numbers into increments of twelve, and column bets split the numbers into columns. The payoff for dozen and split bets is 2 to 1.[57]

Punto banco, another popular game in Egyptian casinos, is closely related to the card game baccarat. The came can be played on a table similar to a blackjack table with one dealer, or it can be played on a larger, kidney-shaped table with three dealers. The object of the game is to bet on the winner of two hands—the player or the bank. "Cards are dealt to both hands by the dealer according to a set of rules and the winner is the hand closest to a total of nine. Both table versions of the game are identical in this."[58]

Egyptians also enjoy strategic games such as chess. Currently, the Egyptian national team is considered the strongest on the African continent, with Imed Abdelnabbi leading the team. The current Junior African Champion, fourteen-year-old Ahmed Adly, also hails from Egypt and provides a hopeful future for continued success of the national chess team.[60]

Computer and video gaming are popular among the 4.2 million Internet users in Egypt, as evidenced by Egypt's participation in the Electronic Sports World Cup (ESWC). Started in the 1990s, the Electronic Sports World Cup brings together the best electronic gaming champions from around the world to square off in a world-class tournament. Each country's finalists are determined through preliminary rounds held throughout the year in that country. The finalists are then brought together in a central location "for an international event commanding several hundreds of thousands of dollars. All the champions are invited to participate free of charge. The ESWC covers their accommodation costs and provides them with all of the IT equipment needed to take part in the competition."[61] The Electronic Sports World Cup is considered the best and most popular event in its field.

Although not necessarily considered a game or toy, it is important to note that Egyptian children are fond of television, which is certainly a viable form of entertainment for many in Egypt. Children are especially fond of the American shows *Candid Camera* and *Third Rock from the Sun*.[62]

Hobbies in Egypt are varied. Many children enjoy watching and participating in sports such as soccer, and teenagers enjoy music, dancing, and attending nightclubs. Outdoor activities such as scuba diving, boating, swimming, and other beach-related activities are also popular. One hobby, however, has grown into a thriving business and has helped shape and define the culture and, quite literally, the flavor of Egypt—cooking.

Jordan

Situated northwest of Saudi Arabia, the country of Jordan is slightly smaller than Indiana and has a population nearing 6 million, which is relatively small compared to other Middle Eastern countries. Research regarding toys, games, and the play culture of Jordan is largely lacking. With Internet users totaling a little over 450,000, however, it is logical to conclude that Internet and computer games have not reached a notable level of popularity in the country. Jordan's lack of participation in the Electronic Sports World Cup further supports this theory.

As far as toys and games are concerned, however, the country of Jordan took a tough stand against the use of violent toys that could be used to aid in the training or recruitment of children under the age of 18 for military purposes. According to the Amman Declaration on the Use of Children as Soldiers, which was adopted April 10, 2001, the country took a stand against "[the creation of] a culture of militarisation and violence, including through toys, computer games, violent films and cartoons, and media images."[63]

Card games are enjoyed by Jordanians. Two of the most popular are trix and basra. Trix is a "compendium game played with the 52-card pack, slightly similar to Barbu," and basra is categorized as a fishing game.[64]

Traditional hobbies in Jordan have had staying power as evidenced by the industry and craft of embroidery, which originally was a way for young Jordanian girls in villages to prove their domestic prowess and attract suitable bridegrooms. "This is one of the most important traditional crafts of Jordanian women and one which has, in recent years, been incorporated into high fashion. Elegant gowns and jackets have been created using traditional needlework together with rich, Middle Eastern fabrics and these designer collections are frequently modeled on the catwalks of Jordan's hotels."[65]

Israel

Israel is situated between Egypt and Lebanon, bordering the Mediterranean Sea. Israel's Arab Children Friends Association (ACFA) has been a driving force in the educational and play culture of Arab-Palestinian children in Israel. Founded in Haifa, Israel, in 1986, the ACFA "is committed to increasing the knowledge of Arab-Palestinian children about their culture and history, improving the scholastic performance of Arab-Palestinian pupils, and providing opportunities for Arab-Palestinian children to express their artistic skills."[66] As a result, the ACFA publishes popular children's magazines in Israel. These magazines include the bimonthly magazines *Al-Hayat Lilatfal* and *Al-Hayat Lilasafeer*, as well as *Kaus Kusah Encyclopedia*, the *Palestinian Folk Encyclopedia for Children*, and a 480-page collection of biographies titled *Min Aalm Alfikre Wal-Abad Al Arabi*.[67] The *Al-Hayat Lilatfal* magazine, published since 1986, was the first magazine for Palestinian children in Israel, and *Al-Hayat Lilasafeer* is "the only magazine for children in the Arabic language in Palestine and Israel."[68]

Toys in Israel have a strong American influence. Dora the Explorer, Star Wars, and Power Rangers action figures as well as Fisher Price, Little Tykes, and LeapFrog toys can easily be found in the twenty or more Toys R Us stores located throughout Israel. With the store's strong presence in Rehovot, Ramat-Gan, Petah-Tikva, Kiryat Shmona, Bat-Yam, Ashod, Jerusalem, Rishon Le-Zion, Kfar Saba, Eilat, Tel-Aviv, Gan-Shmuel, Haifa, Beer Sheeva, and Beerot Itzhak, it is clear that American toys are popular with Israeli children of all ages.[69]

Traditional toys and games, however, are also still enjoyed by children in Israel. The matching game perfect pair, for example, is a typical memory game. It uses "40 cards with various 'holy object' pictures" that are matched up to "develop memory, visual coordination and knowledge of Judaism."[70] Hebrew coloring books exploring the Hebrew alphabet, daily activities, the seasons, playground activities, and colors are also popular.[71]

Electronic and computer games are also popular in Israel. With a third of the population using the Internet, and with Israel's participation in the Electronic Sports World Cup, electronic and Internet games are becoming more popular in the country. The three games slated for

ESWC preliminary tournaments in Israel in 2006 include Counter-Strike, Quake IV, and Pro Evolution Soccer 5.[72]

The most popular card game in Israel appears to be Israeli whist. In this four-player game, played with a traditional fifty-two-card deck, the dealer is chosen at random; each player is dealt thirteen cards, and game play moves clockwise. The dealer is the first to bid in two phases of bidding. "A bid in the first phase consists of a number of tricks from 5 to 13 and a suit or 'no trumps,' so that possible bids would be 'six clubs,' 'eight hearts,' 'nine no trumps,' etc. A bid of more tricks outranks any bid of fewer tricks. Also, when comparing bids for the same number of tricks, the five denominations rank in the same order as at Bridge: no trumps is highest, then spades, hearts, diamonds, clubs (lowest)."[73]

Players choose to either bid or pass. Play continues until all players have chosen to pass, at which time "the last (and highest) bidder becomes the declarer and the trump suit (if any) for the hand is determined by the declarer's final bid. There is now a second phase of bidding in which the other three players, starting at declarer's left and going around clockwise, state how many tricks they will each try to take."[74]

Palestinian Territories: Gaza and the West Bank

As in Iraq, the political and civil strife in Gaza and the West Bank has affected the toy and play culture of children in the region. The most popular children's game, for example, includes simulated warfare and is called Jews and Arabs, Army versus Militants, or Settlers and Villagers. "After five years of witnessing real warfare played out in their own neighborhoods, most children throughout the Gaza Strip have become experts at imitating the whine of sniper bullets, automatic-weapons fire, grenade explosions, missile strikes. Young boys in the villages and refugee camps have always played war games occasionally, but during the intifada the bloodless battles have become wildly popular."[75]

The rules of this game are not set in stone, and children often switch back and forth between being the aggressors and being the victims. The game involves mimicking warlike behaviors commonly seen in the region. Bullying, harassing, and interrogation are all part of the game. Interrogation sometimes involves degrading the captured player by making the player undress and lie on the ground while the interrogation continues.[76] "Other real-life situations sometimes enter the game: ambulance drivers pleading to pass a checkpoint to save the life of a critically ill patient; or civilians telling the soldiers in vain of their lost relatives, their lost land."[77]

Adults living in the West Bank and the Gaza Strip are horrified by this game, but for many of the children, who lack parks, organized sports, and other safe recreational pursuits, it is the only outlet for their own fear, aggression, and imagination. Psychology Professor Dr. Fadel Abu Hiem speculates that the simulation involved in this type of game is "a way to have some feeling of power in a real-life situation where they [children] are powerless.... If a boy can 'fire' the same weapon as the occupier, if he can imitate the sound of a mortar or rocket which he sees as the Israeli source of power, then he 'owns' that power too and feels more in control. It's also a way to vent anger and act out a symbolic revenge. Children's play always reflects both their environment and their own emotions."[78]

There are organizations in place, however, that act to curb these violent games and introduce another culture of toys and play into the region. UNICEF's Sports for Development program organizes various sports, including volleyball, ping-pong, and others, among boarding schools for girls who, unlike their male peers, are not often allowed to play rough games outdoors with boys.[79]

The United Nations Relief and Works Agency for Palestine Refugees in the Near East (UNRWA) also seeks to bring more traditional play back to children of Gaza and the West Bank. Their mission is to create eleven toy libraries in and around the Gaza Strip that will ultimately serve approximately 3,800 children. These libraries will contain dolls, doll houses, teddy bears, and other toys that children can play with while visiting the facility.[80]

The ACFA is also active in the region, hosting the Brotherhood Summer Camp that brings together Palestinian children from the Gaza Strip with those who live in other regions of the country to participate in outdoor activities so the children can learn more about the lifestyles of those in other regions.[81]

Iraq

The current culture of Iraq, including the toy and play culture as well as the pursuit of hobbies, is largely influenced by the recent overthrow of the former Iraqi leader, Saddam Hussein.

After Hussein was removed from power, toy stores and markets in and around Baghdad, for example, began featuring a dancing Saddam doll. The foot-tall doll, which dances to the *Hippy Hippy Shake*, is dressed in insurgent regalia and "is decked out with hand-grenades, daggers, a walkie-talkie, binoculars and an AK-47."[82] Store owners had originally hidden the dolls behind the counter for fear of retaliation for mocking the former leader, and the doll was sold only to those who asked for it. As fear abated, the doll was displayed in the open and sold to adults and children alike, meeting with great popularity. Other dolls featured at the same time included "dancing Osama bin Ladens, Fidel Castros and George W. Bushes."[83] The dancing bin Laden doll also proved to be popular.

Along with dancing Saddam dolls, Iraqi children have been influenced by an influx of donated toys from American soldiers—mostly Beanie Babies. These small stuffed animals, originally created by the Ty Inc. toy company, have enjoyed a new-found popularity among Iraqi children. Small enough to be tucked into a soldier's gear and economical to ship, American soldiers have distributed hundreds of the small animal toys to children throughout Iraq.[84] These toys have met with great enthusiasm and popularity among Iraqi children. Other American toys that have found their way into small Iraqi hands by way of donation include soccer balls and Frisbees, as well as children's backpacks decorated with various cartoon themes.

Soldiers are not the only ones bringing American toys into Iraq. Reconstruction efforts have built or renovated stores and markets throughout Baghdad. The Disney Island toy store in the Karrada district of Baghdad offers Disney-themed toys as well as remote-controlled cars made in China. Increased spending by Iraqi citizens has helped the store bring in $15,000 a month.[85]

The game culture has also been affected by warfare. According to Iraqi teachers, a new-found violence has found its way into children's games in Iraq. "Teachers say that grades are down and aggression up as districts realign themselves along ethnic and religious divides, the separation seeping even into the games children play. . . . Even in the games they play they'll split into two groups and play Americans and Mujahidin. Most of the time they choose the runty kid to be an American soldier, then they chase him and beat him. It's like they are taking revenge."[86] In addition, many male children in Iraq, left fatherless as a result of warfare, civil strife, or insurgent violence, have been forced to take on the role of provider for the family, sacrificing childhood for work. This is evident in Nineveh Province, where children sell various goods on the street as a way to raise money. This leaves little time for some of the more traditional games, such as informal street soccer, that were often played here.

Even without warfare and civil strife, Internet and computer games have not enjoyed popularity in recent years in Iraq. With a population of more than 26 million, there are fewer than 30,000 Internet users. In addition, video games have not reached the heights of popularity that are present in North America or Europe.

Iran

The second-largest country in the Middle East after Saudi Arabia, and the center of the Shia branch of Islam, Iran is unique in its creation of two dolls opposing the more stereotypical and popular notion of the American Ken and Barbie: Dara and Sara. "Developed and marketed by the Institute for the Intellectual Development of Children and Young Adults, a government agency affiliated with the Ministry of Education, they have been created to promote traditional values . . . and pro-family backgrounds."[87] Dara and Sara, dark-haired eight-year-old twins, are the direct opposite of blonde, buxom Barbie and her boyfriend, yet never husband, Ken. While Barbie and Ken have dominated the Iranian toy market, Iranian adults and the Institute for the Intellectual Development of Children and Young Adults fear that young girls who play with Barbie dolls will grow into women who reject traditional Islamic values. Barbie's buxom image and revealing clothing are considered counter to Islamic beliefs. One Iranian toy seller even commented that "every Barbie doll is more harmful than an American missile."[88]

Dara and Sara are brother and sister, and neither one is involved in a sketchy relationship with someone of the opposite sex. In addition, the buxom image and revealing clothing are gone. The four different versions of Sara each comes with a white headscarf, and both dolls are fully clothed from head to foot. The dolls even have a history and hoped-for future that is traditional and familiar to many Iranian children. Their mother, for example, is a homemaker. "She is their best advisor and helps them out in their troubles. Their father works in the Iran Cultural Heritage Organization."[89] They live in an old house in the country with a cat, chickens, and goldfish, all of which they take care of. Sara enjoys science, plays ping-pong, and hopes to be a teacher, while Dara likes football, wrestles, and wants to be an astronaut or archaeologist.[90] Their background, history, and adventures are told on various audio cassettes that are part of the marketing blitz designed to counter the influence of Barbie and Ken and propel these dolls into the current Iranian toy culture. The dolls have become popular, and the prevalence of Barbie and Ken seems to be waning.

Electronic and Internet games are also popular among the 4.3 million Internet users in Iran. Iran participates in the Electronic Sports World Cup (ESWC) and also competes in the World Cyber Games. The World Cyber Games is similar to the ESWC in that it hosts an annual tournament dedicated to the best cyber gamers around the world. In 2005, the Iranian national final included competitions in Warcraft III, Starcraft Broodwar, FIFA Soccer 2005, and Warcraft 2v2.

Card games are also popular with Iranian youth and adults. Chahar barq and gharat are both fishing games. "Gharat is an unusual fishing game played with a single central pile, in which it is also possible to steal the other players' capture."[91] Blof is a bluffing game much like the American game of Bullshit, and "ghahveh is a trick-taking game which seems to be a descendant of the American game Spades."[92] Other games include hokim, a game whose objective is to win a minimum of seven of thirteen possible tricks, and rok or shelem, "a point-trick game with bidding, possibly from the south of Iran. Aces and tens are worth 10 points, fives are worth 5 and each trick is worth five."[93]

Similar to other countries in North Africa and the Middle East, Iran is active in professional chess. The Iran Chess Federation sponsors tournaments and championships for men, women, adults, and youths, some boasting more than 250 participants.[94]

Iran is also known for its traditional games and its contribution to the game of polo. Polo is believed to have originated in Persia (now Iran) more than 2,000 years ago. "The first recorded game took place in 600 BC between the Turkomans and Persians (the Turkomans won)." In later centuries the young King Sapoor II of Persia learned the game, and "in the 16th century, a polo ground (300 yards long and with goalposts eight yards apart) was built at Ispahan, then the capital, by Shah Abbas the Great."[95]

Traditional games are still played by children in Iran. One game, atali gol matali, originated in the Iranian village of DaVan. In this game one player sits among other players, who are sitting with their legs out straight. While singing the following song, the single player hits the leg of each seated player to the rhythm of the song:

> atali gol matali
> khaje-ye mau mitelavi
> az kauri az bauri
> poshte qelam dasmauli
> dey ahmado joone koret
> to tisha vardaur mo tevar
> berim ba jang-e kau nezar
> kau nezar hee ke hoo ke
> galle-ye shau ram ke
> sivo sot-osh kam ke
> ey bezza vo ey dar koo.[96]

When the lead player sings the word "koo," the player whose leg is tapped must do his or her best to completely cover his or her toes. Legs can be brought up underneath the body, but if the toes are still showing, other players will pinch them, and the toe-covering player will then be out of the game.[97]

Hobbies in Iran also include handicrafts. Iran is noted for the production of handcrafted carpets, with each area of the country producing its own color and style of carpet. Hobbies also include woodcarving, stone carving, metal work, and glassblowing.[98]

Bahrain

A small country covering only 665 square miles, and with a population of little more than 675,000, the country of Bahrain is noted for its scrabble league. With a list of champions dating back to 1987, the citizens of this country have clearly taken their involvement with Scrabble seriously for nearly two decades.[99] Weekly tournaments take place at Yateem Centre, where the 2005 Bahrain Cup was held. That year, the Bahrain Cup pitted an accountant against a car air-conditioning foreman against each other, with the accountant, Ozzie Fernandes, proving victorious.[100] Scrabble is taken so seriously in Bahrain that a "Scrabble tournament among top-level executives—billed as the Clash of the Titans—has been proposed in the current season." The tournament was proposed for 2006 and offered top-level executives the chance to square off against each other over a Scrabble board.[101]

Bahrain is also known for its Brains in Bahrain tournament held in 2002, in which Russian chess champion Vladimir Kramnik matched wits against the computer Deep Fritz. The tournament ended in a 4 to 4 tie. Kramnik and Fritz played a six-game rematch in November 2006 in Germany; the computer edged Kramnik 4–2.[102]

In 2005 Bahrain hosted the International Children's Games in the city of Manama. The games, first started by Slovenian sports instructor Metod Klemenc in 1968, are a way to foster friendship and an understanding of culture through children's games and sports. Events include swimming, table tennis, tennis, handball, running, Judo, basketball, volleyball, cycling, and more.[103]

Card games also enjoy popularity in Bahrain. Games such as teka and fis kut, which are plain trick games; betrinu, a three-card vying game; and chor voli are the most popular.[104]

With approximately 200,000 Internet users, Bahrain is not the leading computer or gaming country in the Middle East, but its citizens do participate to a small degree in the Electronic Sports World Cup. Unlike other participating countries that have preliminary tournaments for various games, however, Bahrain only has a preliminary competition for Pro Evolution Soccer 5.[105]

Saudi Arabia

Bordering the Persian Gulf and the Red Sea, Saudi Arabia has a strong Arab and Muslim population, resulting in strict codes for behavior and dress. Theater and the public cinema do not exist, isolating Saudi Arabian children from many Western trends and fads in dress, music, and in the toy and game industry.[106] Foreign games and toys that do make their presence known in Saudi Arabia may not have staying power, as was the case with Pokemon. Created in 1986 by the Japanese company Satoshi Tajiri, Pokemon was banned by the mufti, "the highest religious authority in the conservative Muslim state," because it was thought to promote Zionism, and because it constituted gambling.[108] "The kingdom's senior cleric, Sheikh Abdul Aziz bin Abdullah, protested that most of the cards figure symbols such as crosses, sacred for Christians and triangles, significant for Freemasons."[109] Another toy that is sometimes restricted, especially during the Christian celebration of Christmas, is the American Barbie doll. Religious police from the Authority for Promotion of Virtue and Prevention of Vice banned Barbies from toy store shelves in December of 2004 to quell corrupting Western influences related to the Christian holiday.[110]

Even with the lack of public cinema and the banning of certain toys and games, Saudi Arabian children are still likely to play with some American toys. There are four Toys R Us stores in Saudi Arabia. The stores are located in the central region of Riyadh, the

> **CELL PHONES**
>
> It is the custom in Saudi Arabia for groups of teenagers to be segregated based on gender. Typically, teenage boys will hang out together, and teenage girls will also hang out together, but the two groups rarely mix. The increasing prevalence of cell phones, however, is changing the dynamic of this gender-based segregation. While the teenagers are not socializing with each other in a formal way, Middle Eastern teenagers do socialize with members of the opposite sex, using their phones as private vehicles for communication. Text messaging has become a huge part of the teen culture. Secretly sending text messages to members of the opposite sex allows for interaction while still upholding the social norm of gender segregation.
>
> Cell phone games are not as prevalent in the Middle East as they are in the United States, or in Japan, the pioneer of the cell phone gaming industry; as more cell phone companies expand into the region, cell phone games are sure to catch on as well. In addition to being popular with teenagers, cell phones are also quite popular with the adult population. They have become such a part of the culture that they are now a normal part of the Saudi wardrobe: "The cell phone has joined the headscarf, the gold-trimmed gossamer robe, the be-jeweled dagger, the dyed goatee and the AK47 as the fashion accessory of choice."[107]

western region of Jeddah 1, the western region of Jeddah 2, and the eastern region of Dhahran.

Saudi Arabia is also a participant in the Electronic Sports World Cup. With an estimated 1.5 million Internet users out of a population of more than 26 million, it is fair to say that the computer and electronic gaming industry is most likely still in its infancy; an increase would be expected as the Internet becomes more accessible throughout the population. Past preliminary tournaments in the country indicate the popularity of Counter-Strike, Warcraft III, Gran Turismo, and Pro Evolution Soccer 5.[111]

In addition to contemporary toys and games, traditional games are still played in Saudi Arabia as well. One game, called the hunter, is similar to American game of hide and seek. In a group of children, one becomes the hunter. The hunter counts from one to ten, while the others run and hide. When the hunter has reached ten, he or she hunts for the other players and tags them once found. Each player must be tagged before the game starts again. If all players are tagged, then the first one tagged becomes the hunter. If the hunter can't tag each player, he or she calls out "clear," and the game begins again.[112]

Another game, kaab, was originally played with the knee bones of sheep. In this game, players gather ten knee bones each. The players then draw a line in the dirt approximately six feet away. Each player places his or her bones on the line. The object is to throw a bone and knock the other players' bones from the line. If a bone is thrown and does not knock a bone from the line, it is kept as a target. A bone that is knocked from the line becomes the property of the player who knocked it away. The person with the most bones wins.[113]

RESOURCE GUIDE

PRINT SOURCES

Braman, Arlette. *Kids around the World Play! The Best Fun and Games from Many Lands.* San Francisco: Jossey-Bass, 2002.

Dunn, Opal. *Acker Backa Boo! Games to Say and Play from around the World.* London: Francis Lincoln Publishing, 2006. This book offers a myriad of games categorized by type, including hand and feet mover games, ball games, and hide and seek games.

Erlback, Arlene. *Sidewalk Games around the World.* Michigan: Milbrook Press, 1998. This book offers sidewalk games played by children around the world. It includes information on Iran and also categorizes games by continent.

Fernea, Elizabeth Warnock. *Children in the Muslim Middle East.* Austin: University of Texas Press, 1995.

Icon Group International. *The 2000 Import and Export Market for Baby Carriages, Toys, Games and Sporting Goods in the Middle East.* San Diego: Icon Group International, 2000. This market report provides insight into various aspects of cultural trends related to toys and games in the Middle East.

———. *The 2000–2005 Outlook for Dolls, Toys, and Games in the Middle East.* San Diego: Icon Group International, 2000. This market report provides insight into various dolls, toys, and games in the current culture of the Middle East.

———. *The 2000–2005 Outlook for Traditional Toys in the Middle East.* San Diego: Icon Group International, 2000. This market report provides insight into various aspects of traditional toys in the Middle East. This report offers a perspective on traditional games that are still culturally accessible.

International Business Publications USA. *Israel Consumer Goods Export-Import Directory: Arts & Crafts, Footwear, Furniture, Cosmetics, Toys.* NP: International Business Publications USA, 2002. This is a business publication that provides Israel's consumer goods export and import directory.

Mohr, Merilyn Simonds. *The New Games Treasury: More Than 500 Indoor and Outdoor Favorites with Strategies, Rules, and Traditions.* Boston: Houghton Mifflin Company, 1997.

Oakley, Ruth. *Games with Sticks, Stones and Shells: Games Children Play around the World.* London: Marshall Cavendish, 1989.

Rossie, Jean-Pierre. *Saharan and North African Toy and Play Cultures: The Animal in Play, Games and Toys.* Stockholm: Stockholm International Toy Research Center, 2003. Rossie is a noted scholar on the toy and play culture of North Africa.

Sierra, Judy, and Robert Kaminski. *Children's Traditional Games: Games from 137 Countries and Cultures.* Westport, CT: Oryx Press, 1995. This book includes traditional games from Algeria and a host of other countries. This is a good resource for information about traditional games that have survived to the present.

Uche, Greg. *African Folktales: Exotic Stories from Africa for Children around the World.* Bloomington, IN: Authorhouse, 2006.

Zaslavsky, Claudia. *Math Games & Activities from around the World.* Chicago: Chicago Review Press, 1998.

WEBSITES

Arab Children Friends Association. http://www.palestine-child.org/.
The Arab Children Friends Association is dedicated to the children of Israel.

Brewer, Douglas and Emily Teeter. *Ancient Egyptian Society and Family Life.* 2001. Fathom Library University of Chicago. November 12, 2005. http://fathom.lib.uchicago.edu/2/21701778/. This site offers information regarding ancient Egyptian society and family life.

Casino City. January 17, 2005. http://www.casinocity.com/. This Website contains rules for casino games from all over the world.

Chess Drum. December 5, 2005. http://www.thechessdrum.net. The Chess Drum is a wonderful reference for chess teams from North Africa and the Middle East.

Dara and Sara. July 27, 2003. KanoonParvaresh. November 17, 2005. http://darasara.kanoonparvaresh.com/. An understanding of Dara and Sara, the Middle East's answer to Barbie and Ken, is extremely important to an understanding of the toy and play culture of the Middle East.

Electronic Sports World Cup. 2006. Games Services Inc. January 18, 2005. http://www.esworldcup.com/2006/?act=preliminary&id_preliminary=SA. This site offers the statistics for various countries that partake in the Electronic Sports World Cup.

Gameclub.com. 2002. Fogware Publishing. January 17, 2006. http://www.game-club.com/index.htm. This site offers a searchable index to game rules from all over the world.

McLeod, John. *Card Games.* December 30, 2001. Card Games. December 4, 2005. http://www.pagat.com/index.html. This site offers information about a myriad of card games from all over the world. The Middle East is certainly represented here.

Toy Trade Fair. February 3, 2006. Libyaonline. http://www.sakerexpo.org/toy/index.htm. This Website offers information on the current Toy Trade Fair in Libya.

NOTES

1. See Andre Dollinger, "Play: Children's Games," December 2003, *Ancient Egyptian Games*, January 22, 2006, http://nefertiti.iwebland.com/timelines/topics/games.htm.
2. See *The Petrie Museum of Egyptian Archaeology*, Petrie Museum, University College London, January 20, 2006, http://www.petrie.ucl.ac.uk/index2.html.
3. See "Ancient Egyptian Sport," 2005, *Egypt State Information Service*, January 22, 2006, http://www.sis.gov.eg/En/Society/Sport/Ancient/090701000000000001.htm.
4. See "Galimoto-Wire Toys," *Sanjuan Education*, January 15, 2006, http://www.sanjuan.edu/schools/barrett/stiles/4.07.htm.
5. See *Mancala*, 2002, Fogware Publishing, January 8, 2006, http://www.game-club.com/cover1/mankrule.htm.

6. See Andy Rabagliati, *Owari Bead Game*, WZI Consulting, January 28, 2006, http://wizzy.com/owari/#Rules.
7. See "Corporate Strategies in Global Toys & Games," June 2005, *Purdue University*, February 1, 2006, http://www2.lib.purdue.edu:2286/mrm/default.asp.
8. See "Algeria to Launch First Ever Children's TV Channel," *Asia Africa Intelligence Wire*, February 17, 2005.
9. Ibid.
10. See "Keep Active with Sport in Algeria," January 2006, *Algeria.com: Information and Destination Guide*, January 18, 2006, http://www.algeria.com/sport/.
11. See Reetha Parthiban, *Sports and Recreation*, Algeria Cultural Profiles Project, December 5, 2005, http://www.cp-pc.ca/english/algeria/sports.html.
12. McLeod (in Resource Guide). For Algeria see http://www.pagat.com/national/algeria.html.
13. *Chess Drum* (in Resource Guide). For Algeria, January 18, 2006, see http://www.thechessdrum.net/Olympiad2002/Algeria.html.
14. McLeod (in Resource Guide). For Algeria, see http://www.pagat.com/national/algeria.html.
15. See "Algeria," June 6, 2006, *World Factbook*, June 6, 2006, http://www.odci.gov/cia/publications/factbook/geos/ag.html#People.
16. See "Land Casinos Morocco," *Gambling Guide: Il Dado*, January 18, 2006, http://www.ildado.com/land_casinos_morocco.html.
17. See Houssa Yakobi, *Card Games in Morocco*, August 11, 2003, National and Regional Card Games Index, December 18, 2005, http://www.pagat.com/national/morocco.html.
18. *Chess Drum* (in Resource Guide). For Morocco, December 18, 2005, see http://www.thechessdrum.net/tournaments/Olympiad2004/Morocco.html.
19. See "Maxitoys Catalogue," January 2006, *Maxitoys Toy Company*, January 28, 2006, http://www.maxitoys.be/home.php?lg=fr&p=BE.
20. See "Play and Folklore," July 2003, *Museum Victoria*, December 14, 2005, http://www.museum.vic.gov.au/playfolklore/pdf/playfolklore_july03_2.pdf.
21. *Tunisia Online*, December 2005, Tunisian Ministry of Economic Development, November 23, 2005, http://www.tunisiaonline.com/society/index.html.
22. See Jean-Pierre Rossie, *Toy Play Culture and Society: An Anthropological Approach with Reference to North Africa and the Sahara*, 2003, Stockholm International Toy Research Center, November 12, 2005, http://filarkiv.sitrec.kth.se/pub2003/tpcands2003/Index.html.
23. Ibid.
24. Ibid.
25. Fernea 1995 (in Resource Guide), p. 448.
26. Ibid.
27. Ibid., pp. 451–452.
28. Rossie 2003 (in Resource Guide), pp. 27–28.
29. Ibid.
30. *Chess Drum* (in Resource Guide). For Tunisia, December 5, 2005, see http://www.thechessdrum.net/Olympiad2002/Tunisia.html.
31. McLeod (in Resource Guide). For Tunisia, December 5, 2005, see http://www.pagat.com/national/tunisia.html.
32. Ibid.
33. *Toy Trade Fair* (in Resource Guide).
34. Ibid.
35. Ibid.
36. See Reetha Parthiban, *Sports and Recreation*, Algeria Cultural Profiles Project, December 5, 2005, http://www.cp-pc.ca/english/libya/sports.html.
37. See Teri Khadja, *Shkouba*, February 4, 2006, http://www.khadijateri.com/shkouba.html.
38. Ibid.
39. *Chess Drum* (in Resource Guide). For Libya, January 16, 2006, see http://www.thechessdrum.net/Olympiad2002/Libya.html.

40. Ibid.
41. See Douglas Brewer, and Emily Teeter, *Ancient Egyptian Society and Family Life*, 2001, Fathom Library University of Chicago, November 12, 2005, http://fathom.lib.uchicago.edu/2/21701778/.
42. See Andre Dollinger, "Play: Children's Games," December 2004, Ancient Egyptian Games, January 22, 2006, http://nefertiti.iwebland.com/timelines/topics/games.htm.
43. See Catherine Soubeyrand, "The Game of Senet," October 2000, *Game Cabinet*, December 17, 2005, http://www.gamecabinet.com/history/Senet.html.
44. Ibid.
45. See Bonnie McMeans, "Toys and Games (Ancient Egypt)," *Appleseed* 1 (Feb 1999): 16.
46. Ibid.
47. See *Camel Boy's Game*, Eureka Project, December 22, 2005, http://www.website1.com/odyssey/week9/NewsFlash03.html.
48. Ibid.
49. Ibid.
50. Fernea 1995 (in Resource Guide).
51. Ibid.
52. Ibid., p. 429.
53. Ibid., p. 430.
54. *Casino City* (in Resource Guide). See "Rules of Roulette," January 17, 2005, http://casinocity.com/rule/roulette.htm.
55. Ibid.
56. Ibid.
57. Ibid.
58. See "Punto Banco: How to Play," *Good Gambling Guide*, February 7, 2006, http://www.thegoodgamblingguide.co.uk/casino/puntobancohowtoplay.htm.
59. See Joyce Carta, "Food," *Tour Egypt*, January 17, 2005, http://www.touregypt.net/featurestories/food.htm.
60. *Chess Drum* (in Resource Guide). For Egypt, December 5, 2005, see http://www.thechessdrum.net/Olympiad2002/Egypt.html.
61. See *About the Electronic Sports World Cup 2006*, Game Services, February 7, 2006, http://www.esworldcup.com/2006/?act=about.
62. See Catherine Harris, "Children in Modern Egypt," September 27, 2005, *Tour Egypt*, January 17, 2005, http://www.touregypt.net/featurestories/children.htm.
63. See "Amman Declaration on the Use of Children as Soldiers," 2005, *Human Rights Internet*, November 11, 2005, http://www.hri.ca/children/reports/amman2001.shtml.
64. McLeod (in Resource Guide). For Jordan see http://www.pagat.com/national/jordan.html.
65. See "Jordan," 2002, *Arab Net*, November 11, 2005, http://www.arab.net/jordan/jn_embroidery.htm.
66. *Arab Children Friends Association* (in Resource Guide).
67. For Arab Children Friends Association publications, see Ibid., January 17, 2005, http://www.palestine-child.org/publications.shtml.
68. Ibid.
69. See *Toys R Us*, January 17, 2005, http://www.toysrus.com/our/intl/intlAsia.cfm.
70. See *Zara Mart*, January 17, 2005, http://www.a-zara.com/pe-Children-89-8906-2840.htm.
71. See Ibid., http://www.a-zara.com/pe-Children+Gifts+-89-8905-2828.htm.
72. See *Israel: Electronic Sports World Cup*, 2006, Games Services, January 18, 2005, http://www.esworldcup.com/2006/?act=preliminary&id_preliminary=IL.
73. McLeod (in Resource Guide). For Israeli whist, see http://www.pagat.com/exact/israeli_whist.html.
74. Ibid.
75. Mohammed Omer, "Give Up or . . . ! The Games Gaza's Children Play," January 2006, *Washington Report on Middle East Affairs*, February 11, 2006, http://www.wrmea.com/archives/Jan_Feb_2006/0601024.html.

76. Ibid.
77. Ibid.
78. Ibid.
79. See Sami Abu Salem, "UNICEF Brings Volleyball to Children in the Gaza Strip," August 2004, *UNICEF*, February 11, 2006, http://www.unicef.org/oPt/voices_children_806.html.
80. See "The Toy Library Project," 2006, *United Nations Relief and Works Agency for Palestine Refugees in the Near East*, February 11, 2006, http://www.un.org/unrwa/emergency/toys/index.html.
81. See "Brotherhood Summer Camp," *Arab Children Friends Association*, December 17, 2005, http://www.palestine-child.org/brotherhood.shtml.
82. See James Joyner, "Dancing Doll Ridicules Saddam," June 30, 2004, *Outside the Beltway*, January 18, 2006, http://www.outsidethebeltway.com/archives/6666.
83. Ibid.
84. See *Alaska Business Monthly* 22 (January 2006): 36(1).
85. See "Baghdad Economy Perks Up as Incomes, Currency Rise," January 24, 2004, *Arabnews*, January 17, 2006, http://www.arabnews.com/services/print/print.asp?artid=38509&d=24&m=1&y=2004&hl=Baghdad+Economy+Perks+Up+as+Incomes%2C+Currency+Rise.
86. James Hider, and Ali Hamdani, "Ethnic Rifts that Colour the Games Little Children Play," October 4, 2005, *Timesonline*, November 17, 2005, http://www.timesonline.co.uk/article/0,,7374-1809880,00.html.
87. See "Dara and Sara—Iran's Islamic alternative to Ken and Barbie," *Islam for Today*, December 17, 2005, http://www.islamfortoday.com/iran02.htm.
88. Ibid.
89. *Dara and Sara* (in Resource Guide).
90. Ibid.
91. McLeod (in Resource Guide). For Iran, see http://www.pagat.com/national/iran.html.
92. Ibid.
93. Ibid.
94. See *Iran Chess*, Chess Federation of Islamic Republic of Iran, February 12, 2006, http://www.iranchess.ir/indexen.htm.
95. See *A Short History of Polo*, Ascot Park Polo Club, February 11, 2006, http://www.polo.co.uk/polo_history.htm.
96. See Nader S. Hasawi, "Traditional Games," 2005, *Davan Information*, November 17, 2005, http://davan.info/davan/games/games.php.
97. Ibid.
98. See *Salam Iran*, October 22, 2003, Embassy of the Islamic Republic of Iran, Ottawa, Canada, February 9, 2005, http://www.salamiran.org/CT/Tourism/travelinfo/practical_info.html.
99. See *Bahrain Scrabble League*, 2006, January 29, 2005, http://mywebpage.netscape.com/bahrainscrabble/main.html
100. Ibid.
101. Ibid.
102. See "Deep Fritz," January 17, 2005, *Wikipedia*, http://en.wikipedia.org/wiki/Deep_Fritz.
103. See "International Children's Games," *Committee of the International Children's Games*, January 17, 2005, http://www.webicg.org/index.html.
104. McLeod (in Resource Guide). For Afghanistan, see http://www.pagat.com/national/afghanistan.html.
105. See *Bahrain: Electronic Sports World Cup*, 2006, Games Services, January 18, 2005, http://www.esworldcup.com/2006/?act=preliminary&id_preliminary=BH.
106. See "Saudi Arabia," 2006, *Travel Document Systems*, November 4, 2005, http://www.traveldocs.com/sa/culture.htm.
107. See Mark Phillips, "Saudi Social Norms: Buy or Cell," August 7, 2005, *CBS News*, February 11, 2006, http://www.cbsnews.com/stories/2005/08/05/listening_post/main763196.shtml.
108. See "Saudi Arabia Bans Pokeman," March 26, 2001, *BBC News*, November 4, 2005, http://news.bbc.co.uk/1/hi/world/middle_east/1243307.stm.
109. Ibid.

GAMES, TOYS, AND PASTIMES

110. Paul Martin, "Religious Police Take after Barbie," *Washington Times*, January 3, 2004, http://washingtontimes.com/world/20040102-112738-9433r.htm.
111. See *Saudi Arabia: Electronic Sports World Cup*, 2006, Games Services, January 18, 2005, http://www.esworldcup.com/2006/?act=preliminary&id_preliminary=SA.
112. See "Traditional Children's Games," *Topics: The Online Magazine for Learners of English*, November 11, 2005, http://www.topics-mag.com/edition11/games-tag.htm.
113. See "Scouts Guide," February 1, 2001, *United States Scouts*, February 12, 2006, http://www.usscouts.org/macscouter/CubScouts/PowWow01/Feb01.pdf#search='bivoe%20ebuma'.

LITERATURE

KATHRYN KNIGHT

In discussing the two regions covered in the following pages, the term "North Africa" (or the *Maghreb*) should be understood to encompass Tunisia, Algeria, Morocco, and Libya. The term "Middle East" refers to all Arab states (Bahrain, Egypt, Iraq, Jordan, Kuwait, Lebanon, Oman, the Palestinian Territories, Saudi Arabia, Syria, Qatar, Yemen, and the United Arab Emirates); Iran; and Israel. The following text begins with a discussion of Arabic popular poetry and prose, followed by a closer look at the literature of each Arab state or country, including many important authors and forms that are unique to those regions. When possible, novel and story titles will be given in English first, followed by the transliterated Arabic name in parentheses.

ARAB STATES: FROM CLASSICAL TO MODERN

Until Napoleon Bonaparte and his army of more than 30,000 men marched into Egypt in July 1798, the Middle East had remained largely isolated from the West; so most classic Arabic literature—all literature written in this area through the early nineteenth century—although rich and varied, was mostly untouched by Western influence. This classical literary period progressed in rather linear fashion, whereas the renaissance, or *al-nahdah,* has a more amorphous quality in regard to its development. One image that may be employed when thinking of the body of Arabic literature is that of an enormous tree. The classical period makes up the tree's trunk: linear, broad, and substantial. Writing that emerged at the onset of al-nahdah and beyond forms the tree's branches and leaves: connected to the past but often wildly different; sometimes springing from or overlapping with other narrative techniques, sometimes moving in a different direction altogether.

As with all cultures, for Arabs the mythical tale was the first fictional form, serving as an explanation for natural phenomena and human experience. In addition, heroic legends and love stories were abundant, both of which were often sung by itinerant bards. The former served to detail great battles, tribal vendettas, and heroism, while the latter, in either chaste or vulgar detail, often had well-known poets as protagonists, many of whom were very popular

LITERATURE

and prolific during the Umayyad period (661–750 CE). Both forms have endured throughout the ages and remain a permanent part of the Arabian cultural canon. Beginning with the Abbasid period (750–1256 CE), the form of the short narrative or "factual anecdote" (*al-khabar*) emerged as an established and distinctively Arabic fictional style; it would grow to become a major narrative technique for Arabic writers. The primary reason for the formation of this style is that Islam forbids dishonesty and deceit, so Muslim authors felt that the overt creation of fiction was not permissible. To work around this, storytellers would narrate a tale that was at least marginally based in truth, but heavily and creatively embellished. Because of this mixture of fact and fiction, both the history and social life of the Abbasids were indirectly documented via these semi-true anecdotes. The Abbasid period also produced, in addition to the al-khabar, one of the earliest collections of fables, *Kalila wa Dimna*. The Persia-born writer Ibn al-Muqaffa used a Persian version of this Indian text to produce an Arabic translation. The immense popularity of the new version was widely admired for al-Muqaffa's simple, pithy language. Many of the fables in *Kalila wa Dimna* resurface in other classical Arabic works, including the famous *Arabian Nights*.

Another literary form that took shape during the Abbasid period was the trickster tale, called *al-maqamat*, or "assemblies." These humorous, uniquely Arabic stories, usually describing the travels of some roguish character, both formally acknowledged the lower and middle Arab classes and served as social criticism: the protagonists and supporting characters were drawn directly from all classes of Abbasid society. Although the poet al-Hamadhani (d. 1008) is credited with inventing this genre, al-Hariri (1054–1122) used the maqamat to play with language, frequently with impressive results. For example, one of his creations manages to use only letters of the Arabic alphabet that have no dots. This literary endeavor is referred to in English as a lipogram, a work that deliberately excludes one or more letters of the alphabet. (One such example from Western literature is Ernest Vincent Wright's *Gadsby*, a novel of more than 50,000 words, none of which contains or requires the letter "e"). Al-Hariri's maqamat are regarded by many as the greatest written creations in Arabic, next to the Qur'an.

The epistle genre emerged in the eleventh century as a distinct literary form with the publication of *The Epistle of Forgiveness*. Written by the famous blind poet Abu l-Ala al-Maarri (973–1057), this story traces a writer's journey to both heaven and hell, during which he converses with many poets, linguists, and literary figures. (Some scholars believe that this work influenced Dante's *Divine Comedy*.) In the century that followed, the Andalusian philosopher Ibn Tufail (1100–85) wrote the very famous philosophical novel *Living Son of the Vigilant* (*Hayy ibu Yaqzan*), which tells the story of a man spontaneously born from mud and raised on an uninhabited island by a gazelle.

Arguably the most famous Arabic literary work (certainly the work best known to Western readers) is *The Arabian Nights*, which has only recently gained status as an extremely important work in the Arab canon of literature. Scholars believe that this collection of stories was derived from several sources, one of which most likely originated in Sasanian Iran under the title "A Thousand and One Nights" (*Hezar afsan*); this was also the title of the first Arabic translation (*Alf laylah wa-laylah*). The tales in the collection are derived from Indian, Persian, and Arabic folklore; scholars estimate that the compilation that modern readers are familiar with was compiled in the early 1500s. Some stories may be derived from (or perhaps are close narratives of) sailor stories and songs, as concluded from the similarity of certain motifs in both *The Arabian Nights* and some Western texts. For example, in *Natural History*, Greek author Pliny (23–79 CE) writes about a "magnetic mountain," an image that also appears in *The Arabian Nights*' "Story of the Third Calendar."

Near the end of the eighteenth century, most of the Arab world was part of the Ottoman Empire, under the Turkish rule of the Mameluke Beys. Although the Mameluke regime was violent, its rulers as well as their subjects were all Muslims. Master and servant were both part of the Islamic Community of Believers, or *Ummah*. Furthermore, the vicious Mameluke regime, made up entirely of Muslims, was also a defender of *Sharia*, the sacred law of Islam, making the regime accepted as sovereign in spite of how it came to power. The Ottoman rulers and their Arab subjects held common views on social and religious beliefs, so little was done by Arabs to resist or run from the Turkish regime. Consequently, until Bonaparte's army marched into Egypt in 1798, most of the Arab world had successfully avoided contact with the West and lived in cultural isolation.

The three-year French occupation of Egypt changed the Arab world forever. The West was no longer isolated from this area, and so began the process of expansion and colonization of the Middle East and North Africa, particularly by France, Britain, and Italy. Political changes were not the only ones to occur: cultural and social change began as well. Napoleon and his army brought with them (from the Vatican) the first Arabic-language printing press, enabling the French occupiers' proclamations to be issued in Arabic. Also the *Institut d'Egypte* was founded, giving the scholars and scientists who followed Bonaparte into Egypt a place to conduct scientific experiments.

Prior to the publication and distribution of Arabic translations of Western novels and short stories in the early twentieth century, the novel as a literary form was unknown to this part of the world. The first novels translated into Arabic and distributed in the Arab world were Victor Hugo's *Les Miserables*, Goethe's *The Sorrows of Young Werther*, Alphonse Karr's *Sous les Tilleuls*, and Bernardin de Saint-Pierre's *Paul et Virgine*. In addition, plays like *Cyrano de Bergerac* by Edmond Rostand and *Pour la Couronne* by François Coppée gained enormous popularity in the 1920s, which endured for generations. Although the popularity of Western fiction was criticized by some as being potentially dangerous to Islamic and Arab moral and cultural values, many also criticized their own classical literature (notably *The Arabian Nights*) for lacking true representation of reality. In spite of reservations regarding Western culture, Arab writers experimented with both the short story and novel. Initial efforts focused primarily on the short story genre, which eventually became the genre most respected and utilized by Arab authors.

In particular, Egypt produced the bulk of early modern Arabic fiction, with such prominent Egyptian writers as Mahmoud Taymur leading the way. Although the basic form of short fiction had been present in Arab culture for twelve centuries, the modern form of the short story as rendered by Western writers seemed very new, particularly because political turmoil and ineffective, uninspiring leadership within the Arab world had distanced eighteenth- and nineteenth-century Arabs from their literary heritage. Furthermore, their extreme and contented cultural isolation from the West kept the development of the short story and novel in Europe and America a relative secret. Yet by the mid-twentieth century, the short story had become the most popular fictional genre in the Arab literary world. Not until the 1970s did the novel take the place of the short story as the major literary fiction form, although many accomplished and highly respected novelists were being published and read before this time. The first real attempt at the modern novel by an Arab author was *Zaynab* (1914), written by Muhammad Husain Haykal. This book received more attention from literary critics than any other piece of fiction by an Arab author until Naguib Mahfouz began writing.

Poetry has presented a different sort of predicament for modern authors. By the nineteenth century, Arabic poetry, like other Arabic literary forms, had suffered under the Turkish rule that controlled almost the entire Middle East. The censorial Mameluke regime stifled artistic creativity, and there was little effort by writers to break free of the dull conventions of their poetry. Prior to this, Arabic verse had been rich and highly aesthetic, and was the most revered art form in the Middle East.

Literature

In addition to the maqamat style of poetry already described, another popular style was used in the collection of poems known as the Hanged Poems (*muallaqat*). The name may be descriptive of the way the poems were once displayed (hung on walls), although the origin of the name has been much debated and may be unlikely. Seven poems make up the muallaqat, all written in the very long *qasida* style, which predates Islam. These poems were compiled, probably in the eighth century, by scholar and poet Hammad ar-Rawiya, and represent both the merits and shortcomings of Bedouin Arabic poetry. Most scholars agree that the poets responsible for these works are Labid, Harith ibn Hilliza, Amr ibn Kulthum, Imru al-Qais, Antara Ibn Shaddad, Tarafa, and Zuhayr. Other notable poets from the Arabic classical period are Farazdaq, Tarafah ibn al-Abd, al-Shanfara, Abu Nuwas, Al-Nabigha, and Bashar ibn Burd.

After Islam emerged in 622 CE, the old style of poetry gradually fell from favor. The new Islamic dogma was antithetical to the pre-Islamic poetic embrace of gambling, sex, and the imbibing of alcohol. Sufism, a mystical religion derived from Islam, produced several notable poets, among the most outstanding of whom are Rabiah al-Adawiyya, Abd Yazid al-Bistami, and Mansur all-Hallaj. One of the most popular poets to emerge from this period is the Persian poet Movlana Jalaluddin Rumi. He was not only a Sufist poet but also a theologian, jurist, and teacher, and the founder of the Mevlevi order of Sufists (known as the Whirling Dervishes). Rumi's most significant work, the *Spiritual Couplets* (*Masnavi-ye Manavi*), was highly influential among both Turkish and Persian poets. Some consider the *Spiritual Couplets* to be nearly as important to Islamic literature as the Qur'an.

In 1801 Napoleon was driven out of Egypt, and in 1805 Muhammad Ali Pasha became Egypt's leader. Under his rule, newspapers, translations, and schools flourished. Egypt experienced a general cultural awakening, and the new printing press introduced by Napoleon made collections of classical Arabic poetry available. Books became inexpensive and available to all who could read them, so Middle Eastern readers were able to reacquaint themselves with their literary heritage, and Arabic poets began writing again.

The first wave of modern Arabic poets was called the neoclassical group. Poets such as Ahmad Shauqi wrote in a style similar to the classical style, although with variations in approach, imagery, and tone. The *qasida* style, a classical rhetoric characterized by an oratorical tone, was often utilized. Like the neoclassical poets in the West, Arabic neoclassical poets wrote about an orderly, easily understood world governed by reason and logic. Nationalism was among the most common themes for the neoclassical poets.

The poet to break from this style of poetry and move toward a kind of Arabic romanticism (albeit a romanticism that lacked the philosophical basis of the West's) was Kahlil Gibran, born in Lebanon in 1883. His style, although closer to prose than to verse poetry, introduced innovative uses for images that had never been seen in Arabic writing. Gibran's writing has an unmistakable character: his use of repetition, vocative voice, interrogatives, and emotional imagery all work together to create his distinctive poetic voice, characterized by the persistent theme that love is redemptive in all ways. By the 1920s, romanticism had become the major Arabic poetic trend.

The next major movement in Arabic poetry was symbolism, which rejected both the extreme rationality of neoclassicism and the lyrical sentimentality of romanticism. Symbolism retained traces of romanticism's tendency to idealize beauty. The poet most responsible for the growth of symbolist poetry was Sa'id Aql. His style carries unmistakable traces of the influence of French poets Paul Valéry and Stéphane Mallarmé, who frequently evoked sensorial experience to embody the ineffable. However, the political upheavals of 1948 abruptly ended the symbolist sensibility, which had been the catalyst for the most extreme change in Arabic poetry.

In the 1950s avant-garde poets, writing in the wake of the defeat of Palestine, chose to move away from the ideas of "Beauty" and the "Ideal," and instead wrote about everyday experience, spiritual confusion, and the general existential problems faced by most of the Arabs living in the twentieth-century Middle East. Yusuf al-Khal was one of the major advocates of this new kind of poetry; he even coined the phrase *al-shi'r al-hadith* (modern poetry) for the Arab world. Al-Khal held radical political and aesthetic opinions and advocated challenging all conventions in language, rhythm, imagery, and experience. Although some poets embraced and benefited from his advice, others felt that al-Khal was attacking classical Arabic literature. In the wake of the 1948 war, it was difficult for many to endure any further attack on Arab culture, even a merely literary one. Al-Khal began publishing *Shi'r*, a poetry quarterly, in 1957. Many disliked the publication—for the same reasons they disliked the poet—and the magazine eventually ceased publication in 1964. Even so, it was the first of a series of avant-garde poetry publications that helped change the perception, tastes, and styles of both Arabic readers and poets.

Western influence, especially the modernist poets', was also of great importance in changing Arabic poetry. In particular, T. S. Eliot's *The Wasteland* and Frazer's *The Golden Bough* inspired modern poets to draw on their mythological and archetypal heritage, particularly on myths and legends dealing with death and fertility. Poetic language and imagery also changed under the use of modernist poets. Phrasing and rhythm were often reduced to an unadorned, sometimes colloquial structure. Experimentation with metaphor was rampant, sometimes with lackluster consequences. One of the more famous poets to write in decidedly metaphorical style was Mahmoud Darwish, whose writing was greatly influenced by the 1948 war.

As daily life in Arab cultures became as modern as the literature, modernist Arabic poetry began to address the theme of the city. Sometimes forbidding and problematic, sometimes bustling with life, sophistication, and independence, the city and urban themes became staples of late twentieth-century Arabic poetry. One of the most interesting uses of the image of the city was made by Palestinian poets. Weighed with tremendous loss and made rootless, they used the image of the Palestinian city to emblemize alternately the victim, the hero, and resistance.

WHAT DO PEOPLE IN THE MIDDLE EAST AND NORTH AFRICA *REALLY* READ?

It is difficult to identify the most popular literature, or best-selling books, in the Middle East and North Africa. Part of the difficulty is with the enterprise of publishing. Much of the book production in this part of the world is government controlled, and Arab authors are frequently censored when they attempt to publish a book in an Arab country. The appearance of just one word or phrase may be enough to keep an entire book of poetry, short stories, or a novel from being published at all. This situation does not exist in every Arab or Maghrebi country, but censorship is still a significant enough problem to pose definite difficulty for authors and readers. Censored books may be published in secret or may be imported and distributed surreptitiously. Copyright laws are not stringent, and pirated books are common. Official publishing statistics, if available, are generally grim: the Arab Human Development Report indicates that even in Egypt, a country that hosts an internationally renowned book fair, roughly twenty-one titles were published for every million people in the late 1990s. To find out what Arab readers are actually reading versus what they are supposedly reading (or if there is a discrepancy at all) is not a simple task.

Literature

The United Nations Educational, Scientific, and Cultural Organization (UNESCO) reported in 1991 that only 1.1 percent of the world's published books come from Arab countries. This often-quoted statistic has recently been used to illustrate the current state of Arab publishing (and implicitly, to illustrate Arab reading habits), even though the information is fifteen years old and was collected during the first Gulf War. Additionally, this same report claims that the books published in Arab countries are overwhelmingly religious (15 percent of the total published). Although this may be accurate in one sense, the word *religious* tends to be used pejoratively, without clearly indicating what makes a book religious—that is, this category encompasses books related to religious debate and criticism, self-help or "feel-good" books, politics, sociology, and so forth. The 2003 Arab Human Development Report also cites these outdated statistics, but confirms the lack of reliable data regarding book publication and readership.

Publishing regulated in nearly all Arab countries, and solid statistics are difficult to gather. The United Nations Development Program did state that in 2005, the Arab country that published the most books was Bahrain, where 132 books were published, 30 of them works of literature (and only 10 deemed to be religious). By comparison, the Deputy Minister of Culture and Islamic Guidance for Cultural Affairs reported that in Iran, 200 million books were published in 2005. In fact, reading and publishing have steadily increased in Iran, and Iranian reading patterns are reported to be somewhat similar to the habits of their Arab neighbors (with Iranian readers reportedly being particularly fond of love stories, poetry, and Harry Potter, in addition to being readers of books on politics).

For Arab publishers, publishing itself is not very profitable, with generally fewer than 3,000 print runs of an individual book title; however, Arab readers are often literate in at least one Western language (such as French and English) and may choose to read a book in its original language rather than in Arab translation. According to a statistic provided by the Frankfurt Book Fair, Arab countries import close to $40 million worth of foreign language books and magazines annually. Book sharing among readers is very common because books are rather expensive; therefore, a book that sells 4,000 copies may well have over 20,000 readers. Publishing statistics from Arab publishers are thus not necessarily indicative of which books are read or how often they are read.

Points of View (*Weghat Nazar*), a literary magazine, and "The Book" ("al-Kitab"), a weekly television program aired on Al-Jazeera, give some indication of what Arab intellectuals are reading—and are perhaps indicative of popular tastes as well. Of the many television programs viewed in Arab countries and the many literary magazines that cover books (ranging from books on international politics to books on religious and social phenomena), many are written by Western authors. Book fairs provide another insight in determining what Arab readers are interested in. Although there are no across-the-board statistics to utilize, reported best sellers at the fairs are most often religious, educational, and political books. It must be stressed, however, that these descriptions are very general. The three best sellers of the 2003 Beirut Arab Book Fair of were Tarif Khalidi's study of Jesus in Islamic texts and tradition (translated from English), a study of late nineteenth- and early twentieth-century South Lebanese Shi'i clerics (translated from French), and a collection of essays by Salim el Hoss (a former Lebanese Prime Minister). According to an article published in 2005, there has been an increased demand for foreign books in Iraq, especially textbooks, books that cover technological and political topics, and translations (some of the more popular authors include Tolstoy, Dostoyevsky, and Gabriel García Márquez).

To find out what the "average" person from Jordan or Oman is reading, more statistics must be collected by booksellers and researchers. As it stands now, we can only glimpse into the tastes and preferences of Arab readers.[1]

LITERATURE

NORTH AFRICA

The term "North Africa" (the *Maghreb*) as used here encompasses Tunisia, Morocco, Libya, and Algeria. The word "Maghreb" is both Western, from the Middle Eastern point of view (in fact, the word is Arabic for "west"), and is "oriental" from the Western point of view.

Muslim armies invaded Egypt during the seventh century, thus beginning the spread of Islam and Middle Eastern culture to the northern countries of Africa. The Ottoman Turks began ruling in the sixteenth century, staying until Napoleon's invasion in the eighteenth century.

Tunisia and Algeria had become somewhat self-governed by the 1800s, although this situation changed abruptly when France invaded Algeria in 1830. The French stayed until 1962, leaving only at the end of eight grueling years of fighting that finally won Algerian independence. Morocco and Tunisia, also under French rule, enjoyed relatively more freedom than the Algerians. Until the Moroccan and Tunisian nationalist movements emerged in the 1920s and 1930s, these countries had been considerably less resistant to their European rulers. Soon after World War II, the nationalist movements gained power and influence and fought successfully to gain Moroccan and Tunisian independence from their occupiers.

Writers from the Maghreb are often categorized by language (French; Arabic; and the Chelha, or Berber, dialects Tamazight, Rifia, and Tachelhit). Many Maghrebi authors are multilingual and have been known to translate their own works or write in more than one language, with Tunisian poet Hédi Bouraoui and Moroccan author Abdelfattah Kilito being just two examples. Spanish is also widely spoken in northern Morocco, and naturally many dialects are spoken and used by popular authors. Topics favored by North African authors include colonization, family structure and traditions, and religion. Very little Maghrebi literature has been translated into English. Although there are few reliable sources listing North African booksellers and publishers, an online Maghreb bookstore is located at http://www.ketabook.com/.

Algeria

The National Library of Algeria (Bibliothèque Nationale d'Algérie), located in Algiers, is the country's national library. Other research centers include the National Archives (Archives Nationales) and the Algeria University Library (Bibliothèque de l'Université d'Algérie).

One of Algeria's most famous authors is Kateb Yacine, best known for his novel *Nedjma*. The book purports to cover the years between 1945 and 1952, although the events are by no means recounted chronologically, nor is the novel really just about post–World War II Algeria. Rather, Algerian, Arabic, and Islamic identities are explored in the novel with a significant focus on tolerance and change. All twentieth-century Algerian writers—including Mouloud Feraoun, Mouloud Mammo, Mohammed Dib (one of Algeria's most prolific authors), and Abdallah Rukaibi—have been greatly influenced by Kateb Yacine.

Other important Algerian authors include Jean Amrouche, Mouloud Mammeri (who founded *Alwal*, a literary publication dedicated to Amazigh culture), Jean Sénac (a protégé of Albert Camus), Tahar Ouettar, Ahlam Mosteghanemi, Leila Sebbar, Rachid Boudjedra, Mohamed Sari, Tahar Djaout, Malika Mokeddem, Assia Djebar, and Merzak Allouache. Djebar and Allouache are also famous as critically acclaimed filmmakers.

Morocco

Morocco's national library, the Bibliothèque Générale et Archives, has branches in the cities of Rabat and Tétouan. Academic libraries can be found at l'Université Mohammed V,

Literature

l'Université Hassan II, and the University of Al-Akhawayn. Other research centers include the Bibliothèque Ben Youssef; Centre Nationale de Documentation; Biblioteca Española; Islamic Educational, Scientific, and Cultural Organization; King Abdul Aziz al-Saoud Foundation Library; and La Source. At least one public library, the Orient Occident Foundation Library, is located in Rabat.

Tahar Ben Jelloun, author and adamant activist opposed to racism and discrimination against North Africans and Palestinians, is best known for his sixth novel, *The Sand Child*. In this book Ben Jelloun explores gender relations, specifically female roles, in Moroccan society. The novel draws on the oral storytelling tradition of North Africa and is narrated by a series of storytellers. The most notable is the Blind Troubadour, believed by critics to distinctly resemble Argentinean author Jorge Luis Borges. Ben Jelloun uses the technique of multiple storytellers and multiple points of view to help explore the problems of reality and objectivity. He was one of the intellectuals and writers who collectively changed the North African approach to writing in French. Mohammed Khair-Eddine, Mostafa Nissaboury, and Abdelkebir Khatibi—all tied to the literary journal *Souffles*—all wrote in French, although their writing took a decidedly unconventional approach to the structure of the language.

Abdel-ilah Salhi was born in 1968 and started writing and publishing poetry while he was still a student. After graduating, he moved to Paris and joined the circle of Arab surrealists. He is responsible for creation of the literary magazine *Israf*, a publication that hugely influenced surrealism and prose poetry in Morocco. Other important Moroccan literary figures include poet Mohammad Bennis and author of short stories Muhammad Barrada, who also headed the Union of Moroccan Writers and lectured for a time at l'Université Muhammad V in Rabat. Other significant authors from Morocco include Driss Charaibi, Abdellatif Laâbi, Mohammed Aziz El-Hababi, Mostafa Nissabory, Khnata Bennouna, Mohammed Berrada, Rabia Mubarak, Mohammed Zefzaf, Abdelhak Serhane, Ahmed Lemsih, and Abdelkarim Ghellab.

Tunisia

Tunisia's national library, La Bibliothèque Nationale de Tunisie, is located in Tunis.

Self-taught writer of short stories Ali al-Du'aji and poets Mustafa Khrayyif and Muhammad Bairam al-Tunisi formed part of the bohemian literary movement that arose in Tunisia during the 1930s and 1940s. Hassouna Mosbahi writes novels and short stories, as well as being a freelance journalist. Muhammad Aziza, a poet, critic, and short story author, often publishes his creative material under the pseudonym Shams Nadir. Mustafa al-Farisi works for both the Tunisian film organization SAPEC, the Tunisian Society of Authors, and the Tunisian Ministry of Information, in addition to being a writer of successful radio plays and short stories. Abu al-Qasim al-Shabbi is responsible for the popularity of avant-garde poetry in Tunisia. Other important poets from Tunisia include Al-Munsif al-Wahaybi and Muhammad Ghuzzi.

Other authors of note to emerge from Tunisia include Albert Memmi, Moncef Ghacem, and Fawzi Mellah.

Libya

The National Library of Libya is located in Benghazi on the Gar Yunis University campus; another library is located at Al Fatah University in Tripoli.

Ibrahim al-Koni, a Libyan author of both novels and short stories, was born in the northern Sahara town of Ghadamis but received his literary education in Moscow. In Moscow he began work as a Libyan News Agency correspondent. Later he edited the Libyan-Polish Friendship Committee's journal *Friendship* and acted as cultural counselor in Libya's embassies in Poland, Russia, and Switzerland. His major works include *The Magi, Gold Ore,* and *The Bleeding of the Stone.*

Ahmad Ibrahim al-Faqih, dramatist, journalist, and short story writer, both founded and worked for newspapers and reviews for a considerable time before the Higher Council for Literature and Art in Libya recognized him in 1966 for his short story collection *No Water in the Sea.* Important poets from Libya include Muhammad al-Faituri.

THE MIDDLE EAST

Egypt

National libraries in Egypt are the Egyptian National Library and Archives in Cairo and the Egyptian National Agricultural Library in Giza. Academic libraries in Egypt may be found in Asuit University, Helwan University, Cairo University, Alexandria University, and Monofeya University. There are many other public libraries and cultural institutions in Egypt, such as the Bibliotheca Alexandrina, which contains six specialized libraries, three museums, a planetarium, an exploratory learning area for children, six art galleries, and seven research institutes, and hosts more than 800,000 people visitors annually. Other important libraries include Al Azhar Alsharef Library, Great Cairo Public Library, Haras Gomhory Library, and Mubarak Public Library. Egypt also has the Egyptian Libraries Network, which links all of the automated libraries in Egypt, regardless of category.

The annual Egyptian Book Fair, which takes place in Cairo and has been held since 1969, is extremely popular; the thirty-eighth annual fair held in February 2006 hosted 623 publishers from seventeen Arab and fifteen European countries.

In the first half of the twentieth century, Egypt was a hotbed of literary creativity and development. Egypt was the dominant producer of poetry criticism. The "prince of poets," Ahmad Shawqi (1869–1932), called Egypt home. Organizations such as the Diwan Group and the Apollo Group were widespread and influential. The Apollo Group even founded a magazine (*Apollo*) in which it published poetry guidelines. Beginning in the 1950s, however, Egypt's influence on poetry decreased, although its writers still played a leading role in prose production, primarily because of the work of Naguib Mahfouz, considered one of the two patriarchs of Arab literature (the other is Abd al-Rahman Munif).

Naguib Mahfouz was born in 1911 in Cairo, and this city serves as the setting for most of his fiction. As a philosophy student in Cairo, he was deeply influenced by positivism, especially the work of August Comte. Before he graduated from the University of Cairo, Mahfouz wrote and published both philosophical articles and short stories in *al-Majalla al-Jadida,* a contemporary periodical edited by Fabian intellectual Salama Musa, who was a significant influence on Mahfouz's scientific and social sensibilities. In 1939 Mahfouz added novels to his repertoire, and in 1941 he was one of five winners of the Ministry of Education's novel-writing competition, although his writing received no substantial acclaim until 1957, when he published *The Trilogy* (*al-Thulathiyya*).

Most of Mahfouz's early work centers around middle-class life in Egypt, both before and during World War II. In his first few novels, Mahfouz wrote about men and women who repeatedly tried to change their lives for the better, although they met tragic ends at

Literature

the hands of both society and the cruelty of fate. All of Mahfouz's writing was done in his spare time, as his regular income came from his work as a civil servant. The real turning point in his career as a writer came with the publication of *The Trilogy*; this also marked a turning point for the Arabic novel as an art form. The three books that make up *The Trilogy* (*Bayn al-Qasrayn, Qasr al-Shawq,* and *al-Sukkariyya*—all street names in Cairo) follow three generations of the same Egyptian family, beginning in 1917 and ending in 1944. Both the development of the characters and the narrative serve as a microcosm for modern Arab society, mirroring generational struggles with religion, politics, and social convention.

After *The Trilogy*'s publication, Mahfouz published nothing for approximately five years. In 1959 he returned to the literary world with the novel, *The Children of Gebelawi* (*Awalad Haratina*), which was published in serialized form in the Egyptian journal *Al-Ahram*. This book, an allegorical novel that tackled the nature of evil, the meaning of life, and many other metaphysical questions, was so controversial that the entire Arab world, except for Lebanon, banned it. This novel was followed by the publication of a series of shorter novels that focused on the spiritual development of just one protagonist (except *Miramar*, which is told from the perspective of four people). These novels are *The Thief and the Dogs* (*al-Liss wa'al-Kilab*) in 1961, *Autumn Quail* (*al-Summan Wa'al-Kharif*) in 1962, *The Search* (*al-Tariq*) in 1964, *The Beggar* (*al-Shahhadh*) in 1965, *Chattering on the Nile* (*Tharthara Fawq al-Nil*) in 1966, and *Miramar* in 1967 (published under the same title in Arabic). These novels were marked by increased lyrical and symbolic characteristics.

In 1970 Mahfouz was awarded Egypt's National Prize for Letters, and in 1972 he was presented with the Collar of the Republic, the highest honor a person can receive from Egypt. In spite of his prodigious and brilliant literary work, Mahfouz's outspoken support for Anwar Sadat's Camp David peace treaty with Israel caused many Arab countries to ban his works, a ban that lasted until he was awarded the Nobel Prize for Literature in 1988. He continued publishing a weekly column in *Al-Ahram* until his death.

Scholars believe that the author Muhammad al-Muwailihi connected modern Arabic fiction to the classical traditions. The narrative of *Isa Ibn Hisham*, a work that he serialized in the journal *Misbah al-Sharq*, references the narrator of al-Hamadhani's popular maqamat, the classical poetry style from the tenth century. Until al-Muwailihi, Arabic authors had been using Western forms of fiction as models from which they created. Al-Muwailihi's work established that the Arab world drew from a rich tradition of fiction, and many authors subsequent to al-Muwailihi followed suit.

Mahmoud Taymur, the short story writer and dramatist, stands with writers such as Mahfouz and Munif as a great pioneer in Arabic literature. Often his writing, like that of his contemporaries, expresses the absurdity of the human experience with both humor and pathos. Short story author Mahmoud Badawi, influenced heavily by Anton Chekhov, was a contemporary of Mahmoud Taymur; however very little is known about Badawi. Still he stands with other groundbreaking Arabic writers who helped Arabic literature break from its shaky beginnings and begin to emerge as solid first-rate literature. Another important Egyptian author is Fat-hi Ghanim.

Young poets who advocated traditional style, the Diwan Group (named for a type of literary criticism), included the writers Ibrahim Abd al-Qadir al-Mazini, Abbas M. al-Aqqad, and Abd al-Rahman Shukri, all of whom wrote in many different genres. Other important poets from Egypt include Ali Mahmud Taha, Hafiz Ibrahim, Ahmad Shauqi, and Ibrahim Naji.

The famous author and antifeminist Tawfiq al-Hakim, who wrote short stories, novels, and plays, received his literary education in both France and at the Berlitz School in Cairo. Because of his extensive knowledge of French literature and his exposure to Western culture, al-Hakim's literature often links the Arab world to the West, as seen in his acclaimed novel, *A Bird from the East.* Moreover, his plays laid the foundation for Arabic theater.

The short story pioneer Yahya Haqqi, who also worked as a diplomat, played a crucial role in the development of Egyptian fiction in spite of the fact that he did not write very much, compared to his contemporaries.

Gamal al-Ghitani is an impressive writer who also has drawn on the roots of Arabic literary history to develop his fictional style. His writing is full of political and social criticism, some of which led to his imprisonment.

Fifty bookshops are listed on the Egyptian Tourism Ministry Website, and there were 281 active members of the Egyptian Publishing Association in 1998. It is very likely that there are many more bookstores and publishers, although an updated, more comprehensive statistic was not available. A small sample of Egyptian booksellers and publishers follows, as listed on the Website www.tradearabia.com:

Bookshops and Publishers in Egypt

Alam El Feker Bookshop	Middle East Observer
Book Center	Rose El Youssef Establishment
Dar Al Hilal Establishment	Telezone Egypt
Dar El Maaref	World of Tourism
International Marketing Center	

Jordan

The National Library of Jordan is located in Amman. Academic libraries are located at Amman University, Al-Isra University, Mu'tah University, Irbid National University, Yarmouk University, and the University of Petra. Public libraries in Jordan include the libraries located within the British Council and the U.S. Embassy, and the University of Jordan Public Library, Abdul Hameed Shoman Public Library, and the Municipality of Amman Public Library.

Jamal Abu Hamdan, born in 1938, began writing as a journalist, publishing articles in both *Al-Ra'i* and *Al-Dustur.* He has written plays, short stories, and two novels, many of which rely on symbolism to reflect the social and political life of Arabs, particularly the conditions in Palestine and other current conflicts in that region. His 1970 short story collection *Many Sorrows and Three Gazelles* brought him wide acclaim in avant-garde circles. Ilyas Farkouh is a fiction writer who has produced several works that have been translated into Western languages. Ghalib Halasa's work not only embodies the modern Arabic novel, but also focuses on the customs and experiences of Bedouin and peasant groups, Arabs who are often overlooked by other Arab authors. One of Jordan's famous poets is Amjad Nasir, who writes experimentalist verse.

Here is a sampling of Jordanian bookshops and publishers as listed on the Website www.tradearabia.com:

Bookshops and Publishers in Jordan

Istiklal Library	Sarah Bookshop
Madaba Oriental Gifts	University Bookshop
Mujamma Bookshop	Wadi Saqra Bookshop
Petra Bookshop	

Israel

The Jewish National and University Library is Israel's national library. Academic libraries are located at Tel Aviv University, Bar-Ilan University, Ben-Gurion University of the Negev,

LITERATURE

the University of Haifa, Hebrew University of Jerusalem, and many other colleges and academic institutions, all linked through the Israel Library Network. The Public Libraries Law of 1975 established the Public Library Council, and requires the Minister of Education and Culture to establish free public library services in all of Israel's provinces. These include the Qiriat Gat Public Library and the Matte Asher Regional Library.

The modern state of Israel is barely sixty years old (having been officially formed in 1948). Because the citizens of Israel did not just pop out of nowhere, some discussion is required of the popular literature that helped shape the culture of the Israelis. This literature is repeatedly referred to as "Hebrew literature." From about 200 CE until recently, Hebrew was primarily a language used only in a religious context; the exception was the secular and religious Hebrew poetry written in Spain and Italy between the tenth and fourteenth centuries by Juda Halevi, Samuel HaNagid, and Immanuel of Rome. Some prose fiction also appeared, although it was not nearly as common as verse writing. Authors who developed Hebrew literature learned it by studying the *Torah* (the Hebrew name for the first five books in the Bible) in seminaries (*yeshivot*), most of which were located in Eastern Europe. Because the first writers of Hebrew literature were taught the language for religious purposes, these authors used biblical Hebrew in their writing, in spite of its archaic vocabulary and awkward syntax. The beginning of a solution to this problem lay in rabbinic literature such as the *Mishna*, the first part of the *Talmud*, a commentary on the *mitsves* (commandments or rules) found in the Torah. In addition to rabbinical investigation of the mitsves, the Mishna also contains history, gossip, jokes, anecdotes, and innuendo—in short, Hebrew prose is slightly more similar to everyday speech than the biblical form found in the Torah. The first person to use this form of Hebrew was Shalom Yakov Abramowitz—or, as he was more commonly known, Mendele Mokher Seforim (Mendele the Book Seller).

During the Geonic period (576–1038) the influential author and scholar Saadia ben Joseph (892–942) began publishing. Born in an Egyptian village, he occupied the chair of Gaon of Sura as an adult. This meant that he was the agreed-upon religious leader of the communities of the Diaspora. His earliest work, *Agron,* is the first Hebrew dictionary, and many scholars consider him one of the first Hebrew grammarians and a founder of Hebrew philology. The esoteric, mystic literature called *cabala,* which speculates on the origins of the universe and its creator, also gradually emerged during this time. One of these mystical works, *The Book of Formations* (*Sefer Yetzirah*), written in the oldest known Hebrew grammar, is the earliest effort by a Jewish mystic to explain the creation of the world. The *Book of Yosipon,* a popular history spanning 539 BCE to 70 CE, was quite popular in the Middle Ages, although it was full of errors and inconsistencies. Translations were available in Arabic, French, English, German, Latin, and Yiddish. Authorship of the *Book of Yosipon* is dubious: initially it was thought that first-century Jewish historian Josephus Flavius was the author, although scholars now generally agree that he was not. An Arabic copy was found in the library of Ibn Hazin (d. 1063), so the book was unquestionably written before the end of the Geonic period.

The mystical doctrine of cabala grew extensively during the Middle Ages, beginning with the thirteenth century. Although mystical books had been written before this time, the thirteenth century saw a renewed interest in Jewish mysticism, with authors such as Isaac the Blind (1190–1210), Abraham Abulafia (1240–c. 1290), Solomon Alkabiz (c. 1529–53), Joseph Caro (1488–1575), and Israel ben Moses Najara (c. 1555–c. 1625).

The Jewish Enlightenment, or *Haskala,* ranged from the 1770s to the late 1880s and was influential in paving the way for Modern Hebrew and Yiddish literature. The Haskala sought to disseminate secular knowledge among Jews so that reform and assimilation into the larger, primarily Christian society could take place. This movement divided the Jews into three factions: the Hasidim, the Rabbinical, and the Maskilim. The Hasidim had direct ties to cabalistic traditions and tended to place great emphasis on prayer. Rabbinical Jews, although vehement opponents of Hasidism, also adhered to tradition and rejected the secular philosophy of the Haskala. The Maskilim advocated and adhered to the ideas promoted by the Haskala, which primarily sought to move Jewish education and lifestyle away from Talmudic teaching and thought.

The philosopher Moses Mendelssohn is widely considered to be the father of the Haskala. Much of his philosophy is influenced by Leibniz-Wolff metaphysics, particularly its principle of sufficient reason (the idea that, for everything that happens, there is a reason). Mendelssohn published *Jerusalem, or on Religious Power and Judaism,* which argued that Judaism was founded solely upon reason and laws, a position that incited some traditionalist Jews to accuse him of heresy. In 1767 he published the book *Phädon,* which sought to argue the soul's immortality. This book was potentially his most popular work and one of the most heavily circulated books in eighteenth-century Europe. He had an intense dislike for Yiddish, and chose to write only in German or Hebrew. In fact, as the Haskala philosophy became more widely practiced in the late eighteenth and nineteenth centuries, the use of Yiddish waned, and European languages (particularly German and French) and Hebrew became the primary spoken languages among European Jews.

Beginning in the mid-nineteenth century, newspapers, journals, and civic organizations (for example, the Society for the Promotion of Culture) disseminated literary and social criticism in both Hebrew and Yiddish, even though the latter was still considered a language strictly for the uneducated. Everything changed, however, at the end of the nineteenth century. The assassination of Russian Czar Alexander II in 1881 generated a huge wave of emigration (the *Aliya*) by the Jewish population of Russia. Alexander II's son and successor, Alexander III, held intensely anti-Semitic views and ruled with extreme prejudice. The pogroms that ensued after the murder of Alexander II were believed to have been sanctioned by the new czar. Because the pogromists received little or no official punishment (and, in some cases, even won sympathy), this view of the new czar was probably not far from the truth. In 1882 Czar Alexander III introduced the "Temporary Edicts," otherwise known as the May Laws, which began an official discriminatory policy that endured for thirty years. Under the May Laws, Jews were banned from towns with populations of fewer than 10,000 people, including the Pale of Settlement, the western border of Russia where permanent Jewish residence was permitted. As life grew increasingly difficult for the Russian Jews, mass emigration to America and Palestine ensued, resulting in the estimated movement of nearly 2 million Jews out of the Russian empire.

New inhabitants of Palestine, most of whom were members of Hibbat Zion (Love of Zion), included writers, scholars, and teachers. Among them was Eliezer Perlman (later changed to Eliezer Ben-Yehuda, 1858–1922), who advocated the use of Hebrew as an everyday language. The idea of using a sacred biblical language was extremely unpopular among orthodox Jews, who felt that such everyday use of Hebrew amounted to heresy. Moreover, the two-thousand-year-old, virtually unchanged language of Hebrew did not always translate well into nineteenth- and twentieth-century concepts. Even so, Ben-Yehuda established two Hebrew-language periodicals, co-initiated the Hebrew Language Committee, and helped begin the seventeen-volume *Complete Dictionary of Ancient and Modern Hebrew,* which was mostly published posthumously by his second wife Hemda. Although he faced intense criticism for his work to promote Hebrew—he was both excommunicated and imprisoned for his ideas about religious leaders and politics—Ben-Yehuda still succeeded in promoting and establishing Hebrew as the official language of the Jews.

Another important writer around this time was Sholem Jacob Abramovich, often called the grandfather of modern Hebrew literature. He wrote in both Yiddish and Hebrew, even when it was still widely believed among Jewish intellectuals that Yiddish was too unsophisticated for

LITERATURE

serious literature or scholarship. Abramovich's writing, especially his work published under the pseudonym Mendele the Bookseller (*Mendele Mokher Seforim*), changed this perception. Books such as *The Magic Ring* (*Dos Vintshfingerl*), *Fishke the Lame* (*Fishke der Krumer*), and *The Mare* (*Di Kliatshe*), all written in Yiddish, used satire and plain, realistic depictions of life in the *shtetl* (village) to both criticize and defend the position of the Jew in nineteenth-century Christian society. His works were extremely popular and utterly new, using a "nonliterary" language that brilliantly utilized satire, allegory, and pathos. Ultimately his popularity and literary skill established the tone for the thematic and stylistic trends of the new Yiddish literature. After twenty years of writing in Yiddish, Abramovich switched back to Hebrew; he translated many of his Yiddish books into Hebrew as well. Using Hebrew, he composed possibly his most famous work, The Travels of Benjamin III (*Mas'ot Binyamin Ha-Shelishi*), sometimes called *The Jewish Don Quixote* in translation.

Another extremely influential Hebrew/Yiddish author is Sholem Rabinovitz, commonly known by his pen name, Sholem Aleichem, which translates from Hebrew as "peace be upon you" (although the overall meaning is truly closer to "how's it going" or "howdy"). Like Abramovich, he began writing in Hebrew, and it wasn't until he started publishing in Yiddish (using the pseudonym) that his writing became exceptional. His humorous stories were often told in the manner of a pseudobiography: Western readers may be familiar with stories such as Daniel Defoe's *Robinson Crusoe*, a story told by a narrator who claims to have "discovered" certain documents, so the printed story claims to be nothing more than a recounting of "facts." Aleichem's character Menakhem-mendl, who first appeared in 1892, narrates this sort of story. Among Aleichem's other well-known and loved characters is Tevye the Dairyman, who inspired the character of Tevye in *Fiddler on the Roof*. In addition to his humorous writing, Aleichem (who achieved international acclaim in his lifetime) wrote novels and one full-length play, *Yaknehoz*. He was a supporter and member of the Zionist movement and also founded *Di Yidishe Folksbibliotek*, a Yiddish literary journal in which many prominent Yiddish authors were published.

I. L. (Isaac Loeb) Peretz began his literary career writing Hebrew poetry, although he became a well-known author through his fiction. While he is considered equally important to the history and development of both early Hebrew and Yiddish literature, Peretz's writing had more realistic qualities than the humoristic styles of Abramovich and Aleichem. Although he also wrote in Yiddish, his intention at first was not to advocate the permanent use of the language; he initially viewed writing in Yiddish as a way to reach a larger audience. Originally a lawyer, Peretz was forced to give up his practice and move with his family to Warsaw, Poland, in 1886. There his literary career flourished. He wrote poetry, novels, plays, and essays, but was most famous for his short stories. "Bontshe the Silent" (Bontshe Shvayg), one of his more well-known stories, showcases his trademark style, a blend of symbolism and realism. He worked primarily with spiritual and moral themes, frequently writing about forgiveness, sacrifice, and purity.

Yosef Haim Brenner (1881–1921) and Schmuel Yosef Agnon (1888–1970) were both considered fathers of modern Hebrew literature. Agnon, whose first name is also written "Samuel Joseph," was the first Hebrew writer to receive the Nobel Prize for Literature in 1966. A native of Eastern Europe, his family immigrated to Palestine in the early twentieth century from Galicia, the region between Poland and Ukraine. Agnon's novels are characterized by their sympathetic portrayals of Eastern European life, written in a style that influenced all subsequent Hebrew authors.

The first wave of Hebrew literature written in Palestine (with works beginning in the 1940s and continuing through the 1950s) was published by the "War of Independence Generation." Hebrew was not just a sacred language to them, but had become their native tongue, due in part to the work of Ben-Yehuda. Authors classed in this generation are Moshe Shamir, Hanoch Bartov, Haim Gouri, and Benjamin Tammuz. Their themes included social realism and nationalism, with a significant focus on the Jewish pioneers and their relationship to Israel.

A. B. Yehoshua, Yoram Kaniuk, Yaakov Shabtai, and Amos Oz were the writers of a new wave of fiction that emerged in the late 1950s and 1960s. These authors moved away from the Zionist tradition of their predecessors, choosing to focus on both the individual and their apprehension regarding Israeli-Arab relations and Zionism in general. New styles in narrative forms emerged during this time, including surrealism, symbolism, psychological realism, and allegory.

Aharon Appelfeld, David Shahar, David Grossman, and Meir Shalev (along with Oz, Yehoshua, and Kaniuk) are some of the better-known authors who wrote in the 1980s and 1990s. They continued to explore literature as a means by which readers could place themselves in the world both as individuals and as part of the world. Other themes explored in recent years include the Arab village (Anton Shammas), Orthodox Jews living apart from society (Yossl Birstein), the Hassidic courts (Haim Be'er), nonbelievers in a time of escalating fundamentalism (Yitzhak Orpaz-Auerbach), Arab immigrants (Sami Michael, Albert Suissa, Dan Benaya Seri), and democracy in a society that remains in nearly perpetual flux (Yitzhak Ben-Ner, David Grossman, and Amos Oz).

Women too figure prominently in the popular literature of Israel. The detective fiction of such authors as Shulamit Lapid and Batya Gur has attained international critical acclaim. Other Israeli female authors include Ruth Almog, Chana Bat-Shahar, Amalia Kahana-Carmon, Shulamit Hareven, and Savion Liebrecht. Amalia Kahana-Carmon, who set the stylistic tone for subsequent female Israeli authors, has written novels, novellas, and short stories that focus on the individual's struggle to accept life and find meaning through self-expression rather than in political or social causes. Other important female authors include Shifra Horn, Michal Govrin, Gila Almagor, and Alona Kimchi.

The current generation of Israeli writers tends to reject using the Israeli experience as a central theme and is more apt to write about alienation, surrealism, or idiosyncrasy. These writers include Orly Castel-Blum, Yehudit Katzir, Etgar Keret, Irit Linor, Mira Magen, and Gadi Taub.

Gershon Shaked, an Israeli author who has written roughly thirty books of criticism, was awarded the Bialik Prize in 1986. The award, named after Israel's national poet, Hayyim Nahman Bialik, is considered Israel's most prestigious literary award. The extremely influential Yizhar Smilansky, who writes under the pen name "S. Yizhar," began publishing both adult and children's fiction in 1938. Most of his writing explores the pioneer spirit (or lack thereof) of the Israeli Diaspora. His masterpiece, the epic novel *Days of Ziklag* (*Days od Ziklag*) detailed people and events from Israel's war for independence. Abraham B. Yehoshua, novelist and playwright, has been described by *The New York Times* as the "Israeli William Faulkner." Etgar Keret, born in Tel Aviv in 1967, began writing fiction in 1992. His publications include fiction for children and adults across many formats, including comics, short stories, and novellas. His work has been translated into sixteen languages, and nearly forty short films have been based on his short fiction. His own film, *Skin Deep,* won an Israeli Oscar. Yitzhaq Shami is one of Hebrew literature's best writer of short stories; one of his most famous works is entitled *Hebron Stories.* Uri Orlev, born Jerzy H. Orlowski in Warsaw, has received the Hans Christian Andersen Author Award. His novels include *The Island on Bird Street, The Lady with the Hat,* and *The Man from the Other Side.*

Rhyme in traditional Hebrew poetry is uncommon. Although parallelism, alliteration, and assonance occur frequently, they are not easy or possible to represent in translation. Books from the Old Testament such as *Psalms, Job, Song of Solomon,* and *Kohelet* (*Ecclesiastes*) serve as excellent examples of classical Hebrew poetic writing. The Hebrew *piyyutim*, liturgical poets from the early Geonic period (576–1038 CE) had tremendous influence on the development of Hebrew literature. Although few records survive from this period; this style of poetry is still recited today by Orthodox Jews.

Two poets who demonstrate the shift from ancient Jewish poetry to the current, modern form are Haim Nahman Bialik (1873–1934) and Saul Tchernichovsky (1875–1943). Bialik, who is considered both Israel's national poet and the poet of the Hebrew renaissance, wrote both epic and lyric poetry. The language of his poetry merges the biblically influenced idiom of his predecessors with conversational Hebrew. Tchernichovsky also wrote dramatic epics, ballads, and lyric poems, although his language was closer to rabbinical Hebrew than Bialik's. Poets who followed include Natan Alterman, Lea Goldberg, Uri Zvi Greenberg, and Avraham Schlonsky, all of whom were writing just before the creation of the state of Israel. The common tonality in the language of this group is an unelevated normal Hebrew. Themes in their poetry range from the development of the Jewish community, city, and nature, to the impact of the Holocaust. Russian futurism, symbolism, and German expressionism all were significant influences on the poetry of this period, so the verse was often melodic and classically structured. Often set to music, some of the poems became part of Israel's national lore.

The group who emerged in the mid-1950s moved away from the classically structured and rhymed verse of poets like Alterman and instead continued to experiment with daily speech patterns, metaphysical images, and irony. Their writing helped to move Hebrew poetry away from describing the collective experience and (like the prose of the same period) began to focus more on the individual. Hebrew poetry today is a polyphony of many different kinds of voices, ranging from direct, free-rhymed slang to restrained sadness. Modern Hebrew poets include Yehuda Amichai, who is one of Israel's most famous poets (his work has been translated into nearly thirty languages), David Avidan, Moshe Dor, Yair Horowitz, Asher Reich, Yona Wallach, Meir Wieseltier, and Natan Zach.

No reliable data are available regarding the number of bookshops in Israel. However, Israel does have both small, independent sellers and major bookstore chains such as Tsomet Sfarim, Sifri, and Steimatzky (according to statistics gathered by the Frankfurt Book Fair).

Palestinian Territories

Academic libraries are located at An-Najah National University and Birzeit University. Public libraries and other educational institutions have either been destroyed or have suffered severe losses due to the conflict between Palestine and Israel. There are still public libraries and cultural centers in Ramallah, Nablus, Jenin, and El Bireh. West Bank libraries operate in Tulkarm, Hebron, and Jericho. In the Gaza Strip, libraries still operate in Gaza City and Rafah. Over the past four years, many of these institutions have been vandalized, looted, or otherwise damaged. The Qattan Centre for Educational Research and Development supports libraries from its offices in Ramallah and Gaza. The mosque libraries are also important, although their holdings are limited to religious literature. Some schools also have a version of a public library, although their holdings are also limited.

Palestinian novelists, beginning with Ghassan Kanafani, truly emerged as important additions to the Arabic literary world in the early 1960s. Kanafani, eventually assassinated for his involvement with the Popular Front for the Liberation of Palestine, wrote extensively about Palestinian refugee men and women as they lived before, during, and in the wake of the 1967 war with Israel. His novels, including the acclaimed *Men in the Sun* (*Rijal fi`l-Shams*), explore finding individual salvation in the face of cultural and political alienation.

Jabra Ibrahim Jabra, who left Palestine in 1948, adds poetry, translation (notably the translation of Shakespeare), and painting to his talents as an author. Although he wrote one short novel in 1948 (*A Cry in the Long Night*, published in 1955 in Baghdad as *Surakh fi Layl*

Tawil), his next novel, *The Ship* (*Al-Safina*), published in 1969, was important for elaborating the ways in which Arab intellectuals confront and cope with contemporary philosophy, culture, politics, and morality. Many of Jabra's novels have melodramatic elements, but overall his writing clearly displays the difficulty faced by twentieth-century Arab intellectuals as Arabic philosophy, culture, and politics began to alternately blend and clash with Western beliefs and ethos. One of his novels, *Mapless World* (*Alam bila Khara'it*), was a joint effort with Abd al-Rahman Munif, another prominent Arab writer.

The novelist and short story writer Liana Badr edited the cultural section of *Al-Hurriyya* while working for the Union of Palestinian Women in Jordan and Lebanon. The latter experience is detailed in her novel *The Sundial* (1979). Other Palestinian authors include Zaki Darwish; Emile Habiby, perhaps most famous for his novel *The Secret Life of Saeed, the Pessoptimist*, which details life for Palestinians in Israel; and Huzama Habayib, originally from Kuwait but who fled the country in 1990 during the first Gulf War. Habayib has published both short stories and translations of nonfiction subjects (before leaving Kuwait, she worked as a teacher of Arabic to non-Arabic speakers and as translator for the newspaper *Al-Watan*). Two important poets from Palestine are Ibrahim Tuqan and Salma Khadra Jayyusi.

Reliable information is not available regarding the number of booksellers or publishers in the Palestinian Territories.

Lebanon

As of this writing, Lebanon has undergone the destruction of life and property in the wake of fighting between Hezbollah and Israeli forces in parts of Lebanon and Israel. Universities, libraries, and bookstores have suffered losses of people, structures, and programs.

Academic libraries are located at the Lebanese University, the American University of Beirut, Lebanese American University, Saint Joseph University, Notre Dame University, Beirut Arab University, University of Balamand, and Haigazian University. There have been nearly thirty public libraries in Lebanon, including two in Beirut (with the goal of providing one library for each of Beirut's twelve districts).

One of the first Arabic authors to attempt a true novel was the Lebanese writer Jurji Zaydan. Although not strictly modern, his novels had none of the supernatural elements of classical Arabic literature. Rather, the predictable characters of Zaydan's novels represent both good and evil, and portray Arab Islamic civilization as it has developed over time. Because of the vast historic subject matter chosen by Zaydan, his use of the novel form was essential, the short story being clearly inadequate to describe historical events of epic proportions. Although many Arabic novelists who came after Zaydan created artistically superior work, his work as an Arabic novelist creating fiction about Arabic history cannot be ignored.

Zaydan was not the only Lebanese writer to tackle the novel as an art form. The first Arab author outside of Egypt who truly explored the form of the novel was Tawfiq Yusuf Awwad (1911–89). In *The Loaf* (*Al-Raghif*), written in 1939, Awwad explored both Lebanese nationalism and social justice. In 1972, he published *Death in Beirut* (*Tawahin Bayrut*), a novel set in 1968, one year after the Arab-Israeli war. Little about the novel is experimental, although his character development progressed from the conventional good-cop/bad-cop characterization present in his first novel to a more complete portrayal of flawed humanity.

Halim Barakat, somewhat more experimental a writer than Awwad, published his first novel, *Six Days* (*Sittat Ayyam*), in 1961. Using symbolism, stream of consciousness, and phrase repetition, Barakat describes the events that transpire over a period of six days in a small coastal town. The townfolk have been warned that they have six days to evacuate before the Israeli army invades and destroys everything. His second novel, *Days of Dust*

Literature

(*Awdat al-Ta'ir ila'l-Bahr*), published in 1967, explores the suffering of the Palestinian people during the 1967 Arab-Israeli war, specifically using a parody of the style found in *Genesis* and themes found in Wagner's opera, *The Flying Dutchman* (the literal translation of '*Awdat al-Ta'ir ila'l-Bahr* is "The Return of the Flying Dutchman to the Sea"). Barakat's third novel specifically focuses on male-female relationships in Arab society. *Traveling between Arrow and Bowstring* (*Al-Rahil bayn al-Sahm wa'l-Watar*), published in 1979, makes use of the language style of *The Arabian Nights* and comments on Egyptian literature and culture (specifically on the political regime of Anwar Sadat) and on the situation faced by Arab women.

Suhayl Idris, editor of *Al-Adab*, one of the most influential Arabic literary journals, also wrote noteworthy novels that drew heavily on his own life experiences. They also explored the political, cultural, and social issues of contemporary Arabic life, among them the general subjugation and repression frequently experienced by Arabic women. His novel *The Latin Quarter* (*Al Hayy al Latini*) focuses on the relationship of a young Arab man and a French woman.

Lebanese women too were writing profusely by the 1950s and 1960s, and many of them gained excellent reputations among Arab authors. Layla Ba'albaki achieved immediate notoriety when she published *I Am Alive* (*Ana Ahya*) in 1958, a novel that both describes and attacks the social constraints that Arab women frequently face. She stands at the front of the feminist movement among Arab authors. Another important Lebanese writer, May Zeyadeh (born Marry Zeyadeh in Nazareth in 1886), moved to Cairo in 1907, where she began publishing her writing in the Egyptian newspapers *Al Mahrousa* and *Al Hilal*. An activist for women's rights, she completed fifteen books of poetry, literature, and translations, even though she wrote during a difficult historical period for women. Layla Usayran, in addition to advocating Arab women's liberation, wrote about the Palestinian resistance movement of the mid-twentieth century, heavily romanticizing the lifestyle and martyrdom of guerrilla fighters. Some critics believe that her work is a political treatise in the thin guise of mediocre fiction. Emily Nasrallah's writing was less political, but still drew heavily on feminist themes, particularly as they related to the twentieth-century Arab woman. Her novels examine the marked contrast between Lebanese village and city living with evocative, lyrical, but altogether unsentimental descriptions of rural and urban life. *The Story of Zahara* (*Hik ayat Zahara*), written and published in 1980 by Hanan al-Shaykh, is believed by some critics to be one of the most well-written of novels by a female Arab author. Hadia Said, the novelist, journalist, and short story author, writes for radio and television, and continues to publish novels. Her most recent novel, published in 2002, is *Red Orchards*. Her first, *Black Orchard*, was awarded a prize by *Al-Katiba*, an esteemed literary review published in London.

Marun Abboud primarily wrote literary criticism, but he was acclaimed both his work as a critic and short-story author. He wrote extensive criticism regarding traditional Arabic poetry, paving the way for more modern poets and critics to create new poetic models and theories. Other important poets from Lebanon include Gibran Khalil Gibran, Ilya Abu Madi, Ilyas Abu Shabaka, Bishara Abdallah al-Khuri (who published under the pseudonym Al-Akhtal al-Saghir), Said Aql, Hasan Abdallah, and Shauqi Abi Shaqra.

Bookshops are mainly located in Tripoli and Beirut, although no exact number is available.

Syria

Al-Assad Library, located in Damascus, is the enormous national library of Syria. It encompasses 22,000 square meters and is nine floors high. Syria's academic libraries are located at Al-Baath University, the University of Aleppo, Tishreen University, and the University of Damascus. Syria has many public libraries, one of which is its national library.

Syrian and Lebanese novelists are difficult to distinguish by region because many writers from Syria moved to Lebanon, where they drew directly from the people and location for their fictional work. Most critics agree that the first Syrian novel was *Greed* (*al-Naham*), written in 1937 by Shakib al Jabiri. This novel is frequently compared to Muhammad Husain Haykal's *Zaynab*. Al-Jabiri's novels are full of European characters, settings, and a tone that is substantially influenced by European romanticism. The first novel to emerge from Syria that is Arabic in both style and attributes, *Blue Painted Lamps* (*al-Masabih al-Zurq*), was written by Hanna Mina in 1954. The book traces in keen detail the lives and work of poor inhabitants of a district in Lattakia, Syria's busy seaport. Drawing on the influence of both Naguib Mahfouz and Maxim Gorky, Mina's writing initiated the heavy stylistic use of Social Realism among Syrian authors.

Another influential writer to emerge from Syria is Muta Safadi, a writer who composed the nationalistic and existential novels *A Professional Revolutionary* (*Tha'ir Muhtarif*) and *The Generation of Destiny* (*Jil al Qadar*). Both novels influenced upcoming Arab writers in terms of both theme and style. Many of Safadi's ideas, especially his prototype of the intellectual, sex-obsessed, and metaphysically lost protagonist, were so admired and imitated that they became a standard feature of Syrian writing.

The other prominent trend in Syrian and Arabic writing during this time was the *nouveau roman*, or "anti-novel." The phrase, coined by Émile Henriot, describes a style of writing that is consistently without style. Authors who produce in the style of the nouveau roman write without regard for conventional plot, chronology, theme, or characters. Syrian author Walid Ikhlasi often employs this technique, as exemplified in his 1965 novel, *Winter of the Dry Sea* (*Shita al-Bahr al-Yabis*). Other authors who experimented with the nouveau roman include Hani al-Rahib, Jurj Salim, and Haydar Haydar.

Other important writers from Syria include Fu'ad al-Shayib and Haydar Haydar, who is one of Syria's most famous authors, lauded for his theatrical—at times suspenseful—writing. Ilfat Idilbi, a self-educated woman, has reached a high level of appreciation within literary circles in Syria. Her novels, often set in Damascus, highlight the stark contrast between old and modern routines and practices, and describe the impact of modernization on the Damascene way of life. Ghalia Qabbani, a Syria-born journalist who now lives in London, typically writes stories that criticize the strict social codes and beliefs of Arabic society, particularly as they relate to women. Jameel Hatmal's reputation extends far beyond his native Syria. When he was 20 years old, Syrian universities had already given his writing an award. Much of Hatmal's fiction focuses on the culture of Syrian city life and has a uniquely Syrian tone. Important Syrian poets include Umar Abu Risha, Mutran Khalil Mutran, Khalil Khouri, and Orkhan Muyassar. Adunis (Ali Ahmad Said) is considered one of the greatest of all Arabic poets.

Reliable statistics were unavailable on the names and number of booksellers and publishers in Syria.

Iraq

The National Library of Iraq is in Baghdad. Academic libraries in Iraq are the Iraqi National Academy of Science Library, The House of Wisdom Library, Baghdad University Central Library, Al-Nahrain University Central Library, Al-Mustansyria University Central Library, University of Technology Central Library, Musel University Central Library, Basrah University Central Library, Babel University Central Library, Anbar University Central Library, Dyalla University Central Library, Salah-Eldin University Central Library, Tikreet University Central Library, Dhuk University Central Library, and Baghdad University college, institution, and research center libraries. There are two national Iraqi libraries: the Iraqi House of Manuscripts and the House of Books and Archives, both run by the Ministry of

LITERATURE

Culture. Iraq has many public and school libraries, and at least one library exclusively for children. Because of the ongoing war in Iraq, the number of libraries continues to diminish. Baghdad once had nineteen public libraries but now has just eight.

Iraqi author Abd al-Rahman Munif, one of the most important and influential of all Arab novelists, is most famous for his book *Mudun al-milh* [Cities of Salt], a five-part novel that covers the political, ethical, and economic history of the second half of the twentieth century in the Gulf countries. It deals particularly with the Arab relationship to oil. Literary theorist Edward Said called this book "the only serious work of fiction that tries to show the effect of oil, Americans and the local oligarchy on a Gulf country." Born in 1933 in Amman, Jordan, to a Saudi father and Iraqi mother, Munif eventually moved to Saudi Arabia, but was stripped of his nationality in 1963 because of his political opposition to the Saudi Arabian royal family. Later he became a naturalized Iraqi citizen. Munif is considered to be one of the two patriarchs of Arab literature (the other being Egyptian Naguib Mahfouz). Munif received the Cairo Award for Creative Narration in 1998. He died in Syria at age 71 in 2003.

Other important Iraqi authors include Jafar al-Khalili, who wrote encyclopedias, essays, criticism, biographies, and journalistic media in addition to fiction; Dhannoun Ayyoub; and Lutfiyya al-Dulaimi, who writes extensively about women in the Arab world. Some important Iraqi poets are Nazik Sadiq Al-Malaika, Muhammad Mahdi al-Jawahiri, Ahmad al-Safi al-Najafi, Maruf al-Rasafi, and Zuhur Dixon. Badr Shakir al-Sayyab is one of the Arab literary world's most respected and loved poets.

Little data were available with regard to booksellers and publishers still in operation in Iraq. As of August 2005, four publishing houses were affiliated with the Ministry of Culture (all situated in Baghdad and government controlled).

Bookshops and Publishers in Iraq
General Federation of Iraqi Women
General Federation of Trade Unions

Iran

Iran has four national libraries: the National Library and Archives and Malek National Library, both located in Tehran; the Central Library of Astan Quds Razavi, located in Mashad; and the Tabriz National Library, located in Tabriz. Iran also has a plethora of public libraries and museums: more than 1,500 libraries and 400 museums and cultural centers operate throughout the country.

Classical Persian literature comprises court, mystic, philosophical, and love poetry, as well as epics, legends, and courtly prose. Pre-Islamic Persian literature mostly consists of religious writing, the most noteworthy of which is the Avesta, the oldest known scripture of Zoroastrianism. The Pahlavi writings of Sasanian and Parthian Iran are the core known writings from early Persian literary sources. Very little is known of this period, although maxims, fragments of *The Memorial of Zarir* (an epic), and *The Book of the Exploits of Ardashir* (a historical romance) were preserved, in addition to the religious texts. As with Arabic literature, the literature of Iran was transformed by contact with the West. The Constitutional Revolution of July 1909 also had widespread effects, bringing about educational reform, establishing the press, and fostering an environment favorable to public debates ranging from politics to religion. Writing became a way to communicate with a newly literate public and a means of spreading knowledge and opinions on social and political issues.

Beginning in the 1960s, nationalist and leftist political movements began gaining strength as a way to oppose the dictatorship of Mohammad Reza Shah. These movements resulted in an outpouring of nostalgic literature that exposed the ambiguity between modernity (i.e., Westernization) and romanticized traditions. Censorship increased, as did the imprisonment and execution of writers. The 1979 revolution brought about a brief period of free expression; however, the religious Cultural Revolution that followed resulted in the same tight censorship and persecution as before. Writers active both before and after the revolution tend to make extensive use of metaphor and the contrasts between realism and surrealism. Cultural nuances, such as dialect, regional politics and culture, figure prominently in their literature, as do gender roles and Iranian history.

The poetry of Iran began in the royal courts, drawing from oral tradition and legends. Poetry also began to change as the Middle East was increasingly exposed to Western culture, although the significant changes in poetry occurred in the 1960s and 1970s, just before the Cultural Revolution of 1979. Iranian poetry can be divided into roughly three different movements: before the revolution, during the revolution, and post-revolution. The first movement, which spans roughly the period between the 1890s and 1930s, is marked by nationalist themes, imitation of Western literary forms, and lauding of nontraditional culture. The second movement, from the 1940s to the 1970s, marked the introduction of Marxism to Iranian intellectuals, and the literature came to play a significant role in the events that led up to the 1979 upheaval. Beginning in the 1980s, feminist themes predominate, and postmodern and experimental forms eventually figure more prominently.

Important Iranian prose authors include the very influential Mahmud Dowlatabadi, who focuses his short stories and novels on social injustice, particularly as it oppresses the working classes of Iran. Simin Daneshvar is Iran's first female prose writer. She also works as a translator (and has translated Chekhov, Shaw, Hawthorne, and Saroyan, among others). Her novel *Savushun* is the first written by a woman in Iran. Shahrnush Parsipur, a novelist and short story writer, focuses her writing on gender and sexuality in Iran. Many of her books have been banned, and she has been imprisoned for her outspoken writing and opinions. Many critics consider the most significant of Parsipur's novels to be *Touba and the Meaning of Night*. The writing of Parsipur and Moniru Ravanipur exemplifies use of the technique of magical realism in Iranian writing. Ghazi Rabihavi, an author of short stories, novels, and plays, experiments with different narrative techniques and tends to focus on marginalized groups as subjects for his stories. Both he and the novelist Shahriar Mandanipour represent postmodern trends in Iranian fiction.

Major classical poets from Iran include Ferdowsi, Omar Khayyam, Sa'adi, Mevlana Jalaluddin Rumi, and Hafez. One of the most influential poets of the modern period is Ahmad Shamlu, the author of twenty volumes of poetry and the translator of such Western poets as Federico Garcia Lorca and Langston Hughes. Yadollah Royai is an extremely important Iranian poet and representative of the Iranian avant-garde in verse. He is more interested in the language of a poem than in imparting a political or social message. Other influential poets include Simin Behbahani, Nader Naderpur, Esmail Khoi, Mehdi Akhavan Saless, and Abbas Kiarostami (the latter also considered among Iran's most influential filmmakers).

According to statistics gathered at the Frankfurt Book Fair, Iran has approximately 1,700 bookshops, although no locations are specified.

THE ARABIAN PENINSULA

Bahrain

The Sheikh Isa bin Salman Al Khalifa National Library is currently under construction in the city of Manama. Bahrain's academic libraries are located at the University of Bahrain, the Arab Open University, and the Arabian Gulf University. The Directorate of Public Libraries,

Literature

a department of the Ministry of Education for the Kingdom of Bahrain, manages nine public libraries throughout the country in Muharraq, Sitra, Riffa, Hidd, Jidhafs, Arad, Salmanya, Isa, and Manama. The museum Beit al-Quran also houses a public library, although its collection focuses primarily on the Qur'an.

Two publishing houses in Bahrain are Al Ayam Publishing and the Al Hilal Publishing and Marketing Group, which manages the Elmia Book Store chain. Bahrain hosts an annual international book fair in Manama.

Some of Bahrain's best fiction authors tend to use experimental forms in their writing. Amin Salih has published a novel, *First Song of A. S.*, and several collections of short stories. Muhamad Abd al-Malik, an author of both short stories and novels, typically writes stories that deal with down-and-out protagonists, although his fiction is not without humor. Qasim Haddad is the most famous poet from Bahrain. Others include Ali Abdallah Khalifa and Ali al-Sharqawi.

Here is a sampling of Jordanian bookshops and publishers as listed on the Website www.tradearabia.com:

Bookshops and Publishers in Bahrain

Al Hilal Bookshop
Al Hilal Corporation
Bookcase (Children's Books Specialists)
Delmon Bookshop
fakhrawi Bookshop

Family Bookshop (Bahrain)
Jashanmal & Sons
National Bookshop Bahrain
Qudrat Ali & Sons

Kuwait

The National Library of Kuwait is located in Kuwait City. Academic libraries are located at Yarmouk University and Kuwait University and in several other private institutions. Al-Maktabah Al-Ahlia, established in 1923, was Kuwait's oldest library until the Central Public Library was built 13 years later, absorbing the entire collection of its predecessor. Kuwait's current system of public libraries has more than twenty branches, mostly in Kuwait City. Many public schools have libraries, all managed by the Libraries Administration at the Ministry of Education.

Kuwaiti author Ismail Fahd Ismail is extremely well-known among Arab readers. He writes criticism, history, novels, and short stories, although some of his most intense activity has been his work with Kuwait's dramatic and cinematic arts. Kuwait's famous poet Su'ad al-Mubarak al-Sabah not only writes verse but is also a human rights and Arab unity activist. Initially a conservative poet, al-Sabah later began publishing more emotional, socially conscious poetry. Another famous poet from Kuwait is Ahmad al-Mushari al-Udwani, whose work is also typified by its critical outlook on social and political issues.

Information about bookstores and publishers in Kuwait is not reliable, although a partial list can be compiled from the Website www.tradearabia.com:

Bookshops and Publishers in Kuwait

Al Batra Bookshop
Dar Al Oloum Library
Family Bookshop Kuwait
Farajalla Press Agency, Ltd.
Gulf Union Company
Hala Stationery Supply Est
Kuwait Department Stores
Kuwait Printing Press
Musaed Bader Al Sayer Est

National Library of Kuwait
Press Agency
Saeed & Samir Bookstore
Spectrum Bookshop
Sultan Publication & Distribution Co.
The Bookhouse Co., Ltd.
The Kuwait Bookshops Co., Ltd.
Tulaitula Bookshop

Qatar

The National Library of Qatar is located in Doha. The University of Qatar is home to Qatar's academic library. The National Council for Culture houses the Department of Public Libraries, which supports the oldest public library in Qatar, Dar al-Kutub al-Qatariyya. This library was created in 1962 when the National Public Library merged with the library of the Ministry of al-Ma'arif (Education); it has several branches throughout the state. The National Council for Culture, Arts, and Heritage is currently building another national library; which will be located adjacent to their main building.

Qatar has several acclaimed authors, such as Jamal Fayiz, a short story writer and novelist; fiction writer, poet, and editor Mumtaz Rashid; and Abdul Qadir al-Emiri. Since the year 2000, Qatar has hosted the Doha Cultural Festival, which features lectures, poetry readings, and art exhibitions. Arab intellectuals and authors from all countries are included, with a specific focus on Qatari culture.

There are no reliable statistics indicating the number of bookstores and publishers in Qatar, although a partial list has been compiled from the Website www.tradearabia.com:

Bookshops and Publishers in Qatar

Abu Karbal Bookshop
Al Almyah Bookshop
Al Arouba Press & Publishing
Al Farabi Bookshop
Al Jahez Library
Al Lujaen Company, Ltd.
Al Mutanabbi Bookshop & Stationary
　(Dar Al Mutanabbi)
Al Ousra Bookshop
Al Shahwani Library
Al Shark Library
Al Ummah Magazine
Alfatah Bookshop
Ali Baba Boutique
Alnahdah Library
Arabian Bookshop
Arabian Est for Commerce
Arabian Library
Dar Al Thaqafah Bookshop
Dar Almutanabi for Pub & Dist
Doha Magazine
English Bookshop
Fahad Bin Jassem Trading Co.
Family Bookshop
Intramas—Qatar
Jarir Book Store
Modern Library
Orient Public Relations
Oryx Publishing & Advertising Co.
Qatar History WLL
Qatar National Library
Ragam Library
School Library
Student Bookshop
Talal Trading Centre
The Centre
The Peninsula
University Bookshop
World of Early Learning
Y K D Group

Oman

University and other school libraries are to be found in Sultan Qaboos University, which is Oman's national library. Muscat College, Sohar University, and the American International School of Muscat also house libraries. Other libraries are the Library of Manuscripts and Documents within Oman's Ministry of Heritage and Culture, the library within the Ifta (the office that answers religious queries specific to Islam), and the Sultan Qaboos Grand Mosque, which contains a library and religious studies teaching center.

The Oman Literary Society supports literature and is currently creating a database of Omani authors. Oman is home to several notable authors, such as poet Sayf al-Rahabi, who writes free verse about contemporary Arabic culture. Another notable Omani is Abdullah al Ryami, who partially founded the avant-garde theatre group A'Shams, where he worked for a time as artistic

LITERATURE

director. Oman is also home to Najma Publications, which publishes modern poetry, novels, and translations. Both he and fellow Omani poet Mohamed Al Harthi were informally banned by the Omani government for expressing critical views of Omani politics on satellite television.

The Website www.tradearabia.com lists the following bookshops and publishers operating in Oman:

Bookshops and Publishers in Oman

Al Fanar Bookshop	Family Bookshop Oman LLC
Al Nahja General Store	Osama Educational Supplies Est
Al Saqafa Bookshop	Three Star Corporation
Book Centre	Ziadfleet Traders & Contractors

Saudi Arabia

The national library of Saudi Arabia is the King Fahad National Library, located in Riyadh. Universities located in Saudi Arabia, all of which have libraries, include Imam Muhammad bin Saud Islamic University, Islamic University Medinah, King Abdul Aziz University, King Faisal Center, King Faisal University, King Khaled bin Abdul Aziz University, King Saud University, Umm Al-Qura University, Dar Al-Hekma College, Jeddah College of Technology, and Riyadh College of Technology. The King Abdulaziz Public Library, open to everyone, is located in Riyadh. Saudi Arabia is also home to many museums and cultural institutions, most funded by oil revenue. Bookstores and public libraries are ubiquitous, although the available materials are selected based on strict religious and political standards.

Authors who have emerged from Saudi Arabia include Abdul Mohsen Musalam, a popular poet, and Khalil al-Fuzayyi, who is both a journalist and writer of short stories. Ghazi al-Gosaibi, who has extensive experience in his country's government, has also published twelve volumes of poetry, all of it typified by a clear, articulate style. Other Saudi Arabian poets of note include Iqbal Qamar, Sohail Saqib, and Tariq Butt.

According to the Website www.tradearabia.com, the following publishers and bookshops operate in Saudi Arabia:

Bookshops and Publishers in Saudi Arabia

Afya Najd Magazine	Makkah Printing and Publishing Co.
Al Esha'a P Press	Maktabat Makkah—Publishing & Distribution
Al Hamad Printing Press	National Printing Press
Al Hasa Modern Press	New National Bookshop
Alnajah Educational	Obeikan Industrial Investment Group
Dar Al Khaleej Stationery	Sahli Bookshop
Jarir Bookstore	Saudi Distribution Co.
Khafji Printing Press	Shadi Publisher House
Konooz Al Marefa	

United Arab Emirates

The Cultural Foundation National Library, located in Abu Dhabi, is the national library for the United Arab Emirates. Many schools are located in the Emirates, with two of the major university libraries located at Al Ain Men's College and United Arab Emirates University. The National Medical Library is another important institution.

Nasir Jubran, Amina Abdallah, Abd al-Hameed Ahmad (a distinguished journalist as well as a short story writer), and Harib al-Dhariri are some of the prominent authors to emerge from the Emirates. Al-Dhariri is the founder of the Short Story Club and director of the Union of Emirate Writers.

The Website www.tradearabia.com lists the following bookshops and publishers operating in the United Arab Emirates:

Bookshops and Publishers in the United Arab Emirates

Abdulla Al Jaroodi Agencies
Abdulla Mohd Ali
Ahmed Abdul Rahim Kazim Bookshop
Al Abdi Books & Publications Est
Al Albany Archeologic Library
Al Amin Book Shop
Al Andalos Bookshop
Al Anwar Enterprises
Al Araka Bookshop
Al Arooba Book Shop
Al Bairooni Cultural Tape Est
Al Balagh Bookshop & Recordings
Al Bikar Stationery
Al Elim Lil Malayen Bookshop
Al Ellm Ulmalayen Bookshop
Al Falah Bookshop LLC
Al Farah Stationery LLC
Al Fikrah Library
Al Forqan Bookshop
Al Gurg Stationery
Al Hadara Bookshop
Al Hilal Office Supplies Est
Al Hoson Printing & Stationery Est
Al Huda Stationary
Al Ittifaq Newspapers Trading
Al Jabr Al Elmiyah Book Shop
Al Jafla Bookshop
Al Jamal Library
Al Karama Bookshop
Al Kayan Bookshop
Al Khamri Commercial Enterprises
Al Madina Technical Center
Al Maqta Books Trading
Al Masar Audio & Publications Center
Al Musalla Star Bookshop
Al Mutanabbi Bookshop
Al Mutanabbi Bookshop LLC
Al Najah Book Shop
Al Qassim Trading
Al Razi Bookshop
Al Risala Recording & General Trading Co.
Al Roman Trading Est
Al Safa Journals & Prints LLC
Al Shahd Publication Distribution
Al Siddique Book Centre
Al Taif Greeting Cards & Gifts
Al Taqdeer Trading Est
Al Taqwa Al Islamiyah Recordings
Al Tawasul Illustrated
Al Wadah Bookshop
Al Wafa Stationery & Book Shop
Al Watan Printing Publishing
Alefba Est
Alexandria Bookshop
Ali Ghanim Bookshop
All Prints Distributors & Publishers
Andrews Bookshop LLC
Anthraper Books
Archies Bookshop
Asfaar Tourism & Travel Magazine
Asian Printing Press
Atlas Industries LLC
Atlas Printing Press
Books Gallery
Corporate Publishing International (CPI)
Dar Al Aman
Dar Al Hikmah Printing, Publishing & Distribution LLC
Donya Entertainment (Ltd Liability Co.)
Dubai Printing Press
Express Print Publishers (Dubai Indl Dir)
Future Bookshop
Gulf Printing & Publishing
Jashanmal National Co.
Magrudy Enterprises
Nabeel Printing & Publishing FZ LLC
New Culture Bookshop
Oriental Printing Group
Pangrosvnor Group
Santiago Gift Exibition
Taymour Stationery Est
Technical Printing Press
Union Printing Press & Stationery
Yousuf Book Binding House
Zabeel Printing Press

Yemen

Yemen's national library is located in Aden, Yemen's former capital. Yemeni collegiate and university libraries are located at Al-Eman University, Al Ahgaff University, Hodeidah University, Hadramout Science University, Queen Arwa University, Saba University, Sanaa

LITERATURE

BOOK FAIRS

At least five major book fairs are held in the Middle East and North Africa. The Jerusalem International Book Fair, a biennial event since 1963, has grown into an enormous attraction. More than 500 publishers from thirty countries participated at the last Jerusalem fair. In addition to featuring books and the business of publishing, the fair hosts annual symposia and various cultural events that focus on a specific theme. The focal point of the most recent fair, held in February 2005, was "dialogue," or the role of writing in culture and history, particularly with regard to how writing can influence one culture's perception of another. The fair also commemorated the fortieth anniversary of German–Israeli relations. German ambassador to Israel Dr. Niels Hansen discussed the Hebrew translation of his book, *Out of the Shadows of the Catastrophe*.

The annual International Cairo Book Fair, the second oldest of the five fairs, is sited in Nasser City and is organized by the Egyptian Book Association. Egypt's government began the fair in 1969 to commemorate Cairo's one-thousandth birthday. For the thirty-eighth and most recent fair, 623 publishers from thirty-two Arabian and international countries participated.

Tunisia hosted its twenty-fourth international book fair between April 28 and May 8, 2006, in El Kram Palexpo. Since 1982, the event has been organized by the Ministry for the Safeguarding of Culture and Heritage. Participants included 672 publishers from twenty-nine countries, including 81 publishers from Tunisia. The Tunisian fair featured more than 100,000 books, most of them written in Arabic or French, although works in English, Italian, German, and Spanish were offered as well. Roughly 200,000 attendees are expected each year.

The Tehran International Book Fair has seen steadily increased participation from publishers and participants since its inception in 1987. During its inaugural year the fair drew participants from nineteen countries and 196 publishers that exhibited nearly 16,000 books. In 2003 the numbers rose significantly, when the fair attracted fifty-five participating countries, 900 publishers, and 75,000 exhibited titles.

As part of its National Cultural Project, Saudi Arabia's Ministry of Higher Education and the Riyadh Exhibition Company agreed to host the first Riyadh International Book Fair, an event that ran from February 22 through March 3, 2006. Approximately 150,000 Arabic titles and 100,000 foreign-language books were exhibited, and nearly 500 publishers participated.

University, Taiz University, and the University of Aden. Yemen has at least one public library, the Yemeni Public Library.

Yemeni short story author Muhammad Abd al-Wali did not set out to be a writer. Instead he went to work for the Yemeni government, as did several of his contemporaries. Most of al-Wali's fiction focuses on the sadder points of human existence. Common themes in his fiction are loneliness, oppression, failure, and contradictory behavior and attitudes. Author Said Aulaqi writes both plays and short stories on a variety of subjects, including North and South Yemen's revolutions. Zayd Mutte Dammaj is a novelist and short story author whose family had close revolutionary ties. His experience allowed him to detail the former Yemeni government's corrupt and unjust conduct. Yemen's Abd-Allah al-Baraduni writes some of the best examples of irony in Arabic, particularly as it relates to social and political circumstances. Poet Abd al'Aziz al-Maqalih is the author of more than thirteen volumes of poetry and more than thirty other works of literature and criticism.

Reliable information was unavailable regarding the number and location of booksellers and publishers in Yemen.

RESOURCE GUIDE

PRINT RESOURCES

Al-Sayyid Marsot, Afaf Lutfi. "Survey of Egyptian Works of History." *American Historical Review* (December 1991): 1422–1434.

Allen, Roger. *The Arabic Novel: An Historical and Critical Introduction.* Syracuse, NY: Syracuse University Press, 1995.

Altoma, Salih J. *Modern Arabic Literature in Translation: A Companion.* London: Saqi, 2005.

Badawi, M. M. *Modern Arabic Literature.* Cambridge: Cambridge University Press, 1992.

Badawi, M. M. *A Short History of Modern Arabic Literature.* New York: Clarendon Press, 1993.

Bergan, Erling. *Libraries in the West Bank and Gaza: Obstacles and Possibilities*. IFLA Council. Updated 2000. http://www.ifla.org/IV/ifla66/papers/170-172e.htm.

Chraibi, Aboubakr. "Texts of the Arabian Nights and Ideological Variations." *Middle Eastern Literatures* 7.2 (2004): 149–157.

Elturk, Ghada. "Palestinian Libraries: Little Pieces of Heaven in Hell." *Progressive Librarian* 21 (Winter 2003): http://libr.org/pl/21_Elturk.html.

Hashmi, Sohail H. "Arab Middle East and North Africa." Pp. 575–577 in Richard C. Martin (ed.), *Encyclopedia of Islam and the Muslim World.* Vol. 2. New York: Macmillan Reference USA, 2004.

Luxner, Larry. "A Nobel for the Arab Nation." *Saudi Aramco World* 40.2 (1989). http://www.saudiaramcoworld.com/issue/198902/default.htm.

Jacobson, David C. *Modern Midrash: The Retelling of Traditional Jewish Narratives by 20th Century Hebrew Authors.* Albany: State University of New York Press, 1987.

Jayyusi, Salma Khadra, ed. *Modern Arabic Poetry: An Anthology.* New York: Columbia University Press, 1987.

Kravitz, N. *3,000 Years of Hebrew Literature.* Chicago: The Swallow Press, Inc., 1972.

Manzalaoui, Mahmoud, ed. *Arabic Writing Today: The Short Story.* Cairo: American Research Center in Egypt, 1968.

Marzolph, Ulrich, and Richard van Leeuwen, eds. *Arabian Nights Encyclopedia,* Vols. 1–2. Santa Barbara, CA: ABC-CLIO, 2004.

Messick, Brinkley. *The Calligraphic State: Textual Domination and History in a Muslim Society.* Berkeley: University of California Press, 1993.

Mozaffari, Nahid, ed. *Strange Times, My Dear: The PEN Anthology of Contemporary Iranian Literature.* New York: Arcade Publishing, 2005.

Nebenzahl, Ora. "Public Library Legislation in Israel: A Study in Public Policy Process." diss., Columbia University, 1996.

Riggan, William. "Hebrew Literature in the 1990s." *World Literature Today* 72.3 (Summer 1998): 477.

Shaheen, Mohammad. *The Modern Arabic Short Story.* Hampshire: Palgrave Macmillan, 2002.

Shaked, Gershon. "Through Many Small Windows, by the Back Door: An Introduction to Postrealistic Hebrew Literature, 1950–80." *Prooftexts* 16 (1996): 271–91.

Stevens, P. R., C. M. Levine, and S. Steinmetz. *Meshuggenary: Celebrating the World of Yiddish.* New York: Simon and Schuster, 2002.

Talattof, Kamran. *The Politics of Writing in Iran: A History of Modern Persian Literature.* Syracuse, NY: Syracuse University Press, 2000.

LITERATURE

Tuczay, Christa A. "Motifs in the Arabian Nights and European Literature: A Comparison." *Folklore* 116 (2005): 272–91.

Woodhull, Winifred. *Transfigurations of the Maghreb: Feminism, Decolonization, and Literatures.* Minneapolis: University of Minnesota Press, 1993.

WEBSITES

@*The Source: The Israel Info-Access Magazine.* 2006. Israel Info-Access, LLC. http://www.thesourceisrael.com/current.

African and Middle Eastern Reading Room. Updated May 18, 2006. The Library of Congress. http://www.loc.gov/rr/amed/.

Ahmad Shamlu. Updated March 9, 2004. Shamlu's Publishing, Inc. http://www.shamlu.com/index.htm. The official Website for the Iranian poet Ahmad Shamlu.

ArabNews Online. Updated August 14, 2006. ArabNews. http://www.arabnews.com/.

Beit Al Qur'an. 2002. http://www.beitalquran.com/. This site serves as a source for information on the Beit Al Qur'an, a museum dedicated to Islamic culture.

Central Bureau of Statistics (Israel). Updated August 14, 2006. The State of Israel. http://www1.cbs.gov.il/reader/cw_usr_view_Folder?ID=141.

Culture & Arts. 2005. Embassy of State of Qatar in Washington, D.C. http://www.qatarembassy.net/culture.asp.

Frankfurt Book Fair. August 2006. German Booksellers and Publishers Association. http://www.frankfurt-book-fair.com/en/portal.php.

Iraqi Libraries Network. Updated April 3, 2006. Bielefield University Library: http://iraklib.ub.uni-bielefeld.de/.

Islamic Philosophy Online. Updated July 30, 2006. Islamic Philosophy Online, Inc. http://www.muslimphilosophy.com/.

Israel Ministry of Foreign Affairs. Updated August 12, 2006. The State of Israel. http://www.israel-mfa.gov.il/.

Jewish Virtual Library. 2006. American-Israeli Cooperative Enterprise. http://www.jewishvirtuallibrary.org/.

Khelladi, Aïssa. *Algérie Littérature/Action.* Updated May10, 2001. http://www.algerie-litterature.com/.

Kjeilen, Tore. *Encyclopedia of the Orient.* 2006. http://i-cias.com/e.o/index.htm.

The Literature of Morocco: An Overview. Updated May 13, 2001. The Literature and Culture of Morocco in the Postcolonial Web. http://www.scholars.nus.edu.sg/landow/post/morocco/literature/litov.html.

LiMag: Littératures du Maghreb. Updated November 5, 1998. http://www.limag.com/.

Maghrebi Arts. National Institute for Technology and Liberal Education. http://www.maghrebi-studies.org/.

MENALIB: Middle East Virtual Library. Updated June 23, 2005. ULB Halle. http://ssgdoc.bibliothek.uni-halle.de/vlib/html/.

MENIC: The Middle East Network Information Center. 2004. University of Texas at Austin. http://menic.utexas.edu/menic.html.

Middle East & Islamic Studies Collection. Updated November 19, 2004. Cornell University http://www.library.cornell.edu/colldev/mideast/.

Middle East World Newspapers and Magazines. Updated August 14, 2006. Worldpress.org. http://www.worldpress.org/newspapers/MIDEAST/.

Ministry of Information, Sultanate of Oman. Updated August 14, 2006. Omanet. http://www.omanet.com/english/home.asp.

National Council for Culture, Arts, and Heritage (Qatar). http://www.nccah.com/english.asp.

Newspapers and News Media. 2006. ABYZ News Links. http://www.abyznewslinks.com/. This site contains links to many newspaper and media outlets of the Middle Eastern world.

PEN American Center. Updated August 3, 2006. PEN American Center. http://www.pen.org/index.php. This site has a great deal of information about past, present, and future literature by authors around the world, including those from the Middle East.

Statistics Algeria. Updated April 8, 2002. National Office of Statistics. http://www.ons.dz/English/indexag.htm.

Teissier, Bruno. *Bibliomonde*. 2006. L'Association BiblioMonde. http://www.bibliomonde.net/.
Trade Arabia. Updated August 14, 2006. Al Hilal Publishing & Marketing Group. http://www.tradearabia.net.
Universities and Research. Updated September 15, 2005. Arab World. http://www.library.ucla.edu/libraries/url/colls/mideast/pages/arabpages/arresrch.html.

NOTE

1. Sources for the remainder of the chapter include Eugene Rogan, "Arab Books and Human Development," *Arab Studies Quarterly* 26.2 (2004): 67–79; Azar Mahloujian, "Phoenix from the Ashes: A Tale of the Book in Iran," www.iranchamber.com/podium/history/o40702_tale_of_book_iran.php; Mona Mahmoud, "Iraqi Publishers Compete with Foreign Literature," *USA Today*, August 25, 2005; *Arab Human Development Report 2003* and *Arab Human Development Report 2004*, United Nations Development Programme; and Frankfurt Book Fair, http://www.frankfurt-book-fair.com/en.

LOVE, SEX, AND MARRIAGE

RIHAB KASSATLY BAGNOLE

Many aspects of the Middle Eastern and North African lifestyle have been altered by years of Western domination of these regions. Most of these countries acquired their independence during the twentieth century and were affected by new ideas that came to them through the mass media. Access to local television stations became available to most Middle Easterners and North Africans around the mid-twentieth century, and many of them can now view international stations by using inexpensive satellite dishes. Around the turn of the current century, access to Western programs and trends also became available through the Internet, the use of which is spreading via Internet cafés and making its way quickly into the homes of the people in the region.

During the twentieth century, some aspects of the legal system of many Middle Eastern and North African countries thoroughly changed to conform more closely to Western ideas. This has been the case with laws concerning trade and commerce. The region, however, is trying to maintain its moral values and is resisting foreign ideas that deal with women by adhering and reinforcing cultural laws that are mostly controlled by Shariah, Islamic law governing family relations, marriage, and divorce. Some judiciary establishments are responding more quickly to the changes in their society and are adapting their laws accordingly. For example, in Tunisia, which became a republic in 1957, women have not been required to obey their husbands since 1993, and the country is amending family laws to make the bonds of matrimony more applicable in court. Other countries are experiencing an unprecedented, creative use of their existing laws; examples include the remarkably unorthodox marriage contracts in Egypt, Iran, and Saudi Arabia (discussed later).

Marriage in the Middle East and North Africa is the most important goal in the lives of young people. They dream about it, prepare for it, and arrange to achieve it. Although more women are getting an education, working outside their homes, and planning to change legislative rules that limit their lives, only through marriage can a woman elevate her status and acquire the respect of her society. Marriage allows her more freedom and power, granted according to her husband's rank in society. His success elevates her position, regardless of her background or education. Therefore, her essential role is to support her husband and take care of their children. On the other hand, the husband fulfills the expectations of his

LOVE, SEX, AND MARRIAGE

WEDDING COSTS AND RESPONSIBILITIES

A wedding in the Middle East and North Africa is expensive. Although the family of the bride now helps with the costs and sometimes providing a house, furniture, or both, these are usually the groom's responsibilities. The wedding involves the following:

- A present from the groom and his family to seal their intention, which is called *raboun*, *shabkah*, or *heddiyah*. It consists of gold items that include a ring and a bracelet, and may include a necklace and earrings if the groom is financially able. The fiancée wears her jewelry to show off her self-worth and the status of her future husband. She keeps these items if the groom decides to break the engagement and returns them if she changes her mind.
- A cash dowry called *mahr* consisting of the *mouqaddam*, which is paid by the groom in advance or deferred to a later time, and the *mouakhkhar*, which is paid to the bride in case of divorce. The amount of mahr is indicated in the marriage contract, and the mouqaddam can be used in full or in part to furnish the couple's lodging or to buy some of the bride's trousseau, known as *gihaz*. The gihaz consists of the bride's personal possessions and may extend to bedroom and kitchen items.
- The engagement party, which is the responsibility of the bride's family. It can be extensive or restricted to close family members and friends.
- The wedding party, which is the responsibility of the groom. Nowadays, many urban wedding parties are taking place in hotels and clubs.

society by marrying a woman who is able to bear him children, especially boys who will carry on his family name and assets.

All Middle Eastern and North African countries are patriarchal societies. Only a man can provide a family name for his children, and his consent confers their legitimacy. He is also the guardian of the family wealth and the beneficiary of his father's estate. Therefore, it is customary that the man and his family are the ones who choose a wife for the man; they initiate their intent by proposing to the desired bride-to-be and her family, who in turn can accept or refuse the offer.

Marriage for Middle Easterners and North Africans, then, does not simply concern the bride and the groom; it is an affair that greatly impacts their families, too. Whether in the urban or rural areas, the two families will become, in many ways, one extended family. Therefore, harmony between the two sides is essential for the marriage to succeed.

Family is the most respected social unit in the region. To become a member of a family means to belong to a group whose collective behavior affects all its members. The Arabic word *aila* (family) refers to a family unit of father, mother, and children, or the extend group of kin. The family members of the spouse also become members of the extended family, which can be either *ahl*, if the spouse is not a relative, or *qarayeb*, if the spouse is one of the cousins.

Consanguineous marriages (marriages between blood relatives) are customary in the Middle East and North Africa. While it is a widely practiced custom in rural areas, fewer urban people tend to marry their relatives. However, most people prefer that the spouse comes from the same ethnic background or has the same religious belief; when this happens, the match is more likely to be acceptable to the families and chances for future problems are reduced. Not conforming to the family traditions may deprive the couple of celebrating their union publicly, may ostracize them, and in some extreme cases may get them killed.

Romantic relationships are frequent in urban settings for many Middle Easterners and North Africans. While the countryside still adheres to the traditional ways and expectations, the cities tolerate freer lifestyles and allow more opportunities for meetings with the opposite sex. Some young men prefer to live a modern lifestyle and migrate to a city where they can continue their education, find better job opportunities, and make the acquaintance of the opposite sex. The advantage of greater anonymity in the urban setting gives the youths a chance to escape the traditions of their parents and find "love" marriages. They can even contract temporary or secret marriages, which are permitted in some countries, without informing their parents. For the woman, a love affair without a marriage contract may not be an option, and the relationship may last for only a very short time, in the vain hope that it may develop into a marriage. This type of relationship is common among the elites, the educated, and those of moderate Muslim or non-Muslim communities.

The concept of a premarital sexual relationship is not accepted in the Middle East and North Africa because a woman's virginity is highly valued. Her hymen symbolizes honor and purity. As a bride, the woman is still expected to bleed on her wedding night to legitimize her marriage and acquire the approval and respect of her in-laws. A woman who loses her virginity to another man before the wedding, however, can fake bleeding through a common procedure that restores the hymen. Similarly, doctors who are willing to perform secret abortions to save women from being disgraced or killed are available in many parts of the region as well. Some couples, nevertheless, opt for premarital sex even if it is risky.

Adoption is a rare occurrence in the Middle East and North Africa. A child must keep its original lineage and blood heritage. However, there is no law against foster parenting as many children as one desires. Single men and women are permitted to take on foster children from an orphanage in their community or from families that agree to relinquish their children to them. The biological parents may also give up a child or children to a childless relative who can better afford to care and raise their offspring. These fostered children are usually aware of the arrangement between their biological and fostering parents, and they usually honor their parents' agreements when they come of age. The fostered children of a family cannot inherit from the family, but there is no law against them marrying each other.

The age of marriage is rising in most Middle Eastern and North African countries because of education and for economic reasons. The following describes love, sex, and marriage in various Middle Eastern and North African countries in the early years of the twenty-first century.

REGIONS

Algeria, Morocco, and Tunisia

Algeria, Morocco, and Tunisia are located at the western end of North Africa, separated from Europe by the Mediterranean Sea. They received their independence from France and Spain (the latter controlled a small part of southwestern Morocco) in 1962, 1956, and 1956, respectively. They are commonly known as *al-Maghreb al-Arabi* (the Arab West).

The People's Democratic Republic of Algeria has an area of 919,595 square miles with a population of 32,854,000. The birth rate is 13.2 per thousand, and life expectancy is 71.2 years for males and 74.3 years for females. The marriage rate is 7.0 per thousand. The largest ethnic groups are Arab (59.1%), Berber (26.2%), Bedouin (14.5%), and other (0.2%). Religious affiliation is mostly Muslim (99.7%) and Christian (0.3%). The literacy rate is 76 percent for males and 59.7 percent for females. The official language is Arabic.[1]

The Kingdom of Morocco has an area of 274,461 square miles with a population of 30,230,000. The birth rate is 14.6 per thousand and life expectancy is 67.5 years for males and 72.1 years for females. The largest ethnic groups are Berber (45%, of which Arabized 24%), Arab (44%), Moors (from Mauritania) (10%), and other (1%). Religious affiliation is mostly Muslim (98.3%), Christian (0.6%), and other (1.1%). The literacy rate is 61.1 percent for males and 35.1 percent for females. The official language is Arabic.[2]

LOVE, SEX, AND MARRIAGE

The Republic of Tunisia has an area of 63,170 square miles with a population of 10,038,000. The birth rate is 15.7 per thousand, and life expectancy is 73.0 years for males and 76.4 years for females. The marriage rate is 6.4 per thousand. The largest ethnic groups are Arab (67.2%), Bedouin Arab (26.6%), Algerian Arab (2.4%), Berber (1.4%), and other (2.4%). Religious affiliation is mostly Muslim (98.9%), Christian (0.5%), and other (0.6%). The literacy rate is 85.2 percent for males and 69.0 percent for females. The official language is Arabic.[3]

The minimum legal age for marriage is 21 for males and 18 for females in Algeria, 15 and 18 in Morocco, and 20 and 18 in Tunisia. It is common for people in this region to marry their relatives. This type of marriage is not always arranged; it may very well be the choice of the marrying partners. Although there is an increase in education among both sexes, marriages between relatives still exist in some urban settings and are increasing in the rural settings of Algeria.[4]

People who decide to extend their options to a nonrelated partner can meet in a variety of places: at work, at public venues, or in college. Their intimate relationships however, should be kept secret from their parents. Although more young people are having premarital sex, most girls prefer to stay chaste. In a survey conducted by the BBC in 2005, a young Algerian woman pointed out that when she met her husband in college, she did not tell her parents. She used to ignore him outside the walls of the university for fear that someone would see her talking to him. She did not have sex with him because she was afraid he would think her promiscuous. The young woman kept her virginity until they got married.[5]

It is customary for the marrying couple to have an engagement period before the wedding. The bride and the groom start to know each other and prepare their new house. The sum of money needed for the wedding comes mostly from the groom, who is also expected to bring gifts for his bride to show his generosity. He should also find an occasion to give a gift to the mother of his bride and to her unmarried sisters.

Before the wedding, the bride's family hosts a party where close relatives and friends help her in the preparation for the big day. They enjoy a variety of foods such as couscous, a selection of *tajines*, and many kinds of delicious desserts, such as baklava, semolina cookies, and gazelle horns. The guests also transfer the bride's personal items to her new house.

During the last decade, many women refrained from displaying proof of their virginity, either because they did not agree with this custom or because they were not virgins. In a 2004 study, 90 percent of a group of urban women in Morocco indicated the importance of virginity for marriage. However, the majority of them did not approve of the traditional public display of hymenal blood to prove their virginity. Two-thirds of them had had sexual experience before marriage, and 39 percent had lost their virginity before marrying.[6]

Berber women are much less obsessed with their virginity. Proof of virginity, however, is included in the wedding ceremony to show that the bride comes from a decent family, which was able to monitor her sexual activity. The bride places a red-stained piece of fabric in a plate and passes it around for everyone to witness her purity. No one is supposed to ask if the blood is real or simply a red solution that can be bought especially for that purpose.

The wedding celebration, according to the Berber tradition, lasts several days, with a special focus on each day. It includes a day for the ritual bath and another for the application of henna. On this day, female friends and relatives of the bride draw elaborate designs, including the name of the husband-to-be, on the woman's body, hands, and feet. Female guests also instruct the bride on sexual matters and childbirth.

The colors yellow and red are frequently used by the Berber bride. In some tribes, such as the Tafilalet, the bride wears a red veil for three days during the wedding ceremony, and only her husband is allowed to see her. Before she enters her new residence, it is customary for the bride and her wedding party to tour the new house three times.

If there is a divorce, a Berber woman may remarry on the same day, but not with the lover who caused her separation from her husband. The former husband has the right to restrict her new marriage, and makes his request public in front of the lineage council. If the ex-wife ignores his request, he may seek revenge by killing both of them.

The women of the Maghreb are joining efforts to end discrimination and inequality. In 2004 Moroccan women gained the right for self-guardianship and the right to compose their own marriage contracts. They have persistently demanded reform in family law.[7] Tunisian women also aspire to shift divorce and child custody into the civil code and are working to impede polygamous marriages.[8]

Polygamy, in fact, is prohibited only in Tunisia, and both spouses face a penalty of up to a year in prison and a fine if they knowingly enter into a polygamous marriage. The laws in Algeria and Morocco require justification and prior notification of existing wives. In all three countries, it is possible for a woman to marry a foreigner, and in Tunisia she maybe able to give her citizenship to her children.

Homosexuality is considered sinful and shameful, and is illegal under the law in all three countries. Algeria, Morocco, and Tunisia have condemned sexual relationships between people of the same sex. For example, Article 489 of the Algerian penal code punishes homosexuality with imprisonment ranging from six months to three years, or fines of 120 to 1,200 dirhams ($12 to $132). Islamic extremists in the Maghreb insist on severe punishment for same-sex partners. A member of the religious board in the Moroccan capital city Rabat recently called for the death penalty for gay people. It is remarkable, however, that homosexuals are sheltered and protected by the owners of some clubs and bars. These social establishments have sometimes favored gays because they are loyal customers and support the trade by buying what these businesses supply. Some managers stretch their protection even further by hiring special guards to watch for potential incursions by the police. It is notable that there is no law against two men living, traveling, or staying in a hotel together as long as they stay out of trouble. They are safe as long as they keep their relationship secret and avoid attracting attention through their clothes and manners.[9]

Libya

The Socialist People's Libyan Arab Jamahiriya has an area of 679,369 square miles with a population of 5,853,000. The birth rate is 27.2 per thousand, and life expectancy is 74.1 years for males and 78.6 for females. The largest ethnic groups are Arab (87.1%), Berber (6.8%), and other (6.1%). Religious affiliation is mostly Muslim 96.1 (percent), Christian (2.7%), and other (1.2%). The literacy rate is 92.3 percent for males and 71.8 percent for females. The official language is Arabic.[10]

The minimum legal age of marriage in Libya is eighteen for males and fifteen for females. Early marriage declined sharply in Libya between the early 1970s and the mid-1990s. The number of married women ages fifteen to nineteen dropped from 40 percent to 1 percent. Twelve percent of women who got married in 1995 were between the ages of 20 and 24, and 11 percent were between the ages of 35 and 39. Some 40 to 50 percent of these women were married to their blood relatives.[11]

Egypt

The Arab Republic of Egypt has an area of 997,739 square miles with a population of 70,457,000. The birth rate is 23.8 per thousand, and life expectancy is 68.2 years for males and

LOVE, SEX, AND MARRIAGE

> ### CLITORIDECTOMY
>
> Clitoridectomy is the medical term for one form of female circumcision. It involves the removal of any of the prepuce of the clitoris, the clitoris, and/or the labia. It is believed that this excision ensures cleanliness and chastity, and minimizes the passion of women.
>
> The procedure is usually performed on girls between the ages of four and seven and is carried out either by a physician, midwife, or a designated woman from the community. Young girls are usually tricked into going through it together, thinking they are celebrating a festive event. Clitoridectomy is a dangerous procedure and can result in life-threatening hemorrhage or infections. It can also cause other problems, such as infertility, psychological trauma, sexual trauma, and other psychological problems. Of recent, many mothers have refused to circumcise their daughters and are determined to discard this custom from their communities.

73.3 years for females. The largest ethnic groups are Egyptian Arab (84.1%), Sudanese Arab (5.5%), Berber (2.0%), Bedouin (2%), Roma or Gypsy (1.6%), and other (4.8%). Religious affiliation is mostly Muslim (84.4%), Christian (15.1%), and other (0.5%). The literacy rate is 67.2 percent for males and 44.8 percent for females. The official language is Arabic.[12]

The Egyptian views on love, sex, and marriage vary from the upper class to the middle and lower classes. Upper-class women are more privileged and open in their relationships with men. They are allowed to meet their partners in clubs or private homes and participate in mixed parties. Many of them are educated in Western schools and universities, speak foreign languages, and have been influenced by Western lifestyles. They do not practice clitoridectomy, and a female is not threatened with death if she violates sexual taboos.

Clitoridectomy is rarely practiced among middle-class women; although it is now banned by the government, it is still practiced by the lower classes and in rural areas. Local statistics compiled in 1994 estimated that between 70 and 90 percent of Egyptian women were circumcised.[13] A more recent survey conducted by an international group puts the figure even higher. In October 1995, hospitals were banned from conducting any types of female circumcision.

Egyptian middle-class parents support their sons' relations with girls, but they are more reluctant for their daughters to have friendships with males. Engaged couples are often allowed to walk together or meet in public areas. It is important for them to remain in public places for fear of causing gossip. Some families insist on chaperoning the courting couple to ensure they do not have a sexual relationship before their wedding day.

The custom of marrying a relative is becoming rare among the educated classes in Egypt. However, the tradition is still widely preferred in the *Said* (Upper Egypt). Saidi families prefer marrying their daughters to their cousins, especially those on the father's side. Recent studies indicate that 55 percent of people from rural areas are married to their relatives.[14]

Although the state and the church ban marriages of girls younger than fifteen, many rural females still get engaged at a younger age. A girl's father may promise her to the groom before she reaches puberty. In rare instances, the arrangement is sealed with the father of the groom without consulting the man in question himself.

The family may also find a suitable husband for their daughter through the good offices of a *khatibah*, a woman mediator who acts as a matchmaker. She promotes suitable men and women and convinces both sides that they are best for each other. She arranges family visits, bargains for the mahr and gifts, and helps with the preparations for the wedding. The khatibah usually does not charge a specific fee and leaves this matter to the generosity of the involved families. Her reward depends on the bride's age, beauty, and assets. For example, it may take more time and effort for the khatibah to find a husband for a woman who is over twenty, divorced, or unattractive. In these cases, the mediator's role is to convince the potential groom and his family of the woman's special characteristics or aptitudes. Such an arrangement may prove successful for customary marriages.

Some people, on the other hand, may choose to practice *zawaj urfi*, a secret marriage with just two witnesses and a contract for proof. There are at least 30,000 urfi marriages each year in Egypt, a phenomenon that is increasing among university students.[15] Such a marriage ends by tearing up the contract. If the wife gets pregnant, she can prove the legitimacy of her child by presenting the contract to court. It becomes more complicated in cases where the wife looses the contract, and the husband denies his involvement. In 2005 the Family Court of Appeals in Cairo accepted DNA testing in a paternity case. The parliament is currently discussing a new law that would make DNA tests mandatory in paternity cases.

The divorce rate is relatively high in Egypt, and it is easier for a man to divorce than for a woman. Unlike his wife, a husband is not limited by conditions when he seeks divorce. He can repudiate his wife by repeating the Islamic performative *Inti Taleq* (you are divorced) three times. The husband must then register the divorce and inform his wife about it. He terminates his marriage contract as soon as he registers the divorce, while she becomes free of her obligations as a wife when she receives the divorce papers.

Unlike the husband, the wife needs a judicial decree from the court to dissolve her marriage officially. A recent law allows Egyptian women to seek a unilateral, no-questions-asked divorce, making Egypt the second country in the Arab world, after Tunisia, to give women divorce rights similar to those of men.[16]

A study published by the National Center of Social and Criminological Research indicates that during the last quarter of the twentieth century, 95 percent of the total number of divorce cases in Egypt occurred among those who were illiterate, and 33 percent of those were initiated by women. These rates have declined with the increase in the level of education. The number of divorce cases was higher in urban areas and lower in the conservative parts of the country (Upper Egypt). For women the main causes of divorce were polygamy, conflicts with the husband's family, financial problems, and sterility. For men the reasons were incompatibility and conflicts with the wife's family.[17]

Recent statistics indicate that about 290,000 people divorce each year. In Cairo, where about one-fifth of Egypt's more than 70 million people live, roughly 15,000 women file for divorce annually.[18] Under the new law, court-supervised mediation is required before a divorce is granted, and the wife must return any cash or property that she received from her husband in exchange for their marriage. The husband, however, can still end his marriage quickly whenever he chooses under the broad divorce powers given to men.

Homosexuality is not allowed in Egypt, and state police have been known to raid the bars where gay people meet. A raid on the Queen Boat, a popular gay floating disco hang-out on the Nile in the Zamalek district of Cairo, resulted in the sentencing of twenty-nine men to hard labor for two to four years. Fear of prosecution is leading homosexual individuals to ask for asylum in the United States. In 2003 a man who was sentenced to prison for one year and three month was granted asylum in the United States through the help of human-rights groups.[19]

Jordan

The Hashemite Kingdom of Jordan has an area of 34,495 square miles with a population of 5,182,000. The birth rate is 28.1 per thousand, and life expectancy is 70.6 years for males and 72.4 years for females. The largest ethnic groups are Arab (97.8%), Circassian (1.2%),

HONOR CRIMES

Honor is the pride of Middle Easterners and North Africans. To many of them, the concept depends heavily on the behavior of the females in their families. A well-behaved woman reflects well on the ability of the male members of her family to control her. Her father, brother, cousin, and husband are permitted by the law to imprison her, torture her, or even kill her if they think that she is having premarital sex or sex with someone other than her husband. The United Nations agency for children, UNICEF, indicates that while Jordan had an average of 23 "honor killings" a year in 1997, 52 "honor killings" occurred in Egypt, and 400 in Yemen; more than two-thirds of all the murders in Gaza and the West Bank in 1999 were also "honor killings."[22] Many human-rights organizations and individuals are concerned about such crimes against women. They are calling for treating such cases as crimes.

and other (1.0%). Religious affiliation is mostly Muslim (93.5%), Christian (4.1%), and other (2.4%). The literacy rate is 90.1 percent for males and 85.1 percent for females. The marriage rate is 10.0 per thousand. The official language is Arabic.[20]

The minimum marriage age in Jordan is 16 for males and 15 for females. The consanguinity rate in marriage has decreased to 30 percent of all marriages, largely as a result of increased education: the higher the education level of women, the lower the marriage rate between relatives. This type of marriage is more common in rural, as compared to urban, settings.[21]

Dating without the consent of the family or premarital sex can be a very risky situation in Jordan. A single or married woman whose activities arouse her family's suspicion about her having premarital or adulterous sexual relationships may be killed. Honor killing is considered a cleansing reaction to restore the family reputation. In most cases, the sexual activities of a woman destroy her reputation and damage the name and honor of all her family. In 2002 there were 15 honor killings out of a total of 125 murders in the country. The Jordanian penal code does not penalize a man for killing an adulterous female in his family. Under the existing law, husbands who are found guilty of committing honor killings often receive sentences of less than six months, and rarely do any of the victim's family file a complaint against the crime.[23]

Polygamy is allowed in Jordan without judicial permission. In most divorces women retain custody of the children until they reach puberty.

Israel

The State of Israel has an area of 8,367 square miles with a population of 6,677,000. The birth rate is 21.7 per thousand, and life expectancy is 77.5 for males and 81.5 for females. The largest ethnic groups are Jewish (76.2%), and Arab and other (23.8%). Religious affiliation is mostly Jewish (76.2%), Muslim (15.7%), Christian (2.1%), Druze (1.6%), and other (0.2%). The literacy rate is 96.9 percent. The marriage rate is 6.2 per thousand. The official languages are Hebrew and Arabic.[24]

Among the Israeli Arab community, consanguinous marriage rates are significantly decreasing. The frequency has dropped from 52.9 percent in the period 1961–70 to 32 percent in the period 1991–98. Of these, marriages with paternal cousins have decreased while maternal first-cousin marriages have risen.[25]

Only religious marriages are legal in Israel. Religious courts have been established for each of the major religions in Israel. There are Jewish rabbinical courts, Islamic Shariah courts, Christian religious courts, and Druse courts. Couples of any particular faith are required to marry according to the tenets of that religion, and then only according to the specific custom recognized by the government to be legally binding. The jurisdiction of the religious courts is exclusive in some areas of domestic relations and exists concurrent with that of civilian courts in others.

The marriages of Israeli Jews are conducted according to Orthodox Jewish *halaka*. Some secular Israelis choose to travel abroad and have civil marriages. Some groups are calling for a change to institutionalize civil marriages. These marriages are legally binding in Israel, although not recognized by the rabbinate as Jewish.

The celebration of a Jewish wedding lasts seven days, during which friends and family give parties in honor of the newlyweds. A prenuptial agreement is common and should be stated publicly during the ceremony.

Although the fundamental right to marriage and a family is protected in Israel under law, current policy forbids certain people from marrying. For example, a divorced woman who does not have a *get*, a document that allows her to remarry, from her ex-husband cannot remarry in Israel. The children of the *agunot*, or woman without a get, are considered *mamzerim*, or illegitimate.

Jewish law allows a man to divorce a woman without her consent. He, however, is required to pay her the sum of money specified in the marriage contract. He is also prohibited from remarrying his ex-wife after she has married another man.

The population of homosexual people in Israel is on the rise because, in addition to Israelis, Palestinian gays are escaping their life-threatening situation in Gaza and the West Bank and moving to Israel. In 2003, there were 350–450 gay Palestinian men, mostly under the age of twenty-six, who were living illegally inside Israel. These men claimed they had been sent to Palestinian "reform schools" because they had been considered criminals.[26]

Lebanon and Syria

The Lebanese Republic has an area of 4,016 square miles with a population of 3,577,000. The birth rate is 19.3 per thousand, and life expectancy is 69.9 years for males and 74.9 years for females. The largest ethnic groups are Arab (84.5%), Armenian (6.8%), Kurd (6.1%), and other (2.6%). Religious affiliation is mostly Muslim (55.3%), Christian (37.6%), and Druze (7.1%). The literacy rate is 93.1 percent for males and 82.2 percent for females. The marriage rate is 8.5 per thousand, and the divorce rate is 1.2 per thousand. The official language is Arabic.[27]

The Syrian Arab Republic has an area of 71,498 square miles with a population of 17,794,000. The birth rate is 28.9 per thousand, and life expectancy is 68.5 years for males and 71.0 years for females. The largest ethnic groups are Syrian Arab (74.9%), Bedouin Arab (7.4%), Palestinian Arab (3.9%), Kurd (7.3%), Armenian (2.7%), and other (3.8%). Religious affiliation is mostly Muslim (86%), Christian (8%), Druze (3%), and nonreligious (3%). The literacy rate is 93.1 percent for males and 82.2 percent for females. The marriage rate is 9.5 per thousand, and the divorce rate is 0.8 per thousand. The official language is Arabic.[28]

The minimum legal age of marriage in both countries is eighteen for males and seventeen for females. Lebanon and Syria are considered lenient in terms of sex segregation. Many elementary schools are mixed but, except for private schools, boys and girls are separated in middle school. Most public universities are co-ed institutions. Students usually enroll in neighborhood schools but can travel to other cities for higher education. For economic reasons and cultural traditions, unmarried men and women are expected to live with their parents even if they are well educated and have jobs. They are permitted to live away from their parents if they are pursuing their education in a university located in a different city from where their parents live. Once they graduate, they go back to their family home. Living alone is not illegal, but a young woman will risk tarnishing her reputation through the gossip of her neighbors. They may suspect her actions because she has no one to monitor her movements.

In cities like Damascus, and even more so in Beirut, there are plenty of cafés, clubs, public gardens, restaurants, theaters, and other venues where men and women may meet. In cities with a shore line, the corniche along the sea is a romantic favorite of young people. They can walk together, exchange occasional kisses, and find secluded areas away from the watching eyes of someone who may recognize them. Mountains, such as Jabal Qasioun in Damascus, are also a favorite spot for a rendezvous. The youths can stay in their cars, sheltered in a private spot. In an effort to reduce prostitution, the Syrian secret police may occasionally check the identification of secluded passengers.

There are no laws against spousal rape in Lebanon and Syria. An ordinary rapist can be punished with a sentence of at least fifteen years, but if he agrees to marry the victim, he faces no punishment. Christians, Muslims, and other religious groups are subject to their respective religious laws regarding personal status issues of marriage, divorce, and inheritance. For Muslims, personal status law is based on the government's interpretation and application of Shariah law.

Husbands and wives can claim adultery as grounds for divorce; however, criminal law discriminates against women in this regard. A man can only be accused of adultery if his actions occur in the home he shares with his wife; a woman, on the other hand, is adulterous regardless of venue. If a woman attempts to file for divorce based on adultery, her husband must admit to the crime, or she must provide an eyewitness. Women usually do not file for divorce based on adultery.

Polygamy is legal, but it is practiced by only a small number of Muslim men. A stipulation in the marriage contract may restrict the husband's right to marry polygamously. In this case, polygamy can be grounds for divorce. In a divorce, the wife can have custody of her children until a boy is nine and a girl is eleven in Syria; custody rules vary from one sect to another in Lebanon (ages seven and nine for Sunni, two and seven for Shiah, and seven and nine for Druze).

Iraq

The Republic of Iraq has an area of 167,618 square miles with a population of 27,818,000. The birth rate is 33.1 per thousand, and life expectancy is 67.1 years for males and 69.5 years for females. The marriage rate is 7.3 per thousand, and the divorce rate is 1.3 per thousand. The largest ethnic groups are Arab (64.7%), Kurd (23.0%), Azerbaijani (5.6%), Turkmen (1.2%), Persian (1.1%), and other (4.4%). Religious affiliation is mostly Muslim (96.0%), Christian (3.2%), and other (0.8%). The literacy rate is 55.9 percent for males and 24.4 percent for females. The official language is Arabic.[29]

Iraq uses a modified Shariah law to review family cases. Both men and women can apply for divorce. The couple has to go for a six months' counseling before finalizing their separation. The wife is usually granted the custody of her children until they are ten years old regardless of gender.[30]

Polygamy in Iraq is allowed only by judicial permission when financial ability and lawful benefit can be proven. The husband can divorce his wife by uttering "taleq" three times. It is common for the woman and her children to keep the residence and any items—including the car—that would be necessary to maintain their lifestyle.

Iran

The Islamic Republic of Iran has an area of 631,659 square miles with a population of 695,515,000. The birth rate is 17.1 per thousand, and life expectancy is 68.3 years for males and 71.1 years for females. The largest ethnic groups are Persian (34.9%), Azerbaijani (15.9%), Kurd (13.0%), Luri (7.2%), Gilaki (5.1%), Mazandarani (5.1%), Afghan (2.8%), Arab (2.5%), and other (13.5%). Religious affiliation is mostly Muslim (95.6%), Zoroastrian (2.8%), Christian (0.5%), and other (1.1%). The literacy rate is 83.5 percent for males and 70.4 percent for females. The marriage rate is 10.2 per thousand. The official language is Farsi (Persian).[32]

> **PREMARITAL SEXUAL PRACTICES**
>
> One young Iranian man responded to a BBC questionnaire about sex in the Middle East this way: "Even though we live in an Islamic country, having a pre-marital sex is quite common between young people my age (19 years old). I am a university student and all my friends have sex with their girlfriends. Our intimacy is in secret and hidden from everybody. Hymen reconstruction surgery is quite common between young girls prior to marriage here as well."[31]

Courtship in Iran is restricted because the government promotes segregation of the sexes. Although it is hard for Iranian boys and girls to spend private time together, they can still see each other in restaurants and cafés. They arrive at the location separately so they not risk being arrested by the police, who may check out their relationship.

A man and a woman are not allowed to be together if they are not related by blood or marriage. Therefore, people who are attracted to each other may use *zawaj mutah* to satisfy themselves. Zawaj mutah is a temporary marriage that is by definition contracted specifically for sexual pleasure. The basic principle of zawaj mutah is the exchange of money for sex, which is limited to the time and amount accepted by both sides. However, only a man is allowed to initiate this type of "marriage" and trade sex for money with one woman at a time. As soon as the contract has ended, each of the partners is free to contract someone else. In the case of pregnancy, the father must assume his responsibility by registering the child under his name. Such marriages are spreading among youths because they are legal, although they are undesired by the youths' parents, and a zawaj mutah relationship protects the people involved from jail, fine, torture, and embarrassment.

To reduce the number of divorces, the government in Iran has made a model marriage contract available and obliges the marrying couple to secure the court's permission to divorce. The model contract grants the divorced wife half the property acquired during the marriage when her husband seeks divorce without her being at fault. Another article in the contract permits the wife to divorce on grounds that are required by Shariah law.[33]

In 1994 a divorced Iranian woman became eligible to monetary compensation for the years she had worked as a housewife and mother in her husband's home. Another law that followed it in 1997 required courts to calculate the unpaid mahr (including any differed mouqaddam and mouakhkhar) payments according to an index updated for inflation.[34]

A divorced woman can have custody of daughters under the age of seven and sons under the age of two. Thereafter, the children transfer to the father, and in the case of his death, to his male kin. During the Iran-Iraq war, however, war widows were granted the right to raise their children and to keep their husband's salary, pension, or other living expenses without the interference of his male kin.[35]

The punishment for homosexual conduct between two men varies from beating, to death. For lesbian conduct, a woman gets a hundred lashes from a whip.[36]

Bahrain and the United Arab Emirates

These countries are located on the Persian Gulf across from Iran. They are part of what is commonly called *bilad al-Khalij*, the Gulf countries. They gained their independence from Britain in 1971.

The Kingdom of Bahrain has an area of 278 square miles with a population of 2,409,000. The birth rate is 18.5 per thousand, and life expectancy is 71.5 years for males and 76.5 years for females. The marriage rate is 7.8 per thousand, and the divorce rate is 1.3 per thousand. The largest ethnic groups are Bahraini Arab (63.9%), Indo-Pakistani (14.8%), Persian (13.0%), Filipino (4.5%), British (2.1%), and other (1.7%). Religious affiliation is mostly Muslim (82.4%), Christian (10.5%), Hindu (6.3%), and other (0.8%). The literacy rate is 91.9 percent for males and 85.0 percent for females. The official language is Arabic.

The United Arab Emirates (UAE) has an area of 32,280 sq miles with a population of 4,690,000. The birth rate is 15.1 per thousand, and life expectancy is 72.5 years for males and 77.6 years for females. The marriage rate is 3.0 per thousand, and the divorce rate is 8 per thousand. The largest ethnic groups are Arab (48.1%), South Asian (35.7%), (Filipino 3.4%), white (2.4, 1.0%), and other (5.4%). Religious affiliation is mostly Muslim (76%), Christian (11%), Hindu (7%), and other (6%). The literacy rate is 70.5 percent for males and 30.1 percent for females. The official language is Arabic.[37]

Men and women in Bahrain and the UAE are wealthy and keep up-to-date on the latest technology. Although traditionally their societies have been against dating, their youths are finding ways to meet socially. The malls are one of the most frequent places to search for mates. Young men go around seeking out women, who respond to their suggestions. They sneak their mobile phone numbers to the women, who may call the eager men if they like them. It is also common for teenage males to dial random numbers until they hear a woman's voice and start conversing. Such a relationship may stay restricted to phone calls and may also develop into meetings. These meetings remain secret because the parents of both partners must not be aware of the romantic liaisons of their children. These societies do not allow their children to experiment with love and sex, and some parents allow only consanguineous marriages. Such a restriction is especially common among the elite families. However, they may permit their children to leave the country to study or visit abroad.

It is possible for a man in Bahrain or the UAE to have a polygamous relationship or to divorce without notifying his wife. In extreme cases a woman finds out only by chance that she has been divorced. In one case, a woman from the UAE who was not able to conceive found out from a relative that her husband had divorced her and had taken a second wife.[38]

Kuwait

The State of Kuwait has an area of 6,880 square miles with a population of 2,847,000. The birth rate is 19.5 per thousand, and life expectancy is 75.9 years for males and 77.9 years for females. The divorce rate is 2.6 per thousand. The largest ethnic groups are Arab (74%), Kurd (10%), Indo-Pakistani (8%), Persian (4%), and other (4%). Religious affiliation is mostly Muslim (83%), Christian (13%), Hindu (3%), and other (1%). The literacy rate is 84.7 percent for males and 81.0 percent for females. The official language is Arabic.[39]

Meeting members of the other sex is becoming more difficult in Kuwait. The current Islamist movement is stressing *raqabah* (censorship), especially for their youths. While advisory committees for the implementation of Shariah are asserting the role of women in the moral upbringing and religious education of their youths, the state police are keeping a close eye on women's behavior. For example, in the summer of 1999, police arrested more than 150 women as they were leaving private parties that had included both men and women. These women were charged with prostitution because they were not related to the gathered men. In 2000 a young woman was beaten by a group of Muslim extremists while she was meeting a nonrelated male friend in a secluded area.[40]

Violence against women, including domestic violence, is not a criminal offense in Kuwait, and the authorities have ignored complaints and requests for help from housewives. Men have the right to punish their women because men are considered their women's protectors and maintainers, as well as the individuals responsible for the women's acts.

Abortion is illegal, and women who violate the code of sexual conduct can be arrested and imprisoned. During the period 1986–88, forty-two women were arrested at a maternity hospital for giving birth to illegitimate children. Eleven of them were jailed for more than two years, seventeen were forced to marry their lovers, and fourteen were placed under the guardianship of male family members, who became officially responsible for their sexual misconduct. During the same period at least sixteen cases of rape were reported, all of which were denied by the alleged partners.[41]

Qatar and Saudi Arabia

The State of Qatar has an area of 4,412 square miles with a population of 7,730,000. The birth rate is 15.6 per thousand, and life expectancy is 70.9 years for males and 76.0 years for females. The largest ethnic groups are Arab (52.5%), Persian (16.5%), Indo-Pakistani (15.2%), black African (19.5%), and other (6.3%). Religious affiliation is mostly Muslim (83%), Christian (10%), Hindu (3%), nonreligious (2%), and other (2%). The literacy rate is 80.8 percent for males and 83.7 percent for females. The marriage rate is 3.4 per thousand. The official language is Arabic.[42]

The Kingdom of Saudi has an area of 830,000 square miles with a population of 23,230,000. The birth rate is 29.7 per thousand, and life expectancy is 73.3 years for males and 77.3 years for females. The largest ethnic groups are Arab (88.1%), Persian (16.5%), Indo-Pakistani (5.5%), black African (1.5%), Filipino (1.0%), and other (3.9%). Religious affiliation is mostly Muslim 94 (percent), Christian (3.5%), and nonreligious/other (1.5%). The official language is Arabic.[43]

Most marriages in Qatar and Saudi Arabia are arranged between people of the same background. It is common for two lineages to be married to each other, and often they marry from among other Gulf Arab countries (Bahrain, Kuwait, Oman, Saudi Arabia, and the UAE). To marry someone from outside the region requires permission from the government, which is rarely given in Saudi Arabia. However, an individual who does this may lose all the subsidized benefits in his country.

A woman remains a member of her father's lineage, but her children associate more with their father's lineage. In case of a divorce, the woman can take her children with her to her father's house and keep them until adolescence. Both men and women can ask for divorce, and, in the case of a polygamous husband, the wife is granted an immediate divorce.

In addition to the customary marriage contract, *nikah*, there exist a union called *misya*, which is increasing in Saudi Arabia. In *misyar* marriages the woman does not have the same

> **AN AMNESTY INTERNATIONAL APPEAL**
>
> It is risky for a woman in Qatar to marry a foreigner without the permission of her parents. Twenty-nine-year-old Hamda Fahd bin Jasem al-Thani, a member of an elite family in Qatar, left a voice message for the Amnesty International in January 2006 asking for help. She claimed her parents were holding her prisoner in her bedroom because she had married forty-two-year-old Sayed Saleh of Egypt. Her family would not let her free unless she asked for a divorce.
>
> Hamda met her husband first in 2000. They fell in love, and he wanted to ask for her hand in marriage from her father in 2001. Fahd bin Jasem refused to see him and sent him a message rejecting his proposal. Saleh tried again and received the same reply. The couple then eloped and married secretly in Egypt.
>
> On November 5, 2002, nine days after their marriage, Hamda was abducted in Cairo by Qatari officers and was sent back to her country. In Qatar she was detained for nearly six months at the al-Sayliyah prison and then transferred to her family's house.
>
> Amnesty International wrote to Qatar's emir and issued a worldwide appeal for Hamda al-Thani's release and planned to report the case to the UN's Committee against Torture.[44] In June 2006, Hamda attempted to escape from her family home; during this attempt she injured her leg. Following the intervention of the Qatari Human Rights Committee, she was admitted to the hospital. While there, her family was prohibited from visiting. At the end of her treatment, the paperwork necessary for Hamda to receive a passport was completed. On October 17, 2006, Hamda al-Thani flew to Egypt to rejoin her husband.[45]

rights as the traditional wife. Most misyar brides stay with their parents but consummate their marriage on a visitation basis. It is estimated that seven of ten marriage contracts are misyars. The majority of women in misyar partnerships are divorced or widowed. For men, a misyar partnership is usually a polygamous marriage. A survey conducted by the *Arab News* in Saudi Arabia of men and women between the ages of twenty and forty indicated that 60 percent of the men would consider misyar marriage for themselves, but only a few of them found such a marriage acceptable for a female relative. The survey showed that only a few women over forty would consider such a marriage for themselves, largely because of the lack of rights for the woman.

Young people are increasingly interested in misyar marriages because a misyar relationship gives them a legal way to have sexual relations. A college teacher explains it this way: "I overheard one of my son's friends talking about marriage and girls, and he asked 'why buy the cow when the milk is free?' They were talking about their ability to have sex without the difficulties and expenses of a standard marriage." In the opinion of this teacher, the misyar marriage legalizes the why-buy-the-milk-when-the-cow-is-free syndrome.[46]

Oman and Yemen

The Sultanate of Oman has an area of 119,500 square miles with a population of 715,000. The birth rate is 24.0 per thousand, and life expectancy is 73.2 years for males and 75.4 years for females. The largest ethnic groups are Omani Arab (48.1%), Indo-Pakistani (31.7%), other Arab (7.2%), Persian (2.8%), Zanzibari (2.5%), and other (7.7%). Religious affiliation is mostly Muslim (87.4%), Hindu (5.7%), Christian (4.9%), Buddhist (0.8%), and other (1.2%). The literacy rate is 83.0 percent for males and 67.2 percent for females. The official language is Arabic.[47]

The Republic of Yemen has an area of 214,300 square miles with a population of 20,043,000. The birth rate is 43.2 per thousand, and life expectancy is 59.5 years for males and 63.3 years for females. The largest ethnic groups are Arab (92.8%), Somali (3.7%), black African (1.1%), Indo-Pakistani (1.0%), and other (1.4%). Religious affiliation is mostly Muslim (98.9%), Christian (0.2%), and other (0.2%). The literacy rate is 70.5 percent for males and 30.1 percent for females. The official language is Arabic.[48]

Although the minimal legal age of marriage in Oman and Yemen is fifteen for men and women, these countries have seen a decline in marriage before nineteen years of age. Recent statistics indicate that 61 percent of women in Oman and 59 percent of women in Yemen are marrying between the ages of twenty and twenty-four. Of these, those with high school diplomas marry at an older age than those with no formal education.[49]

People in Yemen and Oman believe in the separation of the sexes. As a result, many individuals depend on their families to arrange their marriages. A marriage often becomes the affair of relatives and friends as well. When they find a suitable bride, the father and mother consult with their son, who may have known about the girl or her family. In many cases, she is a cousin or another close relative.

The groom's family visits the bride's, and they bargain over the price that must be offered for her hand. Once the two families arrive at an agreement, they decide the wedding date.

The father of the groom and the bride read the *fatihah*, which is considered an oral wedding contract and blessing. From this moment on, it is customary for the groom to bring gifts for his bride-to-be. These gifts are topped off by a *nafaqah* (a spending allowance) for as long as the bride stays at her family's home before the wedding day.

The wedding festivity usually lasts five days. Each day serves as a different ritual that involves the families of the newlyweds: the initial visit to the bride (an introductory meeting), the mahr day (a business meeting to decide the monetary aspects of the marriage), the *katb al-kitab* (a gathering to unite the couple religiously and legally), the henna day (a celebration to prepare the bride physically), the *zafaf* or *dakhla* (the wedding). The bride is expected to wear different dresses each day; she keeps a white dress for the last ceremony, where she and the groom are displayed on a dais surrounded by friends and relatives.

RESOURCE GUIDE

PRINT SOURCES

AbuKhalil, Asad. "A Note on the Study of Homosexuality in the Arab/Islamic Civilization." *Arab Studies Journal* 1.2 (1993): 32–34.

Adeney, Miriam. *Daughters of Islam: Building Bridges with Muslim Women.* Downers Grove, IL: InterVarsity Press, 2002.

Ahmed, Leila. *Women and Gender in Islam.* New Haven, CT: Yale University Press, 1992.

Al-Mughni, Haya. *Women in Kuwait: The Politics of Gender.* London: Saqi Books, 1993, 2001.

AlMunajjed, Mona. *Women in Saudi Arabia Today.* New York: St. Martin's Press, 1997.

Altorki, Soraya. *Women in Saudi Arabia: Ideology and Behavior among the Elite.* New York: Columbia University Press, 1986.

Badran, Margot. *Feminists, Islam, and Nation: Gender and the Making of Modern Egypt.* Princeton: Princeton University Press, 1995.

Barakat, Halim. *Society, Culture, and State.* Berkeley: University of California Press, 1993.

Beck, Lois, and Nikki Keddie, eds. *Women in the Muslim World.* Cambridge, MA: Harvard University Press, 1978.

Bowen, Donna Lee, and Evelyn A. Early. *Everyday Life in the Middle East.* Bloomington: Indiana University Press, 1993.

Carapico, Sheila. "Women and Public Participation in Yemen." In Suha Sabbagh (ed.), *Arab Women: Between Defiance and Restraint.* New York: Olive Branch Press, 1996.

Esfandiari, Haleh. *Reconstructed Lives: Women and Iran's Islamic Revolution.* Washington, D.C.: Woodrow Wilson Center Press, 1997.

Esherick, Joan. *Women in the Arab World.* Philadelphia: Mason Crest, 2005.

Farsoun, Samih K., ed. *Arab Society: Continuity and Change.* London: Dover, 1985.

"Female Illiteracy in the Arab World." *Society* 42.6 (2005): 6.

Fernea, Elizabeth, and B. Bezirgan, eds. *Middle Eastern Women Speak.* Cambridge, MA: Harvard University Press, 1978.

Goldberg, Ellis, Resat Kasaba, and Joel Migdal, eds. *Rules and Rights in the Middle East: Democracy, Law and Society.* Seattle: University of Washington Press, 1993.

Haddad, Reem. "Breaking Silence." *New Internationalist* no. 382 (2005): 35.

Hartley, Delinda. "Women in the Arab World." *Washington Report on Middle East Affairs* 23.7 (2004): 70.

Hopkins, Nicholas S., and Saad Eddin Ibrahim, eds. *Arab Society: Class, Gender, Power, and Development.* Cairo: American University in Cairo Press, 1997.

Mernisi, Fatima. *Beyond the Veil: Male-Female Dynamics in a Modern Muslim Society.* Cambridge: Cambridge University Press, 1975.

Mir-Hosseini, Ziba. *Islam and Gender: The Religious Debate in Contemporary Iran.* Princeton: Princeton University Press, 1999.

Moghadam, Valentine M. *Modernizing Women: Gender and Social Change in the Middle East.* Boulder, CO: Lynne Rienner, 1993.

Monger, George P. *Marriage Customs of the World: From Henna to Honeymoons.* Santa Barbara, CA: ABC-CLIO, 2004.

Moors, Annelies. *Women, Property and Islam: Palestinian Experiences, 1920–1990.* Cambridge: Cambridge University Press, 1995.

Mordecai, Carolyn. *Weddings, Dating & Love Customs of Cultures Worldwide, Including Royalty.* Phoenix, AZ: Nittany, 1998.

Murphy, Brian M. *The World of Weddings: An Illustrated Celebration.* London: Paddington, 1978.

Obermeyer, Carla Makhlouf, ed. *Family, Gender and Population in the Middle East.* Cairo: American University in Cairo Press, 1995.

Pearl, David, and Werner Menski. *Muslim Family Law.* London: Sweet and Maxwell, 1998.

Poya, Maryam. *Women, Work and Islamism.* London: Zed Books, 1999.

Sabbagh, Suha, ed. *Arab Women: Between Defiance and Restraint.* New York: Olive Branch Press, 1996.

Underwood, Carol. "Islamic Precepts and Family Planning: The Perceptions of Jordanian Religious Leaders and Their Constituents." *International Family Planning Perspectives* 26 (2000): 110.

United Arab Emirates: "Raped Woman Sentenced to Death by Stoning." *Off Our Backs* 30 (2000): 4.

Walther, Wiebke. *Women in Islam: From Medieval to Modern Times.* Princeton, NJ: Markus Wiener, 1993.

WEBSITES

ArabNews Online. August 14, 2006. Saudi Research & Publishing Co. http://www.arabnews.com/. A daily Saudi Arabian newspaper that includes recent amendments to family laws, unusual wedding stories, and divorces.

BBC. August 14, 2006. British Broadcasting Co. http://www.bbc.co.uk. A source for information about controversial issues including sex, homosexuality, and laws that discriminate against minority groups in the Middle East and North Africa.

Huda. *Wedding Customs of the Muslim World.* 2006. New York Times Company. http://islam.about.com/blworldweddings.htm. A Website that deals with religion and spirituality, including Islam and Judaism. It discusses wedding ceremonies from traditional and contemporary points of view.

Middle East. 2002. Emory University. http://www.law.emory.edu/IFL/region/mideast.html. A Website managed by the school of law at Emory University. It provides a summary of Middle Eastern and North African laws on sex, marriage, and divorce.

The Middle East Forum: Promoting American Interests. 2006. Middle East Forum. http://www.meforum.org. The *Middle East Forum* and the *Middle East Quarterly* provide cutting-edge discussions, essays, and articles on Middle Eastern and North African cultures.

Middle East Research and Information Project. July 31, 2006. MERIP. http://www.merip.org. The *Middle East Research and Information Project* analyzes, reports, and provides information on critical issues, including information about the family, women, and homosexuality in the Middle East and North Africa. This newspaper has search functions for articles and discussions on the chosen topic.

Muslim Matrimonials and More. July 2006. Zawaj. http://www.zawaj.com. Muslim wedding customs and interesting discussions of family, sex, and women's issues from a Muslim point of view.

Population Reference Bureau. August 10, 2006. Population Reference Bureau. http://www.prb.org. The Population Reference Bureau includes valid statistics, datasheets, reports, and articles on issues of marriage, divorce, and sex.

Wedding Traditions and Customs around the World. 2004. Euroevents & Travel. http://www.worldwedding traditions.com/. This Website provides short summaries of wedding traditions and customs from a variety of countries around the world.

VIDEOS/FILMS

Arab Diaries, 3: Love & Marriage (2000). Directed by Samia Chala and Muriel Aboulrouss. First Run Icarus Films.
Crimes of Honour (1998). Directed by Shelley Saywell. First Run Icarus Films.
Death of a Princess (2005). Directed by Antony Thomas. WGBH Educational Foundation; PBS Video.
Divorce Iranian Style [Talaq] (1998). Directed by Kim Longinotto and Ziba Mir-Hosseini. Women Make Movies.
Family Ties (1986). Directed by Nadia Hijab and Luke Colin. Falls Church, Virginia: Landmark Films.
Haram: Yemen, The Hidden Half Speaks (2003). Directed by Fibi Kraus and Gudrun Torrubia. Women Make Movies.
Human Rights and Islam (1995). SAGA.
Permissible Dreams (1983). Directed by Atiat El-Abnoudi. Women Make Movies.
The Perfumed Garden (2000). Directed by Yamina Benguigui. First Run Icarus Films.
Satin Rouge (2002). Directed by Raja Amari. Zeitgeist Video.
The Syrian Bride (2005). Directed by Eran Riklis. Koch Lorber Films.
Veils Uncovered (2002). Directed by Nora Kevorkian. Canada.
Wedding in Galilee [Noce en Galile] (1993). Directed by Michel Khlefi. Kino International.
Women and Islam (1993). Directed by Farheen Umar.
Women in the Middle East: The Price of Change (1982). Directed by Marilyn Gaunt. First Run Icarus Films.

NOTES

1. See *Encyclopedia Britannica 2006 Book of the Year* (Chicago: Encyclopedia Britannica, 2006), p. 508.
2. Ibid., p. 650.
3. Ibid., 714.
4. H. Hamamy, L. Jamhawi, J. Al-Darawsheh, and K. Ajlouni, "Consanguinity Marriages in Jordan: Why is the Rate Changing with Time?" *Clinical Genetics* 67.6 (June 2005): 515.
5. *BBC* (in Resource Guide), accessed June 6, 2006, http://news.bbc.co.uk/1/hi/world/middle_east/4708461.stm.
6. See Bernhard Venema, and Jogien Bakker, "A Permissive Zone for Prostitution in the Middle Atlas of Morocco," *Ethnography* 43.1 (Winter 2004): 52.
7. See Zinab Touini-Benjelloum, "A New Family Law in Morocco: Patience is Bitter, But Its Fruit Is Sweet," accessed June 7, 2006, www.arabwomenconnect.org.
8. See "North Africa: Religion Holds Back Rights of Muslim Women," *Women's International Network News*, 24.2 (Spring 1998): 66.

9. See *Index on Censorship* 34.3/01 (August 2005): 154–165.
10. See *Encyclopedia Britannica*, p. 627.
11. See Hoda Rashad, Magued Osman, and Farzaneh Roudi-Fahimi, "Marriage in the Arab World," September 2005, accessed June 1, 2006, *Population Reference Bureau* (in Resource Guide).
12. See *Encyclopedia Britannica*, p. 565.
13. See http://bmj.bmjjournals.com/cgi/content/full/313/7052/249, accessed June 7, 2006.
14. See Andrea B. Rugh, *Family in Contemporary Egypt* (Cairo: American University in Cairo Press, 1985), p. 144.
15. See Allegra Stratton, "Secrets and Marriages," *New Statesman* 134.4730 (2005): 15.
16. See http://www.library.cornell.edu/colldev/mideast/divrua.htm.
17. See A. Azer, "Laws as an Instrument for Social Change: An Illustration from Population Policy, Law and Social Change in Contemporary Egypt," ed. Nelson and Koch, *Cairo Papers in Social Science* 2.4. (Cairo: American University in Cairo Press)
18. See http://www.library.cornell.edu/colldev/mideast/divrua.htm, accessed June 10, 2006.
19. See Mike Hudson, "Escaping Abuse Overseas," *Advocate* no. 939 (2005): 36.
20. See *Encyclopedia Britannica*, p. 614.
21. See Hamamy et al., p. 511.
22. See Nick Pelham, "Battle of the Sexuality," *BBC* (in Resource Guide), June 26, 2000, accessed July 5, 2006, http://news.bbc.co.uk/2/hi/middle_east/806642.stm.
23. See http://www.irinnews.org/S_report.asp?ReportID=46677&SelectRegion=Middle_East, accessed June 12, 2006.
24. See *Encyclopedia Britannica*, p. 606.
25. See H. Hamamy et al., p. 515.
26. See Charity Crouse, "Out and Down and Living in Israel," *Gay & Lesbian Review Worldwide* 10.3 (May/June 2003): 24.
27. See *Encyclopedia Britannica*, p. 624.
28. Ibid., p. 706.
29. Ibid., p. 603.
30. See Jan Goodwin, *Price of Honor, Muslim Women Lift the Veil of Silence on the Islamic World* (Boston: Little Brown and Company, 1994), p. 246.
31. See *BBC* (in Resource Guide), http://news.bbc.co.uk/1/hi/world/middle_east/4708461.stm.
32. See *Encyclopedia Britannica*, p. 602.
33. See Haleh Esfandiari, *Reconstructed Lives: Women and Iran's Islamic Revolution* (Washington, D.C.: Woodrow Wilson Center Press, 1997), p. 43.
34. See Maryam Poya, *Women, Work and Islamism* (London: Zed Books, 1999), pp. 101–102.
35. Ibid., p. 101.
36. See Hudson, "Escaping Abuse Overseas," p. 36.
37. See *Encyclopedia Britannica*, p. 720.
38. See Goodwin, *Price of Honor*, p. 153.
39. See *Encyclopedia Britannica*, p. 620.
40. See Al-Mughani (in Resource Guide), pp. 159–160.
41. Ibid., p. 189.
42. See *Encyclopedia Britannica*, p. 676.
43. Ibid.
44. See http://peacefulmuslimah.blogspot.com/2006/05/married-foreigner-prisoner-for-love.html, accessed June 15, 2006.
45. See *Amnesty International*, "Qatar: Further information: Fear for Safety: Hamda Fahad Jassem Al-Thani," Oct 20, 2006, http://web.amnesty.org/library/Index/ENGMDE220032006?open&of=ENG-QAT.
46. See http://www.arabnews.com/?page9&section=0&article=64891, accessed June 20, 2006.
47. See *Encyclopedia Britannica*, p. 665.
48. Ibid., p. 735.
49. See Rashad et al., "Marriage in the Arab World," *Population Reference Bureau* (in Resource Guide), p. 4.

MUSIC

RIHAB KASSATLY BAGNOLE

Music is indispensable to Middle Eastern and North African peoples because it is deeply integrated into the mystical and secular aspects of their lives and has a special effect on their well-being. The three most common religions that are embraced by almost 99 percent of the population in the region (Judaism, Christianity, and Islam) all use music as part of their rituals. The amplified Islamic call to prayer in Egypt, the private reading of the Torah in Israel, and the celebratory Christian chants in Syria exemplify the necessity of music for personal and communal purposes. On a secular level, a taxi driver, a shopkeeper, a restaurant owner, and others use music regularly to keep themselves and their customers cheerful and sane.

Middle Eastern and North African music is based on various melodic modes called *maqamat*. Each *maqam* (mode) is a melody type, characterized by features such as center tone, range, progression, melodic formulae, rhythmic patterns, and ornamentations. The maqam forms a stylistic base for each composition and gives it a designated musical key. Each maqam consists of a variety of tones that may include quarter and eighth tones to form a scale. These tones create intricate compositions and improvisations called *taqasim* that allow the musicians to demonstrate their skills and virtuosity as players of specific instruments. A virtuoso solo may form an introduction to a song or a section between two stanzas.

The most commonly used musical instruments in the Middle East and North Africa are the *qanoun* (a stringed instrument); the flute; the *buzuq* and *oud* (lutes); the *darabaka*, *dumbek*, and *tabla* (types of drums); the tambourine; and the cymbals. Other instruments such as the *rababa* (a one-string instrument), the *mijwez and mizmar* (flutes), and the *gerbeh* (bag pipe) are used for music that incorporates Bedouin influences.

For most of the twentieth century, singers such as Asmahan, Farid al-Atrache, Muhammad Abd al-Wahab, Nazem al-Ghazali, and Um Kulthoum were considered the enchanters par excellence of the Arabic-speaking countries of the Middle East and North Africa. These early stars were followed by a younger generation, including Abd al-Halim Hafez, Najat al-Saghira, and Warda al-Jazairiah, who maintained the idea of *tarab* (enchantment) that prevailed in Arabic music, and whose unique voices complemented modern instruments such as the electronic keyboard and the saxophone. Both generations depended on the *qasida* (strophic

Music

MUSICAL INSTRUMENTS

Middle Easterners and North Africans use similar instruments for their music. Sometimes they refer to them by different terms and vary them according to their preferences. The following describes some widespread types of instruments.

Stringed Instruments. The buzuq is a hybrid instrument associated with Gypsy music. It is a long-necked, fretted string instrument, with two strings that are played with a plectrum.

The oud is an ancient instrument documented on old Akkadian seals. It developed around the ninth century to include four or five strings. Today, the oud has five double strings, of which the three highest pairs are made of gut or nylon, and the two lowest are made of silk covered with copper wire. They are played with a trimmed plectrum. The Iranian *tar* is a similar instrument, with three double courses of strings, while the *setar* has four. The *tanbur* has a longer arm and only three strings. Also common is the Iranian *dotar*, which has two strings, and the Moroccan *lotar*, with three to four strings.

The qanoun is a classical instrument famous in Arabic music. It is a plucked box zither with a trapezoidal-shaped body. It settled into its current basic form around the eleventh century. It sits flat in front of the musician, who plucks the triple-grouped, twenty-six rows of strings with a plectrum on each index finger. Comparable instruments are the Iranian *santur*, which can be plucked or hammered, and the *tanbura*.

The rababa is a spiked fiddle that accompanies Bedouin music. It has a quadrilateral sound box covered with skin and a single horsehair string. It is played with a horsehair bow. Some versions have two strings or more, and they are known as *jawzah*, *guenbri*, *ginbri*, *hajouje*, *anzad*, *kamanjah*, and *kaman* (violin).

Percussion Instruments. The *daff* and *riq* are percussion instruments that are similar to a tambourine. They consist of a round frame covered on one side with goat or fish skin, with pairs of metal discs set into the frame or under its head. When the instrument is struck, the discs produce a jingle that accentuates the rhythm. A large daff with loud cymbals is also called a *mazhar*; a daff without cymbals is called a tar or *bendir*.

The darbuka, dumbek, and tabla are clay or brass goblet-shaped drums, with sheep, goat, or fish skin heads, played as percussion instruments. The drum is placed either under the left arm or between the legs and struck in the middle for the strong beats and on the edge for the sharp in-between beats.

Other type of drums include the *mirwas*, a small double-sided hand drum; the *naqqarah*, a double kettle-shaped drum made of pottery; the *jahlah*, a clay pot played with both hands; the *qasah*, a double kettle-shaped drum; and the *tabol*, a wooden drum covered with skin and played with wooden sticks. Another unique percussion instrument is the *mihbaj*, a large wooden mortar and pestle used to grind coffee and played by the Bedouin.

Wind Instruments. *Mijwiz, maqroun*, mizmar, and *zammara* are terms used for various types of woodwind instruments. They are all played by blowing through a circular opening in the end and manipulating the fingers over the holes down the front of the tube to produce specific sounds. The smaller size mijwiz is known also as a *minjayrah, mitbiq, mizwid, ghaytah, raita*, and *zukrah*. Other versions of the same instrument are the *arghul* and *yarghul*, which have holes on only one of the tubes while the other tube gives an accompanying drone sound.

The *nay*, or flute, is the generic Arabic name for the open-ended cane or reed instruments with five or six holes in the front and one hole underneath the tube. Its origin goes back to the Sumerian civilization. The sounds are produced by blowing. This instrument is especially suitable to express both joy and yearning. Other versions of the nay are the *qasabah*, *salamiyyah*, and *khallol*.

poem), *ughniya* (song), and other regional musical structures to affect the mood of their listeners and infuse them with emotions. Most of their musical compositions stayed within the boundaries of the regional musical scales and customary melodies in order to satisfy the taste of the majority of their audiences. Any sort of creativity that prompted a change to supplement the primary musical basis was carefully modified to produce a pleasing reaction from their enthusiastic listeners. Famous poets, songwriters, and composers also used regional vocabulary familiar to a variety of people regardless of their class, education, and background in order to acquire additional devotees to support them. For example, Um Kulthoum, who maintained her songs grounded in the region's Islamic tradition of rendering Arabic text, was highly admired in Iraq. Similarly, the Syrian Egyptian Farid al-Atrache, who innovated his tunes by adding Western flavors, was greatly esteemed in Algeria and Tunisia.

These deceased influential legends are still popular around the Arab world. The music of Abd al-Wahab (d. 1991), Asmahan (d. 1944), Farid al-Atrache (d. 1974), Um Kulthoum (d. 1975), and others is heard on everyday programs on many Middle Eastern and North African radio and television stations. These legends have maintained their status as "perfect enchanters," and many people prefer their songs to those of contemporary singers. For example, in a recent interview conducted by the newspaper *al-Ahram* in Egypt, Mohamed, a restaurant worker, claims that all the new songs sound the same: "There is no art left in them, no soul. One musician pops up after another, and simply copies the work of those who have had success in the past. It's all rubbish."[1]

Not surprisingly, many famous singers have begun their careers by imitating the legendary artists. For example, Warda and Afaf Radi have imitated Asmahan, Aziza Galal copied Leila Murad, Fadia el-Hage styled herself after Fairuz, and Mayada el-Hinawy emulated Um Kulthoum. Others who tried to establish original musical trends had a hard time convincing people of their talent because they were always compared to the former icons.

Access to satellite radio, television channels, and the Internet has altered the usual progression for recent artists and inspired contemporary variations in Arabic music. The exposure to Western pop music has opened up new horizons for Middle Eastern and North African artists and has created more sophisticated musical tastes among their audiences, especially the young, who have been becoming increasingly accustomed to different tonalities, modes, and instruments. The limited beats and melodies of traditional music can no longer satisfy these audiences or reflect their contemporary experience. Therefore, many current artists have incorporated a variety of international styles in order to develop unique musical compositions that correspond more closely to their increasingly more cosmopolitan lifestyles.

In addition, many of the contemporary songs are released with music videos and are produced by large production companies; these include Rotana, which is based in Dubai, United Arab Emirates, and is controlled by the Saudi prince Walid bin Talal; and Alam el Phan, which is based in Cairo, Egypt, and managed by chief executive Muhsin Jaber. Such production companies use their satellite channels, Rotana TV and Mazika TV, respectively, to advertise and commercialize their artists and sell their creative products around the world. Both companies compete to promote new moneymaker talents and the interests of well-known performers, who appeal to prevailing tastes, to ensure their marketability at home and abroad. Smaller companies, such as Free Music, owned by Nasr Mahrous, and High Quality Record Company, owned by Tarek Abdullah, have adopted a different strategy because of their comparatively limited budgets. They have implemented a strategy that aims to involve talented musicians who can satisfy groups of people that want variety or conventional presentations. In addition, many Western-based companies have realized the potential gains from Middle Eastern and North African

Music

WALID BIN TALAL

Egyptian record companies in the Arab world have become somewhat alarmed because they are losing ground to Walid bin Talal, the Saudi Arabian who owns Rotana. Other record companies have accused him of wanting to monopolize the entertainment scene in the Arab countries. In addition to controlling 75 percent of the total Arab music market and signing many popular singers with his company, Rotana, bin Talal secured a deal with Fanoun, the owner of Alam el Phan, a competing company, which gave him the rights to one-third of all films produced in Egypt until 2004. In 2004, Walid bin Talal added 180 new artists to his company. Rumors have circulated that bin Talal's lavish gifts, such as a BMW given to each newcomer at Rotana's annual party, have tempted the young artists to switch their alliance to Rotana.[2]

music, and they are capitalizing on recording and producing pop music from the region; examples of these companies include Ark 21, of Mondo Melodia, and Putumayo World Music.

Although some songs and musical compositions prevail simultaneously in their country of origin and in many other Middle Eastern and North African countries, each of these countries supports its own music, which is most popular among its local people and may have attracted international fans. The following introduces a few of the most popular music styles and talents of each nation.

AL-MAGHREB AL-ARABI: THE ARABIAN WEST

Algeria

Rai (opinion) is a folk music style that originated in Oran, western Algeria, in the late nineteenth century. It was primarily concerned with the feelings and struggles of ordinary people. Sheikha Rimitti, whose real name was Saadia Bediaf (1923–2006), was known as the "Mother of Rai" because she was the first woman who sang this optimistic and satirical music in public. Her songs reflected her thoughts on moral and societal issues. She talked about joy, pain, and the forbidden issues in her life. For example her *Charrak Gatta* [Lacerate] of 1954 was an attack against the virtue of virginity and an invitation for women to rethink their morality. Ultimately, the Algerian government banned her music in the 1960s.

In the 1980s rai music evolved and gained great popularity. Artists in Oran started to combine *shabi* (folk) music with Bedouin, Spanish, French, jazz, and Arabic sounds; they also began incorporating Western instruments and studio techniques into the production of their rai. The Algerian government recognized this modernized local style as one of the country's native music styles right after the Oran music festival of 1985.

Young rai singers, such as Hasni, Khaled, Mami, and Nouria preceded their names with *cheb* (young), for men, or *chebba*, for women, to contrast themselves with the elder *sheikh* (old) or *sheikha* singers. Many rai singers such as Abdo, Anour, Fadila, Rashid Taha, Sahraoui, and Zahouania have their own styles and followers, who enjoy the special talent of each singer. The following introduces the most famous of the rai artists, all of whom are popular for their distinctive voices, music, and ingenuity.

Cheb Khaled

Khaled (known as the "King of Rai") was born Khaled Haj Ibrahim in 1960 in Sidi-el-Houri, a suburb of Oran in Algeria. He started singing at the age of fourteen and got involved with rai music in the early 1980s. His first album, *Khaled*, which included his first hit, "Didi," was recorded partly in Brussels, with the aid of producer Michael Brook, and partly in Los Angeles, with Don Was, in 1992. "Didi" rocketed to the top of the French Top 50, making it the first song recorded in Arabic to chart in France, and soared to the top of the list of hit songs in India, Israel, Egypt, and Saudi Arabia. This album sold over 1.5 million copies worldwide.[3] Khaled's second album, *N'ssi N'ssi* [Forget, Forget], was released the year after. Don Was produced four tracks; French producer Laurent Gueneau and British producer Richard Evans produced one track each; and French composer, arranger, and producer Philippe Eidel, produced and arranged the remaining five tracks. In 1996 Khaled released *Sahra*, which was also co-produced by many individuals, including Don Was, French composer Philippe Eidel, reggae producer Clive Hunt, French singer Jean-Jacques Goldman, and the hip-hop rap duo from Marseille IAM; this album included the hit song "Aicha."[4]

Cheb Mami

Cheb Mami (known as the "Prince of Rai") was born Khelifati Mohamed in Saida, south of Oran in Algeria. He started singing as a teenager, and his career flourished in the late 1980s. After his participation at the Oran Rai Festival in 1985, he released several renowned albums. His 1990 CD, *Let Me Rai*, was the first to be recorded in Los Angeles, followed by *Saida* [Happy] in 1994. Neneh Cherry and Paula Abdul produced *Saida* in Los Angeles; it became a successful album, selling 100,000 copies in France and winning a Double Golden Disc and a Golden Disc award in Algeria and Morocco, respectively.[5] Cheb Mami achieved crossover success with the hip-hop remix of his track "Parisien du Nord" on his album *Meli Meli* [What Is Happening to Me], produced in 1999. His duet collaboration with Sting in 1999, which in 2000 went rocketing to the top of singles charts around the world, established Mami as an international artist. It also marked the "Desert Rose" duet as the first Eastern-Western singing collaboration. Another successful hit, "Le Rai C'est Chic" [*Rai* Is Fashionable], from his 2001 album, produced by Nile Rodgers, propelled Mami to international stardom. Mami continued his collaborations with Middle Eastern, North African, and Western artists such as Charles Aznavour, Bob Marley, Enrico Macias, Hakim, and Samira Said.

Morocco

Gnawa music is one of the most celebrated styles in Morocco. This genre originated in Africa and was carried by the Berbers to Morocco. The Berber musicians are known for their healing of physical injuries and emotional disorders through music and dance: they drive away evil phantoms and encourage good spirits to protect their patients. The hypnotic gnawa uses low-toned rhythms and melodies, hand-clapping and cymbals, and local language to set the mood and achieve the desired result.

Recent gnawa musicians have been modifying their music to incorporate current feelings and concerns and have been commercializing their performances. For example, one of the local singers, Hassan Hakmoun, choreographs special spectacles for tourists who want to experience gnawa and trance. Other famous singers have adopted different styles that have popularized their music.

Najat Aatabou

Najat Aatabou grew up in the poor Berber village of Khmisset in the central Atlas Mountains. She started singing at family gatherings and weddings against her family wishes when she was a teenager. She left her home when her brothers announced that she had put the family to shame. She moved to the Casablanca where she recorded her first hit, "J'en ai marré" [I Have Had Enough], which is also sung in Arabic and has sold an unprecedented half a million copies in Morocco. Many hits were to follow, such as "Shoufi Ghirou" [Find Someone Else], "Souvenir," and "Hadi Kadba Beyna" [You Lie to Me].

Aatabou was the first woman to release a CD in the Moroccan market. Her songs mix Berber and Arabic, and deal with messages about morality and life's dramas. As her popularity has spread throughout the Maghreb, Aatabou has become particularly aware of her importance to women in the region. She encourages them to claim freedom, and to insist on their responsibly and self-respect.

Aatabou sings with an orchestra that includes the bendir (drum), dumbek (drum), lotar (stringed instrument), oud (lute), tar (tambourine), and violin. As her songs have evolved from the themes of heartbreak and loneliness into truthful tales of urban romance, she has included more instruments, such as bass and electric guitars, synthesizer, a variety of drums, and congas.[6]

Samira Said

Samira Said grew up in Rabat, where she began performing at an early age. She blended qualities of Moroccan music with contemporary Arabic sounds and sang her songs with a strong voice that earned her the status of a star.

Said established herself as one of the favorite singers of the Middle East and North Africa after she went to Egypt in the early 1980s. She worked with such renowned composers as Mohamad Sultan, who composed "Al Hob Elli Ana Aichah" [The Love That I Live], which demonstrated her vocal capability and excellent presentation. By 1983 Said had proven that she could perform classic music in the manner of Um Kulthoum, and she had many leading songwriters and composers working with her. In the 1990s she began to incorporate elements of rai, jazz, and Western pop into her songs. Her album *Youm Wara Youm*, which contains dance beats, Arabic ululation, scratching, and other creative musical sounds mixed with her powerful voice, was one of the best-selling albums in the region and abroad. She was also nominated for the BBC World Music Award after the release of *Youm Wara Youm* in 2002 by Ark 21.[7]

Tunisia

The music of Tunisia has been strongly influenced by the musical styles of Algeria and Morocco. One of the most popular genres is the classical Arabic repertoire of songs.

Amina Annabi

Amina Annabi was born in the 1962 in Carthage, Tunisia. Her professional career began in France, and she was the first of the younger female singers to cross over to the international stage. Her songs include both traditional Tunisian and Arab classical forms.

Annabi released her debut album *Yalil* [Oh Night] in France in 1989. This successful album, which fused an eclectic range of musical styles, earned her the Best Female Singer of the Year French award in 1991. Annabi's famous song "Le Dernier Qui A Parlé" [Who Has The Last Word], which mixes European pop with North African rhythms and West African melodies, placed first in the Eurovision Song Contest. Other songs incorporate pop, electronic, and jazz beats with the dance melodies of Tunisia.

AL-MASHRIQ AL-ARABI (THE ARABIAN EAST)

Libya

Various genres of music are popular in Libya. There is *al-Andalusi* music, known also as *maluf* (familiar), shabi (folk), and Arabic classical music. Another style is *huda*, the rhythm of which is said to mimic the feet of a walking camel. Two of the most famous musicians in Libya are Mohammed Hassan and Ayman al-Attar. The musical instruments used in Libya include the *zukrah* and *mizwid*, tambourine, darbuka, and oud. Clapping is also common in folk music.

The Tuareg, who live in the southern Saharan part of the Libyan Desert, have their own distinctive music. The Tuareg women, who are the musicians of their tribes, play the stringed *anzad* and a variety of drums.

Egypt

Al-jeel (generation) is modern, high-tech Egyptian dance music, originally created by Egyptians and Libyan expatriates in Cairo. It consists of a fusion of Nubian, Bedouin, and Egyptian rhythms. The influential early producer of al-jeel music, Hameed Sharay, came from Libya in the early 1970s when the Libyan leader Muammar Gaddafi imposed a system of Islamic socialism that excluded Western ideas. In Cairo, Sharay discovered stars such as Hanan and Ehab.

Al-jeel developed as an Egyptian alternative to foreign pop. It draws on shabi music and establishes a modern presentation that involves synthesizers, contemporary romantic lyrics, and good-looking singers, who can charm audiences with their sweet voices.

Al-jeel simplified the classic scales of regional music to complement up-to-date lyrics and vocal nuances that reflect the sound of the younger singers. Such music became fashionable in urban venues in the late 1980s, especially when handsome Amr Diab appeared on the Egyptian stage, jumping around in front of crowds sometimes in excess of 50,000 people.

Amr Diab

Amr Diab was born in 1961 as Amro Abd Al-Bassit Abd Al-Aziz Diab in Port Said, Egypt. He started singing at the age of six and graduated from the Cairo Academy of Art in 1986. His first successful album, *Ya Tareeq* [Oh Path], followed immediately, and in the 1990s he became the first Arab artist to make a music video. Amr Diab was also the first young Arab singer to perform at the Kennedy Center in Washington, D.C. (the only other Arab artists ever invited were Fairuz and Wadi al-Safy). In 1996 Diab released his hit album *Nour al-Ain* [Light of My Eye], which made him internationally famous. The album, accompanied by a lavish music video produced by Alam el Phan, became the best-selling album ever released by an Arab artist. In 1997 Diab won three awards (Best Video, Best Song, and Artist of the Year) at the Annual Arabic Festival in Egypt, and the following year, he received a Triple Platinum Award for the sales of "Nour al-Ain," the song that won him the Worldwide Music Award in Monaco. Diab also signed for Pepsi Cola commercials and recorded with Middle Eastern and international singers, including Khaled and the Greek singer Angela Dimitriu. He joined the Rotana group in 2004.

Hakim

Hakim was born in 1962 in the village of Maghagha in Minya, and he started performing in the Minya area when he was fourteen. In the early 1980s Hakim moved to Cairo to study and made his debut with "Nazra" [Glance] in 1991. This song was included in an album by the same name produced by Hamid El-Shaeri and Sonar Ltd./Slam Records. "Nazra" sold out in Egypt and was followed by "Nar" [Fire] in 1994.

Hakim was chosen to represent Egypt at the Festival des Allumées in Nantes, France. He was also nominated for the Kora Award for Best North African Singer in 1996, a prize he won in 2000. He has sold more than six million records locally and became the first of the young Egyptian artists to develop into a worldwide celebrity.

In 1998 Transglobal Underground, the British world dance fusionists, remixed some of Hakim's work for a new version called *Hakim Remix*. This made him an instant celebrity in Europe and launched a series of his international remixes and American releases. Hakim's *Yaho* [Hey You] album, which sold more than a million copies in the Middle East, was produced by Ark 21/Mondo Melodia and has sold over a million copies in America. This success was followed by other albums and new collaborations with internationally known producers such as American Narada Michael Walden, Puerto Rican Olga Tanon, and Frenchman Sodi. Hakim also released *El Youmein Dool* [These Days] in 2004, which included a duet track with the American soul/funk singer James Brown.[8]

Jordan

The music of Jordan has a strong Bedouin influence. One of the popular styles is *zajal* (improvised rhymed poetry), which is recited in colloquial Arabic. It is a rural genre with elaborate rhythms that focuses on the themes of family, love, and honor. It is usually accompanied by all or some of the following instruments: rababa, mizmar, mijwez, *ney gerbeh*, oud, and drum.

One of the famous Jordanian singers is the Bedouin singer Omar al-Abdullat, who is known for his song "Hashemi." He has been singing since 1988 and has represented Jordan in many international music festivals. He has also performed in the United States and Europe, and composed for other artists, including the Syrian Asala Nasri and a number of Jordanian artists.

Omar Badwan, a graduate of the Jordanian National Music Conservatory, has performed internationally and won the Golden Prize in the 2000 Cairo Song Festival. Other famous performers include singers Ghada Abbasi and Ibrahim Khalifa, musicians Ayman Tayseer and Hani Naser, and composers Omar Faqir and Khalid Asad. The first winner of the *Middle East Superstar* series in 2003 was also a Jordanian, Diana Karazone. The show is the staged Arabic version of *American Idol*. Karazone, a student of aviation sciences at Amman Private University impressed the audience with her interpretations of the songs of Um Kulthoum. She signed the release of her first album, *Diana Karazone Arab Superstar*, with Warner Music and Music Master International in the same year.

Recognized musical entities include the National Jordanian Music Institution, Jordanian Music Center (*Muntada Huwa al-Fan*), National Music Conservatory (NMC, part of Yarmouk University), and the Jordanian Music Council. There is also an annual Jordanian music festival called the Jarash Festival, which has been taking place in the ancient city of Jarash for more than twenty-five years.

Israel and the Palestinian Territories

The music of Israel and Palestine reflects strong influences from both local and foreign inspiration. Besides Hebrew, the popular musical flavors in Israel are Arabic and Greek. A number of musicians are known for their hybrid and native Arabic and Jewish genres. For example, Ofra Haza (1957–2000), known as the "Madonna of the East," introduced Eastern and Western instrumentation, orchestration, and dance beats mixed with her mezzo-soprano voice and multilingual lyrics in several of her songs. Her talent and innovative approach won her several awards for albums, such as *Shaday* and *Yemenite Songs*, which increased her international appeal.

Other famous singers in Israel are Lior Narkis, with his hits "Lekhol Ekhad Yesh" [Everyone Has] and "Millim Laahava" [Words for Love]; and Zehava Ben, who is famous for her "Shir Lashalom" [Song for Peace]; and "Ma Yihye" [What Will Be] from 1994. The following highlight other popular Israeli and Palestinian singers.

Sarit Hadad

Sarit Hadad was born to immigrant parents, who moved to Israel from Kavkaz, located in the Chechen Republic of Ichkeria (CRI). She learned to play drums, guitar, and organ, and started performing at the age of eight. She then joined a youth music group and started performing with them when she was fourteen.

Hadad was discovered by Avi Gueta, a top Israeli music manager, who released her first album when she turned sixteen. Since then, Hadad has performed across Israel and around the world, drawing thousands of fans to her performances. During this time, her music has ranged from ballads to pulsating dance grooves, always with a *Mizrahi* (Eastern) musical flavor, which deals with the themes of love and prosperity. Her latest album features a duet with the group Subliminal and Israel's leading rapper, set against a Persian fusion musical track.

Hadad remains popular in Israel, and her album, *Hagiga* [Celebration] has sold more than 40,000 copies. In addition, Hadad has eleven triple-platinum albums to her credit. She has also released a high-quality, polished music video titled *Rak Ata* [Only You], which is also popular in her country.[9]

Shiri Maimon

Shiri Maimon was born in Haifa, Israel, in 1981. She was the first runner-up in *Kochav Nolad* [A Star Is Born], the Israeli version of *Pop Idol*. She also represented Israel in the 2005 Song Contest in Kiev, where she sang "Hasheket Shenishar" [The Silence That Remains] in Hebrew and English.

Maimon released her first album in 2005 and sold 20,000 copies. Since March 2006 Maimon has been starring in the soap opera *Yeladot Raot* [Bad Girls] on the Israeli music channel 24, showing off her talent by singing the role of Maya Gold, a talented singer and star of the Monokol Record Company.

Svika Pick

Svika Pick was born in Wroclaw, Poland, in 1951. He started to perform at the age of fifteen and studied music at the Conservatory of Ramat Gan in Tel Aviv. He is best known in Israel for a long list of pop hits produced throughout the 1970s. He changed his style in the nineties and became famous for his dance music hits.

Pick has participated seven times as a singer in the Israeli preliminary of the Eurovision Song Contest (*Kdam*), and he has composed many hits for the competitors of the contest.

For example, his song "Diva," performed by Dana International, won the Eurovision Song Contest in 1998. In 2002 he composed "Light a Candle" for Sarit Hadad, who represented Israel in Eurovision 2002. In 2003 he composed the song "Hasta la Vista" for Oleksander, and in 2005, Pick was one of three judges in the musical talent reality show *Kokhav Noland*.

Simon Shaheen (Palestinian)

Simon Shaheen was born 1955 in Tarshiha, a small village in Galilee, to a musically talented father, who passed on the Arab musical tradition to him. Shaheen started playing the oud when he was five, and at seven years old, he started learning the violin and Western music at the Rubin Conservatory. In 1978 Shaheen graduated from the Academy of Music in Jerusalem; he moved to New York in 1980, where he continued his musical training at Columbia University and the Manhattan School of Music. In 1982 Shaheen founded the Near Eastern Music Ensemble, followed by the band *Qantara* [Arch] in 1995. He also joined numerous experimental and fusion collaborations and performed in a variety of international events. He received the National Heritage Award in 1994. Shaheen was also appointed to the Presidential Advisory Board for World Music at the John F. Kennedy Center.

The music of Simon Shaheen can be described as a mixture of Arabic pop, jazz, classical, and world music. One of his most famous musical compositions, performed with *Qantara*, is "Blue Flame," which debuted in 2001. It stayed on the CMJ (*Critical Musicology Journal*) world music charts for several weeks. The piece combines Arabic genres with American jazz, Western folk, and classical music of Eastern Europe and Spain.

Lebanon

Popular music in Lebanon can be divided into folk music that is accompanied by a *dabkeh* beat and the urban pop music that has *raks sharqi* (belly dancing) rhythms influenced by Western music. The following represent both genres.

Fairuz and the Rahbanis

The most important living vocal legend is Fairuz (known as the "Soul of Lebanon"), who was born Nuhad Haddad in Beirut in 1934. She made her solo debut in the early 1950s and initiated a yearly performance at the Baalbeck Festival in 1957. Fairuz's significance as a popular icon, which has spanned the second half of the twentieth and early twenty-first centuries, relates to the wide spectrum of her repertoire that includes songs in classical Arabic and local dialect.

Fairuz's chief composers have been her husband, Assi Rahbani; his brother, Mansour; and her son, Ziyad. These three arranged a variety of regional musical styles, including the *muwashshahat* (poetic form originating in Islamic Spain), dabkeh (line dance/community dance) songs, and *mawawil* (vocal improvisation), which were also included in a variety of musicals starring Fairuz.

The Rahbani brothers, trained in Western and Arabic music, adapted a variety of folk tunes and popular songs from many countries and blended them with segments from Middle Eastern and North African tradition, Arabic folk music, and Western classical music. Most of the Rahbanis' compositions are short and concise, with no more than two maqam (melodic modes) modulations and rare taqasim improvisations. They employed a modified

Western-style orchestra, which includes a piano, accordion, flute, and regional instruments such as the buzuq, darabaka, and riq. The Rahbanis also complemented the beauty of Fairuz's voice with brilliant lyrics that corresponded to their excellent compositions.

After the death of Fairuz's husband, her son, Ziyad, started composing her songs and musical productions, and backed up her voice with jazz and contemporary Western tunes. He also reissued an album of his father's compositions named *Ila Assi* [To Assi] that re-orchestrated his father's arrangements in a more contemporary style. This young composer has attracted the younger generation as well as the older one with his fresh version of Fairuz's music. He mixes his mother's classical lyrics with manipulated maqams and presents controversial and satirical plays that honestly depicted the struggle of the nation.

Fairuz is still heard on radio and television around the Middle East and North Africa. Her latest appearances included the Baalbeck Festival in 1998, Las Vegas in 1999, and the Beiteddine Festival in Lebanon in 2000.

Nancy Ajram

Nancy Ajram (known as the "Sun of Arabic Song") was born in 1983 in Beirut. She made her debut at the age of fifteen singing one of Um Kulthoum's songs and winning the *Nujoum al-Mustaqbal* (the Stars of the Future) contest. Her first album was produced in 2000, but it was her album *Ya Salam* [How Nice] of 2003 that contains her song "Akhasmak Ah," which made her an instant hit.

Ajram is considered one of the most famous pop singers. She has performed in many Arab countries and was also featured in several Coca-Cola and Damas Jewelry commercials. She was also a guest on one of the episodes of *Superstar*, a Middle Eastern version of *Pop Idol*, and was named as the best Arabic singer by the magazine *Zahrat el Khalij* for both 2003 and 2004. She was also considered in the Arabic version of *Newsweek* as one of the most influential personalities in the Arab world in 2005. Her albums are a hit around the world, with estimated sales of over 3 million copies for *Ya Salam* in 2003, 3 million for *Ah Wu Nuss* [One Ah and a Half] in 2004, and 5 million copies for *Ya Tabla Wa Dalla* [Rhythm and Allure] in 2006.

Haifa Wehbe

Haifa Wehbe (known as an ultimate sex symbol) was born in 1976 in Beirut. She first attracted attention to her beauty when, at the age of sixteen, she won a beauty contest in south Lebanon. In 1995 she won the Most Beautiful Young Woman in Lebanon award, which put her in instant demand for fashion shows. She signed with Rotana, the Saudi production company that produced her first album, *Howa al-Zaman* [Only Time], in 2005. Wehbe was also one of the fourteen Arab celebrities who participated in the hit reality show *al-Wadi* [The Valley], which featured weekly live performances. This artist also became the newest face for Pepsi commercials in 2005. She is famous for her 2006 song "el-WaWa" [The Pain].

Syria

Syria's music production companies are small and limited in number. As a result, musical groups began attracting Western companies to produce Syrian music. For example, France's Harmonia Mundi produced the famous Ensemble al-Kindi of Aleppo. The renowned singer

Music

Sabri al-Moudallal, one of the few left who has kept traditional Syrian music alive, is included with the Ensemble al-Kindi and has a self-titled CD produced by IMA (Institute du Monde Arabe).

The traditional tarab (enchantment) style of music is much admired in Syria. Open-air restaurants regularly engage an oud player or singer to enchant their customers. Some of the younger singers introduce certain aspects of tarab at the beginning of their songs, then progress to dance rhythms. The following are singers of both genres.

Asalah Nasri

Asalah Nasri was born in 1969 and started singing with her father, Mustapha Nasri, at the age of eight. She is one of the most popular young singers in Syria and throughout the Arab countries. Nasri's songs are backed up by an orchestra with a variety of traditional Middle Eastern instruments, such as the darbuka, tambourine, oud, and qanoun. She also uses the violin, piano, and electric guitar. Her strong, flexible voice allows her to vary her performance between traditional songs, which employ long poems, and short *aghani* (songs). She is known for her *mawwal* (improvisation), which shows the excellent qualities and the high range of her voice.

George Wassouf

George Wassouf was born in 1961 in Kafroun near Homs. He started singing at the age of twelve for different occasions such as marriages and parties at hotels and theaters, and he was called the "Miracle Child." The composer George al-Khouri discovered Wassouf when he was singing at one of these events and promoted him around the region in concerts and radio performances. At the age of sixteen, Wassouf started singing at Lebanese festivals and became known as "Sultan el Tarab." Many songs, including "Hawa Sultan" [Love of the Sultan], "Rohi ya Nesmah" [Go Breeze], "Hilef el Amar" [The Moon Has Sworn], and "Law Naweit" [If You Are Determined] have made him popular throughout the region. The Lebanese studio el-Fan has popularized George Wassouf, who has produced more than thirty albums and performed concerts around the world. The song "Hilef el Amar" scored a massive hit in the Arab world.

In 2002 Sultan el Tarab released his album *Salaf Wi Dein* [Loan and Debt], which became a huge success in both the Arab world and abroad.

Sabah Fakhri

Sabah Fakhri was born in Aleppo, Syria, in 1933 and started performing at the age of ten. He studied at the Damascus Conservatory with traditional teachers of the Mevlevi Sufi order, including Shaykh Ali al-Darwish and Shaykh Umar al-Batsh. He started singing with the National Syrian Radio Orchestra in 1950 and became known for his superb vocal technique. His songs are of the traditional genres of *muashshahat* (strophic song), *qasida* (poem), *dawr* (vocal genre sung in colloquial Arabic), *qadd* (a light popular song genre originating in Aleppo), and mawwal (vocal improvisation). Fakhri's repertoire of classical music is popular around the Arab countries. Some of his most famous songs include "Ya Mal al-Sham" [Damascene Beauty], "Al Rosana" [Roseanne], and "Qadduka el Mayyass" [Your Swaying Figure]. His latest international recording was with Ark 21/Mondo Melodia in 2000.

Other popular singers are Johnny Salem, Kanana al-Qasir, Linda Barakat, Hussam Madaniyya, Muhannad Mushlih, Husayn Duwayri, and Ali Dawli. Most of their tracks air on the Damascus-based radio, FM al-Madina.

Iraq

The most admired music in Iraq is a combination of old and new styles. Rising singers are always compared to the late phenomenon, Nazem al-Ghazali, who was one of the most admired singing giants of the twentieth century in the Middle East and North Africa. His romantic voice and poems expressing themes of love and yearning had become part of the Iraqi classic repertoire. Singers such as Kazem al-Saher have elaborated on this prevailing genre.

Kazem al-Saher

Kazem al-Saher was born in 1961 in Nainawa in northern Iraq. He started playing music when he was ten years old, and he was accepted into the Baghdad Music Academy at the age of twenty-one. In 1987 al-Saher made the first video for his song, "Ladghat El Hayya" [The Snake Bite], which was broadcast on Iraqi television. A year later, he had a hit with "Abart al-Shatt" [I Crossed the Ocean], which made him a household name.

In general, al-Saher's repertoire ranges from long romantic ballads to more political work and from shabi pop to Arab classical. In 1989 he established himself as a classical singer with the hour-long song "La Ya Sadiki" [No, My Friend], which used old Iraqi traditional maqams. By 1998 he had earned the title *fanan* (artist) in addition to his fame as a pop star.

Al-Saher performed his song "Tathakkar" [Remember] in America for Congress and the United Nations, and he won a UNICEF award for it. He also recorded a tribute to the Pope with the Italian Symphony Orchestra and allowed a remix (by fusionists Transglobal Underground) of his song "La Titnahad" [Do Not Sigh], which was taken from his 2000 release album *El Hob El Moustahil* [The Impossible Love]. This album was the first of his to be given an official American release through Mondo Melodia, and it sold an unprecedented number of albums for a Middle Eastern artist. He has also collaborated with famous Arab poets, such as the Syrian Nizar al Qabani, and international singers, such as Sarah Brightman.

Iran

The classic poetry of Rumi and Hafiz has survived the influence of popular Western music. The popular music that started to take place before the Iranian revolution was cut short with the change of regimes and the restrictions imposed by the Islamic government. Many musicians left the county and continued their performances abroad. Others stayed and were banned from performing or touring to promote their musical genres.

Googoosh

Googoosh was born Faegheh Atashin in 1950 in Tehran. She began performing with her father at a young age and made her first film at the age of seven. In the 1970s Googoosh was at the height of her film and music career and was widely admired by Iranian men and women. In addition to listening to her music, women liked her fashionable appearance and vibrant personality. Googoosh was banned from public performance after the Iranian

Music

> ### PUBLIC CONCERTS
>
> After several years of banning public concerts, Kuwait has recently resumed granting permits for well-known Arab pop singers, despite opposition from the Islamic morality police.[11]
>
> Islamists have also asked that unrelated men and women be seated separately at concerts given by Arab singers held during a festival each February. In recent years, Bahrain has also seen Islamist protests against pop concerts. Some protests have turned violent. One outcry led to the cancellation of the Arabic version of the reality TV show *Big Brother* that was being filmed in one of the Gulf states.[12]

revolution of 1979. She kept silent for almost twenty years and was not permitted to leave the country until 1997.[10]

Googoosh has since reestablished her position as a pop diva in North America, and she has started performing her old and new songs in concerts and at cultural events. Lyrically and musically, her songs are notable because she collaborated with the best Iranian poets and composers. These songs, although rooted in Persian melodies that are often mixed with a dance beat, blend Eastern and Western elements. For example, some of her songs use an electric guitar, have rumba or flamenco rhythms, or follow French *chanson* style.

Googoosh is now a national icon because she represents the struggle and pain of the Iranian people. In the last few years, the Iranian authorities have softened their hardline stance on pop music, and while the sale of pop music CDs is still illegal, possession of them is now allowed.[13]

AL-KHALIJ AL-ARABI (THE ARABIAN PENINSULA)

Khaleeji music is a style of Persian Gulf–area folk music, played with polyrhythms in the countries of the Arabian Peninsula. The style is strongly influenced by African music.

Bahrain, Kuwait, and Qatar are also known for the *fidgeri* repertoire of vocal music, originally sung by pearl divers. The two main genres of fidgeri are *Bahri* and *Adsani*. The singer and his chorus use the mirwas (drum), jahlah (drum), and hand clapping as their instruments. Some of the popular singers of fidgeri are Ahmad Butabbaniya and Salem Allan.

Bahrain

The small island nation of Bahrain is known along with Kuwait for the vocal *sawt* music. It is a complex form of urban music performed with oud, mirwas (a drum), and violin, and it is influenced by African, Indian, and Persian music.

One of the most popular musicians and singers of Bahrain is Ali Bahar and his band al-Ekhwa al-Bahrainiya (Bahraini Brothers). The band, established in the early 1970s under the name Al-Sakhra (Rock), became al-Ekhwa al-Bahrainiya in the 1980s. The style of this band is mostly influenced by the music of the Middle East. Ali Bahar released his latest album *Damal Ayon* [Tears] in 2005.

Other popular entertainers include Sultan Hamid, Khalid al-Sheikh, the Bahraini hip-hop performer DJ Outlaw, and the band Osiris. A female singer, Hind, is a popular new performer who has just released her new album *El Ghroub* [Dusk], produced by Rotana.

Qatar

Most Qataris enjoy listening to khaleeji music in the traditional Bedouin musical style. This music dominates the capital, Doha, and the rest of the country. The Qatari Gulf

Folklore Center is one of the preeminent centers for the study of popular folk music of the Persian Gulf.

United Arab Emirates

Some of the most famous performers are Aitha al-Manhali, Samar, Reem, Rouwaida, Abdallah Belkhair, and Ahlam, the first female pop star in the Gulf. To encourage singing talents from around the world, a man from Dubai started a Website to encourage people to post their voices and have the audience rate them.[14]

Saudi Arabia

The traditional, basic structure of music in Saudi Arabia remains little changed in modern times. Men and women have separate singing groups. Both have a lead singer, a *mutrib* (male singer) or *mutriba* (female singer), who heads the group that consists of around twelve chorus members and drummers. The drummers play various sizes of the daff, the *zir ardhi* (a shallow clay drum played on the ground with a stick), the *zalafa* (a multihandled drum), the *tanaka* (a large rectangular tin played as a hand drum), and the mihbaj (mortar and pestle) to accent the end of each rhythmic phrase.

The folk songs consist of simple repeated melodies overlying complex repeated hypnotic rhythms. The melody usually stays in a single mode and is repeated throughout a series of verses, sung in colloquial Arabic. At times, the singer embellishes the melody with ornamentation. Some singers play the oud, with an occasional accompanist on violin.

Today's popular wedding male and female singers—such as Riyadh's Noura al-Jassas and Mary Said, and Jeddah's Sarah Musaifir—favor electronic quarter-tone keyboards, which can also replicate *zagharid*, or ululation, the traditional women's trilling cry of celebration. Some of these singers record with large orchestras, release compact discs, and appear in music videos. These videos often reflect the music in their modesty and simplicity.

Oman

Omani music is influenced by the music of many other neighboring countries, including Egypt, Iran, Saudi Arabia, the United Arab Emirates, and Yemen. Omani music relies on the strong rhythms provided by the drumbeats. Most of the melodies are based on the Arabic maqam.

One popular Omani folk music is the *lewa,* which uses the mizmar as its primary instrument. The Omani Center for Traditional Music is the main musical culture center and promotes instruments such as the mizmar, oud, rababa, and tanbura.

Yemen

The poetic songs of Sanaa, the capital of Yemen, have maintained the original roots of traditional music. A solo singer is usually accompanied by the oud and percussion instruments to highlight the rhythms. Music styles in Yemeni folk music are fluid in rhythm, with a wide variety of metrical patterns derived from poetic language. Some of the instruments used in Yemen are the tabol, mizmar, and *khalloul.* Some of the most famous Yemenite musicians are Hasan al-Ajami, Ousama al-Attar, Mohammad al-Harithi, Ahmad Fathey, Ahmed Al-Hubaishi, and Ahmed Ushaysh.

MUSIC

The music of Yemen is also known abroad through the popular Arab performers and the Yemenite Jews who became musical stars in Israel during the twentieth century: Zohar Argov, who died in 1987, and Zion Golan, who is still singing in Jewish Yemeni dialect. In 2003 UNESCO called this musical genre of Sanaa a masterpiece of the oral and intangible heritage of humanity.[15]

RESOURCE GUIDE

PRINT SOURCES

Al-Mahdi, Muhammad Salih. *Music in Muslim Civilization.* London: Al Furqan Islamic Heritage Foundation, 2002.

Bessman, Jim. "Arabic Music Moves West." *Billboard* 113.32 (2001): 1.

Danielson, Virginia. *The Voice of Egypt: Umm Kulthum, Arabic Song, and Egyptian Society in the Twentieth Century.* Chicago: University of Chicago Press, 1997.

Hammond, Andrew. *Pop Culture Arab World! Media, Arts, and Lifestyle.* Santa Barbara, CA: ABC-CLIO, 2004.

Maalouf, Shireen. "Mikha'il Mishaqa: Virtual Founder of the Twenty-Four Equal Quartertone Scale." *Journal of the American Oriental Society* 123.4 (2003): 835–840.

McGrath, Cam. "New Museum Honours Diva of Arabic Music." *Middle East* 324 (2002): 46.

Meijer, Roel, *Alienation or Integration of Arab Youth: Between Family, State, and Street.* Richmond, Surrey: Curzon, 2000.

Motavalli, Jim. "The Light for the Heart." *Nation* 274.3 (2002): 36–37.

Olsen, Poul Rovsing. *Music in Bahrain: Traditional Music of the Arabian Gulf.* Moesgaard: Jutland Archaeological Society: Moesgaard Museum; Bahrain: Ministry of Information, 2002.

Racy, A. J. *Making Music in the Arab World.* New York: Cambridge University Press, 2003.

Schnee, Daniel. "Arabic Concepts for Improvisation." *Canadian Musician* 27.6 (2005): 29.

Shiloah, Amnon. *Music in the World of Islam: A Socio-cultural Study.* Detroit: Wayne State University Press, 2000.

Sinclair, David. "Global Music Pulse." *Billboard* 106.19 (1994): 61.

Percak, Suzanne. "Arabic Music in the Heartland." *Washington Report on Middle East Affairs* 24.4 (2005): 58.

Van Nieuwkerk, Karin. *"A Trade Like Any Other": Female Singers and Dancers in Egypt.* Austin: University of Texas Press, 1995.

Zuhur, Sherifa, ed. *Colors of Enchantment.* Cairo: American University of Cairo Press, 2001.

———, ed. *Images of Enchantment.* Cairo: American University of Cairo Press, 1998.

WEBSITES

Al Bawaba. August 16, 2006. http://www.albawaba.com. Source for the latest news on singers and musicians.

Arab Culture and Civilization. 2006. National Institute for Technology and Liberal Education. http://arabworld.nitle.org. This site offers information on popular music and links to other good Websites that provide information on music.

Farraj, Johnny. *Arabic Maqam World.* May 9, 2005. http://maqamworld.com. A noncommercial educational Website that promotes Arabic music and instruments.

Islamic and Middle Eastern Music and Dance. http://www.sfusd.k12.ca.us/schwww/sch618/Music/Islam_Music_&_Dance.html. The Islamic and Middle Eastern cultural site provides specific information on Middle Eastern secular and religious music, including theory and history.

Kontanis, Mavrothis. *Oud Café.* http://www.oudcafe.com/index.htm. A great site for those interested the oud. It includes instructional pages ranging from tips to how to play the oud and theoretical information.

Ludvigsen, Børre. *Al Mashriq—The Levant.* 2006. Ostfold College. http://almashriq.hiof.no/. Run by Ostfold College, Halden, Norway, and mirrored at AUB in Lebanon, this site has extensive information about the culture of Lebanon and the Middle East. The section on Arabic music describes and illustrates the instruments used in Middle Eastern music.

Marcus, Scott. *UCSB Middle East Ensemble.* 2006. University of California–Santa Barbara. http://www.music.ucsb.edu/mee/instruments.html. Run by the Friends of Middle Eastern Music Association (FOMEMA) at the University of California–Santa Barbara; provides information on Arabic music.

Parfitt, David. *The Oud.* 2004. http://www.oud.eclipse.co.uk/arabmod.html. This site provides a great basis for understanding Middle Eastern modulation practices.

Rotana. 2006. Rotana. http://www.rotana.net. Producers and distributors of Arabic music. Good source for latest hits.

Turath.org: A Resource for World Arts. 2005. http://www.turath.org. Maintained by UCLA; provides articles, information about events, and interviews. It is an extensive Website that seeks to educate and sponsor enthusiasts in Arabic music.

Whitaker, Brian. *Al-Bab: An Open Door to the Arab World.* January 10, 2006. http://www.al-bab.com. Privately managed. It offers links to a variety of other interesting sites loaded with information on the culture and arts of the Middle East and North Africa.

MAGAZINES

Al-Ahram Weekly. August 10, 2006. http://weekly.ahram.org.eg. A weekly Egyptian magazine that provides good coverage of Egyptian and Arab artists.

Al Jadid Magazine. 2006. http://www.aljadid.com/. A quarterly magazine based in California and edited by Elie Chalala. It provides information on entertainment in the Middle East and North Africa.

Global Rhythm. August 16, 2006. First World Entertainment, Inc. http://www.globalrhythm.net/. A New York–based monthly magazine that covers world music and arts.

Saudi Aramco World. August 2006. http://www.saudiaramcoworld.com/. Source for articles on Arabic music.

Sound on Sound. August 2006. PB Associates. http://www.soundonsound.com. A music recording magazine with articles on a variety of musical types. Based in Cambridge, England, and independently owned

Yemen Times. August 14, 2006. Yemen Times. http://www.yementimes.com. Source for information about Yemen and khaleeji music.

VIDEOS/FILMS

Rai Story: From Cheikha Rimitti to Cheba Djenet, vol. 5 of *Women Pioneers Collection* (Arab Film Distribution, 2004). Directed by Madeleine Verschaffelt and Ahmed Rachedi.

Um Kulthum: A Voice Like Egypt (Arab Film Distribution, 1998). Directed by Michal Goldman.

RECORDINGS

Ahlam. *Ahsan.* ALA (Khalij, Arabian Gulf).
Ajram, Nancy. *Ah W Noss.* EMI (Lebanon).
Alama, Ragheb. *Ragheb Alama Greatest Hits 1996–2005.* EMI (Lebanon).
———. *Tab Leh.* Ark 21, 2002 (Lebanon).
al-Attar, Ayman. *Bahibak.* MMI (Libya).
al-Jassmi, Husain. *Al Jassmi 2004.* VMP, 2004 (Bahrain).
al-Saher, Kazem. *Entaha Almeshwar.* ROT (Iraq).
Annabi, Amina. *Nomad: The Best of Amina.* Mondo Melodia, 2001 (Tunisia).
Ben, Zehava. *Beit Avi.* Musicrama, 2003 (Israel).

MUSIC

Desert Roses & Arabian Rhythms, vol. 1 and 2. Mondo Melodia, 2001.
Diab, Amr. *The Very Best Of.* EMI (Lebanon).
Fakhri, Sabah. *Ya Hadi al-Eiyss.* LPD (Syria).
Hadad, Sarit. *Ashlayot Metukot.* Musicrama, 2004 (Israel).
Hakim. *Kolo Yoross.* EMI (Egypt).
———. *Talakik.* Mondo Melodia, 2002 (Egypt).
Karazone, Diana. *El Omr Mashi.* MMI (Jordan).
Khalaf, Aline. *Best of Aline Khalaf.* EMI (Lebanon).
Khaled. *Didi.* Cohiba, 1992 (Algeria).
———. *Sahra.* Plygram Record, 1997 (Algeria).
Mami, Cheb. *Dellali.* Ark 21, 2001.
Nasri, Asala. *Ady.* ROT (Syria).
Nawal. *Nawal.* EMI, 2004 (Khalij).
Ruby. *Ruby with the Tatou Band.* KNG (Egypt).
Said, Samira. *Youm Wara Youm.* Ark 21, 2002 (Morocco).
Samar: Music from Yemen Arabia. Rounder Select, 1999 (Yemen).
Shaheen, Simon. *Blue Flame.* Mondo Melodia, 2001 (Palestine).
Toufic, Walid. *Top Hits—Arwa Al Aghani.* EMI (Lebanon).
Wassouf, George. *Wassouf Remixed.* MMI (Syria).
Wehbe, Haifa. *Howa el-Zaman.* EMI (Lebanon).
Yemen Traditional Music. 2005 (Yemen).

EVENTS

Al-Bustan Festival, Lebanon. The festivals of Baalbeck, Beiteddine, Byblos, and Al-Bustan are focal events of both national and international artistic expression held each year starting in February.
al-Rabat Festival, Morocco. This festival has been held each July since 1998.
Arab Heritage Festival. http://arabic.meetup.com/45/events/. This Website covers all the details for the festival held annually in New York.
Arabic Music Retreat, Fares Center for Eastern Mediterranean Studies, Cabot Intercultural Center, Tufts University, 160 Packard Avenue, Medford, MA 02155. http://farescenter.tufts.edu. Annual retreat offers an intensive hands-on learning experience focusing on music of the Arab world; held at Mt. Holyoke College in Massachusetts.
Arabic Music Retreat, Arab American Arts Institute, P.O. Box 296, Accord, MA 02018-296. http://www.simonshaheen.com/. Explains the annual Arabic music retreat held at Mount Holyoke College in Massachusetts. The camp program consists of seven days of intensive work in Arabic chamber and large orchestra performance.
Cairo International Song Festival, Cairo International Convention & Exhibition Centre, Nasr Road, Nasr City, Egypt. The Cairo Opera House has hosted this annual music festival dedicated to Arabic music since 1991.
Dearborn Arab International Festival. http://www.americanarab.com/festival/. An annual festival held on Father's Day weekend.
Festival al-Mahaba, Syria. This festival includes invited musicians and singers.
International Carthage Festival, El-Manzeh Olympic Stadium, Carthage, Tunisia. http://www.festival-carthage.com.tn/main.htm. The International Carthage Festival started in 1964. It includes music awards.
Jarash Festival, Jordan. Annual festival celebrating international folklore; held every July since 1981.
Mahrajan Al-Fan: Festival of Arab Arts, Symphony Space, W 95th St & Broadway New York, NY 10025. http://www.worldmusicinstitute.org/WMICAL/MAIN.ASP. Mahrajan Al-Fan is an annual event held in New York.
Middle Eastern Music and Dance, 3244 Overland Ave., No. 1, Los Angeles, CA 90034. http://www.middleeastcamp.com/. Covers all the details for this annual Middle Eastern music camp held at

Mendocino, California. The camp provides professional training for beginners and advanced musicians in vocal and instrumental music.

World Music Festival, Chicago, IL. http://egov.cityofchicago.org/. This festival has been an annual event since 1999.

NOTES

1. See Assir, Serene, "Big Bucks, Big Labels," *Al-Ahram Weekly on Line* (in Resource Guide), December 30, 2004–5, January 2005, no. 723, accessed June 22, 2006, http://weekly.ahram.org.eg/2004/723/fe1.htm.
2. See http://www.zawya.com/printstory.cfm?storyid=ZAWYA20040801071442&SecMain/pag Homepage&l=000000040801 (accessed June 22, 2006).
3. See http://www.rfimusique.com/siteEn/biographie/biographie_6027.asp (accessed June 22, 2006).
4. See Paul Tingen, "Khaked, Algerian Rai Music," *Sound on Sound* (in Resource Guide), October 1997, accessed June 22, 2006, http://www.soundonsound.com/sos/1997_articles/oct97/khaled.html.
5. See http://www.rfimusique.com/siteEn/biographie/biographie_6108.asp (accessed June 23, 2006).
6. See http://www.najataatabou.com/index.php?nav=static&pagina=about_najat (accessed June 24, 2006).
7. See http://www.bbc.co.uk/music/world/reviews/said_youm.shtml (accessed June 25, 2006).
8. See http://www.answers.com/main/ntquery;jsessionid=1naw395goeglp?tname=hakim-egyptian-singer&sbid=lc01a (accessed June 25, 2006).
9. See Loolwa Khazoom, "Sabra Madonna: Meet Israel's Pop Diva," *Forward*, posted September 10, 2004, accessed June 25, 2006, http://www.forward.com/main/article.php?ref=khazzoom20040909235.
10. See Hadani Ditmars, "Arts Abroad: World Tour for a Diva Long Banned from Singing," *New York Times*, August 9, 2000, accessed June 25, 2006, www.newyorktimes.com.
11. See http://www.arabnews.com/?page=4&section=0&article=53273&d=22&m=10&y=2004 (accessed July 2, 2006).
12. See Marc Lynch, "'Reality is Not Enough': The Politics of Arab Reality TV," *Transnational Broadcasting Studies* 15, accessed July 2, 2006, http://tbsjournal.com/Lynch.html.
13. See Hadani Ditmars, "Let Googoosh Sing," *Media Reviews, A Virtual TV for the Persian Diva*, accessed June 25, 2006, www.googoosh.tv/medrev/asalon.html.
14. See http://www.khaleejtimes.com/CityHome.asp?xfile=data/citytimes/2006/June/citytimes_June17.xml&section=citytimes&col=(accessed July 3, 2006).
15. See "UNESCO Second Proclamation of Masterpieces of the Oral and Intangible Heritage of Humanity," November 2003, http://www.unesco.org/culture.

PERIODICALS

LYNN BARTHOLOME

There is little doubt that the Middle East dominated the news of 2006. It began in January when ailing Israeli leader Ariel Sharon exited the political arena in a coma; later that month Hamas candidates swept to power via the Palestinian ballot box. In February, caricatures of the Prophet Muhammad published in Danish newspapers led to protests in the streets of Muslim nations across the region and beyond. While the violence in Iraq seemed to increase in intensity each day, there was a glimmer of hope in March when American journalist Jill Carroll was released by her captors, who had kidnapped her from off the streets of Baghdad months earlier. In April, there were bombings in Egypt and just a few weeks later, the death in Iraq of al Qaeda leader, Abu Musab Zarqawi by U.S. bombing raids left us with frightful yet graphically compelling images.

In July, two Israeli soldiers were captured; this unfortunate event pitted Israel against militants of Hezbollah, and set into motion the nationwide bombardment of Lebanon by Israel. Hezbollah responded by hitting northern Israel with a torrent of rocket fire. As autumn arrived, more and more reporters referred to the situation in Iraq as a civil war and the world began to accept that maybe this was so. In November, more than 200 died in one day in Baghdad's Sadr City; calls began to mount for an American withdrawal. President George W. Bush could no longer ignore these calls, for they came in the form of a crushing defeat for his administration and the Republicans in the U.S. midterm elections.

The possibility of a civil war rose again in Lebanon when Government Minister Pierre Gemayel was murdered in late November, and questions about Syria's influence and interference in Lebanese affairs came under scrutiny once more. The death of a member of one of Lebanon's foremost families led to protests at his funeral, which later developed into ongoing protests in the streets of Beirut.

In December, the hasty execution of Saddam Hussein left many with more questions than answers about what would come next. As the final days of 2006 drew to a close, U.S. and Coalition forces were once again battling a resurgent Taliban in the hills of Afghanistan. Some of them, in their second and third straight tours of duty, wondered what the next year would bring.[1] They did not have long to wait. The year 2007 has brought additional strife to the region and, sadly, many more American casualties. It has also brought a change of war policy to the Bush administration. This new policy has not been tested yet, nor has it been approved by the legislative branch of the U.S. government.

While we in the West take for granted the freedom of speech and expression that we are born with, it is interesting to note that much of the news and information that Middle Easterners and the populace of North Africa receive is frequently monitored and/or censored by individual governmental regimes. Even in Israel, where governmental curbs are more relaxed than in many of the neighboring Muslim nations, story content is sometimes influenced or controlled by government policy or opinion. In several Islamic countries, state-run agencies own and control the very presses the news is printed on. As recently as December 2006, reporters and writers have been jailed for publishing material that censors believed was insulting to Islam.

Although news and information are vital in shaping our perception of the universe and all that is within it, it is also essential to remember that the information we receive may be skewed in such a manner that a truly unbiased outlook may not be possible. The following summaries describe the role of print journalism in the political, economic, social, and cultural milieu of the Middle East and North Africa.

ALGERIA, MOROCCO, AND TUNISIA

Algeria

The languages spoken in Algeria include Arabic (the official language), French, and the Berber dialects. Approximately 74 percent of males and 49 percent of females aged fifteen and over can read and write (61.6 percent total literacy).[2]

Algeria has one of the most aggressive and independent presses in the Arab world, despite pressure from the government and attacks by Islamic extremists. Daily national newspapers are published in both Arabic and French and locally in the cities of Algiers, Oran, and Constantine.

The national daily newspaper *El Khabar* [The News] is published in Arabic and French, with selected sections in English. The paper started in 1988, after the fall of Algeria's one-party system, which had previously controlled the press. *El Khabar* is independent and has no party affiliation. Its critical reporting has at times caused run-ins with the Algerian government. The paper's sensationalistic style has led to comparisons with the tabloid press.

Other Arabic papers published in Algeria include *Ech Chaab*, *El Voum*, and the government periodical, *Journal Officiel*. French-language newspapers include *El Moudjahid*, *La Tribune*, and *Liberte*. *El Massa* [Evening] was founded in 1985 and is the first Algerian paper published in an evening edition.

El Watan [The Homeland], a French-language paper begun in 1990, reflects Algeria's shift from a one-party state toward democracy. The publication promotes democracy and covers the Algerian opposition, and is a candid voice against censorship and corruption. It has been suspended and its journalists jailed on several occasions.

Regional publications in Algiers include the general interest *Algiere Post* (English), the sports periodicals *El Heddaf* (Arabic) and *Le Buteur* (French), and the business journal *Le Maghref* (French).

In the city of Constantine the general interest publication *An Nasr* is published in Arabic, and the populace of Oran is served by the French publications *Lit Voix de l'Oranie* and *Le*

Quotidien d'Oran. The business and economics magazine *The Economist* is also published nationally in English.[3]

Morocco

Arabic is the official language in Morocco; French is often the language of business, government, and diplomacy. Berber dialects are also present in isolated regions.

Fifty-seven percent of males and 31 percent of females aged fifteen and over are literate (43.7 percent total literacy).

There are roughly two dozen newspapers published in Rabat, Casablanca, and Tangier; they are written in both French and Arabic. Most of these, however, are vehicles of Morocco's political parties; the others are owned by or sympathetic to the government.

The high rate of illiteracy keeps readership low and continues to make television the primary instrument for the dissemination of news and information.[4]

Four French-language magazines are widely circulated nationally. They are the satirical publication *La Gachette du Maroc, La Verite, La Journal Hebdomidaire,* and *Tel Quel*. The general interest English newspaper *Morocco Times* is currently published in Casablanca. A sports publication, *Le Journal du Sport,* is published in French. Business newspapers include *Frances News Hebdo, La Vie Eco,* and *L'Economiste* [*The Economist*]. A contemporary women's magazine, *Femmes du Maroc,* is becoming increasingly popular. The publication focuses on women's issues, fashion, and contemporary life.[5]

Attajdid is a conservative newspaper with close ties to Morocco's Justice and Development Party. In 2005, *Attajdid* published an article by its editor-in-chief, Lhassan Sarrat, claiming that the 2004 Indian Ocean earthquake and resulting tsunami was God's punishment for sexual tourism, homosexuality, and child trafficking in Southeast Asia. Editor Sarrat asserted that the only way to avoid such catastrophic disasters was to follow the teachings of Islam. He further stated that Morocco would be the next destination for this "tourism of debauchery." The statements sparked controversy and opposition. The paper then distanced itself from the article by declaring that the piece expressed only the opinion of the author.[7]

MAGAZINE BANNED OVER RELIGIOUS JOKES

The Committee to Protect Journalists (in New York) has publicly decried the banning in Morocco of an independent magazine and the charges brought against its director and a reporter. These charges stem from an article analyzing popular jokes about religion, sex, and politics.

Driss Ksikes, the publisher and director of the weekly magazine *Nichane*, and reporter Sanaa al-Aji were charged with denigrating Islam under Article 41 of Morocco's Press and Publication Law 2002.

Ksikes and al-Aji face three to five years in prison and fines ranging from 10,000 to 100,000 dirhams (equivalent to $1,100 to $11,000) under penalty of the press law. Their trial was set for January 8, 2007.

"We understand that *Nichane* may have offended people by publishing these jokes," says Committee to Protect Journalists executive director Joel Simon, "but that cannot be a justification for banning a magazine and threatening journalists with jail. We call on the Prime Minister to rescind the ban and on the legal authorities to halt the prosecution at once."

The Arabic-language magazine *Nichane* is a sister publication of the independent French-language weekly, *Tel Quel*. Both magazines are owned by the Tel Quel Group headed by Ahmed Reda Benchemsi.

In February 2006, another weekly Moroccan publication came under fire for offending religious beliefs. *Le Journal Hebdomadaire* accused government authorities of organizing protests against it for having published a photograph of the controversial Danish cartoon of the Prophet Muhammad that sparked widespread discontent in the Muslim world.[6]

PERIODICALS

Tunisia

The official language of Tunisia is Arabic. Languages of commerce are Arabic and French. Approximately 79 percent of males and 51 percent of females aged fifteen and over can read and write (66.7 percent total literacy).

Although Tunisia has recently introduced some press freedoms and has freed a number of political prisoners, human-rights advocates maintain that authorities tolerate little or no dissent. President Ben Ali and the Constitutional Democratic Rally (RCD) have controlled the country since 1987, when President Habib Bourguiba was declared unfit to govern because of senility.

Tunisian press codes define parameters for coverage and specify large fines and prison sentences for violators. Publications are scrutinized by government officials and self-censorship is encouraged. The media are prohibited from discussing censorship and government corruption. Editions of foreign periodicals, including French and pan-Arab publications, are seized on a regular basis. Still, there are several privately run newspapers and magazines, including two opposition party journals.

National newspapers owned by the ruling RCD party are *La Presse* and *Al-Horria*. Additional daily publications include *Nouvelles de Tunisie, Assabah,* and *Le Quotidien*.[8]

LIBYA

Arabic, Italian, and English are all widely understood languages in major Libyan cities. Eighty-eight percent of males and 63 percent of females aged fifteen and over can read and write (76.2 percent total literacy).

The government of Colonel Muammar Gaddafi controls the press. Newspapers and periodicals are published by the Jamahiriya News Agency (JANA), government secretariats, the Press Service, and trade unions. The media rights organization Reporters Without Borders claims that press freedom is "virtually nonexistent" in Libya. The state owns and virtually controls the media; government officials prohibit publication of opinions contrary to government policy. Few visas are issued to foreign journalists.

JANA publishes a daily newspaper, *Al-Fajr al-Jadid* [New Dawn], in Tripoli. Other general interest Libyan news periodicals include *Al-Shams, Al-Jamahiriyah,* and *Al-Zahf Al-Akhdar*.[9]

EGYPT

Arabic is the official language of Egypt. English and French are widely understood by the educated classes. Sixty-four percent of males and 39 percent of females aged fifteen and over are literate (51.4 percent total literacy).

The Egyptian press is one of the most influential and widely read in the region. Media criticism of the government is a routine occurrence, but there are press laws in place that dictate stiff fines and/or prison sentences for libeling the president, state institutions, and foreign heads of state. The government's Supreme Press Council supervises these laws.[10]

Al-Ahram, the daily newspaper published in Cairo, is one of the oldest papers in the Arab world, and is considered Egypt's most influential periodical. Founded in 1875 by

Lebanese-Christian brothers Salim and Bisharah Taqla, it became a daily publication in 1881. *Al-Ahram* was initially known for its independence and objectivity, despite harsh British censorship and control of the paper's international news. *Al-Ahram*'s dominance waned shortly before Egyptian independence.

In the late 1950s *Al-Ahram* came under the influence of the Egyptian government. Egyptian President Gamal Abdel Nasser eventually nationalized the press, thus turning the newspaper into an effective governmental mouthpiece. Mul Hassanein Heikal, a friend of Nasser, was appointed editor. Heikal had a profound effect on the periodical and on Middle Eastern journalism in general. He was an eloquent writer and brilliant editorialist, and built the paper's reputation. Heikal was removed from his post as editor during the presidency of Anwar El-Sadat, but his contributions continued to be evident. *Al-Ahram*'s circulation averaged one million copies per day at the turn of the twenty-first century.[11]

Egypt Today is the leading current affairs magazine in Egypt and the Middle East. It is also the oldest English-language publication of its kind in the country. The magazine is published monthly in Cairo, and is available on newsstands, by subscription, and in Egypt's finest hotels and resorts. Target readers are "A-class" Egyptian nationals and foreign residents in Egypt with an interest in regional affairs. The magazine's circulation is between 11,000 and 14,500 copies in Egypt alone, but it reaches a much broader audience through a free Website. *Egypt Today* is a private independent publication, and supports itself on advertising and circulation income. It receives no subsidy from any governmental or private interest.[12]

Cairo Magazine is another major English-language source of news and cultural information about Egypt. Its stated mission is to cover the richness and variety of life and culture in Cairo and around Egypt. The publication is committed to maintaining the editorial independence that will allow it to provide its readers with consistently accurate coverage of news, current affairs, culture, and lifestyles.[13]

Other Egyptian English-language publications include the *Egypt Daily News, The Egyptian Gazette*, the *Cairo Observer* (a pro-government publication), and *The Egyptian Mail*, a Saturday edition of *The Egyptian Gazette*. The *Daily Star Egypt* is the country's only independent English-language daily; it comes bundled with the *International Herald Tribune*.

Arabic-language periodicals are plentiful and varied in subject and source. *Al Watan Al Arabi* is a weekly political magazine. A state-owned literary magazine, *Akhbar al-Adab*, is produced weekly in Cairo; *Al Kawakeb* is a government-sponsored film weekly. Other government-sponsored periodicals published in Egypt's capital include *Al-Mussawar, Aker Sa'a, Al-Gomhuria, Akhbar al-Yom*, the Islamist weekly *Al-Ahrar*, and the government-owned business weekly *Al-Ahram al-Iqtissadi* and cultural weekly *Al Qahira*.

Independent and/or opposition publications include *Al Arabi, Al-Wafd, Al-Shaab* (the Al-Shaab party organ), the newsweekly *El Fagr*, and the left-wing weekly *Al-Ahali*.

Publications designed for targeted audiences abound in Egypt. *Hawa* is a government-owned weekly directed to women, and *Cartoon* is an independent satirical weekly. *Aquidati* is a religious magazine published in Cairo; *Watani* is a weekly Sunday newspaper published in both Arabic and English.[14]

JORDAN

Arabic is the official language of Jordan. English is widely understood among upper and middle classes.

Ninety four percent of males and 80 percent of females aged fifteen and over are able to read and write (86.6 percent total literacy).

PERIODICALS

TAKING ON MIDDLE EASTERN BAD GUYS WITH SUPER POWERS

A 39-year-old Cairo University economics professor has created the first home-grown comic book superheroes from the Middle East. Ayman Kandeel says it is a dream he has had since childhood. Although translated versions of American comics have long been available in the Arab world, Kandeel feels that readers in his country need positive role models of their own.

Kandeel is the founder of AK Comics; sales have increased steadily since the company's beginnings in 2003. His heroes include Rakan, who tries to protect the innocent as he wanders the war-ravaged lands of a medieval Islamic world. Other champions live in a Middle Eastern world of the near future—a world that has overcome its political differences following a 55-year war, and is now united against extremism.

Another character is Jalila, a Wonder Woman–like heroine who defends the City of All Faiths, where Jews, Christians, and Muslims coexist peacefully. Although peaceful, this city is threatened by terrorists of the United Liberation Front and the Army of Zios. Jalila acquired her powers when she was exposed to radiation from a nuclear blast at Dimondona (reminiscent of Dimona, the site of Israel's nuclear weapons facility).

In many respects, Kandeel's superheroes closely resemble their Western counterparts. Their major differences are key elements that are inspired by Middle Eastern events.

The comics premiered in the United States but had difficulty finding an audience, so they were introduced in Egypt where they now sell at the rate of 8,000 copies per issue. Egypt's number one air carrier, Egyptair, has also signed a deal with Kandeel to purchase 10,000 copies a month to distribute to airline passengers.

The artwork is outsourced to a studio in Brazil, as Egyptian practitioners presently lack the technical know-how. The company does have artists in training and hopes to centralize production in Cairo in the near future.

Scholars believe that the comics have the potential to change children's attitudes. As Adel Abdel Moneim, an assistant director at the Netherlands-Flemish Institute in Cairo noted, "you are educated in society and school to look at other religions in a different way and you are trained to treat women in a different way, and this is what these comics could change. They could build a new generation that has a new perspective." A significant concept behind the superhero series is the promotion of gender equality through strong female role models.[15]

The Jordanian press has traditionally been under the control of the government. The government sets "the tone" for the major daily newspapers. In 2003 it repealed legislation that mandated jail terms for potentially damaging the king's reputation or for inciting strikes, criminal activity, and illegal gatherings.[16]

Petra is the state-run news agency, operated by the Information Ministry. The government owns major shares in two of Jordan's largest dailies, *Al-Ray* [The Opinion] and *Al-Dustour* [The Constitution]. Most newspapers and magazines, however, are privately owned. The country now has several literary magazines, as well as scientific and topical periodicals.[17]

ELLE MAGAZINE LAUNCHES MIDDLE EASTERN EDITION

"Head-To-Toe black robes rarely make it into the pages of women's fashion magazines. But *Elle* magazine is changing that with the launch of its first Middle Eastern edition."

The publication, which is on newsstands in Jordan, Lebanon, and Morocco, mixes glossy photos of stylish clothes with fashion advice for readers who wear loose-fitting abayas or chadors in public but want to look chic underneath and indoors. Layouts include models with violet head scarves and long black embroidered robes with Ferragamo sandals. Desiree Sadek, publisher of *Elle*'s Middle East edition, believes they can mix the East and the West in fashion.

Although women in most Muslim countries cover their heads and bodies in public, a growing number of them are wearing elegant, fashionable, even revealing attire underneath. Not only do young Middle Eastern women have a global understanding of fashion, many also have both the appetite and the money to spend on clothing and accessories. In countries like Lebanon, the clothing on the pages of *Elle* can be worn on the street; in others, like Saudi Arabia, the garb is reserved for private gatherings of women. Accessories—from designer shoes to handbags, scarves, sunglasses, and jewelry—are permitted almost everywhere.

Advertisers in *Elle* include Christian Dior, Cartier, and Giorgio Armani. These retailers will be adapting their message to fit the milieu of the Middle East. The magazine, currently originating in Beirut, will also be introduced over the next few months in Syria, Egypt, Dubai, Kuwait, and Saudi Arabia.

For *Elle,* the biggest gamble is its introduction to Saudi Arabia. Although Saudi Arabia offers the largest market in the Middle East because of its young population, it is also the most conservative market. Government censors black out all images of unveiled women—and this is more lenient than the past procedure of outright removing the offending pages. The Saudi Arabian edition will have more conservative stories, photos, and ads.[18]

Other Arabic-language dailies include *Al-Ghad* and *Al-Arab al Yawn*. *Al Hadath* is a political weekly published in Amman. The independent weekly *Al-Hawadeth* is produced in Amman as well.

Jordan Times is the English-language daily paper. *The Star* is an English-language political, economic, and cultural weekly.[19]

ISRAEL AND THE PALESTINIAN TERRITORIES

Hebrew is the official language of Israel, while Arabic is used officially by its Arab minority. English is the most commonly used foreign language. Ninety-seven percent of males and 93 percent of females aged fifteen and older can read and write (95% total literacy).

Tel Aviv is the center of newspaper publishing in Israel. Although periodicals were associated with the government and political parties in the past, most are now independently

Periodicals

owned and run. Many are written in Hebrew; a considerable number are also published in English, Yiddish, German, Arabic, Russian, Polish, French, Bulgarian, and Romanian. This is due, in part, to the continual immigration of new citizens from around the world. There are literally hundreds of other periodicals, more than half of which are published in Hebrew.[20]

The media watchdog group Reporters Without Borders described Israeli media in 2005 as "robust and independent." However, it also alleged that the army regularly obstructed the movement of some Palestinian and foreign journalists. There have also been reports that the content of these journalists' stories has been monitored.[21]

Ha'aretz [The Land] is Israel's oldest daily newspaper and is considered to be of highest quality. Published in Tel Aviv since 1923, it was originally founded in Jerusalem in 1919 as an independent liberal paper in the tradition of Russian-Hebrew journalism.

Ha'aretz's influence is unparalleled in Israel. It has maintained an independent stance, at times criticizing the government and illuminating state abuses. Its readership includes a broad cross section of the Israeli populace, ranging from government leaders to common laborers. The publication is noted for its even and thoughtful appraisal of international, national, and regional news; its cosmopolitan flair; and its lack of bias in reporting. The paper is not aligned with any political party and is applauded for its independence. It has foreign correspondents throughout the world.[22]

Two other daily general interest centrist papers are *Yedioth Aharonot* and *Ma'ariv*. Both are produced in Tel Aviv, and both are also published in English. A *Ma'ariv*-affiliated weekly, *Kol Ha'Zman*, is published in Jerusalem.

Yedioth Aharonot [Latest News] is a Hebrew-language tabloid. Since the 1970s it has been the most widely circulated paper in Israel. One of the first privately owned Israeli publications, it was founded in 1939. In 1948, a group of the paper's journalists and staff members left to form another newspaper, *Yedioth Ma'ariv*, now known as *Ma'ariv*. Thus began an ongoing battle between the two publications for circulation and prestige, which resulted in an incident in the 1990s when both papers were discovered to have bugged each other's phones.[23]

Ma'ariv [Evening] is the most popular evening tabloid. It gives fair coverage of the diverse opinions found in Israeli society by publishing side-by-side the differing views of journalists and guest columnists from opposite ends of the political and social spectrum. It does, however, have a predominantly center-left orientation, as expressed by the views of its senior writers.[24]

Hebrew-language periodicals also include *Globes*, a daily business journal (also published in English), *Hatzofeh*, a right-wing religious publication produced in Tel Aviv, and *Kol Ha'ir* [Voice of the City], a liberal weekly from Jerusalem.

Israel has one of the world's most technologically literate populations. Around 3.7 million people had Internet access by 2006. Thus, online news sites are flourishing in Israel. These include *Jerusalem Newswire*, *Bitter Lemons*, a Palestinian-Israeli online weekly, *Ha'ayal Hakoreh*, and *One*, a Hebrew-language sports Website. The *Ynet News* site is a huge hit, with tabloid-style format and celebrity news articles that have Israeli readers begging for more.[25]

The Jerusalem Post is the largest English-language daily in Israel. It was established in 1932 as *The Palestine Post*; it adopted its current name in 1950. Published each morning except Saturday, the paper emphasizes foreign news, and gives particular attention to Arab-Israeli relations. In recent years its daily circulation has increased to roughly 11,000 in Israel and 26,000 in the United States. The *Post*'s French-language edition has a readership of more than 3,000 in France. The newspaper's successful weekend edition is the foundation for a successful international publication called *The Jerusalem Post Weekly*.

Through economical headlines and careful editing, *The Jerusalem Post* has built a solid reputation for thorough and informative coverage. The paper was sold in 2004 when two firms each purchased a 50 percent share. The new owners are CanWest Global Communications, a

Canadian newspaper publisher, and Mirkaei Tikshoret, a diversified international media firm.[26]

Other English-language periodicals include the *Jerusalem Report*, an independent biweekly publication, the *Jerusalem Times*, a biweekly newsmagazine, and the *Palestine Israel Journal*, a pro-peace quarterly.[27]

Because television is the key source for news and information in the Palestinian Territories, there is not a wealth of Palestinian print periodicals. The largest-circulation Palestinian daily paper is *Al-Quds*, published in Jerusalem. *Al-Ayyam* is a Ramallah-based daily, and *Al-Hayat Al-Jadidah* is the Palestinian National Authority daily. *Al-Sennara* is an independent Arab weekly and *Al-Talia* is an Arab-oriented communist weekly. Both are published in Jerusalem.

International watchdog groups regard media in the Palestinian Territories as being generally more independent than in the remainder of the Arab world. However, journalists risk harassment or attack by armed activists or militant groups. Members of Reporters Without Borders report that threats, violence, and killings of journalists increased dramatically in 2005 because of political instability.[29]

> **ONLINE FASHION MAGAZINE SET TO DEBUT IN ISRAEL**
>
> *Extrovert Magazine* is the world's "first laptop fashion magazine." It provides global coverage of everything going on in the worlds of fashion, music, art, film, culture, and design. It is already a big hit in cities such as Los Angeles, Berlin, London, and Tokyo. It will soon come to computers in Israel.[28]

LEBANON AND SYRIA

Lebanon

Arabic is the official language of Lebanon. Other languages spoken in the country include English, French, and Armenian. Ninety-one percent of males and 82 percent of females aged fifteen and older are literate (86.4 percent total literacy).

In addition to the wide variety of foreign newspapers and magazines produced in Beirut, also published in Lebanon are periodicals in Arabic, English, French, and Armenian. Arabic dailies include *An-Nahar, As-Safir, Al-Mustaqbal,* and *Al-Diyar*. Criticism of government officials and policies is common and is found in dozens of newspapers and magazines.

An-Nahar [The Day] is a leading daily Arabic-language newspaper. It was first published on August 4, 1933, as a four-page, hand-set publication. It is currently regarded as one of Lebanon's newspapers of record with a liberal political stance. It strongly opposes any Syrian occupation of Lebanon. The publication is banned in Syria. An editor of *An-Nahar*, Gebran Tueni, was elected to Parliament in 2005 to represent a Beirut constituency. He was later assassinated on December 12, 2005, in a car bomb explosion near Beirut. Tueni, a vehement opponent of the Syrian government, had just returned from Paris, where he had fled to escape assassination threats.[30]

As-Safir [The Ambassador] is an Arabic-language paper first published in 1974 as a political daily. Financed with the aid of Libyan funding, it provided an independent voice for left-wing political factions after the Arab defeat by Israel in the June 1967 war. Its initial aim was to be "the newspaper of the Arab world in Lebanon, and the newspaper of Lebanon in the Arab world." This slogan is still printed on the paper's masthead.[31]

Al Akhbar is a relatively recent addition to the Lebanese daily news scene. It came into being during the 2006 Israeli war on Lebanon, publishing its first issue on the day that a

Periodicals

U.N.-brokered ceasefire took effect. The political stance of the paper is liberal, democratic, and opposed to U.S. intervention in the Arab region. It clearly supports the radical Shiite group, Hezbollah. Many of *Al Akhbar*'s articles and writings defend those Hezbollah practices that are in full compliance with Syria's and Iran's regional policies.[32]

The Daily Star is an independent, pan-Middle East English-language daily that explores politics, business, local news, arts and culture, and the star scene. It is edited in Beirut, and is published alongside the *International Herald Tribune*. Founded in 1952, it was created to serve the growing number of foreign nationals brought by the oil industry. By the 1960s, it was the leading English-language newspaper in the Middle East. After ceasing publication twice during the Lebanese Civil War, it resumed printing in 1996 with modern presses, experienced foreign journalists, and an energetic staff. It now appears in all Middle Eastern countries except Kuwait. In 2006, the newspaper announced that it will soon be available in print in the United States. Another English-language periodical, *Monday Morning*, is a weekly magazine focusing on current events.[33]

For French-language readers, *L'Orient-Le Jour* is the "Lebanese daily newspaper of French expression." *Femme Magazine* is the leading French-language periodical focusing on fashion, beauty, cuisine, health, and society. *La Revue du Liban* is a weekly magazine that provides French readers with information and political and cultural commentary. It is also the first online Lebanese weekly magazine.[34]

Syria

Syria's official language is Arabic. Kurdish, Armenian, Aramaic, and Circassian are widely understood. French and English are somewhat understood by the upper classes.

Eighty-six percent of males and 56 percent of females aged fifteen and over can read and write (70.8 percent total literacy).

The government and the Baath party own and control most of Syria's print industry. Criticism of the president and his family is banned, and the domestic and foreign press are severely censored. Journalists practice self-censorship and foreign reporters rarely receive recognition. Right after Bashar al-Assad became president in 2000, there seemed to be an initial burst of press freedom. For the first time in forty years, private publications were licensed. New publications included a satirical journal and political party papers. A subsequent press law was imposed with new restrictions; periodicals can now be suspended for violating content rules.[35]

Arabic-language publications include *Al-Baath*, the Baath party paper, *Al-Fida*, a government-controlled weekly, *Al-Thawra*, a government daily, and *Tishreen*, a semi-official daily produced in Damascus. Also published in Damascus is the sports periodical *Al-Maukef Al Riadi*.

Syria Times is the major English-language daily. It is published by the same government-owned company that produces *Tishreen*. In 2003 *Syria Times* received international attention for its harsh condemnation of the U.S.-led war against Iraq. Another English-language publication is *Syria Today*, a newsletter magazine.[36]

Iraq

Languages spoken in Iraq include Arabic, Assyrian, and Armenian. Kurdish is the official language in Kurdish regions. Seventy-one percent of males and 45 percent of females aged fifteen and over are literate (58 percent total literacy).

Since the overthrow of Saddam Hussein in 2003, there has been a major transformation of the Iraqi media. Instead of a few tightly controlled and regulated outlets, Iraqis now have their choice of hundreds of publications. Traditionalist, conservative, and conformist in nature, diverse political views are now beginning to be aired. Religious divisions are also making themselves evident in the media. Additionally, several journalists and media staffers have fallen victim to violent acts at the hands of insurgents and even Coalition military forces. The financial situation of publishing companies has also been put in jeopardy due to an unstable security situation. In the northern territories, Kurdish factions operate their own media outlets.[37]

Well-known Arabic-language papers include *Al-Sabah*, sponsored by the state-run Iraqi Media Network, and *Al-Mada*, a privately owned daily produced in Baghdad. *Al-Zaman* is a London-based daily, printed in both Baghdad and Basra, which contains some English-language pages. *Al-Manarah* is a daily printed in Basra.

IRAN

Fifty-eight percent of the Iranian population speak Persian or one of the Persian dialects. Twenty-six percent speak Turkic or Turkic dialects. Other languages include Kurdish (spoken by 9%), Luri (spoken by 2%), Balochi (spoken by 1%), Arabic (spoken by 1%), Turkish (spoken by 1%), and others (spoken by 2%). Seventy-eight percent of males and 66 percent of females aged fifteen and over can read and write (72.1% total literacy).

> ### IRAN: REFORMIST DAILIES TEMPORARILY BANNED
>
> On February 18, 2004, the Committee to Protect Journalists (CPJ) condemned the suspension of two Iranian reformist daily papers on that date by Tehran's Press Court. The suspensions came just before Iran's controversial parliamentary elections.
>
> The dailies *Yas-e-No* and *Shargh* both received notification that the Court had ordered them temporarily closed. The move came after both publications printed portions of an open letter from reformists who had resigned from Parliament. The letter criticized Iran's spiritual leader, Ali Khamenei, and questioned whether he was involved in the decision to bar several reformist candidates from running for parliamentary seats. Iranian authorities consider criticism of Khamenei unacceptable; thus, it rarely appears in Iranian newspapers. Both papers were high-profile reformist dailies.
>
> Although the Court's orders termed the suspensions "temporary," most newspapers in Iran that the Press Court has banned have never reopened.[38]
>
> Although *Yas-e-no* has not reopened, the ban on *Shargh* was lifted on February 28, 2004, and the newspaper resumed publication the following month. However, the Iranian government again shut the paper down on September 11, 2006. It is not clear whether this second banning of *Shargh* will be permanent.[39]

Daily newspapers and periodicals are published primarily in Tehran and must be licensed, as required by press laws adopted in 1979. The struggle for influence and power is often played out in the Iranian media. Although the press is still relatively free—one of the notable achievements of former President Mohammad Khatami—political conservatives have recently turned their focus to press freedom, and pro-reform publications have been closed and reformist writers and editors jailed.

Although there are more than twenty national dailies, few Iranians buy a newspaper everyday. Sports periodicals are the biggest sellers. One such publication is *Iran Varzeshi*, a Persian-language paper published in Tehran. Widely circulated general interest periodicals include *Ettela'at, Resalat, Jomhuri-ye-Eslami*, and *Kayhan*.

HAMSHAHRI SOLICITS HOLOCAUST CARTOONS TO TEST WESTERN FREEDOM OF EXPRESSION

On February 13, 2006, *Hamshahri*, one of Iran's top five newspapers, published an international call for cartoons about the Holocaust in English and Farsi on its Website and on page 31 of the print version of the paper. The publication questioned whether the West would be as supportive of freedom of expression if the subject were Nazi genocide rather than caricatures of the Prophet Muhammad, under the headline, "What Is the Limit of Western Freedom of Expression?"

The contest came in the wake of widespread Muslim protests over drawings of the Prophet Muhammad, and a few months after conservative Iranian President Mahmoud Ahmadinejad declared that Israel should be "wiped off the map" and that the Holocaust was a myth.

The drawing of the Prophet—Islam's most revered figure—depicts him wearing a turban shaped like a bomb. The first caricatures appeared in a Danish newspaper in September 2006. They were then reprinted in publications in Europe and the United States as a show of solidarity for freedom of expression. Islam maintains that representations of the Prophet are banned because they could lead to idolatry.

The call for submission of cartoons even went out to Israelis. The announcement stated that "in the wake of the publication of the profane cartoons in several European newspapers, *Hamshahri* is going to measure the sanctity of freedom of expression among the Westerners."

The contest ended on November 1, 2006, and Abdellah Derkaoui, a Moroccan cartoonist, claimed the first prize. The selected cartoons were reproduced in a catalog and put on public display.[42]

Kayhan [Universe] is an influential newspaper in Iran, published by the Kayhan Institute. Because it is directly supervised by the Office of the Supreme Leader, it is regarded as the most conservative Iranian periodical. Its offices are located in Tehran.

The Kayhan Institute also publishes special foreign editions of the newspaper, including the English-language *Kayhan International*, the Persian-language *Kayhan-e-Havaee* [Kayhan by Air], and an Arabic version of *Kayhan*. All of these are meant for international distribution. The Institute also produces special interest magazines for women (*Zan-e-Rouze* [Today's Woman]), children (*Kayhan-e Bache-ha* [Children's Kayhan]), and sports fans. *Kayhan Caricature*, a humor magazine run by cartoonists, was shut down in 2003.[40]

Hamshahri is a reformist Persian-language newspaper published in Tehran. The publication was founded by Gholamhossein Karbaschi. It is the first color-daily newspaper in Iran and includes more than sixty pages of classified advertisements. Currently, *Hamshahri* can only be distributed inside Tehran.

The *Tehran Times* is an English-language daily newspaper established in 1979. It is run by the state and leans toward theocratic principles. It has been critical of and steadily opposed to the administration of George W. Bush. For stories outside of Iran, it uses national news service sources such as the Associated Press, Reuters, and the Agency for the French Press. Other English-language papers circulated in Iran include the *Iran Daily* and the *Iran News*.[41]

KUWAIT

Although Arabic is the official language of Kuwait, English is widely spoken. Eighty-two percent of males and 75 percent of females aged fifteen and over are literate (78.6 percent total literacy).

Kuwait enjoys some of the most candid newspapers in the Arab world; they are often quite aggressive in their coverage of politics, the government, and world events. Although journalists do have great freedom, they use restraint when reporting on stories relating to the emir and other top royals. A press law forbids blasphemous references to God and the Prophet Muhammad. Prison sentences are mandated for transgressors. The center of journalistic efforts is Kuwait City.

Arabic-language newspapers include the privately owned independent dailies *Al Qabas* and *Al Watan,* the pro-government dailies *Al Rai Al Aam* and *Al Seyassah,* and the center-left paper *Al Taleea.* English-language periodicals include the pro-government *Arab Times* and the family magazine *Kuwait This Month. The Kuwait Times,* a pro-government broadsheet established in 1961, was the first English-language daily newspaper in the Persian Gulf. It provides in-depth reporting on local events, business news, editorials, features and entertainment, and sports.[43]

BAHRAIN

Languages spoken and written in Bahrain include Arabic, English, Farsi, and Urdu. Eighty-nine percent of males and 79 percent of females aged fifteen and over are literate (85.2 percent total literacy).

Several weekly and daily papers are published in Arabic; a small number are in English. Most press is privately owned and not subject to censorship as long as the ruling family is not criticized or insulted. Some self-censorship is practiced.

Daily Arabic papers include *Akhbar Al Khaleej* [Gulf News], *Al-Ayam* [The Days], *Al-Wasat,* and *Al Meethaq.* Another daily distributed in Bahrain but originating in the United Arab Emirates (UAE) is the *Khaleef Times.* There are eight circulated weeklies that have more pronounced political views than the dailies. Among the largest are *Al-Adwaa* [Lights], produced in Bahrain's capital city, Manama, and *Al-Bahrain ath-Thaqafya* and *Huna al-Bahrain,* published by the Ministry of Information. Three additional weeklies are *Al-Mawakif, Oil and Gas News,* and *Sada al-Usbou',* which circulates in several Gulf states.

Fifteen periodicals are currently distributed in Bahrain. Many of these are business and tourism related. These include *Bahrain This Month, Discover Bahrain, Gulf Construction, Gulf Panorama, Al-Hayat at-Tijariyaor* [Commerce Review], *Al-Hidayah* [Guidance], *Al-Musafir al-Arabi* [Arab Traveler], *Shipping and Transport News International,* and *Travel and Tourism News—Middle East.*

Although the press environment is relatively relaxed and free of strict controls, several issues have arisen in recent years. In November 2001, Hafez El Sheikh Saleh, a journalist with the daily *Akhbar al Kahleej,* was charged with betraying national unity and producing written information in opposition to the National Charter and constitution. Saleh was banned from traveling abroad and forced to discontinue journalistic ventures. Also in 2001, Bahrain prohibited the London-published Arabic daily *Azzaman* from being printed in the country because the periodical had criticized the Emir of Qatar, thereby violating provisions of press and publications law. In March 2002, the government of Bahrain blocked several Websites judged to contain offensive content, lies, and questionable subject matter. One of these sites was run by Islamic fundamentalist Abdel Wahab Hussein, who is a member of the political opposition group, the Bahrain Freedom Movement, and by *Al-Manama,* an online newspaper. Finally, in May 2002, Bahrain refused to allow Qatar-based Al-Jazeera TV to cover municipal elections.[44]

The Gulf Daily News is an English-language paper published daily in Bahrain. It was founded in March 1978, by Al Hilal Group. Until the founding of *Bahrain Tribune, The Gulf Daily News* was Bahrain's only English daily. It was created to provide news to English-speaking residents of Bahrain—to the British, Americans, Filipinos, Pakistanis, and Indians. Initially pro-government, the periodical now includes Islamists as well as liberals on its staff, and employs several reporters who focus on local issues.[45]

UNITED ARAB EMIRATES (UAE) AND OMAN
United Arab Emirates

Arabic is the official language of the United Arab Emirates (UAE). Other languages include Persian, English, Hindi, and Urdu. Seventy-nine percent of males and 80 percent of females aged fifteen and over are literate (79.2 percent total literacy).

The news media are concentrated in Dubai, Abu Dhabi, and Al-Shariqah. Several newspapers are published in both Arabic and English. A 1988 law stipulates that publications be licensed; foreign publications are censored before distribution. Self-censorship is practiced when reporting on government policy or the ruling family.[46]

Newspapers include the private Dubai-based dailies *Al-Bayan* and *Khaleej Times*. The *Emirates News* is a pro-government English-language newspaper. Another English-language publication, *Gulf News*, was founded in 1978 as a tabloid paper; new management in 1985 relaunched it as a broadsheet, and circulation has grown steadily ever since.[47]

Oman

The official language of Oman is Arabic. Other languages include English, Baluchi, Urdu, and Indian dialects. Eighty-seven percent of males and 74 percent of females aged fifteen and over can read and write (80.5 percent total literacy).

Although there is government censorship of the Omani press and most newspapers are state-run, several independent Arabic-language papers are published on a daily or weekly basis. *Al-Watan, Al Shabiba,* and *Oman* are the Arabic-language papers produced in Muscat. There are also several English-language publications, including the daily *Times of Oman, Oman Daily Observer,* and *Oman Tribune,* and an independent weekly, *The Week*.[48]

QATAR

Arabic is the official language of Qatar, with English commonly used as a second language. Seventy-nine percent of males and 80 percent of females aged fifteen and over can read and write (79 percent total literacy).

As media restrictions in Qatar became generally more relaxed in 1996, the satellite television network Al-Jazeera was founded by a member of the ruling family. The outspoken news channel is received throughout much of the Muslim world. It has become known internationally since broadcasting speeches of Osama bin Laden and his followers in 2001.[49]

Even though the Qatari press is considered one of the freest in the region, its leading newspapers still have strong links to the royal family and other notables. Arabic-language dailies include *Al-Watan* [The Homeland], *Al-Rayah* [The Banner], and *Al-Sharq* [The East]. English-language publications include *The Peninsula* and *Qatar Tribune*.

The Gulf Times is the oldest surviving English-language newspaper in Qatar. Founded in 1978; its first issue was a black-and-white tabloid. In 1995 it converted from a tabloid to a broadsheet, and its content increased. The paper dominates the English-language market with an 80 percent share. *The Gulf Times* is known for reporting on controversial topics. It was the first Gulf publication to examine the mistreatment of child camel jockeys. This led to reform of the camel racing industry in several Gulf states.[50]

SAUDI ARABIA

Arabic is the official language of Saudi Arabia. Seventy-two percent of males and 50 percent of females aged fifteen and over are literate (62.8% total literacy).

Saudi Arabia has one of the most tightly controlled media environments in the Middle East. Newspapers are created by royal decree. Ten dailies and dozens of magazines are published. Pan-Arab papers are available but are subject to heavy censorship. Publications tend to follow the direction of the Saudi Press Agency, the state-run news agency that determines whether to publish or refrain from publishing sensitive subject matter.[51]

By 2003, however, there were slight signs of a new openness by the Saudi press. Some formerly taboo topics began to receive press coverage. The September 11 attacks on the United States and the occurrence of domestic militancy could be responsible for this new, more straightforward style of reporting.

Daily Arabic-language newspapers include *Al-Riyadh, Al-Jazirah,* and *Al-Sharq al-Awsat,* which are pro-government and based in Riyadh. *Okaz* is a daily based in Jeddah. Also produced in Jeddah is *Al-Muslimoon,* a religious weekly. The paper is considered one of the main information sources for the Muslim world. It offers readers all the political, cultural, and social news that affects Islam.[52] The pro-government paper *Al-Watan* is produced in Abha.

English-language publications include the *Saudi Gazette* and the *Arab News,* the latter being a leading source of news presented from an Arab perspective. It has been published since 1975 and is available as both a daily and a Website. It is published simultaneously from Jedda, Riyadh, and Dhahran. The printed version is distributed in Bahrain, Europe, Kuwait, the Near East, North Africa, Oman, Qatar, Saudi Arabia, the United Arab Emirates, and the United States. Total circulation in 1998 topped 51,768.[53]

YEMEN

The official language of Yemen is Arabic. Fifty-three percent of males and 26 percent of females aged fifteen and over are literate (38 percent total literacy).

The modern Republic of Yemen has changed considerably since the merging in 1990 of the traditionalist North Yemen and the Marxist South Yemen, following years of border wars and conflict. Peace fizzled out in 1994, which led to a short civil war that ended in defeat for the southern separatists. Yemen thus remains unified today, although some friction continues. Southerners maintain that the northern part of the state is economically advantaged.[54]

Since 1990 more than eighty-five innovative newspapers and journals have come into being. These publications represent diverse political, economic, social, and cultural organizations.[55] The Ministry of Information still controls most printing presses and funds the publication of some newspapers. Subject matter is strictly monitored; newspapers have been prosecuted for suspect story content.

Prominent Arabic-language daily newspapers include the government-owned *Al-Thawra* and the independent *Al-Ayyam. Fourteenth October* is another paper produced in Aden. Also based in Aden is the Socialist Party weekly *Al-Thawri.*

PERIODICALS

> ## SUSPENDED SENTENCE FOR EDITORS IN THIRD CARTOON CASE
>
> On December 14, 2006, a primary court in Sanaa, Yemen, convicted two local journalists of insulting the Islamic religion and ridiculing the Prophet Muhammad by republishing some Danish cartoons in February 2006. Judge Mohammed Rubaid delivered guilty verdicts against Akram Sabra, managing editor of the weekly *Al-Hurriyah*, and against assistant editor Yehya al-Abed.
>
> The journalist received suspended sentences that include four months of jail time, the closing of the paper for one month, and a one-month public writing ban imposed on the defendants. By suspending the sentences, no part of the verdict will be implemented, although it will go on record. The judge ordered the editors to publish the court's decision in all official newspapers at their own expense and as soon as possible.
>
> In less than one month, three local newspapers and their editors have been convicted of insulting Islam. The three newspapers, including the *Yemen Observer*, republished some of the Danish cartoons in the context of criticizing them. The *Yemen Observer* was fined 500,000 riyals (equivalent to $2,530) by Judge Sahl Hamza, but the paper was allowed to remain open and the editor did not receive a prison sentence. The editor of *Al-Rai Al-Aam*, Kamal Al-Olufi, was convicted on November 25 and sentenced to a year in prison, the closing of the newspaper for six months, and a ban on public writing for the same period of time.
>
> The Yemeni Journalists Syndicate, the International Federation of Journalists, Reporters Without Borders, and the Committee to Protect Journalists have all condemned the trials and the verdicts. They called for the president of Yemen, Ali Abdullah Saleh, to intervene and overturn the verdicts—especially the implementation of Al-Olufi's jail sentence. They have also called for the reopening of the newspaper, closed down by the prosecutor.
>
> Yemeni journalists have been outraged over the deterioration of press freedom in Yemen. A member of the board of the Journalists Syndicate, who is also a seasoned editor, stated, "I am afraid that a police-policy government seems to be dominating the situation."[56]

The *Yemen Times* is the most widely read independent English-language newspaper in Yemen. It is published twice weekly on Mondays and Thursdays, and has its own printing press, advertising department, and news service. The paper has correspondents across the country. It supports freedom of the press and respect for human rights, political pluralism, and democracy. In the economic sector, it supports liberalization and amicable interaction with other nations. The publisher and chief editor, Professor Abdulaziz Al-Saqqaf, states, "We use the *Yemen Times* to make Yemen a good world citizen."[57]

Another independent English-language paper, the *Yemen Observer*, was embroiled in controversy in 2006. In February, Chief Editor Mohammed Al-Asaadi was arrested on charges of offending Islam. The paper had published the Danish cartoons considered blasphemous caricatures of the Prophet Muhammad. In a trial that began on February 23, 2006, prosecution attorneys called for Al-Asaadi to be sentenced to death, for the paper to be closed, and for all its assets to be confiscated. Al-Asaadi denied all of the charges;

his defense team argued that publication of the cartoons had been accompanied by articles condemning them. Two other Arabic-language publications were also charged. On December 6, 2006, the Capital South West Court found the *Yemen Observer* guilty of republishing the Danish cartoons. Editor Al-Asaadi was fined 500,000 riyals (equivalent to $2,530), although the paper was allowed to continue publication and Al-Asaadi was spared having to serve time in jail.[58]

RESOURCE GUIDE

PRINT RESOURCES

"*Attajdid* Newspaper: Article Banned over Religious Jokes." *Morocco Economics* (2005, January 31). http://www.arabnews.com/ansub/Daily/Day/050131/2005013123.html.

Bowen, Donna Lee, and Evelyn A. Early. *Everyday Life in the Muslim Middle East*. Bloomington, IN: Indiana University Press, 2002.

Boyd, Douglas. *Broadcasting in the Arab World: A Survey of the Electronic Media in the Middle East*, 3rd edition. Ames, IA: Iowa State University Press, 1999.

"Court Convicts *Yemen Observer*." *Yemen Times* (2006, December 6). Available: http://www.yementimes.com.article.shtml?i=1005&p=local&a=a.

Dehqan, Sadeq. "Children's Press Festival Showcases Achievements." *Iran Daily* (November 19, 2005). http://www.irandaily.ir/1384/2429/html/art.htm.

Dor, Daniel. *Intifada Hits the Headlines: How the Israeli Press Misreported the Outbreak of the Second Palestinian Uprising*. Bloomington, IN: Indiana University Press, 2004.

Eickelman, Dale F., and Jon W. Anderson. *New Media in the Muslim World: The Emerging Public Sphere*. Bloomington, IN: Indiana University Press, 2003.

"*Elle*'s Middle Eastern Edition Balances Fashion and Tradition: Wearing Designer Labels Indoors." *The Wall Street Journal* (2006, June 20): B1.

Held, Colbert C. *Middle East Patterns: Places, People, and Politics*. Boulder, CO: Westview Press, 2006.

Kamalipour, Yahya R., and Hamid Mowlana, eds. *Mass Media in the Middle East*. Westport, CT: Greenwood, 1994.

Karimi, Nasser. "Iranian Newspaper, *Hamshahri*, Calls for Holocaust Cartoons to Test Purported Western Freedom of Expression." *Al-Jazeerah* (February 13, 2006). http://www.aljazeerah.info/News%20News%20Archives/Febriaru/13.

Maher, Joanne, ed. *Regional Surveys of the World: The Middle East and North Africa 2002*, 48th edition. London: Europa Publications, 2001.

McAlister, Melani. *Epic Encounters: Culture, Media, and U.S. Interests in the Middle East, 1945–2000*. Berkeley: University of California Press, 2004.

Moaveni, Azadeh. "Silencing the Voices of Dissent: Inside the Forced Shutdown of Iran's Most Popular Reformist Paper, *Shargh*." *Time.com*. http://www.time.com/time/world/article/0,8599,1533773,00.html.

"Morocco: Magazine Banned over Religious Jokes." *Nieuwsbank* (December 23, 2006). http://www.nieuwsbank.nl/en/2006/12/23/1003.htm.

Rosett, Claudia. "Gebran Tueni, RIP: My Conversations With the Latest Victim of Syrian Terror." *The Wall Street Journal Opinion Journal* (December 14, 2005). http://opinionjournal.com/cRosett/?id=110007675.

Sakr, Naomi. *Women and Media in the Middle East: Power through Self-Expression*. London: I.D. Tauris, 2004.

Schemm, Paul. "Taking on Mideast Bad Guys—With Super Powers." *San Francisco Chronicle* (October 14, 2004). http://www.sfgate.com/cgi-bin/article.cgi?f=/c/a/2004/10/14/DDGQR8S6UD22.UTL.

Sumner, Jeff, ed. *Gale Directory of Publications and Broadcast Media*. Vol. 5, 136th edition. Farmington Hills, MI: Gale Group, 2002.

PERIODICALS

"Suspended Sentence for Editors in Third Cartoon Case." *Yemen Observer* (December 14, 2006). http://www.yobserver.com/article-11383.php.

2004 Committee to Protect Journalists. "Iran: Reformist Dailies Temporarily Banned." http://www.cpj.org/news/2004/Iran20Feb04na.html.

"2006, the Year in Review News." *Associated Press* (2006, December 31). http://www.aptn.com/80256FEE0057BF4AE/(httpHomepageMainStories)/5A9E63D33F57.

Zahlan, Rosemarie Said. *The Making of the Modern Gulf States: Kuwait, Bahrain, Qatar, the UAE, and Oman*. London: Unwin Hyman, 1989.

WEBSITES

ABYZ Newslinks. http://abyznewslinks.com (a comprehensive country-by-country list of newspapers).
Al-Akhbar. http://al-akhbar.com (a daily newspaper).
Al-Alyam. http://www.alayam.com (a daily newspaper).
Al-Muslimoon. http://www.alkhaleejiahv.com.sa/srpc/muslimoon (a weekly newspaper).
Arab News. http://www.arabnews.com (a daily newspaper).
As-Safir. http://www. assafir.com (a daily newspaper).
Bahrain Press, Media, TV, Radio, Newspapers. http://www.pressreference.com/A-Be/Bahrain.html (a list of media sources in Bahrain).
BBC News Country Profiles. http://news.bbc.co.uk/hi/english/world/middle_east/country_profiles (extensive profiles of countries).
Cairo Magazine. http://www.cairomagazine.com (an English-language publication).
CIA. The World Factbook 2001. http://www.cia.gov/cia/publications/factbook/ (a country-by-country list of statistics).
Daily Star. http://www.dailystar.com.lb/ (a daily newspaper).
Egypt Today. http://www.egypttoday.com (an English-language newspaper).
Encyclopaedia Britannica Online. http://www.britannica.com (online versions of several encyclopedia publications).
Extrovert Magazine. http://www.extrovertmagazine.com (an online fashion magazine).
Femme du Maroc. http://femmesdumaroc.com (a Moroccan fashion magazine).
Gulf News. http://www.gulfnews.com (a daily newspaper).
Gulf Daily News. http://gulf-dailynews.com (a daily newspaper).
Ma'ariv. http://www.nrg.co/il (an Israeli daily evening newspaper).
Online Newspapers. com. http://www.onlinenewspapers.com (a comprehensive country-by-country list of newspapers).
Reporters Sans Frontieres, Middle East Archives 2002. http://www.rsf.fr (site of the journalists watchdog group, Reporters Without Borders).
UNESCO Institute for Statistics. http://www.uis.unesco.org (world statistical data).
United Nations Commission on Human Rights. "Child Camel Jockeys in the United Arab Emirates." June 2001. http://www.antislavery.org/archive/submission/submission2001-UAF.htm.
Worldpress.org. www.worldpress.org/profiles/ (detailed country profiles).
World Press Review. http://www.freemedia.at/wpfr/world.html (a list of publications worldwide).
Yedioth Ahronot, Ynet News. http://www.ynetnews.com (an Israeli daily newspaper).
Yemen Observer. http://www.yobserver.com (a daily English-language newspaper).
Yemen Times. http://www.yementimes.com (a daily English-language newspaper).

NOTES

1. "2006, the Year in Review News," Associated Press, 2006 (in Resource Guide).
2. See *BBC News Country Profiles: Algeria*, August 24, 2006, http://news.bbc.co.uk/1/hi/world/middle_east/country_profiles/790556.stm.

PERIODICALS

3. See *Algeria Newspapers,* August 24, 2006, http://www.abyznewslinks.com/alger.htm.
4. See *Encyclopaedia Britannica Online,* September 23, 2006, http://www.britannica.com.
5. See *Femmes du Maroc,* December 25, 2006, http://www.femmesdomaroc.com.
6. "Morocco: Magazine Banned over Religious Jokes," 2006 (in Resource Guide).
7. "*Attajdid* Newspaper: Article on Sexual Tourism and Tsunami Reflects Opinion of Its Own Author," *Morocco Economics,* January 31, 2005, http://www.arabicnews.com/ansub/Daily/Day/050131/2005013123.html.
8. See *BBC News Country Profiles: Tunisia,* August 24, 2006, http://news.bbc.co.uk/1/hi/world/middle_east/country_profiles/791969.stm.
9. See *BBC News Country Profiles: Libya,* August 24, 2006, http://news.bbc.co.uk/1/hi/world/middle_east/country_profiles/819291.stm.
10. See *BBC News Country Profiles: Egypt,* August 24, 2006, http://news.bbc.co.uk/1/hi/world/middle_east/country_profiles/737642.stm.
11. See *Encyclopaedia Britannica Online,* September 24, 2006, http://www.britannica.com.
12. *Egypt Today,* April 12, 2006, http://www.egypttoday.com/Aboutet.aspx.
13. *Cairo Magazine,* December 28, 2006, http://www.cairomagazine.com.
14. *Worldpress.org—Egypt Profile,* November 28, 2006, http://www.worldpress.org/profiles/Egypt.cfm.
15. Schemm, 2004 (in Resource Guide).
16. See *BBC News Country Profiles: Jordan,* August 24, 2006, http://news.bbc.co.uk/1/hi/world/middle_east/country_profiles/828763.stm.
17. *Encyclopaedia Britannica Online,* "Jordan," September 23, 2006.
18. "*Elle*'s Middle Eastern Edition Balances Fashion and Tradition," 2006 (in Resource Guide), p. B1.
19. *Onlinenewspapers.com,* "Jordan Newspapers," December 26, 2006, http://www.onlinenewspapers.com/jordan.htm.
20. *Encyclopaedia Britannica Online,* "Israel," September 23, 2006, http://www.britannica.com.
21. See *BBC News Country Profiles: Israel*, July 23, 2006, http://news.bbc.co.uk/1/hi/world/middle_east/country_profiles/803257.stm.
22. *Encyclopaedia Britannica Online,* "Ha'aretz," October 10, 2006, http://www.britannica.com.
23. *Yedioth Ahronot, Ynet News,* December 24, 2006, http://www.ynetnew.com/home/0,7340,L-3082,00.html.
24. *Ma'ariv,* December 26, 2006, http://www.nrg.co/il.
25. *ABYZ News Links,* "Israel Newspapers and News Media," December 29, 2006, http://www.abyznewslinks.co/israe.htm.
26. *Encyclopaedia Britannica Online,* "The Jerusalem Post," September 23, 2006, http://www.britannica.com.
27. *BBC News Country Profiles: Israel,* July 23, 2006, http://news.bbc.co.uk/1/hi/world/middle_east/country_profiles/803257.stm.
28. *Extrovert Magazine,* June 30, 2006, http://www.extrovertmagazine.com.
29. *BBC News Country Profiles: Israel,* July 23, 2006, http://news.bbc.co.uk/1/hi/world/middle_east/country_profiles/803257.stm.
30. Rosett, 2005 (in Resource Guide).
31. *As-Safir,* December 22, 2006, http://www.assafir.com.
32. *Al-Akhbar,* December 21, 2006, http://www.al-akhbar.com/.
33. *Daily Star,* December 19, 2006, http://dailystar.com.lb/.
34. *La Revue du Liban,* December 29, 2006, http://www/rdl.com.lb.
35. *BBC News Country Profiles: Syria,* December 22, 2006, http://news.bbc.co.uk/2/hi/middle_east/country_profiles/801669.stm.
36. *Worldpress.org—Syria Profile,* November 28, 2006, http://www.worldpress.org/profiles/Syria.cfm.
37. *BBC News Country Profiles: Iraq,* December 24, 2006, http://news.bbc.co.uk/2/hi/middle_east/country_profiles/791094.stm.
38. 2004 Committee to Protect Journalists, "Iran: Reformist Dailies Temporarily Banned," July 26, 2006, http://www.cpj.org/news/2004/Iran20feb04na.html.
39. Moaveni, 2006 (in Resource Guide).

Periodicals

40. Dehqan, 2005 (in Resource Guide).
41. *BBC News Country Profiles: Iran,* December 24, 2006, http://news.bbc.co.uk/2/hi/middle_east/country_profiles/790877.stm.
42. Karimi, 2006 (in Resource Guide).
43. *Worldpress.org—Kuwait Profile,* November 29, 2006, http://www.worldpress.org/profiles/Kuwait.cfm.
44. *Bahrain Press, Media, TV, Radio, Newpapers,* November 30, 2006, http://www.pressreference.com/A-Be/Bahrain.html.
45. Ibid.
46. *Encyclopaedia Britannica Online,* "United Arab Emirates Media and Publishing," December 1, 2006, http://www.britannica.com.
47. *Gulf News,* December 30, 2006, http://gulfnews.com/aboutus/gulfnews/index.html.
48. Oman, *ABYZ New Links,* December 10, 2006, http://www.abyznewslinks.com/oman.htm.
49. *Encyclopaedia Britannica Online,* "Qatar," December 18, 2006, http://www.britannica.com.
50. United Nations Commission on Human Rights, "Child Camel Jockeys in the United Arab Emirates," (in Resource Guide).
51. *BBC News Country Profiles: Saudi Arabia,* December 27, 2006, http://news.bbc.co.uk/2/hi/middle_east/country_profiles/791936.stm.
52. *Al-Muslimoon,* November 17, 2006, http://www.alkhaleejiahv.com.sa/srpc/muslimoon.
53. *Arab News,* December 31, 2005, http://www.arabnews.com.
54. *BBC News Country Profiles: Yemen,* December 27, 2006, http://news.bbc.co.uk/2/hi/middle_east/country_profiles/784383.stm.
55. *Encyclopaedia Britannica Online,* "Yemen," December 29, 2006, http://www.britannica.com.
56. "Suspended Sentence for Editors in Third Cartoon Case," 2006 (in Resource Guide).
57. *Yemen Times,* December 29, 2006, http://www.yementimes.com/view.shtml?about.
58. "Court Convicts *Yemen Observer,*" 2006 (in Resource Guide).

LITERATURE

LITERATURE: Men and women come out in numbers to peruse the collections during the annual Hebrew Book Week. © Israel images / Alamy.

LOVE, SEX, AND MARRIAGE

LOVE, SEX, AND MARRIAGE: Bride-to-be at a traditional henna ceremony before the wedding, Morocco. © Orit Allush / Alamy.

LOVE, SEX, AND MARRIAGE: A young bride in Fez, Morocco, wears a luxuriant traditional veil over her kaftan. © dk / Alamy.

LOVE, SEX, AND MARRIAGE: A gold merchant counts gold rings from India in Muscat's Mutrah souq (market) in Oman. Gold jewelry is given to wives and as a bride's dowry in Arab societies from Morocco to Iraq. © Mike Nelson/epa/Corbis.

MUSIC

MUSIC: A blind man plays the oud in Tripoli. The oud is one of the most commonly used musical instruments in the Middle East and North Africa. © Art Directors / Helene Rogers.

MUSIC: Iranian pop diva Googoosh waves to the crowd during a concert at the Air Canada Center in Toronto, 2000. Googoosh broke years of silence to perform her first concert in 21 years. © AP Photo/CP, Kevin Frayer.

PERIODICALS

PERIODICALS: Jihad Hussein, 10, looks through an edition of AK Comics at a children's book fair in Cairo, Egypt, 2004. AK Comics is the first Middle Eastern superhero comic series and features such themes as terrorism, the Israeli-Palestinian conflict, and the threat of nuclear war. © AP Photo/John Moore.

RADIO AND TELEVISION

RADIO AND TELEVISION: U.S. First Lady Laura Bush (left), and Egypt's First Lady Suzanne Mubarak (right) stand by the puppet Khokha, while touring the set of *Aalam Semsem*, or *Sesame World*, the Egyptian version of the popular American children's show *Sesame Street*, 2005. © AP Photo/Hasan Jamali, Pool.

RADIO AND TELEVISION: The English language branch of Al Jazeera prepare for their first broadcast in the Doha news room in Qatar, 2006. © AP Photo/ Hamid Jalaudin.

SPORTS AND RECREATION

SPORTS AND RECREATION: Moroccans Lahcen Ahansal (left) and his brother Mohamad Ahansal, arrive respectively first and second in the 20th Marathon des Sables in Tazzarine, Morocco, 2005. © Pierre Verdy/AFP/Getty Images.

SPORTS AND RECREATION: Afghan boys try to catch a kite during a kite flying competition in Kabul, Afghanistan, 2007. Until very recently, these types of competitions were banned. © AP Photo/Rafiq Maqbool.

THEATER AND PERFORMANCE

THEATER AND PERFORMANCE: Iranian children gather in Tehran to watch a puppet show during a feast to mark the World Puppet Theater Day, 2004. © Behrouz Mahri/AFP/Getty Images.

THEATER AND PERFORMANCE: Egyptian actors perform a play called *Fairouz, Did You Ever Cry?*, relating to the last war in Lebanon, during the 18th Cairo International Festival for Experimental Theater, 2006. © Behrouz Mahri/AFP/Getty Images.

TRANSPORTATION AND TRAVEL

TRANSPORTATION AND TRAVEL: The ancient rock-carved city of Petra at night. Petra draws more visitors annually than any other attraction or historical site in Jordan. Courtesy of Shutterstock.

TRANSPORTATION AND TRAVEL: Tel Aviv is Israel's fast-moving center known for its shopping, cafes, night life, an expansive drive-through safari park, a sprawling promenade extending to Jaffa, and glorious beaches. Courtesy of Shutterstock.

RADIO AND TELEVISION

RIHAB KASSATLY BAGNOLE

Radio and television are natural extensions of the oral tradition common to Middle Eastern and North African cultures. Inhabitants of countries in the region like to listen, watch, and discuss news of local and international events. By arguing their opinions, Middle Easterners and North Africans not only fulfill their need to share and unite with others around them, but they also spread the news and related speculation. Given this fascination with the spoken word, radio and television offer natural outlets for mass communication in a region rich in oral tradition.

In 1991 the British Broadcasting Corporation (BBC) estimated that Middle Easterners and North Africans owned 73.5 million radio receivers and 36.1 million television sets.[1] While many families today use one television per household, most of them own more than one radio. Some may have a radio in each room or have individual transistor models for easier access. Radios are also favored among bus and taxi drivers, shopkeepers, and many office employees to keep themselves and their customers informed through the latest news and entertainment programs.

For more than a century, radio and television have been considered Western phenomena requiring certain stylistic and artistic traditions. Almost all radio and television station equipment is imported into the region and installed by Western or Japanese companies. These foreign manufacturers include production training for local specialists, who assemble and service their equipment. The manufacturers also have sponsored other programs to train radio and television experts and create technical and artistic producers.

In many countries of the Middle East and North Africa, broadcasting networks also serve as an extension of political agendas, and they function under direct government supervision. This control varies in its format and potency from one country to the next. For example, the rulers of Libya, Syria, and Yemen have taken full control of broadcasting because they have recognized the instrumental role of radio and television in communicating political messages and encouraging public support. Consequently, they resort to jamming stations that attack their policies: one example of this was the jamming of the Voice of Arab Syria that originated from Iraq in 1976. Other countries, such as Jordan, Kuwait, and Qatar, have adopted a more relaxed policy that allows a degree of freedom of broadcasting and does not limit the role of the media to that of providing support for the government.

RADIO AND TELEVISION

> ### WESTERN BROADCASTS IN THE MIDDLE EAST
>
> Many Western broadcasters are interested in marketing their services to listeners in the Middle East and North Africa. CNN has declared that the BBC will close its radio broadcast services to Bulgaria, Croatia, Czech Republic, Greece, Hungary, Kazakhstan, Poland, Slovakia, Slovenia, and Thailand by March 2007 to fund a new Arabic television station. The Arabic channel is part of a £30 million (US$53 million) package to enhance the BBC World Service and boost its audiences. The BBC Arabic Television Service will provide a tri-media service in Arabic, using TV, radio, and online broadcasts. The channel will initially broadcast 12 hours a day and will be available to everyone in the Middle East who has a satellite or cable connection.[2]

Broadcasting may also be delivered from Western countries, which aim to promote their own policies, serve their political visions, and circulate their strategies in the region. For example, the British station of al-Sharq al-Adna (the Near East Arab Broadcasting Station) started in Palestine in 1942 as part of the Allied radio effort during World War II and moved to Cyprus when the British left Palestine in 1948. A few years later, it replaced its shortwave transmitter with a medium-wave transmitter, and to counteract the patriotic message of the Egyptian Voice of the Arab radio station in 1956, it changed its name to Voice of Britain. Such stations stop broadcasting, as was the case with Voice of Britain in 1957, when they loose their listeners or change their political strategies.

Most broadcasting systems in the Middle East and North Africa are subsidized by governments and partially financed by advertising. Radio broadcasting was initiated in many countries on a commercial basis and was originally funded by local or foreign individuals and businesses. For example, private radio stations that began broadcasting services in the mid 1920s in Algeria and Egypt were profit-oriented stations based on marketing program products and selling commercial messages. They also authorized foreign companies, such as the British Marconi Company, which operated on Egyptian radio from 1934 to 1948, to receive benefits from introducing the system.

Television started in some Middle Eastern and North African countries in the 1950s and spread to the rest in the 1960s and 1970s. This visual medium was accepted throughout the region, including even in the most conservative Islamic states such as Saudi Arabia. Some of these countries adopted the German (PAL) color system while others used the French Sequential Color and Memory (SECAM) system. In countries such as Syria and Egypt, the government facilitated the availability of television sets for many viewers by importing cheap sets, allowing installment payments over time for medium- and low-income citizens, and manufacturing the appliances locally as soon as a contract with the foreign company permitted.

Television viewers in the Middle East and North Africa enjoy seeing and listening to the Koran, which kicks off daily programming in most countries of the region. Their television channels include local and foreign programs whose contents relate to, challenge, or entertain the public. Many local programs are inspired by a foreign format but are adapted to fit the traditions, values, and ideology of the region. Sometimes such productions can stir cultural and political opinions. For example, an episode of Al Jazeera's most popular political talk show, *The Opposite Direction*, asked whether reality TV and music video clips should be seen as an American-Saudi conspiracy to destroy Arab and Islamic political unity.

Reality shows are popular among the audiences in the Middle East and North Africa. Some of them are accepted and enjoyed, while others are rejected and eliminated. For example, *Ala al-Hawa Sawa* [On the Air Together], a Saudi MBC program that is an Arabized mix of

The Dating Game and *The Bachelorette*, with female contestants surveying a variety of suitors to reach the end goal of an arranged marriage, is a hit because it reflects cultural aspects related to the local society. On the other hand, a welcoming kiss by a Saudi man on the cheek of a Tunisian woman during the first episode *al-Rais* [The Leader], MBC's adaptation of *Big Brother*, caused Bahraini Islamists to launch a campaign against the show. The charge of indecency forced MBC to cancel the program after only a few episodes so as not to cause cultural tensions.

Western influence also emanates through the spread of new technologies. Since the 1991 Gulf War, broadcasting has changed, and the use of satellite television has increased in the region. The wealthy Gulf countries launched their own satellite television channels between 1992 and 1994. Other countries, including Jordan, Tunisia, Morocco, and Algeria, entered the competition as early as 1993. By early 2000 almost all countries had joined the satellite wave, and every country has become a transmitter of its own values, culture, and ideology.

The residents of the region receive many foreign ideas through satellite services as well. Foreign networks can reach the homes of millions of Middle Easterners and North Africans for a small fee to the broadcasting provider of foreign networks. For example, Orbit Satellites, which was established by a Saudi group in Rome in 1994, services the Middle East and North Africa. It carries a variety of television and radio networks, including CNN, Disney entertainment, sports channels, and the Discovery Channel. Such channels have introduced innovative ideas that inform the viewers of recent news, views, and opinions, and have opened new horizons for them.

> ## TV SYSTEMS AROUND THE GLOBE
>
> There are several standards for television systems that have been adopted around the world. The most common ones are the NTSC, PAL, and SECAM. The NTSC (National Television System Committee) is an established standard used in North America and Japan. This system has the ability to display up to 525 lines of resolution displayed at 30 frames per second. PAL (Phase Alternating Line), a standard used almost everywhere else in the world, has the ability to display 625 lines of resolution. It was developed in Germany and is used in much of Western Europe and Asia, as well as throughout the Pacific and southern Africa. PAL has a higher resolution than NTSC with 625 lines, but refreshes at only 25 frames per second. SECAM (*Séquential Couleur Avec Mémoire* or Sequential Color with Memory) was developed in France and is used in France, Eastern Europe, Russia, the Middle East, and northern Africa. This system uses the same resolution (625 lines) and frame rate (25 per second) as PAL, but the way SECAM processes the color information is not compatible with PAL. While any SECAM country can display PAL tapes in full color, not all PAL countries can display all SECAM tapes in color. Only if the tapes are true SECAM and not MESECAM can PAL VCRs display SECAM.

Thus, among the changes that have been sweeping throughout the Middle East and North Africa at the dawn of the twenty-first century are the many developments associated with communications and broadcasting. The following presents detailed descriptions of broadcasting in individual countries.

ALGERIA, MOROCCO, AND TUNISIA

Algeria has 7.38 million radios (244 receivers per 1,000 persons) and 3.33 million televisions (110 receivers per 1,000 persons). In 1962 Algeria acquired its independence from France, whose influence has been felt in many spheres, including broadcasting.[3]

Radio and Television

France started radio broadcasting in Algeria with the channel France Cinq (Channel Five) in 1937. Its programs were relayed straight from Paris. The *Emissions des langue Arabe et Kabyle* (ELAK) expanded this service in 1940 to include an Arabic channel followed by a Berber (Kabyle) channel in 1948. The French and Arabic channels operated with 100-kilowatt transmitters for the French and Arabic channels and 20-kilowatt transmitters for the Kabyle channel.[4] These channels were supplemented later but have remained the primary channels in modern Algeria.

The French organization *Radiodiffusion Television Française* (RTF) started television broadcasts to the cities of Algiers, Blida, Constantine, and Oran in 1956 and immediately started transmitting its programs in French directly from Paris. In 1963 the Algerian government assumed control over RTF and changed it to RTA. It was not until 1970, however, that the RTA was reorganized to launch a cultural revolution, which has stressed Arabizing its programs and has included more locally made productions. In the 1970s, satellite technology allowed the current stations to reach additional locations.

In 1973 Algeria started switching to color television and began operating with the German PAL system. The RTA divided its responsibilities among several entities: ENTV (National Enterprise of Television) for news programming, ENPA (National Enterprise of Audiovisual Production) for the production of entertainment and cultural programs, ENRA for radio programming, and the TDA for television equipment. Since then, the United States has become the primary supplier for programming on Algerian television. For example, series such as *Dallas*, *Beauty and the Beast*, and *Kate and Allie* were popular in the 1980s.

Since 1971, Algeria has been enhancing program productions in several ways. One of its local dramatic TV series, for example, won an award for the best dramatic series at the Fifth Cairo International TV and Radio Market and Festival (CAMAR TV) in 1999. The Algerian government has recently taken steps to reform ENTV as well. In December 2002 it signed an agreement with Khalifa TV, a privately owned Algerian station broadcasting in France, to incorporate new communication methods.

Another independent station, the Arab News Network (ANN), owned by the Algerian Rafik Khalifa, broadcasts in Arabic from studios in London. ANN was launched in 1997 to reach the Middle East, North Africa, and Europe. ANN presents a variety of programs, including news bulletins; political, economic, and social analysis; talk shows; and music 24 hours a day. The talk show *Kanadeel wa Muajahai* [Illumination and Confrontation] is favored among moderate listeners, while programs such as *Cinema 2000* and *Olympica and Musica*, a pop music show, cater to people with different tastes.

Morocco has 6.92 million radios (243 receivers per 1,000 persons) and 4.72 million televisions (166 receivers per 1,000 persons). Morocco acquired its independence from France in 1956.[5]

The first radio broadcast emanated from Radio Maroc in Rabat in 1928. It aired from a medium-wave transmitter in both French and Arabic. In 1947 the French and Arabic programs separated their production and transmission facilities. Soon after, the main programs were broadcast in Arabic, with the secondary in French, and then in Berber, Spanish, and English.

Morocco was the first country in the Maghreb (the region that includes Algeria, Morocco, and Tunisia) with privately owned radio stations. Around the middle of the twentieth century, an American launched Radio Tanger, and a Frenchman established *Radio Africa*. In addition, the Voice of America (VOA), among other stations, began operating on a lease basis. These were followed by other commercial radio stations such as Médi 1.

Today, the radio system in Rabat includes three networks plus nine regional stations in Tangier, Casablanca, Laayoune, Marrakech, Agadir, Fez, Oujda, Tetouan, and Dakhla that use nineteen studios and twelve mobile units.[6] They broadcast on three language channels: the main national one is in Arabic, operating on shortwave; the second is international broadcasting, broadcasting on medium-wave with FM stations using French, Spanish, and English; and the third broadcasts in various Berber dialects.

Television was started in 1950 by two French firms, which were bought by the firm TELMA a year later. In 1960 the government acquired the equipment and assumed control over the local television. It operated as the Radio Diffusion Television of Morocco (RTM), which was financed by a combination of state budget allocations, fees from users, and advertising revenues.

In 1970 Morocco became the first African nation to own an earth station. Color was introduced in 1972 using the French SECAM system, with local programming coming from Rabat and Casablanca. In 1990 Rabat had two studios, four mobile units, fifteen video mobile units, and fifteen mobile film units, while Casablanca had two studios and two mobile units.

Morocco is considered the first in the Maghreb to have independent commercial television. In 1989, 2M International went on the air. It was the only privately owned station in the country until 1996; at that time, the government took over the management of the station as part of the Moroccan Broadcasting Network. This station specializes in movies from France, Egypt, and the United States. It also includes music videos, sports, and live interviews. Its programs necessarily cater to middle-class and wealthier households because of the extra fee for its services.

By the beginning of the 1990s Moroccans were buying locally made satellite dishes. The government allowed the production of these receivers but controlled their use by issuing special satellite dish permits to each buyer. The procedure was instituted to protect the local international channel. Around 200,000 to 300,000 satellite dishes had been installed by 2001.

Tunisia has 1.51 million radios (158 receivers per 1,000 persons) and 1.89 million televisions (198 receivers per 1,000 persons). Tunisia became independent from France in 1956.[7]

The first broadcasting in Tunisia appeared on the air from the Tunis Kasbah Station, developed by French amateurs in 1924. This French Radio Tunis (RTF) received official authorization in 1937. An Arabic service was added in the 1950s. The French station carried programs straight from Paris, such as jazz from the Champs Elysées, and the Arabic station broadcast popular Egyptian music that was widely available on discs.

In 1966 Tunisia had six radio transmitters, including medium-wave, shortwave, and FM. The country added seven AM, one shortwave, and eight FM transmitters in 1986. Until late 2003 the state had a monopoly on radio broadcasting. The first private radio station was Mosaique FM. It broadcasts music from the region, news, and interviews. Some popular programs are *Dhohket Jaloul*, *Venus*, and *Best of Trahwijah*.

Television service was introduced in 1966. It depended on local and imported programs that offered entertainment and information in Arabic and French. The programs included series such as the French *Dossier*, the British *Anna Karenina*, and the American *Grizzly Adams*. Egyptian and Lebanese films and series have also been popular for the Arabic services.

The state-run Tunisian Radio and Television Establishment (ERTT) still operates two national TV channels. Egyptian and pan-Arab satellite TV stations also compete with the local channels and command large audiences. Tunisians can also receive other TV channels such as al-Mustaqillah TV and Zeitouna TV via satellite. A popular private station is Hannibal TV, which was the first private television station in Tunisia. The animated show *Ninja* has been a hit among children, and the weekly documentaries of *Rawaat El Khalk* [Beautiful Creation] and *L'amour de la Nature* [Love of Nature] are admired among nature lovers.

RADIO AND TELEVISION

LIBYA

Libya has 1.43 million radios (273 receivers per 1,000 persons) and 717,000 televisions (137 receivers per 1,000 persons). Libya gained its independence in 1951.[8]

The first radio broadcast appeared on a medium-wave transmitter from a station in Tripoli in 1955, followed by another station in Benghazi. These two stations joined together in an official organization called Radio Libya in1957. The stations then expanded their services and started broadcasting from transmitters in Tripoli, Benghazi, Tobruk, and al-Baida. By 2002 Libya had three main radio stations (AM, FM, and shortwave).

During the first two decades of independence, the American Wheelus Air Force Base, a few kilometers east of Tripoli, was the main source of telecast entertainment. The programming included local news and a mixture of shows from American networks. A Libyan television service started in 1968, providing local programs and shows from the United States, Egypt, and other Arab countries.

The Libyan government started and designated Libyan Jamahiriya Broadcasting (LJB) under the authority of the Department of Information and Culture in 1969. By 2002 this had increased to twelve television stations plus one low-power repeater, among them a main Arabic channel, a secondary channel, and a children's channel. The main Arabic channel begins transmitting at 6:00 AM and signs off at 1:00 AM throughout the week, except on Fridays when it signs off at midnight. Another channel transmits various programs including documentaries, translated foreign movies, news, public discussions, and instructional programs from Benghazi. Some of the programs that are popular on this channel are *The Brady Bunch*, *The Untouchables*, and the BBC series *The World at War*. The special children's channel, Al-Qanat al-Saghira [the Little Channel], transmits daily for a few hours of educational, recreational, cartoon, and games programming. Another channel transmits English and French programs, including documentaries, news, serials, films, and music.

Libya does not permit private broadcasting, but most parts of the country have access to Italian, Tunisian, and other international stations via satellite. The government, however, fought such influences by jamming two international stations and knocking TV, radio and other communication channels off the air in 2005.

EGYPT

There are 21 million radios (339 receivers per 1,000 persons) and 12.2 million televisions (189 receivers per 1,000 persons) in Egypt.[9] In 1991 there were 18 million radio receivers and 8 million television sets.[10]

Egypt is considered the leader and the most influential developer of broadcasting in the region. Radio Cairo, which started broadcasting from the Marconi station in 1934, was heard in many surrounding countries, and its main station was popular among the Egyptian expatriate community working in neighboring countries. Since the revolution in 1952, Egyptian radio has started its own broadcasts and added more local programs. Some of the programs that were added to the main program include the European program, the Sudan program, the Palestine Broadcast, the Middle East program, and the musical program.

In the early 1960s a central, high-efficiency broadcasting complex was built and is still in use. It includes production studios, engineering services, and administrative offices established to supply a support network to various transmitters. Local radio services, however, could also operate without using the central complex; for example, the Alexandria Local Service operated until the late 1980s.

Television in Egypt went on the air in 1960 under the Radio Corporation of America (RCA), which established the first television broadcast facility. A year later, another channel presented cultural programs and a variety of information shows about local and foreign civilizations. Color TV was introduced in 1973, and a new color television production service opened in 1974.

Egypt started its own satellite system for international broadcasting in 1990. The Egyptian Space Channel (ESC) transmitted its programs on Arabsat. The 24-hour service load consists of news, entertainment, religious, and health programs. ESC was followed by Nile TV, which was originated by Hassan Hamid in 1993. Nile TV broadcasts in Arabic, French, English, and Hebrew. It presents cultural, variety, sports, and dramatic programs, as well as news reports from the region and around the world. Some of the popular programs are *Around the World*, *Egypt in a Week*, *The World in Seven Days*, and *Africa Report*.

> **IDEOLOGICAL SYMBOLS ON THE SMALL SCREEN**
>
> Female Muslim television hosts have been complaining that they lost their place in front of the camera when they adopted the Islamic veil. The BBC reports that a ten-year employee with Egyptian television is preparing to sue the government if she does not recover her place on screen. Apparently the government fears that such public display of Islamic symbols will play against the ideology of the present moderate rulers.[11]

The state owns and operates most of Egypt's broadcast media, but a few private television stations are now on the air. Al-Mehwar, owned by a group of businessmen, has been operating since late 2001, while Dream 1 and Dream 2, owned by Egyptian tycoon Ahmed Bahgat, have been broadcasting since November 2001. The government also created a "media city" outside of Cairo in the late 1990s where media outlets can rent facilities to produce and broadcast shows.

JORDAN

Jordan has 1.85 million radios (372 receivers per 1,000 persons) and 417,000 televisions (84 per 1,000 persons).[12] Jordan became independent from Britain in 1946.

In 1948 the Hashemite Broadcasting Service (HBS) took over the Palestine Broadcasting Service, which had been established by the British in Ramallah for radio broadcasting. In 1956 another radio station began transmitting from Amman, followed by a new station in 1959. By 1992 radio broadcasting in Jordan was transmitting in Arabic, English, and French on FM, and on medium, short, and long waves. Arabic programming has been dominated by talk shows that involve communication between radio hosts, listeners, and public officials. It also includes news, music, culture, sports, and children's programs.[13] Some of the recent popular programs are *Sabah al-Kheir* [Good Morning], which airs on the main station, and talk shows that are transmitted from the FM station in Irbid.

Television appeared in Amman as a commercial enterprise in 1964 and was soon expanded to include Irbid and Nablus. The government established its official Jordan Television (JTV) in 1968. Jordan Television broadcasts on two channels. The main Arabic channel carries news, series programming, music, children' programs, religious programs, sports, and movies. The foreign channel includes news in French, Hebrew, and English; documentaries; British and American sitcoms; and some local talk shows.

Jordan Television is the country's only broadcast channel. It is a public service funded by license fees and commercial revenue. This channel covers local and international news and provides a variety of Arabic programs, including news reports, family entertainment, documentaries, cultural and educational programs, and sporting events. News and various feature films are also broadcast in English and French. Some of the local programs include *Yawm Jadeed* [A New Day], which covers social issues, health, and religion; *Yisid Sabahak* [Happy Morning], which features various local events across the kingdom and spotlights local talents, artists, national occasions, and accomplishments; and *Isalu Ahl al Thikir* [Ask Religious People], which concentrates on Islam by responding to questions.

In February 1993, Jordan launched its Jordan Satellite Television channel, transmitting 20 hours of programs a day. This station reaches many countries in the region, southern parts of Europe, Turkey, western Iran, North America, and several countries in northern Africa.

ISRAEL AND THE PALESTINIAN TERRITORIES

Israel has 3.21 million radios (526 receivers per 1,000 persons) and 2.04 million televisions (335 receivers per 1,000 persons).[14] Israel declared its independence in 1948.

In 1936 Kol Yisrael began broadcasting programs and eventually expanded to become one of the largest radio stations in the world. Since 1993, Kol Yisrael has consisted of seven stations. These stations emphasize culture, news, current events, and popular music; youth programs and rock music; Arabic news and entertainment programs; classic music; and shows in Hebrew, English, French, Russian, Yiddish, Romanian, and Spanish. Funding for these stations comes from fees paid by listeners and from commercial advertising.

Television in Israel started in 1965 as an educational tool. By 1969 Israel Television (ITV) included news, educational and children's movies, talk shows, cartoons, and British and American entertainment programs. Another channel became commercial in 1993 and was followed by the development of other privately owned cable television services throughout the country.

Since the beginning of the 1990s, sophisticated studios have spread outside of Jerusalem and Tel Aviv; these are located all around Israel and compete with other private stations. Israeli law obliges private channels to provide 20 percent of their programs from local productions. Cable broadcasting includes thematic local channels focusing on children, science, family, sports, movies, and imported international programs.

An Arabic-language satellite TV channel, launched in 2002, targets the Arabic-speaking audience in Israel and surrounding countries. Its programming includes news, which represents 60 to 70 percent of its programs, as well as talk shows, children's programs (live or recorded), dramatic series, soap operas, and films in Arabic. This channel also features programs aired on other Israel Broadcasting Authority (IBA) channels, such as *Politika*, with Arabic subtitles.

The British introduced radio to Palestine in 1936; it broadcast in English, Hebrew, and Arabic. Many Palestinian stations came on and off the air from various neighboring countries: the Palestinian Service of Radio Cairo from Egypt (1954), the Palestinian Program (1962), the Palestinian Broadcast from Syria (1964), and Corners on Radio from Kuwait (1970) are among the many stations that promoted the Palestinian cause and interests.

Although no cable television serves the Palestinians in the West Bank, the Palestine Satellite Channel (PSC) is operated by the Palestinian Broadcast Corporation (PBC), under the authority of the Ministry of Information of the Palestinian National Authority. The channel is a 24-hour station that focuses on news, current affairs, films, documentaries, soap operas, and music. The main television office and studios were burned in 2001, and PSC has since been operating from temporary headquarters in Ramallah and Gaza. In 2005 the PBC and the PSC were unified into a single corporation, the Palestinian TV and Radio Broadcasting Corporation, affiliated with the Information Ministry.

LEBANON AND SYRIA

Lebanon has 2.46 million radios (687 receivers per 1,000 persons) and 1.2 million televisions (335 receivers per 1,000 persons).[15] Lebanon gained its independence from France in 1941.

Radio Levant was established in Lebanon by the French in 1936. In 1946 the station became the Lebanese Broadcasting Station, and by 1961 the government had created a monopoly over radio transmission. The programs were broadcast regularly in Arabic, Armenian, English, French, and Spanish. An FM transmitter started up in 1965. The Lebanese radio receives its budget from the Ministry of Information, and only public advertising is allowed on the radio.

Many radio stations appeared illegally after the beginning of the civil war (1975–90). For example, the Voice of the Nation, Voice of the Mountains, Voice of the People, and Voice of Free Lebanon were all rebel stations, supporting different political groups. Some of these broadcast stations are still active (i.e., the Voice of Lebanon in the Christian sector of Beirut) because of their loyal listeners.

Television in Lebanon was established by a private business, the Lebanese Television Company (CLT), in 1959. Another company, the Lebanese and Near East Television Company, began operating three channels in 1962. Both companies adopted the SECAM color system. More than 50 percent of the programs were imported from the United States, France, and Egypt. The two Lebanese companies merged and formed Tele-Liban in 1972. This system broadcast Arabic programs on two channels, and French and English on another.

In 1985 the Lebanese Forces Militia launched the Lebanese Broadcasting Corporation (LBC). It became popular and funded itself with advertising revenue. Another privately owned station, Al-Mashreq TV, followed in 1990, focusing on Arabic programming. A third station, NTV, appeared in 1991 and emphasized thematic programs such as children's shows, women's shows, health programs, comedies, and soap operas.

There are also two religious stations in Lebanon: one is Middle East Television, which focuses on Christianity; the other is Al-Manar TV, which focuses on Islam. Al-Manar TV is controlled by the Shiite fundamentalist movement Hezbollah, which holds a number of elected positions in the Lebanese government. Al-Manar TV presents a combination of religious programming, international and local news, sports, politics, society, culture, and

---

THE TOP TV SHOWS

Following are some of the television shows popular among the citizens and expatriates of the Middle East and North Africa.

- From LBC (based in Lebanon): *Al Wadi*, a reality show with fourteen celebrity contestants from different Arab countries filmed while they live together. The host is entertainer Haifa Wehbe.
- *Miss Lebanon*, a reality show that follows the contestants and documents their lives as they prepare for the contest.
- *Spotlight*, a show that introduces the latest happenings in the world of cinema in Lebanon, the Middle East, and around the world. The host of the show is Elise Farah.
- *Kalam El Nass*, a show that deals with controversial topics and allows discussion between the public and different leaders.
- From Al-Arabiya (based in Dubai): *Special Mission*, a show that investigates and addresses controversial topics such as politics, the economy, and religion.
- *Rawafed*, a show that introduces the lives of cultural and artistic celebrities. The show is presented by Ahmad Ali Al Zein.
- From Dandana TV (based in America): *Gossip*, a show that tackles the gossip that evolves around film and music stars in a humorous way.
- *Be the One*, a show that searches for Middle Eastern talent.
- From TAC TV (based in America): *Leilat El Omer*, a show that interviews newlywed couples at their wedding reception.

children's shows. The network includes live talk shows and dialogue programs with a variety of perspectives.

The Future TV Network was founded in 1993 as an independent channel in collaboration with MBC, the Saudi Arabian network now based in Dubai. The channel presents local and international news broadcast in Arabic, English, French, and Armenian. It also offers American movies, Spanish soap operas, Lebanese comedy shows, and Arabic children shows.

The National Broadcasting Network (NBN) covers local, regional, and international news. It is owned by Nabih Berri, the head of Amal, a Shiite organization. NBN's programs include news, features, fashion, astrology, and sports.

Syria has 4.5 million radios (276 receivers per 1,000 persons) and 1.09 million televisions (67 receivers per 1,000 persons).[16] Syria acquired its independence from France in 1946.

Expansion of the radio system did not take place until 1965 when Syria boosted its old system with several radio transmitters, a move that enabled broadcasting to all Syrian towns. In the 1980s five shortwave transmitters with sophisticated antenna systems were installed to target the expatriate Syrians residing in Europe, North America, and Latin America. Since 1992, transmitters have been broadcasting to the nation and the neighboring countries.[17] The programs on Syrian radio are broadcast in Arabic, French, English, Russian, German, Spanish, Portuguese, Hebrew, Polish, Turkish, and Bulgarian. They transmit from the central studios in Damascus, under the supervision of the government.

Television in Syria began in 1960 with the help of the Radio Corporation of America (RCA) through an agreement between Syria and Egypt. Four studios operated in Damascus, Aleppo, and Homs, producing news, interviews, and local programs. In 1970 the Ministry of Information for Radio and Television installed various transmitters and relay stations around Syria. The government also started to produce a German-brand television set, Syronex, and distributed these sets within the country at a subsidized price.

Since 1992, two national stations, one in Arabic and one providing programming in several foreign languages, have been broadcasting. Both of them have depended on government sources and commercial advertisers for funding. The Arabic station is concerned with news, public affairs, folk stories, children's shows, and educational programming. The other channel includes commercial programming; entertainment in Arabic, English, and French; and local and imported shows. For example, the American show *Dallas* and the Lebanese show *Alo Hayati* have been among the popular series.

The Syrian Ministry of Information also operates Syria Satellite TV. This 24-hour channel is broadcast from Damascus and reaches most of the Middle East, Europe, the United States, South America, and North Africa. It delivers Arabic language programming, which includes news, sports, music, popular movies, and comedy shows. In 2000 the network added a daily news bulletin in Hebrew. In 1999 the Syrian television system won more than twenty awards for programs and TV films at the Fifth Cairo International TV and Radio Market and Festival (CAMAR TV).

IRAQ

Iraq has 5.03 million radios (222 receivers per 1,000 persons) and 1.88 million televisions (83 receivers per 1,000 persons).[18] Iraq acquired its independence from Britain in 1932.

Following the U.S.-led coalition's attack on Iraq, the United States sponsored the Iraqi television station Al-Iraqiyah. It began broadcasting in 2003 and started satellite broadcasting in the same year. In 2004 the U.S. Defense Department awarded the Harris Corporation a 12-month contract to manage the Iraqi Media Network, including Al-Iraqiyah. The Lebanese

Broadcasting Corporation (LBC) worked with Harris to provide training and programming. In January 2005, Harris was awarded a second contract—this time it was for three months at a cost of US$22 million. The scope of the contract includes training, programming support, systems integration, and deployment work for the country's public television and radio broadcasting organization.

Al-Iraqiyah offers shows from other Arab states as well as some original shows including the daily news hour and a weekly show entitled *Steps*, which presents interviews with political figures discussing plans for the transition of sovereignty and the future of Iraq. In 1999 Iraq radio and television won five trophies in the field of radio in the Fifth Cairo International TV and Radio Market and Festival (CAMAR TV).

IRAN

Iran has 17.9 million radios (281 receivers per 1,000 persons) and 10.4 million televisions (163 receivers per 1,000 persons).[19]

The first radio station was established in 1940 with shortwave and medium-wave transmission. It became the National Iranian Radio (NIRT) in 1971 and was changed to Voice and Profile of Islamic Republic (VPIR) during the Islamic Revolution in 1979. By 1971 there were thirty radio stations in different cities.

There are two major national radio networks in Iran. The first one broadcasts diverse programs, including news, arts and literature, Islamic education, Friday prayer, economics shows, and sports. The second broadcasts live and taped parliamentary sessions, religious education, and prayers. There are three other stations that broadcast recitations from the Koran.

Television was introduced as a private enterprise in 1958. The stations in Tehran and Abadan have depended on funding from advertising. The American-educated owner, Iraj Sabet, also brought Radio Corporation of America (RCA) television to the country.[20] This private television network became Iranian Television (ITV) in 1971, and by 1975 ITV had expanded to become National Iranian Television and Radio.

After the Islamic revolution, all American programs and series were replaced with local, Japanese, English, and German programs. One of the popular Japanese shows was *Oshin*. Iran allows some international programs on the state-controlled channels and has eliminated others. For example, Iranians can watch the Olympic games but without the women's swimming and gymnastic events, which are censored.

KUWAIT

Kuwait has 1.4 million radios (624 receivers per 1,000 persons) and 1.09 million televisions (486 receivers per 1,000 persons).[21] It gained its independence from Britain in 1961.

Radio broadcasting started in 1951, and facilities were enhanced rapidly after 1961. Kuwait's radio broadcasting stations include AM, FM, and shortwave services. Before the invasion by Iraq in 1990, Kuwait had five radio stations with FM, mediumwave, and shortwave transmitters. The five stations were reestablished after the liberation.

Television started as a private enterprise right after independence. The system was switched to the PAL color system in 1974. In 1993 several VHF (very high frequency) and UHF (ultrahigh frequency) transmitters located at the al-Mouqawa, Faylaka, and al-Moujamaa channels started operating. Almost 25 percent of the First Channel programs, which cater to the indigenous population, are locally produced, and 75 percent are imported from the neighboring countries. The Second Channel imports 85 percent of its programs.[22]

Today in Kuwait there are thirteen television broadcasting stations plus several satellite channels. The Kuwaitis can also receive live coverage of important news from the Arab State Broadcasting Union (ASBU), World Wide TV Network (WTN), Reuter TV, the British Broadcasting Corporation (BBC) TV, Eurovision, and Cable News Network (CNN).

BAHRAIN

Bahrain has 49,000 radios (76 receivers per 1,000 persons) and 256,000 televisions (402 receivers per 1,000 persons).[23] It gained its independence in 1971.

The government started broadcasting its national Arabic radio news, music, and entertainment from a studio near the capital, Manama, in 1955. The Ministry of Information added another English-language radio service in 1977. This station generated its income from advertising by international companies that were interested in reaching the large audience in Saudi Arabia, which could hear these ads on the Bahraini radio.

In 1972 the American company RTV International signed a two-year contract with the Bahraini government to operate a small advertising channel. It also acquired permission to build a studio that used the PAL color system; this construction was completed in 1973. The company produced local news and interviews, and imported programs from America, England, and Egypt. In 1976 the government assumed operation of the channels and expanded the service to the surrounding region.

In the early 1990s Bahraini television operated about 85 hours a week on the Arabic and the English channels. It offered imported programs and wire news. The Voice of America was also permitted on the island, followed by satellite-delivered Egyptian programming on the Arabic channel, Cable News Network (CNN), and the British World Television Service.

Bahrain Radio and Television became a public corporation in 1993. The new system, which includes three radio stations and five television services, was launched by the Bahraini Amir, Sheikh Isa bin Salman al-Khalifa.

QATAR

Qatar has 250,000 radios (432 receivers per 1,000 persons) and 503,000 televisions (869 receivers per 1,000 persons).[24] It acquired its independence in 1971.

The government started Voice of Qatar in 1968. In 1993 Radio Qatar started using several large transmitters in al-Arish, al-Khaisa, and al-Markheya to broadcast its programs, and it expanded its studios to include a large radio complex. The new system operated on AM and FM using Arabic, English, French, and Urdu. It included a variety of Arabic and religious programs, drama, sports, educational features, and governmental announcements.

Until 1970 Qatar had no television service of its own. It depended on the broadcasting of Arabian American Oil Company TV (ARAMCO) in Saudi Arabia for news and entertainment. In 1974 the government built a three-studio complex and acquired a new color transmitter for its national Qatar Television. More studios were soon added, and another channel was launched in 1982.

Today Qatar has one of the most famous satellite channels: the Al Jazeera network. The Al Jazeera Satellite Channel (JSC) started broadcasting for 6 hours a day in 1996; it increased its daily broadcasting hours to 12 hours by 1997, and to 24 in 1999.

Al Jazeera grew out of a failed joint venture between the BBC and the Saudi company Orbit in 1996. The Emir of Qatar, Sheikh Hamad bin Khalifa al-Thani, initially funded JSC, which has been the only 24-hour station in the region dedicated to news, news analysis, talk shows, and documentaries. One of the most popular shows on Al Jazeera is *The Opposite Direction*, a talk show hosted by Faisal Al Qasim, a Syrian presenter who invites guests with opposing ideologies to debate their views on air. He also invites home viewers to call in and give their opinions or ask questions.

A recent article in the Athens, Ohio, *News* that described a Ohio University professor of journalism who had presented lectures to Al Jazeera employees in Qatar indicates that this station is determined to become one of the best reporting channels in the world. The channel uses the latest technologies, and brings in specialists and experts to teach its employees the latest strategies needed to compete in local and international markets.[25]

UNITED ARAB EMIRATES

The United Arab Emirates (UAE) has 1.03 million radio sets (318 receivers per 1,000 persons) and 948,000 television (292 receivers per 1,000 persons) receivers.[26] The UAE consists of seven individual emirates: Ajman, Abu Dhabi, Dubai, Fujairah, Ras al-Khaima, Umm al Qaywayn, and Sharjah. They acquired their independence from Britain and established their union in 1971. Since then, the government has been operating a radio and television system that includes broadcasts by individual Emirates.

The British were the first to attempt radio broadcasting from Sharjah. After independence, the government owned the radio service and established four radio stations that broadcast in Arabic, French, English, and Urdu.

There are four radio stations, one each in Abu Dhabi, Dubai, Ras al-Khaima, and Sharjah, with the main transmitter in Abu Dhabi. It is equipped with a powerful transmitter and broadcasts the national radio service, which is rebroadcast throughout the nation using a low-power transmitter.[27] The first Arabic radio broadcasting from Abu Dhabi Radio started in Abu Dhabi in 1969 and became the United Arab Emirates Radio, also broadcast from Abu Dhabi beginning in 1971. This station has been known as the Voice of the United Arab Emirates since 1976.

Dubai also operates stations in Arabic and English. The Arabic station is dedicated to music, with brief segments of news and features. It operates from 6:30 AM until 12:30 AM. The foreign language station operates on FM from 6:30 AM until 12:30 AM, with a concentration on popular Western music.

The first television transmissions started in Abu Dhabi in 1969, even before the formation of the United Arab Emirates. PAL color system transmission started in 1974. A second national Arabic channel, which resembles the Western channel in terms of programming, was added in the late 1980s. The daily programming at that time consisted of Koranic reading, cartoons, and *Iftah ya Simsem* [Open Sesame].

Abu Dhabi Satellite TV was launched in 2000, managed by the Emirates Media Incorporation (EMI). Its funding has come from the government through the Ministry of Information and Culture. Today, Abu Dhabi television produces 90 percent of its own programs, including political shows, current affairs, culture, entertainment, drama, and documentary features. It broadcasts throughout the Middle East, North America, and Europe.

Dubai's television initiative started in 1972 with one channel, which was soon followed by two more in Arabic and English. The Arabic channel carries locally produced programs, which include humor, sports, documentaries, serials, news, plays, and films. The second channel was designated for the expatriate community. It carries imported entertainment including films, children's programs, soap operas, and films.

Dubai TV is a government-owned satellite channel operated by the UAE Department of Information. As part of a larger media network, Dubai TV's programming is varied and includes coverage of news, sports, finance, and business in addition to family shows. Dubai TV was the first station in the region to broadcast its programming via satellite to Europe and North America.

Al-Arabiya is another Arabic-language satellite news channel based in Dubai. It was launched in 2003 by a group of Arab investors including Sheikh Walid al-Ibrahim, a brother-in-law of Saudi Arabia's King Fahd and owner of MBC, and Lebanon's Hariri Group. Al-Arabiya is owned by MBC and was created to compete with Al Jazeera in news broadcasting.

There are also three major cable networks in the region. They are the BBC, Star TV Plus, and MTV. The first is preferred among expatriates, the second is admired among Asian expatriates, and the third is popular among the youth in the region.

The Emirates have also built an impressive media city. Dubai Media City (DMC) was launched in Dubai in 2000. Dubai invested almost $800 million in the media city and its production and transmission facilities. It includes broadcast facilities for major broadcasters such as CNN, BBC World, Voice of America (VOA), Showtime Arabia, Middle East Broadcasting Center (MBC), Ten Sports, Taj Television, ARY Digital Network, and Geo TV.

Another massive creative city complex is underway in Fujairah. It will house television and radio stations and hopes to attract local, regional, and international firms that specialize in media, design, technology, and training. It was launched by Fujairah Media and is expected to be ready by 2007.

SAUDI ARABIA

Saudi Arabia has 7.18 million radios (326 receivers per 1,000 persons) and 5.81 million televisions (264 receivers per 1,000 persons).[28] It acquired its independence (unification of the kingdom) in 1932.

Radio service was not accepted in Saudi Arabia till 1949. Broadcasting Service in Saudi Arabia (BSSA) belonged to and was created as a monopoly by the Ministry of Information. It has five radio networks: two Arabic services, two religious services, and a foreign language service in English and French. The first two are located in Riyadh and Jeddah, the second two are in Mecca and Jeddah, and the last one broadcasts from Dammam.

Saudi Arabia has acquired three additional radio stations: Al-Arabiya, a 24-hour Arabic news channel; Panorama FM, an Arabic-speaking entertainment radio channel; and MBC FM, another Arabic-speaking entertainment radio channel. It also owns three national television channels, which are controlled by the Ministry of Information. One broadcasts in Arabic, the second programs in English, and the third is dedicated to sports.

Another network is Al-Ikhbariya, which was launched in 2004. This was the first Saudi state-owned TV network to feature women anchors. The programs of Al-Ikhbariya include local and international news and live debate shows.

Satellite television has never been formally legalized in the kingdom, but it is widely popular among the Saudis and foreigners who live there. According to a 2003 international poll, 91 percent of Saudis watch satellite television, and nearly two-thirds (63 percent) have Internet access.[29]

One of the major Saudi broadcasting centers in the Middle East is the Broadcasting Corporation of the Middle East Broadcasting Center (MBC). It was launched in 1991 from

London by a group of businessmen and shareholders under the direction of its chairman and CEO, Sheikh Waleed Bin Ibrahim al-Brahim. MBC broadcasts news of domestic and international events, popular programs from the Middle East, and shows from the United States and the United Kingdom.

MBC moved to Media City in the United Arab Emirates in 2002. The 24-hour service is divided as following: MBC 1, an Arabic entertainment and news channel; MBC2, a movie channel concentrating on Hollywood movies with Arabic subtitles; and MBC 3, specializing in cartoons and children's shows. A fourth channel, MBC 4, offers a mixture of reality shows such as *Nanny 911* and *Wife Swap*, as well as American and British comedy and drama series such as *Malcolm in the Middle*, *Scrubs*, and *Alias*; news and current affairs programming from the American networks ABC and CBS; game shows such as *Jeopardy* and *Wheel of Fortune*; and magazines such as *Insider* and *Inside Edition*. One of the channel's most popular programs is the talk show *Oprah*.

Local television programs in Saudi Arabia have started to prove themselves by winning awards. In 1999 the Saudi Arabian director, Miriam Mohammed, won the Grand Prize at the Cairo TV Market and Festival for her script for the Saudi Arabian–based TV series that she also directed. The series was called *The Woman Who Faces the Challenge*.

OMAN

Oman has 1.49 million radios (621 receivers per 1,000 persons) and 1.35 million televisions (563 receivers per 1,000 persons).[30] It acquired its independence from Britain in 1951.

Radio Sultanate of Oman began local broadcasting in July 1970 from a small station at Bait al Falaj in Ruwi, near Muscat, when Sultan Qaboos bin Said came to power. In the following year, transmissions began from a second location in Salalah.

In 1972 a new medium-wave station started broadcasting, and in 1979, the Muscat and Salalah stations were linked by satellite. The number of Arabic transmission hours increased to 24 hours a day in 1998. Since then, Arabic programs have been broadcast via Radio Sultanate of Oman's own channel on the Arabsat satellite, Egyptian Nilesat, and Hot Bird 4 satellite as well as via the Internet. English FM programs are broadcast 15 hours each day from Muscat, Salalah, and Thumrait. In April 1999 FM English-language programs began broadcasting via Arabsat 2 satellite as well.

Sultanate of Oman Television began broadcasting for the first time from Muscat in November 1974, and then separately from Salalah in November 1975. In 1979 the two stations at Muscat and Salalah were joined by satellite link to form a unified broadcasting service. Oman TV's broadcasts are transmitted through a network of stations spread across the country. At present, Oman TV broadcasts its programs around the world through its Website and via the following satellites: Arabsat 2A, Arabsat 3A, Arabsat 2B, Nilesat 101, and Hot Bird 4.

Many of the films and serials produced by Oman TV have won prizes at international festivals, for example, at festivals in Bahrain and Egypt in 1999 and 2000, respectively.

YEMEN

Yemen has 1.17 million radios (65 receivers per 1,000 persons) and 5.1 million televisions (283 receivers per 1,000 persons).[31] It became independent in 1967. North Yemen and South Yemen were unified in 1990.

Between 1976 and 1990, television broadcasting in northern Yemen was the responsibility of the Yemeni Public Corporation for Radio and Television. A similar organization, the

Radio and Television Authority, was established in the south in 1988. With the unification of Yemen, these were merged in 1990 to form the Public Corporation for Radio and Television, which operates under the Ministry of Information.

The government-owned Yemen Satellite Channel includes programs from Yemen's two terrestrial channels. Most of their programs are in Arabic, but they include news broadcasts in English. Yemen TV also presents dramas, documentaries, religious shows, and a variety of public announcements, especially about health.

Japan has recently provided nine programs to Yemen. These programs include *Animation, Living in the Nuclear Age, Junior High School Science: Chemistry, Face of the Earth, We Love Nature,* and *Project X,* which depicts Japanese innovators working in various industries in Japan.[32]

RESOURCE GUIDE

PRINT SOURCES

Boyd, Douglas. *Broadcasting in the Arab World*, 2nd edition. Ames: Iowa State University Press, 1993.

Fakhreddine, Jihad. "Pan-Arab Satellite Television: Now the Survival Part." *TBS* 5 (Fall/Winter 2000). Available from http://www.tbsjournal.com/Archives/Fall00/Fakhreddine.htm.

Ghadbian, Najib. "Contesting the State Media Monopoly: Syria on Al-Jazira Television." MERIA 5.2 (June 2001). Available from http://meria.idc.ac.il/journal/2001/issue2/jv5n2a7.html.

Gher, Leo A. "New and Old Media Access and Ownership in the Arab World." *International Communication Gazette* 61.1 (1999): 59–88. Available from http://gaz.sagepub.com/cgi/content/abstract/61/1/59. Hafez, Kai, ed. *Mass Media, Politics, and Society in the Middle East.* Cresskill, NJ: Hampton 2001.

Kamalipour, Yahya R., and Hamid Mowlana, eds. *Mass Media in the Middle East.* Westport, CT: Greenwood, 1994.

Kraidy, Marwan M. "Arab Satellite Television Between Regionalization and Globalization." *Global Media Journal* 1.1 (Fall 2002). Available from http://lass.calumet.purdue.edu/cca/gmj/OldSiteBackup/SubmittedDocuments/archivedpapers/fall2002/Kraidy.htm.

———. "Transnational Television and Asymmetrical Interdependence in the Arab World: The Growing Influence of the Lebanese Satellite Broadcasters." *TBS* 5 (Fall/Winter 2000). Available from http://www.tbsjournal.com/Archives/Fall00/Kraidy.htm.

WEBSITES

Middle East Broadcasters Association. MEB. http://www.mebshow.com. This Website is privately owned and focuses on information about the growth and development of broadcasters in the pan-Arab region.

Middle East Review of International Affairs. MERIA. http://meria.idc.ac.il/whatis.html. MERIA is a privately owned Web publication that deals with issues from the region. MERIA produces its work in conjunction with the Global Research in International Affairs (GLORIA) Center.

FESTIVALS AND CONFERENCES

Annual Cairo TV Market and Festival, Egypt. http://www.tbsjournal.com/Archives/Fall99/Reports3/TV_mkt/tv_mkt.html.

MEB Annual Conference and Exposition, Lebanon. http://www.mebshow.com.

Middle East Broadcasting Conference, Dubai. http://www.abu.org.my/public/documents/AMEABUCABSAT mar06.pdf.

NOTES

1. Boyd 1993 (in Resource Guide), p. 11.
2. See http://www.cnn.com/2005/WORLD/europe/10/25/bbc.arabic/index.html?section=cnn_world.
3. See *Encyclopedia Britannica 2006 Book of the Year* (Chicago: Encyclopedia Britannica, 2006), pp. 818–819.
4. See Yahya Mahamadi, "Algeria," in Boyd (in Resource Guide), p. 206.
5. See *Encyclopedia Britannica* 2006, pp. 820–821.
6. See Claude-Jean Bertrand, "Morocco," in Boyd (in Resource Guide), p. 244.
7. See *Encyclopedia Britannica* 2006, pp. 822–823.
8. Ibid., pp. 820–821.
9. Ibid., pp. 818–819.
10. Boyd (in Resource Guide), p. 15.
11. See Magdi Abdelhadi, "Egypt TV 'Bans Veiled Presenters,'" September 6, 2003, http://news.bbc.co.uk/2/hi/middle_east/3087220.stm.
12. See *Encyclopedia Britannica* 2006, pp. 820–822.
13. See Muhammad Ayis, Mohamed Najib El-Sarayrah, and Ziyad D. Rifai, "Jordan," in Kamalipour and Mowlana 1994 (in Resource Guide), p. 133.
14. See *Encyclopedia Britannica* 2006, pp. 820–821.
15. Ibid., pp. 820–821.
16. Ibid., pp. 822–823.
17. See Arvind Singhal and Vijay Krishna, "Syria," in Kamalipour and Mowlana 1994 (in Resource Guide), p. 265.
18. See *Encyclopedia Britannica* 2006, pp. 820–821.
19. Ibid.
20. See Abbas Malek and Mehdi Mohsein Rad, "Iran," in Kamalipour and Mowlana 1994 (in Resource Guide), p. 83.
21. See *Encyclopedia Britannica* 2006, pp. 820–822.
22. See Fayad E. Kazan, "Kuwait," in Kamalipour and Mowlana 1994, p. 153.
23. See *Encyclopedia Britannica* 2006, pp. 818–819.
24. See *Encyclopedia Britannica* 2006, pp. 822–823.
25. See Garrett Downing, "OU Profs Train Reporters at Famed Arab News Network," *Athens News*, October 19, 2006, p. 9.
26. See *Encyclopedia Britannica* 2006, pp. 822–823.
27. See Anantha Babbili and Sarwat Hussain, "United Arab Emirates," in Kamalipour and Mowlana 1994 (in Resource Guide), p. 301.
28. See *Encyclopedia Britannica* 2006, pp. 822–823.
29. See *Carnegie Endowment*, "Statistics on Arab Media," December 2004, http://www.carnegieendowment.org/files/New_chart.pdf.
30. Ibid.
31. Ibid.
32. See http://www.yementimes.com/article.shtml?i=851&p=local&a=13.

SPORTS AND RECREATION

KATHLEEN J. O'SHEA

THE MIDDLE EAST

Team sports are increasingly becoming a part of Arab life, as the region experiences a very high profile throughout the world. With worldwide attention since the September 2001 attacks, governments are actively pushing participation in sporting events, and many countries are bidding to host these to help attract cash, rich tourists, and corporations to the region. Though sport is being encouraged at government levels for genuine sports-related reasons—and is being pulled by new participants/consumers—all the region's states recognize the leverage that sport gives for attracting foreign business and international visitors.[1]

Millions of dollars are pouring into infrastructure projects, and these efforts are paying off. In 2006, for instance, Qatar hosted the 2006 Asian Games, which now involves participation from forty-four countries and regions.

The sport-business market in the Middle East offers companies access to Western, Arab, and Asian sporting competitions. These markets, in at least ten Middle Eastern countries, are at a commercially interesting stage. The ten principal sport-business markets are Bahrain, Egypt, Iran, Israel, Jordan, Kuwait, Lebanon, Qatar, Saudi Arabia, the United Arab Emirates (UAE), and even Turkey. Cash-rich regions are directing funds into infrastructure developments and are pitching for international events. Arab stars and teams are beginning to be noticed on world stages.

Sports that are typically for the wealthy—such as golf, sailing, powerboat racing, rallying, and horseracing—are booming. There are well over 100 sports federations/associations at national levels for Olympic sports, football, basketball, horseracing, rugby, volleyball, golf, motor sports, and water sports. Several pan-Gulf and Arabian organizations represent regional sports interests.

For major sports, at least ten Middle East countries have national teams, professional campuses, youth and amateur leagues in football, (called "soccer" in the United States), basketball, and volleyball. There is a strong club culture for these sports. For individual sports, facilities for golf, tennis, athletics, swimming, shooting, sailing, etc. are up to world-class standards in these regions. Significantly, in all sports, infrastructure developments are

SPORTS AND RECREATION

THE ASIAN GAMES

The First Asian Games took place in New Delhi in 1951, with eleven countries participating in just six sports. The 15th Asian Games, held at Doha, Qatar, in 2006, hosted forty-four countries and regions participating in thirty-nine competitive sports. The number of women athletes has been steadily rising over the years, and about 2000 female athletes participated in 2006. The Asian Games have come a long way since 1951 to become the second-largest sports event in the world after the Olympic Games, with athletes representing half the world's population.[2]

occurring in such countries as Egypt, Lebanon, Qatar, Saudi Arabia, and UAE.

All major sports have both national and pan-Arabian competitions (the latter representing the qualifying phases of world events such as the World Cup and the Olympic Games). Federations for popular sports report growing levels of local participation for three reasons: (1) government programs and investments are driving developments; (2) media exposure fuels consumption, with cable/satellite coverage advancing; and (3) Arab youth are much like those in more developed nations—that is, sport is emerging as a consuming interest, influenced by role models and increasing penetration of global brands through television.

Sports Websites list many publications. Circulation for such established titles as *Gulf News* is high, while *BBC World Service*, *BBC Middle East Section*, *BBC Sports*, and *BBC TV News* are increasing their exposure, primarily through their Websites. Every nation has local and national radio stations, and television is adopting Western standards and practices for its sports coverage. Apart from national networks, dedicated satellite channels provide coverage, including six regional networks, plus METV, Pan-Arab Television, TVSAT, and global networks such as BBC Sport, MBCTV, and CNN Sport.

An important trend in building sports coverage is for national stations to form alliances with global players; an example is the partnering of Lebanese Broadcasting Corporation International, its country's first private television station, with Star Sports to provide live coverage of all Asian Cup football matches in 2000. Over 1,500 media personnel from forty-two countries reported live from Lebanon.[3]

A key development has been the launching of dedicated sports Websites for the region, including major generic sites such as MidEastNet.com, ArabSport.com, EgyptianSport.com, IranMania.com, IraqSport.com, and Lebanese-football.com. About three-quarters of these sites are in Arabic or Hebrew, and most of the rest are available in English.[4]

ALGERIA

Soccer is the most popular and widely played professional and recreational sport in Algeria. Teams qualified to participate in the World Cup championships in 1982 and 1986 and won Africa's Continental Championship in 1990.

Generally, only men are allowed to attend matches. However, Algerian women are making great strides in the world of sports. For the first time, a Women's National Championship for football took place in 1999, being played prior to the Algerian Cup Final for Senior Men in front of 80,000 fans of both sexes. Casbah FC, a women's team from Algiers, played a game in public despite receiving death threats. The National Association for the Promotion and Development of Women's Sport was also established in 2000, hosting a conference on women and sport with the theme "Dimensions and the Future of Women's Sports in the New Millennium."[5]

Although traditional Algerian society does not encourage women to pursue competitive sports, Algeria has produced a woman track champion, Hassiba Boulmerka. In 1991 Boulmerka won gold in the 1,500-meter race at the Tokyo world track and field championships, becoming the first woman from an Arabic or African nation to do so. It was an historic achievement for women in her homeland, but it was also the subject of much debate in her own country. While some viewed Boulmerka as a heroine, others denounced her as a heretic for having run with bare legs, contrary to the Muslim belief that in public women should be covered from head to toe. Boulmerka answered, stating that she was a practicing Muslim but also an athlete, and that the traditional Islamic women's clothing would slow her speed. She followed up her performance in Tokyo with Olympic gold in the 1,500-meter race at the 1992 Games. "I screamed for joy and for shock, and for much more. I was screaming for Algeria's pride. . . . I screamed finally for every Algerian woman, every Arabic woman," remarked Boulmerka after the 1991 Tokyo world championships.[6]

Algerian men have also gained worldwide recognition for their accomplishments in track and field. In 1999 the Algerian team came in third at the African Games, and Algerian athletes have participated in the Olympic Games since 1964. Although they have won medals in boxing, their major success has been in long-distance running. Basketball, volleyball, and handball are also popular sports.

MOROCCO

Football, a game originally introduced by French colonists, is by far the most popular spectator sport and is enjoyed by all ages. The largest stadiums are found in Casablanca and Rabat. Whenever there is a big match, the streets are deserted because everyone is indoors watching the game on television or in local cafes. In 1970 Morocco was the first African nation to play in the World Cup. In 1986 the national team—the Atlas Lions, controlled by the Federation Royale Marocaine de Football—was the first African team to win a group at the World Cup, finishing ahead of Portugal, Poland, and England.[7] Morocco has won the African Nations Cup once, in 1976, and it was runner-up in 2004.

Since the early 1980s, track and field has become the second most popular sport in the country. Moroccan champions include Hicham El Guerrouj, who set a world record for the 1,500-meter race in 1998, and Nezha Bidouane, the women's world champion in the 400-meter hurdles. At the 1984 Olympic Games, two Moroccans won gold medals in track and field events; one of them—Nawal El Moutawakel in the 400-meter hurdles—was the first woman from an Arab or Islamic country to win an Olympic gold medal.

Morocco has also produced several excellent tennis players; Younes el Aynaoui, Karim Alami, and Hicham Arazi have competed at Wimbledon and at the U.S. Open tournaments.

Golf is growing in popularity in Morocco. There is a Moroccan Federation for Golf; the honorary president is the late King Hassan II, an avid golfer, who created one of the most coveted tournament prizes, known as the Hassan II Challenge Cup.

The Marathon Des Sables, a world-famous 145-mile foot race across the Sahara sands each year, is a grueling test of strength, endurance, and will. The six-day run through the desert in southern Morocco each year involves nearly 800 focused athletes—some famous and some who want to meet a personal challenge that drives them to the extreme. The field of competitors comes from all over the world and has included former gold-medal Olympians, polar explorers, executives, scientists, and high-school students. They have come from over thirty countries worldwide to compete against other hardy adventurers, against the elements, and against themselves.

Sports and Recreation

The actual course of the race remains a secret until the day before the Marathon begins, but in past years the event has been staged in the rough terrain south of the city of Ouarzazate. Temperatures in the region reach as high as 125° F, and Sahara sandstorms are common. Contestants are required to be self-sufficient. They are allowed to carry a lightweight backpack with all the clothing, food, and supplies they will need for the week. Marathon officials supply only a nine-liter ration of water each day.

Another popular sport is rowing; there are several rowing clubs that hold annual regattas in the Atlantic coast cities of Rabat and Casablanca. Car rallying is also a favorite sport, and the Atlas Rally through Spain and Morocco is an important international event.

The mountains of the High and Middle Atlas are snow covered for part of the year and provide good skiing. The long coastlines of the Atlantic and Mediterranean make a variety of water sports possible such as swimming, sailing, surfing, water skiing, and scuba diving. Climbing, trekking, and whitewater rafting or canoeing are all possible in Morocco's four mountain ranges. Finally, with the worldwide fame of Arabian horses, it is not surprising that riding is also a popular sport.

In the last few years, Moroccans have become more acquainted with seeing women competing in boxing, football, rugby, or track tournaments. "Thankfully, Moroccan women athletes are now in a much better situation than in the past," said Moroccan former sprinter Nezha Bidouane, who ended her 15-year career in early 2005.[8] The 37-year-old retiree is one of the most titled women in African and Arab athletic history. She twice won the 400-meter hurdles gold medal—in 1997 at the World Athletics Championships in Athens and four years later in Edmonton—and she won the silver in 1999 in Seville.

Besides their performances in different sports categories, women in Morocco have also managed to make their way into the world of sports management. TAS Casablanca, a second division football club, was until last year run by a woman, Samira Zaouli. The Royal Moroccan Aerobic and Fitness Federation is under the command of Selma Bennani, and the Moroccan Association for Sports and Development is presided over by Nawal El Moutawakel.

Through her landmark triumph in the women's 400-meter hurdles at the 1984 games in Los Angeles, El Moutawakel paved the way for her countrywomen to use their sporting prowess and eventually bring in further victories. An Olympic pioneer in her country and continent, El Moutawakel became a member of the International Olympic Committee (IOC) in 1998, only a year after the late King Hassan II appointed her Secretary of State for Sport and Youth.

Tunisia

The development of modern sports in Tunisia contributed to the formation of a national identity following the independence movement from France. Since 1987, under President Ben Ali, a new national identity has developed, rooted in traditional culture and modeled on pre-Islamic forms, allowing traditional sports to play a role in building Tunisian identity.

The national sports obsession for Tunisians is football, with its national team, nicknamed Les Aigles de Carthage (The Eagles of Carthage), controlled by the Fédération Tunisienne de Football. This team recently won the title "Champions of Africa" and qualified for the World Cup in Germany, a phenomenal accomplishment for a country of fewer than 11 million people.

Over the past decade, Tunisia earned a reputation for excellence in handball by making progressively stronger showings at international tournaments. The sport is gaining such popularity in Tunisia that sports journalist Sami Akrtmi now calls it "the second sport of our country." His point was proven when Tunisia hosted the 19th World Handball Championship.[9]

LIBYA

Football is the most popular sport in Libya. Professional teams are members of the Libyan Arab Jamahiriya Football Federation and are members of international and African football federations as well. Students play in organized teams, from elementary school until university.

Libya first participated in the Olympics in 1968. However, after the establishment of the Libyan Arabic Republic, there was a period of nonparticipation, and Libyans did not again take part in the Olympics until 1992, when a small number of athletes represented the country in Barcelona.

Libyans have enjoyed racing horses and have competed in chariot races, including Fantasias (displays of special riding skills) for over 3,000 years. In the South, a particular form of camel racing, *mehari*, where two riders compete, is a popular sport that highlights the skill and fearlessness of the riders more than the speed of the camel.

EGYPT

Among the most-watched sports in Egypt are basketball, handball, squash, and tennis. The most-played, most-watched sport in Egypt, however, is football. Egyptian football clubs, especially Al Ahly and Al Zamalek, are known throughout the Arab World and Africa, and they enjoy the reputation of long-time champions of the sport regionally.

Egyptian football fans, players, and officials planned and organized the African Cup of Nations during 2006 in the best way possible to prove to the world that they were capable of hosting and organizing big international events. Egypt had hosted this tournament before, in 1959 and in 1974, but participation from other countries was very limited. With this major event, *Egypt 2006,* the country hosted millions of people from all over the world. Besides hosting the successful event, Egypt won its fifth football championship, beating Cote d'Ivoire in the final, 4–2.

A very attractive aspect of *Egypt 2006,* in addition to the football, was the African cheerleading during the matches. Africans are known to invent the best and craziest ways of cheerleading in the world. Coloring their faces and wearing strange outfits, they filled the stadiums where their teams were playing. Some teams also took magicians with them to the matches to lead the fans and frighten the other teams. This tradition in African sports has become a major attraction in any tournament.[10]

Squash, handball, judo, karate, and horse racing have been major sports and have established important traditions, as well. Egyptian and Pakistani players have dominated the world of squash since the inaugural Open Squash Championships in the 1930s. Today, young Egyptian players have also dominated the sport's amateur and young-professional tournaments. The majority of these players emerged from the families who looked after the British Officer Clubs in their countries. As young boys, they would act as ballboys and court minders who watched the service personnel play and then took to the courts when their masters did not require them.

The one major exception was F. D. Amr Bey, the best player in the world from 1933 until he retired, undefeated, in 1938. An amateur who beat all the pros of the time, he held down a series of important government posts, eventually becoming the Egyptian Ambassador to the court of St. James in London. In this capacity, he single-handedly brought the existence of squash to the attention of the general public for the first time. As a top diplomat winning the British Open Championship, he was big news in both England and his home country.[11]

SPORTS AND RECREATION

In 2003 sports for women and Egyptian squash, in particular, took another leap forward, as Egypt played host to the 10th World Junior Women's Squash Championship—a 13-day event that gathered 128 players and sixteen teams from around the world: "This is a huge event and another challenge for Egyptian squash," Mohamed El-Menshawi, President of the Egyptian Squash Association (ESA), told the press.[12]

El-Menshawi—the youngest-ever national federation president at 35—recalled the history of Egyptian squash: "Some years ago, the dormant giant that had once been elite Egyptian squash awoke, shook itself and took the youthful road to long-term success," he began. "Some great names from Egypt grace the annals. But the production line stopped 20 years ago, and it wasn't until the beginning of the 1990s that real time, effort and expenditure were invested in some future stars. . . . Egyptian women's squash has shown great progress lately," El- Menshawi said.[13] There may not yet have been the number of landmark titles that the older age groups won, but young players such as Omneya Abdel-Qawi and her teammates have already made their mark and there are strong foundations for the women's future.

The support for women's squash in recent years—both from the Egyptian Federation and the Al-Ahram organization—has started to show signs of returns. Of the 128 players competing in the game, 9 are Egyptian. "It's wonderful for the girls," said World Squash Federation (WSF) technical director, Jackie Robinson, commending what she called a "brilliant" idea: "and good to see women in Egypt coming through in this part of the world. It's good to take the championship to different parts of the world."[14]

Clearly, the role of women in Egyptian sports is growing significantly, largely through the efforts of Dr. Sahar El-Hawari, who has raised women's sports profile, despite contending with religious, social, and financial obstacles. In fact, the tremendous global development of women in sports is often symbolized by the progress made in Egypt.[15] A 10-day Arab women's football tournament, which came into being largely because of El-Hawari, head of the Goethe Institute in Cairo, was first played in Alexandria in 2006. El-Hawari helped spread the game to the rest of the region, and after forming a women's committee at the Union Arab de Football Association (UAFA) persuaded officials to organize an official tournament.[16] In recognition of her role in supporting the participation of women in sport and her efforts in establishing the first female football team in the region, El Hawari was awarded the IOC Award for Women and Sport for the Year 2000.

The Egyptian Olympic Committee formed a Women's Commission, and the election law of all national sport federations was amended to stipulate the necessity of having at least one woman on each board. Women now have the right to be members of the National Olympic Committee, and they now can serve as members on all administrative councils of clubs, sport federations, and youth centers not only by election, but also by nomination.[17]

The Egyptian Handball Federation (EHF) was founded in 1957 and joined the International Handball Federation in 1960. The 1990s proved golden for the Egyptians: in June 1991 the Egyptian national team earned the silver medal at the Mediterranean Games in Athens, and in September of the same year, Egypt claimed the African Nations Cup title—after two decades of absence—in the championship held in Cairo.

In 1993 the Egyptian national junior's team won the world championship for the first time in Egyptian history. Egypt was ranked sixth in the world championship in Iceland in 1995, and in the Olympic Games of 1996 Egypt placed sixth and preserved its standing in the world championship in Japan in 1997.

Horse racing may have had its roots in Egypt in about 1500 BCE, and some events continue in Egypt today. The breeding of Arabian horses also remains a popular endeavor, with the Arabian Horse Festival continuing to be the focal attraction of Arabian horse breeders worldwide. The event, organized annually in November by El-Zaharaa station, is located in the Cairo suburb of Ain-Shams.

The Egyptian Judo Federation was officially established in 1963 under the name of the Egyptian Judo & Karate Federation. When aikido and sumo joined the federation, the official name became The Egyptian Judo, Aikido & Sumo Federation. Since 1964 Egypt has taken part in all official judo tournaments on all the African and worldwide levels. In fact, the headquarters of the Arab Judo Federation is located in Egypt.

JORDAN

Leading professional sports include football, basketball, and motor sports. Sport enthusiasts in Jordan also enjoy hiking, diving, mountain climbing, and horseback riding.

The Jordan Football Association (JFA) was founded in 1949 and in 1958 became affiliated with Fédération Internationale de Football Association (FIFA) and with the Asian Football Confederation in 1975. Important developments for Jordanian football have included the construction of a headquarters, training and fitness center, and the qualification to the 2004 finals of the Asian Cup. The Jordan national team had jumped from 131st place on the FIFA ranking list in 1999 to 47th place by the end of 2004.

The second most popular sport, basketball, has recently received an increase in financial resources from the Jordan Basketball Federation (JBF) and from private sectors. The JBF has been led by Honorary President Prince Hamzah since 1999. Focus has been on improved teaching and coaching of young players, as well as performance-based incentives for national teams at various levels.

The popularity of motor sports is due, in part, to the interest of the late King Hussein, a sports enthusiast, who started racing as a hobby in 1955. The first Jordan International Rally was held in 1981; in 1982 the Rally became part of the Middle East championships.[18]

The Royal Automobile Club of Jordan, a private, nonprofit club established in 1953, assists motorists and organizes all motor sports activities in the Kingdom. With an army of trained volunteers and marshals at its disposal, the Royal Automobile Club takes pride in organizing one of the most eagerly anticipated events of any kind on the country's social and sporting scene. During the early days, the Marka Airport track provided the venue for the sport, but a stunning track in 1998 at the Royal Automobile Club injected new life into the sport, and today events are also held at the SOFEX track as well as through the streets of the capital, Amman.

The support from the general community is considerable, with up to 10,000 spectators annually attending the Super Special Stage, which provides a spectacular launch for the rally on the outskirts of Amman. The result is a fantastic return for investors and sponsors alike, as well as significant exposure for Jordan.

Since joining the Federation Internationale De L'Automobile (FIA) Middle East Championship in 1982, the Jordan Rally has become a favorite among drivers and spectators alike. The 2004 event was particularly pleasing for the local fans, with home favorite Amjad Farrah becoming the first Jordanian to win.

ISRAEL

More and more Israelis are participating in sports, ranging from tennis and squash to jogging, soccer, and basketball. Particularly popular are beach and water sports, including swimming, diving, surfing, and sailing. Israel has regularly participated in the Olympic

Games since 1952, winning its first medals at the 1992 Barcelona games. The 1998 World Cup final between France and Brazil attracted an all-time record television rating of 48.3 percent of viewers.[19]

Throughout the early years of the State, sports were inextricably linked to political parties, but the apolitical Academic Sports Association (ASA), founded in 1953, had nine branches and 5,000 members. This worldwide organization still exists today, providing college and university students with opportunities to participate in team sports.

The tone for the modern era was set in the first half of the twentieth century by Chief Rabbi Abraham Kook, who emphasized the importance of sports and insisted that only a healthy body can ensure a healthy soul. In 1932 the first Maccabiah (the international Jewish Olympics, which takes place every four years sanctioned by the International Olympic Committee) was held in what was then Palestine, attracting 500 Jewish athletes from twenty-three countries. The 15th Maccabiah of 1997 drew a record-breaking 5,500 sportsmen and sportswomen from Jewish communities in fifty-four countries to compete in over fifty sports. The Maccabiah is now the third-largest sporting event worldwide, after the Olympics and the World University Games; it is the biggest Jewish event of any kind.

Most Maccabiah participants are eager amateurs, not professional competitors. However, there have been some notable exceptions, such as Marc Spitz, who won six gold medals as a teenager in the 1965 Maccabiah swimming competitions. Spitz went on to win four gold medals in the Mexico Olympics of 1968 and an all-time record of seven Olympic gold medals in Munich in 1972.

The opportunity to compete in Europe has been most significant in basketball and football, Israel's two most popular spectator sports. Israel has been more successful in basketball. Maccabi Tel Aviv won the European Cup club competition in 1977 and 1981; the first of these triumphs is generally considered to be the single greatest Israeli sporting achievement.

Although the Israeli basketball has never returned to the glory of the 1970s and 1980s, the national team regularly reaches the quarterfinals of the European Basketball Championships (as it did in 1997), and Maccabi Tel Aviv usually reaches the final 16. In 1996 Maccabi Tel Aviv's Doron Sheffer was the first Israeli to be drafted by the U.S. National Basketball Association (NBA) after three successful college seasons with the University of Connecticut. Although he was drafted, ultimately he was not offered an NBA contract, and he spent the remainder of his career with Maccabi Tel Aviv.

The Football Association, the first pre-state sporting federation established in 1928, was the first of fourteen umbrella sports organizations to be founded. These sporting organizations absorbed hundreds of leading sportsmen who immigrated when anti-Semitism intensified in Central and Eastern Europe and the USSR during the 1930s. Israel's most impressive football achievement came in 1970, when the country qualified for the World Cup finals in Mexico for the first—and so far the only—time.

Israel's club teams have competed in the major European competitions since 1993 and seem set to have a promising future with some excellent achievements by the Under 16 and Under 18 national teams. The Under 16 team won the bronze medal in the European Championships in Austria in 1996 and also reached the final 16 in 1998 and the Under 18 team reached the final 8 in 1996.

Track and running competitions are also popular in Israel. The regular annual marathons at Tel Aviv, Jerusalem, the Dead Sea, and the Sea of Galilee attract thousands of runners, and tens of thousands participate in the shorter "fun runs." The Jerusalem March attracts 15,000 "walkers" annually.

With access to four bodies of water—the Mediterranean Sea, the Red Sea, the Dead Sea, and Lake Kinneret—swimming is Israel's most popular participation sport. An estimated 50 percent of the country's residents go swimming at least several times a year, and with over 40,000 qualified divers, Israel also has the highest per capita number of divers in the world.

At the professional level, Israel has enjoyed some notable achievements in swimming in recent years. In 1997 the country's first medal in a major international competition was awarded in the European Swimming Championships in Spain. In the 1996 Olympics, Israel won its first swimming final when the 4 × 100-meter medley relay team finished eighth. The same team finished fifth in the European Championships. In other water sports, Israel hosted two major world championships in recent years: the World 470 Sailing Class Championships (Tel Aviv 1997) and the World Windsurfing Championships (Haifa 1996).

Beach sports have always been popular in Israel, particularly a locally developed game called "mascot" rackets, which is a cross between tennis and table tennis. Volleyball has emerged as a popular sport in recent years, as well.

Racquet sports also enjoy popularity in Israel. With tennis, Israel has not only enjoyed success at the international tournament level; it has also pioneered the concept of tennis as an educational medium to help children from disadvantaged neighborhoods. A network of Tennis Centers from Karat Shone in the north to Sakhalin in the south enables thousands of schoolchildren from all socioeconomic sectors to take tennis lessons. The children learn the sport as well as discipline and manners, an integral facet of modern tennis.

Cricket was introduced to the region by the British during the Mandatory Period in the 1950s, when South African and Indian immigrants established the Israel Cricket Association (ICA), which today is composed of 16 teams, including a special league for those who do not play on the Sabbath. The ICA was a founding member of the European Cricket Council. Elected as an Associate Member of the International Cricket Council (ICC), Israel has competed in all six ICC trophies, winning outstanding victories in 1990 and 1994. Israel was also accepted into the European Rugby Federation in 1996.

Several games exist for pre-teen and teen males and females. "Release" is a game played by male and female teens, designed to teach agility and discovery. Requiring only a ball and an open area, the object of the game is to escape the opponents' circle and to discover the player without a home circle. The game is finished when all players are in their home circles and the "homeless" player has been discovered.

"Shelter" is another game for male and female pre-teens and teens, the object of which is to survive being hit by the ball as it is thrown in the "active zone." The game requires six or more players (two teams) and uses a ball and an open field.

"The Wall" has as its object throwing a ball toward a specific object (or designated area marked "the wall.") The game requires six or more players (two teams) to use agility and teamwork to catch the ball thrown to them by team members so that by the time the game has expired (usually 15 minutes), one of the two teams has had all its members standing behind the wall of the opposing team. There is a neutral area one meter wide into which no player from either side may enter. The distance between each wall and the neutral area is determined by the age of the players.

Israel is also a world leader in sports rehabilitation, having consistently won medals in the Paralympics (Olympics for the handicapped) and the Transplant Olympics (Olympics for persons who have undergone organ transplants).

Located on the coast south of Netanyahu, the Wingate Institute is the country's most prestigious sports institution. The leading athletic and swimming stars train there, and top soccer clubs and international athletes from Europe often come to Wingate for winter training camps. The Wingate Institute is also a world leader in sports medicine, with a department that investigates the physical and psychological stresses that sports place on the body and mind. The Wingate Test, carried out worldwide, is a blood test that determines an individual athlete's anaerobic lung capacity. The Institute also has a residential high school for some forty talented sports students in disciplines such as swimming and judo.

Government allocations to sports through the Ministry of Education and Culture amounted to US$25.7 million in 1999. Of this figure, $5.7 million was used for policing sports events, mainly football matches. Of the remaining $20 million, about 50 percent was allocated to municipalities and local authorities, who use the funds to maintain and operate existing facilities, support local sports teams, and arrange tournaments between schools and community centers. The remaining 50 percent is disbursed to other bodies and institutions. However, sports at the national and municipal levels are struggling to find funding.

Some success has been enjoyed in encouraging the private sector to invest in sports sponsorship and advertisement. Nonetheless, Israeli sports are caught in a vicious circle, with its relative lack of success ultimately discouraging businesses. For example, the Israel Tennis Open Championship was discontinued in 1997, when ten companies withdrew their sponsorship.

Yet sporting success is imperative; today, it is one of the single most important expressions of international prestige after economic success. Nobody is more universally admired than a sports champion. At present, Israel has all too few such heroes.[20]

The problem is even greater for women in sports. Women's basketball is a flourishing sector, and major matches can attract several thousand spectators. However, Israel's sports are still male dominated in terms of funding and participation. Research has shown that only about 25 percent of the participants in competitive sport are women, a much lower number than in the Western world and lower than the average in the world as a whole.[21]

In 1985 the women's basketball team made the finals of the Acacia and was scheduled to play the American team in the country's premiere basketball stadium at Yard Elijah. Days before the final, however, the women's venue was changed to a far less prestigious one. The team, terribly insulted by this slight, convinced the American team to join them in boycotting the game. As a result, the Israel Basketball Association disbanded the team, though the decision was ultimately rescinded.

LEBANON

The most popular sport in Lebanon is football, played and watched mostly by men. Basketball is also very popular, with Lebanon having hosted both the Asian and Arab League Basketball Cups. Many people enjoy swimming, volleyball, ping-pong, and fishing.[22]

Nejmeh Sporting Club is considered as one of the most distinguished football teams in Lebanon. In 1945 several Beirut men decided to establish a football club that would not only compete but also promote moral standards, contributing to a strong Lebanese society. This first provisional committee of the Nejmeh Club applied for a license to the Lebanese government in 1945; the license was finally issued on April 28, 1947.

A major break came in 1970 with the rise of the "golden team" at Nejmeh Club, composed of the best players in Lebanon (Mohammad Hatoum, Hassan and Mahmoud Shatila, Habib Kammouneh, Zein Hashem, Jamal El Khatib, and Youssef El Ghoul). This team led the way to a decade of glory for Nejmeh, particularly in the1970s, when Nejmeh dominated the Lebanese scene and gained worldwide respect with a series of international matches.

In the late 1970s and the 1980s, the civil war spread hatred among the Lebanese people and destroyed much of Lebanon's infrastructure. Lebanese football in general and the

Nejmeh Club specifically suffered much from this war, particularly when the championship was suspended for twelve years, from 1975 to 1987. At the end of the war, the Nejmeh Club re-emerged with the rise of new generations of Lebanese players who restored the championship title to the club in 2000.

Another milestone in the club history was in 2003, with the election of a new board of directors, which immediately set many objectives—strengthening the club's first football team, rehabilitating the club stadium, and establishing a long-term plan to transform the club into a self-dependent organization. Today the Nejmeh team has regained the lead position in Lebanese Football out of a field of at least 11 other teams.

The new board has also sought to strengthen ties with the large fan base in Lebanon and the rest of the world. To this end, the club president, Mr. Fanj, gave instructions to enhance the club's presence on the World Wide Web and to provide support to the club's Web site.

In recent years, Lebanon has hosted the Asian Cup and the Pan-Arab Games, and the country will host the Winter Asian Games in 2009. To meet the needs of these international competitions, Lebanon maintains state-of-the-art athletic facilities, which in turn encourage local sporting activities. Lebanon sends athletes to both the winter and summer games of the Olympics and Special Olympics.

The Beirut International Marathon has been an annual event since 2003, drawing top runners from Lebanon and abroad. Shorter races are also held for youth and less serious competitors. Race day is promoted as a fun, family event, and it has become a tradition for many to participate in costumes or outlandish clothing.

SYRIA

Syria actively participates, nationally and internationally, in sporting competitions, hosting many sporting events, including the Pan Arab Games of 1976 and 1992 and the Mediterranean Games in 1987. Syria won its first gold medal in the Olympic Games in 1996, when Ghada Shouaa won the heptathlon, a track and field event.

Syria has an excellent national sports establishment with basketball and football leagues. The Syrian Basketball Association has been a member of FIBA, the international basketball organization, since 1948. The Army Club is one of its most successful football teams. All major cities have world-class sporting arenas and complexes, consisting of stadiums, olympic-sized swimming pools, playgrounds, gardens, and training facilities for its world-class athletes.

The women's football team has competed for the 2006 Cup of the Arab Ladies First Football Championship, organized by United Arab Emirates' Football Union. Chairman of the Championship's Higher Organizing Committee, Mohammed Hilal al-Kaabi, said that this seven day championship aims to improve communications and fraternal ties among Arab sportswomen: "The United Arab Emirates is trying hard to make this event a success," he noted.[23]

IRAQ

Football is Iraq's most popular sport, and the Iraq Premier Football team remains the pride of the country. During the 1970s and 1980s, Iraq's national team was a competitive force throughout the Middle East and Asia, competing in the 1986 World Cup in Mexico.

The league continued playing even during the 1980–88 Iran-Iraq War, and during the 1991 Persian Gulf War. But just before the U.S.-led invasion of Iraq in 2003, the league had shut down for two seasons (2001–02) because of violence and lack of money. In 2004 the league began playing again. "Despite all the hard circumstances, we are playing football and challenging the terror," said Hameed Salman, the coach of Al Shurta, a team based in Baghdad that has until recently dominated the sport in Iraq. One major piece of Iraqi soccer is still missing: the fans. Before the war, even minor games would attract 40,000 fans. Now, the biggest matches draw 15,000 or fewer because of widespread violence, Salman says.[24]

The Iraqi Football Association was formed on October 8, 1948, and was the third sports union to be founded in Iraq after the Track and Field Athletics Federation and the Basketball Federation. The Iraqi national team's greatest accomplishment came when they qualified for the 1986 World Cup in Mexico, having played all their matches outside of Iraq because of the Iran-Iraq War. The team was run by Saddam Hussein's eldest son Uday Saddam Hussein, who had taken over as president of the Iraqi Football Association in 1984.

Iraq's football team earned a trip to the Olympics in 2004 for the first time ever. In fact, the country sent thirty participants to these Olympics, a sevenfold increase over any previous Olympic competition.

Ahmed Al-Samarrai, President of the National Olympic Committee of Iraq, has recently noted the inadequacy of domestic sports facilities in Iraq, with only one stadium, which was constructed in 1986. Al-Samarrai has indicated that under the Saddam Hussein administration, very little attention was given to sports because of the economic sanctions.[25]

Other popular sports for men continue to be basketball, boxing, swimming, horseback riding, and weightlifting; Assud Shaker is a well-known weightlifter.

While sports in Iraq are mostly played by men and boys, Iraq has recently launched a national women's football team. Girls also enjoy volleyball and tennis.

IRAN

Sports in modern Iran are prevalent in almost every field found worldwide, but football is by far the most popular. Particularly in the past ten years, with the privatization of ownership of football clubs and the beginnings of Iran's Premiere Football League, many Iranian players now compete in major European leagues. Iran has reached the World Cup finals three times, most recently qualifying for the World Cup 2006. This feat is particularly impressive, since adequate football facilities are limited.

Football was an unknown sport in Iran until British workers introduced the game in the 1930s. As the number of club teams increased in the 1950s and 1960s, the need for a national league became apparent, and ever since 1960, with the exception of a few years, a nationwide football league has existed in Iran. Shahin FC, Pas, and Taj are all Tehran teams established in the mid-1940s, which even to this day have a great following. In the last two or three decades, however, football has become more of a national sport, and teams other than from Tehran have received notice. So have the Irani professional leagues that have been established: the Azadegan League, the Iranian Premier League, and the Persian Gulf Cup.

By the 1970s, Iran had established itself as one of Asia's top teams, winning the Asian Cup in 1968, 1972, and 1976, qualifying for the 1972 and 1976 Olympics, and, most importantly, qualifying for World Cup 1978 in Argentina.

During the Iranian Revolution and the Iran-Iraq War, the importance and popularity of football was downplayed, but the national team has made a comeback in recent years, qualifying for the World Cup in 1998 and 2006.

Next to football, wrestling probably holds the most popularity among Iranians. In fact, many refer to Greco-Roman and freestyle wrestling as the national sports of Iran. Wrestling is also the oldest sport to be practiced among the Iranians; its roots penetrate deep into the history of the nation. Iranian folkloric heroes were wrestlers, the most famous of them being Rostam. Modern international free and Greco-Roman styles are predominant, but many traditional styles are also still in favor, including the most famous of the traditional wrestling styles, Pahlavani wrestling.

Ever since the First World Championship in 1951, Iran has managed to obtain a high rank in world wrestling. By the year 2000, the Iranian team had been World Champion three times (1961, Yokohama; 1965, Manchester; 1998, Tehran) and three times the vice champion (1971, 1973, 1995). It has also held third place nine times between 1951 and 1971. By the year 2000, Iranian wrestlers had managed to win five Olympic gold medals, 10 silver medals, and 13 bronze medals. They had also won 28 gold World Championship medals, 30 silver medals, and 30 bronze medals. In 2006 Iran placed second overall at the world freestyle wrestling meet. The team captured one gold metal, one silver metal, and two bronze metals.[26]

Other countries have acknowledged Iran's leadership in promoting wrestling throughout the world. So far, three Iranians have been FILA bureau members, and two have served on its committees. Iran has also been one of the founders of Asia's wrestling confederation.

Obtaining its current status has not been achieved easily. Currently, wrestling is being taught scientifically at the sports universities, coaches are being trained at the Wrestling Institute, and champions are trained at the House of Wrestling. Iran has valued its officials as well, and the number of its international referees is more than any other country in the world.

Martial arts have also become increasingly popular over the last 20 years, because of their relatively low cost and high rate of individual benefit.

Because Iran is home to many mountainous regions, skiing and climbing sports are also very popular. The Tochal resort is the world's fifth highest ski resort, over 3,730 meters at its highest station. This resort, completed in 1976, before the overthrow of the Shah, is only 15 minutes away from Tehran's northern districts.

Iranian women have participated in international events in many sports, including karate, chess, shooting, chess, and aerobic gymnastics. There is also a Women's Sports Association for Disabled Persons in Iran, and women with disabilities participated in international shooting, athletics, chess, and volleyball competitions during 2000.

Women's sports have strong partnerships with other sectors such as government organizations, universities, schools, and media. These links help women workers improve their physical and sport activities. To increase the meaningful and visible role of women as leaders and decision makers, a woman has been selected as "The General Manager of Women's Sports Associations Joint Affairs."[27] Although some inroads have been made, of late, women's sports have been under scrutiny by the current government regime. The president of the Iranian women's sports federation, Faezeh Hashemi, recently launched an attack against the current Iranian president, Mahmoud Ahmadinejad. Hashemi, whose father was defeated by Ahmadinejad in the last presidential election, stated that "some forces currently in power would like women to abandon sports." Furthermore, she claimed that her organization, the Muslim Women's Sport Foundation (MWSF), had been squandering government funds.[28]

In May 2006 the supreme leader of Iran, Ayatollah Khamenei, vetoed a ruling by President Ahmadinejad that would have allowed women to attend major sporting events.

The president claimed that lifting the ban would "promote chastity." The ayatollah argued that the participation of women at sporting events would have violated Islamic law; it is forbidden for a woman to look at the body of a male stranger.[29]

AFGHANISTAN

The regime of the Taliban and the destruction of war have taken serious tolls on Afghanistan sports. Sports infrastructures are almost nonexistent. The few stadiums in the country are damaged and do not meet international standards. For example, there is no proper running track in all of Afghanistan, there are very few gymnasiums, and opportunities for women to practice sports remain extremely limited. However, there are movements suggesting the recognition that sports can offer a unifying element to Afghan society.[30]

Unlike football, which was largely driven underground by the Taliban, cricket survived the rule, though it first had to be cleared by the Orwellian Vice and Virtue police, who suspected the game of American associations. The Afghanistan national team played its first game in 2000, with the players drawn from the 22 regional sides that comprise the national league.

Buzkashi, the national sport of Afghanistan, dates back to the days of Genghis Khan, when the Aryans could sweep up a goat while riding a horse at full gallop. The sport, played from horseback, translates literally to "goat grabbing," though the goal today of a Buzkashi player is to grab the carcass of a calf, get it clear of the other players or pitch it across a goal line. The fierce competition requires that riders wear heavy clothing and head protection, since players may use any force short of tripping the horse in order to thwart scoring attempts. The two forms of the game, Tudabarai and Qarajai, require specially trained horses and players who train for years.

In Tudabarai, the easier of the two forms, the rider must get possession of the carcass and then carry it away from the starting circle in any direction, staying clear of other riders. The task in Qarajai is more complex, since the player must carry the calf around a marker and then return it to the team's designated scoring circle. Winners are awarded prizes and earn great respect as honored members of Afghan society. The game has become more widely known through its depictions in films such as *Rambo III* and *Caravans* (after the book by James Michener) as well as the novel *Les Cavaliers* by French writer Joseph Kessel.

In 1994 the Taliban regime banned hobbies such as kite flying and bird keeping, in the belief that such pastimes were unIslamic. However, Afghans can now pursue these activities without fear of punishment.

Kite fighting is particularly popular in Afghanistan. It was recently brought to the attention of a wider audience through Khaled Hosseini's celebrated 2003 novel, *The Kite Runner*. In this sport, participants attempt to outmaneuver their opponents in order to cut the strings of their kites. Kites cost from 2000 afghanis (just a few cents) for tiny children's kites no bigger than a magazine to 100,000 afghanis (less than $2) for large kites, usually handled only by the most experienced flyers.

Kite fighting is a two-person affair. One person, the "charka gir," holds the wooden spool around which the wire, or "tar," is wound. The second person—called the "gudiparan baz," or kite flyer—actually controls the movement of the kite in the air. Afghan kite fighting often depends on the quality of the wire, or string, and how it is prepared. First, glass is finely ground and combined with an adhesive to make a thick paste. The wire is then coated with this paste to make it strong and sharp. After drying, the wire is wound around the spool. Kite fighters often wrap a piece of leather around their fingers to protect themselves from the taut wire, which can easily cut to the bone.

When an opponent's kite is cut free, it flutters away into the sky. Such kites are said to be "azadi rawest," or "free and legal," and can be retrieved by neighborhood children to fly another day. Each neighborhood also crowns its own "sharti," or kite-fighting champion.

Afghans have elevated kite flying—or "gudiparan bazi"—to an art. Kabul's streets are filled with shops selling kite-flying equipment, and the skies above cities are filled each day with hundreds of colorful kites fluttering in the wind.

Some other popular sports played in Afghanistan include wrestling (Palwani), boxing, martial arts, basketball, soccer, bicycle racing, and archery. In summer 1995 several body-building clubs also opened in Kabul.

KUWAIT

Kuwaitis have competed at the national and international levels in the country's two most widely played and enjoyed sports, football and golf. The National Football Team has achieved remarkable success at both international and Arab levels. The first football team, the Alahi club, was established in 1947, followed by Jazeerah and then Al Hilal.

Oil revenues have enabled the government to support sports generously, and the country boasts a number of stadiums capable of hosting international competitions. Over the last 25 years, Kuwait has had outstanding success in international soccer, equestrian sports, and swimming.

In 1968 the country first participated in the Summer Olympic Games, but it has never competed at the Winter Games. Kuwait won its first Olympic gold medal in Moscow in 1980.

The government has been eager to support sports institutions. In 1992 sports came under the auspices of the Public Authority for Youth and Sport, which is concerned with the physical and psychological development of youth. This authority is also concerned with the development, support, and spread of sport in Kuwait according to the international Olympic principles.

In addition, sport activities are included as part of school curricula. Youth centers have been established and sport teams formed. The number of sport clubs has increased from eight in 1956 to twenty in 1998. Each of these clubs contains an Olympic swimming pool, a multipurpose indoor sports hall, tennis and squash courts, and grounds for other sports. Similarly, the number of sport unions reached fifteen in 1998. The number of youth centers increased from two in 1963 to nine in 1998, with 8,313 members. In addition to youth centers, there are five women's centers serving almost 5,000 women a month.

The government cares not only for youth sport development and the organization of sport camps to develop their physical and mental abilities, but also for the encouragement of entertainment and cultural activities for children, women, and the disabled. In 1994 the Kuwait Disabled Sport Club was founded, and its membership reached 923 in 1998. Likewise, the Girls Sporting Club offers the practice of almost all sports for women and encourages them to participate in foreign championships. Kuwaiti women are now encouraged to practice some sport and participate in championships.

The country combines the traditional sports of nomadic Arabian society with contemporary sports of Western origin. Traditional sports of enduring popularity include camel racing and horse racing.

In April 2006 Kuwait held the first regional camel race, using robots as riders, after child jockeys were banned from the lucrative sport following criticism in the region by human rights groups. Teams from the six Gulf Arab states participated in the race outside the capital,

Sports and Recreation

Kuwait City. "We hope this sport, part of our cultural heritage, will be spared from suspicion," said Kuwait's Energy Minister, Sheikh Ahmad al-Fahd al-Sabah, who opened the five-day championship.[31]

Falconry is enjoyed primarily by wealthy sheikhs, although the overhunting of game and, after 1990, the presence of unexploded land mines in the desert has reduced its practice. Other sporting activities include ice skating, bowling, darts, table tennis, and martial arts.

Bahrain

Football, grand prix racing, basketball, and camel racing are all popular sports in Bahrain. The Bahrain Football Association (BFA), the governing body of football in Bahrain, was founded in 1957, has been a member of FIFA since 1966, and is also a member of the Asian Football Confederation. The same year that it was founded, the first two official national football clubs were established: the Al Khalifa team in Muharraq and the National team in Manama. The two teams play against each other, and also against visiting foreign teams and those of the British forces based on the island. The country's best performance came in the 2002 preliminary round of the World Cup, with victories over Iran and Iraq. In 2004 the national team was honored by the FIFA as the most improved team.

The Grand Prix made history as the first Formula One Grand Prix to be held in the Middle East. The idea of the Bahrain International Circuit was first suggested by Sheikh Salman Al Khalif and funded by the prime minister and then followed by Sheikh Salman. The Bahrain Grand Prix is a Formula One championship race that first took place at the Bahrain International Circuit on April 4, 2004.

Basketball in Bahrain is not very old; it was first recognized in 1946, with the Ferdousi Club, followed by the Ittifaq Club in 1956. The first official league schedule was played in 1977. For the past two years the local confederation decided to merge the two divisions, division one and division two, to form a unified championship for the teams. There are two domes used for playing basketball; though they are also used for a number of different sports, each has a capacity of approximately 5,000 spectators.

Fishing, camel racing, water sports, ice skating, running, horsemanship, and motor sports are all very popular in Bahrain. Chess, bridge, scrabble, swimming, cricket, tennis, squash, golf, tennis, gymnastics, and bowling are popular recreational sports as well.

Although Bahraini children enjoy modern pastimes such as video games and amusement parks, they still play traditional games as well. Girls play *al-sashay*, in which they jump over the hands and feet of their friends; *al-kerdiyah*, in which they act out stories using rag dolls; and *al-khabash*, in which they bury beads and challenge their friends to find them. Boys play *al-lomsabaq*, in which they race tiny handmade boats, as well as more common games such as *al-lityal*, or marbles, and *al-bilbool*, which is top spinning. Both boys and girls play *al-khaishaisheh*, or hide-and-seek.

In 1976 the Supreme Council for Youth and Sports was established under the patronage of the now King H.M. Shaikh Hamad Bin Isa Al Khalifa. The Council encouraged and promoted all kinds of activities and sports in Bahrain, with particular emphasis on youth sports.

Currently pursuing a "sports for all" mandate under the chairmanship of Crown Prince, Salman bin Hamad Al Khalifa, The Supreme Council for Youth and Sports works closely with Shaikh Fawaz Bin Mohammed Al Khalifa, president of the General Organization for Youth and Sports, to develop sport training and identification programs for Bahrain's youth population. In just four years, Bahrain has developed Arab champions in both female and male track and field, swimming, sailing, and shooting.

For the first time, the Institution of Youth in Bahrain is forming a committee for women's sport, headed by a woman. Another first occurred at the Sydney 2000 Olympic Games, when a young girl from Bahrain participated in the swimming competitions. At just 12 years of age, she was both Bahrain's swimming champion and the youngest female participant in the event.[32]

QATAR

Qatar has promoted itself as one of the world's leading sports destinations and continues to expand existing infrastructure and build new facilities. With the announcement that the 15th Asian Olympic Games would be hosted by Qatar in 2006, new sporting facilities were quickly being developed. The country has hosted many international sports stars such as Pete Sampras, Tim Henman, Boris Becker, Colin Montgomerie, and Seve Ballesteros.

The youth and sports movement in Qatar began privately in the early 1950s and continued in a small way until the Qatar National Sports Federation was formed in 1961 by an administrative decision, the first of its kind, to organize the establishment of a formal sports organization. This decision heralded a host of other such decisions, laws, and directives. Existing facilities in Qatar are excellent, particularly Khalifa Stadium, which seats 45,000 spectators.

The Qatar National Olympics Committee (QNOC) was established in 1979 to oversee the activities and participation of Qatar's national teams in international, regional, and continental competitions. Its mission, to make sport and physical recreations available to men, women, and children, fosters harmonious development in true Olympic spirit, in accordance with the Olympic charter.

Horse racing and falconry, two of the oldest sports in the country, remain major activities. Camel racing is one of the traditional sports of the Gulf area. The Horse Race and Equestrian Club has organized many championships, including the Qatar Desert Marathon in 1997.

Sports enthusiasts in Qatar also enjoy golf, diving, boating and sailing, water sports, and deep-sea fishing.

SAUDI ARABIA

Sporting events include traditional games and contests from the past, as well as the integration of international sports, including football, volleyball, table tennis, fencing, martial arts, and track and field.

Football has gained enormous popularity in Saudi Arabia in the past few decades and is now considered the national sport. Thousands of football fans, in cities and towns all over the country, flock to watch their teams compete. The Saudi Arabian football team has one of the best records among all the teams in Asia. The team has been a finalist of the Asian Cup five times in succession since 1984, and it qualified for the 1984 Olympic finals and the 1994 World Cup finals. In 1989 the National Youth Team won the National Youth Soccer Cup held in Saudi Arabia.

Since becoming an official participant in the Olympic Games in 1965, Saudi Arabia has constructed numerous modern sports complexes for international and local competitions. Much of the growth and interest in modern sports resulted from the 1974 establishment of the General Presidency of Youth Welfare (GPYW), an organization that seeks to make sporting, recreational, and cultural facilities and events more accessible to young Saudis. In 1992 Prince Faisal Bin Fahd established the Saudi Squash Federation, aimed at publicizing and developing the squash game throughout the kingdom.

More traditional sports such as falconry, horse racing, and camel racing remain popular. The Arabian horse, whose bloodline dates back 5,000 years, is regarded by many experts as the world's best-pedigreed animal. Camel racing has changed since times when thousands of camels sped across the open desert. Now races take place on racetracks, though gambling is illegal.

The King's Camel Race, started in 1974, has become one of the world's largest camel races. More than 2,000 camels and their riders compete, and between 20,000 and 30,000 spectators come to enjoy the race.[33]

The role of women in sports remains limited, but there are movements toward change. Maha Fitaihi, the wife of Jidda's mayor and a prominent women's activist, said, "We don't want a civil war—we just want this to be an evolutionary change." Fitaihi learned firsthand the risks of over-publicizing her activities in 2005, when she organized a basketball tournament for girls. Within days, religious figures contacted local leaders to put a stop to it, insisting that girls were forbidden to play sports. Fitaihi scrapped the event.[34]

OMAN

The most popular sports in Oman include football (the national game of Oman), bullfighting, hockey, volleyball, basketball, rugby, handball, and horse racing.

In 1971 The Muscat Rugby Football Club was founded. The constitution, drawn up by a six-man committee, was adopted on August 9, 1971. In 1985 the club was asked to move from its home at Wattayh, and moved to its new home at Al Khuwair. The playing field of sand and gravel was carved out of a major sand dune. Over the years, the club has competed in both the Asian Cup and the Gulf Cup with much success, winning both the first and second team cups on a number of occasions. Perhaps the highlight of the club's achievements has been the three Dubai Sevens crowns, in 1981, 1982, and 1991. In 1996 the club celebrated its twenty-fifth anniversary.

Al Quraiyya, one of seven games indigenous to Oman, was introduced to the public at Seeb Stadium by the Ministry of Sports Affairs' Committee for Traditional Sports. Twenty players, in two teams of ten each, are involved in this sport.

Al Yous (also known as *Bu Halan*), *Al Halein*, *Sayyad*, and *Al Doha* are highly popular in Dhofar and the Batinah. Though the sports seem simple, they require much agility. *Al Halein* involves two teams of eight players each, with six on the field and two in reserve. The game is played in a circle of 3.5-meter radius. The game is very popular in the Batinah, Dakhliyah, and Dhahirah regions.

Sayyad is played on a 20-meter-long court, similar to one for tennis, in halves of 15 minutes. Players from one team are split further to form two sub-teams that stand at either end of the court, with the opposition placed between the two sub-teams. Players from the first team strike at members of the other team with two tennis balls. Players from the second team who are struck by the ball have to leave the court. If all the members of the second team have been struck before the end of the half, the first team has the option of calling the second team back onto the court and then replaying the entire sequence until the end of the half. At the end of the allotted 15 minutes the roles are reversed, with the second team now trying to hit members of the first team with the tennis balls. The team that manages to clear more of the opposition from the court is the winner.

Al Doha is played in a court made of two concentric circles and involves two teams of six members each. While the players of the first team stand in the inner circle, about three meters in diameter, the opposition stands in the outer circle, about seven meters in diameter. Players inside the inner circle try to pull players from the outer circle, inside. With positions being changed at intervals of seven minutes, the team that has managed to pull more of its opposition into the inner circle wins the game. *Al Doha* is quite popular in the Batinah, Dakhliyah, and Dhahirah regions.

Bullfighting attracts not only Omani citizens but also expatriates and tourists. Some people believe there is a direct connection between the sport in Oman and bullfighting in Spain and Portugal. Bulls in Oman are divided into three species: the Omani bull (a pure Omani breed, found in northern and central provinces of Oman), the Dhafari bull (found in Dhafar Province), and the Marine bull (brought from overseas to the Sultanate of Oman).[35]

For cultural, social and religious differences, women are still unable to participate in Olympic events. In fact, adherence to strict Islamic code forbids women to display their bodies and compete in sports before a male audience.[36]

YEMEN

The Yemen national football team is controlled by the Yemen Football Association, founded in 1962. Yemen has never appeared in the World Cup or the Asian Cup. The only appearance by any Yemeni team in the Asian Cup was that by South Yemen in 1976.

Yemen's team was suspended by FIFA on August 12, 2005, in the wake of numerous unsuccessful pleas from both FIFA and the AFC for the Yemeni Ministry for Youth and Sport to stop meddling in the running of the National Football Association. FIFA recently announced the provisional lifting of the suspension. Today the Yemen Football Association is once again entitled to participate in FIFA competitions.[37]

The Yemen Boxing Federation was formed in 1990, shortly after the Yemen Unity. The federation members very ambitiously wanted to revolutionize the art of boxing in Yemen, but the Ministry of Youth and Sport did not much care for such games. The ministry was not enthusiastic about individual games such as boxing, swimming, wrestling, karate, kung-fu, and judo, not providing enough compensation to finance minimal training demands.[38]

RESOURCE GUIDE

PRINT SOURCES

Coakley, J., and E. Dunning, eds. *Handbook of Sports Studies.* London: Sage Publications, 2000.
Foer, Franklin. *How Soccer Explains the World.* New York: Harper, 2004.
Goldschmidt, Arthur, Jr. *Concise History of the Middle East*, 8th edition. Boulder, CO: Westview Press, 2005.
Radnedge, Keir. *The Illustrated Encyclopedia of Soccer.* New York: University Publishing, 2001.
Stevenson, T. B. "Football in Yemen: Rituals of Resistance, Integration, and Identity." *International Revolution for the Sociology of Sport.* 32.3 (1997): 251–265.
Sugan, John. *Football for Peace: Teaching and Playing Sport for Conflict Resolution in the Middle East.* Aachen: Meyer & Meyer Verlag, 2006.
Wagg, S. "Mr. Drains, Go Home: Football in the Societies of the Middle East." Pp. 163–178 in Stephen Wagg, ed., *Giving the Game Away: Football, Politics, and Culture on Five Continents.* London: Leicester University Press, 1995.

SPORTS AND RECREATION

WEBSITES

Al-Bawaba: Middle East Information, Media, and Technology. http://www.albawaba.com/
Arab Net: Arab News. http://www.arab.net/magic_carpet/global.html.
Ashton, Chris, "The Middle East: Opportunities in the Business of Sport." http://www.sportbusiness associates.com/sports_reports/middle_east.htm (accessed May 10, 2006).
Columbia University Libraries. Middle East and Jewish Studies. http://www.columbia.edu/cu/lweb/indiv/mideast/cuvlm/index.html.
From Montreal to Kumamoto—Women and Sport Progress Report 2002–2006. http://www.iwg-gti.org/e/progress/index.htm06.
Iran Sports Press. Updated 2006. http://www.iransportspress.com/.
The Middle East Media Guide. Media Source. Updated 2006. http://www.middleeastmediaguide.com/consumer.htm.
The Middle East Network Information Center. Center for Middle Eastern Studies at the The University of Texas at Austin. http://menic.utexas.edu/.
The Middle East Research and Information Project: March 2000-2006. http://www.merip.org/.

VIDEOS/FILMS

Breaking Down Barriers with Table Tennis Balls. The Population Council in Cairo: Ishraq Project. (Egypt, 2003). Directed by Glenn Tepper. http://www.popcouncil.org/me/egypt.html.
Child Camel Jockey in the U.A.E.s–Modern Day Slavery. (England, 2004). Home Box Office Documentary. http://www.ansarburney.org/videolinks/video-hbol.html.
The Soccer Academy. (USA, 2004). Directed by Christine Coppola. This television series, distributed throughout North Africa and the Middle East, is a soccer, travel, and adventure show for kids, teens, and adults.
Street Life in Tehran—Tehran: The 25th Hour. (Iran, 1999). Directed by Seifollah Samadian. This short film documents the Iranian National Football Team's qualification in the World Cup in 1998, a day of celebration that became known as "Sweet Saturday."

EVENTS

The Amman Dead Sea Ultra Marathon, Jordan. The DSUM is held annually on the second Friday of April, from Amman to the Dead Sea. It is the main fund-raising event for the SCNP, which provides neurological patients with medical aid and covers the costs of necessary surgeries for the needy.
Bahrain International Racing Circuit. This yearly racing schedule includes the Gulf Air Bahrain Grande Prix, the BIC National Race Championship, and the Chevrolet Bahrain Drag Racing Championship.
Camel Races at Nad Al Sheba Racecourse, Dubai. Season runs from October to March. Hours 8 AM to 2 PM.
Dubai Classic (golf).
The Dubai Cup (horse racing).
Dubai Rugby Sevens.
Dubai Tennis Championships, held annually.
FIFA World Youth Championships, held annually.
Formula One: Turkish Grand Prix.
Kirkpinar Oiled Wrestling Festival.
The Marathon Des Sables, Morocco.
Men's and women's ATP Tennis (the international governing body of men's and women's tennis): Doha, Qatar; Dubai, U.A.E; Casablanca, Morocco.
Qatar, Class I Powerboat Race.

Qatar Masters (PGA).
The UAE Desert Challenge, Dubai.

ORGANIZATIONS

Afghan Sports Federation (ASF), Fairfax, VA, USA. http://www.afghansportsfederation.org/about.htm. ASF is a nonprofit organization, established in 1998. It is run by Afghan individuals, for the benefit of amateur sports among Afghan youths and adults, both men and women at every level of excellence in the region, the United States, and the world.

The Egyptian Handball Federation Athletic Associations/Organizations, National Federations, El Estade El Bahary Street, Nasr City, Cairo, Egypt.

Egyptian Judo & Aikido Federation, Olympic Federations Complex, Cairo Stadium's Authority, Nasr City, Cairo, Egypt. www.egyptsport.gov.eg/judoeg.htm.

The Egyptian Squash Association, 20 El Irak Street, Mohandseen, Agoza, Giza, Egypt. http://www.squashegypt.com/.

Federation Internationale de Football Association (FIFA). http://www.fifa.com/en/index.html. FIFA was founded in the rear of the headquarters of the Union Française de Sports Athlétiques at the rue Saint Honoré 229 in Paris on May 21, 1904. In May 2006, the organization's home moved to Zurich, Switzerland. ***National affiliates:*** Afghanistan Football Federation (AFF) (foundation year 1933, affiliated since 1948); Algerian Football Federation (FAF) (foundation year 1962, affiliated since 1963); Bahrain Football Association (BFA) (foundation year 1957, affiliated since 1966); Egyptian Football Association (EFA) (foundation year 1921, affiliated since 1923); Iran Football Federation (IFIFF) (foundation year 1920, affiliated since 1945); Iraqi Football Association (IFA) (foundation year 1948, affiliated since 1950); Israel Football Association (IFA) (foundation year 1928, affiliated since 1929); Jordan Football Association (JFA) (foundation year 1949, affiliated since 1958); Kuwait Football Association (KFA) (foundation year 1952, affiliated since 1962); Lebanese Football Association (F.L.F.A) (foundation year 1933, affiliated since 1935); Libyan Football Federation (LFF) (foundation year 1962, affiliated since 1963); Oman Football Association (O.F.A.) (foundation year 1978, affiliated since 1980); Pakistan Football Federation (PFF) (foundation year 1948, affiliated since1948); Qatar Football Association (Q.F.A.) (foundation year 1960, affiliated since 1970); Saudi Arabian Football Federation (SAFF) (foundation year 1959, affiliated since 1959); Tunisia Football Federation (FTF) (foundation year 1956, affiliated since 1960); Turkey Football Federation (TFF) (foundation year 1923, affiliated since 1923); United Arab Emirates Football Association (UAEFA) (foundation year 1971, affiliated since 1972); Yemen Football Association (YFA) (foundation year 1962, affiliated since 1980).

The General Organization of Youth and Sports (Bahrain), Manama, Bahrain. http://www.goys.org.bh/.

Moroccan Federation for Golf, Royal Golf Rabat, Route des Zaers, Rabat, Dar es Salaam, Morocco.

Israel Cricket Association. http://www.cricinfo.com/db/NATIONAL/ICC_MEMBERS/ISR/. The ICA has been an associate member of the International Cricket Council since 1974 and was a founding member of the European Cricket Council in 1996.

International Working Group on Women and Sport. http://www.iwg-gti.org/e/progress/index.htm.

Kuwait Disabled Sport Club, Attn. Mr. Fahad Alradan, P.O.BOX 44866, HAWALLI 32062. Email: Kuwaitdisabled@kuwait.net.

Qatar Fencing Federation. www.qatarfencing.com.
Qatar Football Federation. www.qatar-football.com.
Qatar Golf Federation. www.qatargolfassociation.com.
Qatar Marine Sports Federation. www.qmsf.org.
Qatar Motor Federation. www.qatarmotorfederation.com.
Qatar Swimming Federation. q-swimming-a@yahoo.com
Qatar Tennis Federation. tennis@qatarolympics.org.
Qatar Taekwondo & Karate Federation. www.qtkf.org.
Qatar Wrestling Federation. www.qwfonline.net.

Sports and Recreation

The Royal Automobile Club of Jordan (RACJ). http://www.racj.com.jo/main.php. The RACJ is a private club established in 1953 as a nonprofit organization.

The Saudi Squash Federation. http://www.saudi-sq-fed.org/history.htm. The Saudi Squash Federation was established in 1992.

United Arab Emirates Football Association (UAEFA). http://www.uaefootball.org/.

NOTES

1. Chris Ashton, "The Middle East: Opportunities" (in Resource Guide).
2. See *15th Asian Games DOHA 2006*, "History of the Games," www.dohaasiangames.org.
3. Chris Ashton, "The Middle East: Opportunities" (in Resource Guide).
4. Chris Ashton, "The Middle East: Opportunities" (in Resource Guide).
5. See Daisuke Sato, "Sport and Identity in Tunisia," *International Journal of Sport and Health Science*, 3 (2005): 27–34.
6. See Nancy Foley, www.sportsillustrated.cnn.com/siforwomen/top_100/70 (accessed April 25, 2006).
7. See BBC Sport Online, www.news.bbc.co.uk/sport3/worldcup2002/hi/history/newsid_2012000/2012894.stm (accessed April 26, 2006).
8. See International Working Group on Women and Sport (IWG), "High Performance Sport," www.iwg-gti.org/e/montreal/challenge/perform.htm (accessed June 30, 2006).
9. See "Tunisia Earns Reputation as International Handball Power," *Magharebia: The News & Views of the Maghreb*, www.magharebia.com/cocoon/awi/xhtml1/en_GB/features/awi/features/2005/04/07/feature-01 (accessed April 26, 2006).
10. "Tour Egypt," www.touregypt.net/featurestories/africancup.htm (accessed April 25, 2006).
11. See "Squash: The Ball-Boy Servants Who Watched, Waited—and Conquered," www.pponline.co.uk/encyc/0659.htm (accessed April 25, 2006).
12. See Inas Mazhar, "Evolution of Squash," *Al-Ahram Weekly*, www.weekly.ahram.org.eg/print/2003/652/sp3.htm (accessed June 30, 2006).
13. Ibid.
14. Ibid.
15. See Tatjana Haenni, ed., "Dealing with Social Problems: Women's Football from a Global Perspective," *Al-Ahram*, 791 (April 2006): 20–26, www.fifa.com/documents/fifa/ publication/symposium.
16. Ibid.
17. See Ahmed Enan, "Woman and Sport Progress Report 2002-2006," *International Working Group of Sports and Women*, www.canada2002.org/e/progress/worldwide/chapter3_africa.htm (accessed May 3, 2006).
18. See "The Royal Automobile Museum," http://www.royalautomuseum.jo/main.asp?fl=link (accessed April 25, 2006).
19. See Simon Griver, "Sports in Israel 1999," Jewish Virtual Library, http://www.jewishvirtuallibrary.org/jsource/Society_&_Culture/sports.html.
20. See Simon Griver, "Sports in Israel," Israel Ministry of Foreign Affairs, http://www.mfa.gov.il/mfa/mfaarchive/1990_1999/1999/6/sports%20in%20israel (accessed April 25, 2006).
21. See Israeli Foreign Ministry, www.jafi.org.il/education (accessed April 25, 2006).
22. See "Sports and Recreation." www.cp-pc.ca/english/lebanon/sports.html. (accessed April 26, 2006).
23. See "Syria to Participate in Arab Ladies First Football Championship," www.syrialive.net/sports/2006 (accessed April 28, 2006).
24. See Zaid Sabah, "After 2 Canceled Seasons, Soccer Teams Bouncing Back," USATODAY.com (accessed July 13, 2006).
25. See "Prime Minister Junichiro Koizumi Receives a Courtesy Call from President Ahmed Al-Samarrai of the National Olympic Committee of Iraq (NOCI)," http://www.mofa.go.jp/region/middle_e/iraq/issue2003/assistance/assist0404-2.html (accessed April 15, 2006).
26. See *Payvand's Iran News*, "Iran Stands Second at World Freestyle Wrestling Meet," September 29, 2006, http://www.payvand.com/news/06/sep/1330.html.

27. See "Woman and Sport Progress Report 2002–2006." *International Working Group of Women and Sport*, www.canada2002.org/e/progress/worldwide/chapter3_asia.htm (accessed April 26, 2006).
28. See "Iran's Sportswomen Adapt to Religious Custom," *BBC News*, August 16, 2004, http://newsbbc.co.uk/2/hi/middle_east/3570040.stm.
29. See "Iran Women Sports Ruling Vetoed," *BBC News*, May 8, 2006, http://news.bbc.co.uk/2/hi/middle_east/4751033.stm.
30. See http://www.af/resources/mof/recosting/draft%20papers/Pillar%201/Culture,%20Media%20and%20Sports%20-%20Annex.pdf (accessed July 13, 2006).
31. See "Robots Ride in Camel Races," www.iol.co.za/index.php?set_id=1&click_id=116&art_id=vn20060206095905725C117343 (accessed April 18, 2006).
32. "Bahrain," *International Working Group on Women and Sport*, www.canada2002.org/e/progress/worldwide/chapter3_asia.htm.
33. See "The Riyadh Camel Races," www.toursaudiarabia.com/races.html.
34. See Hassan M. Fattah, "Women's Place in Society Evolving Fast in Saudi Arabia," *The New York Times*, 25 December 2005.
35. See Ahmed Al-Rebaiei, "Bullfighting in Oman, Inherited Tradition," www.middle-east-online.com (accessed April 15, 2006).
36. See Regan Good, "Women's Share at Olympics Drops," www.womensenews.org/article.cfm/dyn/aid/824 (accessed May 1, 2006).
37. See "FIFA Lifts Ban on Yemen," www.meo.tv/english/yemen/?id=14986 (accessed May 1, 2006).
38. See "The First Amateur Boxer in Sana'a: 'We did not find enough support, so we left training.'" *Yemen Times*, www.yementimes.com/99/iss04/sports.htm (accessed May 1, 2006).

THEATER AND PERFORMANCE

ANN TIPPETT AND MICHAEL DOOLIN

Drama as we know it is not a native Arab art. The dramatic art of Greece, from which the Western theater derives, remained unknown to this region of the world[1] until imitations of European theater were introduced into the Arab world during a nineteenth-century Middle East renaissance. Before the nineteenth century, the force of religion, comedic presentations, and storytelling took the place of the customary theatrical arts for more than five centuries.

Similar to the ritual, or passion, plays staged in the West to promote religion were the Arab world's Taziya, literally translated as "consolation." Performed during the first ten days of the first month of the Islamic calendar (Muharram), the Taziya plays had as their main purpose the representation of the suffering and death of Muhammad's descendants and followers. The Taziya culminated on the tenth day with the anniversary of the death of Imam Hussein, grandson of Muhammad. These plays were performed to the accompaniment of music and with varying degrees of theatricality in theaters and mosques and in the open air. Scholars' first attempts in the late 1880s to record the Taziya in Persian and other languages do no justice to the plays' sometimes deadly impact on their fevered, excited audience.[2]

The popularity of comedy was another important element in the history of Middle Eastern theater. The shadow plays, many of which were written and performed in Arabic, were enacted with colored figures manipulated by wires behind a transparent screen. The stories were told as broad comedies, intending to show the worst foibles of humankind, mostly related to sex. An especially popular form of this theatrical entertainment was known as *karagoz*, in which a single performer would be wrapped in a tent-like structure and manipulate puppets overhead. Karagoz always featured the simpleton hero, an Everyman in a kind of Punch and Judy show, who would try to outsmart pretentious hypocrites.[3]

Another form of Middle Eastern premodern drama was known in Arabic as that presented by the *hakawati*, or storyteller. In Turkish such a performance would be given by the *meddah* (praise giver) or *mukallit* (imitator).[4] A man accompanying himself on musical instruments would elaborately gesture and pantomime at appropriate moments in the basic performance of this kind of theater. The form endures to this day, and ranges from contemporary dramatists who incorporate hakawati as a Brechtian distancing mechanism, to a prominent Palestinian theatrical troupe who call themselves "The Hakawati Troupe." The

THEATER AND PERFORMANCE

> ### THE INTERNATIONAL THEATER INSTITUTE
>
> Currently eight Middle Eastern countries participate in the International Theatre Institute (ITI), an initiative of the United Nations Educational, Scientific and Cultural Organization (UNESCO), Founded in 1948, the ITI is an international nongovernmental organization (NGO) supported by UNESCO's Division of Arts and Cultural Enterprise. The ITI aims to "promote international exchange of knowledge and practice in theatre arts (drama, dance, music theatre) in order to consolidate peace and solidarity between peoples, to deepen mutual understanding, and increase creative cooperation between all people in the theatre arts."[5] Countries participating to date include Egypt, Iran, Iraq, Israel, Jordan, Kuwait, Morocco, and the Palestinian Territories.
>
> As a supplement, ITI created *The World Theatre Directory* online. Each entry includes information on ITI members, a brief account of each country's recent theatrical developments, and detailed data on such topics as festivals, theaters, theater training, resource centers, and publications.

Palestinian company, established in 1984, continues the time-honored tradition of traveling around the country, telling powerful stories to fellow citizens.

These forms were unrivaled until European classical drama was introduced to the Arab world during the nineteenth-century cultural renaissance. Thus began the sometimes painful merger of both traditions. From Shakespeare to Shaw, Molière, and Wilde, Middle Eastern actor-managers and translators battled the Anglo-Saxon tradition. Interestingly, the formulaic European comedy of manners became one of the most popular transplants.

Today, drama is prosperous in the more stable countries of the Middle East, while in other countries it barely struggles to overcome basic obstacles. Because drama is the most public of all literary genres, a performance—the act of impersonation in front of an audience—makes it immediately the focus of censorship. The most extreme forms of censorship currently prevail in Saudi Arabia (which currently supports no undertakings of drama or theater) and in Iraq, which historically had a strong culture and tradition of live theater, but now enjoys very little theatrical activity in face of the current occupation and civil chaos.

Some ancient forms of popular theater still thrive. In Iran, the Taziya (the Islamic drama) is still performed and is considered the most important part of the Iranian theater. The puppet theater community is very active in Iran, as well as in some other countries. The preservation and continuance of puppet theater are so important in Iran that it has official support from the government and in the school, and Iran hosts the International Puppet Theater Festival every two years.

Some of the more beleaguered countries in the Arab world continue the tradition of using theater as an educational and therapeutic means of helping to ease wounds of illiteracy, war, and repression. This special kind of theater is more prevalent in countries such as Lebanon, Palestine, Sudan, and in Iraq. Many of these efforts begin by reaching out to children through the tradition of puppet theater.

Not surprisingly, the more politically stable countries have the financial and educational resources that allow their drama and theater artists to grow and thrive. Theater festivals abound in many countries. In some countries, the festivals focus on exploring experimental, nontraditional forms of drama and theater. Egypt, Algeria, Iran, Israel, and Jordan all host a variety of day- or week-long celebrations of experimental drama and theater. Countries such as Lebanon, Oman, and Qatar currently celebrate established theatrical efforts with well-renowned international festivals.

In conclusion, in the Middle East the arts of theater and performance are in transition. Dramatic writers and artists continue challenging themselves to develop drama within a

European intellectual framework without sacrificing their cherished traditional culture and language. Popular traditional entertainment forms such as puppet theater and storytelling continue in some countries but are in danger of extinction in others. The result is a mixed art form that in many places is still seeking an authentic voice.

THE MAGHREB REGION

The region known as the Maghreb includes Morocco, Western Sahara, Algeria, and Tunisia. The term usually also encompasses Libya, and sometimes extends to Mauritania, too.

Theater in this large, diverse region has a rich, varied history dating back nearly three thousand years. Some of the oldest known theater buildings in this part of the world date from the Romans and are found in Libya, Algeria, and Tunisia. The Maghreb has been historically influenced by the Middle East, especially through the Islamic empire's western al-Andalus, known as the Muslim Spanish province. Between the eighth and fourteenth centuries, social and cultural exchange in this region resulted in the adoption of the Arabic language and classical system of education and Islamic law. The Maghreb absorbed the *qasida*, the Arabic poetic form, and developed the Arab-Hispanic-Romance form of poetry known as *zajal*, which is often sung.

Additional influence came from the Ottoman empire, reaching a peak in the sixteenth and seventeenth centuries. From the Ottomans the region received its rich tradition of oral narration and storytelling, particularly the *ortaoyuno*, an improvisational theater in the round, and the *karagoz,* a shadow puppet theater. By the eighteenth century Turkish popular culture had become firmly embedded in the tradition; itinerant poet troubadours accompanied by the stringed musical instrument, the *saz*, were common.

More recent influences have come from the French Colonial period in Algeria, Morocco, and Tunisia, spanning roughly the mid-1800s through the mid-1900s.

Morocco

The Kingdom of Morocco is the farthest west of the North African countries known as the Maghreb. Both ancient and modern theater traditions survive and flourish today in Morocco, specifically in the city of Marrakesh.

For those interested in modern theater, Marrakesh hosts many events, including the annual ten-day Festival National des Arts Populaires de Marrakech, a folklore festival of Moroccan music, theater, and dance. It draws performers from all over Morocco and is held in May or June on the grounds of El Badi Palace.

For those interested in experiencing more ancient theatrical traditions, Marrakesh is also home to the Magic Circles of Djemaa el-Fna. Beginning early every morning, circles—*halgah* in Moroccan Arabic—are formed of dozens or hundreds of onlookers. Performance theater is alive in each circle, and may include storytellers, snake charmers, dentists performing public extractions, or children paired in boxing matches. Especially popular is the street theater in which two or three individuals play-act freeform slapstick skits involving country Arabs and country Berbers, reiterating familiar stories that have endured for more than a millennium. As each evening ends, halgahs form around smaller entertainment groups that include dancers, singers, and drummers featuring trained monkeys.

Two writers who played central roles in fostering and expanding the Middle Eastern/North African theater tradition are Ahmad Tayyib al-Ilj (b. 1928), who successfully transferred Molière's *Tartuffe* as *Wali Alla* in 1968, and the renowned playwright, producer, and actor al-Tayyib al Siddiqui (b. 1938), who presented original plays that explore the older traditions of itinerant poets.[6]

Algeria

Founded by the French in 1838, this country became independent in 1962. Theater here flourished primarily during the nineteenth-century cultural renaissance and has produced a number of well-known playwrights.

Kateb Yacine (1929–89) wrote in French until the early 1970s, when he began to write his *theatre de combat* in the vernacular form of Arabic. His first play was *Le cadaver encercle*, a drama of colonization and alienation filled with surrealist imagery. Later works include *L'Homme aux sandals de cauotchouc*, a play that juxtaposes the French, Americans, and Vietnamese during their war in Vietnam, and *Mohammed, prends ta valise*, a play showing the class complicity between the French bourgeoisie and the Algerian bourgeoisie.[7]

Slimane Benaissa (b. 1943), playwright, actor, and director, lived in Algeria until 1993 when terrorist threats forced him to move to France. His more than a dozen plays and three novels focus on the world of political violence and religious intolerance, while he examines controversial topics such as terrorism, torture, Arab-Israeli relations, and the structures of women's dress in Arab countries.[8]

The importance of theater in Algeria can be illustrated by noting that in 2004, the town of El Eulma celebrated one century of municipal theater with a three-day celebration highlighting the town's colonial theater building, and launched a search for new local acting talent to appear in ongoing performances.

Tunisia

This central-Mediterranean country has been a melting pot of different civilizations for nearly three millennia, and has a rich cultural heritage. Tunisia made the earliest gestures in the region of establishing dramatic tradition. Several theater troupes were founded and performed regularly before independence in 1956, and in 1964 an Arab Theater Festival was established.[9]

Much of the theater activity in Tunisia can be credited to the government. The Ministry of Culture set up the National Theatre (the Palace of Kheireddine), regional drama centers in El Kef and Gafsa, and the National Puppet Center. The government is also intimately involved with the ongoing preservation of the ancient port city of Carthage, which is the site of many festivals. The well-preserved Roman amphitheater here is home to performances at the International Festival of Carthage (July) and the internationally known Carthage Drama Festival (November).

Regional theater workshops and smaller festivals abound. Hammamet's beautiful Dar Sebastian (House of Sebastian), located in the International Cultural Center, hosted a series of workshops in February and March 2006. The Constantine Regional Theatre brought together troupes from Africa, the Middle East, and Western Europe, which featured more than 70 theater shows and international symposia on theater and cultural dialogue. Fourteen Tunisian theater groups took part.[10]

Sudan

The ongoing civil war in this country has ravaged the population and already-skimpy resources available. Miraculously, in the midst of this chaos, there still exists a functional International Theatre Institute, whose project, "Theatre between the Frontiers," has been at work on both sides of the civil war. An ITI workshop discussed and studied various theater-related questions that need answers to provide a meaningful theater experience in Sudan. Among the topics: the role of theater in a radically polarized environment; the resistance of theater to manipulation and ideology; and the creation of necessary links to performance traditions in the country.

The tradition of using theater to ease the wounds of war goes back decades in Sudan. One of the best-known projects was Small World Theatre, started in the early 1980s. It used puppets to encourage social change and transmit cultural awareness. More recently, a March 2005 workshop sponsored by the Sudan Center for Theatre Research—*Playing Against (the) Weapon(s) Culture*—brought together more than 500 playwrights, dramatists, actors, NGO representatives, and peace activists to study the use of theater as a way to battle the increasing availability of small arms and other portable weapons.[11]

The use of theater to transmit important information—particularly in areas that have relatively low literacy rates—continues here. A theater work camp sponsored by the Intercultural Development Agency was held in July 2006. The two-week camp concentrated on HIV/AIDS prevention and care.[12]

A large UNICEF-supported children's rights project, *Theatre for Life— Sudan,* is working with community activists across the country to develop a nationwide network of children's theater groups. The first step is training activists in the principles of participatory theater as a means of researching such issues as child safety, conflict, individual and group rights, HIV/AIDS, and female genital mutilation. Once the activists are trained, they will return home and set up child-centered theater groups in their communities. It is hoped that as many as 450 of these can be created over time. The children are expected to be both the authors and the beneficiaries of this project. The children's groups will select topics of interest and use an open-ended forum theater style of improvisation to discuss and explore the topics. Group storytelling games will then generate a plot, leading to the creation of a play for presentation to the children's community. While the children learn basic theater and performance skills, it is hoped that the added prime program goals of community mobilization and child development will also be achieved.

EGYPT

With its ancient history, cosmopolitanism, strong Islamic traditions, modern pan-Arab political and intellectual history, and relative freedom, Egypt is the cultural capital of the Arab world.

Although it has struggled economically, the country is home to a very wide variety of theatrical productions, venues, and resources. Many other regions in the Arab world can thank Egyptian touring theater companies for helping to form their own local theater companies. Egyptian drama was among the first to successfully combine Western and Arabic literary traditions, owing to the work of two pioneers.

The first, Ahmad Shawqi (1868–1932), pioneered the modern Arabic literary movement, most notably by introducing the genre of poetic verse drama to the Arabic literary tradition. The second major pioneer, Tawfiq Al-Hakim (1898–1997), occupied the overarching role of sole founder of an entire literary tradition that made drama a respected Arabic literary genre. Prior to him, prose plays had been primarily lightweight comedy or farce, while verse had been used by such noted poets as Ahmad Shawqi for heroic drama. Al-Hakim, however, wrote only in prose—a flexible, high-quality prose, often interspersed with colloquial Arabic.

Al-Hakim won fame as a dramatist with *Ahl al-kahf* (1933) [The People of the Cave]. This play was ostensibly based on the story of the Seven Sleepers of Ephesus, but is in fact a study of the human struggle against time. This work introduced Al-Hakim's series of "dramas of ideas," or symbolism. They include *Shahrazad* (1934), based on *The Thousand and One Nights,* as well as the plays *Al-Malik Udib* (1939) [King Oedipus], *Pijmaliyun* (1942) [Pygmalion], and *Sulayman al-Hakim* (1934) [Solomon the Wise]. His output of more than fifty plays also includes many based on Egyptian social themes, such as *Sirr al-muntahirah* (1937) [The Secret of the Suicide Girl] and *Rusasah fi al-Qalb* (1944) [A Bullet in the Heart]. His boldest drama was the lengthy *Muhammad* (1936), which was not intended for performance. Other notable pre-revolutionary playwrights include Mahmad Taymur (1894–1973) and Ali Ahmad Bakathir (d. 1969).[13]

After the Egyptian Revolution of 1952, a new generation of playwrights emerged, including Numan Ashur (d. 1987), Alfred Faraj (b. 1929), and Yusef Idris (1927–91).[14]

Egypt is also home to the Cairo Opera House, one of the best-known and best-loved performance venues in this part of the world. The original Cairo Opera House was built in 1869 by Khedive Ismail, the ruler of Egypt, to celebrate the inauguration of the Suez Canal. When built it was considered "state of the art." Unfortunately, the 850-seat structure was constructed almost entirely of wood, and burned to the ground in 1971. In 1983 the Japanese government helped to fund and build an educational and cultural center on the grounds of the original opera house, and the New Cairo Opera House officially opened in October 1988. This new facility includes a 1,200-seat main theater, the 500-seat Small Hall, and the 600-seat Open Air Theatre. This complex also contains an art gallery, opera museum, and music library. It is home to the Cairo Symphony Orchestra, the Cairo Ballet Company, the Cairo Opera Company, the Cairo Opera Choir, and the National Arabic Music Ensemble, and hosts dozens of performances, workshops, and symposia of various types every year.

The oldest independent theatrical group in Egypt is El-Warsha, Arabic for "workshop." The group's creative process is largely driven by experimentation, an interest in diverse activities, and a team structure open equally to professionals, students, and workers. By the end of the 1980s the group had concentrated mostly on staging European dramas from the likes of Pinter, Kafka, and Handke. The group then turned to renewing ancient Egyptian traditions of performance—shadow puppets, storytelling, and stick-fighting (*tahtib*). More recently the group has been reviving classical tales from Upper Egypt. It has organized a drama festival in concert with a theatrical group from Amman, Jordan, and has begun the Arab Arts project, a network dedicated to improving communication and exchange among various arts and cultural groups in the region.[15]

The Experimental Theatre Festival, an annual event held every September in Egypt, provides an opportunity for new theatrical performances and ideas to be presented to the public. The ten-day event draws performers, playwrights, and other theater professionals from all over the world.

JORDAN

The Hashemite Kingdom of Jordan is a small country with limited natural resources, but Jordan's significance stems partly from its strategic location at the crossroads of what most Christians, Jews, and Muslims consider the Holy Land. At the beginning of the century, theater was produced in the form of historical and religious plays, including a number of translated ones. These plays were performed in schools and churches, in cities and villages, and in Bedouin zones.

Today Jordan is an active member of UNESCO's International Theatre Institute (ITI), and specializes in celebrating its theater through festivals. One of the most important is the annual Amman International Theatre Festival. First held in 1994, it runs for eight days in early April and features a variety of stage performances, workshops, meetings, and seminars. It is the only festival in the Middle East and North Africa organized by an independent theater company, Amman's Al Fawanees Theatre Company, which "provides a venue for artistic exchange among independent and experimental Arab troupes [and] aims to encourage alternatives to the present environment in which artists work in the Arab world."[16]

The Jerash Festival, held at the end of July and beginning of August in this extremely well-preserved ancient Roman city in the heart of the Levant, about 40 miles north of Amman, is unquestionably Jordan's liveliest and most spectacular cultural event. Begun in 1981 by Queen Noor Al-Hussein, the festival is the prime showcase for Jordanian performing artists, and features not only stage plays, but orchestra performances, ballet, handcrafts, and art shows as well.

Other festivals include the annual mid-December Jordan Theatre Festival, the biannual spring Youth Theatre Festival, and the Jordan Children's Festival that alternates biannually with the Arabian Song Festival.

A very popular tourist destination is the Roman Theater in Amman, located in the very center of Amman's old town area. This 6,000-seat stone theater was built between 169 and 177 CE, and was restored in 1957. The Odeon, a much smaller and better-preserved theater, is located next to the Roman theater. It was built in the early part of the second century. Theatrical productions are still mounted in both of these theaters.

ISRAEL

The division of the former British mandate of Palestine and creation of the state of Israel in the years after the end of World War II have been at the heart of Middle Eastern conflicts for the past half century. After the Nazi Holocaust, pressure grew for international recognition of a Jewish state, and in 1948 Israel came into being. Although it took some time to establish itself, theater in Israel today is energetic, abundant, and comparatively easy to find.

There are active theater departments in virtually all of Israel's major universities, including the University of Hasifa, Tel Aviv University, the Hebrew University of Jerusalem, and the Beit Zvi School of Drama. Together they account for dozens of productions and for the training of hundreds of actors and other theater professionals every year.

The Jerusalem Performing Arts Lab, founded in 2003 and headquartered in a large converted warehouse on the grounds of the old Jerusalem railroad station, nurtures an experimental framework that caters to both established and emerging artists. Its goal is to be at the very cutting edge of the performing arts. Project participants are selected from across the nation, and are provided with rehearsal space, a living stipend, production budgets, and professional guidance. The Performing Arts Lab's productions are staged on site before the public. An important aim of the Lab is to help participants establish collaborations and affiliations with such other groups as regional or international festivals, theaters, and artistic institutions. The Lab also sponsors performances in various disadvantaged neighborhoods to bring the message of theater to groups who might otherwise be denied it, and to bring members of lower socioeconomic groups to the complex. The organization also hosts school visits, and encourages children to participate in rehearsals and workshops.[17]

THEATER AND PERFORMANCE

Professional companies can be found in all of Israel's major cities, often associated with a large physical theater. Some of the best known are the Habimah National Theatre in Tel Aviv, which seats about 1,520 people in a three-hall complex, and the Cameri Theatre, established more than 60 years ago as Israel's first Hebrew-language repertory theater and now dubbed the "theater of social responsibility." Also in Tel Aviv are the Haifa Municipal Theatre, the Be'er Sheva Theatre, a Children's and Youth Theater, the Arab Theatre (a professional Arab-language theater), and the Gesher Theatre, founded in 1991 to provide an artistic outlet for new immigrants from the former Soviet Union.

The Acco Festival for Alternative Theatre is perhaps the best-known Israeli theatrical event, and is easily one of the most popular cultural events in the region. It began in 1979 and takes place in and around the ancient port overlooking Haifa bay, spilling over into the area's archeological sites and streets of the old city. The goal of the Acco Festival is to enable the performance of artistic composition seeking new, original, and alternative language of expression. The Festival for Alternative Theatre runs for five days during September or October. The 2005 festival featured more than 300 performances of forty productions covering a very wide swatch of theater, including stage and street theater, puppet theater, Arab plays, Arab-Jewish productions, and performance art. Many of the productions could be classified as experimental and provocative.

Another major Israeli theater event is the International Theater Workshop in Tel Aviv. Begun in 1998, this nearly three-week-long event in July draws world-renowned artists and teachers to conduct master classes and workshops for Israeli performance artists. The idea is to provide a creative environment situated outside the mainstream theatrical institutions, where new modes of artistic expression can be developed.

THE PALESTINIAN TERRITORIES

Theater in the Palestinian Territories has come to exemplify one of the goals of theater the world over and from all times: to entertain and educate. Much of the theater here is dedicated to either bringing enjoyment to the oppressed or keeping cultural awareness alive.

Before the 1948 war that followed the creation of the state of Israel there were many theater troupes in Jerusalem. However, after the war, Palestinian intellectuals moved to other Arab countries. Their departure, coupled with strict military censorship within Israel and (after 1967) in the Palestinian Territories, made highly problematic the founding of—let alone sustaining of—a theater tradition. The Palestinian playwrights who remained composed plays that relied on the symbolic power of the staged re-enactment of incidents of tyranny, cunning, and revolt. Plays included including the works *Thawrat al-zanj* [The Zanj Revolt] and *Shamsun wa-Daliah* [Samson and Delilah] by Muin Basisu (1927–84) and *Qarqash* by Samih al-Qasim (b. 1939).[18]

Adopting the Arabic word for "storyteller" as its name, the El-Hakawati Company was founded in 1977 and is based in East Jerusalem, the only Palestinian theater group to be formed in the Palestinian Territories. For the first six years of its existence, the six-person company had no permanent home, and operated from any temporary accommodation it could find and afford.

Nevertheless, El-Hakawati performed all over the West Bank, often bringing its audiences the first live theater they had ever experienced. The group staged its productions in refugee camps and towns and villages, using any available structure that could be adapted as a theater—school buildings, chambers of commerce offices, clubs—and when nothing else was to be found, they performed in the open air. In the manner of its storyteller precursors, El-Hakawati mixes contemporary events with Arab folklore in its dramatic projections of Palestinian identity. The group's productions, combining elements of mime, carnival allegory, and satire, are collective works of all the members, who may improvise, often extensively, in performance.[19] El-Hakawati became the first Palestinian theatrical group to become financially self-supporting, and its productions became world-renowned.

A good deal of Palestinian theater is directed to children, the group who are most seriously affected by the nearly constant political and social turmoil that has characterized this land for many decades. Nearly all theater is funded and carried out by private nongovernmental organizations.

For example, Ashtar is a nonprofit NGO established in Jerusalem in 1991, primarily as a theater training program oriented toward school students, with a secondary goal of bringing live theater to the public. In 1995 it expanded its activities and set up a second base in Ramallah. While many of its performances are on the stages of its own facilities, the organization routinely takes its shows on the road, delivering performances in the area's many very small villages and refugee camps. Its training component works with high schools and universities in a multilevel fashion to bring theater knowledge to both students and teachers. It organizes drama training workshops and starts drama clubs in the schools, and works to create productions that the students can present. Ashtar also runs a comprehensive training program for teachers that treats drama as an important part of the school curriculum, and develops various theater skills alongside the theater training program, holding courses in lighting, set, makeup, and costume design.[20]

The Popular Theatre in Palestine Project, on the West Bank and in Gaza, is a unit of the U.S. humanitarian organization CARE. It is used as a development tool to promote a more civil society and emphasizes individual and community rights.

The Palestinian National Theatre, in Jerusalem, produces and presents educational, artistic, and entertainment programs that attempt to reflect the aspirations of the Palestinian people. Created in 1984 by El-Hakawati Theatre Company, it works to upgrade and rekindle interest in the arts at the national level by preserving Palestinian culture and folklore while actively searching for new ideas and innovation in Palestinian self-expression. The organization concentrates on programs and presentations oriented to children and youth. One of the best-known of these targeted activities is the International Puppet Festival, held annually for more than a decade. The Festival includes not only professional performances, but also workshops and puppet plays that allow children and young people to actively participate in this unique form of theatre.[21]

Al-Kasaba Theatre and Cinematheque, established in 1970 in Jerusalem and physically located in Ramallah, is dedicated to enhancing the cultural exchange between local, Arab, and international cultures. The theater hosts performances and training, and creates and produces its own theatrical works. It is widely regarded as having the only professional-grade, fully equipped, multipurpose venue in the entire Palestinian Territories. The larger of its two halls seats more than 370 people and has a 12 × 14–meter stage. The smaller hall seats up to 300 and has a 12 × 10–meter stage. The facility also includes a 100-square-meter gallery and meeting hall that accommodates workshops and seminars.[22]

The Freedom Theatre is dedicated to providing live theater and other cultural activities to the children of the Jenin refugee camp. The theater was originally begun in 1987 by the Israeli Arna Mer Khamis, and was generously funded through her Right Livelihood ("Alternative Nobel") award in 1993. The theater was destroyed in 2002 during fighting with Israeli armed forces, and was reconstructed in 2005. The project aims to provide children a safe, secure environment in which to temporarily adopt the roles of others, to discover through theater arts their own internal feelings and to open up perspectives and new possibilities.[23]

LEBANON

Bordered by Syria and Israel, since 1991 Lebanon has made steady progress toward rebuilding its political institutions and regaining national sovereignty after the end of a devastating 16-year civil war. Before the civil war the tradition of theater in Lebanon was alive and well with the 1960 founding of the National Theatre. In the decade that followed, a number of troupes emerged, including those of Munir Abu Dibs, Roger Assaf, and the Rahbani Brothers (greatly aided in the performance of their operettas by the spectacularly beautiful voice of the world-famous singer, Fayruz).

Although the civil war largely destroyed theater in Lebanon, it had begun a resurrection when, in February 2005, the assassination of former Prime Minister Rafik Hariri threatened to throw the country into turmoil again. Fortunately this did not happen. While theater is still not fully reestablished in Lebanon, it has a good foothold and is reemerging as a powerful cultural force.

There are now a number of theater festivals held in the country, and as stability returns, many more are expected to appear. The Baalbeck International Festival, in July and August, is held in the massive complex of Roman temples in this ancient city, and includes theater performances, musical events, and opera. The Ayloul Festival Forum, held every two years in September, is an experimental multimedia contemporary arts festival in Beirut that features cutting-edge plays and exhibits.

Although the small town of Freikeh is not well-known, even to Lebanese, it is gaining a reputation for its annual (September) Freikeh Festival of Theatre, Visual Arts, and Cinema. The festival offered one of the country's very few avant-garde theater companies before the civil war, and the current festival is reviving that tradition.

The Al Bustan Festival, held in Beirut every February and March, includes more than 30 performances of theatre, opera, dance, and concerts over a five-week period. In some years it also includes puppet theater performances.

The Al Madina Theatre, established in 1994, grew from the drive and dream of well-known Lebanese actress Nidal al Achkar, who spearheaded the effort to reconstruct and reopen the old Saroulla Cinema in the heart of the pre–civil war Hamra district, once Beirut's premiere theater and café area. After years of effort, al Achkar finally succeeded in restoring the stately old building, which now is home to a professional theater company. The Al Madina Theatre hosts numerous Arabic, French, and English productions, from both the classic and modern repertory.

Lebanon has long prided itself on being at the edge of the movement to fight conservatism in theater, and as the society continues to stabilize, more and more plays are being presented dealing with very controversial subjects. Two recent plays serve as examples. *Women's Talk,* inspired by American Eve Ensler's *The Vagina Monologues,* adds other important topics such as rape, domestic violence, and sexual harassment, which Arab women are discouraged from discussing in public. Another play, *The Secret Life of the Woman,* deals primarily with women's right to express their sexual desires and needs. Both plays featured strong, direct language uncommon in Lebanon. Both enjoyed considerable success.

Particular mention must be made of two important Lebanese artists who composed significant works. Within the émigré (mahjar) environment of the United States, Mikhail Nuaymah (1889–1975) published *Al-Aba wa-al-banun* (1916) [Fathers and Sons], a play set within the Christian Lebanese community. Another contributor to the literary tradition of Lebanese drama is the renowned symbolist poet, Said Aql (b. 1912), who is clearly reflecting his well-known concern with the Phoenician aspect of Lebanese nationalism in composing a verse drama on the theme of Qadmus (1944).[24]

SYRIA

This country of nearly 20 million people shares borders with Turkey, Israel, Lebanon, Jordan, and Iraq, and has a theater tradition dating to Roman times. It claims to have the world's oldest continuously inhabited city, Damascus. Syria offers theatrical resources on many levels. It features one of the oldest performance arts in the world, one of the best preserved Roman theaters in the area, active festivals, and internationally noted playwrights and artists.

A performance art form, once believed to have virtually died out in Syria, is now staging a modest comeback. *Al-Hakawati* is a Syrian term for an expert storyteller who combines the additional arts of the poet, comedian, historian, and actor. The root is *hikayah*, a fable or story, or *haka*, to tell a story. The term *wati* implies expertise in a popular street art. The hakawati has analogues in Egypt—the *sha'ir*—and in Iraq, where the storyteller is known as *qisa khown*. The storyteller's performance is simple yet powerful. There is no stage, no curtain, no special lighting. Usually the storyteller is just an older man facing a crowd in the café, reading a book. The story is usually one of the popular heroic epics from Arab history—tales of the Ethiopian invasion or of the Hilal tribe's eleventh-century migration from Arabia across North Africa are common. Readings can last an hour or more, and are often accompanied by shouts and encouraging comments from members of the audience who are intimately familiar with the tale being told. Serial readings that run several days are common. This unusual form of performance art may yet die out, although a few examples still endure in the coffeehouses of Damascus.[25]

One of the best preserved Roman theaters in the world is at Bosra, 140 kilometers south of Damascus. Unlike many other Roman theaters, typically built into hillsides, the one at Bosra is freestanding. When it was in use, the structure was faced with marble and draped in silk. During performances the audience of 15,000 was sprayed with perfumed mist to keep them cool and comfortable. A fortress and moat built around the theater—probably during the Omayyad and Abbasid periods—defended and protected it, and account for its excellent state of preservation today.

The theater at Palmyra, although not as well preserved as the one at Bosra, is also worth noting. Built around the second century CE, it accommodates far fewer patrons and features a marketplace and banquet hall as part of the site. Much of the column-lined original main street of the settlement—the Great Colonnade—is still intact.

The career of the pioneer Syrian dramatist, actor, and troupe manager, Abu Khalil al-Qabbani (1841–1902) illustrates the repression experienced in Syria during the Renaissance. In the early 1870s he was encouraged by the Ottoman governor Subhi Pasha and later by the famous reformer Midhat Pasha (1822–83), to put on some plays inspired by the tales of Harun al-Rashid, found in the *Thousand and One Nights*. The conservative religious establishment in Damascus, already deeply suspicious of the permissibility and probity of this new medium, was aroused to a fury by the appearance on stage of Harun al-Rashid, the caliph in disguise. A decree from Istanbul soon ordered the theater to close, and al-Qabbani and his troupe moved to Egypt.[26] Syrian theater critics such as Sharif Khazandar see the beginning of contemporary Syrian drama occurring with the foundation of the National Theater Troupe in 1958.

Another internationally recognized Syrian playwright is Sadallah Wannous (1940–96), who for many years directed the nation's Music and Theatre Administration. He began his career as playwright in the early 1960s, authoring several one-act plays. Even this early work illustrates Wannous's fundamental theme: the relationship between the individual and society and its various authorities. This focus later expanded to the possibilities of resistance and the chances that an individual might have to successfully stand up to governmental oppression in the corrupt political environment of the Arab world as Wannous saw it. He wrote numerous plays—all exploring the basic themes noted above—and many with an experimental feel not unlike the work of Bertolt Brecht. Wannous has also been compared to leaders of documentary theater such as Weiss. He often used the ancient hakawati storytelling form from nineteenth-century Syria, to which Arab audiences passionately related. Some of Wannous's best-known works are *Night Party for June 5* (1968), his first political play; *The Rape* (1990), and *Mirage Epic* (1996), his last play. He is credited with originating the idea for an Arab Festival for Theatre Arts, in 1969. This concept was later realized in Damascus and continues to this day. Wannous died in 1996 of cancer.[27] Other prominent Syrian playwrights include Muhammad al-Maghut (b. 1934), Walid Ikhlasi (b. 1935), and Mamduh Adwan (b. 1941).[28]

The Damascus Theatre Festival, a biannual ten-day event in the capital, is coordinated by the country's Ministry of Culture. Although some performances are given in the northern city of Aleppo, most activity occurs in the Damascus opera house, a complex that stretches over more than 45,000 square meters to include the National Theatre House and the High Institute for Theatre and Music Studies. A typical season includes fifteen to twenty plays by both Arab and foreign troupes, and seminars, lectures, and workshops for actors, playwrights, and other theater professionals.

The Spring Children's Theatre Festival is a new addition to the theater life of Damascus. As with other Syrian festivals, it is supervised by the Ministry of Culture. Syrian playwrights are being encouraged to create plays directed toward children and to work with the Ministry to produce these works.

IRAQ

Appearing during the Hellenistic period (fourth century to second century BCE), village theater and storytelling were the earliest forms of theater in this area now know as Iraq. In the 1920s and 1930s, Egyptian theater troupes generated interest in theater beyond the traditional religious and historic plays. Theater of the modern era owes a great deal to Yusuf al-Ani (b. 1927) and Haqqi al-Shibli (1913–85). Shibli studied in Egypt before returning to found his own troupe.[29]

The state of theater in this beleaguered country is currently scattered at best, and nearly nonexistent at worst. Since the 2003 invasion by U.S.-led forces and the fall of Saddam Hussein, theater has taken a back seat to survival for most Iraqis.

As Iraqi actor Ahmed Janabi, noted in a September 2005 interview with Al Jazeera, "It is well-known that Iraq is still suffering from the absence of basic services and security. That definitely has paralyzed theatre. How can we work without lights? How can we expect people to come to [the] theatre when they do not have petrol for their cars? How can we expect people to risk their lives coming to [the] theatre?"[30]

When asked to predict the role of Iraqi artists in years to come, Janabi said: "Stories of what happened to our country in the last two years will keep the Iraqi artists busy for decades to come. The mission of Iraqi artists is to support their people's rise. We are living in a time of great disappointment. We hoped for a better life but we have got nothing but bitterness, suffering and pain. The artists, I believe, are facing a significant mission, as they have to be an active component of their society, working together with their fellow Iraqis to restore security and peace of mind in order to be able to carry on.... [But] we are looking forward to a better working environment for Iraqi artists."[31]

Theater is a strong drive, however, and even in the chaotic conditions of Baghdad, it finds a way to survive, if not thrive. In mid-April 2006, the Happy Family Children's Theatre Group managed to hold an 11-day variety show featuring many young actors and dancers. Hundreds of families—men, women, and children—enjoyed this children's theater extravaganza, braving the nearly continuous assaults and bloodshed common in today's Baghdad.

Iraq once had a strong cultural tradition of live theatre. It will return.

IRAN

Known as Persia until 1935, Iran was one of the greatest empires of the ancient world. Its individual identity has been maintained for a very long time within the Islamic world by retaining its own language and adhering to the Shia tradition of Islam.

Religious tradition is very important in Iran. An important part of this religious tradition is the *Taziya*, (sometimes given as "Taziyeh"), the Islamic drama of Iran. This complex dramatic form has its roots in many areas, including Zoroastrianism, Mithraism, mythology, folklore, and the more traditional forms of Iranian entertainment. Hundreds of Taziya dramas have been written since the form was first recorded in the mid-1800s. The main plot of them all concerns the suffering and death of Imam Hussein, the grandson of Muhammad, the Prophet of Islam. Hussein and his family were slaughtered on the plain of Kerbala near Baghdad in 680 CE by soldiers of the caliph, Yazid. This is the seminal event in all Taziya theater; which is essentially the drama of mourning.

Performances of the Taziya can be found throughout Iran, given by both professional troupes and amateurs. Many small towns and villages have built *hoseinieh*—special buildings

PUPPET THEATER

Puppet theater is one of those magical styles of live theater that is difficult to perform and perhaps even more difficult to find. Yet puppet theatre is very much alive and well in Iran, and has been for a very long time. This unusual art form is widely known and performed in the country, and is officially supported at the highest levels of the Iranian government. In early 2004 the Iranian Institute for Intellectual Development of Children and Young Adults approved a comprehensive plan to increase the understanding and development of this unique art form. The plan calls for upgrading the knowledge of art teachers through workshops and the creation of professional theater centers in various part of the country; the production of educational texts; the inauguration of traveling performance groups and workshops; and the development of both short- and longer-term programs to expose more Iranians to puppet theater. For many years an Iranian has served on the governing board of the International Marionette Union. The University of Tehran offers a popular Bachelor of Arts degree in Puppet Theater.

For nearly twenty-five years, Iran has hosted the International Puppet Festival. Held every two years in September in the capital city of Tehran, this week-long celebration of puppet theater includes many dozens of performances, workshops, guest speakers, and small conferences, all staffed and attended by puppet aficionados from around the world, all dedicated to the understanding and advancement of this unique mode of performance theater. Hundreds of submissions are judged early in the year; the competition to appear and perform at this well-known festival is intense.

dedicated to these performances during the month of Muharram, the first month of the Islamic calendar. The ninth and tenth days of this month are especially important, when performances may last all day. Ashura—the tenth day of Muharram—is the anniversary of the death of Imam Hussein.

Although Taziya is often viewed more as mourning than as theater by spectators and participants, the form has many theatrical conventions. Players do not normally memorize their roles, relying instead on *tumer*—handheld script about eight inches long and two inches wide. Parts are not presented in a common script as they are in Western theater. Rather, the players work from cues on their individual script. The so-called good characters (the ones on the side of Imam Hussein) chant their lines in classical Persian musical modes, and dress in green. The "bad" characters simply say their lines and dress in red. Men dressed in black with veiled faces play the roles of women. There are usually a number of roles for children, all of whom dress in black but are unveiled, whether they play male or female characters.[32]

Tehran also hosts a major theater festival every year, the Fajr Theatre Festival, usually at the end of January. Now entering its twenty-fifth year, this ten-day event typically receives between 150 and 200 submissions from more than fifty-five countries, and includes plays performed both on stage and on the street. The 2005 festival, as an example, featured troupes from Iran, Germany, The Netherlands, Japan, Romania, Switzerland, Spain, France, Hungary, Slovenia, and the Russian Federation. More than seventy foreign drama groups participated in the 2005 event. The festival historically draws 5,000 to 10,000 people per day.

BAHRAIN

Arguably the most Westernized of the oil-rich Persian Gulf countries, Bahrain has a small but thriving theater scene. With a population of fewer then 800,000, many of them Westerners, theater here flourishes in the Western tradition, often performed in European as well as Arabic languages.

Bahrain is often the host country for the Gulf Theatre Festival, a large regional theater gathering that has prospered since its inception in 1997. The eight-day 2006 Festival, which began in late January, was held in the Bahrain Art Amphitheatre. The annual event drew more than 200 participants from Persian Gulf drama groups representing Bahrain, Saudi Arabia, the United Arab Emirates (UAE), Kuwait, and Iraq, among others. In addition to plays, the Festival featured workshops and seminars on lighting, staging, costumes, and other subjects.

The country also hosts a cooperative venture with France every year. Among the many events included are musical performances and workshops, poetry readings, movie festivals, and a week-long workshop on theater practices in collaboration with the Bahrain Director of Theatre. A number of plays are performed during this workshop, in both Arabic and French.

KUWAIT

The National Council for Culture, Arts, and Letters (NCCAL), founded by the Kuwaiti government in 1973, is responsible for enhancing the arts, stimulating interest in them, and encouraging research and development in those areas in the country. The Council supervises the publication of a number of books dedicated to various aspects of the arts, including *World Theatre, World Culture,* and several others. The Higher Institute for Theatrical Arts exists to provide special facilities and support for Kuwaiti actors, dancers, and musicians.[33]

Examples of Kuwaiti writers who are nurtured by the Institute include Saqr al-Rashud and Abd al-aziz Surayyi.[34]

Kuwait has a long history of amateur theater, dating to the first amateur plays performed in 1922. There are a number of active theater groups in the country, including the Kuwaiti Players, which presents about ten productions a year. The Kuwaiti Little Theatre, established in 1948 in Ahmadi, was virtually destroyed by the 1990 invasion by Iraq, but has since reconstituted itself and is back to producing several full-scale musicals and dramas every year, in addition to presenting its traditional pantomime show at the end of the year.

QATAR

This small Persian Gulf country has an active theater community, thanks in large part to the Qatari National Council for Culture, Arts, and Heritage. This autonomous body has an independent budget whose focus is the sponsorship and support of a very wide variety of arts for the country. The Culture and Arts Department of the Council is directly concerned with theater. The Department supports theatrical works performed by private troupes, hosts scholars of Arab theater who give lectures and workshops, sends trainees to attend courses abroad, and encourages academic studies of theater.

Perhaps best-known of the Department's troupes are the highly respected Doha Players. Begun in 1954, this amateur group is made up largely of expatriates employed by the oil industry. Until 1979 they performed only a few productions a year, always in borrowed space. A gift of land from the Emir, along with prodigious fundraising, allowed the organization to build its own theater, and to expand it in 1985. On March 19, 2005, a suicide car bomber rolled into the theater compound in the middle of a *Twelfth Night* performance and detonated himself. The explosion largely destroyed the theater and associated buildings, killed the play's director, and injured many more. The Players regrouped, and in December 2005 they performed their annual pantomime production, this time at the National Theatre. Productions of *The Importance of Being Earnest* and *Oliver!* were scheduled for the first half of 2006.[35]

The Qatar National Theatre was inaugurated in 1982 as the state's official theater, which seats about 550 people. In 2004 the government of Qatar launched a full-scale renovation of the facility. The structure itself was generally kept intact, but stage, engineering, lighting, sound, electrical, and most other systems were completely gutted and brought up to twenty-first-century standards. A complete portable, professional-quality video system was added, which allows productions to be not only completely recorded, but also broadcast live by Qatar TV.

The annual Eid al Fitr Festival in October, which celebrates a traditional Muslim holiday, encompasses five days of theater plays, street performances, pantomime, comedy theater, high-wire and "living statue" acts, musical acts, and much more.

UNITED ARAB EMIRATES (UAE)

This is a federation comprising six states that merged in 1971 to form the UAE: Abu Dhabi, Ajman, Al Fujayah, Ash Shariqah, Dubai, and Umm al Qaywayn. The UAE population of about 2.6 million enjoys a per capita income roughly equal to that of leading Western European nations, largely because of the federation's oil revenue.

Most of the limited theater activity in the UAE is centered on Dubai. The Dubai Drama Group, a very active amateur company in existence since 1974, has produced and staged well over 100 productions, including Shakespeare's *Henry V* and *Merchant of Venice,* Agatha Christie plays including *Witness for the Prosecution* and *Black Coffee,* classics such as *The Importance of Being Earnest* and *Lysistrata,* and traditional year-end pantomime shows. A typical season may have as many as four productions.

Dubai's first purpose-built community theater (the first of its kind in the Gulf region), the Dubai Community Theatre and Arts Centre (DUCTAC), was begun in 2004 and opened in early 2006. It is built on the roof of the Mall of the Emirates and will likely become the center of culture for Dubai and the entire region. It consists of a 550-seat, two-level theater; a flexible-seat studio theater for an audience of 150; rehearsal space for plays and various types of dance; a music school; an art gallery, library, and café; and sixteen studios and classrooms for art, theater, sculpture, photography, creative writing, calligraphy, and pottery. The $6.5 million project has largely been funded through donations.

SAUDI ARABIA

One of the most devout and insular countries in the Middle East, Saudi Arabia has emerged from underdeveloped desert kingdom to become one of the wealthiest nations in the region, owing to vast oil resources.

There is no officially sanctioned theater in this country. It is remotely possible that there could exist an "underground" theater, but given the country's political and social conditions, it is difficult to imagine how that theater could survive.

OMAN

It is a goal in Oman to keep ancient traditions alive while nurturing new talent. The policy of the Sultan of Oman is to "protect the Sultanate's heritage for future generations, develop new talent in the arts, and promote Oman's attractions to the outside world."[36] Official government statistics in 2005 indicated 50 to 75 professionals, 100 to 125 practitioners, and 100 to 150 amateurs were active in Omani theater arts. Those active in theater arts included actors, directors, writers, critics, and various stage professionals.[37]

Encouragement is given to the theater to focus on social issues, developing the talents of young graduates and theater-lovers. Government guidelines issued in 1996 created a number of theater groups across the sultanate. The impressive Falaij Theatre near Barka is a UNESCO-assisted project. Muscat theater groups include Al Sahwa Theatre Group, Muscat Free Theatre Group, Majan Artists' Theatre Group, Thought and Art Theatre Group, Al Ahli Theatre Group, and Modern Arts Theatre Group. The three main theatre groups in Dhofar are the Salalah Theatrical Arts Group, the Ubar Theatre, and the Land of Frankincense Theatre Group.[38]

The country sponsors the Omani Theatre Festival every two years, which has become a major cultural event for the country. This nine-day event features a number of stage performances, competitions of various types, critical reviews, workshops, and seminars. Awards are presented to the best actor, best actress, best producer, and best scriptwriter, and for the best setting in a ceremony at the conclusion of the festival.

In 1999 the Omani government, with help from UNESCO, converted the 230-year-old Felaij Castle to a cultural center, featuring state-of-the-art lighting and acoustics for its 500-seat open-air theater, and an opera stage with revolving mobile tower. The theater, just 40 minutes from Muscat, has since become a major draw for Omani tourism, and allows many different types of performances to be staged, including plays, operas, ballet, and musical attractions, among others.

YEMEN

Yemen, a country of about 22 million, is bordered by Saudi Arabia, Oman, the Red Sea, and the Arabian Sea/Gulf of Aden. It is one of the poorest countries of the Arab world. At this writing in mid-2006, Yemen is on many nations' security watch list, and travel to and within Yemen is strongly discouraged by many countries in North America, Europe, and Asia. It has a reputation as a very dangerous place.

Although the country has a theater tradition dating back several thousand years, and is the birthplace of the world's oldest written story—the Epic of Gilgamesh—there has been little active theater in Yemen in recent times, and there is some indication that theater may be officially discouraged.

The Social Health Assessment, Research, and Education (SHARE) Institute, a nongovernmental organization working in the region, uses theater to inform the public about the negative health aspects of female genital mutilation. The Ebhar Foundation, another NGO, has launched an initiative called the "Portable Doll Theatre for Children." This traveling doll theater is being used to combat domestic violence against children.[39]

RESOURCE GUIDE

PRINT RESOURCES

Allen, Roger. *An Introduction to Arabic Literature.* Cambridge, England: Cambridge University Press, 2000.

Chalala, Elie. "Farewell to Sadallah Wannous, Noted Arab Playwright." *Al Jadid.* 3.18 (May 1997). http://www.aljadid.com/theatre/FarewelltoSadallahWannousaNotedArabPlaywright.html.

Landau, Jacob, M. *Studies in the Arab Theater and Cinema.* Oxford, England: Oxford University Press, 1958.

The Middle East Journal, published quarterly by the Middle East Institute, http://www.mideasti.org/programs/programs_journal.html.

Yousif, Salaam. "The People's Theater of Yusuf Al-Ani." *Arab Studies Quarterly* (ASQ), 19 (1997).

Zuhur, Sherifa, ed. *Colors of Enchantment: Theater, Dance, Music, and the Visual Arts of the Middle East.* Cairo: American University in Cairo Press, 2001.

WEBSITES

al-hakawati. Accessed May 15, 2006. http://www.al-hakawati.net. This Website tells the story of Arab culture through folk and fairy tales; biographies of Arab personalities and artists; and features on the arts, architecture, history, countries and their cities, nature and the environment, and traditions of the Arab world.

Allen, Roger. "Drama." *An Introduction to Arabic Literature.* Cambridge University Press. http://arabworld.nitle.org/texts.php?module_id=7&reading_id=41&sequence=1.

Arab World. http://arabworld.nitle.org. The Al-Musharaka Initiative of the National Institute for Technology and Liberal Education (NITLE) developed this site with funds from the Andrew W. Mellon Foundation. It is intended to serve as a resource for all who would develop a better understanding of the Arab world. The principal intended audience consists of students, faculty, staff, and alumni of the liberal arts colleges served by NITLE, although the site is open to all visitors. A relevant section of the site is a reproduction of the famous play by Syrian playwright Sadallah Wannous,

THEATER AND PERFORMANCE

The King Is the King (Al-Malik huwa al-Malik) with an introduction by Roger Allen. Another is a 2002 essay by Deborah Foloran, "The Oral Narrator: Oral Narrating and Performing Traditions on the History of Modern Middle Eastern and Maghrebian Theater and Drama," NITLE, July 10, 2006.

Israeli Theatre. Departments of Theatre and Theatre Schools, University of Haifa. http://research.haifa.ac.il/~theatre/links.html.

Sandak, Moti. *All About Jewish Theatre.* A Website to promote and enhance Jewish Theatre and performing arts worldwide. http://www.jewish-theatre.com/.

VIDEOS/FILMS

Deadly Currents. (film, 1997). Directed by Simcha Jacobovici; produced by CITY-TV, The Ontario Film Development Corporation, Téléfilm. A documentary about the history of the conflict between Jews and Arabs over the lands of the Middle East, focusing on the intifadah. The film's attempt to give meaningful form to violence and confusion is mirrored in interspersed performances by dancers, theater groups, protest singers, and a remarkable street performer.

EVENTS

Acco Festival for Alternative Theatre: Haifa. Ticket agencies: Main distributor: Graber 04-8384777; Haifa box-office 04-8662244; Tel Aviv – Castel 03-6045000. http://www.accofestival.co.il/home_eng.html.

Amman International Theatre Festival, P.O. Box 850749, Amman 11185, Jordan. Tel-Fax: 009626 5857353. E-mail: aitf@nol.com. Website: http://www.arabttc.org/our_partners.html. Held annually in April

Ayloul Festival Forum, Theatre Al-Madina: Clemenceau, near Downtown Beirut. Phone: +961 (0) 3 75 02 85. Fax: +961 (0) 1 34 70 31. E-mail: ayloul@cyberia.net.lb. Website: http://guides.hotelbook.com/sisp/index.htm?fx=event.detail&event_id=38894. Held annually in September.

Baalbeck International Festival. Baalbeck, Jordan. http://www.baalbeck.org.lb/. Held annually in July/August.

Carthage Theatre Days Festival. Tel: (21617) 843 856. Fax: (21617) 285 342. Email: CNCC@Email.ati.tn. Website: www.jtcfestival.com.tn. An Arab-African international festival organized in Tunis once every two years to present theater performances, it includes a competition, seminars, and exhibitions.

Experimental Theatre Festival: Cairo, 12 Gomhuriya St. (Gomhuriya Theatre), Cairo. Phone: +20 2 391 3956. Website: http://uk.holidaysguide.yahoo.com/p-travelguide-36825-action-describe-experimental_theatre_festival_cairo-i. Held annually in September

Fajr Theater Festival: Tehran. Website: www.theater.ir. Held annually at the end of January, this ten-day event typically has 150–200 submissions from more than fifty-five countries and includes both stage and street play performances.

Freikeh Festival, Freikeh Beit-Chabab. Phone: +961 (0) 3 40 50 88. Website: http://guides.hotelbook.com/sisp/index.htm?fx=event&event_id=38538. Festival of avant-garde theatre, cinema, and the visual arts, held annually in September.

International Festival of Carthage: Carthage: Email:info@tourismtunisia.com. Phone: 216 1 731 332. Held annually in July/August.

Jerash Festival, Jerash, Jordan. http://www.jerashfestival.com.jo/. Held annually at the end of July and beginning of August

ORGANIZATIONS

AL-JANA/The Arab Resource Center For Popular Arts, P.O. Box: 114/5017, UNESCO Beirut 1108 2010, Lebanon. Tel./Fax: (009611) 8199970, Cell: 3-839917. E-mail: arcpa@cyberia.net.lb. Website: www.oneworld.org/al-jana. Al Jana is a registered, nonprofit Lebanese NGO involved in the promotion of active learning and creative expression, working with low-income communities in Lebanon.

Arab Education Forum. Regional Office: 32 Shaker Bin Zeid St., Shmeisani, Amman, Jordan. P.O. Box 926701 Amman 11190. Tel.: 962 6 5694861. Fax: 962 6 5694862. Mobile: 962 79 5618889. Email: aeforum@go.com.jo. Website: www.almoultaqa.com. The Arab Education Forum is a project that aims to develop a network among original and inspiring educational and community initiatives in the Arab world that are rooted in the culture.

The Arab Theatre Training Center, 850749 Amman, 11185 Jordan. E-mail: info@arabttc.org. Website: http://www.arabttc.org. The Arab Theatre Training center is an offshoot of the Arab Project for Theatre and Arts.

Darat Al Funun. Jabal Aluwaibdeh, Amman, Jordan, P.O. Box: 910406. Phone: 962 6 4643251/2. Fax: 4643253. E-mail: darat@cyberia.jo. Website: www.daratalfunun.org. Darat Al Funun is a home for the arts and the artists of Jordan and the Arab world.

High Institute for Theatre and Cultural Animation, Charia Al Mansour, Addahbi – B.P.1355, Rabat, Morocco. Tel.: 212-7-72.17.02. Fax: 212-7-70.34.23.

The International Theatre Institute (ITI), UNESCO, 1 rue Miollis, 75732 Paris CEDEX 15 France. http://www.iti-worldwide.org/index.php?lang=en. An international non-governmental organization (NGO), founded in Prague in 1948 by UNESCO and the international theatre community.

Makan, Jabal Luweibdeh, Nadim Mallah St. P.O. Box 317, 11821 Amman, Jordan. Tel.: 4631969–0795588393. Fax: 5921980. E-mail: ola@makanhouse.net. Makan is a cultural house founded for the purpose of showcasing contemporary art in its various forms, by providing a space for expression and interaction among young emerging artists in Jordan.

Masrah Al-Madina, Clemenceau St., Beirut, Lebanon. Tel.: 01-371963/4. Fax: 01-347104. E-mail: masmad@cyberia.net.lb. Website: www.almadina-theater.com.

Middle East Institute, 1761 N Street, NW, Washington, DC 20036-2882. http://www.mideasti.org/index.html. Since 1946 the Middle East Institute has been an important conduit of information between Middle Eastern nations and American policymakers, organizations, and the public.

Palestine National Theater. Email: info@pnt-pal.org. Website: http://www.pnt-pal.org/. A Palestinian nonprofit cultural institution in Jerusalem.

Young Arab Theatre Fund, 19 Square Sainctelette, 1000 Brussels, Belgium. E-mail: tfetouh@yatfund.org; tfetouh@hotmail.com. Website: http://www.yatfund.org/. YATF is a production fund to assist young, independent directors and theater groups.

NOTES

1. Landau 1958 (in Resource Guide), pp. ix–x.
2. Ibid., 6.
3. Allen 2000 (in Resource Guide).
4. Landau 1958 (in Resource guide), p. 3.
5. See *World Theater Directory*, UNESCO, July 8, 2006, http://www.iti-worldwide.org/amt/index.php
6. Allen, "Drama: Recent Trends Elsewhere in the Arab World," in *An Introduction to Arabic Literature* (in Resource Guide).
7. See *Books and Writers*, "Kateb Wacine" April 21, 2006, http://www.kirjasto.sci.fi/kateb.htm.
8. See Benaissa, *Contemporary African Data Base*, May 1, 2006, people.africadatabase.org/en/person/15213.html.
9. Allen, "Drama: The Magrib," in *An Introduction to Arabic Literature* (in Resource Guide).
10. See Tunisia On-Line News, "Theater Workshops in Hammamet Promote Cultural Exchange," http://www.tunisiaonlinenews.com/mars06/060306-1.html.
11. See "Small World Theater Sudan," May 12, 2006, http://smallworld.org.uk/sudan.htm.
12. See Kabissa, "IDA Announces Two International Theater Work Camps," May 13, 2006, http://www.kabissa.org/members/theater_work_camp.html.
13. Allen, "Drama: The Achievements of Tawfiq al-Hakim" in *An Introduction to Arabic Literature* (in Resource Guide).

14. Ibid.
15. See Culturebase.net, http://www.culturebase.net/artist.php?44.
16. See http://www.alfawaneesw.com/program12.htm (accessed April 30, 2006).
17. See *Jewish Theater*, "The Performing Arts Lab Launched in Jerusalem," http://www.jewish-theatre.com/visitor/article_display.aspx?articleID=171 (accessed April 3, 2006).
18. Allen, "Syria, Lebanon, and Palestine" in *An Introduction to Arabic Literature* (in Resource Guide).
19. See "El-Hakawati on Stage," *Saudi Aramco World*, http://www.saudiaramcoworld.com/issue/198806/el-hakawati.on.stage.htm (accessed May 14, 2006).
20. See "ASHTAR for Theater and Training," http://www.ashtar-theatre.org/about/about.html (accessed May 12, 2006).
21. See PNT: Palestine National Theater, http://www.pnt-pal.org/insidepages.php?action=fullnews&id=140 (accessed April 30, 2006).
22. Al Kasaba Theatre and Cinematheque, http://www.alkasaba.org (accessed May 13, 2006).
23. See "The Freedom Theater,"http://www.thefreedomtheatre.org.
24. Allen, "Syria Lebanon and Palestine" in *An Introduction to Arabic Literature* (in Resource Guide).
25. Barbara Nimri Aziz, "The Last Hakawati," *Aramco World*, http://www.arabicnews.com/ansub/Daily/Day/041118/2004111807.html.
26. Allen, "Beginnings in Syria and Egypt." in *An Introduction to Arabic Literature* (in Resource Guide).
27. Chalala. 1997 (in Resource Guide).
28. Allen, "Syria Lebanon and Palestine," *An Introduction to Arabic Literature* (in Resource Guide).
29. Allen, "Iraq and Gulf Sates," in *An Introduction to Arabic Literature* (in Resource Guide).
30. See Ahmed Janabi, "Iraqi Actor Hopes for Theatre's Revival," *Occupation Magazine*, http://www.kibush.co.il/show_file.asp?num=7913.
31. Ibid.
32. See Peter J. Chelkowski, "Indigenous Theatre," *The Iranian*, http://www.iranian.com/Arts/Taziyeh (accessed April 15, 2006).
33. Kuwait Information Office, "National Council for Culture, Arts and Letters (NCCAL)," http://www.kuwait-info.com/sidepages/culture_nccal.asp (accessed April 30, 2006).
34. Allen, "Iraq and Gulf States." *An Introduction to Arabic Literature* (in Resource Guide).
35. See "Doha Players," http://www.dohaplayers.com.
36. See Ministry of Information Sultanate of Oman, "Heritage, Culture and the Media," http://www.omanet.om/english/oman2002/media.asp?cat=om02 (accessed May 12, 2006).
37. See UNESCO, "Culture, Status of the Artists, Oman," http://portal.unesco.org/culture/en/ev.php-URL_ID=24639&URL_DO=DO_TOPIC&URL_SECTION=201.html.
38. Ibid.
39. See Child Rights Information Network (CRIN), "Yemen: Ebhar to Launch Child Doll Theatre," http://www.crin.org/resources/infoDetail.asp?ID=6987 (accessed May 11, 2006).

TRANSPORTATION AND TRAVEL

HOLLY WHEELER

While Westerners may group all the Middle Eastern countries together, the nations making up this region have more differences than similarities. While generally they do share a common language and religion, diversity is the rule rather than the exception. Diverse cultural traditions, conservative or modern views, and varied topography separate these countries into distinct identities. From the gorgeous blue of the Mediterranean Sea, the buoyancy of the Dead Sea, and the vast deserts of Saudi Arabia, to the mountains of Iran, Jordan's archaeological sites, and Israel's religious sites, the Middle East has much to offer visitors. This area is home to cradles of civilizations, archaeological wonders, and the holiest sites of the world's major religions. Forever changed by the discovery of oil, this area of the world is often dismissed as too volatile to visit. While security is a concern in some areas, travel is becoming safer in most areas, and tourism is rapidly developing in all countries. People from all over the world are traveling to the Middle East, visiting countries from the smallest, Bahrain, with only six of its thirty-three islands inhabited, to the largest, Saudi Arabia, gargantuan by comparison.

Of the world's top tourist destinations, Saudi Arabia is ranked highest in the Middle East, but five additional countries in the region—Egypt, Bahrain, Syria, Lebanon, and Oman—have earned the label of "emerging tourism destination" by the World Tourism Organization (WTO). Travel to countries with this designation is growing at a rate double that of the world average, with an increase of at least 100,000 international arrivals each year.[1]

Transportation systems in the Middle East are fairly well established, with a few locations and border crossings subject to change depending on political situations. Generally, all countries can be reached by air, most by land, and some by sea. All countries in the region have internal bus and taxi services, and half have rail service. The most popular form of transportation in most areas is bus, but Egypt's rail service is a close second; the exception is in the Arabian Peninsula, where cars are the most popular mode of transport.

Driving in the Middle East is challenging at best. While roads are generally paved, multiple roundabouts and the lack of marked lanes make driving in the region confusing. Night driving is particularly challenging because many cars aren't equipped with headlights, and herds of animals and sometimes people are apt to wander into and across roads. Additionally, traffic is heavy, accident rates are high—with Iran having highest accident rate in the world, according to the *Iran Daily*[2]—and drivers often have little regard for rules of the road. Toyota sells more cars in the region than do other car manufacturers, with sales topping 325,000 in 2005; the second most popular car manufacturer in the Middle East, GM, sold about half that, with Nissan following with approximately 75,000 cars.

Bicycles are not a popular mode of transportation in the region because of its high temperatures. Generally, Middle Easterners see bicycling as a leisure activity, not a mode of transport; erratic drivers may be a danger for cyclists, and spare parts are often difficult to find. Bikes are often used along the corniches along coasts and at the oases in countries such as Egypt. Bicycling is also considered the best way to see the sights at the Sea of Galilee, where a trip around the lake takes about four hours. A leading Lebanese environmental group, Greenline, is working on a plan to increase bicycle use as a viable mode of transportation throughout that country.

Motorcycles aren't very popular in the Middle East except in Iran. Some people speculate that in Tehran, with a population of some two million and increasing car traffic clogging the roads, motorcycles could outnumber cars in the future; already, drivers often use them to weave between pedestrians and gridlocked cars. Motorcycles are available for rent in many countries, and some, including Jordan and Oman, offer motorcycle tours.

While tourists may expect to see herds of camels when visiting the Middle East, the camel population has decreased dramatically. In countries like Saudi Arabia and Yemen, camels are used most often as photo props and tourist attractions, or sometimes for pleasure riding. The Bedouin in Jordan usually have small herds that they will rent out for walks and desert excursions, and Egyptian companies will rent camels to those wanting an authentic desert experience among Giza's pyramids.

Like camels, donkeys pulling carts are not as popular as they once were, although they are sometimes used in rural areas and even in larger cities. In Egypt, though, donkey carts, called *caretas*, are readily used to navigate old areas of cities and are the preferred mode of transport for the Siwans in the Siwa Oasis.

Summer temperatures are very hot throughout of the Middle East, but the period November to March is the best for visitors in terms of temperature. Non-Muslim visitors should make sure not to travel during Ramadan or other religious holidays since businesses are usually closed, and public transportation is clogged.

Given the good year international tourism had in 2004, with some 763 million reported arrivals, it is not surprising that growth was reported in just about all areas of the world, especially in the Middle East, which reported a total of 35.4 million visitors, up 18 percent from the previous year.[3] With the development of permanent tourism infrastructures, public and private investments, and the building of new hotels and resorts, the Middle East is demonstrating its readiness to meet the demands of being the fourth most visited location in the world.[4] Egypt's tourism grew the most in the region, with an increase of more than 2 million visitors in 2004 for a total of 8 million.[5] All countries in the region have ministries of tourism, or their equivalent, except Kuwait, Iraq, and Yemen, although the latter is under construction. Many countries are working hard to upgrade facilities to meet demands; for example, the Bahrain-based Baisan Institute of Hospitality Management, focused on hospitality, management, travel, and tourism, has opened hospitality training centers in Saudi Arabia, Kuwait, Jordan, and Egypt and has plans for development in Oman and UAE, thus demonstrating the region's commitment to developing tourism.

People from the Middle East visit other destinations in the Middle East more than any other areas in the world by an overwhelming majority. In 2003, 17 million Middle Easterners traveled away from home, with 13 million of them visiting regional destinations.[6] Africa and

Europe are tied as the second-choice destination for Middle Eastern travelers, receiving 1.5 million visitors each.[7]

REGIONS

North Africa

Tunisia's seven major international airports—Tunis-Carthage, Monastir Habib Bourguiba, Djerba-Zarzis, Tozeur-Nafta, Sfax-Thyna, 7 Novembre Tabarka, and Gafsa-Ksar—served some 11.7 million passengers in 2004, with Tunis-Carthage and Monastir Habib international airports together serving 61 percent of the total passengers.[8] Tunis Air is the country's national carrier, which flies to destinations in Africa, Europe, and North America. Domestic service is limited to flights from Tunis to Gefsa, Jerba, and Sfax.

Libya has five airports with regular international flights—Tripoli, Benghazi, Sebha, Tobruk, and Al-Kufra—with Tripoli and Benghazi as the country's most popular airports. Tripoli International Airport offers regular service to Syria, Saudi Arabia, Belgium, Turkey, the Netherlands, and Italy. Before the economic sanctions imposed by the United States from 1986 to 2004 and by the United Nations from 1992 to 2003, Tripoli's airport saw 3 million passengers a year; in 2006, though, it served only half that, but traffic was gradually increasing, according to Tripoli International Airport Director Milad Matouk.[9] Construction began in 2006 on upgrades to the airport to reach a 5 million passenger capacity with a 2.5-year projected completion date. Continued construction is planned to reach a total capacity of 12 million.[10] While Benghazi International Airport currently serves multiple international destinations, plans are in the works for an entirely new airport that would help increase the city's tourism potential. Libyan Arab Airlines, the country's national carrier, and the newly established Afriqui Yah Airlines fly to European, African, and Middle Eastern destinations, with plans for the latter to fly directly to New York City by 2009.

Morocco is home to eight international airports, with Mohammed V and Marrakech-Menara International Airport the busiest. Mohammed V, 30 kilometers south of Casablanca, is the country's main airport in terms of size and volume, with regular service to most European and Middle Eastern countries; service is also provided to North and West Africa, with most domestic flights routed through Mohammed V. The majority of Marrakech-Menara Airport's flights are charter flights to London, Geneva, and Paris, among other destinations. Royal Air Maroc (RAM) is the national carrier. It flies from its hub city of Casablanca to destinations throughout Europe, the Middle East, and Africa. Because there is only one other domestic airline, RAM dominates the industry; with no competition, its international flights are not necessarily inexpensive.

Rail service exists in North Africa, with expansions planned in both Libya and Morocco. Running approximately 2,475 kilometers north and south throughout the country, Tunisia's train network offers frequent service, with branches off the main route to other areas in the country. It is also connected to train networks in Morocco and Algeria. Tunis has two additional train systems: a suburban train line between the center of the city and its suburbs, and a tram network. The latter has five routes running to various areas around the city.

Libya is currently working on developing two main rail lines: a 2,178-kilometer coastal line running from Emfsaid to Ras-Ejdeer and a 992-kilometer southern line from Elhesha to Brak and on to Sebha. One line was completed in 2004; the rest of the lines were planned to be fully operational by 2006 and serve an annual capacity of 5 million passengers.[11]

Transportation and Travel

Morocco's rail system—linking its major cities—is one of the most modern in Africa. Taking the train is the transportation mode of choice for Moroccans traveling to cities that are on a line. The two main lines run from Tangier to Marrakech and from Oujda to Marrakech, with plans to extend the line south to Agadir.

Tunisia's road network, some 31,000 kilometers in all, is well maintained, with 50 km/hr speed limits on highways and 90 km/hr limits on highways. Drivers generally follow the rules and drive safely. While Tunisia shares land borders with Algeria and Libya, they are usually closed to foreigners. It is possible to rent a car through an internal agency, but the cost can be prohibitive. Public transportation offers bus, train, and taxi services covering just about the whole country. Buses run throughout the country, with most routes beginning or ending in Tunis. Taking the bus is the transportation mode of choice for long-distance travel in the country. Towns also offer regional services, which may be the only public transportation in smaller towns. Taxi service is available in most large areas, and, although it is possible to walk throughout most cities and towns, taxis are popular in the summer because temperatures are so high. Because wait times for buses can be long, taxis are a popular choice. Long-distance shared taxis, *louages*, are often more practical for visitors than buses because the buses leave when full. Additionally, *caleches*, horse-drawn carriages, are popular in Gabes, Houmt, Nabeul, and Tozeur.

Libya shares borders with Chad, Sudan, Egypt, Tunisia, Niger, and Algeria, but the most commonly used land borders for travelers are those with Egypt. The Sudanese border is open only for Libyans and Sudanese; the border with Chad is closed. The country's 83,200 kilometers of roads, just over half of which are paved, have speed limits of 100 km/hr on highways, 85 km/hr on main roads, and 50 km/hr inside cities, but speeding is prevalent. Driving at night can be hazardous since camels and sand deposits pose difficulty. While the country has no significant bus service within towns, Tripoli does have international bus service to Middle Eastern cities. Minibuses known as micros crisscross most towns and leave when full. Tripoli and Benghazi have bus depots, but micros in other cities congregate at shared taxi stations and offer roughly the same routes for half the price. Hailing a micro from the street is possible as well. Most car rental agencies don't operate in Libya, but local companies do, mostly from the lobbies of major hotels. Yellow-and-white shared taxis can be found anywhere in Libya with paved roads. This is the mode of choice for long stretches between tourist sites, so they fill up quickly, especially on the coast. The black-and-white private taxis are more expensive than the shared taxis, but destinations are more flexible.

Morocco's land border with Algeria is closed, so its only open border is with Mauritania; crossing that boarder requires a four-wheel-drive vehicle. Morocco's highways reach all major destinations, with 100 km/hr speed limits on open roads, 120 km/hr on highways, and 40–60 km/hr within cities and towns. Driving in Morocco is not without its challenges since mountain roads are dangerously narrow, passengers and bicyclists swerve into traffic, and cars traveling under 20 km/hr aren't required to have lights, even in the dark, further complicating driving. Additionally, minor roads are narrow, and lighting is mostly absent except on approaches to large towns; people, donkeys, and sheep wandering into roads cause problems as well. Car rentals are offered by local and international companies in large cities, but they are not inexpensive. Rates are fixed for *grande taxis* in Morocco, which link towns to each other and leave only when full. While *grande taxis* can be found mostly outside large hotels, *petit taxis* can be hailed from the streets or found at taxis stands. Used in bigger towns and cities, these small taxis are metered but are not permitted to go beyond the city limits.

The only point of entry into Morocco via bus is by ferry from Spain; travelers can arrive this way from destinations as far away as London since buses run daily from Morocco to Spain and on to other European destinations. Internally, the country's bus service network is dense and competitive: service is provided by the national carrier, Compagnie de Transports Moroccans, in addition to multiple private companies. Local networks are not always in the best repair, but traveling the country by bus is the cheapest public transportation option. Additionally, night buses are quicker and cooler over long distances. Morocco's train company also runs buses through Supratours to complement the train network in outlying areas. Remote areas of Morocco's Atlas Mountains are served by *camionettes*, or pickup trucks, but often wait time is considerable. Additionally, Marrakech is also served by caleches, the horse-drawn carriages. One increasingly popular mode of transportation in Morocco is the camper vans that arrive via ferry.

Bicycling has not been popular in North Africa, but that may be changing. Except in the height of summer or winter, conditions for bicycling in Tunisia are favorable. While Tunisia's reputation among cyclists is good, riders do have to share the road with heavy traffic. Because trains can accommodate bikes, it is easy to split up longer trips around the country. Although Libya's roads are flat and well surfaced, bicycling can be hazardous since traffic is fast, roads have no bicycle lanes, and drivers don't often look for bicyclists as they drive. However, mountain biking in Morocco is increasing in popularity as are bicycle rentals: many streets in the medinas, or the non-European parts of cities, such as those in Marrakech and Agadir, are long and narrow, making them perfect for bicycles. However, as in Libya, riding can be hazardous because of traffic and inconsiderate drivers. For enthusiasts, though, thousands of kilometers of trails, or pistes, await exploration.

Reaching North Africa by ferry is easy and popular. Service runs between Tunisia, Italy, Spain, and France; Libyan ports currently receiving cruise liners are Tripoli, Benghazi, El Khoms, and Derna. Additionally, ferry service to Morocco runs from southern Spain and France.

Of the international tourist arrivals in 2004, visitors to North Africa increased 8 percent over the previous year, with 12.8 million visitors, who generated US$6.1 billion.[12] Tunisia and Morocco saw the greatest increases, 17 percent and 16 percent respectively; Tunisia took in US$1.5 billion and Morocco US$3.2 billion.[13] With ancient ruins, gorgeous golf courses, and medinas nestled up against the *ville nouvelle*, the new areas of towns, North Africa has more to offer its tourists than camels and heat.

Clustered along the coastline in an area called *zone touristique*, Tunisia's beaches are its biggest draw. The white sand and blue Mediterranean draw travelers and locals to beaches at Sidi Ali el-Mekki, Raf Raf, and Cap Serrat, while the best beaches in the south are at Sidi Marhes on Jerba. In addition to the glorious sand, most resorts in these areas offer bars, restaurants, pools, shops, games, and a variety of water sports including diving, parasailing, water skiing, snorkeling, and paddle boats.

Tunis and Carthage are the country's major cities. Tunis's medina is a labyrinth of alleys and tunnels boasting souvenir shops, local markets, and workshops, with its focal point being the Zitouna Mosque, the ninth Great Mosque. Its central prayer hall was built of some 200 columns salvaged from Roman ruins in Carthage. The medina also has multiple mosques, including Kasbah, Hamuda Passa, and Youssef Sahib, but they are closed to non-Muslims. With some sections dating back to the thirteenth century, the medina's *souqs* are divided by area according to commerce and are named after the trade or founding community: Souq des Libraries (the booksellers' souq), Souq el-Attarine (the perfume makers' souq), Souq el-Trouk (traditionally the Turkish tailors' souq but now mostly dedicated to souvenirs), and the Grand Souq des Chechias, which in the seventeenth century was dedicated to one of the country's biggest industries: the annual making of some 1 million red skull caps (fezzes in the West). The Bardo Museum is the country's finest museum, most famous for its mosaics that once adorned Roman Africa's villas. Among the highlights are prehistoric monuments, day funeral masks from Carthage, fresco fragments, a sixth-century cruciform baptismal font, an Islamic museum, marble statuary from Carthage, Roman statues, and its extensive collection of mosaics, the most famous of which is of the Cyclops.

Carthage and Dougga are the most significant of the ancient cities in Tunisia; they have much to offer those interested in archaeology and history. Bursa Hill was Carthage's spiritual heart, with most of its important structures located there. The Musée National de Carthage boasts mosaics, Roman sculptures, Punic domestic objects, and lamps dating to the fourth century BCE, among other exhibits. Once one of the largest theaters in the Roman empire, Carthage's amphitheatre is now in ruins, but its scope is dramatic: it once could hold 40,000 people. The La Malga Cisterns showcase the second-century pipe network that supplied water for the city in Roman times. Additional draws for visitors include the Damous el-Karita Basilica, Roman villas, the Antonine Baths, and the Punic ports. Dougga's remains are in superb condition, including a renovated theater, built in 188 CE, which consisted of nineteen tiers and held 3,500 people. The capitol of Dougga has 20-meter-high walls, with fluted columns supporting the portico. Its walls enclose some twenty-one temples, which once housed statues of Jupiter, Juno, and Minerva that are now on display in the Bardo Museum. The Licinian Bath complex's walls are largely intact and include the Cyclops Bath, named after the mosaic on display at the Bardo Museum. Other ruins of significance include the temples of Pluto, Minerva, and Saturn; the Arch of Septimius Severus, the House of the Gorgon, and the Cisterns of Ain el-Hammam.

The medina's walls in Soussa enclose some twenty-four mosques and historical landmarks, including the Great Mosque; Sofra Cistern, with its 55 kilometers of tunnels, including graves in its catacombs; Zaoula Zakkak's octagonal stone minaret, and Ribat, the oldest monument in the medina. Designed as a fort, the top of its seventy-six-step spiral staircase offers dramatic views of the area. Bougaffar beach is crowded in the summer with public and private events and a variety of sports. Just 14 kilometers north of the city is the luxury marina complex of Port el-Kantaoui, a favorite area for locals and visiting Arabs. This custom-built village is home to a variety of hotels, restaurants, and souvenir shops, with much to offer its visitors, including mock pirate ships, glass bottom boats, a zoo, gardens, a golf course, diving schools, and a floating restaurant.

Home to the Berbers, the Grand Erg Oriental is one of the Sahara's most expansive seas of sand. The erg (sand sea) begins some 50 kilometers into Algeria. This is the Sahara of day dreams, with its shifting orange sands and excursions via camel. It's not an area to explore without a guide: as in other desert areas, getting lost is too easy. Oases found on the northern perimeter provide cafes and magical dunes from which to watch the sunset.

From the Atlantic and Mediterranean coasts, the Atlas Mountains, the western Sahara, and the magical cities of Casablanca and Tangier, Morocco is a diverse country of blended cultures, offering much to its people and visitors. In 2004 Morocco attracted 5.5 million foreigners, up 18 percent from the previous year, who spent over the equivalent of US$3.5 billion.[14] France is the country's first source for tourists, with Spain running a close second.[15] Morocco has plans to attract as many as ten million tourists by 2010; to help achieve that goal, six new seaside resorts are planned.[16]

Casablanca and Rabat are the Atlantic coast's most significant cities. Popularly known as "Casa," Casablanca is a juxtaposition of tradition and modernity. Hassan II Mosque, the ancient medina, and Quartier Habous are among the most frequented sites. Hassan II Mosque is one of the largest in the world, with a 25,000 worshipper capacity inside and room for an additional 80,000 outside. Although its marble column and zellij tile work are beautiful, its minaret is its most noticeable feature: at 210 meters, it is the tallest in the world and is visible for miles. At night its laser beams illuminate the sky and point toward Mecca.

Hassan II is comparatively high tech since it has a centrally heated floor, electric doors, and a retractable roof. It is also one of the few Islamic religious buildings open to non-Muslims. Two of the medina's original four gates still stand today, along with its restored clock tower, the Chleuh Mosque, and the remains of eighteenth-century fortifications. The sqala's (fortress's) stunning panorama of the sea and the daily markets, which include barbers, public letter writers, and jewelers, often draws visitors. The Quartier Habous, or "the district of holy men," is another area not to be missed. Built in the 1930s, this area was an attempted solution to an ongoing housing shortage. In addition to its architecture, the bazaars, craft shops, mosques, and bakeries are draws. Other points of interest to visitors are the Jewish Museum of Casablanca, the only museum in the city; the corniche; the public beaches; and the shops and restaurants along the seafront.

Rabat is the country's capital with the medina, *ville nouvelle*, Kasbah des Oudaias, Hassan Tower, and Chellah Necroplis among the city's highlights. The walled medina is packed with souqs, where one can purchase food next to bootlegged CDs and Western clothing, while the *ville nouvelle* is home to restaurants, cafés, a cathedral, and a museum. Flanked by two towers and a horseshoe arch, Kasbah des Oudaias overlooks the Atlantic Ocean from the oldest part of the city. Here, one can visit the oldest mosque in the city and stroll through the Andalusian Gardens. *Le Tour Hassan*, or Hassan Tower, is Rabat's most famous landmark. Originally, its minaret was intended to reach 60 meters, which would have made it the tallest in the world at the time of its construction, but its construction was halted at 44 meters in 1199 when the sultan died. Although the tower still stands, most of the adjacent mosque was destroyed by a 1755 earthquake. The Chellah Necropolis, built on the site of the ancient Roman city of Sala Colonie, is a gorgeous location not to be missed by visitors. A platform provides an excellent location from which to view the ruins. The group of buildings makes up the mausoleum of Mohammed V, father of Moroccan independence, which includes a mosque, a museum, burial vaults, and Mohammed V's sarcophagus.

The blue of the Mediterranean Sea contrasts with the rocky red cliffs of the Rif Mountains along the northern coast of Morocco. Sporting a history filled with questionable activities, including money laundering, prostitution, gun running, and smuggling, Tangier, the region's

STAR WARS

Tunisia is no stranger to movie crews, having been the site for such films as *Indiana Jones: Raiders of the Lost Ark* and *The English Patient*, but no movie filmed there is more famous than *Star Wars*. George Lucas chose multiple Tunisian locations for his first film in the series, *Episode IV: A New Hope*. Homes in Matmata that had been dug downward into the sandstone provided the location of Luke Skywalker's home; the interior of his home was shot in one of the inner courtyards of the city's Sidi Driss Hotel. The disco scene was also filmed in Matmata's dug-out structures. Mos Espa is a village that was constructed in the middle of the desert for the first film, but it was left standing for use in subsequent films. Chott el-Jerid provided the backdrop for Luke's contemplation of two suns while standing at the edge of a crater, but perhaps the most famous location is Sidi Bouhiel. Now known locally as "*Star Wars* Canyon," it is the location where the Jawas parked their sand crawlers, R2D2 wandered, and Luke was attacked by raiders. In fact, Lucas was so drawn to the scenery and locales that he named Luke's home planet Tatooine after the identically pronounced name of the Tunisian city of Tatouine, and he returned to the country to film parts of *Episode I: The Phantom Menace* and *Episode II: Attack of the Clones*. Ong Jemal provided Darth Maul's lookout, and Ksar Haddada was the location for the Mos Espa slave quarters in *Phantom Menace*. Guided tours of the sites are popular and easily accessible.

major city, has been an artistic retreat for famous writers and artists such as Truman Capote, Alan Ginsberg, William Burroughs, Jack Kerouac, and Tennessee Williams. With Grand Socco as the gateway to the medina, Tangier's medina climbs up a hill to the north of the city. Renamed Place du 9 Avril 1947 to commemorate Mohammed V's speech in support of independence, this modern square is full of snake charmers, shops, storytellers, musicians, and food vendors. Religious buildings of significance in this area of the city are the Church of the Immaculate Conception and the Grande Mosque. Behind its walls, the Kasbah is the highest point in the city and houses Dare el-Makhizen, the former sultan's palace. The Kasbah's mosque's octagonal minaret, the Museum of Moroccan Arts, and the Sultan's Gardens are also attractions of interest. The *ville nouvelle*'s Terrasee de Paresseux, or Idler's Terrace, is popular with locals for evening walks and with tourists for its views of the port, Gibraltar, and Spain. The beaches in Tangier are nice to walk near but swimming is not recommended since the waters are polluted. Another attraction is the Old American Legation Museum, a five-story mansion filled with maps, furniture, and paintings, which was given to the United States in 1821 by Morocco, the first nation to recognize the United States politically. The Musée de la Foundation Lorin and the Museum of Moroccan Crafts and Antiquities are also of interest to visitors.

Fez is the oldest of Morocco's imperial cities, consisting of Fez el-Bali, the historic center of the city; Fez el-Jadid, the imperial city of Merinids; and the modern districts established by the Protectorate. Fez el-Bali still retains its old walls and encloses mazes of twisting alleys, hidden souqs, museums, and tanneries in what is believed to be the largest adjoining car-free area in the world. Because space is finite, businesses are tiny—some only a few meters in size. Merinid tombs overlook the palace and necropolis. Fez el-Jadid, also known as New Fez or White Fez, is home to the narrow, tall buildings of the Mellah, or Jewish Quarter; the Ibn Danan Synagogue; and Dar el-Makhzen, a palatial complex. Its wide streets are home to shops and restaurants. Fondouk el-Nejjarine, one of the most renowned buildings in the city, houses the Museum of Wood, the craft for which Morocco is famous. Zaouia of Moulay Idriss II is the country's most venerated shrine, where pilgrims gather at the end of each summer to receive a blessing at the tomb. Kasbah Cherarda, known formerly as Thursday Fort, is formed from a system of fortifications that include the seventeenth-century walls and gateways enclosing a university annex and a hospital. The Borj-Nord fortress, north of the medina, offers a gorgeous panorama of the city.

Had the third-century Roman settlement of Volubilis not been demolished in the eighteenth century so that its building materials could be used to construct Moulay Ismail palaces, it might have been one of the most well-preserved Roman sites in the world. While many of the remains have been moved to Rabat's archeology museum, Volubilis is not to be missed. Its triumphal arch, forum, and basilica are impressive, and its mosaics are in excellent condition. The ruins of the houses of Euphebus, Orpheus, and Dionysus are its most significant ruins.

Moulay Idriss is the country's holiest city and is structured around the Moroccan saint's tomb from which the city draws its name. Although tourism isn't generally welcomed since the city is an important pilgrimage destination, it is possible for non-Muslims to hire guides; the nearby hills also provide a great view of the city, from which the city's shrine and minaret are visible.

Marrakech is one of Morocco's greatest tourist attractions, with many sights located within the medina's monumental walls: 19 kilometers long, 2 meters thick, and up to 9 meters high. The Koutoubia is the tallest building in the city, with its 70-meter minaret visible for miles. Its prayer hall can hold up to 20,000 people, and walking around the mosque's gardens is a local favorite. Place Jemaa el-Fna is an enormous square in the city that serves as Marrakech's core. With its snake charmers, acrobats, jugglers, food vendors, musicians, and shops, this traditional showcase of Morocco's culture is popular with both locals and visitors; it is the former site of the beheadings of criminals, who received the death penalty until the nineteenth century. The souqs, organized by trade, provide the opportunity to watch artisans at work. The city's most famous palace, Palais el-Badi, located in the Kasbah, is in ruins but is home to a 90-meter central pool surrounded by sunken orange groves and a maze of underground dungeons, storerooms, and corridors. Other places of interest in Marrakech include the mosques; the Saadian dynasty tombs; Dar Si Siad, which houses the Museum of Moroccan Arts; and the gardens throughout the city.

Agadir is the country's premier resort city, which sees thousands of visitors a year.

Rebuilt after a 1960 earthquake, the city is modern and clean. Its sheltered beaches, water sports, golf, tennis, camel riding, and food from most countries attract visitors from all over. Its modern nightlife is full of clubs and laser light shows, which attract the young and young at heart alike.

Although the western Sahara, whose boundaries are still disputed, has a long and violent history, it is the part of the country that many people want to visit because of its desert landscapes and oases similar to those found in Tunisia's Sahara.

The 350-kilometer-long Middle Atlas Mountains are covered by a great cedar forest and are home to Berber tribes. Scenic small towns, including Sefrou, Azrou, and Taza, provide excellent bases for day hikes through mountains, caves, and gorges. The water tumbling from ledge to ledge to drop 100 meters into Wadi el-Abid Canyon draws Moroccans and visitors alike to Cascades d'Ouzoud. While the High Atlas Mountains are not as accessible as the Middle Atlas range, the steep valleys and high rises provide opportunities for hiking and mountain climbing. Most people would not think about going skiing in a desert country like Morocco, but Oukaimeden ski resort provides excellent accommodations for skiers during the winter months. In addition to skiing and snowboarding, visitors can relax in the resort and restaurants. For a little variety, it is even possible to bypass the ski lift and ride a camel or donkey to the top of the mountain.

Although Libya has been difficult to visit, especially for non-Muslims because of visa restrictions, the government hopes to greatly increase its current half-million visitors a year.[17] In fact, Libyan authorities have signed contracts to develop large-scale holiday complexes planned for completion by 2010, with further plans to fully develop the country's tourist potential by 2018.[18] Tripoli, Sabratha, Leptis Magna, Benghazi, and Ghadames are the most significant of the country's cities.

Tripoli is the country's most visited city, with visitors drawn to this harbor city's castle, medina, and museums. Assai al-Hamra, the city's castle, has evolved into a citadel with 13,000 square meters of serpentine alleyways, courtyards, and houses. The whitewashed medina is enclosed in the ruins of fourth-century fortified walls; it is home to some thirty-eight mosques, of which Ahmed Pasha Karamanli is the largest; a nineteenth-century Ottoman clock tower; the Arch of Marcus Aurelius; a Turkish prison; and multiple souqs. The Jamahiriya Museum is Tripoli's most important, with its comprehensive outline of Libyan history from the Neolithic period to the current day arranged chronologically through the forty-seven galleries. Among the highlights are rock art and artifacts from revolutionary Libya in addition to Phoenician, Greek, and Roman Islamic artifacts including mosaics, stone lions, pillars, columns, and statues. Although the beaches aren't tranquil or clear, the city's water park has a wave machine, and water slides popular with water lovers.

The ruins at the ancient cities of Sabratha and Leptis Magna are among the country's premier attractions. Built of soft sandstone, Sabratha is full of significant sites. The Punic and Roman museums contain mosaics, frescoes, and objects recovered from Sabratan tombs. Archaeological highlights include a Byzantine wall; the temples of Serapis, Hercules, and Isis; the columns of Temple Liber Pate; the Basilica of Justinian; and the former centerpiece of the ancient city, the Forum. Leptis Magna's ruins are more well-preserved than those in Sabratha because they were built of limestone, which is more resistant to weathering than is Sabratha's sandstone. While restoration is ongoing, multiple sites are draws for tourists, including the Temple of Nymphs, the Basilica, the Old Forum, the Byzantine Gates, the Arch of Septimius Severus, the Monumental Arches, and the Hadrianic Baths. The monumental Great Colonnaded Street, once 20 meters wide and 400 meters long, led from the port to the Temple of Nymphs and was lined with shops and porticos.

Libya's second city, Benghazi, was the principle city of the East. Its old town hall, Souq al-Jreed, Freedom Square, and Greek Orthodox Church are common stops for tourists. The Commonwealth War Graves Cemetery and the Osman Mosque are also highlights. The old city of Ghadames is full of covered alleyways and has only seven main streets. Each is a self-contained town, complete with a mosque, schools, communal square, markets, and houses.

The ever-shifting sand and the rock formations of the Sahara make this desert a natural draw for visitors. Exploration using a four-wheel-drive vehicle or camel is a must, as is a guide. Wadis, oases towns, gorgeous landscapes, and rock carvings from almost 1,200 years ago make this mysterious area a romantic destination for visitors.

Egypt

With a recorded history dating back to approximately 3200 BCE, Egypt is a famous cradle of ancient civilization. Most of the country's development centers along the mighty Nile River and on its delta, while approximately 90 percent of the country remains unsettled desert. As is true with other countries in the region, Egypt is working on updating and renovating facilities and services to ease an overburdened network of road, air, and rail traffic.

The country has multiple airports, including those in Aswan, Luxor, Hurghada, and Sharm El-Sheikh, where a new terminal will be completed by May 2007, which together handle approximately 10 million passengers annually.[19] However, airports in Cairo and Alexandria are the country's main hubs. Cairo International Airport is the country's main airport, with the capacity to handle approximately 9 million passengers, just about what the country is currently processing. To keep up with increasing traffic and to ease current congestion, renovations are currently underway to upgrade the airport, including expanding the current two terminals and building a new terminal with the capacity of twenty-three aircraft, thereby increasing the airport's capacity to 20 million passengers; this project has a 2007 expected completion date.[20] The government-owned EgyptAir is the airport's main airline, with an extensive network connecting passengers to international destinations throughout Europe, North America, Africa, and the Far East, and to domestic locations including Luxor, Aswan, and Al Ghardaqah. The airport is also served by various international carriers, including Air France, Alitalia, British Airways, and Lufthansa.

Egypt's second largest city, Alexandria, is home to two international airports: Al-Nozha and Borg Al-Arab, the former of which is set to be closed. Both airports have been plagued by problems that have prevented Alexandria from being the tourist hub for which it has potential. To meet demand for passenger and cargo transport, Borg Al-Arab will be upgraded by 2008. In 2002, 440,000 people visited Alexandria via air, but with upgrades to the airport and industrial expansions in the area, projections indicate that as many as 1 million people will arrive annually via air by 2014.[21]

In 2003, 1.4 million passengers traveled over Egypt's nearly 9,500 kilometers of train tracks daily, excluding the Alexandria and Cairo metros.[22] The state-owned Egyptian Railways operates trains between outlying areas and major cities, but habitually demand outweighs supply. First- and second-class cars are air conditioned and in good repair, but the cheaper third-class cars, the only transportation choice for the nation's poor, have traditionally lacked seats, emergency brakes, windows, and fire extinguishers; some of these issues contributed to the February 2002 incineration of nearly 400 people who were not able to use the extinguishers to put out a fire on the train or could not get out through the barred windows.[23] These trains have been considered unsafe, and in 2003 were called "inhuman" by the Railway Authority;[24] however, little has been done to change their condition in recent years. These cars seat only 50, but an average of 200 passengers travel in each car, cramming into luggage racks and sitting or standing in the aisles. An estimated 10,000 people a day ride on the tops of these cars—such is the demand for this mode of transportation.[25] Car upgrades in recent years have made little dent in the problems of third-class trains, but the metro systems in Cairo and Alexandria and their outlying areas have helped relieve some of the pressure on the overburdened rail and road systems. In 1989, 42 kilometers of metro track opened in Cairo, and the Metro quickly became the transportation mode of choice for many. Designed to carry 60,000 passengers in each direction per hour, the system has received steady upgrades in facilities to keep up with the demand.[26] By 2003 the inexpensive Metro consisted of 65.5 kilometers of track linking Giza, Cairo, and Qalyabia, with two lines running from Helwan to the Cairo suburbs of El-Marg and Shvora, then on to Mouneb via El-Kheima, and transporting 1.8 million people a day.[27] Alexandria's Metro consists of 32 kilometers of track, 22 kilometers of which are for the regional metro service and 16 kilometers of which are for light rail using six lines.

The government has committed to upgrading and renovating all modes of public transportation to increase efficiency and customer service and to decrease congestion on overburdened routes. Among those planned changes to the rail service are adding an additional four lines to the Cairo Metro; adding an additional line to the Metro in Alexandria to cover a wider area of each city; and developing new stations near hotels, parking areas, malls, theaters, and apartment complexes.[28] Additionally, new technology is being explored to make traveling easier, including online ticket reservations, automated ticket machines, and prepaid payment cards.

Egypt shares open borders with Israel at Éclat and Tuba; at Ababa, Jordan; and at the sometimes open Rajah crossing to the Gaza Strip, which is subject to closings depending on the volatile political situation. Direct bus routes run from Cairo to Libya, but currently no land borders are open with Sudan, which can be reached only via Wadi Halfa using a ferry. With a network of approximately 45,500 kilometers of roads, Egypt's road system is highly developed and comprehensive, although overcrowded. According to the Egyptian State Information Service,[29] 115.85 billion passengers traveled on the roads between 2003 and 2004, up 2.3 billion from the previous year, in some 2 million cars and buses. Although Nissans are popular in the country, they will be much more prevalent in the future since Nissan plans to invest US$60 million in the next two years, with an additional US$40 million by 2010, to increase production sevenfold and convert Egypt into its Middle Eastern–North African production hub. Egypt's driving issues are similar to those of other countries in the region, with hazardous drivers, speeders who ignore the posted speed limits of 100 km/hr on highways and 90 km/hr in other areas outside towns, and in the less populated areas, cars without headlights and people wandering into the roads.

The extensive bus network in Egypt runs through just about every city, town, and village in the country using four basic types of buses: general public buses, minibuses, microbuses, and long-distance luxury or deluxe buses. Two state-owned companies run approximately 8,000 public buses in different states of disrepair, with some vehicles as much as 20 years old,

> ### ROAD ACCIDENTS
>
> Like other countries in the Middle East, Egypt suffers from tragically high accident rates. In 2000, the Egyptian government launched an innovative and controversial insurance plan. By increasing tolls on roads by 75 pilasters (U.S. equivalent of 13 cents), the government planned to provide a negotiable compensation to families of those killed in road accidents.[31] The government also planned to pay for the treatment for people injured in highway accidents. An additional plan that would do the same for people injured in all-too-frequent rail accidents was proposed in 2002.

and serve 5 million passengers a day.[30] The demand for buses is much higher than the supply, so buses are often overcrowded; service can be chaotic since the buses rarely come to a complete stop, requiring passengers to jump on and off as other passengers crowd the aisles and sometimes hang out the doors. Government-owned minibuses seat approximately twenty-six passengers each; minibuses leave the stops when full and travel established routes. Standing is technically not allowed on minibuses, but the regulation is not always enforced. Privately owned microbuses, which carry approximately fourteen passengers each, numbered almost 9,000 in Cairo, with a total of 20,000 in the greater Cairo area, in 2003.[32] About 2 million Cairenes use microbuses daily because they are reliable and fast. Microbuses operate in just about all the large cities, and competition between companies is fierce, with new routes being introduced regularly. Sometimes microbuses are difficult for visitors to use because destinations are not always clearly marked. Deluxe buses operate between all major areas of the country, including Upper Egypt, the Mediterranean Sea region, and the Red Sea coast; additionally, they run to several international destinations in neighboring countries, including cities in Libya and Jordan. These buses are relatively cheap but are more expensive than standard buses.

Taxis, pickups, and *servees* are other forms of transportation widely available in Egypt. Taxis are convenient and run in most cities. They are all shared, and travelers should consult a travel guide for adequate fares before traveling since prices should not be discussed with the drivers, who may state inflated rates. Smaller towns and villages often use pickup trucks as local taxis, in which people cram into the covered back end or even hang off the back or roof. Servees don't have specific departure times, but they run along set inter- and intracity routes, mostly from buses and train stations, and leave when full. They are usually less expensive than are buses or trains.

Egypt is experiencing a boom in tourism that generated the equivalent of US$6.1 billion in 2004 from 8 million international visitors.[33] While Western visitors may think the only important site in Egypt is the pyramids at Giza, a trip to Egypt encompasses much more, including archaeological exploration, tombs from ancient Egypt, modern shopping, and beach resorts. Old Cairo, known as Coptic Cairo to visitors, is rich in history. After exploring Old City Jerusalem's cobbled narrow alleys and stone walls, visitors can wander through excavations of the Roman Towers and the Coptic Museum and visit the famed Ben Ezra Synagogue, the oldest in the country, and the Mosque of Amr ibn al-Al, the remains of the country's first mosque, before heading toward the souq.

Islamic Cairo is an open-air museum packed with a dense population living in quarters not upgraded for centuries. Egypt's Ministry of Culture is trying to conserve the area and increase its tourism by restoring and refurbishing structures. Because authorities worry that its name will scare away tourists, the government now calls Islamic Cairo "Fatmid Cairo." Along its narrow streets, merchants, people, and donkey carts jostle for passage. Among the famous religious monuments are the Al-Azhar Mosque, which claims to be the world's oldest university, and one of the most sacred Islamic sites in Egypt, the Mosque of Sayyidna al-Hussein. It is possible to climb Mosque Madrassa's minaret as well as the red minaret of the Mosque of Mohammed Ali, which dominates the Cairo skyline and sits on the Citadel complex with the Mosque of An-Nasir Mohammed. Known as the City of the Dead, the Northern Cemetery is home not just to the dead. Traditionally, family tombs included a room where family members could stay overnight to remember their loved ones, which left space available for free access for those needing it. The cemetery now has gas, water, electricity, and even a post office; on Fridays, it is filled with picnickers and visitors paying their respects. Those who want to shop will find treasures of all kinds at the Khan al-Khalili markets, as well as carpet and clothing at Al-Ghouriyya; for those interested in law and justice, the quirky Police Museum houses an Assassination Room documenting the various attempts on President Nasser's life, among other exhibits.

Downtown Cairo is not old, so it does not offer the archaeological wonders and antiquities found in other areas of the cities, but it is teeming with life and people. In an area full of restaurants, cafés, theaters, shops, gardens, and hotels, tourists have much to choose from. A panoramic view of the city can be found from the top of the 187-meter Cairo Tower, and the country's first train station, Ramses Station, is always an attraction for visitors. The Egyptian Museum is the museum to visit in the country. Located in downtown Cairo, the museum is home to more than 120,000 relics from almost every ancient Egyptian period. So many treasures are in storage that the museum opened a "Hidden Treasures" exhibit to showcase hundreds of items on a rotating basis that otherwise would not be displayed. Plans are in the works for renovations and a new museum at Giza. A description of the museum's content would be enormous, and at least a two-day visit is necessary to appreciate all it has to offer. Highlights include triads and statues of the Old Kingdom, the Royal Mummy Room's glass-encased mummies, ancient Egyptian jewelry, and the amazing Tutankhamen Galleries, with their 1,700 items of the pharaoh's treasure. Virtually intact when discovered in 1905, the Yuyu and Thuyu rooms exhibit ornate sarcophagi, mummies, death masks, and a chariot.

As the sole surviving wonder of the ancient world, Giza's Pyramids have been *the* symbol for the country. More than 2,500 years old at the time of the birth of Jesus Christ, part of their allure is the mystery of how they were built and what their purpose was intended to be beyond that of functioning as tombs. One pyramid at a time closes on a rotating basis to allow for restoration work, so any visit will only provide the opportunity to visit two of the three pyramids. The oldest and largest of the pyramids on the complex is that of the Great Pyramid of Khufu, rising 146 meters above the sand when it was completed in 2570 BCE. The Pyramid of Khafre looks larger that that of Khufu because of its location on higher ground, but it is 136 meters tall, with the third pyramid, the Pyramid of Menkaure, rising 62 meters. Inside the pyramids themselves there isn't much to see—mostly passageways and rooms— but the experience of climbing inside them and seeing their sheer size is well worth the effort.

The Sphinx's purpose is still a mystery, but its appearance is known around the world. Unfortunately, it, too, has been a victim of time, wear, and vandalism. It lost its nose between the eleventh and fifteenth centuries and its beard in the ninth century; currently, scientists are puzzled as to what is causing erosion from the inside out. Pollution and rising ground water are the most likely culprits, and scientists continue to work on restoration attempts.

Although it is the most well known, Giza isn't the only location in the country where pyramids stand. Although not as well preserved or as large as those at Giza, the pyramids of Abu Sir are home to four complexes in differing states of decay. Saqqara houses eleven pyramids, including the Step Pyramid and the Pyramids of Unas and Teti, in addition to some of the deepest tombs in the country, those of the Saite and Persians; a group of Greek philosopher statues known as the Philosopher's Circle; and the Mastaba of Ti—the grandest and most detailed private tomb in the area. Danshur's Bent Pyramid received its name because of its unique shape, and the world's oldest true pyramid is the North Pyramid, better known as the Red Pyramid because of the red tones of its limestone.

Luxor has been a destination for tourists dating back to the Greek and Roman periods. Three areas—Luxor proper on the east side of the Nile, the town of Karnak to the north, and Thebes on the west side of the Nile—actually comprise what tourists call Luxor. Most of the city's restaurants, hotels, and sites are on the east bank, including the corniche's Luxor Museum, the Mummification Museum, and the Luxor Temple. The Luxor Temple was once home to a three-kilometer-long avenue of sphinxes running north to Karnak, many of which are still standing while others are still buried under the city of Thebes. The temple was built on an unexcavated site and contains such treasures as Amenhotep III's sanctuary, forecourt, and hall; the East Tower of the Pylon; the Great Court of Ramses II; fourteen papyrus columns forming the colonnade of Amenhotep III; the chapels of Serapis, the Theban Triad, Khons, and Mut; and reliefs, shrines, statues, and an obelisk. The Valley of the Kings is a canyon once home to stone sarcophagi of pharaohs, of which sixty-two tombs have been excavated so far. Tombs discovered here include those of Ramses I–IV, VI, and IX; Merneptah; Horeheb; Tuthmosis Siptah; and Tutankhamen, the valley's most famous. Revealed during twentieth-century excavations, King Tut's tomb is not particularly spectacular now, but it once housed four chambers packed with treasures, including statues, furniture, chariots, weapons, and musical instruments; man of these are currently on display in museums in Egypt and Great Britain. After the pyramids at Giza, the Temple of Karnack is considered by many to be the most spectacular architectural accomplishment in the history of Egypt. The Temple is actually three main temples—Mut, Montu, and Amun—enclosed by brick walls and surrounded by smaller temples; outer temples was built and enlarged over 1,300 years. Although the site is in ruins, columns, halls, pylons, and reliefs remain.

Alexandria's waterfront on the Mediterranean is the city's major geographical feature, with cinemas, restaurants, and shops located nearby. Visitors flock to such sites as the Greco-Roman Museum's 40,000 relics; the largest known Roman burial site in Egypt, the Catacombs of Kom Ash-Shuqqafa; the newly constructed giant Bibliotheca Alexandria; and the Mahmoud Said Museum. Ongoing excavations at the waterfront have revealed sphinx bodies, columns, capitals, a fifth-century wooden pier, a shipwreck dating to between 90 BCE and 130 CE, and a black granite Isis statue.

Other points of interest in Egypt include Port Said, the Red Sea, and Sinai. Port Said's major draw is the Suez Canal, where watching ships line up to enter is an amazing site. Colonial architecture from the nineteenth century, museums, and gardens are also attractions for visitors. Tourists flock to Egypt's 800-kilometer-long Red Sea coast to sun themselves on its beaches, view its coral and some 1,000 species of marine life, snorkel, and dive. The area also has more resorts and hotels being built than anywhere else in the country. While people flock to the resorts on the Mediterranean and Red Sea coasts, Sinai is more than beaches and reefs, although both are beautiful. Ras Mohammed National Park, Sharm El-Sheikh, Naama Bay, and Bedouin camel rides in nearby Nuweiba are also of interest to visitors.

Stretching over 2.8 million square kilometers, Egypt's western desert is home to five isolated but thriving oases popular with tourists and locals. Egyptians themselves often visit the same sites as visitors, but they also frequent Aswan for its winter resorts, white sandy beaches near deep turquoise waters in Marsa Matruh, and the beaches near Lake Timsah.

Jordan

The status of aviation in Jordan is high, and even the head of state is a highly qualified pilot of both military and commercial aircraft. Royal Jordanian is the national airline, with flights to most major European and Middle Eastern cities. In the last three years, the aviation industry in Jordan has seen upgrades in aircraft types and numbers as well as the addition of new destinations like Detroit and Barcelona. Queen Alia International Airport (QAIA) airport, home of Royal Jordanian, replaced the Amman-Marka International Airport (AMCA) as Jordan's largest in 1983. This modern facility, 32 kilometers south of Amman, is capable of handling 5 million passengers a year, with possibilities for future expansion and growth to serve potentially 10 million passengers annually.[34] Although QAIA replaced it as Jordan's major airport, AMCA is the base for the Royal Jordanian subsidiary Royal Wings. Aqaba, Jordan's third airport and gateway to the Red Sea, can comfortably handle 1.5 million passengers a year. Because of its size, the country has only one internal route—from Amman to Aqaba.

It's not surprising that a country as small as Jordan has no internal train service. The Ottoman-built Hejaz railway is the country's only train service, running from Damascus to Amman and back, but it makes no stops in Jordan. As a result, Jordan's main cities are clogged with a variety of cars, taxis, and buses. In 2004, Jordanians registered 614,614 cars, an 8 percent increase from the previous year.[35] Because of a lack of internal air and train transport, the main forms of public transportation are public minibuses, private buses, and taxis, both service and private. Public buses, the normal mode of transport for the locals, usually leave stops when full, can be hailed along the route, and are both efficient and relatively inexpensive; they cater to locals traveling to and from work, so visitors usually are better served by hiring private taxis or cars.

The service taxi is a common form of transportation that runs along set routes without fixed stopping locations. Privately owned, these taxis aren't scheduled and fill up quickly. While all taxis have meters, they aren't always used, so a price to the desired destination should be agreed upon before departing. While hiring taxis for a day is usually cheaper than a daily car rental, a car rental is usually more cost effective for long distances.

The Desert Highway is one of Jordan's three main highways; south of Amman, this highway detours by all major tourist attractions. The Dead Sea Highway is the quickest way to travel between Amman in the north and Aqaba in the south. The 5,000-year-old King's Highway is often considered the most interesting of the highways, but it is the most difficult and time consuming to travel. It traces the route of pilgrims, merchants, and monarchs as it passes through most of Jordan's main attractions. With increasing urbanization, economic growth, and rising numbers of vehicles, Jordan's major cities are congested. Like other Middle Eastern countries, driving in Jordan can be challenging at times since the 90 km/hr to 110 km/hr speed limits are rarely obeyed on Jordan's 8,500 kilometers of paved highways.

Jordan's tourist industry suffered tremendous setbacks in 1967, when the country lost the West Bank and the religious and historical towns of Bethlehem, Jericho, and Jerusalem, and again in 1990, with the Iraqi invasion of Kuwait; however, the 1994 peace agreement with Israel produced record highs in tourism in 1995. Despite the continued violence in Israel and Palestine and the ongoing war in Iraq, Jordan has been experiencing steady increases in tourism; for example, in 2004, 5.6 million people visited the country, an increase of just over a million people from the previous year.[36] The 2004 tourism generated the equivalent of US$2.7 billion, 20 percent of which was generated from Jordanians, 25 percent from other Arabs, and 29 percent from other foreigners.[37] Jordan's rock-carved city, Petra, draws more visitors annually than any other attraction or historical site in the country—over 300,000 visitors in 2004 alone, almost double the number of visitors in the previous year.[38] More than 2,000 years ago, the Nabateans made Petra their capital, from which they established an expansive trade network. Lost from the fourteenth century to early in the nineteenth century, and despite the few extant free-standing buildings, the condition of the structures carved into the mountains is staggering. Petra is naturally protected by a series of canyons formed by the Wadi Mousa River and is hidden behind an almost impenetrable barrier of mountains, so visitors must enter through the Siq—a long narrow gorge also carved by the Wadi Mousa. Visitors can hire horses to take them from the entrance of the Siq to the entrance of the city, a distance of about one kilometer, but once one enters the city, the only transportation available is by camel or donkey. Petra boasts dozens of sacred sites with the Khasneh (the Treasury) being its most famous monument and the most photographed site in the whole country. The second most remarkable site is E-Deir, a monastery, dating to the first century. The garden temple complex, obelisk tomb, Nabatean sacrificial site, royal tombs, colonnaded streets, Petra Church, the Roman Theater, and the Petra Museum are also tourist attractions in Petra.

The ancient cities of Umm Qais, Jerash, Pella, and Mt. Nebo draw visitors for their archaeological wonders. Located in the hills of the northwest corner of Jordan, Umm Qais was "discovered" by Western explorers in 1806 but was not excavated until 1982. Occupied as early as the seventh century, Umm Qais boasts a fourth-century Roman baths complex, a Roman theater, a well-preserved underground Roman mausoleum, a classical Acropolis, and the Central Church, which dates to the Byzantine period. Jerash, although occupied by humans for 6,500 years, was hidden under the sand for centuries. The past 70 years of restoration have revealed paved and colonnaded streets, the Temple of Zeus, Hadrian's Arch, the Temple of Artemis, and a dozen churches. Overlooking the Jordan Valley and the Sea of Galilee, the city of Pella is a favorite of archaeologists because excavations have revealed ruins from the Greco-Roman period, including Byzantine churches, a medieval mosque, and a traditional Roman gate. Boasting a view of the Jordan Valley, Dead Sea, Jerusalem, and Bethlehem, Mt. Nebo, Jordan's most revered spot, is the presumed site of Moses's death and burial; it sees over 100,000 visitors annually.[39]

The modern cities of Amman and Aqaba are favorite destinations of travelers. Jordan's capital, the rapidly developing Amman, is no more than five hours from anywhere in the country. Because Amman is new, having been rebuilt from ruins in 1875, it lacks the ancient architecture so famous in Jordan's other tourist sites, but it is home to one of the largest Roman amphitheaters in the Middle East. Amman's citadel, Jebel al-Qala, is a walled complex with an impressive series of buildings, including Umayyad Place, an extensive complex of residential buildings, and the castle, Al-Qalah, a superb example of Greek architecture just north of the ruins of the Temple of Hercules. Home to 110 species of soft coral, 120 species of hard coral, and at least 1,000 species of fish, the indigo-colored Gulf of Aqaba is a world-renowned tourist paradise. The coastal city of Aqaba draws visitors to its wide assortment of beaches and water sports, including diving and snorkeling, its rare marine life, virgin coral reefs, and friendly sea creatures like dolphins and turtles. For the non-water-sports fan, this gorgeous gulf can be toured in a glass-bottomed boat.

While climbers are attracted to Wadi Rum's sheer granite cliffs and hikers to its open, ancient valleys, it is probably best know for its connection with T. E. Lawrence, the British officer based in Wadi Rum during Great Arab Revolt of 1917–18. Much of the famed *Lawrence of Arabia* was filmed in Wadi Rum. The village of Rum is home to several Bedouin tribes that live in scattered camps as well as the headquarters of the famous Desert Patrol.

Closed off for years in a military zone along Jordan's western border, the area opposite Jericho was reopened following the 1994 peace treaty with Israel. This important archaeological discovery on the east bank of the Jordan River has been identified as the Biblical Bethany-beyond-the-Jordan, where John the Baptist preached and baptized during the early part of his ministry as well as the site where the Prophet Muhammad crossed the Jordan River en route to Jerusalem and heaven. Built in the sixth and seventh centuries, the city of

Jericho includes the Byzantine Church, said to have been built to commemorate the baptism of Jesus, as well as other churches, Corinthian capitals, baptismal pools, caves for monks, and lodges for pilgrims.

Along the eastern coast of Jordan is the Dead Sea, the lowest spot on the earth at 4,100 meters below sea level. The water, four times saltier than normal water, is the Dead Sea's main attraction. Virtually nothing can sink in the Dead Sea, and visitors can float effortlessly on its surface. The chemical composition of the water is only part of the attraction to this area. The filtered sun rays, oxygen-rich air, and the shoreline's black mud, rich with minerals, are also major tourist draws. This popular holiday spot is packed on Fridays and public holidays.

Israel and the Palestinian Territories

Israel's current transportation minister, Shaul Mofaz, is continuing the work of the previous minister to, revolutionize the transportation industry in Israel. Tel Aviv's Ben Gurion Airport is the country's main international gateway, receiving 7.5 million people in 2004.[40] Eliat Airport offers international and domestic flights as well as charter and private flights. In 2005 it saw a 30 percent increase in passengers.[41] Other airports in Israel include Oveda, which served 48,130 passengers in 2003; Haifa Airport, which served 70,659 passengers in 2003, most of which were domestic travelers; Rosh Pina Airport, with 80,000 passengers; and Dov Hoz Airport, with approximately 652,750 passengers in 2004.[42] Major airlines link Israel to countries around the world; the country is linked internally as well, with domestic flights connecting Eliat, Haifa, Jerusalem, Masada, Rosh Pina, and Tel Aviv.

Israel's rail network has domestic lines linking Tel Aviv to a variety of suburbs, but historically rail transport has been slower than traveling by car, so rail has not been the transportation mode of choice. However, the rail network is undergoing a revolution, with plans to upgrade the network considerably. Newly opened express lines and new stations are already completed. Work is in progress on a high-speed line running between Tel Aviv and Jerusalem, which Mofaz considers a high priority despite growing budgetary concerns.[43]

Although Israel has open borders with Jordan and Egypt, it is not possible to cross them in taxis or hired cars, although buses do run through the crossings. The approximately 16,903 kilometers of roads in Israel have a tough time keeping up with the sheer density of cars on them, which is at three times the accepted norm for developed countries.[44] In order to cope with the sheer number of vehicles on the roads, the transportation minister has placed a high priority on upgrading existing highway systems and constructing new roads. Currently, the Hyundai automobile corporation is experiencing the most rapid growth in Israeli markets.

Israel's Egged Bus Company is the largest in the world, offering frequent service across the country. Because the bus network is so extensive, it is the public transportation mode of choice for Israelis. In only two areas is the bus service not the best choice: near the Red Sea and in Bethlehem. Buses run along the Red Sea, but fares are excessive, and not all destinations can be reached via bus, making car rental the best option for this area. Bethlehem can be reached by bus, but currently bus travel is not allowed within the city. A new station closer to sites within the city is in the planning stages.

Taxis serve all cities in Israel and can take passengers anywhere in the cities as well as between cities. The Israel institution of *sherut*, or shared limo, is a popular option for both locals and visitors. Seating seven to ten people, sherut follow local and intercity bus routes; fares are often more than the bus, but less than a private taxi.

When traveling to Israel, it is important to take the current political climate into consideration since the area is volatile and subject to change. Currently, if visitors plan to visit Israel, Lebanon, or Syria, Israel must be visited last since it is not possible to enter Syria or Lebanon with an Israeli passport stamp. Tourism is steadily increasing in Israel, with visitors arriving from all corners of the world. Europeans and North Americans comprise 56 percent and 32 percent of all tourists, respectively.[45] Three million visitors were expected in 2006, but there was concern that the country's tourism industry would not support that number of visitors. The country can handle about 2.4 to 2.7 million visitors; the biggest concern is with a shortage of hotels.[46]

Most of the sites frequented by visitors and natives alike are religious in nature, and several cities are important to the world's major religions. Jerusalem is the third holiest city of Islam and the holiest for Judaism and Christianity. Its old city is surrounded by four kilometers of walls; eight gates provide access to different quarters of the city and the Ramparts Promenade, which provides an overview of the Old City. In the southeast corner of Jerusalem's Old City sits the 141,640-square-meter Temple Mount, one of the most renowned religious sites for both Islam and Judaism. Historically, it served as a holy site for at least ten ancient religions. Tradition indicates this is the Biblical Mount Moriah, where Abraham was asked by God to sacrifice Isaac, his son. After the Mosque of the Prophet in Medina and the Kaaba in Mecca, the Dome of the Rock and the Al-Aqsa Mosque complex is Muslim's third holiest site—the majestic gold dome covers what Muslims believe to have been the altar where Abraham almost sacrificed Ishmael. Additionally, it is the location where God took Muhammad on his journey from the Holy Mosque in Mecca to heaven, according to Muslim tradition.

The Jewish Quarter of Jerusalem's Old City's most significant site is the Western Wall, sometimes referred to as the Wailing Wall in reference to expressions of Jewish sorrow over the destruction of Judaism's holiest shrine, the Temple Mount. At 67 meters long and 18 meters tall, only this small part of the original 488-meter retaining wall still stands. Pilgrims from around the world tuck prayers into the wall's cracks because many people view the wall provides a direct connection to God. Other areas of interest in the Jewish Quarter include the Cardo, the Burnt House, and multiple museums and synagogues. The Armenian Quarter of the Old City is home to a small Armenian Christian population, with the St. James Cathedral serving as the spiritual center. While most Christians believe Mt. Zion is the location of the Last Supper, the Syria Orthodox Convent believes its location is on that famous site.

The Christian Quarter surrounds the Church of the Holy Sepulcher, believed to be the place of Jesus' crucifixion, burial, and resurrection. Via Dolorosa, "The Path of Sorrow," is the route on which Jesus bore his cross from the site of his condemnation to the site of the crucifixion. Each event on this walk has a chapel of commemoration, which make up the Stations of the Cross. Other religious sites of interest include the Lutheran Church of the Redeemer, St. Alexander's Church, and the Church of St. Anne, which commemorates the birthplace of Jesus' mother, Mary.

The largest and most heavily populated quadrant in the Old City is that of the Muslim Quarter, reached through the Damascus Gate. This area is home to a bustling souq, Bab Al-Sil Silah Street, Crusader period architecture, Tomb of Lady Turkan, and Zedekiah's cave, which extends far beneath the Quarter.

Near the Old City are located multiple religious spots of interest, including Mount Zion, traditionally considered to be the site of the Last Supper and the Tomb of David; the Basilica of the Dormition Abbey, commemorating the death of the Virgin Mary; and the most ancient part of the city, the city of David, which is politically sensitive and much disputed. Running between the Old City and the Mount of Olives is the Kidron Valley, venerated by Christians as the path of Jesus' last walk. Additional religious points of interest include the Chapel of Christ's Ascension, the first church to commemorate that event; the Church of the Pater Noster, the church commemorating the first recitation of the Lord's Prayer,; tombs of the prophets; the Church of All Nations; the Russian Church of Mary Magdalene; and the Garden of Gethsemane.

West Jerusalem is a tourist haven because of its restaurants, dance clubs, and shops. Each of its some twenty neighborhoods offers visitors distinctive local flavors. Other areas of interest include Zion Square, the area's largest mall; Mea Shearim, where Jewish books and religious items are cheaper than anywhere else in the world; and the architectural masterpiece, Givat Rum, the Israeli Supreme Court. Additionally, East Jerusalem is home to the skull-shaped rock formations of Garden Tomb, the Basilica of St. Stephen, and St. George's Cathedral, among other points of interest.

According to the Ministry of Tourism, Israel has more museums per capita than any other country in the world, with its most famous, the Israel Museum, located in Jerusalem.[47] The largest and most comprehensive in Israel, it boasts an impressive collection of antiquities and sculptures, ancient and modern art, and archaeological tools and weapons. Its most significant exhibit is the Shrine of the Book, which displays the Dead Sea Scrolls. Also located in Jerusalem are Israel's largest Holocaust Museum, Wofson Museum, and the Underground Prisoners' Museum.

The hotspot for cultural interests, Tel Aviv is the country's fast-moving center because of its shopping, cafés, night life in several historical neighborhoods, an expansive drive-through safari park, the sprawling promenade extending to Jaffa, and beaches offering a variety of water sports. Among its most famous museums are the Eretz Yisrael and Beit Ha-Tfutzot, the Diaspora Museum.

Situated on a small peninsula extending into the Mediterranean and rising up the steps of the slopes of Mt. Carmel, Haifa has long housed multiple religious minorities. Because of its steep topography, cable cars are the best, albeit more expensive, way to see Haifa. Known locally as "Carmel's Eggs," the cable cars run up and down the northwest slope of Mount Carmel. The golden dome of the Baha'i Shrine dominates the skyline, while the monastery of the Carmelite order stands high on a promontory overlooking Haifa Bay. Revered as sacred ground by Jews, Christians, and Muslims, Elijah's Cave draws the faithful from all three religions. Haifa's beaches are also popular with locals on the weekends.

Galilee is an enormous attraction for tourists, with pilgrims descending by the thousands down a massive metal staircase into the Jordan River to visit the site where it is believed that John baptized Jesus. Nazareth, in southern Galilee, is important to Christians as the site of Jesus' early life and the traditional home of Mary and Joseph. Most of the city's sites are near the recently repaired souq, including Mary's Well, which is believed to contain water with the power to heal; St. Joseph's Church, located on top of the cave believed to have been Joseph's home; the Basilica of the Annunciation, which was built on the spot where the archangel Gabriel heralded the birth of Jesus in Mary's home; and the former seat of Talmudic study in the second and third centuries, among others. The new village of Nazareth was created as a magnet for tourists. Stone houses and synagogues were built using the same materials and techniques of the first century CE: the new Nazareth village is believed to look just as it did 2,000 years ago during the time of Jesus. Tiberias is another spot frequented by visitors and locals along the Sea of Galilee.

The shore of the Sea of Galilee, also known as Lake Kinneret, is home to multiple hotels, restaurants, bed and breakfasts, and hot baths, where visitors can bike, hike, or take a ferry across the Sea. Among the New Testament sites are the Church of the Primacy of St. Peters; the Mountain of the Beatitudes, the location where Jesus is believed to have delivered his sermon on the Mount and chosen his disciples; and the Church of the Bread and the Fish, believed to be the location of Jesus' biblical feeding of 5,000 people with five loaves of bread and two small fish.

Transportation and Travel

The still-disputed plateau known as the Golan Heights, which borders Syria, is home to Tzfat, with its serpentine side streets, the old city, and various religious sites, including the cave said to be the burial location of Shem, Noah's son. The largest settlement in the Golan is Katzrin, with its ancient excavations from the fourth century and fine wineries.

By a peaceful border drawn down its center, the Dead Sea is partially in Israel and partially in Jordan. Its Israeli coast is 65 kilometers long and holds the same properties as does its counterpart in Jordan. The beaches of Kalya in the north are the least visited by tourists, while Qumran, the site where the Dead Sea Scrolls were discovered, is visited often by Israelis and tourists. Ein Feshka is popular with locals because it is the only Dead Sea resort with attached fresh water ponds. Only a few minutes' hike from the Dead Sea, waterfalls and rare desert wildlife are found in the Ein Gedi Oasis.

Eilat is revered by some for its weather, coral reefs, and nightlife but despised by others as being too touristy. Regardless, Eilat is one of the most popular locations for Israelis on summer holiday. With its expansive underwater world filled with coral and marine life, water sports, including diving and snorkeling, are popular. For those preferring not to get wet, the Coral World Underwater Observatory is a good option since are the several glass-bottom boats. People-watching is a prominent pastime along the promenade that overlooks the Gulf of Aqaba.

The struggle for the West Bank is historic and unpredictable, so travelers need to take note of current relations between Israel and the Palestinian Territories. Bethlehem and Jericho are the most heavily visited areas of the West Bank. Bethlehem's Basilica of the Nativity, the oldest continually used church in the world, marks the location traditionally believed to be that of Jesus' birth. Other sites of interest include St. Catherine's Church, the Tomb of Rachel, and the sprawling market. Visiting the holy city of Bethlehem isn't as easy as it once was because of the recent Israeli-constructed 8-meter wall separating the city from nearby Jerusalem. To access Bethlehem, visitors have to pass through a security checkpoint similar to those at airports, which could take up to an hour.[48] Residents and business people complain about the damage the barrier has caused to the city's tourism industry, which accounts for 70 to 80 percent of its economy.[49]

Believed to be the world's oldest city, Jericho, located in the middle of the Judean Desert, was the first city to fly the Palestinian flag. Settled more than 10,000 years ago, Jericho is also the world's lowest city at 250 meters below sea level. Although summer temperatures are stifling, winter temperatures are pleasant, explaining its popularity as a winter resort for those on vacation. Unfortunately, ancient Jericho is little more than a heap of ruined walls. The Greek Orthodox Monastery sits on the edge of a cliff in the Jericho Mountains to the west, which many believe to be the site where the Devil tried to tempt Jesus, as recounted in the New Testament. The Jericho Synagogue is one of the oldest in the world.

Stretching 46 kilometers long and 16 kilometers wide along the Mediterranean Sea, the Gaza Strip is one of the most densely populated areas in the world. The area is well known for the volatile history of Israeli occupation and uprisings. Israeli citizens can travel there only after receiving special permission, while foreign visitors can visit without problems. Gaza City's most impressive archaeological structure is its Great Mosque. The seventeenth-century fortress Al-Redwan Castle, the Gold Market, and the souq are also points of interest.

Lebanon

The recent conflict between Lebanon's Hezbollah and Israel has affected much of Lebanon's transportation infrastructure, resulting in widespread destruction and rendering future plans and developments uncertain.

Located only eight kilometers from downtown Beirut, the Beirut Rafic Hariri International Airport saw 1.60 million passengers use it in 2004.[50] The airport underwent extensive renovation after the 1982 Israeli invasion, which included a new terminal, the ability to receive thirty aircraft at the same time, and the capability to handle 6 million passengers annually. Future plans for improvement include developing the capability to handle 16 million passengers annually by 2035.[51] Middle East Airlines is Lebanon's national carrier, with a network connecting Beirut to most European capitals, the main cities in the Persian Gulf, and several destinations in North Africa. Because the country has only one civilian airport, there are currently no domestic flights in Lebanon.

Lebanon has very little train service. The full length of the track is 401 kilometers, with just a few sections operable since the civil war. Fifty meters of track from Sin al-Fil to Enbete is operable and has been used to transport freight, but doing so is more expensive than using road transport. Recently, Syria has initiated talks to discuss revitalizing two tracks: the one from Riyaq to Aleppo and the one from Tripoli to Aleppo.

The only open land border in Lebanon is with Syria, since the Lebanon-Israel border is closed for the foreseeable future. The country has approximately 8,000 kilometers of roads in varying condition, and one of the highest car ownership rates in the Middle East. Home to 1.2 million cars alone, Beirut, in particular, has severe traffic problems, most of which will be addressed by the newly launched Urban Transport Development Project, funded by the World Bank, to upgrade the road system to help ease transportation problems.[54]

EFFECTS OF THE HEZBOLLAH-ISRAELI CONFLICT ON TRAVEL ROUTES

On July 12, 2006, the Shiite Muslim militant group Hezbollah crossed into Israel, killed three Israeli soldiers, and abducted two others. Considered a terrorist group by Israel and the United States, Hezbollah is backed by both Iran and Syria. It operates freely in southern Lebanon because the Hezbollah party currently holds 23 of the 128 seats in Lebanon's parliament; as a result, the Lebanese government lacks the capacity to extend its authority south into Hezbollah strongholds.[52] Israeli Prime Minister Ehud Olmert called Hezbollah's cross-border raid an attack of war, which prompted retaliation by Israeli forces.[53]

Israel imposed a full blockade of Lebanon by air, sea, and land, using warships to cut off its ports, bombing its roads, and attacking its bridges and airports, thereby stranding tourists, impacting residents, and frustrating aid efforts. Worst hit was Beirut's Hariri International Airport, thought to be a Hezbollah weapons and money transport site. These attacks left craters in the runways and diverted flights; the future of the airport is unknown.

Also targeted by Israel was the main north-south coastal highway between Beirut and Damascus, Syria, along with four of the highway's bridges, to stop the flow of weapons from Syria and money from Iran. Traffic was paralyzed and highways were left in shambles.

Lebanon's bus system covers most major destinations in the country, with additional service outside Lebanon. The main routes are from Beirut to three Syrian cities: Damascus, Aleppo, and Lattakia. Service runs at least three times a day, seven days a week, with service on the Beirut-Damascus route running every hour. Additionally, a daily service runs from Tripoli to Riyadh, Saudi Arabia, via Damascus and Amman, Jordan. Beirut, itself, is the bus transport center of the country, with three main bus hubs, each serving different areas of the country. Minibuses are a bit cheaper than the already cheap bus, but they are less comfortable.

Transportation and Travel

Most of Beirut's taxi fleets are old and decrepit, but some taxi companies boast new vehicles. Taking a taxi in Lebanon is easy, and two options are available. A taxi can function as a servee—a service taxi following a fixed route, leaving when full and dropping off and picking up passengers along the route. It may be necessary, though, to take more than one service taxi if a destination isn't along a straight route. Individuals using a taxi may also pay for any empty seats, effectively turning the vehicle into a private taxi, and then it can take the passengers anywhere they desire. The other option is to take one of the private taxis, which are metered.

With more than 4 million visitors in 2004 alone, Lebanon is a treasure trove of ancient caves, sarcophagi carved into rock, monasteries, churches, mosques, traditional houses, and Roman ruins.[55] More than 1.3 million international visitors arrived in Lebanon in 2005, spending the equivalent of $US1.3 billion.[56] As Lebanon's capital, Beirut is its most visited city. Full of vendors, parks, picnickers, and sports enthusiasts, Beirut's corniche boasts amazing coastal views and an opportunity for tourists to watch locals going about their daily lives. A cave-set group of rock formations called Pigeon Rocks is a popular night time spot, and the Souk el Barghout, or Martyr's Place, offers outdoor cafes and throngs of people. Visitors can marvel at archaeological treasures at the often-visited National Museum and enjoy contemporary Lebanese art at the wedding cake look-a-like Sursock Museum.

Baalbek is consistently most visited attraction in the country, with more than 104,000 visitors in 2004.[57] Known as the "Sun City" of the ancient world and formerly one of the wonders of the ancient world, Baalbek is home to the largest and most well-preserved Roman temples in existence. Among the ruins are the Sacrificial Courtyard and temples dedicated to Jupiter, Venus, and Bacchus. Six huge columns mark the well-preserved Temple of Jupiter. Inside, visitors find monumental doorways, ornate decorations, a ceiling of carved stone covered with scenes of gods and goddesses, and friezes with lions and bulls. Only a staircase remains of a fourth temple, dedicated to Mercury.

Among the other major sites in Lebanon are the Jeita Grotto, Tripoli, Sidon, Byblos, and the Chouf Mountains. Discovered in 1836, the grotto at Jeita is divided into an upper dry portion and a lower portion through which an internal river flows. The inside is home to marvelous caves, stalactites, and stalagmites sculpted over time. The Sweets Capital of Lebanon, Tripoli, is the country's second largest city and a popular stop for visitors who want to experience its maze of mosques, souqs, and restaurants. While the fourteenth-century Al-Muallaq Mosque is one not to be missed since it is suspended over a street, the most significant structure in the city is a medieval castle built by the Crusaders; the Citadel of Raymond de Saint-Gilles's entrance is most impressive, with its three imposing gateways and a moat. The port city of Sidon offers an old city with a maze of souqs, old buildings, and mosques. The Chouf Mountains, in the southern part of the Mt. Lebanon range, is home to Beiteddine Palace, the second largest tourist spot in the country, with almost 90,000 visitors in 2004.[58] Resting on top of a hill surrounded by terraced gardens and courtyards, this historical monument is one of the best examples in the country of nineteenth-century Lebanese architecture. Vaulted passageways, fountains, mosaics, intricately carved ceilings, and carved marble abound in this gigantic structure, complete with luxurious rooms, balconies, reception halls, and private apartments.

Other popular spots for visitors and natives are resorts and entertainment centers. The Cedars, a resort settlement in Lebanon's highest mountain range, is named for its ancient grove of cedar trees, the emblem of the country. A resort area in all seasons, it serves as an escape from the heat in the summer and as a magnificent skiing location in the winter. Additional resorts popular for those from both within Lebanon and outside can be found in Raifoun, Faraya, and Faitroch. Journieh and Broummana are popular among the young in

Beirut: the former is home to shops, nightclubs, and restaurants teeming with people; the latter's carnival-like atmosphere makes it particularly popular on the weekends.

Syria

Syria has three international airports—Damascus International, Aleppo International, and Bassel Assad International—and various smaller domestic airports. Because of the time involved to get to and from the airport and to check in, flying within Syria usually does not save any time, other than for the trip from Damascus to Qamishle. Despite this, multiple domestic flights are available. Damascus International Airport is currently constructing a new terminal and is the country's main international airport, serving 1.7 million passengers in 2000.[59] Aleppo International Airport has the capacity to accommodate 1.5 million passengers annually and is undergoing construction on an additional runway. Bassel Assad International Airport is the only international airport on the coast side of Syria and offers fewer flights than the much larger Damascus and Aleppo airports. Plans are in the works for construction of airports in Hassakeh and Raqqa, as well as the creation of an air taxi company to transport small groups of tourists and people traveling on business. Talks are also in progress regarding air transport between Syria and other countries, particularly Iraq. The country's main airline, Syrianair, flies to over forty capitals in Europe, Asia, and Africa.

With 2,753 kilometers of rail lines, Syria's network is modest, but major development is planned. Currently, international service exists between Aleppo and Istanbul, and between Damascus and Jordan. Domestic service runs from Damascus to Aleppo, Deir ez-Zur, and Qamishle; Aleppo has domestic service to Damascus, Lattakia, Deir ez-Zur, and Qamishle. The trains are fairly modern, inexpensive, and punctual, but stations often are located some kilometers from town centers. Multiple plans are in the works to upgrade and develop current stations for tourism by adding hotels, bars, restaurants, and entertainment centers. Plans to develop connections between north-south and east-west tracks and the restoration of old tracks are under way as well.

Syria shares land borders with Turkey, Iraq, Jordan, Lebanon, and Israel; all of the borders are open except the ones with Israel and sometimes the one with Iraq, depending on the political climate. The country's current road system is modern and well paved, and it connects major cities. Its approximately 46,000 kilometers of roads include a major four-lane highway extending from the Jordanian border along the full length of the Damascus-Homs-Hamah-Aleppo axis. Speed limits in built-up areas are 60 km/hr, 70 km/hr on open roads, and 110 km/hr on major highways. Drivers generally follow posted signs and signals, but they often drive aggressively and ignore lane markers. Plans for investing in the transport sector include an additional 8,000-a-day capacity road to connect the Turkish and Jordanian borders, a projected road connecting Tartous to eastern Syria and Iraq, a switchover project in Damascus, and the development of a 300-kilometer highway from the Mediterranean coast to Iraq.[60]

Public transportation is inexpensive and frequent when covering short distances. The shrinking Karnak Company buses are cheaper than other options, and often the cost difference is less than a dollar between this service and that of other bus lines; additionally, various old, battered buses run between towns and are the cheapest mode of transportation, but they are unreliable. Minibuses operate on short routes between cities and carry approximately twenty people each, departing only when full. Nicknamed "stop-stops" because they pick up and drop off passengers anywhere along the route, they don't follow any set schedule and often cause journey times to be longer than with other modes of transportation. Microbuses, actually vans, are used mainly to connect small towns and villages with their larger counterparts. Following set routes, they, too, drop off and pick up passengers en route.

Transportation and Travel

The most preferred form of bus transportation, especially for longer trips, is a luxury bus. Although multiple companies operate services, fares and the quality of service are generally the same; unfortunately, there is no main source of information regarding services. Luxury long-distance buses transport passengers to various locations in the country and to Jordan, Lebanon, Egypt, and several Gulf nations.

Taxis are not as popular in Syria as they are in other Middle Eastern countries. Private taxis and servees can be found in the major towns and cities, but with fares three times those of buses, unless people are in a great hurry, taxis are not the most popular choice.

Drawn by its charm and mystery, tourists and natives visit Syria's largest city and capital, Damascus, which claims to be the oldest continually inhabited city in the world. The old part of the city, closed within its walls, houses most of the city's attractions, including the Omayyad Mosque; the Damascus Citadel, the only citadel in the country not built on a hill or mountain but built as a city within itself, consisting of heavily fortified walls, towers, a moat, and trenches to protect the houses, mosques, and schools inside; Al Azem Palace; St. Paul's Church; and exotic, old souqs. The new city expands beyond the walls of the old city and is home to multiple museums, including the National Museum of Damascus, which exhibits classical antiquities as well as Arab-Islamic and contemporary art; the great Al-Takieh al-Suleimaniyeh Mosque, which houses both a mosque and a market; and a history museum.

Qalaat al-Hosn, Crac des Chevaliers, is one of the country's prime attractions. Well-preserved, the castle's outside wall is composed of thirteen towers and a main entrance, which is separated from the inner walls by a deep moat. The loggia's Gothic façade is impressive, as are the Great Hall, vaulted rooms, baths, and various towers.

One of the chief attractions of the old city of Aleppo is its covered souqs. Several parts of the maze of souqs date to the thirteenth century. The Great Mosque's freestanding minaret and the city's citadel are other main attractions. Al-Jdeida's Christian Quarter's web of streets is slowly being converted into an area full of restaurants, hotels, and bars.

The ruins at Palmyra include the Temple of Bel, the most complete structure in the ruins; colonnades; monumental arches; a restored colonnaded street; the Temple of Baal Shamin, a third-century funerary temple; and an amphitheater. Other areas of archaeological interest are the ruins at Tal Mardikh and Apamea's columns, with the remnants of its colonnade stretching far off into the distance.

Iraq

Iraq's volatile history makes reliable and up-to-date information regarding transportation systems largely unavailable. The first Gulf War (1990–91) left Iraq's transportation industry crippled, and although efforts have been made and completed, with the 2003 invasion of Iraq, it is unclear if those repairs and upgrades are still standing.

Estimates indicate there may be as many as 111 airports in Iraq, but an unknown number have been damaged in the recent war. The main airports are Baghdad International, Basra International, and Mosul International, all of which suffered neglect under Saddam Hussein's rule. Since 2003, the U.S. Agency for International Development (USAID) has invested $47 million to rehabilitate the Baghdad and Al Basrah international airports. The agency reports that the work on the Basrah airport, including rehabilitation of the water and sewage facilities, stripping of the runway, replacement of fences, and rehabilitation of the air traffic control tower, has been completed.[61] Commercial flights between Iraq, Ireland, Russia, and Jordan have recently been reestablished, but since tourists currently cannot obtain visas to visit the country, these flights are mainly used by business people.

TRANSPORTATION AND TRAVEL

Iraq has approximately 24,000 kilometers of rail lines and is linked via rail to Turkey, Syria, and Iran, with several tracks running into Baghdad; of these, the Baghdad-Basrah line carries the most passengers. Baghdad has had plans for a metro system for two decades, and some 1,000 kilometers of metro tunnels are rumored to exist, but to date United Nations inspectors have been unable to find their entrances.[62]

Iraq has an extensive road system, with approximately 45,550 kilometers of highways constructed in the 1970s and 1980s—which have not been sufficiently maintained—and an estimated 735,500 passenger vehicles. The roads are in disrepair because of war. While Iraq shares land borders with Saudi Arabia, Kuwait, Iran, Turkey, Syria, and Jordan, up-to-date border crossing information is unavailable. More than 1,000 of the bridges that cross the Tigris and Euphrates rivers are in differing stages of disrepair, but some rehabilitation progress has been completed. Buses link towns and cities, and taxis are available in major areas.

> ## THE TOMB OF JOSHUA
>
> The Tomb of Joshua's origin continues to be debated. An early commission established that Joshua's remains had been brought to Iraq during the first Jewish exodus, where they were interred as those of a Jewish rabbi, but for centuries Jews and Muslims argued about the origin; eventually, in 1885, Joshua's Tomb became a mosque, based on a decision by Sultan Abdul Hamid. Excavations are ongoing and may yield more information regarding the identity of the occupant. Joshua's tomb is guarded by a snake, which sleeps in the cool hollow of the excavations during the day and guards the entrance to the mausoleum at night. Another snake is currently being trained to replace the current snake when it dies.[63]

In the current political climate, it is easy to forget that Iraq is the historical Mesopotamia, home to the great Tigris and Euphrates rivers, and the cradle of ancient civilizations; when travel is again possible in this country, visitors may be surprised by its beautiful landscapes and architecture.

Baghdad is home to various mosques, a few Christian churches, and several ancient monuments. Of the most significant mosques are the Abu Hanifa Mosque, dedicated to Ibn Thabet al-Kufa, known as Abu Hanifa, whose influence on laws and morality is still present today; Shayka Abdel Kader al-Ghailani Mosque, which contains rooms for pilgrims, a library, and ancient copies of the Qur'an; and the Tomb of Joshua.

Baghdad's most significant museum, the National Museum, was once home to national and worldwide treasures including the Uruk vase, the Harmal Lions, and gold from Nimrod, all displayed in chronological galleries devoted to different historical periods in Iraq. After concerns from art historians and archaeologists, several of these important items were removed before the 2003 bombing of Iraq, but nearly fifty important pieces and multiple lesser but still important pieces are missing. The majestic, blue-tiled Monument of the Martyrs commemorates the civilian lives lost during the Iran-Iraq war; with its 45.72-meter pointed split domes, the monument sits on an expansive marble boardwalk surrounded by water. Baghdad's small, lively streets branch toward the Tigris River, replete with jewelry, rug, and used book souqs; historical meeting places for intellectuals and nationalists; and cafés. Saadun Street is home to the famous Baghdad clock and modern movie theaters, art galleries, hotels, and restaurants.

Among the other ancient locations of significance in Iraq are Najaf, Ur, Uruk, the Tree of Adam and Eve, and Babylon. Najaf is the fourth holy city of Islam, after Mecca, Medina, and Jerusalem. Its cemetery is one of the largest in the world because of the desire of Shia Muslims to be buried there. The restored ziggurat of Ur offers its visitors a panoramic view of the Chaldean desert and the Euphrates 16 kilometers away. A pit of ruins close to the tower boasts possible traces of the flood depicted in the Bible. Gilgamesh, one of the world's best-known heroes of mythology, is said to have ruled Uruk in the twenty-seventh century BCE. Currently, the ancient site is about twenty kilometers from the Euphrates River. The ruins were buried by the Tigris and Euphrates, but they reappeared in the late sixteenth century when the Tigris resumed its original course some distance away from the ruins. Long a top attraction for visitors, the Tree of Adam and Eve is believed to have been planted after the flood by Noah to commemorate the exact spot where a tree had stood in the Garden of Eden. Even though many of the ancient ruins of Babylon had been looted and destroyed by archaeologists, thieves, and locals (who used bricks from the site to build their houses) 30 years ago, partial restorations were completed in 2003 of the Temple of Ishtar, the Nabushcari Temple, ramparts, and the Summer Palace. A square trench surrounding the foundation is all that is left of the famed Tower of Babel, but the Lion of Babylon, brought back from Syria, stands near the place where it was unearthed. This is also the probable location of the ancient hanging garden of Babylon. While difficult to reach, and often mistaken for the Tower of Babel, the Eurmeiminanki, "The House of the Seven Drivers of Heaven and Earth," is worth a visit since its 56-meter ziggurat and part of the temple wall still stand. Located nearby is a sanctuary on the site of the cave said to be the location where Moses was raised.

Other archaeological points of interest include Hatra, Mosul, Nineveh, and Nimrud. The most impressive of Iraq's great archaeological sites is found in Hatra. Excavations are not finished, and over three-quarters of the heart of the city is still buried. Mosul is home to the ruins of a twelfth-century fortress and of the Mosul Museum, whose art and archaeological finds from neighboring areas have so far been protected from looting and bombing. Significant Islamic edifices here include the oldest Muslim religious structure in the city, the minaret on the Umayyad Mosque, and the Nuri minaret, which often compared to Italy's Leaning Tower of Pisa. Muslims believe that the minaret tilted the day the Prophet Muhammad died to salute his rise to Paradise. The archaeological site of Nineveh is located near Mosul; its walls have been partially restored, but most of the site has suffered during the recent decades of war. To the great benefit of the British Museum, Sir Henry Layard caused great devastation to the site by plundering. He pillaged sculpture, winged bulls and lions, reliefs depicting victories of kings, vases, weapons, and an ornamental wood throne. Max Mallowan, husband of the famous writer Agatha Christie, continued research on the site in a more scientific and careful manner. He and his team, including his wife, unearthed palaces, temples, and an ivory head of a woman, all the while trying to limit damage to the site. In 1970 Iraqi archaeologists took over the site.

Iran

Since the breakup of the Soviet Union, Iran has been expanding and improving its transportation network and has designs on becoming a major transit country in three corridors: first, a north-south corridor connecting northern Europe, the former Soviet Union countries, and Iran to the Persian Gulf and then by sea to India. A second plan is for a new Silk Road, linking Tajikistan, Uzbekistan, Iran, Afghanistan, and China. Central Asia, the third corridor, is currently connected via Turkmenistan to highway and rail networks in Iran, but Uzbekistan and Tajikistan desire access to the Persian Gulf through a shorter land route through Afghanistan. Despite these grand plans, development faces considerable obstacles, including political and financial problems.

While great distances between towns exist and flying is the quickest way to travel in the country, air transport composes only 3 percent of domestic passenger transport, carrying 22 million passengers in 2003–04.[64] Although Iran's airports have the capacity for 60 million passengers, planes are few and fill quickly. Eight of the country's thirty airports are suitable for international flights, with Mehrabad International the most prominent. Airport expansion to serve 30 million passengers is under way at Imam Khomeini International Airport. Esfahan, Mashhad, Shiraz, Bandar-e Abbas, Hamadan, Zehedan, and Qeshm are among Iran's other airports. The government-owned Iran Air is the country's official airline, with destinations all over Asia, the Middle East, and Europe. Iran Aseman, Mahan Air, Caspian Airlines, and Kish Airlines also offer a few international flights, generally to other Gulf countries.

Currently, Iran is linked by rail to Turkey, Pakistan, Turkmenistan, and Azerbaijan; approximately 500 kilometers of rail lines have been developed annually since 2000. Trains are efficient, comfortable, and cheap, with daily services to most popular locations. The Trans-Iranian Railway connects the Caspian Sea to the Persian Gulf. The new Bafq-Mashhad Railway reduces the distance between the Persian Gulf and central Asia by approximately 900 kilometers. Tehran also has a growing metro system helping to ease clogged roads; similar transit systems are being built in Mashhad and Esfahan.

Despite the current war in neighboring Iraq, crossing in and out of Iran is easy through borders with Afghanistan, Armenia, Azerbaijan, Turkmenistan, Turkey, Pakistan, and, although not recommended, Iraq. Road transport accounts for 93.2 percent of the domestic travel in Iran.[65] Roads are in good condition, with 110 km/hr speed limits on motorways and 80 km/hr during the day and 70 km/hr at night in built-up areas. Signs are in English, but that does not mean that driving in Iran is easy. Roads are well below the international standard, which is 20–24 km/per 100 sq km; Iran has only 11 kilometers of roads per 100 sq km.[66] According to *Iran Daily*, the number of cars doubles in Iran every 10 years, while the number of roads doubles only every 80 years.[67] Tehran's densely populated and polluted metropolis had 2.8 million cars, but even with the completion of current construction, the city's road networks will only have the capacity for 2.5 million cars. It is estimated that by 2011 the city's traffic will reach complete gridlock.[68] After four decades of domestic dominance in the car manufacturing market, Paykan, Iran's most popular car, ended production in 2005 because the cars were environmental hazards. Import tariffs have been slashed to motivate companies such as BMW and Toyota to export into Iran.

Public transportation is cheap, reliable, safe, and frequent, with long-distance buses running regularly to Azerbaijan, Syria, and Turkey. Most Iranian towns and cities have local bus service, but, because they are usually crowded and taxis are cheap, most visitors don't use them. In addition to the crowding, buses aren't marked in English, routes change without notice, and buses don't leave and return by the same route. Minibuses are primarily used for shorter distances between smaller towns. While they are often faster than buses and only a bit more costly, they aren't as comfortable and leave only when full.

Taxis are the fastest way to get around in Iran for visitors and locals. Shared taxis, or *savaris*, often duplicate local bus services and take up to five passengers. These orange taxis travel between major squares and along major roads in most towns and cities. Fares are fixed by the government. Private taxis can be chartered to go just about anywhere, and it is often possible to hire a driver for the day. The third type of taxi, the agency or "telephone" taxi, must be ordered by telephone or at an agency office. These are more expensive than other taxis, but they are more comfortable, and the drivers often speak English.

Iran offers more geological features than most Westerners realize with its towering mountains, deserts, plains, and coastline. Traditionally, Iran hasn't been a top tourist stop for foreigners, given its history, and while the country ranks among the top destinations in the world, it is last in terms of efforts to attract visitors;[69] however, in October 2004, the government announced plans to privatize the weakly run tourist sector in order increase tourism fifteenfold in the next 20 years by restoring old hotels and repairing transport routes.

Tehran is by far the top spot for those visiting Iran: it hosts roughly 90 percent of all visitors to the country annually.[70] People flock to its museums, historical buildings, the Imam Khomeini Mosque, and bazaar. Once the center of the city, Southern Tehran, although now old and poor, is home to Tehran's best museums. The National Museum is a must for visitors. Inside its grand recessed entrance, visitors will find collections of pottery, ceramics, and stone figures from various excavations; Zanjan's third- or fourth-century Salt Man, thought to have been a miner whose tools, white hair, beard, leg, and boot were preserved by the salt which buried him; and cuneiform inscriptions, glazed tile frieze, and various capitals from Persepolis. Other museums of interest include Golestan Palace, Malek National Museum and Library, National Jewels Museum, Glass and Ceramics Museum, Carpet Museum, Sad Abad Museum Complex, and Niyavaran Palace Museum. Home to the 1953 CIA-led coup d'état overthrowing Mohammad Mossedegh's government and then to 25 years of U.S. support for Mohammed Reza's government, the former U.S. Embassy in Tehran is currently called the U.S. Den of Espionage and is used by the Sepah military, dedicated to defending the revolution. While it is not open to the public, the walls on the outside are full of anti-American slogans and portraits, to which visitors are drawn.

For those interested in outdoor activities, the low-key adventurer will enjoy Park-e Mellat, a favorite in-town getaway for natives to relax and picnic by the lake. Darakeh and Darband's walking trails in the foothills of the Alborz Mountains are also a good choice. For the more ambitious, it is possible to walk up to the summit of Mount Tochal. Mount Damavand is an active volcano, which occasionally spits out sulfuric fumes, and its steep ascent is a challenge for visitors to climb. Unexpectedly for many, skiing in the Alborz ski resorts is also a popular activity.

Although not usually a first stop for travelers, the western part of the country is probably the location of the famed Garden of Eden and has much to offer visitors, including the regional trade and administrative hub, Tabriz, believed by many to be the location of the gates to the Garden of Eden. Popular with the locals, El Goli is a pleasant hillside garden and park nestling up to a huge artificial lake. The pleasant village of Kandovan's Cappadocia-style fairy chimneys; Kaleybar's Babek Castle, Iran's most impressive mountain fortress; the Castle of the Assassin's fifty fortresses; Takht-s Soleiman's crater lake, fire temple, and magnificent setting; Howraman's traditional Kurdish village; and Shush's archaeological site are also of interest to tourists. Hamadan is stretched around a star-shaped square, with six avenues extending outward in the shape of a star. Two of the most visited sites are the Ganjnameh Epigraphs and the Ali Sadr Caves.

Central Iran offers much in the way of attractions both for visitors and natives. Kashan, an oasis along the edge of the desert, offers a busy but relaxing bazaar, traditional houses, the Agha Bozorg Mosque, gardens, and archaeological sites. Tabas is an oasis between the Dasht-e Lut and Dasht-e Kavir deserts and is home to tropical trees and pools; Yazd's old city offers mud brick ruins, wind towers, courtyards, gardens, and the gorgeous Jameh Mosque. As the former capital and former seat of education, Shiraz offers the Arg-e Karim Khani fortress, Regent's Mosque, and the Mausoleum of Shah-e Cheragh. Persepolis is famous for its architecturally significant reliefs, columns, and gateways. Hidden behind high walls, the city's Grand Stairway of carved stone blocks lead into the Persepolic Complex. Xerxes' Gateway, the Palace of 100 Columns, and the Apadana Palace depict Persian history, and the Palace of Darius offers impressive gateways and cuneiform inscriptions.

Isfahan, the former capital of Persia, is 2,500 years old and is one of the most visited cities in the Islamic world; with its museums, bridges, mosques, and gardens, it is truly a city not to be missed. Among other treasures, the Jameh Mosque houses an ablutions fountain used by many to practice for the hajj, and the Taj al-Molk's brick dome is said to be mathematically perfect. The covered bazaar, Bazar-e Bozorg, is one of the highlights of the city, with its winding paths and decorated gateways. Imam Square, 512 meters long and 163 meters wide, and second in size only to Tiananmen Square, has changed little since it was built. The arches are currently being restored and fountains have been added; visitors can eat, shop, and visit its mosques. Covered in blue tiles, the Imam Mosque is considered to be among the most beautiful in the world. Eleven historic, fairy-tale-like bridges cross the Zayandeh River and provide extraordinary views of the city and its inhabitants. The Christian Armenian Quarter is home to excellent restaurants, churches, cathedrals, and the famous shaking minarets of the Manar Jomban Mosque.

The Persian Gulf is far from other tourist destinations in Iran, terribly hot in the summer months, and difficult to reach via buses, but it offers visitors a side of Iran not found elsewhere in the country. Towns along the coast, such as Kangan ad Bandar-e Taheri, offer ruins of fortresses, while Bandar-E Abbas is the country's busiest port. Those seeking solitude will enjoy the mostly uninhabited Hormoz Island, with its famous Portuguese Castle. Kish Island is to Iranians what Hawaii is to Americans—*the* vacation spot, visited by more than 1 million Iranians annually. Visitors are drawn to opportunities to relax and take a break from busy city life. It is also one of the few places where swimming is actually encouraged, although on separate beaches for each sex. Northeastern Iran is snuggled between the Dasht-e Kavi desert and the steppes of Central Asia. For the best views of the area, visit the West Radkan Tower. Up steep ridges and hairpin turns, Views from the Drazno village, reached by taking hairpin turns up to the top of the mountain ridge, are breathtaking. Mashad is the holiest city in the country: its sacred place is where the direct descendant of the Prophet Muhammad died in 817. Currently, the city is Iran's most important pilgrimage center and is visited by more than 12 million people a year. Mashad is also home to the Astan-e Qods-e Razavi, a 75-hectare complex full of mosques, minarets, and courtyards. The Holy Shrine is off-limits to non-Muslims, but the outside is gorgeous.

The Arabian Peninsula

That traditional Bedouin customs and lifestyle have met Western consumerism is obvious throughout the Arabian Peninsula. The seven countries composing the Arabian Peninsula—Bahrain, Kuwait, Qatar, Oman, United Arab Emirates, Yemen, and Saudi Arabia—share much in the way of traditions, transport, culture, and history, but they differ greatly in scenery and access. The Peninsula is home to gorgeous deserts, dense forests, vast wadis, coral reefs, archaeological wonders, and mountains. In the last fifty years, the Peninsula has also moved out of the Third World, experienced a fourfold population increase, and an increase in spending designed to attract tourists. The Gulf Cooperation Council (GCC) even wants to introduce a standard currency for the whole area by 2010. Given its strategic position and valuable resources, the Arabian Peninsula has always been at the center of important trade routes, formerly the main trade routes linking Mesopotamia to the Indus Valley, and is currently in the heart of the oil-rich Gulf.

In terms of travel, the Arabian Peninsula is a crossroads linking the East and the West. Even though air travel is relatively new in some countries, it has developed quickly. Currently, all major European, Asian, and Middle Eastern airlines serve principal cities in the region, and some of the countries have direct flight to the United States, Australia, East Africa, and various locations in the Middle East. Because of the lack of a regional rail system and the fact that it is not always comfortable to cover long distances in buses, most visitors to the Peninsula prefer to fly to their destinations.

Located on Muharraq Island, Bahrain's only international airport is modern and efficient, with 5.2 million passengers passing through it in 2004, an increase of 20 percent over the previous year.[71] The island is connected by two causeways to Bahrain Island.

Kuwait International Airport is not inexpensive to fly into or out of, but it does provide connections to many destinations in the Middle East, Europe, Asia, and the United States. While Kuwait Airlines is the country's national carrier, there are plans to launch a low-fare airline, Jazeera, with thirty flights a week to Bahrain, Beirut, Amman, Dubai, and Cairo.[72]

Qatar's Doha International Airport, home to Qatar Airlines, the national carrier, has one of the newest fleets. It flies to more than seventy destinations, with plans to add new routes to Ho Chi Minh City, New York, Bali, Chennai, India, and Ahmedabad, India.[73] The airport is currently under a three-phase construction project, set to be completed in 2015, which will accommodate 50 million passengers annually.

Yemen's Sanaa airport is home to most of the country's international traffic; flights from other Middle Eastern countries often use the smaller international airports in Aden, Al-Hudayda, Ar-Rayyan, Suyun, and Taizz. Yemenia, the country's national carrier, flies to dozens of destinations across the Middle East, Europe, Asia, and the United States and is the only airline that flies domestically.

Oman's Seeb International Airport completed 34,707 internal flights in 2003. This small airport, the only one in Oman, only offers flights to other countries in the Arabian Peninsula as well as a few domestic flights.

The United Arab Emirates' (UAE) main international airports are in Dubai and Abu Dhabi; Emirates Airlines and Gulf Air are the national carriers, which fly to worldwide destinations. Air Arabia, based in Sharjah, flies to destinations in the Middle East and the Gulf. The UAE has several smaller international airports in Fujairah, Ras al-Khaimah, and at Al-Ain, but there are currently no internal flights in the country. The Dubai Airport is serviced by almost all of the world's leading carriers; it served 21.7 million passengers in 2004 with projections to carry 60 million by 2010.[74] An expansion plan set to be completed by 2007 will increase the airport's current capacity of 22 million passengers to an estimated 70 million.[75]

Saudi Arabia has three main international airports: King Abdulaziz in Jedah, King Kahd in Dammam, and King Khaled in Riyadh as well as twenty-two regional and local airports. Saudi Air is the national carrier for the country and serves destinations across the Middle East, Europe Asia, and the United States; it also operates all domestic flights. In 2004, 34.26 million passengers flew in and out of Saudi Arabia, an increase of 7.6 percent over the previous year, according to the Ministry of Defense and Aviation, with King Abdulaziz transporting a little more than the combined total of King Kahd and King Khaled Airports.[76]

While train travel is not yet possible throughout the Arabian Peninsula, plans are in the works to help reduce traffic congestion and the increasing numbers of accidents by connecting the Arab world with one railway network. Currently, Dubai is at work on a major Metro Rail project set to begin operation in 2008 or 2009; the projection is that the railway will carry 355 million passengers annually.[77] Additionally, Dubai is planning two tram lines that will cater to both the local population and visitors.[78] Saudi Arabia is presently the only country on the Peninsula with operating train tracks providing service between Riyadh and Damman via Al-Hofuf. The kingdom is planning an extensive railway expansion program that includes construction of 950 kilometers of new track, a new 15-kilometer line, and upgrades to the existing lines to ease traffic volumes expected after the construction of the land bridge.⁷⁹ Construction of the land bridge is the cornerstone of the new railway project: it will link the Red Sea to the Gulf and be capable of moving cargo over long distances and transporting passengers quickly between the country's four main centers. It is expected to revolutionize transport in the country.

Turkey is Europe's main land access gateway to the Arabian Peninsula, with bus routes to Kuwait and Saudi Arabia and routes from Greece and Bulgaria by bus, train, and car; travel is also possible from Central Asia by bus or train through Turkmenistan, and by ferry from Iran to Oman or the UAE, but border crossings are often slow. Most countries on the Peninsula are home to high-quality multilane highways. Some of the larger cities on the Arabian Peninsula are experiencing Western-like congestion, and governments are trying to launch plans to ease traffic woes. Unfortunately, driving standards aren't uniform, and accidents are frequent, with parts of Saudi Arabia and the UAE having two of the highest accident rates in the world. Generally, speed limits are 100–120 km/hr on highways and 45–60 km/hr in towns, but not all drivers observe those limits or other driving etiquette. As with other areas of the Middle East, driving at night can be particularly hazardous because some cars don't have headlights, and camels may wander into the roads. Car ownership is high in the Peninsula states: Saudi Arabia alone accounts for 60 percent of the total sales for both Toyota and GM vehicles, with Ford sales skyrocketing as well. The UAE is the second largest market in the Middle East, followed by Kuwait. SUVs are becoming increasingly popular in the area because they are air conditioned, spacious, and usually have four-wheel drive, which is necessary to travel in many areas. Because of the high rates of ownership of personal vehicles, there is little demand for public bus service; however, as congestion results from increased car ownership, many countries are turning to other options such as public buses geared toward commuters and rail services in larger cities. The Peninsula currently has six major bus routes: Saudi Arabia to Bahrain, Saudi Arabia and Bahrain to Kuwait, Saudi Arabia and Bahrain to the UAE via Qatar, and the UAE to Oman and Yemen. It is also possible to travel from a country without much bus service to a neighboring country by taking domestic-service buses to the border, crossing the border, and picking up another domestic service in the other country, thus avoiding waiting for vehicles crossing borders to clear customs, which often can take several hours.

The only land crossing from Saudi Arabia to Bahrain is via the 26-kilometer King Kahd Causeway. Although Bahrain's road system is generally flat and well developed, the habits of the drivers are more of a reason for caution than the roads themselves. Four-to-six-lane highways and major roads are well maintained, but the roads in smaller villages and older sections of larger cities are often twisty and narrow, with confusing roundabouts. Bahrain has bus services to Saudi Arabia, Jordan, Syria, and the UAE. For internal travel, Bahrain has a public bus system that links most of the major towns and resort areas, but the buses are not always reliable and do not always go directly to points of interests for tourists.

Kuwait has approximately 2,000 kilometers of paved roads, and its expressways, which link all the major towns in the country, are in good repair; however, the high vehicle density and a propensity for speed can make driving hazardous. Kuwait's border with Iraq is currently closed, but it does have bus service to Saudi Arabia. Kuwait's bus system is cheap and extensive, but since it was not designed for tourists, the routes do not necessarily coincide with areas of interest; however, it is possible to walk from some stops to tourist locations. Most of the locals who ride the bus are from lower-income homes since car ownership among the middle and upper classes are so high.

Qatar has no international bus service to its neighboring countries, and visitors are not usually able to drive themselves across the Qatar-Saudi border, but there are plans to develop a causeway linking Qatar to Bahrain. Buses were supposed to link Doha with other major towns in the country, but service has been unreliable and infrequent. Recent developments may change that. In 2005, Mowasalat, a government transportation company, began operating a public bus service in Doha from the main bus terminal near Alfardan Center to the city center and industrial area. Buses run every twenty minutes.[80] The bus was immediately successful, carrying more than 2,000 passengers the first day, more than 4,000 the second, and 20,000 in the three days of the first weekend of operation.[81] With Doha's municipality-run buses, passengers were strictly low-income expatriates, but with this new service, that is no longer true. Now the government wants Mowasalat to run buses on the lines that the municipality used to operate.

Yemen has three land border crossings, but only one is open to foreigners. The road system in Yemen is not as developed as the systems in other Gulf countries, but with the increasing number of tourists and budgets to develop areas for tourism, that will most likely be changing in the future. Currently, though, maintenance of roads is a problem because of annual flash flooding. With the distances involved, few tourists opt to travel to neighboring countries by bus; additionally, the buses only go to the border, so tourists have to cross the border and find another bus. Traveling within the country by bus is relatively easy and comfortable, with service to and from almost all major towns. In cities, minibuses run inexpensive service from 6 AM until midnight, but taxis are usually easier for visitors to use.

Currently, it is not possible to cross the land border from Oman to Saudi Arabia, and often the border between Oman and Yemen is not safe because of smugglers and insurgents; however, the Oman border with the UAE has several crossing spots. Oman's bus service within its major cities is reliable and comfortable; the same is true of the service between its major cities.

Crossing land borders into the UAE can be difficult because of visa restrictions, unmanned stations, and confusing stops, so most visitors opt to travel via air into the UAE. Dubai is in the process of improving its internal road network to help ease traffic congestion until the light rail system is operating; construction is planned in late 2007, with an estimated completion date of 2012–15. Plans are in place to open an eight-lane tunnel under the Dubai Airport, a twelve-lane bridge across Dubai Creek, and several major interchanges. As the number of personal cars continues to grow—792,000 in 2003—there is still concern that the rail system will not be able to ease the increasing levels of congestion; as a result, there are plans to develop new water transport services across and along Dubai Creek as well as continued road development, with US$1.5 billion planned for road and bridge construction in 2005 alone.[82] Thirty-nine projects were completed in 2006, including twenty-four bridge and tunnel improvements, costing a total of US$2.5 billion.[83]

Dubai operates buses and minibuses to all the other Emirates. There are dozens of services to Jordan, Syria, Lebanon, and Egypt via Saudi Arabia and Jordan. Abu Dhabi has large municipal buses, but since they follow no fixed routes, they are often not useful for visitors. In June 2005 Emirates Express launched bus services to transport commuters between Dubai and Abu Dhabi. Dubai had several plans in place in 2005 to increase transportation options and ease traffic on clogged roads: possible solar-powered *abras* (small motorboats), water taxi or ferry service between Dubai and Sharjah, expansion of Emirates Express service to other emirates, and a floating pontoon station on Dubai Creek.[84]

Saudi Arabia has land border crossings with Bahrain, Jordan, Kuwait, Qatar, the UAE, and Yemen, all of which are relatively trouble free, except for the border with Yemen, which closes during diplomatic disputes. Saudi Arabia's border with Iraq is currently closed. The road system in Saudi Arabia is extensive and well developed, and some of the most well-traveled routes are eight-lane highways. Under- and overpasses in major cities have helped ease some of the traffic flow on the kingdom's clogged roads. Unfortunately, the country does have one of the highest road fatality rates in the Middle East. Drivers are sometimes so erratic that it is difficult to cross streets in cities. Because of the distances involved, Westerners visiting Saudi Arabia rarely travel to neighboring countries by bus, with the exception of the Dammam to Bah route and the Damman to Qatar route, but service is available from Saudi Arabia to Egypt, Jordan, the UAE, Syria, Kuwait, Qatar, Bahrain, and Turkey. It is easier and faster to fly to most locations in the area. Although local bus services in Riyadh, Jeddah, Damman, and Al-khoba are inexpensive, they are confusing so most visitors do not use them.

Renting cars is an option across the Peninsula. Most international companies have offices in most major cities and airports, but given uncertain border crossings, erratic drivers, potential lack of signage, lack of city parking, out-of-date maps, and confusing roundabouts, car rental may not be the best choice for visitors. Some tour companies, though, offer competitive rates and have drivers available for an extra fee.

Taxis are popular for traveling within most metropolitan areas for both locals and visitors. Operation varies from country to country, as do the different types of taxis. Taxis, also called regular taxis, agency taxis, telephone taxis, special taxis, or private taxis, are found in all main towns or cities; they often coexist with other forms of less-expensive transportation, such as minibuses or shared taxis. Many can be hired affordably for longer trips, depending on the country, and in many cases, taxis are the only way to reach air and sea ports. Cheaper than private taxis, the shared taxis (called servees in Arabic) generally carry four to five passengers at a time, run more frequently and for longer hours than buses, and don't stop as often as buses. While they generally run along a fixed route and charge a flat fee, riders may be able to negotiate a partial fare. Taxis are metered except in Kuwait and Sharjah in the UAE, where fares should be negotiated at the beginning of the trip, but drivers often have to be persuaded to use them. In Bahrain, a new law requires that only natives with good Arabic speaking skills who have passed a tourism course are licensed. Kuwait offers three types of taxis: orange private ones, which can be hailed from the side of the road; orange shared taxis running along set routes; and call taxis, which can only be reached by telephone. Traveling outside the city center in Kuwait is often expensive by taxi. Taxis in Qatar are not the best choice for travelers since the fleet is old and prone to breaking down.

Arabs love their cars, and many of the countries in this region have among the highest rates of personal car ownership in the world. Bahrain has 250,000 vehicles in an area not exceeding 350 square kilometers;[85] Kuwait has 963,499 registered cars, or one car for every 2.86 residents; in 2003, 240,532 cars were registered in Qatar;[86] the UAE registered one car for every two people in Dubai alone;[87] and despite an advanced public transportation system, Saudi Arabia's passion for private cars is perhaps rivaled only by that of the United States.

Travelers to the Arabian Peninsula are attracted to the area's exotic reputation and are delighted with all this mysterious region has to offer its visitors. Water sports such as water-skiing, game fishing, diving, and snorkeling are popular in most areas of the Peninsula. Additionally, diving in the Red Sea from Saudi Arabia is world class, with exceptional views of marine life. Bahrain and Oman also offer opportunities to go dolphin and whale watching. Camel races are popular in both the UAE and Saudi Arabia, with the latter being home to the largest camel market in the world. Swimming in this area can be dangerous, however: low tides make swimming near shore difficult in countries such as Bahrain and Qatar, and rip tides off the coast of the UAE's pristine beaches can also be hazardous. Traditional souqs, although often chaotic, are home to a variety of goods from textiles and gold jewelry to vegetables and animals. Alongside these traditional shopping extravaganzas, many countries now have contemporary malls, extravaganzas in their own right, which illustrates the juxtaposition of the traditional culture and the advancing modern culture. A surprising pastime for the Middle East, ice skating, is popular in Bahrain, Kuwait, and Qatar, with Kuwait home to a professional hockey team and the first rink in the Middle East. Amusement parks are also springing up on the Peninsula: Dubai's Wild Wadi Waterpark offers twenty-three interconnected rides and activities, and Al-Madina Al-Tarfihiya, the City of Entertainment near Doha, provides a complete range of amusements centered around the themes of "Arab World," "International World," and "Future World."

Bahrain's strategic location midway into the Persian Gulf made it a transit center on the ancient caravan routs and contributed to its early wealth built on the pearling industry. Bahrain Island is the largest of the thirty-three islands in the archipelago and consists of 83 percent of the total land are of the country; it is this island most people visit, and the location of most of the country's attractions. Bahrain is connected to Saudi Arabia by the 28-kilometer Kind Fahd Causeway; the causeway itself is a major tourist attraction, with its observation towers and remarkable construction. The early islanders' concern with proper burial is seen in the some 85,000 burial mounds on the island, covering about 5 percent of its total landmass.

Manama, "The Sleeping Place," is a haven for night owls and weekenders thanks to its active night life. It is also home to Bahrain's famous National Museum, which boasts ancient artifacts, contemporary art and culture exhibits, and narratives on contemporary culture. Another important museum in Manama is the Museum of Pearl Diving, which displays the country's heritage relative to this industry, antique weapons, traditional games and costumes, and musical instruments. The largest building in the country is the Al-Fatih Mosque; built in 1984, this mosque is capable of accommodating 7,000 worshippers. Although the Friday Mosque isn't open to tourists, it is worth a visit to admire its mosaic minaret, its most interesting architectural feature. Other sites for visitors on Bahrain Island include Bah Fort; Qala at al, a fort surrounded by a moat that was built as part of a series of defenses along the Gulf shore; the approximately 170,000 A'Ali Burial Mounds, dating from 3000 BCE to 600 CE; Barbar Temple, a complex of second- and third-millennium temples; Bani Jamra, a village famous for its traditional weaving; and the Tree of Life. This mesquite tree is famous not for how old it is but because its source of survival is a mystery. The sixteen islands known collectively as Hawar Islands is home to the Hawar Resort and natural wild life, but Dar Island is more accessible than Hawar Islands and offers sandy beaches and water sports as its main attractions.

The coming years are expected to bring more tourists to this country because of the expected return of the Grand Prix, which Bahrain hosted in April 2004. When excavations are complete of the burial chambers at Sur, the government plans to turn the location into a major tourist attraction. In 2003, the country generated the equivalent of US$2.4 billion, with an expected annual tourism increase of 4.6 percent, which was exceeded in 2005 with an increase of 13 percent.

Visitors to Kuwait expecting to see evidence of its recent upheaval and Iraqi occupation will be surprised instead to see evidence of the country's rapid growth. Although the historic islands of Failaka and Bubiyan are currently closed to visitors for security reasons, and the interior of the country is mostly flat, oil-producing land with few towns and is affected by concerns over undiscovered landmines in the desert, Kuwait City is the country's magnet for tourists. It is home to first-class accommodations, museums, shopping, marine life, traditional souqs, modern malls, and the famous triple towers. Most of the capital's highly visited spots are located along the 10-kilometer-long sculpted corniche, marked by the Kuwait Towers on the north and the Science Center on the south. The country's most famous landmark, the Kuwait Towers with their distinctive green sequins, fulfill a dual purpose: they provide storage for water and house entertainment facilities.

Current visitors won't be able to learn much about the country's past since the collection belonging to the National Museum was destroyed and looted during the Iraqi invasion. Once consisting of four buildings and a planetarium, this museum, the pride of the country, is currently one of the saddest places to visit: it serves as one of the few visible reminders of Iraqi occupation, during which many of the precious exhibits were smashed, set on fire, looted, or stolen. After intense pressure from the United Nations, some of the surviving artifacts were returned to Kuwait, but these are currently being exhibited at the Metropolitan Museum of Art in New York City and the British Museum until restoration is complete.

The artificial Green Island, home to a 700-seat amphitheatre, restaurants, gardens, and a game park, is connected to the mainland by a causeway. Some traditional buildings survived the Iraqi occupation intact, among them Bayt al-Badr, Beit Dixon, and the National Assembly Building, and are draws for visitors. The Masjed Al-Kabir, the Grand Mosque, the largest of Kuwait City's 800 mosques, boasts the country's highest minaret at 74 meters; it can accommodate 5,000 worshippers inside the main hall and an additional 7,000 in the courtyard. The Old City gates, the Beit Lotran Cultural Center, the traditional souq complex, and the Friday Market's shopping extravaganza are other spots of interest.

Other sights of significance include the Liberation Tower, symbol of Kuwaiti liberation and the tallest building in the city; the Science Center, which has the largest aquarium in the Middle East and includes a living reef, a wraparound, floor-to-ceiling shark tank, and underground passages rich in marine life and examples of natural habitat; and the Al-Hashemi Marine Museum, home to the largest wooden boat on earth and a collection of large scales model dhows.

While Qatar has no visible connection to its past, this does not mean modernization has erased its history. Qatar has developed from one of the poorest of the Gulf States, with its income based on pearling, to become one of the richest because of its oil- and gas-producing fields. Qatar's capital, Doha, home to 83 percent of the country's population, continues to grow and to draw tourists. The 13.5-kilometer-long corniche is the highlight of the city; it displays the city's newly constructed bay area and boasts foot and cycling paths, a restaurant complex, and moored dhows. The newly renovated Qatar National Museum was reopened in February 2006. Doha's Fort offers a range of traditional Qatari activities, such as woodcarving, modern painting, weaving, and other local crafts; and Palm Tree Island, in the middle of Doha Bay, offers a seafood market, horseback riding, pools, and a corniche. The beaches on the shore are clean but almost impossible to swim in because of the water's shallowness.

While most of the country's attractions are in Doha, a few sites outside the city are worth a visit. Al-Wakrah and Al-Wakair offer visitors mosques, traditional houses, museums, and old Islamic architecture; Al-Kohr offers a museum, a corniche, an old watch tower, and gardens; Jebel Jassassiyeh is a rocky ridge with rock carvings dating back several thousands of years; Bir Zekreet is a limestone escarpment where the wind has carved away softer sedimentary rock to expose pillars and large mushrooms of limestone; and Al-Shahaniya is famous for its camel races. The most famous attraction in the country is Khor Al-Daid near the Saudi Arabian border. Although the Khor is often described as a lake or sea, it is actually a creek surrounded by silver crescents of sand dunes. While tourists can reach it by four-wheel-drive vehicles, taking an organized tour is the best way to visit.

Yemen's reputation with tourists has suffered in the past as a result of tribal tensions, weak government control of powerful autonomous tribes, and kidnappings. Despite this past, Yemen's recent efforts to attract visitors to its beautiful country—which boasts a desert coastal strip bordering the Red Sea, a mountainous central region, and an eastern desert—have been successful. The expansion and rapid growth experienced in Sanaa, the capital, is evidence of the country's population explosion. In the last three years, Yemen's population has increased tenfold. One of the most ancient sites on the Arabian Peninsula, Sanaa, according to legend, was the city of Shem mentioned in the Bible and built by Noah's son. Although salt is only one of the items in the multitude offered at the Souq al-Milh, the "Salt Market," it is one of the major attractions of the ancient city. Fifty mosques grace Sanaa, of which the Great Mosque is the most significant since it was an important center of learning for centuries. The library is also home to the largest and most famous collection of manuscripts in Yemen.

Wadi Dhahr, Shaharah, Aden, Shibam, and Suqutra are other areas of interest in Yemen. Wadi Dhahr is 14 kilometers from Sanaa; in the center stands the famous Dar al-Hajar. The five-story rock palace, built in the eighteenth century by Imam Yahya as a summer residence, seems to grow out of the rock below and is visible from all sides because it stands alone, rising above all neighboring land masses. The fortified village of Shaharah, located on the top of a mountain, is one of Yemen's highlights, even though it is not easy to reach. Offering stunning views of the country, the village is 2,600 meters up the mountain. To reach it, visitors must charter a local four-wheel-drive vehicle since villagers are wary of strangers after centuries of isolation and will not allow visitors to drive to the mountain top. Shaharah's strategic location was a stronghold during the war against the Ottomans because of its unconquerable location. Two parts of the citadel are on the tops of different mountains, separated by a deep gorge. The famous suspended Shaharah Bridge, constructed completely of rock, connects the two and is one of the favorite sights for visitors to this mountaintop village.

Aden is the country's commercial capital and largest port; according to legend, it is the location where Noah's Ark was built and launched. Spread around the base of extinct volcanoes and joined to the mainland by an isthmus, Aden offers visitors museums, markets, mosques, and beach resorts. The famous Aden Tanks, cisterns believed to date from the first century and numbering among the oldest and greatest feats of engineering in the country, are a considerable draw for visitors. Shibam is a walled city called the "Manhattan of the Desert" because of its tower-like structures rising out of neighboring cliffs. Its famous skyscraper houses are made of adobe on foundations many believe to be several centuries old. Suqutra is one of the country's largest islands and probably the most interesting one because it existed in almost total isolation from the rest of Yemen. Gradually, it is being developed for tourism with locations for the water sports common in the Gulf States.

Oman is a large and geographically diverse country with fertile plains and mountains as well as coastlines. Muscat is the country's capital, but often the name is used to refer to a string of three cities—Muscat, Mutrah, and Ruwi—where most of the country's attractions are located. Formerly walled and currently featuring a stone moat, Muscat is the financial and trade center of Oman, boasting beautiful beaches, public gardens, and parks. Built in the sixteenth century, the forts of Al-Jaladi and Al-Mirani flank the Sultan's Palace. Other museums in Muscat include the Muscat Gate Museum, Bayt Az-Zubair, which displays traditional handicrafts, and the Omani-French Hotel, which exhibits the history of the relationship between France and Oman along with displays of nineteenth-century colonial life in Muscat. Mutrah is the capital's main port and stretches along a corniche made up of mosques and latticed buildings. Mutrah's Fort was also built during Portuguese occupation and stands at the eastern end of the harbor; Al-Riyam and Kalbuh Bay parks provide attractive views of the harbor. The last area of the capital, Ruwi or "Little India," is the commercial and transport hub and home to the National Museum, which houses murals celebrating the country's seafaring heritage, pottery, traditional costumes and jewelry, silver work, and the ornately decorated wooden chests for which the country is famous.

TRANSPORTATION AND TRAVEL

Qurm, the Sharqiya Region, and Wadi Shab are other areas in Oman visited by tourists and locals. Although Qurm consists mostly of shopping areas and residences, it does offer a few other attractions for visitors. The Oman Museum offers a great view along with cultural artifacts; the Grand Mosque is home to the largest carpet in the world. Taking four years and 600 women working 12 million hours to weave, the carpet measures 70 meters × 60 meters, weighs 22 tons, and is comprised of 1,700 million knots. Some of the country's main attractions are found in the Sharqiya region in the corner of the Arabian Peninsula. Qurayat offers a watch tower and a nineteenth-century castle. The Bimmah Sinkhole is known locally as Bayt al-Afreet, or "House of the Demon," because of the blue green water at the bottom of a limestone sinkhole with an unknown depth; swimming and snorkeling are common here. Known as the "gorge between the cliffs," the entrance to Wadi Shab is marked by a vista of mountains opening to the view of a green lake. This popular site is home to grazing gazelles, gorgeous waterfalls, plantations, and aquamarine pools. Swimming is possible in its partially submerged cave.

OMAN'S TURTLE POPULATION

When one thinks of turtles, Oman probably is not the country that comes to mind. Nevertheless, the country is important in two ways to the world's turtle population. The easternmost point of the Arabian Peninsula, Ras Al-Jinz, is an important site for the endangered green turtle. Annually, over 20,000 females return to the beach where they were hatched to lay their eggs. The site is so important that strict penalties are enforced for harming turtles or eggs. The desert island of Masirah, home to 300-year-old grave sites and various wild life, is currently difficult to access because of its remote location, but major hotel chains are negotiating to develop parts of the island's eastern shore for tourism. Presently, the island's wildlife is its major draw as it is home to over 300 species of birds and four species of turtles. It is also the largest loggerhead turtle nesting spot in the world, and 30,000 come ashore each year.

The western Hajar Mountains and Nizwa are the two biggest tourist destinations in the country. The Hajar Mountains boast Jebel Shams, the country's highest mountains; Wadi Ghul, the Grand Canyon of Arabia; and the green mountain, Jebel Akhdar. While Jebel Shams has the highest peaks in the country, its fame comes from the spectacular, deep Wadi Ghul next to it. The plateau level, approximately 2,003 meters in elevation, drops sharply nearly 1,000 meters into the canyon. This canyon must be reached by a four-wheel-drive vehicle or a minibus. Jebel Akhdar sits at 3,048 meters above sea level, with small villages built with stones from the mountain scattered on it. Diverse agriculture with several varieties of fruit trees earns the area it's "fruit bowl of Oman" nickname. Nizwa's watchtower is 46 meters in diameter and soars 35 meters above the rest of the structure's battlements, secret shafts, turrets, and false doors.

According to the WTO, 5.9 million international visitors traveled to the UAE in 2003, spending the equivalent of US$1.4 billion.[88] The UAE is growing rapidly, and its commercial development can be seen clearly in the recent developments of Palm Island, Hydropolis, and Burj al-Arab. Palm Island added 120 kilometers of beach to Dubai's coastline, 2,000 private residences, shopping malls, cinemas, two marinas, and forty boutique hotels. Hydropolis, due to be completed early in 2006, is an underwater hotel, resembling a submarine, that will be navigated by a subaquatic train. Opened in 1999, Burj al-Arab, the world's tallest hotel at 321 meters, is Dubai's most popular tourist attraction and seems to serve as a tribute to consumerism. Floating on its own man-made island, Burj al-Arab boasts opulence, fire-spouting volcanoes, the world's largest atrium, water ballet fountains, and panoramic elevators traveling at a rapid six meters per second. The hotel had an underwater restaurant, but it is currently closed because camera flashes kept killing the fish.

Dubai, the second largest Emirate and one of the world's major trading ports, was built on the edge of a narrow, winding creek that divides the southern section, Bur Dubai, the city's traditional center, from Deira, the commercial center. Khor Dubai, the creek, is the heart of the city. Crossing the creek is done by bridge, car, pedestrian tunnel, or the traditional abras, a small motorboat. The Dubai Museum's underground section houses lifelike exhibits of an ancient souq, a Qur'an school, an oasis, and typical Arab households. Bastakiya Desert, famous for its wind towers, is one of the original trading districts in old Dubai. Jumeira Mosque is the only working mosque in the UAE open to non-Muslims and is a beautiful sight with its delicate minarets and rose-colored sandstone.

Sharjah is the third-largest emirate. Although currently fairly conservative, with rules banning alcohol, revealing clothes, swim suits on public beaches, and the sharing of rooms between unmarried couples, there are rumors that these restrictions may be lifted. A walk around the heart of the city, Khalid Lagoon, is a must because of the hotels, restaurants, old town, museums, art galleries, and souqs. Sharjah is also home to art museums, architecturally significant buildings, Literature Square, Poetry House, Al-Hisn Fort, and the newly created University City, which boasts a sprawling campus, fountains, and manicured lawns.

Abu Dhabi, the capital, occupies 86 percent, of the country's landmass although much of the Emirate is empty desert. The city's Grand Mosque, currently under construction, was originally planned to be the biggest in the world, but its design angered Saudis, so Sheikh Zayed was persuaded to scale back the plan in order that the "biggest and best" title can be retained by Mecca's mosque. The recently completed Abu Dhabi's Conference Palace Hotel is said to be the only seven-star hotel in the world. Landmark buildings in Abu Dhabi include Qasar al-Hosn—White Fort, or Old Fort—the oldest building in the city; the Clock Tower; and the Volcano Fountain, which is actually a giant incense burner. The Cultural Foundation arts complex is the center of the city's cultural life, while the five-kilometer-long corniche is a favorite for locals and tourists alike, owing to its sentinel-like lighting structures overlooking the bay. Another popular tourist spot is Heritage Village, which offers viewers the opportunity to visit pre-oil era replicas of a Bedouin encampment and traditional mosques, shop in a traditional souq, and take a ride on a camel.

Fujairah is a small city, but its pristine, deep blue beaches make this a popular destination for domestic tourism. A popular spectator sport, bull-butting, has been held here for centuries. Tourists are quickly learning of the dramatic scenery and are flocking to Fujairah for its beaches as well as its Heritage Museum, National Park, and Khor Fakkan—the Creek of Two Jaws—which is considered by many to be the most beautiful harbor in the UAE. Its corniche is bounded by fish markets and the port, and lined with palm trees and large grassy picnic areas.

In Saudi Arabia, tensions between its Islamic heritage and the desire to maintain close friendships with the Western world and its influence are evident throughout most of the country. While the country is host to millions of foreigner workers and pilgrims, it has traditionally been difficult to visit because of multiple bureaucratic obstacles. Recent changes have helped ease these problems; with a 17 percent increase in international tourism in 2004, 8.6 million international visitors went to Saudi Arabia and spent the equivalent of US$6.5 billion.[89] Mecca and Medina are Islam's two holiest cities, receiving 2.5 million pilgrims a year, but are off limits to non-Muslims.

The juxtaposition of ultramodern skyscrapers and mud brick ruins demonstrates Riyadh's balance of past and future. Surrounded by deserts, this capital city is home to historical areas and architecturally significant structures, both ancient and modern. The King

Abdul Aziz Historical Area's landscaped paths cover over 360 square kilometers teeming with open-air exhibits. The National Museum has eight galleries exhibiting reconstructed Dilmun tombs, rock art, models of holy mosques, and virtual visits to ancient sites. Riyadh's most significant monument is the Masmak Fortress, one of the few remaining buildings from Old Riyadh; renovated in the 1980s and turned into a museum a decade later, it is home to a labyrinth of rooms, mosques, and courtyards designed to be self-contained during times of siege. Other popular sites for visitors include Al-Saah Square, known by locals as "Chop Chop Square," the site of the city's infamous beheadings; the ornate Al-Thumain Gate, actually a series of nine restored gates leading into the city; the modern sandstone Great Mosque; the new Al-Faisaliah Tower; and the stylish Kingdom Tower.

Jeddah, Madain Saleh, and Jubba are other cities frequented by locals and visitors in Saudi Arabia. Jeddah is the historical crossroads of traders and pilgrims and is perhaps the most interesting of Saudi Arabia's large cities. Currently approximately 1,000 times the size of the original city, Jeddah is the traditional gateway to Mecca. Standing midway between Mecca and Petra in Jordan, Madain Saleh is the crossroads of trade caravans, pilgrims, and explorers. Since Madain Saleh is home to stone-carved temples, the Nabateans chose it as their second city after Petra. The tombs are well preserved, and the sand and rock formations make this city a gorgeous one to visit. Those interested in cave paintings should visit Jubba to view remarkable rock carvings of long-horned buffalo, domesticated dogs, and human fighters believed to date to 5500 BCE. While not as stunning as that in Jubba, the rock art of Bir Hima is still worth a visit. Beautiful landscapes include Elephant Rock, a towering natural rock formation that looks like the animal for which it is named, and Wadi Hisma, which is comparable to Jordan's Wadi Rum with its red stone mountains and stunning sands.

The Rub al-Khali, or the Empty Quarter, is a 655,000-square-kilometer desert with the largest continuous body of sand in the world. With its sand-sculpted dunes rising sometimes to over 300 meters, this large empty space is still home to some locations through which only a few people have ever passed. While the history of the Empty Quarter is not one told in history books, its story has been passed orally through Bedouin tribes. Although it is easy to enter the Empty Quarter, it is equally easy to get lost: a well-planned trip either in a four-wheel-drive vehicle or on a camel is a necessity.

RESOURCE GUIDE

PRINTED SOURCES

Baker, Patricia L. *Iran: The Bradt Travel Guide*, 2nd edition. Guilford, CT: Globe Pequot Press, 2005.
Burke, Andrew, Mark Elliott, and Kamin Mohammed. *Iran*, 4th edition. Oakland, CA: Lonely Planet Publications, 2004.
Camerapix. *Spectrum Guide to United Arab Emirates*. New York: Interlink, 2002.
Cotterell, Paul. *The Railways of Palestine and Israel*. Oxford, England: Tourret Publishing, 1986.
Gordon, Frances Linzee, and Anthony Ham. *Arabian Peninsula*. Oakland, CA: Lonely Planet Publications, 2004.
Ham, Anthony. *Libya*. Oakland, CA: Lonely Planet Publications, 2005.
——— and Abigail Hole. *Tunisia*, 3rd edition. Oakland, CA: Lonely Planet Publications, 2004.
——— and Paul Greenway. *Jordan*. Oakland, CA: Lonely Planet Publications, 2003.
———, Martha Brekhus Shams, and Andrew Madden. *Saudi Arabia*. Oakland, CA: Lonely Planet Publications, 2004.

Transportation and Travel

Hardy, Paula, Mara Vorhees, and Heidi Edsall. *Morocco*, 7th edition. Oakland, CA: Lonely Planet Publications, 2005.

Held, Colbert C. *Middle East Patterns: Places, Peoples, and Politics*, 3rd edition. Boulder, CO: Westview Press, 2004.

Humphreys, Andrew, Gadi Farfour, Siona Jenkins, Anthony Sattin, and Joann Flether. *Egypt*, 7th edition. Oakland, CA: Lonely Planet Publications, 2004.

Lee, Risha Kim, Amelie Cherlin, and Charlotte Houghteling, eds. *Let's Go: Israel and the Palestinian Territories*. New York: St. Martin's Press, 2003.

Maxwell, Virginia. *Istanbul*, 4th edition. Oakland, CA: Lonely Planet Publications, 2005.

Teller, Matthew. *Rough Guide to Jordan*, 2nd edition. NP: Rough Guides, 2002.

Tourret, R. *Hedjaz Railway*. Oxford, England: Tourret Publishing, 1989.

Turkoglu, Sabahattin. *Paukkale Hierapolis*, 2nd edition. Istanbul: Net Turistik Yayinlar, 1986.

WEBSITES

Al-Ahram Weekly Online. http://weekly.ahram.org.eg/index.htm. Searchable English-language weekly newspaper from Egypt.

Bahrain Tourism. http://www.bahraintourism.com/. Government-sponsored tourism site including attractions, hotels, clubs, resorts, and restaurants.

Bahrain Tribune. 2003. Arabian Network Information Services. http://www.bahraintribune.com/. Searchable English-language newspaper.

Embassy of the Hashemite Kingdom of Jordan. Washington, D.C. www.jordanembassyus.org. News, government information, travel information, and links.

GoDubai. http://www.GoDubai.com. Information regarding attractions, hotels, entertainment, shopping, and events. Includes a virtual tour and additional links.

Jordan Tourism Board North America. 2005. Jordan Tourism Board North America. http://www.seejordan.org/index.html. Pictures, travel information, news, articles, links, and video.

Kingdom of Saudi Arabia Ministry of Defense and Aviation. 2002. General Authority of Civil Aviation. http://www.pca.gov.sa.

Kuwait Information. Kuwait Information Office. New Delhi, India. October 31, 2005. http://www.kuwait-info.com/. Information on history, education, tourism, culture, festivals, news, and a photo gallery.

Ministry of Transport. 2005. The Hashemite Kingdom of Jordan. http://www.mot.gov.jo/index.php.

National Information Technology Centre. 2004. The Hashemite Kingdom of Jordan. http://www.nic.gov.jo/. Government database with statistics.

NetIran. 1995–2005. NetIran. http://www.netiran.com/?fn=site. Searchable site including business and travel news.

Oman Daily Observer. Oman Establishment for Press, News, Publication and Advertising. October 31, 2005. http://www.omanobserver.com/. Searchable English-language newspaper with excellent links to government ministries and organizations.

Oman Ministry of Tourism. 2005. Ministry of Tourism. http://www.omantourism.gov.om/.

The Star Wars Traveler. http://www.toysrgus.com/travel/tunisia.html. A map, local pictures, and movie stills, with an explanation of each location used in the movies.

Visitor's Complete Guide to Bahrain. Nov. 5, 2005. http://www.bahrainguide.org/BG4/editorial.html. Visitor's directory, including a picture gallery with search capabilities.

MUSEUMS

Egged Museum of Passengers Traffic, Moshe Dayan St., Egged Bus Station, Holon, Israel. Contains the different types of buses used by this company since the 1920s.

Israel Air Force Museum, Hatzerim Air Force Base, Beersheba, Israel. http://www.fai.org/education/museums/isr_iaf. Maintains an extensive collection of aircraft, some of which are unique to this museum, and a collection of aerial weapons.

Keren Sahar Vintage Auto Museum, Kibbutz Eyal, Tel Aviv, Israel. One of the most amazing collections of vintage cars in the country.

Railway Museum, Haifa East Station, Haifa, Israel. http://www.israrail.org.il/english/general/museum.html. Exhibits detail the history of railroads in Israel and include pictures and coach cars.

Railway Museum, Ramses Square, Cairo, Egypt. No official website, but an article including pictures and a description can be found at http://www.israrail.org.il/english/general/museum.html. The five sections of this museum include over 700 models, maps tracing the development, and a general overview of air industry in Egypt.

NOTES

1. See "Tourism Highlights 2005 Edition," *World Tourism Organization*, http://www.world-tourism.org.
2. See "Ilan Road Crash Claims 5 Lives," *Iran Daily*, October 10, 2005, http://www.iran-daily.com.
3. See "Tourism Highlights 2005 Edition," *World Tourism Organization*, http://www.world-tourism.org.
4. Ibid.
5. Ibid.
6. Ibid.
7. Ibid.
8. See "Airport Identity Card," *Office de l'aviation Civile et des Aeroports*, Tunisia, http://www.oaca.nat.tn/english/index_public_eng_org.htm
9. See "Libya Preparing to Become a Transit Hub," *United World*, January 16, 2006, http://www.unitedworld-usa.com.
10. See "Airport Expansion Will Handle Increasing Traffic," *New York Times*, Summit Communications, http://www.nytimes.com/ads/global/libya2/five.html.
11. See "Railway Lines and Tracks," *Libyan Railway Executive Board*, http://www.libyaninvestment.com/railways/main_railways.php.
12. See "Tourism Highlights 2005 Edition," *World Tourism Organization*, http://www.world-tourism.org.
13. Ibid.
14. See "Tourism to Morocco Keeps Growing," *Afrol News*, March 23, 2005, http://afrol.com.
15. See "Morocco, First Destination for French Tourists," *Morocco Times*, January 1, 2006, http://www.moroccotimes.com.
16. See Pablo Gracia, "Morocco Confirms Large Growth in Tourism," *Afrol News*, September 2, 2006, http://www.afrol.com/articles/13862.
17. See "Libya Tourist Potential by 2018," *Afrol News*, December 21, 2005, http://afrol.com.
18. Ibid.
19. See Amira Ibrahim, "Necessary Makeovers," *Al-Abram Weekly Online* (in Resource Guide), March 3–9, 2005.
20. See Sherine El-Madany, "Into the Fast Lane," *Al-Abram Weekly Online* (in Resource Guide), June 2–8, 2005.
21. See Ibrahim, "A Breath of Fresh Air," *Al-Abram Weekly Online* (in Resource Guide), April 7–13, 2005.
22. See *YearBook 2003*, Egypt State Information System.
23. See Fatemah Faraq, "Lost Souls," *Al-Abram Weekly Online* (in Resource Guide), February 17–23, 2005.
24. See Faraq, "One Way Ticket," *Al-Abram Weekly Online* (in Resource Guide), February 28–March 6, 2002.
25. Ibid.
26. See Reem Nafie, "Trouble Underground," *Al-Abram Weekly Online* (in Resource Guide), June 12–18, 2003.
27. See *YearBook 2003*, Egypt State Information System.
28. See El-Madany, "Into the Fast Lane."
29. See *YearBook 2003*, Egypt State Information Service.

30. See Mustafa El-Menshawy, "Missing the Bus," *Al-Ahram Weekly Online* (in Resource Guide), March 31–April 6, 2005.
31. See Gahan Shahine, "A Mounting Toll," *Al-Ahram Weekly Online* (in Resource Guide), August 24–30, 2000.
32. See El-Madany, "Into the Fast Lane."
33. See "Tourism Highlights 2005 Edition," *World Tourism Organization*, http://www.world-tourism.org.
34. See "Queen Alia International Airport," *Royal Jordanian Airlines*, http://www.rja.com.jo/pc/QAIA.asp.
35. See "Statistical Tables," *Ministry of Transport* (in Resource Guide).
36. See *Hashemite Kingdom of Jordan*, Jordan Ministry of Tourism and Antiquities, http://www.tourism.jo.
37. Ibid.
38. Ibid.
39. Ibid.
40. See "Airports," *Israeli Airports Authority*, www.iaa.gov.il/RASHAT/en-US/Airports.
41. Ibid.
42. Ibid.
43. Ibid.
44. See Daniel Kennemer, "Sheetrit's Big Vision for Israel's Roads and Rails," *Jerusalem Post*, December 11, 2005, http://www.jpost.com.
45. See *Israel Tourism Portal*, Israel Ministry of Tourism, http://www.tourism.gov.il/.
46. See Danny Sadeh, "Three Million Tourists Expected in 2006," *Ynet Travel*, http://www.ynetnews.com.
47. See *Israel Tourism Portal*, Israel Ministry of Tourism, http://www.tourism.gov.il/.
48. See Martin Patience, "Bethlehem Residents Protest Security Terminal," *USA Today*, December 13, 2005, http://www.usatoday.com/news/world.
49. Ibid.
50. See "Yearly International Travel," *Beirut Rafic Hariri International Airport*, Directorate General of Civil Aviation. http://www.beirutairport.gov.lb/home.html.
51. Ibid.
52. See Barbara Starr, John Dause, and Anthony Mills, "Israeli Warplanes Hit Beirut Suburb,"*CNN.com*, July 14, 2006, http://www.cnn.com.
53. See Anthony Shadid and Scott Wilson, "Israel Blockades, Bombs Lebanon while Hezbollah Rains Rocket Fire," *Washington Post*, July 14, 2006, http://www.washingtonpost.com.
54. See Hannah Wettig, "With 1.2m Cars, Why Not Revive the Train System?" *Daily Star*, August 17, 2005, http://www.dailystar.com.lb.
55. See "Frequenting Touristic Sites," *Central Administration for Statistics*, Lebanese Republic Presidency of the Council of Ministers, "http://www.cas.gov.lb; "Tourism Highlights 2005 Edition," http://www.world-tourism.org.
56. See "Tourism Highlights 2005 Edition," *World Tourism Organization*, http://www.world-tourism.org.
57. See "Frequenting Touristic Sites," *Central Administration for Statistics*, Lebanese Republic Presidency of the Council of Ministers, "http://www.cas.gov.lb.
58. Ibid.
59. See *Syrian Ministry of Transportation*, http://www.mot.gov.sy.
60. Ibid.
61. See "Iraq Reconstruction: A Brief Overview," *U.S. Agency for International Development*, September 12, 2005, http://www.usaid.gov/iraq.
62. See "Saddam's Deadly Subway Scheming," *CBS News*, February 21, 2003, http://www.cbs.news.com.
63. See Gilles Munier, *Iraq: An Illustrated History and Guide* (Northampton, MA: Interlink Books, 2004).
64. See "A Four-Year Analysis of Domestic Transportation," *International Transportation*, February 2005, http://netiran.com.
65. Ibid.
66. See "Roads at Dead-End," *Iran Daily*, October 26, 2005, http://www.iran-daily.com.
67. Ibid.
68. Ibid.

69. See "Travel and Tourism," *Iran Daily*, October 11, 2005, http://www.iran-daily.com.
70. See "Tehran Hosts 90% of the Visitors," *Iran Daily*, September 7, 2005, http://www.iran-daily.com.
71. See "Bahrain Air Traffic up 20%," *Bahrain Tribune* (in Resource Guide), October 19, 2005.
72. See "Green Light for Kuwait's First Private Airline," *Bahrain Tribune* (in Resource Guide), October 19, 2005.
73. See "The Airline," *Qatar Airlines*, http://www.qatarairways.com.
74. See "New Projects," Dubai Airport, http://www.dubairport.com.
75. Ibid.
76. See "Yearbook 2004," *Kingdom of Saudi Arabia Ministry of Defense and Aviation* (in Resource Guide), http://www.pca.gov.sa/statistics/yearbook_2004.
77. See "Dh1.4m Lost in Traffic Jams Per Year: Study," *Khaleej Times Online*, July 22, 2005, http://www.khaleejtimes.com/.
78. See Zaigham Ali Mirza, "Trams to Decongest Al Safoof Proposed," *Khaleej Times Online*, September 13, 2005, http://www.khaleejtimes.com/.
79. See "Saudi Railways Organization Announces Saudi Landbridge Project Day, 31st January 2005, London," Saudi Railways Expansion Program, *Saudi Railways Organization*, http://www.saudirailexpansion.com/.
80. See "Public Bus Service to Start on October 27," *Gulf Times*, September 29, 2005, http://www.gulf-times.com.
81. See "Mowasalat Upbeat as Bus Passenger Numbers Jump," *Gulf Times*, October 26, 2005, http://www.gulf-times.com.
82. See "Traffic Becomes Nightmare in Affluent Dubai," *Khaleej Times Online*, November 4, 2005, http://www.khaleejtimes.com/.
83. See *Khalj Times On-line*, "Dh9b Project Executed Last Year," February 18, 2007, http://www.khaljtimes.com.
84. See "Initiatives to Popularise Emirates Bus Service," *Khaleej Times Online*, June 26, 2005, http://www.khaleejtimes.com/.
85. See "Local Issues: Traffic Problems Getting Serious," *Bahrain Tribune* (in Resource Guide), October 19, 2005.
86. See "Statistics—Annual Abstract," *State of Qatar—Planning Council*, http://www.planning.gov.qa/Pup_Statistics_Chap_2004.htm.
87. See "Dh1.4m Lost in Traffic Jams Per Year: Study," *Khaleej Times Online*, July 22, 2005, http://www.khaleejtimes.com/.
88. See "Tourism Highlights 2005 Edition," *World Tourism Organization*, http://www.world-tourism.org.
89. Ibid.

GENERAL BIBLIOGRAPHY

Armbrust, Walter. *Mass Culture and Modernism in Egypt.* Cambridge: Cambridge University Press, 1996.
Armbrust, Walter, ed. *Mass Mediations: New Approaches to Popular Culture in the Middle East and Beyond.* Berkeley: University of California Press, 2000.
Bergen, Peter. *The Osama bin Laden I Know: An Oral History of al Qaeda's Leader.* New York: Free Press, 2006.
Burke, Edmund III, and David N. Yaghoubian. *Struggle and Survival in the Modern Middle East.* Berkeley: University of California Press, 2005.
Clarke, Richard A. *Against All Enemies.* New York: Free Press, 2004.
Danielson, Virginia. *The Voice of Egypt: Um Kulthum, Arabic Song, and Egyptian Society in the Twentieth Century.* Chicago: University of Chicago Press, 1998.
Douglas, Allen, and Fedwa Malti-Douglas. *Arab Comic Strips: Politics of an Emerging Mass Culture.* Bloomington: University of Indiana Press, 1994.
Eagleton, Terry. *The Idea of Culture.* Oxford, Blackwell, 2000.
Fiske, John. *Reading the Popular.* Boston: Unwin Hyman, 1989.
———. *Understanding Popular Culture.* London: Routledge, 1989.
Harrington, C. Lee, and Denise D. Bielby, eds. *Popular Culture: Production and Consumption.* Malden, MA: Blackwell, 2001.
Heine, Peter. *Food Culture in the Near East, Middle East, and North Africa.* Westport, CT: Greenwood Press, 2004.
Humphreys, R. Stephen. *Between Memory and Desire: The Middle East in a Troubled Age.* Berkeley: University of California Press, 2005.
Kamrava, Mehran. *The Modern Middle East: A Political History since the First World War.* Berkeley: University of California Press, 2005.
McAlister, Melani. *Epic Encounter: Culture, Media, and U.S. Interests in the Middle East 1945–2000.* Berkeley: University of California Press, 2005.
Regev, Motti, and Edwin Seroussi. *Popular Music and National Culture in Israel.* Berkeley: University of California Press, 2004.
Rubin, Barry, and Judith Colp Rubin. *Yasir Arafat: A Political Biography.* New York: Oxford University Press, 2005.
Smith, Dan. *The State of the Middle East: An Atlas of Conflict and Resolution.* Berkeley: University of California Press, 2006.
Stein, Rebecca L., and Ted Swedenburg, eds. *Palestine, Israel, and the Politics of Popular Culture.* Durham, NC: Duke University Press, 2005.
Storey, John. Cultural *Studies and the Study of Popular Culture: Theories and Methods.* Athens: University of Georgia Press, 1996.
———. *Inventing Popular Culture: From Folklore to Globalization.* Malden, MA: Blackwell, 2003.

ABOUT THE EDITORS AND CONTRIBUTORS

THE VOLUME EDITOR

LYNN BARTHOLOME is an associate professor at Monroe Community College in Rochester, New York, where she teaches courses in popular culture, philosophy, humanities, and English literature. Her teaching awards include the SUNY Chancellor's Award for Excellence in Teaching, The Wesley T. Hanson Teaching Excellence Award, the Michigan Association of Governing Boards Distinguished Faculty Award, the NISOD Award for Outstanding Teaching and Leadership in the Two-Year School, and the Ferris State University Teaching Excellence Award (funded by the Michigan Legislature). She is a past president of the Popular Culture Association and currently serves as the executive chair of Popular Culture and American Culture Associations. She is the author of numerous books and articles. Her next writing project is on the Hebrew myth of Lilith, the purported first wife of Adam. She is an accomplished harpist and knitter, and when not teaching, she enjoys spending time with her two bassets, Socrates and Crosby, and her dachshund, Frida.

THE GENERAL EDITOR

GARY HOPPENSTAND is Professor of American Studies at Michigan State University and the author of numerous books and articles in the field of popular culture studies. He is the former president of the national Popular Culture Association and the current editor-in-chief of *The Journal of Popular Culture*.

THE CONTRIBUTORS

RIHAB KASSATLY BAGNOLE is a visiting assistant professor of art history at Ohio University in Athens, Ohio. She grew up in Syria and has lived in Egypt and Saudi Arabia. She has also visited many other Middle Eastern and North African countries, where she learned the customs and practices of the indigenous peoples. She has participated in many international events, exhibiting her photography, performing and choreographing Middle Eastern dance, and speaking about the cultures of the region. Her research deals with art and entertainment in the Middle East, and the effects of Western media on transforming Middle Eastern art. Rihab also taught Middle Eastern dance at Denison University in Granville, Ohio.

About the Editors and Contributors

STASIA J. CALLAN is Professor of English at Monroe Community College, Rochester, New York. Winner of the SUNY Chancellor's Award for Excellence in Teaching (1997), she is a mythologist with extensive myth/culture research and teaching in different countries. She is a specialist in writing across the curriculum and a published writer of professional and personal essays as well as essays on folk and ballroom dancing.

MICHAEL DOOLIN is an adjunct associate professor at Monroe Community College in Rochester, New York. He teaches in the English, geosciences, and business departments. He is the author of *The Success Manual for Adult College Students: how to go to college (almost) full time in your spare time, and still have time to hold down a job, raise a family, pay the bills and have some fun!*

MARY FINDLEY teaches in the English, Humanities and Social Science Department at Vermont Technical College. Her background is in Gothic literature. Her research focuses on Stephen King; the prevalence of the vampire in literature, culture, and film; and what horror's manifestation in popular culture reveals about the American psyche. She is on the governing board of the Popular Culture Association, is the creator and chair of the Stephen King Area of the Popular Culture Association and The Vampire in Literature, Culture and Film area of the Popular Culture Association. She is published in *Spectral America: Phantoms and the National Imagination* (2004) and in the forthcoming *The Films of Stephen King:* Carrie *to* Secret Window.

ROSEMARY GALLICK is Professor of Art, Northern Virginia Community College. She holds an M.F.A. from Pratt Institute and a Master's of Communication from Cornell University. Professor Gallick is an active member of the Popular Culture Association and the American Culture Association. She has published and presented numerous works on art and popular culture. Professor Gallick is also included in *Who's Who of American Women* (2004–2006) and *Who's Who among America's Teachers* (2000–2006).

MATTHEW R. HACHEE is a doctoral candidate in the history of modern philosophy at Michigan State University and is currently serving as coordinator of Honors Studies at Monroe Community College in Rochester, New York. He has a master's degree in contemporary political philosophy and a bachelor's degree in religion and philosophy from Adrian College.

ELIZABETH D. JOHNSTON teaches at Monroe Community College in Rochester, New York. She received her Ph.D. in British literature from West Virginia University, and she has published and presented papers on subjects as diverse as Elizabeth Barrett Browning's critical reception, the representation of women in reality television, and gender ideology in HBO's dramatic series *Rome*.

KATHRYN KNIGHT received a B.A. in English from North Carolina State University and her master's in library science from the University of North Carolina at Chapel Hill. She is currently a librarian for Wake County Public Library System.

SUSAN BOOKER MORRIS teaches philosophy, visual culture (film, popular culture, and art), race and gender theory, and Eastern religions in the Humanities Department at Ferris State University in Michigan. She is currently writing a book on Eastern philosophies in popular film and a biography of the Canadian singer/songwriter Ferron.

KATHLEEN J. O'SHEA is Professor of English at Monroe Community College in Rochester, New York. She is a recipient of the Chancellor's Award for Excellence in Teaching and the NISOD Award for Teaching Excellence.

ANN TIPPETT is Assistant Professor of English at Monroe Community College in Rochester, New York. She teaches *Introduction to Shakespeare* classes and an honors class titled *Introduction to Dramatic Literature*. She is a recipient of the NISOD Award for Teaching Excellence.

About the Editors and Contributors

HOLLY WHEELER is an assistant professor in the English/Philosophy Department at Monroe Community College in Rochester, New York. She teaches courses in college and advanced composition, mythology, children's literature, detective fiction, and short stories. Her writing and research interests include detective fiction and representations of women as action/super heroes on television.

HEATHER L. WILLIAMS is Assistant Professor of English at Monroe Community College. Her areas of academic specialty and research include children's and adolescent literature, fantasy literature, world mythology, and rhetorical theory. She has presented in each of these areas at various scholarly conferences, including several for the Popular Culture Association/American Culture Association.

INDEX

Aatabou, Najat, 209–210
Abboud, Marun, 174
Abramowitz, Shalom Yakov (Mendele Mokher Seforim; Mendele the Book Seller), 168, 169–170
Abu Hamdan, Jamal, 167
Afghanistan
    buzkashi (national sport) in, 276
    kite fighting, 276–277
    sports in, 276–277
    the Taliban and sports in, 276
Africa, indigenous dances in, 53
Agnon, Schmuel Yosef (Samuel Joseph), 170
Ajram, Nancy, 215
al-Abdullat, Omar, 212
al Achkar, Nidal, 296
al-Aji, Sanaa, 227
al-Baraduni, Abd-Allah, 183
Aleichem, Sholem (Sholem Rabinovitz), 170
Alexandria, 11
Algeria
    architecture in, 6–7
    broadcasting in, 248
    the Casbah, 6
    fashion and appearance in, 68–69
    food and food production in, 112
    French influence on architecture in, 6–7
    French influence on broadcasting in, 248
    French influence on fashion in, 69
    geography of, 6
    the Great Mosque in Oran, 7
    languages and literacy in, 226
    libraries, 163
    literature in, 163
    men's clothing styles, 69
    national chess team, 136
    obesity in, 69
    Oran's architecture and buildings, 7
    periodicals in, 226–227
    radio and TV receivers in, 247
    soft drink consumption in, 112
    sports facilities, 7
    sports in, 264–265
    toys, games, and pastimes in, 136
    urbanization in, 6
al-Ghazali, Mazem, 217
al-Ghitani, Gamal, 167
al-Hakim, Tawfiq, 166–167, 291–292
al-Hamadhani, 158
al-Hariri, 158
Ali (Pasha), Muhammad, 160
Ali, Princess Wijdan, 32
al-Jabiri, Shakib, 175
al-Koni, Ibrahim, 165
al-Maarri, Abu I-Ala, 158
al-Maqalih, Abd al'Aziz, 183
al-Muwailihi, Muhammad, 166
al-Qabbani, Abu Khalil, 297
al-Rashid, Harun, 297
al-Sabah, Su'ad al-Mubarak, 178
al-Saher, Kazem, 217
al-Shaykh, Hanan, 174
al-Wali, Muhammad Abd, 182
Amnesty International and women's rights, 200
Annabi, Amina, 210
Apollo Group, 165
Aql, Said, 297
Arab art, role of class distinction in, 38
The Arabian Nights, 158
Arabian Peninsula. *See also* Bahrain; Kuwait; Qatar; Oman; Saudi Arabia; United Arab Emirates; Yemen

357

Index

Arabian Peninsula (*continued*)
    air travel in, 335–336
    Bedouins in, 335
    border crossings, 337
    bus service in, 337
    car ownership in, 337, 339
    car rentals in, 339
    ferry service, 337
    planned new rail service for, 336
    railway service in, 336–337
    road systems in, 337
    taxi services, 339
Arabic nationality, influence on architecture, 1–2
Architecture and housing
    in Alexandria, 11
    in Algeria, 6–7
    of Algiers, 6–7
    Babylon, rebuilding of, 17
    in Baghdad, 17
    baths, public, 18–19
    Bedouin influence on Kuwaiti souq (market) architecture, 21
    in Beirut, 16
    Bibliotheca Alexandrina, 11
    in Cairo, 10
    of Casablanca, 8
    the Casbah, 6
    the Casbah des Oudaia, 8
    changes in commercial and retail, 20
    climate and, 5, 10
    courtyards, 5
    cross-cultural struggles and, xii
    dugout structures in Tunisia, 313
    effort to create new, 2–3
    in Egypt, 8–12
    Eilat Princess Hotel, 14
    El Khoury, Pierre, 16
    ethnic traditions versus Western styles and materials, 1–2
    "façade architecture," 11
    Fathy, Hassan, 10
    fortified adobe villages (ksour), 7
    French influences on Algerian, 6–7
    furniture and, 5
    in Gaza Strip, 14–15
    gateways, 8
    government-subsidized housing in Algeria, 6
    Great Mosque of Qairawan, 6
    hammams, 4, 18–19
    Hassan II Mosque, 8
    historic preservation in Libya, 9
    historic preservation in Morocco, 7–8
    housing forms of nomadic people, 19
    "indigenous structural environments," 10
    in Iran, 18–19
    in Iraq, 16–18
    in Isfahan, 18–19
    Islamic traditions and Saudi Arabian, 22–23
    in Israel, 12–14
    Israeli housing projects, 13
    iwans, 3, 18
    in Jerusalem, 12–13
    in Jordan, 12
    Kaaba (Mecca), 23
    Kempinski Hotel Emirates Palace, 20
    in Kuwait, 21–22
    Kuwait State Mosque, 21
    in Lebanon, 16
    madrassas, 3
    Makiya, Mohamed Saleh, 17–18
    Mamluk townhouses, 10
    "men's only" gathering spaces in Kuwait, 21
    in Middle East, 5–6
    minarets, 3, 4, 8
    mix of old and new, 2
    in Morocco, 7–8
    Mosque of the Prophet Muhammad (Medina), 23
    mosques, 4. *See also individual mosques*
    Mövenpick Resort and Spa, 12
    nomadic people and housing forms, 19
    non-symmetrical layout of residences, 5
    in oasis settlements, 19
    in Oran, 7
    in Palestinian Territories, 14–15
    popular contemporary, 1–3
    of Rabat, 7–8
    reed houses of Iraq, 17
    resort, 11–12
    row houses, 11
    in rural Egypt, 10–11
    rural Iranian, 19
    in rural Libyan communities, 9
    in Saudi Arabia, 22–23
    screening-off of women's areas, 5
    sirocco winds and, 6
    Souq Al-Hijaz, 22
    souq architecture updated, 20, 22
    souqs (souks; markets), 3, 9
    sports facilities in Kuwait, 21
    in Tel Aviv, 13
    "tin can cities" (bidonvilles), 7
    tourism and, 11–12
    in Tunis, 6
    in Tunisia, 5–6

INDEX

Turkish influences on North African, 6
urban housing styles in Iran, 18
urban structures, types of common, 2–5
utilization of traditional elements of, 18
walls and urban plans, 8
in West Bank, 14–15
and Western construction techniques and materials, 2–3
Western influences on Egyptian, 11
Western influences on new, 20
windstorms and, 5

Art
Ali, Princess Wijdan, 32
Allah and the Wall of Confrontation, 31
anti-Semitism and, 33
arabesque design elements in, 29
Asad, Nuha, 38
Assyrian, 35
Azia, Ebtisam Abdul, 38
British School of Archaeology (Baghdad), 36
calligraphy and, 33
calligraphy and art in North Africa and Middle East, 27
ceramics, design themes in, 29
Chagall, Marc, 33
Christian pilgrimages to the Holy Land and, 34
class distinctions, role in Arab art, 38
the computer and spread of, 31
cuneiform writing, 35
Diab, Rashid, 31
in Dura-Europos, 34
in Egypt, 29–31
El Sahali, Ibrahim, 31
Ewer in the Form of a Bird, 29
exhibitions, 30
Faces with One Feature, 38
Fallaha, Natalie, 34
Fondation Arabe pour L'Image (FAI) in Beirut, 32
Forouhar, Parastou, 37
General Presidency of Youth Welfare and art in Saudi Arabia, 37
geometric motifs, 28, 29
Hammurabi's Code of laws and, 35
high culture versus low culture in Arab art, 38
human imagery in, 28, 30
icon controversy, 28
International Cairo Biennial exhibition, 30
in Iran, 36–37
in Iraq, 35–36
Islamic influences on, 28–29, 31
in Israel, 33
Israeli culture and popular art, 33
jewelry, 29
Jewish influences on, 33
in Jordan, 31–32
Kartoum School of Fine and Applied Arts, 31
in Lebanon, 33–34
looting of archaeological sites, 36
Makan—The House of Expression, 32
Mbarak, Ricardo, 34
metal usage, 28–29
metal working and, 33
National Museum (Damascus), 35
Nazi persecution and Israeli art, 33
in Palestinian Territories, 34
Persian influences on Iraqi, 35
Photo Cairo, 30
photography in Egypt, 30
photography in Jordan, 32
photography in United Arab Emirates, 38
popular, defined, 27
prohibition of images of the Prophet(s), 28, 34
"radical" Israeli art, 33
religion and politics and, xii
repression of artistic expression in Iran, 37
Royal Society of Fine Arts (RSFA), in Jordan, 32
royal tombs, 29–30
sacredness of script in, 27
in Saudi Arabia, 37
Saudi Arabian Society for Culture and the Arts, 37
School of Fine Arts, Cairo, 30
sculpture, 34
Sharif, Hassan, 38
Sharjah Art Museum, 38
sponsorship of artistic endeavors, 30–31
in Sudan, 31
Sumerian, 35
in Syria, 34–35
Tutankhamen's tomb, 30
in United Arab Emirates, 37–38
United Nations Charter and, 30
video and, 38
Western influences on, 33
Wijdan (Princess Wijdan Ali), 32
Asad, Nuha, 38
The Asian Games, 264
Aulaqi, Said, 182

359

INDEX

Awwad, Tawfiq Yusuf, 173
Azia, Ebtisam Abdul, 38

Ba'albaki, Layla, 174
Badr, Liana, 173
Bahar, Ali, 218
Bahrain. *See also* Arabian Peninsula
    A'Ali Burial Mounds, 340
    Al-Fatih Mosque, 340
    book publishing in, 162
    bookshops and publishers in, 178
    Brains in Bahrain tournament, 149
    broadcasting in, 256
    clothing manufacture and exports, 83–84
    Dar Island, 340
    demographics, 198
    divorce without notice, 198
    fashion and appearance in, 83–84
    fashion industry in, 84
    fiction writers in, 178
    Hawar Islands, 340
    languages and literacy in, 237
    libraries in, 177–178
    literature in, 177–178
    Manama, 340
    marriage and sexual relationships in, 198
    music in, 218
    non-nationals in, 83
    obesity in, 84
    pearl diving museum, 340
    periodicals in, 237–238
    radio and TV receivers in, 256
    road system in, 337
    sports in, 278–279
    theater in, 300
    toys, games, and pastimes in, 149–150
Baizai, Bahram, 101–102
Bakhtyari people, housing forms of, 19
Baladi. *See* Belly dance (baladi)
Balochi people, housing forms of, 19
Barakat, Halim, 173–174
Bathhouses (hammam)
    Jordanian, 74
    Turkish, 78
Bedouin people
    al-Abdullat, Omar, 212
    in Arabian Peninsula, 335
    and Arabic poetry, 160
    clothing among, in Saudi Arabia, 86
    influence on souq (market) architecture in Kuwait, 21
    influences on Jordanian music, 212
    khaleeji style music and, 218
    and Wadi Rum, 322
    women's dress, 82
    and works of Ghalib Halasa, 167
Belly dance (baladi), 47–49, 54
Benaissa, Slimane, 290
Ben Jelloun, Tahar, 164
ben Joseph, Saadia, 168
Ben-Yehuda, Eliezer (Eliezer Perlman), 169
Berber people
    divorce among, 191
    the Grand Erg Oriental, 312
    home in Middle Atlas Mountains, 315
    influence on popular music, 209
    male veiling among Tuaregs, 66
    in Morocco, 112
    wedding customs, 190–191
Bey, F. D. Amr, 267
Bialik, Haim Nahman, 172
Bidouane, Nezha, 266
bin Talal, Walid, 208
Body art, 63
Book fairs, 182
Books
    censored, 161
    imported, 162
    pirated, 161
    publishing of, 161–162
    Western authors, 162
Bori spirits
    defined, 56
    exorcising, 56–57
Boulmerka, Hassiba, 265
Broadcasting. *See* Electronic media (including radio, television, and computers)
Burnt City (Shahr-e Sokhte), ancient textile industry in, 81

Cairo
    architecture in, 10
    Mamluk townhouses, 10
Calligraphy
    Jewish, 33
    sacred tradition of, 29
Camel racing, 267, 277–278, 279
Carpets
    design elements and creation of, 29
    hobby of handcrafting, 149
    world's largest, 343
Casablanca, architecture and housing in, 8
Casbah, the, 6
Ceramics, design themes in, 29
Chagall, Marc, 33

INDEX

Chess
  in Algeria, 136
  Brains in Bahrain tournament, 149
  in Egypt, 144
  Gibraltar Grand Masters, 137
  in Iran, 149
  Kramnik, Vladimir, versus Deep Fritz computer, 149
  in Libya, 141
  in Morocco, 137
  in Tunisia, 140
Children
  adoption, 189
  foster parenting and, 189
The Children of Gebelawi (*Awalad Haratina*), 166
Christianity
  icon controversy, 28
  pilgrimages to the Holy Land and art, 34
  sculpture as idolatry, 34
Church of the Holy Sepulcher (Jerusalem), 324
Clothing. *See also* Fashion; Textiles
  Egyptian market for, 72
  Egyptian variations on Western, 73
  high fashion in Beirut, 75–76
  Israeli exports of, 74
  Jordanian exports of, 73
  in Kuwait, 82–83
  Lebanese love of fashion, 77
  Lebanese spending on, 76, 77
  manufacture and export in Bahrain, 83–84
  manufacture in Mauritania, 66
  in Middle East, 62–64
  in Morocco, 67–68
  in North Africa, 62–64
  regulation of women's, 81, 86
  Saudi Arabian expenditures for, 86–87
  in Syria, 79
  traditional in Oman, 87–88
  Tunisian exports of, 70
Committee to Protect Journalists (New York City), 227
Commonwealth War Graves Cemetery (in Benghazi), 316
Cosmetics. *See also* Perfume
  Dead Sea products from Israel, 74–75
  economic sanctions in Iraq and, 80–81
  home made in Iraq, 80
  makeup use, 64–65
  trade show in Turkey, 79
  use in Egypt, 71
  use in Iraq, 80–81
  use in Morocco, 68
  use in Oman, 88
  use in Palestinian Territories, 75
  use in Saudi Arabia, 87
  use in Turkey, 78–79
  use in United Arab Emirates, 85–86
Cosmetic surgery
  in Iran, 82
  in Iraq, 81
  in Lebanon, 76
  in Middle East and North Africa, 65
  in Turkey, 78

Dammaj, Zayd Mutte, 182–183
Dance
  African indigenous, 53
  ancient religion and, 47
  awalim versus ghawazee performers, 48
  ban on couple dancing, 53
  basic human need and, 45
  baths (hammams), 4
  battle dance (tahtib), 54–55
  belly dance (baladi), 47–49, 54
  bori demon-dancing, 56–57
  cultural values and, 52–53
  the debkeh (debke) in the Levant, 50–51
  delivering blessings (guedra), 55
  Dubai Mall, 20
  evolution of, xii–xiii, 45–46
  ghawazee professional dancers, 48
  hammams, 4
  harems and, 46
  for healing, 56–57
  homes, 4–5
  hora (Israeli), 51
  Ibn Battuta Mall, 20
  imitations of sema for tourists, 50
  impact on world-wide, 57
  klezmer music and, 51
  in Middle East, 46–53
  modern forms, 46
  Moroccan tea tray, 55–56
  music played for the dabkeh, 50–51
  in North Africa, 53–57
  role in society, 57
  and Salome, 46
  sword dance of Arab warriors (razha), 54
  Saudi sword dance (al ardhah), 52–53
  the sema, 49–50, 53–54
  tourism and belly dancing, 48
  tourism and indigenous, 57
  trance dance (Zar), 56
  in tribal communities, 45
  Whirling Dervishes, 49–50, 53–54

361

INDEX

Dance (*continued*)
    women and, 46
    women's hair, 51–52
Daneshvar, Simin, 177
Dead Sea
    description of, 323
    tourism in region of, 12
    water, food production, and, 118
Diab, Amr (Amro Abd Al-assit Abd Al-Aziz Diab), 211
Diab, Rashid, 31
Diwan Group, 166
Dolls. *See also* Toys, games, and pastimes
    Barbie dolls, negative Iranian reaction to, 148
    Barbie, Moroccan, 137
    fashion dolls, 65, 73
    Fulla, 65, 82
    Sara and Dara, 65, 148
    in Tunisia, 138–139
    Yasmine, and Nada, 65
Dom people. *See also* Gypsies
Dowlatabadi, Mahmud, 177
Dubai. *See also* United Arab Emirates
    Al Maha Desert Resort, 20
    commercial building in, 20
    Dubai Mall, 20
    fashion event, 85
    Jumeira Mosque, 344
    residential parks and towers in, 20
    textile city, 85
    tourist attractions in, 344
    urban architecture in, 2
Dura-Europos, 34

Egypt
    abaliy, 142
    air travel in, 316
    al-Azhar Mosque, 318
    Alexandria, 316
    Alexandrian library, new, 320
    ancient games in, 141
    arranged marriages, 192
    art in, 29–31
    awalim (women performers) in, 48
    ball games, 142–143
    battle dance variation on saidi dance, 54–55
    Ben Ezra Synagogue (Cairo), 318
    beverages, 115
    Bibliotheca Alexandria (new), 320
    bookshops and publishers in, 167
    border crossings, 317
    broadcasting in, 250–251
    bus service, 317–318
    Cairo, 318–320
    circumcision, female, 192
    City of the Dead (cemetary), 319
    class differences and views on marriage and sexual relationships, 192
    clitoridectomy (female circumcision), 192
    comic books in, 230
    cooking as a hobby in, 144
    consumption of sweets, 115
    Coptic Cairo (Old Cairo), 318
    cosmetics use in, 71
    demographics, 191–192
    eating out in urban areas, 115
    the Egyptian Museum, 319
    Electronic Sports World Cup (ESWC), 144
    fashion and appearance in, 71–73
    Fatmid Cairo (Islamic Cairo), 318–319
    film directors, 98
    films in, 97–99
    first Arabic printing press, 159
    first films in, 97
    French occupation of, 159
    ghawazee professional dancers, 48
    Giza, pyramids of, 319
    Great Pyramid of Khufu, 319
    headdress (hijab) use in, 72
    holidays and foods in, 115–116
    Hollywood production model, 97
    imported clothing in, 72
    International Cairo Biennial exhibition, 30
    Islamic Cairo (Fatmid Cairo), 318–319
    jewelry in, 30
    Karnack, Temple of, 320
    languages and literacy in, 228
    libraries in, 165
    list of films from, 98–99
    literature in, 165–167
    Luxor, 320
    Luxor Temple, 320
    Mahfouz, Naguib, 165–166
    marriage and sexual relationships in, 192–193
    melodrama and music in films in, 97–98
    and modern Arabic fiction, 159
    Mosque of Mohammed Ali, 319
    Mosque of Sayyidna al-Hussein, 318–319
    Napoleon Bonaparte's invasion and literature, 157
    national bread shortage, 116

INDEX

nightclub scene, late nineteenth century, 48
oases in western desert, 320
oil companies and contemporary art in, 30–31
Old Cairo (Coptic Cairo), 318
periodicals in, 228–229
photography in, 30
popular genres in films from, 97–98
Port Said, 320
the poultry industry and avian influenza, 116
pyramids of Abu Sir, 319
pyramids of Giza, 319
pyramids of Saqqara, 319
radio and TV receivers in, 250
Radio Corporation of America (RCA) and broadcasting in, 251
rail travel in, 316–317
the Red Sea, 320
road accidents in, 318
royal tombs, 29–30
rural settlements in, 10–11
saidi folk dance variation (tahtib), 54–55
seega, 142
safety concerns and third-class rail cars, 317
senet, 141
the Sphinx, 319
sports played as hobbies, 141–142
Step Pyramid, 319
Suez Canal, 320
toys, games, and pastimes in, 141–144
Tutankhamen's tomb, 30
urban housing shortages, 10
urbanization in, 10
Valley of the Kings, 320
veil use in, 72
views on marriage and sexual relationships, 192
western desert, 320
Western equipment and broadcasting, 251
Western fashion in, 72
wigs in ancient, 71
Electronic media (including radio, television, and computers). *For computer games, see also* Toys, games, and pastimes
    2M International, 249
    Abu Dhabi Satellite TV, 257
    adaptation of foreign formats, 246
    Al-Arabiya, 258
    in Algeria, 247–248
    Algerie Premiere, 136
    Al-Ikhbariya, 258
    Al-Iraqiyah, 254–255
    Al Jazeera Satellite Channel (JSC), 256–257
    Al-Manar TV, 253–254
    Al-Mashreq TV, 253
    Arab News Network (ANN), 248
    in Bahrain, 256
    Bahrain Radio and Television, 256
    BBC Arabic Television Service, 246
    in Berber language (Kabyle), 248
    Broadcasting Corporation of the Middle East Broadcasting Center (MBC), 258–259
    Broadcasting Service in Saudi Arabia (BSSA), 258
    cable television, 252, 258
    Cairo International TV Radio Market and Festival (CAMAR TV), 254, 255
    cell phones and cell phone games in Saudi Arabia, 150
    censorship of, 255
    children's TV programming, 136
    color TV, 251
    commercial broadcasting, 246
    delivered from Western countries, 246
    Dubai Media City (DMC), 258
    Dubai TV, 258
    earth stations, 249
    in Egypt, 250–251
    Electronic Sports World Cup (ESWC) participation, 144
    Emissions des langue Arabe et Kabyle (ELAK), 248
    equipment for, 245
    Extrovert Magazine, an online fashion magazine, 233
    the First Channel, 255–256
    foreign originating broadcasts, 248
    foreign programming, 249, 250, 253, 254, 259
    French founding of radio broadcasting in Algeria, 248
    French influences on, 248
    French Radio Runis (RTF), 249
    Fujairah Media, 258
    Future TV Network, 254
    government subsidies for, 246
    government supervision of, 245
    Hannibal TV, 249
    Hashemite Broadcasting Service (HBS), 251

INDEX

Electronic media (*continued*)
    the Internet and computer games, 136, 138, 144
    Internet usage in Israel, 232
    in Iran, 255
    in Iraq, 254–255
    Iraqi Media Network, 254–255
    Islamic Revolution and Iranian broadcasting, 255
    Islamic veil and appearance on TV, 251
    in Israel, 252
    Israel Television (ITV), 252
    jamming of broadcasts, 245, 250
    Japanese programming, 260
    in Jordan, 251–252
    Jordan Television (JTV), 251–252
    Kabyle language (Berber language), 248
    Kol Yisrael, 252
    Koranic readings, 257
    in Kuwait, 255–256
    in Lebanon, 253–254
    Lebanese Broadcasting Corporation (LBC), 253
    in Libya, 250
    Libyan Jamahiriya Broadcasting, (LJB), 250
    local customs and Western-style programs, 246–247
    local radio services in Egypt, 250
    media critics, 251
    Middle East Television, 253
    Mohammed, Miriam, 259
    Moroccan Broadcasting Network, 249
    in Morocco, 248–249
    Mosaique FM, 249
    National Broadcasting Network (NBN), 254
    Nile TV, 251
    in Oman, 259
    "The Opposite Direction" talk show, 257
    oral tradition and, xiv, 245
    Orbit Satellites, 247
    Palestine Satellite Channel (PSC), 252
    in Palestinian Territories, 252
    Palestinian TV and Radio Broadcasting Corporation, 252
    pan-Arab broadcasting stations, 249
    political agendas and, 245
    popular TV shows, 253
    private broadcasting, 255
    private broadcasting ban, 250, 251
    in Qatar, 256–257
    Radio Africa, 248
    Radio Cairo, 250
    Radiodiffusion Television Française (RTF), 248
    Radio Diffusion Television of Morocco (RTM), 249
    radio France Cinq, 248
    Radio Levant, 253
    Radio Libya, 250
    Radio Maroc, 248
    Radio Qatar, 256
    Radio Sultanate of Oman, 259
    Radio Tanger, 248
    reality shows, 246–247
    rebel stations, 253
    receiver ownership in Middle East and North Africa, 245
    religious programming, 253–254
    RTV International, 256
    Sabah al-Kheir ("Good Morning"), 251
    satellite television, 247, 249, 251, 252, 254, 256, 257, 258, 260
    in Saudi Arabia, 258–259
    the Second Channel, 256
    Sultanate of Oman Television, 259
    in Syria, 254
    Syria Satellite TV, 254
    television shows, most popular, 253
    television, spread of, 246
    television system standards, 247
    in Tunisia, 249
    Tunisian Radio and Television Establishment (ERTT), 249
    2M International, 249
    in United Arab Emirates, 257–258
    Voice of America, 256
    Voice of Britain, 246
    Voice of Qatar, 256
    Voice of United Arab Emirates, 257
    Western broadcasters and North Africa and Middle East, 246
    Western equipment and broadcasting, 251, 254, 255
    Western influences on, 247
    Wheelus Air Force Base and broadcasting in Libya, 250
    in Yemen, 259–260
    Yemeni Public Corporation for Radio and Television, 259–260
    Yemen Satellite Channel, 260
El-Hawari, Dr. Sahar, 268
El Khoury, Pierre, 16
El-Menshawi, Mohamed, 268
El Moutawakel, Nawal, 266

INDEX

El Sahali, Ibrahim, 31
Embroidery
    Jordanian, 73, 145
    in Saudi Arabia, 86
European society, fascination with the Middle East in, 61

Fahd, Ismail, 178
Fairuz (Nuhad Haddad Rahbani), 214
Fakhri, Sabah, 216
Fallaha, Natalie, 34
Farmanara, Bahman, 102
Fashion and appearance. *See also* Clothing; Cosmetics; Cosmetic Surgery; Textiles
    in Algeria, 68–69
    in Bahrain, 83–84
    Bedouin dress in Saudi Arabia, 86
    body art, 63
    and brand names in Kuwait, 83
    challenges to women's dress codes in Iran, 81–82
    clothing, 62–64
    consumer spending in Kuwait, 83
    consumer spending in Saudi Arabia, 86–87
    cosmetic surgery in Iraq, 81
    cosmetic surgery in Lebanon, 76
    cosmetics use, 64–65, 68, 78–79, 85, 87
    cultural and historical contexts influencing, 64
    designers in Mauritania, 66
    and Dead Sea cosmetics, 75–76
    dress codes and, xiii, 81
    Dubai Fashion event, 85
    Dubai Textile City, 85
    economic conditions and fashion in Yemen, 88
    economic sanctions and cosmetics in Iraq, 80–81
    in Egypt, 71–73
    embroidery in Jordan, 73
    entertainment restrictions and shopping in Saudi Arabia, 86
    facial beauty in Iran, 82
    factors influencing, 62
    fashion consciousness in Egypt, 71
    fashion designers in Iraq, 80
    "Fashion in Africa" project, 70
    fashion industry in Israel, 74
    fashion industry in Syria, 79
    fashion magazines and, 66
    fashion trade shows in Bahrain, 84
    Femme Magazine, 234
    foreign influence on Moroccan, 68
    frankincense (*Boswellia sacra*), 88
    French fashion influence in Algeria, 69
    Fulla, Yasmine, and Nada dolls, 65
    fundamentalist vigilantes and hijabs in Iraq, 80
    Gulf Beauty Exhibition, 86
    Hair and Beauty Exhibition, annual in Tripoli, 71
    hair styles, 64
    headdress (hijab) use in Egypt, 72
    headgear in Turkey, 77
    head scarves, meanings of, 77–78
    high fashion in Beirut, 75–76
    henna and body art, 63
    influence of local celebrities on Egyptian culture, 73
    influences on, xiii
    in Iran, 81–82
    in Iraq, 79–81
    in Iraq after 1990, 80
    Islamic fundamentalism and women's dress in Iran, 81
    in Israel, 74–75
    Israeli-Palestinian Territories beauty pageant, 75
    Istanbul as fashion hub, 78
    in Jordan, 73–74
    in Kuwait, 82–83
    in Lebanon, 76–77
    in Libya, 70–71
    limited shopping in Yemen, 88
    makeup, 64–65
    male beauty pageants, 66
    mass media and Iranian fashion trends, 82
    in Mauritania, 66–67
    in Morocco, 67–68
    obesity, 65, 69
    obesity in Bahrain, 84
    in Oman, 87–88
    perfumes in Saudi Arabia, 87
    in Qatar, 84–85
    regulation of women's dress in Iran, 81
    religious dress, banning in Turkey, 77
    in rural Turkey, 78
    Saint Laurent, Yves, 69
    Sara and Dara dolls and, 65
    in Saudi Arabia, 86–87
    shopping malls in Bahrain, 84
    shopping mall, world's largest, 84
    in Syria, 79
    trade show exhibition, Beirut Fashion 2006, 76–77

INDEX

Fashion and appearance (*continued*)
    traditional Iraqi dress, 80
    in Tunisia, 69–70
    Tunisian fashion events, 70
    turbans, use in Oman, 87
    in Turkey, 77–79
    Turkish baths (hammam), 78
    in United Arab Emirates, 85–86
    veiling and Islamic women, 63
    veiling of men, 66
    veils and scarves in Libya, 70
    veil use in Yemen, 88
    Western fashions in Egypt, 72
    Western ideas of beauty and, 65
    Western influences on, 61–62, 70, 74, 79
    in Western Sahara, 66
    Western style shopping malls and, 62
    women's clothing in Libya, 70
    in Yemen, 88
    Zamani, Mahla, 81
Fathy, Hassan, 10
Fertile Crescent, defined, 116–117
Film(s)
    Arab Cinema, 97
    attitudes toward, 95–96
    availability of films in U.S., 103
    Baizai, Bahram, 101–102
    banning and restrictions of, 96
    cinematography in Iranian, 101
    complications affecting, 95
    contemporary culture and Iranian, 101
    in Egypt, 97–99
    Egyptian directors, 98
    Egyptian film list, 98–99
    Farmanara, Bahman, 102
    first feature-length in Saudi Arabia, 95
    Hollywood production model, 97
    influences limiting, xiii
    in Iran, 100–103
    Iranian directors, 101–103
    Islamic resistance to production of, 95–96
    Islamic Revolution and Iranian, 101
    in Israel, 99–100
    Israeli film directors, 100
    Kiarostami, Abbas, 102
    list of Israeli films, 100
    low production and distribution, 97
    Makhmalbaf, Mohsen, 102
    Makhmalbaf, Samira, 103
    Mehrjui, Daryush, 103
    melodrama and music in, 97–98
    poetic stories in Iranian, 101
    popular genres in Egyptian, 97–98
    production in the Middle East and North Africa, 95
    for propaganda purposes, 96
    since 2000, 103–104
    Sun Cinema, 100
    trends in Israeli, 99–100
Fitaihi, Maha, 280
Food and food production
    agricultural cooperatives in Israel, 13
    alcoholic beverages, 123
    in Algeria, 112
    approaches to, in Iran, 121
    Australian Wheat Board and kickbacks to Saddam Hussein's regime, 121
    beverages, 115, 124, 125
    breads, 119, 122
    caviar, Iranian, 122
    changes in Algerian, 112
    cooking as an Egyptian hobby, 144
    couscous, 113, 114
    deserts, Egyptian, 114
    dolmas, 120
    in Egypt, 114–116
    Egyptian national bread shortage, 116
    electricity and Moroccan diets, 113
    ethnic influences on, xiii
    in Fertile Crescent versus Levant, 116–117
    first "fast food," 111
    food courts, 111
    food franchises, 110
    fresh water and agricultural production, 108–109
    ful, 114
    grains and bread in Turkey, 119–120
    grocery shopping, 115, 118
    guests and cuisine in Iran, 122
    Gulf Cooperation Council (GCC) and water supplies, 109
    Halal foods, 107–108
    hazelnuts, 120
    holidays and foods, 115–116
    international trade and, 109–110
    in Iran, 121–122
    in Iraq, 120–121
    irrigation and desalination efforts and, 109
    in Israel, 117–118
    in Jordan, 117
    kibbeh, 119
    koshary, 114
    Kosher foods, 108
    in Lebanon, 118–119

INDEX

in Libya, 113–114
local food shortages, 117
low-or zero-level alcohol malt beverages, 123
"mad cow" disease and meat imports to Saudi Arabia, 123
malnutrition in Palestinian Territories, 118
mansaf, 117
market for food in Middle East and North Africa, 110
in Morocco, 112–113
multinational influences on Israeli, 117
Oil-for-Food program (Iraq), 121
in Oman, 123–125
in Palestinian Territories, 118
pigeons in rural Egypt, 115
politics and food shopping, 115
popular Iranian, 122
the poultry industry and avian influenza, 116
pre-packaged foods, 111
rationing of, in Iraq, 121
religion and, xiii
religious celebrations and Omani, 125
religious doctrines and, 107–108
in rural Egypt, 114–115
in rural Libya, 9
in Saudi Arabia, 123
shifts in Israeli food consumption, 117–118
shish kebabs, 117
snack foods in Turkey, 120
soft drink consumption, 110, 111
street vendors and, 120
sweets, 115
in Syria, 119
taxes and, in Lebanon, 119
in Tunisia, 113
in Turkey, 119–120
urban Iranian, 122
violence and Western style restaurants, 119
water and, 108–109
water, food production, and the Dead Sea, 118
weekly souqs (markets) and, 115
Western influence on, 110–111
Western-style supermarkets, 115
wheat domesticated in Turkey, 119
Football (European)
African Nations Cup, 265, 267
Les Aigles de Carthage, 266
in Algeria, 264
the Army Club, 273
Atlas Lions, 265
in Egypt, 267
El-Hawari, Dr. Sahar, and women in, 268
in Iran, 274
the Iranian Revolution and, 274
in Iraq, 273–274
in Israel, 270
in Lebanon, 272
in Morocco, 265
National Youth Soccer Club (Saudi Arabia), 279
Nejmeh Sporting Club, 272–273
played by children, 136
in Saudi Arabia, 279
in Syria, 273
in Tunisia, 266
women's teams, 273, 274
World Cup, 266, 274
in Yemen, 281
Forouhar, Parastou, 37
France, occupation of Egypt and impact on culture, 159
Frankincense (*Boswellia sacra*), 88

Games, toys, and pastimes. *See* Toys, games, and pastimes
Gaza Strip (Gaza). *See* Palestinian Territories
Ghadames, architecture of, 9
Ghawazee. *See* Gypsies
Ghrib people, evolution of toys and games among, 138
Gibran, Kahlil, 160
Googoosh (Faegheh Atashin), 217
Gypsies
Ghawazee in Egypt, 48
professional female dancers among, 48

Habayib, Huzama, 173
Hadad, Sarit, 213
Hakim, 211–212
Hakmoun, Hassan, 209
Halal foods, 107–108
Halasa, Ghalib, 167
Hamdouchi, Hichem, 137
Hammam. *See* Bathhouses (hammam)
Haqqi, Yahya, 167
Hatmal, Jameel, 175
Hausa people, bori demon-dancing, 56–57
Haza, Ofra, 213
Healing, dances for, 56–57

Index

Heikal, Mul Hassanein, 229
Henna and body art, 63
Hiem, Dr. Fadel Abu, 146
Hijab, defined, 62
HIV/AIDS, theater about, 291
Hobbies. *See* Toys, games, and pastimes
Honor crimes, 194

Idilbi, Ilfat, 175
Idris, Suhayl, 174
Insanity, bori dancing as treatment for, 57
Interior design
    furniture little used, 5
    guest reception rooms, 5
    surface design in homes, 5
    traditional for madrassas, 3
International Theater Institute, 288
Iran
    air travel in, 332–333
    architecture in, 18–19
    art in, 36–37
    Barbie dolls, negative reaction to, 148
    beverages in, 122
    book publishing in, 162
    border crossings, 333
    breads in, 122
    broadcasting in, 255
    bus service in, 333
    Castle of the Assassin, 334
    caviar from, 122
    challenges to women's dress regulations in, 81
    cinematography in films from, 101
    Constitutional Revolution (July 1909) and literature in, 176
    contemporary culture and film in, 101
    Cultural Revolution (1979) and literature in, 177
    cuisine in, 122
    eating out in urban areas, 122
    fashion and appearance in, 81–82
    film directors, 101–103
    films for propaganda in, 96
    films in, 100–103
    food and food production in, 121–122
    Fulla doll popularity in, 82
    Garden of Eden, probable location, 334
    geography of, 18
    guests and cuisine in, 122
    Imam Mosque, 335
    Iranian Revolution and sports in, 274
    Isfahan (Eşfahān), 335
    Islamic Revolution and broadcasting in, 255
    Kish Island, 335
    languages and literacy in, 235
    libraries in, 176
    literature in, 176–177
    Mashad, 335
    motorcycle usage in, 308
    Mount Damavand (volcano), 334
    music in, 217–218
    National Museum, 334
    nostalgic literature of the 1960s, 176–177
    oasis settlements, 19, 334
    Palace of Darius, 334
    periodicals in, 235–236
    Persepolis, 334
    Persian Gulf, 335
    poetry in, 177
    press freedom in, 235
    prose authors, 177
    puppet theater in, 299
    radio and TV receivers in, 255
    rail service in, 333
    regulation of women's dress in, 81
    religious tradition and theater in, 299
    repression of artistic expression in, 37
    road system in, 333
    rural life in, 19
    sports in, 274–276
    Sufist poets, 160
    Sun Cinema, 100
    taxis in, 333
    Taziya dramas, 299–300
    Tehran, 334
    testing Western freedom of expression, 236
    textiles in ancient Burnt City (Shahr-e Sokhte), 81
    theater in, 299–300
    tourism in, 333–335
    travel in, 332–333
    urbanization in, 18
    Zoroastrian scripture, 176
Iraq
    air travel in, 330
    ancient history of, 35
    archaeology in, 36
    architecture in, 16–18
    art in, 35–36
    Australian Wheat Board and kickbacks to Saddam Hussein's regime, 121
    authors from, 176
    Babylon, 332

INDEX

Babylon's architecture, 17
Baghdad, 331
Baghdad's architecture, 17
   bookshops and publishers in, 176
   border crossings, 331
   broadcasting in, 254–255
   as cradle of civilization, 331
   domestic architecture, 16–17
   the Eurmeiminanki, 332
   fashion and appearance in, 79–81
   food and food production in, 120–121
   foods purchased by foreign military in, 110–111
   foreign influences on architecture in, 17
   fundamentalism and fashion in, 79–80
   geography of, 16, 35
   Hussein, Saddam, theater after fall of, 298
   invasion of Kuwait, 36
   languages and literacy in, 234
   libraries in, 175–176
   literature in, 175–176
   looting of archaeological sites, 36
   Makiya, Mohamed Saleh, 17–18
   modern history of, 35–36
   Monument of the Martyrs, 331
   Mosul, 332
   music in, 217
   Najaf cemetery, 331
   National Museum, 331
   Nineveh, site of, 332
   Oil-for-Food program, 121
   periodicals in, 234–235
   radio and TV receivers in, 254
   rail service in, 331
   rationing of food in, 121
   reed houses, 17
   road system in, 331
   after Saddam Hussein, 235
   sports in, 273–274
   Summer Palace (Babylon), 332
   Temple of Ishtar (Babylon), 332
   theater in, 298–299
   Tigris and Euphrates river, 331
   Ur, discoveries in, 35
   Ur, ziggurat of, 331–332
   urbanization in, 16
   vigilantes and hijabs (head scarves), 80
   war and sports in, 273–274
   war and travel in, 331
   war, architecture, and housing in, 16
Isfahan (Eşfahān)
   architecture in, 18–19
   attractions in, 335

Islam
   art and, 28–29
   banning of public concerts and, 217–218, 218
   and cosmetics, 65
   cosmetic surgery and, 65
   fundamentalism and Iranian fashions, 81
   fundamentalism and Iraqi fashions, 79–80
   fundamentalists and clothing, 62–63
   Great Mosque of Qairawan, 6
   Hassan II Mosque, 8
   the hijab, defined, 62
   holy sites, 23
   and human imagery in art, 28
   influence on architecture, 1–2
   influence on cosmetics use in Morocco, 68
   influence on Egyptian fashion, 72
   influence on fashion in Algeria, 68
   Kaaba (Mecca), 23
   Kuwait State Mosque, 21
   literary forms and, 158
   the madrassa and, 3
   minarets, 3, 4
   Mosque of the Prophet Muhammad (Medina), 23
   mosques, 4
   and pre-Islamic poetry, 160
   prohibition of images of the Prophet(s), 28
   prohibition of trance dance, 56
   religious broadcasting and, 253–254
   resistance to film production, 95–96
   response to cartoons seen as denigrating, 240–241
   response to perceived denigration of, 227
   Shariah law and sports in Iran, 275–276
   spread of, 27–28
   in Sudan, 31
   Sufi. *See* Sufi and Sufism
Israel
   Abramowitz, Shalom Yakov (Mendele Mokher Seforim; Mendele the Book Seller), 168, 169–170
   air travel in, 323
   Al-Aqsa Mosque, 324
   Aleichem, Sholem (Sholem Rabinovitz), 170
   American influence on toys in, 145
   ancient culinary traditions, 117
   Arab Children Friends Association (ACFA), 145

INDEX

Israel (*continued*)
    Arab Israelis, 145
    architecture in, 12–14
    Armenian Quarter (Jerusalem), 324
    art in, 33
    and artists fleeing Nazi persecution, 33
    Baha'I Shrine, 325
    ben Joseph, Saadia, 168
    Bethlehem (in Palestinian Territories), 326
    Book of Yosipon, 168
    border crossings and taxis or hired cars, 323
    broadcasting in, 252
    bus services in, 323
    cabala, 168
    Chagall, Marc, 33
    Church of the Holy Sepulcher, 324
    City of David section of Jerusalem, 324
    culture and popular art in, 33
    demographics, 194
    Eilat, 326
    Eilat Princess Hotel, 14
    Elijah's Cave, 325
    emigration to Palestine, 169
    Dead Sea Scrolls, 325
    Dome of the Rock, 324
    divorce in, 195
    film directors, 100
    film(s) in, 99–100
    food and food production in, 117–118
    food shopping in, 118
    Galilee, 325
    Garden of Gethsemane, 325
    geography of, 12
    gets and divorce in, 195
    Haifa, 325
    Hebrew adopted as an everyday language, 169, 170–171
    Hebrew dictionary, first, 168
    Hebrew in Jewish prose, 168
    Hebrew literature, 168
    Hebrew poetry written in Spain and Italy, 168
    homosexuality in, 195
    the hora and, 51
    housing projects, 13
    illegitimacy and children in, 195
    immigration and, 13
    Jerusalem, 324
    Jerusalem architecture, 13–14
    Jewish Enlightenment (*Haskala*), 168–169
    Jewish Quarter (Old City of Jerusalem), 324
    kibbutzim, 13
    Kook, Chief Rabbi Abraham, 270
    languages and literacy in, 231
    libraries in, 167–168
    list of films from, 100
    literature in, 167–172
    Maccabiah games, 270
    marriage and sexual relationships in, 194–195
    May Laws, 169
    Mendelssohn, Moses, 169
    moshavs, 13
    Mountain of the Beatitudes, 325
    Mount Carmel, 325
    Mount of Olives, 324
    Mount Zion, 324
    music in, 212–214
    and Nazareth, 325
    Pale of Settlement, 169
    periodicals in, 231–233
    pogroms, 169
    Qumran, 326
    radio and TV receivers in, 252
    rail service in, 323
    refugees and 1948 war, 14–15
    religious law (*halaka*) and civil law in, 195
    roads in, 323
    rural life, 13
    Sea of Galilee (Lake Kinneret), 325
    Seforim, Mendele Mokher (Mendele the Book Seller; Shalom Yakov Abramowitz), 168, 169–170
    shared limos (*sherut*), 323
    shifts in food consumption, 117–118
    Shrine of the Book (Dead Sea Scrolls displayed), 325
    sports in, 269–272
    taxi services, 323
    Tel Aviv, 325
    Tel Aviv architecture, 13
    Temple Mount, 324
    theater in, 293–294
    themes in modern popular literature in, 171
    tourism in, 14, 324–326
    toys, games, and hobbies in, 145–146
    trends in films in, 99–100
    urbanization in, 13
    Via Dolorosa (Path of Sorrow), 324
    Wailing Wall (Western Wall), Jerusalem), 324

INDEX

wars and art in, 33
water and agriculture in, 118
weddings in, 195
the West Bank and travel, 326
Western (Wailing) Wall, Jerusalem, 324
women writers from, 171

Jabra, Jabra Ibrahim, 172–173
Janabi, Ahmed, 298–299
Jericho Synagogue, 326
Jerusalem
    architecture in, 13–14
    Christian Quarter, 324
    Dead Sea Scrolls, 325
    Jewish Quarter, 324
    Muslim Quarter, 324
    religious sites in, 324–325
    Western (Wailing) Wall, 324
    West Jerusalem, 325
Jewelry, in Islamic societies, 29
Jews
    emigration to America and Palestine, 169
    Hebrew literature, 168–172
    klezmer music of Eastern European, 51
    May Laws, 169
    Pale of Settlement, 169
    Yiddish literature, 169
Jinn, defined, 56
Jordan
    air travel in, 320–321
    Amman, 322
    the Arab-Israeli wars and, 32
    architecture in, 12
    art in, 31–32
    arts promotion in, 32
    Bedouin influence on music in, 212
    Bethany-beyond-the-Jordan, 322
    bookshops and publishers in, 167
    broadcasting in, 251–252
    bus services in, 321
    clothing industry and exports, 73
    communal bathhouses, 74
    the Dead Sea, 323
    the Dead Sea Highway, 321
    demographics, 194
    the Desert Highway, 321
    E-Deir (monastery), 322
    embroidery, 73, 145
    fashion and appearance in, 73–74
    food and food production in, 117
    geography of, 12
    Gulf of Aqaba, 322
    Jerash, 322
    Jericho, 322–323
    Jordan International Rally (auto race), 269
    Jordan River, 322
    King's Highway, 321
    lack of rail service in, 321
    languages and literacy in, 229
    libraries in, 167
    literature in, 167
    local food shortages, 117
    marriage and sexual relationships in, 194
    Mt. Nebo, 322
    music in, 212
    periodicals in, 230–231
    Petra, 321–322
    radio and TV receivers in, 251
    refugees in, 31–32
    Roman Theater (Amman), modern use of, 293
    rural dress in, 73
    the Siq, 322
    spas and health centers, 74
    sports in, 269
    taxis in, 321
    theater in, 292–293
    tourism in, 12, 321–323
    toys, games, and hobbies in, 144–145
    Umayyad Place, 322
    Umm Qais, 322
    urbanization in, 12
    Wadi Rum, 322
    the West Bank, 32
    water and agricultural production, 118
Joshua, tomb of, 331

Kanafani, Ghassan, 172
Karazone, Diana, 212
Keret, Etgar, 171
Khaled (Khaled Haj Ibrahim), 208–209
Khamis, Arna Mer, 295
Kiarostami, Abbas, 102
Kook, Chief Rabbi Abraham, 270
Kosher foods, 108
Ksikes, Driss, 227
Kuwait. *See also* Arabian Peninsula
    Al-Hashemi Marine Museum, 341
    architecture in, 21–22
    Bedouin influences on architecture in, 21
    bookshops and publishers in, 178
    brand name consciousness in, 83
    broadcasting in, 255–256
    clothing expenditures in, 82
    consumer spending in, 83

INDEX

Kuwait (continued)
    dress among Bedouin women in, 82
    fashion and appearance in, 82–83
    geography of, 21
    Green Island, 341
    housing in, 21
    impact of 1990 Iraq invasion, 21–22
    Kuwait City, 340
    Kuwait State Mosque, 21
    Kuwait Towers, 340
    languages and literacy in, 236
    Liberation Tower, 341
    libraries in, 178
    literature in, 178
    "men's only" gathering space, 21
    oil revenue in, 21
    radio and TV receivers in, 255
    road system and driving in, 337
    sports facilities in, 21
    sports in, 277–278
    theater in, 300–301

Lebanon
    air travel in, 327
    architecture in, 16
    art in, 33–34
    Baalbek, 328
    Beirut, 328
    Beiteddine Palace, 328
    border crossings, 327
    broadcasting in, 253–254
    bus service in, 327
    cedar groves, 328
    Citadel of Raymond de Saint-Gilles, 328
    civil war and architecture in, 16
    civil war and broadcasting in, 253
    civil war and periodicals in, 234
    civil war and sports in, 272–273
    civil war and theater in, 296
    cosmetic surgery in, 76
    dabkeh in, 50
    demographics, 195
    El Khoury, Pierre, 16
    fashion and appearance in, 76–77
    food and food production in, 118–119
    Hezbollah-Israeli conflict and periodicals in, 234
    Hezbollah-Israeli conflict and travel routes, 326, 327
    international games held in, 273
    Jeita Grotto, 328
    languages and literacy in, 233
    love of fashion in, 77
    libraries in, 173
    literature in, 173–174
    marriage and sexual relationships in, 195–197
    music in, 214–215
    national dance of (dabkeh), 50
    periodicals in, 233–234
    Pigeon Rocks, 328
    poets, 174
    political unrest in, 33–34
    polygyny (polygamy) in, 196
    popular foods in, 118–119
    radio and TV receivers in, 253
    rail service in, 327
    resorts, 328–329
    Roman ruins, 328
    seasonings, favorite, 118
    sports in, 272–273
    taxes and food in, 119
    theater in, 296–297
    war and fashion industry in, 76
    women writers in, 174

Levant
    versus Fertile Crescent, 116–117
    folk dance in, 50–51

Libya
    agriculture in, 9
    air travel in, 309
    architecture in, 8–9
    Assai al-Hamra castle, 315
    Benghazi, 316
    border crossings, 310
    broadcasting in, 250
    bus service, 310
    camel racing (mehari), 267
    chess, professional, 141
    Commonwealth War Graves Cemetery, 316
    demographics, 191
    fashion and appearance in, 70–71
    first beauty pageant, 70
    food and food production in, 113–114
    geography of, 8
    government control of press in, 228
    historic preservation in, 9
    hobbies in, 141
    Jamahiriya Museum, 315
    languages and literacy in, 228
    Leptis Magna ruins, 316
    markets (souqs) in Tripoli, 9
    marriage in, 191
    music in, 211
    Osman Mosque, 316

Index

periodicals in, 228
popular beverages in, 114
radio and TV receivers in, 250
rail service in, 309
road system, 310
Roman ruins, 315–316
rural life in, 9
Sabratha ruins, 315–316
Sahara Desert, 316
sports in, 267
tourism in, 9
toys, games and hobbies in, 140–141
Toy Trade Fair (Tripoli), 140
Tripoli, 315
Tuareg music, 211
Westernized clothing use in, 70
women's clothing in, 70

Literature. *See also* Poetry
    Abbasid period, 158
    Abboud, Marun, 174
    Abramowitz, Shalom Yakov (Mendele Mokher Seforim; Mendele the Book Seller), 168, 169–170
    Abu Hamdan, Jamal, 167
    Agnon, Schmuel Yosef (Samuel Joseph), 170
    al-Baraduni, Abd-Allah, 183
    Aleichem, Sholem (Sholem Rabinovitz), 170
    in Algeria, 163
    al-Ghitani, Gamal, 167
    al-Hakim, Tawfig, 166–167
    al-Hamadhani, 158
    al-Hariri, 158
    Ali (Pasha), Muhammad, and, 160
    al-Jabiri, Shakib, 175
    al-Koni, Ibrahim, 165
    al-Maarri, Abu I-Ala, 158
    al-Maqalih, Abd al'Aziz, 183
    al-Muwailihi, Muhammad, 166
    al-Sabah, Su'ad al-Mubarak, 178
    al-Shaykh, Hanan, 174
    al-Wali, Muhammad Abd, 182
    antifeminist, 166
    "anti-novel" (*nouveau roman*) style, 175
    the Apollo Group, 165
    The Arabian Nights, 158
    Aulaqi, Said, 182
    Awwad, Tawfiq Yusuf, 173
    Ba'albaki, Layla, 174
    Badr, Liana, 173
    in Bahrain, 177–178
    banning of *The Children of Gebelawi* (*Awalad Haratina*), 166
    Barakat, Halim, 173–174
    Ben Jelloun, Tahar, 164
    ben Joseph, Saadia, 168
    Ben-Yehuda, Eliezer (Eliezer Perlman), 169
    best-selling books, lack of data, 161–162
    Bialik, Haim Nahman, 172
    bohemian literary movement in Tunisia, 164
    book fairs, 182
    censored books, 161
    censorship of Iranian, 177
    censorship under Mameluke regime, 159
    changing motifs in, xiii–xiv
    The Children of Gebelawi (*Awalad Haratina*), 166
    classic Arabic, 157–159
    Dammaj, Zayd Mutte, 182–183
    Daneshvar, Simin, 177
    detective fiction in Israel, 171
    Diwan Group, 166
    Doha Cultural Festival, 179
    Dowlatabadi, Mahmud, 177
    in Egypt, 165–167
    epistle genre, 158
    experimental fiction forms, 178
    factual anecdote (*al-khabar*) style, 158
    Fahd, Ismail, 178
    feminist movement in, 174
    fiction authors in Bahrain, 178
    first Arabic printing press, 159
    first novels translated into Arabic, 159
    French occupation of Egypt and, 159
    Gibran, Kahlil, 160
    Habayib, Huzama, 173
    Halasa, Ghalib, 167
    Hanged Poems (*muallaqat*), 160
    Haqqi, Yahya, 167
    Hatmal, Jameel, 175
    Hebrew, first wave written in Palestine, 170–171
    Hebrew, history of, 168–170
    Hebrew, modern, 170–171
    Idris, Suhayl, 174
    Idilbi, Ilfat, 175
    imported books, 162
    International Cairo Book Fair, 182
    in Iran, 176–177
    in Iraq, 175–176
    Islam and forms of, 158
    in Israel, 167–172
    Israeli poetry, 171–172

INDEX

Literature (*continued*)
   Jabra, Jabra Ibrahim, 172–173
   Jerusalem International Book Fair, 182
   Jerusalem, or on Religious Power and Judaism, 169
   Jewish Enlightenment (*Haskala*), 168–169
   in Jordan, 167
   Kanafani, Ghassan, 172
   Keret, Etgar, 171
   in Kuwait, 178
   Lebanese women and, 174
   in Lebanon, 173–174
   in Libya, 164–165
   Maghreb, 163
   Mahfouz, Naguib, 165–166
   Mendelssohn, Moses, 169
   Mina, Hanna, 175
   modern Arabic fiction, 159
   in Morocco, 163–164
   move toward romanticism in, 160
   Munif, Abd al-Rahman, 176
   mythical tales, 157–158
   Napoleon Bonaparte's invasion of Egypt and, 157
   Nasrallah, Emily, 174
   nostalgic, of Iran in 1960s, 176–177
   nouveau roman ("anti-novel") style, 175
   novel, first Syrian, 175
   novels, Arabic, 173–174, 175
   in Oman, 179–180
   in Palestinian Territories, 172–173
   Parsipur, Shahrnush, 177
   Peretz, I. L. (Isaac Loeb), 170
   Persian, classical, 176
   Phädon, 169
   poetry, Egyptian, 166
   poetry, history of in North Africa and Middle East, 161
   pirated books and, 161
   and popularity of Western fiction, 159
   pre-Islamic Persian, 176
   Qabbani, Ghalia, 175
   in Qatar, 179
   Riyadh International Book Fair, 182
   Royai, Yadollah, 177
   Rumi, Mevlana Jalauddin, 49, 160
   Safadi, Muta, 175
   Said, Hadia, 174
   Salhi, Abdel-ilah, 164
   in Saudi Arabia, 180
   Shaked, Gershon, 171
   Shami, Yitzhaq, 171
   Shamlu, Ahmad, 177
   Shawqi, Ahmad, 165
   Smilansky, Yizhar (S. Yizhar), 171
   Spiritual Couplets, 160
   symbolism in, 160
   in Syria, 174–175
   Taymur, Mahmoud, 166
   Tchernichovsky, Saul, 172
   Tehran International Book Fair, 182
   The Travels of Benjamin III, 170
   trickster tales (*al-maqamat* or "assemblies") form, 158
   The Trilogy (*al-Thulathiyya*), 165
   Tufail, Ibn, 158
   in Tunisia, 164
   Tunisian international book fair, 182
   Umayyad period, 157–158
   in United Arabv Emirates, 180–181
   Usayran, Layla, 174
   Western influence on, 159, 176
   Western authors, 162
   women and Israeli, 171
   Yacine, Kateb, 163
   Yehoshua, Abraham B., 171
   in Yemen, 181–183
   Yiddish, 169, 170
   Yizhar, S. (Yizhar Smilansky), 171
   Zaydan, Jurji, 173
   Zeyadeh, May, 174
   Zoroastrian scripture, 176

Madrassas, 3
Maghreb literature, 163
Maghreb region. *See* Algeria; Morocco; Tunisia
Mahfouz, Naguib, 165–166
Maimon, Shiri, 213
Makhmalbaf, Mohsen, 102
Makhmalbaf, Samira, 103
Makiya, Mohamed Saleh, 17–18
Mami (Khelifati Mohamed), 209
Markets. *See* Souqs (souks; markets)
Marrakech, architecture and housing in, 8
Marriage and sexual relationships
   abortion, 199
   adoption, 189
   adultery, 196
   age of marriage, 189, 190
   Amnesty International, 200
   arranged marriages, 192, 199, 201
   in Bahrain, 198
   Berber wedding customs, 190–191
   case of Hamda Fahd bin Jasem al-Thani, 200
   clitoridectomy, 192

consanguineous marriages, 188, 190, 192, 198
custody of children, 196–197, 197, 199
dating and courtship, 196, 197, 198, 199
divorce, 191, 193, 195, 196, 197, 198, 199
in Egypt, 191–193
families and, 188
family consent and dating, 194
female circumcision (clitoridectomy), 192
foster parenting, 189
goal of marriage for young people, 187–188
homosexuality, 191, 193, 195, 198
honor crimes, 194
hymen reconstruction surgery, 197
illegitimacy and children, 195
in Iraq, 196–197
in Israel, 194–195
in Jordan, 193–194
in Kuwait, 199
in Lebanon, 190–192
in Libya, 191
marriages between blood relatives, 188, 190, 192, 194
matchmakers (*khatibah*), 192–193
misyar marriages, 199–200
in North Africa, 189–191
in Oman, 200–201
parental consent and, 189, 200
paternity cases, 193
patriarchal nature of, 188
patriarchal societies and, xiv
polygamy (polygyny), 191, 194, 196, 198
premarital sex, 189, 190, 194, 197
in Qatar, 199–200
rape, 196, 199
religious courts and, 194–195
romantic relationships and, 188
in Saudi Arabia, 199–200
secret marriages (*zawaj urfi*), 193
Shariah (Islamic law) and, 187, 196, 197
in Syria, 190–192
temporary marriages (Zawaj mutah), 197
in United Arab Emirates, 198
in urban settings, 188–189
violence against women, 199
virginity and, 189
virginity, tradition of proving, 190
weddings, costs and responsibilities, 188, 201
wedding customs, 190, 195, 201
Western influences on, 187

women's rights and family law, 191, 193, 200
in Yemen, 200–201
Mauritania
fashion and appearance in, 66–67
fashion designers, 66
obesity once revered in, 67
Mawlawiyah, meditation dance of, 49–50
Mbarak, Ricardo, 34
Mehari (camel racing), 267
Mehrjui, Daryush, 103
Mendelssohn, Moses, 169
Mesopotamia. *See* Iraq
Metal working
and Jewish art, 33
from Ur, 35
Mevlevi Order of Sufi, meditation dance (sema) of, 49–50
Middle East. *See also individual nations*; Levant
attitudes toward films in, 95–96
best-selling books, lack of data, 161–162
cosmetics use, 64–65
cultural values and dance in, 52–53
dance in, 46–53
defined, xi
driving challenges in, 307–308
evolution of dance, xii–xiii, 46–47
food market in, 110
hairstyles, 64
honor crimes in, 194
introduction of films into, 96
perfumes and their origin, 64
popular contemporary architecture in, 1–3
popular destinations in, 307
September 11, 2001 and, xi–xii
traditional roles of food in, 107
women's hair dance in, 51–52
Mina, Hanna, 175
Mohammed, Miriam, 259
Morocco
Agadir, 315
air service in, 309
architecture in, 7–8
border crossings, 310
broadcasting in, 248–249
bus service, 310
car rentals, 310
Casablanca, 312
the Casbah des Oudaia (Kasbah des Oudaias), 8, 313
Chellah Necropolis, 313
cosmetics use in, 68
electric power and diet in, 113
fashion and appearance in, 67–68

375

INDEX

Morocco (*continued*)
    ferry service, 310
    Fex (city of), 314
    fez hats in, 67
    food and food production in, 112–113
    foreign influence on fashion in, 68
    fortified adobe villages, 7
    forts (casbah, kasbah), 314
    gambling in, 137
    geography of, 7
    government support for development, 7
    Hassan II Mosque, 312–313
    Hassan Tower (Rabat), 313
    historic preservation in, 7–8
    indigenous people in, 112
    Kasbah des Oudaias (Casbah des Oudaia), 8, 313
    languages and literacy in, 227
    libraries in, 163–164
    literature in, 164
    Marrakech, 314–315
    Middle Atlas Mountains, 315
    Moulay Idriss, 314
    museums, 314, 315
    national chess team, 137
    nightlife in, 8
    Old American Legation Museum, 314
    Palais el-Badi (in Marrakech), 315
    periodicals in, 227
    Place Jemaa el-Ena (in Marrakech), 314–315
    Quartier Habous (in Casablanca), 313
    Rabat, 313
    radio and TV receivers in, 248
    rail service in, 309, 310
    road network, 310
    rural culture in, 137–138
    sports in, 265–266
    Tangier, 313–314
    taxis, 310
    tea tray dance, 55–56
    theater in, 289–290
    tourism in, 8
    toys, games, and pastimes in, 136–138
    tribal defense needs and village architecture, 7
    urban culture in, 136–137
    Volubilis, 314
    water resources in, 113
    Western fashions in, 67
    Western influences on foods in, 110–111
    Zaouia of Moulay Idriss II (Shrine of Moulay Idriss II), 314

Mosques, 4
    Al-Aqsa Mosque (Jerusalem), 324
    al-Azhar Mosque, 318
    Al-Fatih Mosque, 340
    Al-Takieh al-Suleimaniyeh Mosque, 330
    Astan-e Qods-e Razavi, 335
    Chleub Mosque, 313
    Grand Mosque (Abu Dhabi), 344
    the Great Mosque in Oran, 7
    Great Mosque of Qairawan, 6
    Great Mosque (Sanaa), 342
    Hassan II Mosque, 8, 312–313
    Imam Mosque, 335
    Jumeira Mosque (Dubai), 344
    Kuwait State Mosque, 21
    of Mohammed Ali (Cairo), 319
    Omayyad Mosque, 330
    Osman Mosque, 315
    of the Prophet Muhammad (Medina), 23
    of Sayyidna al-Hussein, 318–319
    in Soussa, 312
    Sultan Qaboos Grand Mosque (Muscat), 343
    Zitouna Mosque (the ninth Great Mosque), 311
Munif, Abd al-Rahman, 176
Music
    Aatabou, Najat, 209–210
    Ajram, Nancy, 215
    "Akhasmak Ah," 215
    al-Abdullat, Omar, 212
    al-Atrache, Farid, 207
    in Algeria, 208–209
    al-Ghazali, Mazem, 217
    "Al Hob Elli Ana Aichah," 210
    al-jeel style, 211
    al-Saher, Kazem, 217
    Annabi, Amina, 210
    Bahar, Ali, 218
    in Bahrain, 218
    banning of public concerts, 218
    Bedouin influences on Jordanian, 212
    Berber influences on, 209
    bin Talal, Walid, 208
    the buzuq, 206
    the daff, 206
    the darbuka, 206
    Diab, Amr (Amro Abd Al-assit Abd Al-Aziz Diab), 211
    "Didi," 208–209
    drums, 206
    the dumbek, 206
    in Egypt, 211–212

Index

Egyptian recording companies and control of popular music, 208
Eurovision Song Contest, 210
Fairuz (Nuhad Haddad Rahbani), 214
Fakhri, Sabah, 216
fidgeri repertoire of vocal, 218
gnawa style of music, 209
Googoosh (Faegheh Atashin), 217
Hadad, Sarit, 213
"Hagiga" ("Celebration") album, 213
Hakim, 211–212
Hakim Remix, 212
Hakmoun, Hassan, 209
"Hashemi," 212
Haza, Ofra, 213
"Hilef el Amar," 216
huda style, 211
improvisation (*mawwal*) in vocal, 216
international styles and, 207
in Iran, 217–218
in Iraq, 217
Islamists and public concerts, 218
in Israel, 212–213
the Jarash Festival, 212
"J'en ai marré," 210
in Jordan, 212
Karazone, Diana, 212
Khaled (Khaled Haj Ibrahim), 208–209
khaleeji style, 218
klezmer, 51
Kochav Nolad contest, 213
Kulthoum, Um [Umm], 207
in Lebanon, 214–215
legendary artists, 207
lewa style, 219
in Libya, 211
Maimon, Shiri, 213
Mami (Khelifati Mohamed), 209
melodic modes (*maqamat*), 205, 207
the mijwiz, 206
musical instruments commonly used, 205, 206
Nasri, Asalah, 216
the nay, 206
new media and, 207
"Nour al-Ain" album, 211
in Oman, 219
Oran Rai Festival of 1985, 208, 209
the oud, 206
in Palestinian Territories, 212–213, 214
percussion instruments, 206
Pick, Svika, 213–214
played for dabkeh dances, 50–51
poets and, 207
prayer and, 205
the qanoun, 206
Qantara, 214
in Qatar, 218–219
the rababa, 206
the Rahbanis (Assi Rahbani, Mansour Rahbani, and Ziyad Rahbani), 214–215
rai music, 208–209
recording companies and, 207–208
religion and, 205
the riq, 206
Rotana, 208
"Saida" album, 209
Said, Samira, 210
"Salaf Wi Dein" album, 216
in Saudi Arabia, 219
sawt style, 218
scales in, 205
Shaheen, Simon, 214
stringed instruments, 206
in Syria, 215–217
the tabla, 206
tarab (enchantment) style music, 216
"Tathakkar," 217
among Tuareg people, 211
in Tunisia, 310
Um [Umm] Kulthoum, 207
in United Arab Emirates, 219
uses of, xiv, 205
vocalists, popular, 205, 207
Wassouf, George, 216
weddings singers, 219
Wehbe, Haifa, 215
Western popular music influences on, 207
wind instruments, 206
"Yaho" ("Hey You") album, 212
"Yalil" album, 210
"Yeladot Raot" ("Bad Girls") soap opera, 213
in Yemen, 219–220
Yemenite Jews in popular Israeli, 220
"Youm Wara Youm" album, 210

Napoleon Bonaparte and Egypt, 157, 159
Nasrallah, Emily, 174
Nasri, Asalah, 216
Nomads and nomadic cultures. *See also* Bakhtyari people; Balochi people; Bedouin people; Berber people
    clothing among, 66, 86
    housing forms, 19
    in Morocco, 112

377

INDEX

North Africa. *See also individual countries*
    ancient dance traditions, 46
    attitudes toward films in, 95–96
    best-selling books, lack of data, 161–162
    cosmetics use, 64–65
    dance in, 53–57
    demographics, 189–190
    evolution of dance in, xii–xiii, 46–47, 53
    ferry service, 311
    food market in, 110
    Great Mosque of Qairawan, 6
    hairstyles, 64
    honor crimes in, 194
    literature in, 163
    makeup use, 64–65
    popular contemporary architecture in, 1–3
    sword dance of Arab warriors (*razha*), 54
    tourism in, 311
    traditional roles of food in, 107
    travel and tourism in, 309–306
    Western influences on food in, 110–111
Nuaymah, Mikhail, 296–297

Obesity
    in Algeria, 69
    in Bahrain, 84
    in Mauritania, 67
    in Oman, 125
    prevalence of, 65
Oman. *See also* Arabian Peninsula
    beverages, 124
    bookshops and publishers in, 180
    broadcasting in, 259
    carpet, world's largest, 343
    cosmetics and fragrance use in, 88
    demographics, 200
    everyday meals in, 124
    fashion and appearance in, 87–88
    food in, 123–125
    frankincense (*Boswellia sacra*), 88
    Grand Mosque (Sultan Qaboos Grand Mosque, Muscat), 343
    Hajar Mountains, 343
    languages and literacy in, 238
    libraries in, 179
    literature in, 179–180
    marriage and sexual relationships in, 201
    Muscat, 342
    music in, 219
    obesity in, 125
    Oman Museum, 343
    periodicals in, 238
    radio and TV receivers in, 259
    rich culinary tradition, 125
    Ruwi, 342
    soft drinks in, 124
    sports in, 280–281
    traditional games in, 280–281
    travel to and in, 338
    turban use in, 87
    turtle population, 343
    Wadi Ghul, 343
    weddings in, 201
Opera, in Egypt, 292
Operation Desert Straw, 124
Oral tradition and broadcasting, 245
Ottoman Empire
    cultural isolation under, 159
    rule of Mameluke Beys, 158–159

Palestinian Territories
    architecture in, 14–15
    art in, 34–35
    Bethlehem, 326
    broadcasting in, 252
    Brotherhood Summer Camp, 147
    cosmetics use in, 75
    creation of Israel and theater in, 294
    fashion and appearance in, 75–76
    food and food production in, 118
    Gaza Strip, 326
    geography of, 14
    history of, 34
    infrastructure needs, 15
    Israeli-Palestinian Territories beauty pageant, 75
    Jericho, 322–323, 326
    Jericho Synagogue, 326
    literature in, 172–173
    malnutrition in, 118
    music in, 212–213, 214
    novelists from, 172–173
    periodicals in, 233
    radio and TV receivers in, 252
    refugee camps in, 14–15
    refugee crisis, 14–15
    simulated warfare games in, 146
    textile industry and, 75
    theater in, 294–296
    tourism in, 15, 326
    toy libraries in, 147
    toys, games, and pastimes in, 146–147
    war and libraries in, 172
    the West Bank, 326
Parsipur, Shahrnush, 177

Index

Pastimes and hobbies. *See* Toys, games, and pastimes
Peretz, I. L. (Isaac Loeb), 170
Perfume
    frankincense (*Boswellia sacra*), 88
    imported into United Arab Emirates, 85–86
    origins, 64
    in Saudi Arabia, 87
Periodicals
    AK Comics, 230
    Akhbar al Kahleej newspaper, 237
    Al-Ahram newspaper, 228–229
    al-Aji, Sanaa, 227
    Al Akhbar newspaper, 233–234
    Al-Baath party newspaper, 234
    in Algeria, 226–227
    Al-Muslimoon weekly, 239
    An-Nahar newspaper, 233
    Al-Sabah newspaper, 235
    As-Safir newspaper, 233
    Attajdid newspaper, 227
    in Bahrain, 237–238
    banning of reformist dailies in Iran, 235
    Cairo Magazine, 229
    Cairo Today magazine, 229
    censorship and self-censorship of, 226, 227, 228, 234, 235, 237, 238, 239
    comic books, 230
    Committee to Protect Journalists (New York City), 227, 240
    The Daily Star newspaper, 234
    Danish cartoon controversy, 236, 240–241
    in Egypt, 228–229
    Egypt Today magazine, 229
    El Khabar newspaper, 226
    Elle magazine's Middle Eastern edition, 231
    El Watan newspaper, 226
    English language, 227, 229, 231, 234, 237, 238, 239
    Extrovert Magazine, 233
    fashion magazines, 66, 231
    Femme Magazine, 234
    first monthly magazine for Algerian women, 69
    French-language newspapers, 226, 234
    government control of, 228, 230, 234, 239
    The Gulf Daily News, 237–238
    The Gulf Times, 238–239
    Ha'aretz (*The Land*) newspaper, 232
    Hamshahri newspaper testing Western freedom of expression, 236
    Hawa magazine, 229
    Hebrew language, 232
    Heikal, Mul Hassanein, 229
    Internet, censorship of content on, 237
    in Iran, 235–236
    in Iraq, 234–235
    Islamic sensitivities and, 227
    in Israel, 231–233
    The Jerusalem Post newspaper, 232–233
    in Jordan, 229–231
    Kayhan newspaper, 236
    Ksikes, Driss, 227
    in Kuwait, 236–237
    Kuwait This Month magazine, 237
    The Kuwait Times newspaper, 237
    in Lebanon, 233–234
    in Libya, 228
    Ma'ariv (*Evening*) tabloid, 232
    in Morocco, 227
    the *Morocco Times*, 227
    Nichane magazine, 227
    in Oman, 238
    online fashion magazine, 233
    online news services in Israel, 232
    in Palestinian Territories, 233
    press industry, xiv
    in Qatar, 238–239
    Reporters Without Borders, 228, 232, 233, 240
    Saleh, Hafez El Sheikh, 237
    Sarrat, Lhassan, 227
    in Saudi Arabia, 239
    the Saudi Press Agency, 239
    Shargh newspaper, banning of, 235
    sports magazines, 227, 235
    "superheroes" and comics, 230
    in Syria, 234
    Syria Times newspaper, 234
    The Tehran Times newspaper, 236
    television and, 233
    in Tunisia, 228
    in United Arab emirates, 238
    violence against journalists, 233
    women's magazines, 227, 229, 234
    Yas-e-No newspaper, banning of, 235
    Yedioth Aharaonot (*Evening*) tabloid, 232
    in Yemen, 239–241
    The Yemen Observer and cartoons denigrating Islam, 240
    The Yemen Times newspaper, 240
Persia. *See* Iran
Petra, 321–322

Index

Photography
    in Egypt, 30
    in Jordan, 32
    in United Arab Emirates, 38
Pick, Svika, 213–214
Plastic surgery. *See* Cosmetic surgery
Poetry
    al-Hamadhani, 158
    al-Hariri, 458
    Ali (Pasha), Muhammad, 160
    Apollo Group, 165
    avant-garde poets, 161
    Bedouin influence on, 160
    censorship of, under Mameluke regime, 159
    criticism, 165
    Diwan Group, 166
    in Egypt, 165, 166
    Gibran, Kahlil, 160
    Hebrew forms of, 171–172
    Hebrew, modern, 172
    in Iran, 177
    Iraqi, 176
    in Israel, 171–172
    Jabra, Jabra Ibrahim, 172–173
    Lebanese, 174
    modernist, 161
    movements in Iranian, 177
    move toward romanticism, 160
    in Palestinian Territories, 172–173
    Peretz, I. L. (Isaac Loeb), 170
    pre-Islamic, 160
    rhyme uncommon in traditional Hebrew, 171
    of Rumi, Mevlana Jalauddin, 49, 160
    in Saudi Arabia, 180
    and Sufism, 160
    symbolism in, 160
    Western influence on, 161
Polo, origin of, 149

Qabbani, Ghalia, 175
Qatar. *See also* Arabian Peninsula
    bookshops and publishers in, 179
    broadcasting in, 256–257
    demographics, 199
    Doha, 341
    Doha Cultural Festival, 179
    fashion and appearance in, 84–85
    governmental permissions for marriage, 199
    Khor Al-Daid, 341
    languages and literacy in, 238
    largest shopping mall in the world, 84
    libraries in, 179
    literature in, 179
    marriage and sexual relationships in, 199–200
    misyar marriages in, 199
    music in, 218–219
    periodicals in, 238–239
    radio and TV receivers in, 256
    sports in, 279
    tourist attractions in, 341
    travel to and in, 337–338
    women and rights to marry in, 200

Radio. *See* Electronic media (including radio, television, and computers)
Rahbani Brothers, 296
the Rahbanis (Assi Rahbani, Mansour Rahbani, and Ziyad Rahbani), 214–215
Rossie, Jean-Pierre, 138
Royai, Yadollah, 177
Rugs. *See* Carpets
Rumi, Mevlana Jalauddin, 49, 160

Safadi, Muta, 175
Said, Hadia, 174
Said, Samira, 210
Saint Laurent, Yves, 69
Saleh, Hafez El Sheikh, 237
Salhi, Abdel-ilah, 164
Sarrat, Lhassan, 227
Saudi Arabia. *See also* Arabian Peninsula
    al ardhad (sword dance), 52–53
    alcoholic beverages in, 123
    American influence on toys in, 150–151
    architecture in, 22–23
    art in, 37
    banned toys in, 150
    Bedouin dress in, 86
    bookshops and publishers in, 180
    broadcasting in, 258–259
    bus service in, 339
    and the Coca-Cola Company, 124
    demographics, 199
    embroidery in, 86
    Empty Quarter (Rub al-Khali), 345
    fashion and appearance in, 86–87
    first feature-length film in, 95
    food in, 123
    geography of, 22
    governmental permissions for marriage, 199
    Islamic holy sites, 23

INDEX

Islamic traditions and architecture in, 22–23
Jeddah, 345
languages and literacy in, 239
libraries in, 180
literature in, 180
low- or zero-level alcohol mast beverages in, 123
"mad cow" disease and meat imports to, 123
Masmak Fortress, 345
Mecca, 344, 345
Medina, 344
Mosque of the Prophet Muhammad (Medina), 23
misyar marriages in, 199
music in, 219
National Museum, 345
oil and art in, 37
and Operation Desert Straw, 124
periodicals in, 239
radio and TV receivers in, 258
regulation of women's dress in, 86
Riyadhy, 344–345
road system in, 338–339
soft drinks in, 124
Souq Al-Hijaz, 22
sports in, 279–280
tourism and, 307
tourist attractions in, 345
toys, games, and pastimes in, 150–151
traditional games in, 151
travel to and in, 338–339
Script and penmanship. *See* Calligraphy
Sculpture, idolatry and, 34
Sexual relationships. *See* Marriage and sexual relationships
Shaheen, Simon, 214
Shahr-e Sokhte. *See* Burnt City (Shahr-e Sokhte)
Shaked, Gershon, 171
Shami, Yitzhaq, 171
Shamlu, Ahmad, 177
Sharif, Hassan, 38
Sharjah, art in, 38
Shawqi, Ahmad, 165, 291
Smilansky, Yizhar (S. Yizhar), 171
Soccer. *See* Football (European)
Souqs (souks; markets)
design of, 3
origins of, 3
in Tripoli, 9
Spiritual Couplets, 160
Spitz, Marc, 270

Sports. *See also individual sports*
in Afghanistan, 276
the Alahi club, 277
in Algeria, 264–265
the Asian Cup, 273
the Asian Games, 264
in Bahrain, 278–279
basketball, 269, 270, 278
beach sports, 271
Beirut International Marathon, 273
Bey, F. D. Amr, 267
Boulmerka, Hassiba, 265
boxing, 281
broadcast coverage of, 264
bullfighting, 281
buzkashi (national sport of Afghanistan), 276
camel racing, 277–278, 279, 280
camel racing (*mehari*), 267
cheerleading, African, 267
climbing sports, 275
cricket, 271, 276
in Egypt, 267–269
El-Hawari, Dr. Sahar, 268
El-Menshawi, Mohamed, 268
El Moutawakel, Nawal, 266
facilities for, in Algeria, 7
facilities for, in Kuwait, 21
falconry, 278, 279, 280
Fitaihi, Maha, 280
as games and hobbies, 141
games for pre-teens and teens in Israel, 271
golf, 265
government support for, 272, 277, 278, 279
growth of organized, xiv
handball, 266, 268
handicapped athletes and, 271, 277
horse racing, 267, 268–269, 279, 280
in Iran, 274–276
in Iraq, 273–274
Islamic (Shariah) law and, 275–276
in Israel, 269–272
the Jerusalem March, 270
in Jordan, 269
Jordan International Rally (car race), 269
kite fighting, 276–277
Kook, Chief Rabbi Abraham, 270
in Kuwait, 277
Kuwait Disabled Sport Club, 277
lack of facilities in Palestinian Territories, 15

381

INDEX

Sports (continued)
- in Lebanon, 272–273
- in Libya, 267
- Maccabiah games, 270
- Maccabi Tel Aviv, 270
- Marathon Des Sables, 265
- martial arts, 269, 275
- *mehari* (camel racing), 267
- in Morocco, 265–266
- motor sports, 269
- Muscat Rugby Football Club, 280
- Olympic Games, 265, 266, 268, 270, 273, 274, 275, 277, 279, 281
- in Oman, 280–281
- organized, 263–264
- Pahlavani wrestling, 275
- Pan-Arab Games, 273
- the Paralympics, 271
- polo, 149
- in Qatar, 279
- riding, 266
- rowing, 266
- Royal Automobile Club of Jordan, 269
- rugby, 280
- in Saudi Arabia, 279–280
- *sayyad*, 280
- skiing, 266, 275
- Spitz, Marc, 270
- sports federations/associations, 263
- sports markets in the Middle East, 263
- squash, 267–268
- swimming, 136, 270–271
- in Syria, 273
- team sports and Arab life, 263
- tennis, 265, 271
- traditional games in Bahrain, 278
- traditional games in Oman, 280–281
- the Transplant Olympics, 271
- in Tunisia, 266
- UNICEF's Sports for Development program, 146
- Websites and, 264
- weight lifting, 274
- Wingate Institute, 271
- wrestling, 275, 277
- women in, 264–265, 266, 268, 272, 273, 274, 275, 277, 279, 280, 281
- in Yemen, 281

Sudan
- art in, 31
- civil war and theater in, 290–291
- demographics of, 31
- theater in, 290–291

Sufi and Sufism. *See also* Whirling Dervishes
- Mawlawiyah, 49–50
- meditation dance (sema) of, 49–50, 53–54
- Mevevi Order of, 53–54
- Rumi, Mevlana Jalauddin, and, 49, 160

Synagogues in Egypt, 318

Syria
- air travel in, 329
- Aleppo, 330
- Al-Takieh al-Suleimaniyeh Mosque, 330
- art in, 34–35
- Baath party control of print industry, 234
- border crossings, 329
- broadcasting in, 254
- bus service in, 329
- censorship of reporting in, 234
- Crac des Chevaliers (Qalaat al-Hosn), 330
- Damascus, 330
- demographics, 195
- fashion and appearance in, 79
- fashion industry after lifting of ban on imports, 79
- first novel of, 175
- food in, 119
- languages and literacy in, 234
- libraries in, 174–175
- literature in, 174–175
- marriage and sexual relationships in, 195–197
- music in, 215–217
- National Museum (Damascus), 35
- Omayyad Mosque, 330
- Palmyra, 330
- periodicals in, 234
- radio and TV receivers in, 254
- rail service in, 329
- roads in, 329
- souqs, 330
- sports in, 273
- tarab (enchantment) music in, 216
- taxis in, 330
- Temple of Bel, 330

Taymur, Mahmoud, 166
Tchernichovsky, Saul, 172
Tel Aviv, architecture in, 13
Television. *See* Electronic media (including radio, television, and computers)
Television system standards, 247
Textiles. *See also* Carpets; Clothing
- in Burnt City (Shahr-e Sokhte), 81

INDEX

Dubai Textile City, 85
in Palestinian Territories, 75
Theater
    Acco Festival for Alternative Theatre, 294
    Ahl al-kiahf (*People of the Cave*), 292
    al Achkar, Nidal, 296
    Al Bustan Featival, 296
    Al Fawanees Theatre Company, 293
    in Algeria, 290
    Al-Hakim, Tawfiq, 291–292
    al-Ilj, Ahmad Tayyib, 289
    Al-Kasaba Theatre and Cinematheque, 295
    Al Madina Theatre, 296
    al-Qabbani, Abu Khalil, 297
    al-Rashid, Harun, 297
    al-Siddiqui, Al-Tayyib, 289–290
    Amman International Theater Festival, 293
    ancient Egyptian performance traditions, renewal of, 292
    Aql, Said, 297
    Arab Festival for Theater Arts, 298
    Arab Theater Festival, 290
    Ashtar, 295
    Ayloul Festival Forum, 296
    Baalbeck International Festival, 296
    in Bahrain, 300
    Benaissa, Slimane, 290
    Bosra, Roman theater in, 297
    Cairo Opera House, 292
    CARE and theater project, 295
    Carthage Drama Festival, 290
    censorship and, 288, 294
    changes in, xiv–xv
    children's theater (Egypt), 291
    children's theater (Palestinian Territories), 295
    children's theater (Yemen), 303
    comedy in, 287
    commemorating Imam Hussein, 287, 299
    Constantine Regional Theater, 290
    Damascus Theatre Festival, 298
    Doha Players, 301
    Dubai Community Theatre and Arts Centre (DUCTAC), 302
    Dubai Drama Group, 301–302
    as an educational and therapeutic device, 288
    in Egypt, 291–292
    Eid al Fitr Festival, 301
    El-Hakawati Company, 294–295
    El-Warsha, 292
    European classical drama and, 288
    Experimental Theater Festival (Egypt), 292
    Fajr Theatre Festival, 300
    Falaij Theatre, 302
    Felaij Castle and, 302–303
    Festival National des Arts Populaires de Marrakech, 289
    festivals, 288
    the Freedom Theatre, 295–296
    Freikeh Festival of Theatre, Visual Arts, and Cinema, 296
    French influences on, 290
    Gulf Theatre Festival, 300
    Habimah National Theatre (Tel Aviv), 294
    hakawati (storyteller), 287–288, 297
    history of, in Maghreb Region, 289
    about HIV/AIDS, 291
    International Cultural Center (Tunisia), 290
    International Puppet Festival (Palestinian Territories), 295
    International Theater Institute, 288
    International Theater Workshop (Tel Aviv), 294
    in Iran, 299–300
    in Iraq, 298–299
    in Israel, 293–294
    Janabi, Ahmed, 298–299
    Jerash Festival, 293
    Jerusalem Performing Arts Lab, 293
    in Jordan, 292–293
    karagoz shows, 287
    Khamis, Arna Mer, 295
    in Kuwait, 300–301
    Kuwaiti Little Theatre, 301
    Kuwaiti Players, 301
    in Lebanon, 296–297
    Magic Circles of Djemaa el-Fna, 289
    modern use of Roman Theater (Jordan), 293
    in Morocco, 289–290
    mourning drama, 299–300
    music and traditional drama, 287
    National Puppet Center (Tunisia), 290
    Nuaymah, Mikhail, 296–297
    the Odeon, 293
    in Oman, 302–303
    Omani Theatre Festival, 302
    opera, 292
    Ottoman Empire and, 289
    Palestinian National Theatre, 295

Index

Theater (*continued*)
    in Palestinian Territories, 294–296
    Palmyra, Roman theater in, 297
    Playing Against (the) Weapon(s) Culture workshop, 291
    Popular Theatre in Palestine Project, 295
    Portable Doll Theatre for Children, 303
    puppet shows, 287
    puppet theater, 299
    in Qatar, 301
    Qatar National Theatre, 301
    Rahbani Brothers, 296
    Roman theaters, 289, 293, 297
    in Saudi Arabia, 302
    Secret Life of the Woman, 296
    Shawqi, Ahmad, 291
    Small World Theater, 291
    Spring Children's Theatre Festival (Damascus), 298
    storytelling, 287, 297
    in Sudan, 290–291
    Sudan Center for Theater Research, 291
    in Syria, 297–298
    Taziya dramas, 287, 299–300
    "Theater between the Frontiers" (Sudan), 290–291
    Theater for Life—Sudan, 291
    in Tunisia, 290
    "underground" theater possible in Saudi Arabia, 302
    UNESCO's International Theatre Institute (ITI), 293
    UNESCO support for, in Oman, 302
    UNICEF sponsored children's rights project, 291
    in United Arab Emirates, 301–302
    Wannous, Sadallah, 298
    Western origins of, 287
    Women's Talk, 296
    World Theatre, World Culture (book), 300
    Yacine, Kateb, 290
    in Yemen, 303
Tourism. *See also* Transportation and travel
    Aden, 342
    Aleppo, 330
    in Alexandria, 11
    in Arabian Peninsula, 335–345
    archaeological sites, 332
    artist colonies, 314
    Babel, site of tower of, 332
    Babylon, 332
    in Bahrain, 340
    the Bardo Museum, 311–312
    beaches, 311
    boom in Egyptian, 318
    camel races, 339
    carpet, world's largest, 343
    Carthage, 312
    castles, 315, 328, 330, 334
    Chleub Mosque, 313
    churches, 314
    churches and monasteries, 322
    Crac des Chevaliers (Qalaat al-Hosn), 330
    in Dead Sea region, 12, 74, 323, 326
    diving, 339
    driving challenges in Middle East, 307–308
    in Egypt, 316–320
    Egyptian antiquities, 319–320
    the Egyptian Museum, 319
    the Empty Quarter (Rub al-Khali), 345
    film locations, 313, 322
    forts (casbah, kasbah), 312, 313, 314, 340, 342, 344, 345
    the Grand Erg oriental, 312
    Hajar Mountains, 343
    indigenous dance and, 57
    in Iran, 333–335
    in Iraq, 331–332
    Isfahan (Eṣfahān), 335
    in Israel, 14, 324–326
    Jedda, 345
    Jericho, 322–323
    in Jordan, 12, 320–323
    Joshua, tomb of, 331
    in Kuwait, 340–341
    in Lebanon, 326–329
    Legos, 135–136
    in Libya, 315–316
    Mashad, 335
    Mecca, 345
    in Morocco, 312–315
    mosques, 311, 312, 313, 314, 315, 316, 318–319, 330, 332, 334, 335, 340, 342, 344
    Mövenpick Resort and Spa, 12
    mummies, 320
    museums, 314, 315, 319, 320, 325, 330, 331, 332, 334, 344, 345
    Najaf, 331
    and nightlife in Morocco, 8
    Nineveh, site of, 332
    in Oman, 342–343
    palaces, 315, 328, 334, 342
    in Palestinian Territories, 15, 326
    Petra, 321–322

INDEX

popular destinations in Middle East, 307
pyramids, 319–320
recreation, 339–340
the Red Sea, 320
religious sites, 314, 324–326, 335, 344, 345
and resorts, 11–12, 315, 328, 343, 343–344
Roman ruins, 311, 314, 315–316, 322, 328
the Sahara Desert, 312, 316
in Saudi Arabia, 344–345
security issues and travel to Yemen, 303
shopping, 339
in Sinai Peninsula, 320
souqs in Aleppo, 330
souqs (markets) in Tunisia, 311
Star Wars filming in Tunisia, 313
statistics for, 308–309
Suez Canal, 320
synagogues, 318, 326
in Syria, 330
temples (ancient), 320, 328, 330, 340
and transportation in Middle East, 307
travel in, 315–316
Tripoli, 315
in Tunisia, 311–312
in United Arab Emirates, 343–344
Ur, 331–332
volcano, 334
Whirling Dervishes and, 50, 53
world's tallest hotel (Burj al-Arab), 343–344
in Yemen, 341–342
Zitoura Mosque (the ninth Great Mosque), 311
zone touristique, 311
Toys, games, and pastimes. *See also* Electronic media (including radio, television, and computers)
abaliy, 142
in Algeria, 136
American influence on toys in Iraq, 147
American influence on toys in Israel, 145
American influence on toys in Saudi Arabia, 150–151
American roulette, 143–144
Americans and Mujahidin game, 147
Amman Declaration on the Use of Children as Soldiers, 145
ancient, in Egypt, 141
"animal" games, 139
Arab Children Friends Association (ACFA), 145, 147
archaeological finds and, 133–134

atali gol matali, 149
backgammon, 137
in Bahrain, 149–150
Bahrain Cup (for scrabble), 149
ball games, 142–143
banned toys in Saudi Arabia, 150
Barbie dolls, Moroccan, 137
Barbie dolls, negative Iranian reaction to, 148
Beanie Babies, 147
board games, 136, 141
Brains in Bahrain tournament, 149
card games, 136, 137, 140, 145, 146, 148, 150
casinos and casino games, 143–144
cell phones and cell phone games in Saudi Arabia, 150
changes in, xiii
chess, 136, 137, 140, 144, 149
children's television programming, 136
chkoubba, 140
clapping games, 143
common, 135–136
cooking as an Egyptian hobby, 144
dancing Saddam Hussein doll, 147
Dara and Sara dolls in Iran, 148
dolls, 138–139, 147
education and, 138–139
in Egypt, 141–144
Egyptian tug of war, 141–142
ej-jmel game, 139
Electronic Sports World Cup (ESWC), 144, 145–146, 148, 151
fashion dolls, 65, 73
foot grabbing, 141, 142
Fulla doll, 65, 82
galimoto, 135
gambling casinos in Morocco, 137
Ghrib people, evolution of toys and games among, 138
Hamdouchi, Hichem, 137
handball, 134
handcrafting carpets as hobby, 149
Hiem, Dr. Fadel Abu, 146
history of Egyptian, 141
the hunter (game), 151
International Children's Games, 150
the Internet and computer games, 136, 138, 144, 144–145, 145–146, 148, 150, 151
in Iran, 148–149
in Iraq, 147–148
in Israel, 145–146

INDEX

Toys, games, and pastimes (*continued*)
  in Jordan, 144–145
  kaab, 151
  in Libya, 140–141
  mancala, 135
  matching games, 145
  in Morocco, 136–137
  Old Mother Tambo, 139
  origins of games, 134
  origins of toys, 133
  owari, 135
  poverty and, 138
  punto banco, 144
  quarante de roi, 140
  racing and other sports, 141
  and religious festivals, 142–143
  ronda, 137
  Rossie, Jean-Pierre, 138
  scrabble in Bahrain, 149
  seega, 142
  senet, 141
  simulated warfare games, 146, 147–148
  soccer played by children, 136
  song and singing games, 139, 141–142, 149
  sports played as hobbies, 140, 141, 144
  strategy games, 140
  swimming, 136, 138
  teeta, teeta, teeta, 139
  toy-carrying soldiers and, 134
  toy libraries in Palestinian Territories, 147
  Toy Trade Fair (Tripoli), 140
  traditional games in Iran, 149
  traditional games in Saudi Arabia, 151
  traditional toys, 133–134, 137–138, 145
  in Tunisia, 138–140
  violence and toys, 134
  violence, war, and, 145, 147–148
  Western influence on, 137, 145
  whist, 146
  World Cyber Games, 148
  wrestling, 141
Track and field sports
  in Algeria, 265
  Beirut International Marathon, 273
  Bidouane, Nezha, 266
  Boulmerka, Hassiba, 265
  in Israel, 270
  Marathon Des Sables, 265
  in Morocco, 265
Trade and international relations
  food production and, 109–110
  water issues and, 109

Transportation and travel. *See also* Tourism
  air service in Lebanon, 327
  air travel in Egypt, 316
  air travel in Jordan, 320–321
  air travel in North Africa, 309
  in Arabian Peninsula, 335–339
  bicycle travel in Middle East, 308, 311
  border closings and crossings, 310
  bus services, 310
  bus services in Egypt, 317–318
  bus services in Lebanon, 327
  camels and other animals and, 308
  car rentals, 310, 339
  diverse traditions and, xv
  ferry service, 310, 311
  Hezbollah-Israeli conflict and travel routes, 327
  horse-drawn carriages (caleches) in Tunisia, 310
  in Iran, 332–333
  in Iraq, 330–331
  in Israel, 323–324
  in Jordan, 320–321
  in Lebanon, 327–328
  in Libya, 309, 310
  long-distance shared taxis in Tunisia, 310
  in Morocco, 309, 310–311
  motorcycle usage, 308
  in North Africa, 309–316
  Port Said, 320
  rail service in Egypt, 316–317
  rail service in Jordan, 321
  rail service in Lebanon, 327
  rail service in North Africa, 309–310
  road accidents in Egypt, 318
  roadways in Jordan, 321
  safety concerns and third-class rail cars in Egypt, 317
  Suez Canal, 320
  in Syria, 329–330
  systems in Middle East, 307
  taxis, 310
  taxis in Egypt, 318
  taxis in Lebanon, 328
  travel routes and Hezbollah-Israeli conflict, 327
  in Tunisia, 309, 310, 311–312
The Trilogy (*al-Thulathiyya*), 165
Tripoli
  architecture in, 9
  historic preservation in, 9
  souqs (markets) in, 9
  tourist attractions, 315

INDEX

Tuareg people
    male veiling among, 66
    music among, 211
Tufail, Ibn, 158
Tunisia
    air travel in, 309
    architecture in, 5–6
    the Bardo Museum, 311–312
    beaches (in *zone touristique*), 311
    bicycles in, 311
    broadcasting in, 249
    bus service, 310
    Carthage, 312
    Dougga, 312
    family expenditures on food in, 113
    fashion and appearance in, 69–70
    fashion events in, 70
    food and food production in, 113
    geography of, 5
    Ghrib people, evolution of toys and games among, 138
    the Grand Erg Oriental, 312
    Great Mosque of Oairwan, 6
    homes in Tunis, 6
    horse-drawn carriages (caleches) in, 310
    languages and literacy in, 228
    libraries in, 164
    in Libya, 250
    literature in, 164
    mosques in, 311
    music in, 210
    periodicals in, 228
    popular foods in, 113
    private broadcasting to Libya from, 250
    radio and TV receivers in, 249
    rail service in, 309
    road system, 310
    Roman ruins, 312
    shared taxis (long-distance), 310
    songs and singing games in, 139
    souqs (markets), 311
    Soussa, 312
    spending on clothing in, 69
    sports in, 266
    Star Wars filming in, 313
    toys and games in, 138–139
    traditional national dress, 69–70
    Tunis, 311–312
    urbanization in, 5–6
    Western clothing in, 70
    Zitouna Mosque (the ninth Great Mosque), 311

Turkey
    baths (hammam), 78
    cosmetic surgery in, 78
    cosmetics use in, 78–79
    domestication of wheat, 119
    dress in rural, 78
    fashion and appearance in, 77–79
    the fez, 77
    food and food production in, 119–120
    headgear in, 77
    headscarves, meanings of, 77–78
    Istanbul as fashion hub, 78
    snack foods and, 120
    street vendors of food, 120
Turtles, nesting sites, 343

Um [Umm] Kulthoum, 207
United Arab Emirates. *See also* Arabian Peninsula
    Abu Dhabi, 344
    architecture in, 19–20
    architecture in Dubai City, 2
    art in, 37–38
    bookshops and publishers in, 181
    construction projects, 19
    divorce without notice, 198
    Dubai, 344
    Dubai Museum, 344
    economic development in, 20
    founding of, 37–38
    Fujairah, 344
    Grand Mosque (Abu Dhabi), 344
    guest workers, 19
    languages and literacy in, 238
    libraries in, 180
    literature in, 180
    Jumeira Mosque, 344
    Khalid Lahgoon, 344
    marriage and sexual relationships in, 198
    periodicals in, 238
    polygamy in, 198
    popular musical performers in, 219
    Qasar al-Hosn (White Fort; Old Fort), 344
    Shamal winds, 19
    Sharjah, 344
    theater in, 301–302
    tourism in, 20, 343–344
    travel to and in, 338
Usayran, Layla, 174

Violence, targeting Western style restaurants, 111

INDEX

Wannous, Sadallah, 298
Wassouf, George, 216
Water
    and agricultural production in Israel and Jordan, 118
    competition for, 109
    Gulf Cooperation Council (GCC) and, 109
    international relations and, 109
    local decisions and, 109
    new demands on supply of, 108–109
    and power resources in Morocco, 113
    and region's ability to support itself, 108
Weddings, costs and responsibilities, 188. *See also* Marriage and sexual relationships
Wehbe, Haifa, 215
West Bank, the. *See* Palestinian Territories
Western Sahara, fashion and appearance in, 66
Whirling Dervishes (Mawlawiyah; Mevlevi Order of Sufi)
    founding of, 49
    imitations of the sema, 50
    meditation dance of (sema), 49–50, 53–54
    tourists and, 50, 53
Wijdan (Princess Wijdan Ali), 32
Women
    Aatabou, Najat, 209–210
    adultery and, 196
    Annabi, Amina, 210
    awalim (performers), 48
    Bedouin dress for, 82
    belly dancing, 47–49, 54
    bori demon-dancing, 56–57
    censorship of participation in Olympic Games, 255
    clothing, 62–64
    clothing for, in Algeria, 68–69
    clothing for, in Libya, 70
    clothing for, in Morocco, 67
    dance and, 46
    divorce without notice, 198
    in Egyptian sports, 268
    El-Hawari, Dr. Sahar, and participation in sports, 268
    El-Menshawi, Mohamed, on Egyptian squash and, 268
    and feminist movement in literature, 174
    first beauty pageant in Libya, 70
    first monthly magazine for Algerian, 69
    fundamentalist vigilantes and hijabs in Iraq, 80
    ghawazee dance performers, 48
    guedra (dance delivering blessings), 55
    hair dance, 51–52
    the hijab, 62, 72
    honor killing and, 194
    hymen reconstruction surgery, 197
    Islamic veil and TV appearances of, 251
    Islamist movements and, 199
    and Israeli sports, 272
    Lebanese writers, 174
    limits on rights of, in Qatar, 200
    living away from parents before marriage, 196
    magazines for, 227, 229
    national dress for, in Oman, 87–88
    obesity among Omani, 125
    obesity once revered in Mauritania, 67
    polygamy (polygyny), 191, 194, 196, 198
    and popular literature in Israel, 171
    premarital sex, 197
    rape and, 196
    regulation of dress in Iran, 81
    regulation of dress in Saudi Arabia, 86
    rights of and demands for equality, 191
    risks associated with dating or premarital sex in Jordan, 194
    Said, Samira, 210
    screening-off of residential areas for, 5
    Secret Life of the Woman, 296
    sports and, 264–265, 268
    traditional Iraqi dress for, 80
    trance dance (Zar), 56
    Tuareg musicians, 211
    Um [Umm] Kulthoum, 207
    veiling of, 63
    veil usage in Yemen, 88
    violence against, 199
    Women's Talk, 296

Yacine, Kateb, 163, 290
Yehoshua, Abraham B., 171
Yemen. *See also* Arabian Peninsula
    Aden, 342
    broadcasting in, 259–260
    civil war in, 239
    Danish cartoon controversy, 240–241
    Dar al-Hajar (in Wadi Dhahr), 342
    demographics, 200–201
    economic conditions and fashions in, 88
    fashion and appearance in, 88
    freedom of the press in, 240–241
    Great Mosque (Sanaa), 342
    languages and literacy in, 239

INDEX

libraries in, 181–182
literature in, 181–183
marriage and sexual relationships in, 201
music in, 219–220
periodicals in, 239–241
radio and TV receivers in, 259
Sanaa, 341–342
security issues and travel to, 303
Shaharah, 342
sports in, 281
theater in, 303
tourism in, 341–342
travel to and in, 338
weddings in, 201
Yizhar, S. (Yizhar Smilansky), 171

Zamani, Mahla, 81
Zaydan, Jurji, 173
Zeyadeh, May, 174
Zoroastrianism, scripture of, 176

LRC - Batavia HS
Batavia, IL 60510